KT-562-582

PHILIP'S
MODERN SCHOOL ATLAS

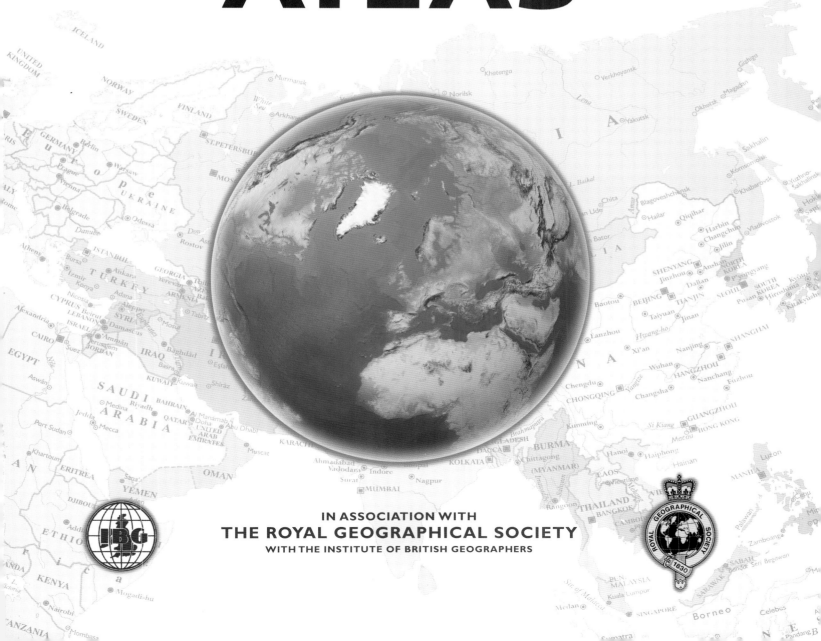

IN ASSOCIATION WITH
THE ROYAL GEOGRAPHICAL SOCIETY
WITH THE INSTITUTE OF BRITISH GEOGRAPHERS

CONTENTS

SUBJECT LIST AND MAP SYMBOLS   3
SCALE, LATITUDE AND LONGITUDE   4
MAP PROJECTIONS   5

REMOTE SENSING   6–16

SATELLITE IMAGERY AND REMOTE SENSING
   INTRODUCTION   6–7
COLOUR COMPOSITES   8
VEGETATION AND LANDFORMS   9
GLOBAL MONITORING   10–11
ENVIRONMENTAL MONITORING   12–13
GEOLOGICAL INTERPRETATION   14
SYNTHETIC APERTURE RADAR   15
DIGITAL ELEVATION MODELS AND LAND USE   16

BRITISH ISLES   17–48

NORTHERN SCOTLAND   18–19
SOUTHERN SCOTLAND   20–21
NORTHERN ENGLAND   22–23
SOUTH AND SOUTH-EAST ENGLAND   24–25
WALES AND SOUTH-WEST ENGLAND   26–27
IRELAND – NORTH   28–29
IRELAND – SOUTH   30–31
BRITISH ISLES *GEOLOGY*   32
BRITISH ISLES *RELIEF OF LAND*   33
BRITISH ISLES *CLIMATE*   34–35
BRITISH ISLES *WATER RESOURCES*   36
BRITISH ISLES *ENVIRONMENT, CONSERVATION AND POLLUTION*   37
BRITISH ISLES *AGRICULTURE AND FISHING*   38–39
BRITISH ISLES *INDUSTRY AND EMPLOYMENT*   40
BRITISH ISLES *ENERGY*   41
BRITISH ISLES *TRANSPORT*   42
BRITISH ISLES *TRADE AND TOURISM*   43
BRITISH ISLES *COUNTIES AND REGIONS*   44–45
BRITISH ISLES *POPULATION TRENDS*   46–47
BRITISH ISLES *STANDARDS OF LIVING*   48

THE WORLD   49–122

THE WORLD *RELIEF OF LAND*   50–51
THE WORLD *COUNTRIES*   52–53
ARCTIC OCEAN AND ANTARCTICA   54–55
EUROPE *RELIEF OF LAND*   56
EUROPE *COUNTRIES*   57
EUROPE *POPULATION*   58
EUROPE *ECONOMIC*   59
EUROPEAN UNION   60–61
EUROPE *CLIMATE AND NATURAL VEGETATION*   62
SCANDINAVIA AND THE BALTIC LANDS   63
BRITISH ISLES   64
BENELUX AND THE RUHR   65
CENTRAL EUROPE   66–67
FRANCE   68
SPAIN AND PORTUGAL   69
ITALY AND THE BALKAN STATES   70–71
EASTERN EUROPE AND TURKEY   72–73
ASIA *RELIEF OF LAND*   74
ASIA *COUNTRIES*   75

ASIA *POPULATION AND WEALTH*   76
ASIA *ECONOMIC*   77
ASIA *CLIMATE AND NATURAL VEGETATION*   78
RUSSIA AND CENTRAL ASIA   79
CHINA AND THE FAR EAST   80–81
JAPAN   82
SOUTH-EAST ASIA   83
SOUTH ASIA   84–85
THE MIDDLE EAST   86–87
ARABIA AND THE HORN OF AFRICA   88
AFRICA *CLIMATE AND NATURAL VEGETATION*   89
AFRICA *RELIEF OF LAND*   90
AFRICA *COUNTRIES*   91
AFRICA *POPULATION AND WEALTH*   92
AFRICA *ECONOMIC*   93
NORTHERN AFRICA   94–95
CENTRAL AND SOUTHERN AFRICA   96–97
AUSTRALIA AND OCEANIA   98–99
OCEANIA *CLIMATE AND NATURAL VEGETATION*   100
OCEANIA *POPULATION AND ECONOMIC*   101
PACIFIC OCEAN   102–103
NORTH AMERICA *RELIEF OF LAND AND CLIMATE*   104
NORTH AMERICA *COUNTRIES, CLIMATE AND NATURAL VEGETATION*   105
NORTH AMERICA *POPULATION AND WEALTH*   106
NORTH AMERICA *ECONOMIC*   107
CANADA   108–109
UNITED STATES   110–111
NORTH-EAST UNITED STATES AND THE ST LAWRENCE   112–113
MEXICO, CENTRAL AMERICA AND THE CARIBBEAN   114–115
SOUTH AMERICA *RELIEF OF LAND*   116
SOUTH AMERICA *CLIMATE AND NATURAL VEGETATION*   117
SOUTH AMERICA *POPULATION AND WEALTH*   118
SOUTH AMERICA *ECONOMIC*   119
SOUTH AMERICA   120–121
SOUTH-EASTERN BRAZIL   122

WORLD THEMES   123–160

THE WORLD *GEOLOGY, VOLCANOES AND EARTHQUAKES*   124–125
THE WORLD *TEMPERATURE AND OCEAN CURRENTS*   126
THE WORLD *PRESSURE, WINDS AND PRECIPITATION*   127
THE WORLD *CLIMATE*   128–129
THE WORLD *CLIMATE STATISTICS*   130–131
THE WORLD *NATURAL VEGETATION*   132–133
THE WORLD *ENVIRONMENTAL CONCERNS*   134–135
THE WORLD *AGRICULTURE*   136–137
THE WORLD *ENERGY AND MINERALS*   138–139
THE WORLD *INDUSTRY AND TRADE*   140–141
THE WORLD *TRAVEL AND TOURISM*   142–143
THE WORLD *STANDARDS OF LIVING*   144–145
THE WORLD *POPULATION DISTRIBUTION*   146–147
THE WORLD *POPULATION TRENDS*   148–149
THE WORLD *LANGUAGES AND RELIGIONS*   150
THE WORLD *INTERNATIONAL ORGANIZATIONS*   151
THE WORLD *HUMAN CONCERNS*   152–153
THE WORLD *SOCIAL AND ECONOMIC STATISTICS*   154–159
THE WORLD *PHYSICAL DIMENSIONS*   160

INDEX   161–184

Published in Great Britain in 2007 by Philip's,
a division of Octopus Publishing Group Limited,
2–4 Heron Quays, London E14 4JP
www.octopusbooks.co.uk

An Hachette Livre UK Company
www.hachettelivre.co.uk

Cartography by Philip's

Copyright © 2007 Philip's
Reprinted 2008

ISBN 978–0–540–09152–2

Philip's World Atlases are published in association with The Royal Geographical
Society (with The Institute of British Geographers).

   The Society was founded in 1830 and given a Royal Charter in 1859 for
'the advancement of geographical science'. Today it is a leading world centre
for geographical learning – supporting education, teaching, research and
expeditions, and promoting public understanding of the subject.

   Further information about the Society and how to join may be found on its
website at: **www.rgs.org**

PHOTOGRAPHIC ACKNOWLEDGEMENTS
All satellite images in the atlas are courtesy of NPA Group, Edenbridge, Kent
(www.satmaps.com), with the exception of the following: p. 17 M-SAT Ltd/Science
Photo Library; p. 49 PLI/Science Photo Library; p. 134 NASA/GSFC.

This false-colour composite image was recorded in June. Glasgow and Edinburgh and other settlements in the Forth–Clyde Valley are clearly visible in blue. The bright red areas are fields of healthy crops. Imagery such as this is used to police EU agricultural subsidies. *(EROS)*

SUBJECT LIST

Acid rain	37
Agriculture	38–9, 136–7, 140
Aid (international)	92, 152
AIDS and HIV	153
Air travel	42, 61, 142
Alternative energy	139
Assisted areas	40
Carbon dioxide emissions	37, 134
Child mortality	149
Climate regions	128
Climate statistics	35, 130–1
Coal/oil/gas	138
Conservation	37
Continental drift	124
Conflicts	153
Debt	92, 152
Deforestation	135
Desertification	135
Drugs	153
Earthquakes	125
Education	48, 61, 145
Electricity	41, 139
El Niño	129
Employment	39, 40, 140
Energy	41, 138
Ethnic groups	47
European Union	60–1
Exports	141
Family size	149
Famine	135
Fishing	39, 136–7
Flood risk	36
Food production	38, 136–7
Foot-and-mouth disease	38
Forestry	37, 39, 137
Fuel	41, 138
Gender development index (GDI)	145
Geology	32, 124
Global warming	134–135
Greenhouse effect	37, 134
Gross domestic product (GDP)	144
Health care	48, 61, 145
Human development index (HDI)	144
Hydroelectricity	139
Illiteracy	145
Industry	40, 61, 140
Internet	141
Languages	58, 150
Latitude and longitude	4
Life expectancy	149
Literacy	145
Manufacturing	40, 140–1
Map projections	5
Migration	47, 152
Monsoon	128
Multinational corporations	141
National parks	37
Natural vegetation	37, 132–3
North Sea fishing	137
Nuclear power	139
Ocean currents	126
Ozone layer	37, 134
Plate tectonics	124–5
Population change	47, 146, 148
Population density	46, 146–8
Population pyramids	47, 146
Precipitation	34, 127
Rainfall	35, 130–1, 135
Refugees	152
Religions	150
Remote sensing	6–16
Renewable energy	41, 139
Research and development	140
Satellite imagery	6–16
Scale	4
Sea-level changes	134
Services	40, 140
Soils	132–3
Standards of living	48, 144
Telecommunications	141
Temperature	35, 126, 135
Time zones	142
Tourism	43, 113, 143
Trade	43, 141
Transport	42, 61
Travel	42–3, 142
Unemployment	40, 61
United Nations	151
Urban population	148
Volcanoes	125
Water pollution	36
Water supply	36, 144
Wealth	48, 61, 144
Wind power	139
Windchill effect	129
World Heritage Sites	37, 143

MAP SYMBOLS

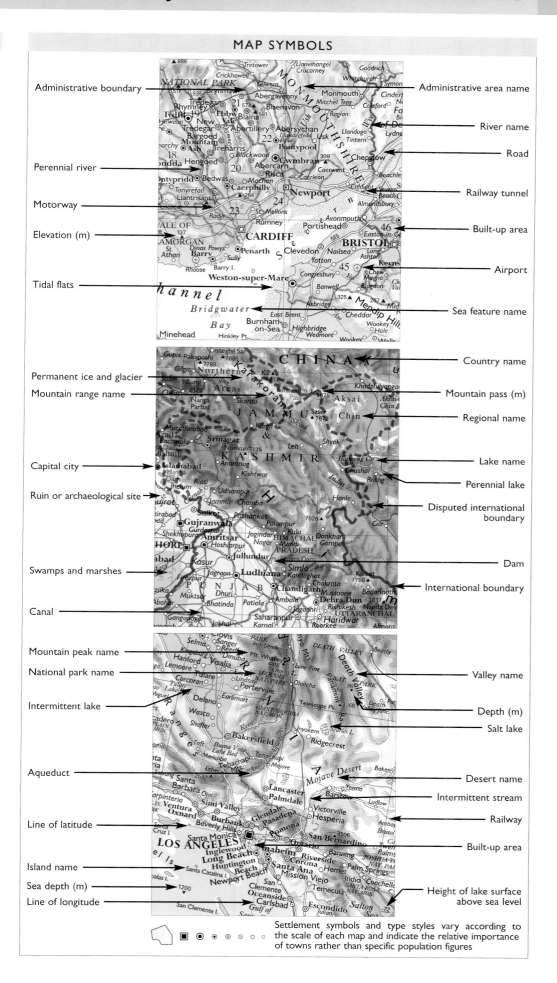

Administrative boundary

Perennial river

Motorway

Elevation (m)

Tidal flats

Administrative area name

River name

Road

Railway tunnel

Built-up area

Airport

Sea feature name

Permanent ice and glacier

Mountain range name

Capital city

Ruin or archaeological site

Swamps and marshes

Canal

Country name

Mountain pass (m)

Regional name

Lake name

Perennial lake

Disputed international boundary

Dam

International boundary

Mountain peak name

National park name

Intermittent lake

Aqueduct

Line of latitude

Island name

Sea depth (m)

Line of longitude

Valley name

Depth (m)

Salt lake

Desert name

Intermittent stream

Railway

Built-up area

Height of lake surface above sea level

Settlement symbols and type styles vary according to the scale of each map and indicate the relative importance of towns rather than specific population figures

SCALE

The scale of a map is the relationship of the distance between two points shown on the map and the distance between the same two points on the Earth's surface. For instance, 1 inch on the map represents 1 mile on the ground, or 10 kilometres on the ground is represented by 1 centimetre on the map.

Instead of saying 1 centimetre represents 10 kilometres, we could say that 1 centimetre represents 1 000 000 centimetres on the map. If the scale is stated so that the same unit of measurement is used on both the map and the ground, then the proportion will hold for any unit of measurement. Therefore, the scale is usually written 1:1 000 000. This is called a 'representative fraction' and usually appears at the top of the map page, above the scale bar.

Calculations can easily be made in centimetres and kilometres by dividing the second figure in the representative fraction by 100 000 (i.e. by deleting the last five zeros). Thus at a scale of 1:5 000 000, 1 cm on the map represents 50 km on the ground. This is called a 'scale statement'. The calculation for inches and miles is more laborious, but 1 000 000 divided by 63 360 (the number of inches in a mile) shows that 1:1 000 000 can be stated as 1 inch on the map represents approximately 16 miles on the ground.

Many of the maps in this atlas feature a scale bar. This is a bar divided into the units of the map – miles and kilometres – so that a map distance can be measured with a ruler, dividers or a piece of paper, then placed along the scale bar, and the distance read off. To the left of the zero on the scale bar there are usually more divisions. By placing the ruler or dividers on the nearest rounded figure to the right of the zero, the smaller units can be counted off to the left.

The map extracts to the right show Los Angeles and its surrounding area at six different scales. The representative fraction, scale statement and scale bar are positioned above each map. Map 1 is at 1:27 000 and is the largest scale extract shown. Many of the individual buildings are identified and most of the streets are named, but at this scale only part of central Los Angeles can be shown within the given area. Map 2 is much smaller in scale at 1:250 000. Only a few important buildings and streets can be named, but the whole of central Los Angeles is shown. Maps 3, 4 and 5 show how greater areas can be depicted as the map scale decreases, down to Map 6 at 1:35 000 000. At this small scale, the entire Los Angeles conurbation is depicted by a single town symbol and a large part of the south-western USA and part of Mexico is shown.

The scales of maps must be used with care since large distances on small-scale maps can be represented by one or two centimetres. On certain projections scale is only correct along certain lines, parallels or meridians. As a general rule, the larger the map scale, the more accurate and reliable will be the distance measured.

LATITUDE AND LONGITUDE

Accurate positioning of individual points on the Earth's surface is made possible by reference to the geometric system of latitude and longitude.

Latitude is the distance of a point north or south of the Equator measured at an angle with the centre of the Earth, whereby the Equator is latitude 0 degrees,

the North Pole is 90 degrees north and the South Pole 90 degrees south. Latitude parallels are drawn west–east around the Earth, parallel to the Equator, decreasing in diameter from the Equator until they become a point at the poles. On the maps in this atlas the lines of latitude are represented by blue lines running across the map in smooth curves, with the degree figures in blue at the sides of the maps. The degree interval depends on the scale of the map.

Lines of longitude are meridians drawn north–south, cutting the lines of latitude at right angles on the Earth's surface and intersecting with one another at the poles. Longitude is measured by an angle at the centre of the Earth from the prime meridian (0 degrees), which passes through Greenwich in London. It is given as a measurement east or west of the Greenwich Meridian from 0 to 180 degrees. The meridians are normally drawn north–south vertically down the map, with the degree figures

in blue in the top and bottom margins of the map.

In the index each place name is followed by its latitude and longitude, and then its map page number and letter-figure grid reference. The unit of measurement is the degree, which is subdivided into 60 minutes. An index entry states the position of a place in degrees and minutes. The latitude is followed by N(orth) or S(outh) and the longitude E(ast) or W(est).

For example:
Helston, U.K.   50°7N 5°17W   **27** G3
Helston is 50 degrees 7 minutes north of the Equator and 5 degrees 17 minutes west of Greenwich, and is on map page 27, in grid square G3.

McKinley, Mt., U.S.A.   63°4N 151°0W   **108** C4
Mount McKinley is 63 degrees 4 minutes north of the Equator and 151 degrees west of Greenwich, and is on map page 108, in grid square C4.

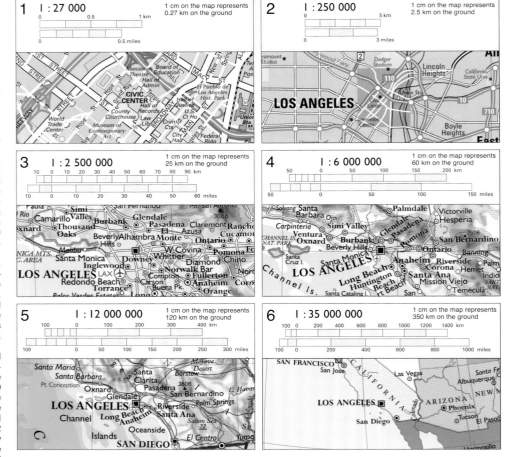

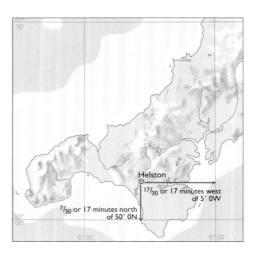

How to locate a place or feature

The two diagrams (*left*) show how to estimate the required distance from the nearest line of latitude or longitude on the map page, in order to locate a place or feature listed in the index (such as Helston in the UK and Mount McKinley in the USA, as detailed in the above example).

In the left-hand diagram there are 30 minutes between the lines and so to find the position of Helston an estimate has to be made: 7 parts of the 30 degrees north of the 50 0N latitude line, and 17 parts of the 30 degrees west of the 5 0W longitude line.

In the right-hand diagram it is more difficult to estimate because there is an interval of 10 degrees between the lines. In the example of Mount McKinley, the reader has to estimate 3 degrees 4 minutes north of 60 0N and 1 degree 1 minute west of 150 0W.

MAP PROJECTIONS

A map projection is the systematic depiction of the imaginary grid of lines of latitude and longitude from a globe on to a flat surface. The grid of lines is called the 'graticule' and it can be constructed either by graphical means or by mathematical formulae to form the basis of a map. As a globe is three dimensional, it is not possible to depict its surface on a flat map without some form of distortion. Preservation of one of the basic properties listed below can only be secured at the expense of the others and thus the choice of projection is often a compromise solution.

Correct area
In these projections the areas from the globe are to scale on the map. This is particularly useful in the mapping of densities and distributions. Projections with this property are termed 'equal area', 'equivalent' or 'homolographic'.

Correct distance
In these projections the scale is correct along the meridians, or, in the case of the 'azimuthal equidistant', scale is true along any line drawn from the centre of the projection. They are called 'equidistant'.

Correct shape
This property can only be true within small areas as it is achieved only by having a uniform scale distortion along both the 'x' and 'y' axes of the projection. The projections are called 'conformal' or 'orthomorphic'.

Map projections can be divided into three broad categories – **'azimuthal'**, **'conic'** and **'cylindrical'**. Cartographers use different projections from these categories depending on the map scale, the size of the area to be mapped, and what they want the map to show.

AZIMUTHAL OR ZENITHAL PROJECTIONS

These are constructed by the projection of part of the graticule from the globe on to a plane tangential to any single point on it. This plane may be tangential to the equator (equatorial case), the poles (polar case) or any other point (oblique case). Any straight line drawn from the point at which the plane touches the globe is the shortest distance from that point and is known as a 'great circle'. In its 'gnomonic' construction any straight line on the map is a great circle, but there is great exaggeration towards the edges and this reduces its general uses. There are five different ways of transferring the graticule on to the plane and these are shown below. The diagrams below also show how the graticules vary, using the polar case as the example.

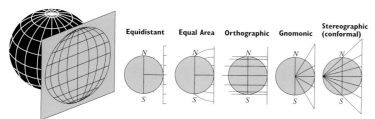

Equidistant | Equal Area | Orthographic | Gnomonic | Stereographic (conformal)

Polar case
The polar case is the simplest to construct and the diagram on the right shows the differing effects of all five methods of construction, comparing their coverage, distortion, etc, using North America as the example.

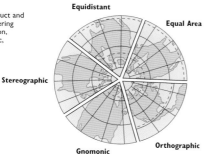

Equidistant
Equal Area
Stereographic
Gnomonic
Orthographic

Oblique case
The plane touches the globe at any point between the Equator and poles. The oblique orthographic uses the distortion in azimuthal projections away from the centre to give a graphic depiction of the Earth as seen from any desired point in space.

Equatorial case
The example shown here is Lambert's Equivalent Azimuthal. It is the only projection which is both equal area and where bearing is true from the centre.

CONICAL PROJECTIONS

These use the projection of the graticule from the globe on to a cone which is tangential to a line of latitude (termed the 'standard parallel'). This line is always an arc and scale is always true along it. Because of its method of construction, it is used mainly for depicting the temperate latitudes around the standard parallel, i.e. where there is least distortion. To reduce the distortion and include a larger range of latitudes, the projection may be constructed with the cone bisecting the surface of the globe so that there are two standard parallels, each of which is true to scale. The distortion is thus spread more evenly between the two chosen parallels.

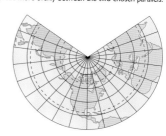
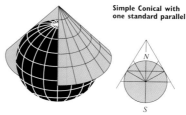

Simple Conical with one standard parallel

Bonne
This is a modification of the simple conic, whereby the true scale along the meridians is sacrificed to enable the accurate representation of areas. However, scale is true along each parallel but shapes are distorted at the edges.

Albers Conical Equal Area
This projection uses two standard parallels. The selection of these relative to the land area to be mapped is very important. It is equal area and is especially useful for large land masses oriented east–west, such as the USA.

CYLINDRICAL AND OTHER WORLD PROJECTIONS

This group of projections are those which permit the whole of the Earth's surface to be depicted on one map. They are a very large group of projections and the following are only a few of them. Cylindrical projections are constructed by the projection of the graticule from the globe on to a cylinder tangential to the globe. Although cylindrical projections can depict all the main land masses, there is considerable distortion of shape and area towards the poles. One cylindrical projection, Mercator, overcomes this shortcoming by possessing the unique navigational property that any straight line drawn on it is a line of constant bearing ('loxodrome'). It is used for maps and charts between 15° either side of the Equator. Beyond this, enlargement of area is a serious drawback, although it is used for navigational charts at all latitudes.

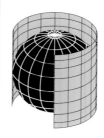

Simple Cylindrical

Cylindrical with two standard parallels

Mercator

Eckert IV (pseudo-cylindrical equal area)

Hammer (polyconic equal area)

The first satellite to monitor our environment systematically was launched as long ago as April 1961. It was called TIROS-1 and was designed specifically to record atmospheric change. The first of the generation of Earth resources satellites was Landsat-1, launched in July 1972.

The succeeding decades have seen a revolution in our ability to survey and map our global environment. Digital sensors mounted on satellites now scan vast areas of the Earth's surface day and night. They collect and relay back to Earth huge volumes of geographical data which is processed and stored by computers.

Satellite imagery and remote sensing

Continuous development and refinement, and freedom from national access restrictions, have meant that sensors on these satellite platforms are increasingly replacing surface and airborne data-gathering techniques. Twenty-four hours a day, satellites are scanning and measuring the Earth's surface and atmosphere, adding to an ever-expanding range of geographic and geophysical data available to help us identify and manage the problems of our human and physical environments. Remote sensing is the science of extracting information from such images.

Satellite orbits

Most Earth-observation satellites (such as the Landsat, SPOT and IRS series) are in a near-polar, Sun-synchronous orbit (*see diagram opposite*). At altitudes of around 700–900 km the satellites revolve around the Earth approximately every 100 minutes and on each orbit cross a particular line of latitude at the same local (solar) time. This ensures that the satellite can obtain coverage of most of the globe, replicating the coverage typically within 2–3 weeks. In more recent satellites, sensors can be pointed sideways from the orbital path, and 'revisit' times with high-resolution frames can thus be reduced to a few days.

Exceptions to these Sun-synchronous orbits include the geostationary meteorological satellites, such as Meteosat. These have a 36,000 km high orbit and rotate around the Earth every 24 hours, thus remaining above the same point on the Equator.

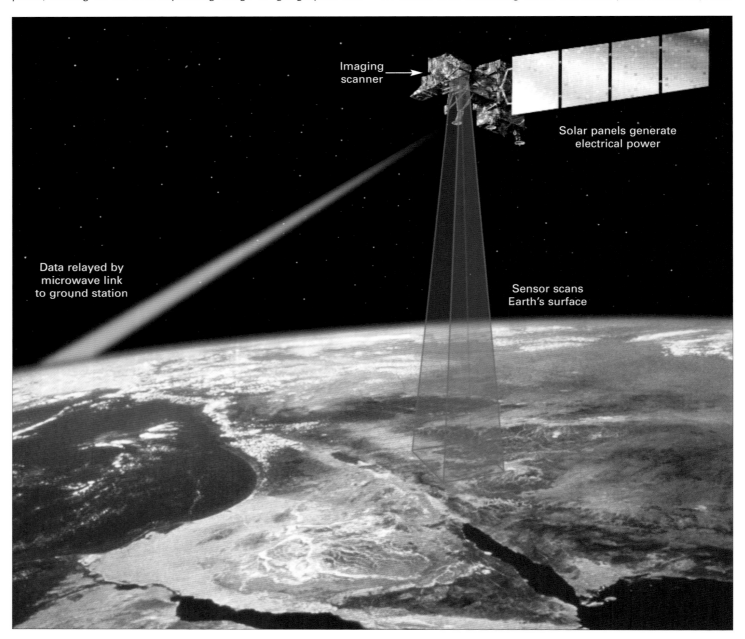

Imaging scanner

Solar panels generate electrical power

Data relayed by microwave link to ground station

Sensor scans Earth's surface

Landsat-7
This is the latest addition to the Landsat Earth-observation satellite programme, orbiting at 705 km above the Earth. With onboard recorders, the satellite can store data until it passes within range of a ground station. Basic geometric and radiometric corrections are then applied before distribution of the imagery to users.

These satellites acquire frequent images showing cloud and atmospheric moisture movements for almost a full hemisphere.

In addition, there is the Global Positioning System (GPS) satellite 'constellation', which orbits at a height of 20,200 km, consisting of 24 satellites. These circle the Earth in six different orbital planes, enabling us to fix our position on the Earth's surface to an accuracy of a few centimetres. Although developed for military use, this system is now available to individuals through hand-held receivers and in-car navigation systems. The other principal commercial uses are for surveying and air and sea navigation.

Digital sensors

Early satellite designs involved images being exposed to photographic film and returned to Earth by capsule for processing, a technique still sometimes used today. However, even the first commercial satellite imagery, from Landsat-1, used digital imaging sensors and transmitted the data back to ground stations (*see diagram opposite*).

Passive, or optical, sensors record the radiation reflected from the Earth for specific wavebands. Active sensors transmit their own microwave radiation, which is reflected from the Earth's surface back to the satellite and recorded. The SAR (Synthetic Aperture Radar) Radarsat images on page 15 are examples of the latter.

Whichever scanning method is used, each satellite records image data of constant width but potentially several thousand kilometres in length. Once the data has been received on Earth, it is usually split into approximately square sections or 'scenes' for distribution.

Spectral resolution, wavebands and false-colour composites

Satellites can record data from many sections of the electromagnetic spectrum (wavebands) simultaneously. Since we can only see images made from the three primary colours (red, green and blue), a selection of any three wavebands needs to be made in order to form a picture that will enable visual interpretation of the scene to be made. When any combination other than the visible bands are used, such as near or middle infrared, the resulting image is termed a 'false-colour composite'. An example of this is shown on page 8.

The selection of these wavebands depends on the purpose of the final image – geology, hydrology, agronomy and environmental requirements each have their own optimum waveband combinations.

GEOGRAPHIC INFORMATION SYSTEMS

A Geographic Information System (GIS) enables any available geospatial data to be compiled, presented and analysed using specialized computer software.

Many aspects of our lives now benefit from the use of GIS – from the management and maintenance of the networks of pipelines and cables that supply our homes, to the exploitation or protection of the natural resources that we use. Much of this is at a regional or national scale and the data collected from satellites form an important part of our interpretation and understanding of the world around us.

GIS systems are used for many aspects of central planning and modern life, such as defence, land use, reclamation, telecommunications and the deployment of emergency services. Commercial companies can use demographic and infrastructure data within a GIS to plan marketing strategies, identifying where their services would be most needed, and thus decide where best to locate their businesses. Insurance companies use GIS to determine premiums based on population distribution, crime figures and the likelihood of natural disasters, such as flooding or subsidence.

Whatever the application, all the geographically related information that is available can be input and prepared in a GIS, so that a user can display the specific information of interest, or combine data to produce further information which might answer or help resolve a specific problem. From analysis of the data that has been acquired, it is often possible to use a GIS to generate a 'model' of possible future situations and to see what impact might result from decisions and actions taken. A GIS can also monitor change over time, to aid the observation and interpretation of long-term change.

A GIS can utilize a satellite image to extract useful information and map large areas, which would otherwise take many man-years of labour to achieve on the ground. For industrial applications, including hydrocarbon and mineral exploration, forestry, agriculture, environmental monitoring and urban development, such dramatic and beneficial increases in efficiency have made it possible to evaluate and undertake projects and studies in parts of the world that were previously considered inaccessible, and on a scale that would not have been possible before.

SELECTED REMOTE SENSING SATELLITES

Year Launched	Satellite	Country	Pixel Size (Resolution)
Passive Sensors (Optical)			
1972	Landsat-1 MSS	USA	80 m
1975	Landsat-2 MSS	USA	80 m
1978	Landsat-3 MSS	USA	80 m
1978	NOAA AVHRR	USA	1.1 km
1981	Cosmos TK-350	Russia	10 m
1982	Landsat-4 TM	USA	30 m
1984	Landsat-5 TM	USA	30 m
1986	SPOT-1	France	10 / 20 m
1988	IRS-1A	India	36 / 72 m
1988	SPOT-2	France	10 / 20 m
1989	Cosmos KVR-1000	Russia	2 m
1991	IRS-1B	India	36 / 72 m
1992	SPOT-3	France	10 / 20 m
1995	IRS-1C	India	5.8 / 23.5 m
1997	IRS-1D	India	5.8 / 23.5 m
1998	SPOT-4	France	10 / 20 m
1999	Landsat-7 ETM	USA	15 / 30 m
1999	UoSAT-12	UK	10 / 32 m
1999	IKONOS-2	USA	1.0 / 4 m
1999	ASTER	USA	15 m
2000	Hyperion	USA	30 m
2000	EROS-A1	International	1.8 m
2001	Quickbird	USA	0.61 / 2.4 m
2002	SPOT-5	France	2.5 / 5 / 10 m
2002	DMC AlSat-1	Algeria (UK)	32 m
2003	DMC UK	UK	32 m
2003	DMC NigeriaSat-1	Nigeria (UK)	32 m
2003	DMC BilSat	Turkey (UK)	32 m
2003	OrbView-3	USA	1.0 / 4 m
2004	Formosat-2	Taiwan	2.0 / 8 m
2004	KOMPSAT-2	South Korea	1.0 / 4 m
Active Sensors (Synthetic Aperture Radar)			
1991	ERS-1	Europe	25 m
1992	JERS-1	Japan	18 m
1995	ERS-2	Europe	25 m
1995	Radarsat	Canada	8–100 m
2002	ENVISAT	Europe	25 m

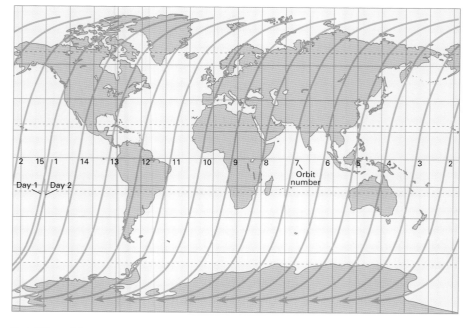

Satellite orbits

Landsat-7 makes over 14 orbits per day in its Sun-synchronous orbit. During the full 16 days of a repeat cycle, coverage of the areas between those shown is achieved.

Natural-colour and false-colour composites
These images show the salt ponds at the southern end of San Francisco Bay, which now form the San Francisco Bay National Wildlife Refuge. They demonstrate the difference between 'natural colour' (*top*) and 'false colour' (*bottom*) composites.

The top image is made from visible red, green and blue wavelengths. The colours correspond closely to those one would observe from an aircraft. The salt ponds appear green or orange-red due to the colour of the sediments they contain. The urban areas appear grey and vegetation is either dark green (trees) or light brown (dry grass).

The bottom image is made up of near-infrared, visible red and visible green wavelengths. These wavebands are represented here in red, green and blue, respectively. Since chlorophyll in healthy vegetation strongly reflects near-infrared light, this is clearly visible as red in the image.

False-colour composite imagery is therefore very sensitive to the presence of healthy vegetation. The bottom image thus shows better discrimination between the 'leafy' residential urban areas, such as Palo Alto (south-west of the Bay) from other urban areas by the 'redness' of the trees. The high chlorophyll content of watered urban grass areas shows as bright red, contrasting with the dark red of trees and the brown of natural, dry grass. *(EROS)*

Western Grand Canyon, Arizona, USA
This false-colour image shows in bright red the sparse vegetation on the limestone plateau, including sage, mesquite and grasses. Imagery such as this is used to monitor this and similar fragile environments. The sediment-laden river, shown as blue-green, can be seen dispersing into Lake Mead to the north-west. Side canyons cross the main canyon in straight lines, showing where erosion along weakened fault lines has occurred. *(EROS)*

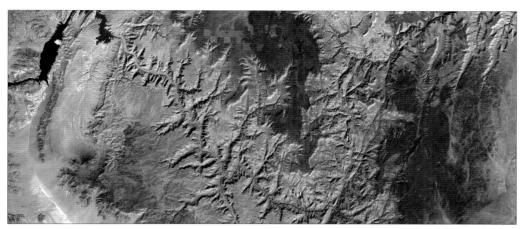

Ayers Rock and Mt Olga, Northern Territory, Australia
These two huge outliers are the remnants of Precambrian mountain ranges created some 500 million years ago and then eroded away. Ayers Rock (*seen at right*) rises 345 m above the surrounding land and has been a part of Aboriginal life for over 10,000 years. Their dramatic coloration, caused by oxidized iron in the sandstone, attracts visitors from around the world. *(EROS)*

Mount St Helens, Washington, USA
A massive volcanic eruption on 18 May 1980 killed 60 people and devastated around 400 sq km of forest within minutes. The blast reduced the mountain peak by 400 m to its current height of 2,550 m, and volcanic ash rose some 25 km into the atmosphere. The image shows Mount St Helens eight years after the eruption in 1988. The characteristic volcanic cone has collapsed in the north, resulting in the devastating 'liquid' flow of mud and rock. *(EROS)*

Niger Delta, West Africa
The River Niger is the third longest river in Africa after the Nile and Congo. Deltas are by nature constantly evolving sedimentary features and often contain many ecosystems within them. In the case of the Niger Delta, there are also vast hydro-carbon reserves beneath it with associated wells and pipelines. Satellite imagery helps to plan activity and monitor this fragile and changing environment. *(EROS)*

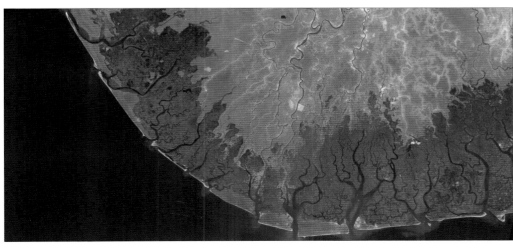

Europe at night

This image was derived as part of the Defense Meteorological Satellite Program. The sensor recorded all the emissions of near-infrared radiation at night, mainly the lights from cities, towns and villages. Note also the 'lights' in the North Sea from the flares of the oil production platforms. This project was the first systematic attempt to record human settlement on a global scale using remote sensing. *(NOAA)*

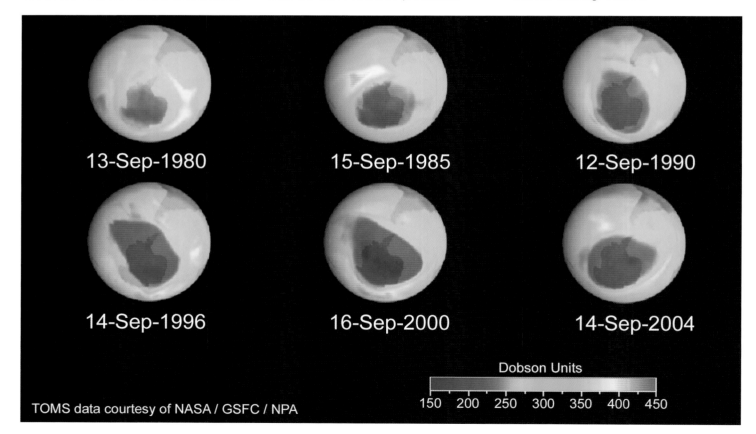

13-Sep-1980   15-Sep-1985   12-Sep-1990

14-Sep-1996   16-Sep-2000   14-Sep-2004

Dobson Units

150 200 250 300 350 400 450

TOMS data courtesy of NASA / GSFC / NPA

Antarctic ozone depletion

The Total Ozone Mapping Spectrometer (TOMS) instruments, first launched in 1978, can measure a range of atmospheric trace constituents, in particular global ozone distributions. Environmental and public health authorities need this up-to-date information to alert people to health risks. For example, low ozone levels result in increased UV-B radiation, which is harmful and can cause cancers, cataracts and impact the human immune system. 'Dobson Units' indicate the level of ozone depletion (normal levels are around 280DU).

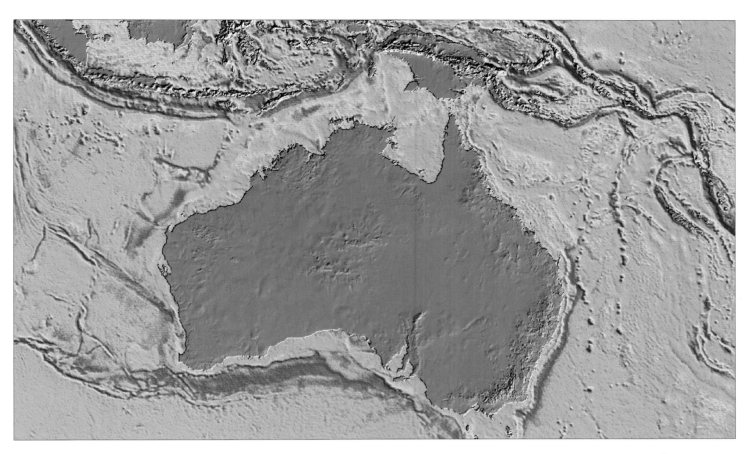

Gravitational fields

The strength of the Earth's gravitational field at its surface varies according to the ocean depth and the density of local rocks. This causes local variations in the sea level. Satellites orbiting in precisely determined orbits are able to measure the sea level to an accuracy of a few centimetres. These variations give us a better understanding of the geological structure of the sea floor. Information from these sensors can also be used to determine ocean wave heights, which relate to surface wind speed, and are therefore useful in meteorological forecasting. *(NPA)*

Weather monitoring

Geostationary and polar orbiting satellites monitor the Earth's cloud and atmospheric moisture movements, giving us an insight into the global workings of the atmosphere and permitting us to predict weather change.

Hurricane Katrina

Making landfall along the US Gulf coast on 29 August 2005, Hurricane Katrina became the most expensive natural disaster ever to strike the USA. Its path was tracked by images such as this. *(NASA/J. Schmaltz, MODIS Land Rapid Response Team)*

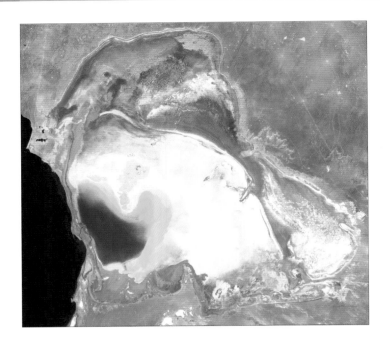

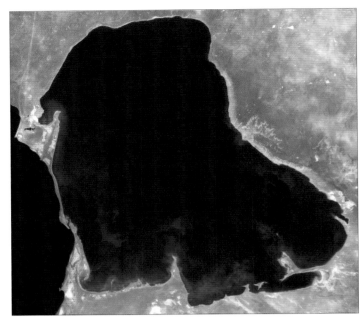

Kara-Bogaz-Gol, Turkmenistan

The Kara-Bogaz-Gol (*above, left and right*) is a large, shallow lagoon joined by a narrow, steep-sided strait to the Caspian Sea. Evaporation makes it one of the most saline bodies of water in the world. Believing the Caspian sea level was falling, the strait was dammed by the Soviet Union in 1980 with the intention of conserving the water to sustain the salt industry. However, by 1983 it had dried up completely (*above left*), leading to widespread wind-blown salt, soil poisoning and health problems downwind to the east. In 1992 the Turkmenistan government began to demolish the dam to re-establish the flow of water from the Caspian Sea (*above right*). Satellite imagery has helped to monitor and map the Kara-Bogaz-Gol as it has fluctuated in size. *(EROS)*

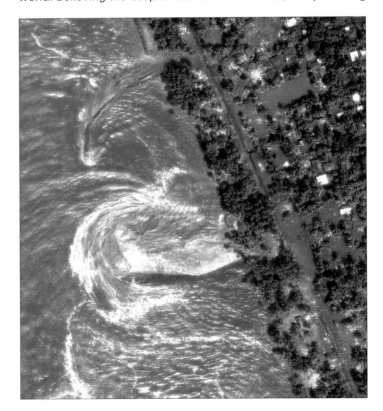

Southern Asia tsunami, Sri Lanka

The turbulent receding waters of the Southern Asia tsunami on 26 December 2004 can clearly be seen in this high-resolution imagery collected by the QuickBird satellite. The area shown here is the holiday resort of Kalutara on the west coast of Sri Lanka, to the south of Colombo. Such imagery enabled rescuers to assess the worst affected areas and direct the overstretched emergency services where most needed. *(DigitalGlobe)*

Lake Amadeus, Northern Territory, Australia

This saline lake system is an important wetland environment situated at the heart of one of the most arid areas in Australia. It supports a wide range of complex habitats and owes its existence to seepage from the central groundwater system. Changes in its extent in an otherwise remote site can be monitored using satellite imagery such as this Landsat ETM scene. *(EROS)*

New Orleans, Louisiana, USA
These two images show the area around the New Orleans Superdome before *(top)* and after *(below)* Hurricane Katrina struck in August 2005. In the lower image, damage to the dome roof can be clearly seen, and the darker areas surrounding the buildings are streets inundated by floodwaters. In the aftermath of the hurricane, satellite imagery played a key role in the assessment of the damage caused and the deployment of emergency services. *(DigitalGlobe)*

Larsen B ice shelf, Antarctica
Between January and March 2002, the 3,250 km² Larsen B ice shelf on the Antarctic Peninsula collapsed. The upper right-hand image shows its area in December 2001 before the collapse, while the lower image shows the area in December 2002 after the collapse. The 200 m thick ice sheet had been retreating before this date, but over 500 billion tonnes of ice collapsed in under a month. This was due to rising temperatures of 0.5°C per year in this part of Antarctica. Satellite imagery is the only way for scientists to monitor fragile environments, such as this, in inaccessible areas of the world.

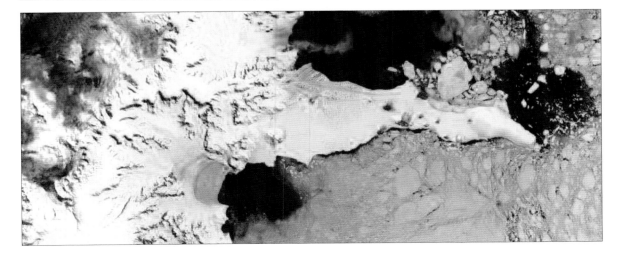

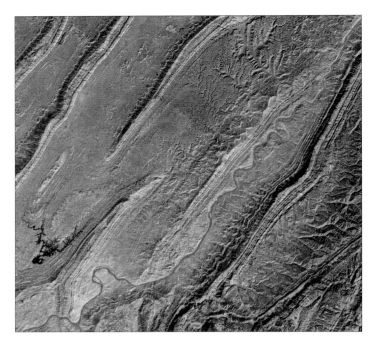

Sichuan Basin, China
The north-east/south-west trending ridges in this image are anticlinal folds developed in the Earth's crust as a result of plate collision and compression. Geologists map these folds and the lowlands between them formed by synclinal folds, as they are often the areas where oil or gas are found in commercial quantities. The river shown in this image is the Yangtze, near Chongqing. *(China RSGS)*

North Anatolian Fault, Turkey
The east–west trending valley running through the centre of this image is formed by the North Anatolian wrench fault. It is the result of Arabia colliding with southern Eurasia, forcing most of Turkey westwards towards Greece. The valley was created by the Kelkit river removing the loosened rock formed by the two tectonic plates grinding together. This active fault has also caused considerable damage further east in the Gulf of Izmit. *(EROS)*

Wadi Hadhramaut, Yemen
Yemen is extremely arid – however, in the past it was more humid and wet, enabling large river systems to carve out the deep and spectacular gorges and dried-out river beds (*wadis*) seen in this image. The erosion has revealed many contrasting rock types. The image has been processed to exaggerate this effect, producing many shades of red, pink and purple, which make geological mapping easier and more cost-effective. *(EROS)*

Zagros Mountains, Iran
These mountains were formed as Arabia collided with Southern Eurasia. The upper half of this colour-enhanced image shows an anticline that runs east–west. The dark grey features are called *diapirs*, which are bodies of viscous rock salt that are very buoyant and sometimes rise to the surface, spilling and spreading out like a glacier. The presence of salt in the region is important as it stops oil escaping to the surface. *(EROS)*

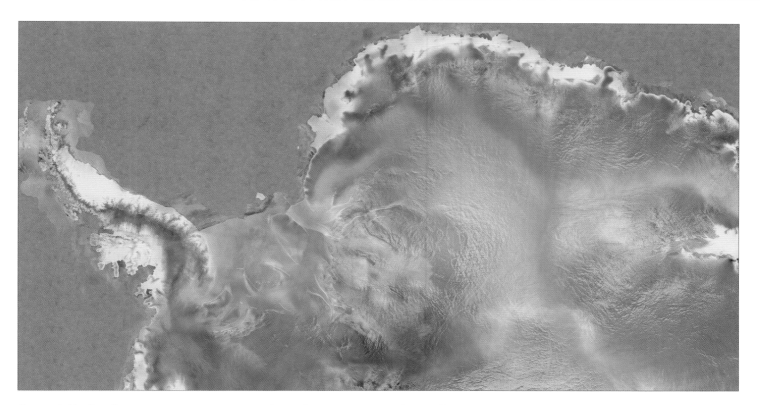

Antarctic Peninsula
Synthetic Aperture Radar (SAR) image brightness is dependent on surface texture. This image of part of Antarctica clearly shows the ice tongues projecting from the Wilkins and George VI Ice Shelves at the south-west end of the peninsula, as well as other coastal ice features. Images can be received, even during the winter 'night', and over a period of time form a valuable resource in our ability to monitor the recession of the ice. *(Radarsat)*

Montserrat, Caribbean Sea
SAR sensors send out a microwave signal and create an image from the radiation reflected back. The signal penetrates cloud cover and does not need any solar illumination. This image of Montserrat shows how the island can still be seen, despite clouds and the continuing eruption of the Soufrière volcano in the south. The delta visible in the sea to the east is being formed by lava flows pouring down the Tar River Valley. *(Radarsat)*

Las Vegas, Nevada, USA
Two satellite images viewing the same area of ground from different orbits can be used to compile a Digital Elevation Model (DEM) of the Earth's surface. A computer compares the images and calculates the ground surface elevation to a vertical precision of 8–15 m, preparing this for thousands of square kilometres in just a few minutes. Overlaying a colour satellite image on to a DEM produced the picture of Las Vegas shown here. *(NPA)*

London, United Kingdom
Lasers based on aircraft or satellites can be used to scan surface elevations to an accuracy of a few centimetres. This extract from a survey of the whole of London shows the City of London (from St Paul's Cathedral in the north-west to the Tower of London and Tower Bridge in the south-east. The very narrow and deep urban canyons and atriums in this area clearly demonstrate the advantages of airborne laser scanning (Lidar), which only requires a single line-of-sight to obtain precise measurements. A basic variant of this technology has been used for several years from satellites to acquire elevation profiles of the surface of Mars. Sensors capable of more detailed scanning are currently under development for Earth-orbiting satellites. *(Precision Terrain Surveys Ltd – www.precisionterrain.com)*

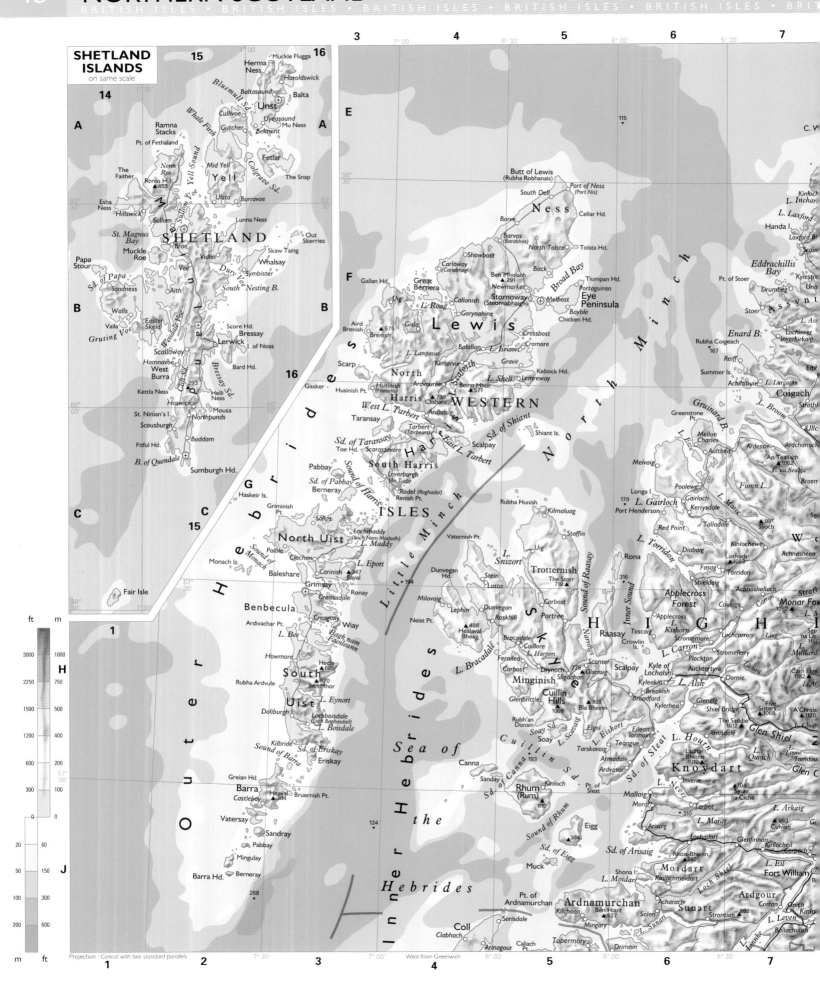

ORKNEY ISLANDS
on same scale

1 : 1 000 000

COPYRIGHT PHILIP'S

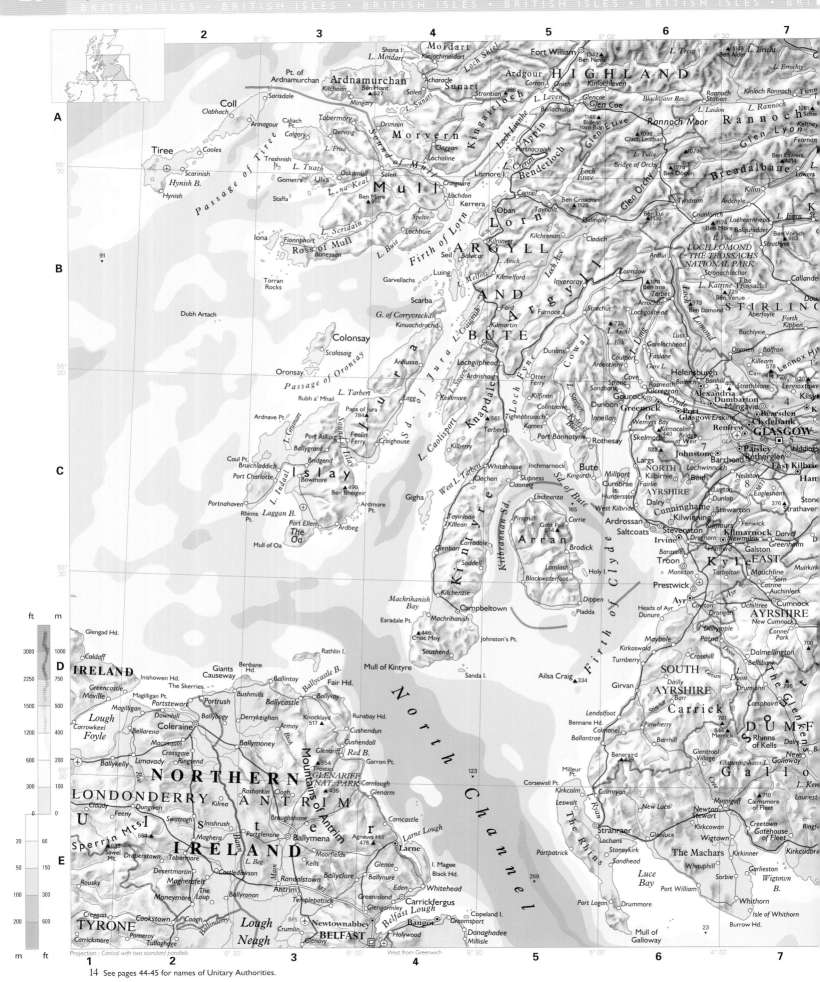

N O R T H

S E A

SCOTTISH
BORDERS

NORTHUMBERLAND
NATIONAL PARK

NORTHUMBERLAND

DUMFRIES
&GALLOWAY

CUMBRIA

DURHAM

TYNE
& WEAR

EDINBURGH

NEWCASTLE-UPON-TYNE

Teesside
Middlesbrough

SOUTH
LANARKSHIRE

COPYRIGHT PHILIP'S

1:1 000 000

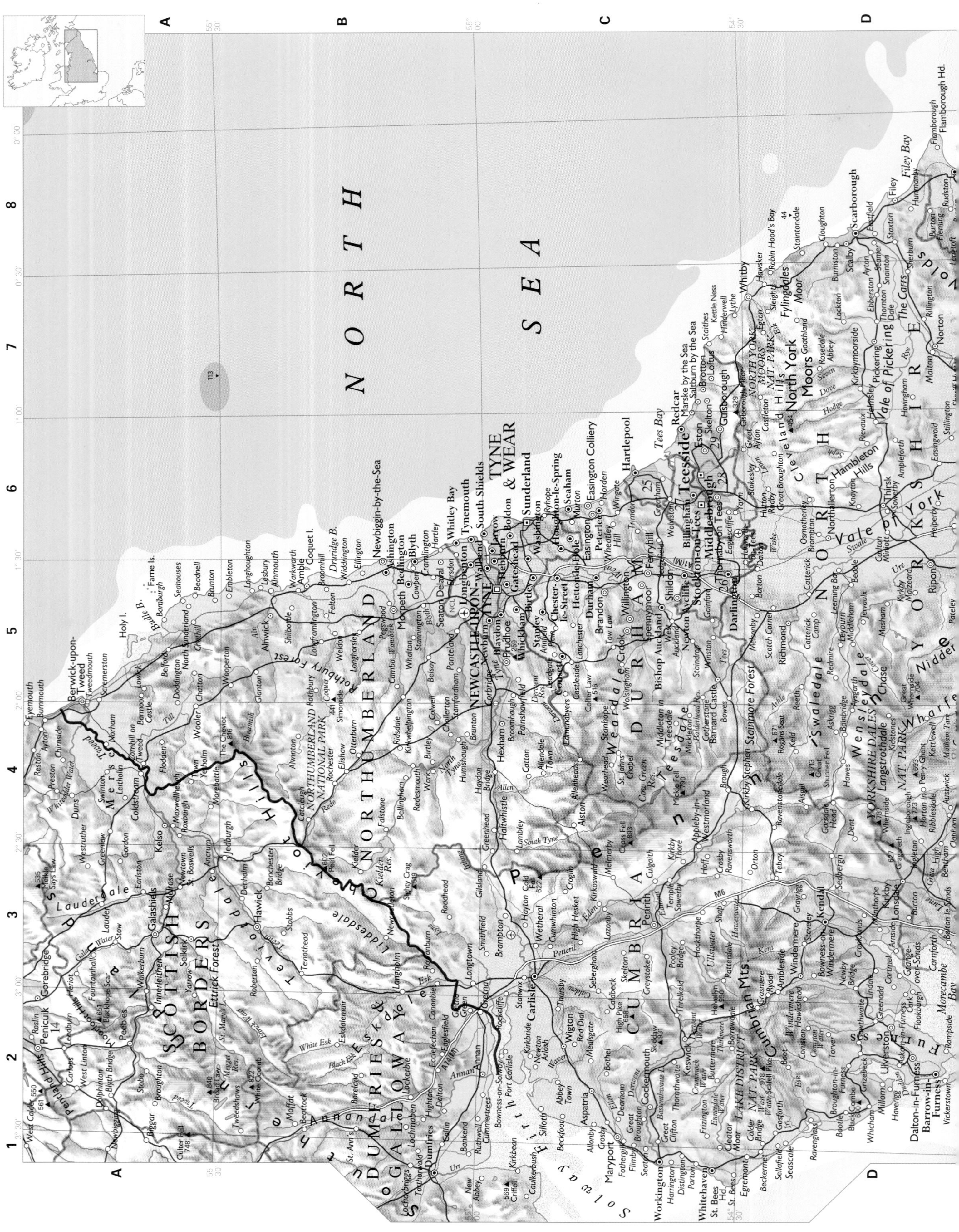

A · B · C · D

NORTH SEA

Major labels:

NORTHUMBERLAND
NORTHUMBERLAND NATIONAL PARK
Rothbury Forest
TYNE & WEAR
DURHAM
CUMBRIA
NORTH YORKSHIRE
NORTH YORK MOORS NAT. PARK
YORKSHIRE DALES NAT. PARK
LAKE DISTRICT NAT. PARK
SCOTTISH BORDERS
DUMFRIES & GALLOWAY
Ettrick Forest
Lauderdale
Liddesdale
Teesdale
Weardale
Swaledale
Wensleydale
Cheviot Hills
Cleveland Hills
Hambleton Hills
Vale of Pickering
Vale of York
Pennines
Cumbrian Mts.

Towns and places:

Berwick-upon-Tweed, Eyemouth, Burnmouth, Ayton, Coldstream, Kelso, Jedburgh, Hawick, Galashiels, Melrose, Selkirk, Peebles, Innerleithen, Biggar, Moffat, Lockerbie, Dumfries, Annan, Gretna, Carlisle, Longtown, Brampton, Wigton, Aspatria, Maryport, Workington, Cockermouth, Keswick, Penrith, Appleby-in-Westmorland, Kirkby Stephen, Kendal, Windermere, Bowness-on-Windermere, Ambleside, Ulverston, Barrow-in-Furness, Dalton-in-Furness, Whitehaven, St. Bees Hd., Egremont, Millom,

Alnwick, Amble, Warkworth, Morpeth, Ashington, Bedlington, Blyth, Newbiggin-by-the-Sea, Whitley Bay, Tynemouth, South Shields, NEWCASTLE UPON TYNE, Gateshead, Sunderland, Washington, Chester-le-Street, Durham, Consett, Hexham, Haltwhistle, Alston, Bishop Auckland, Crook, Spennymoor, Willington, Newton Aycliffe, Darlington, Stockton-on-Tees, Middlesbrough, Billingham, Hartlepool, Peterlee, Easington, Seaham, Redcar, Saltburn by the Sea, Marske by the Sea, Guisborough, Whitby, Robin Hood's Bay, Scarborough, Filey, Thirsk, Northallerton, Richmond, Leyburn, Bedale, Ripon, York, Malton, Pickering, Helmsley, Catterick

Tees Bay, Filey Bay, Flamborough Hd., Holy I., Farne Is., Coquet I.

R. Tweed, R. Tyne, North Tyne, South Tyne, R. Wear, R. Tees, R. Eden, R. Swale, R. Ure, R. Wharfe, R. Nidd, R. Esk

Projection : Conical with two standard parallels

36   See pages 44-45 for names of Unitary Authorities.

COPYRIGHT PHILIP'S

1:1 000 000

West from Greenwich

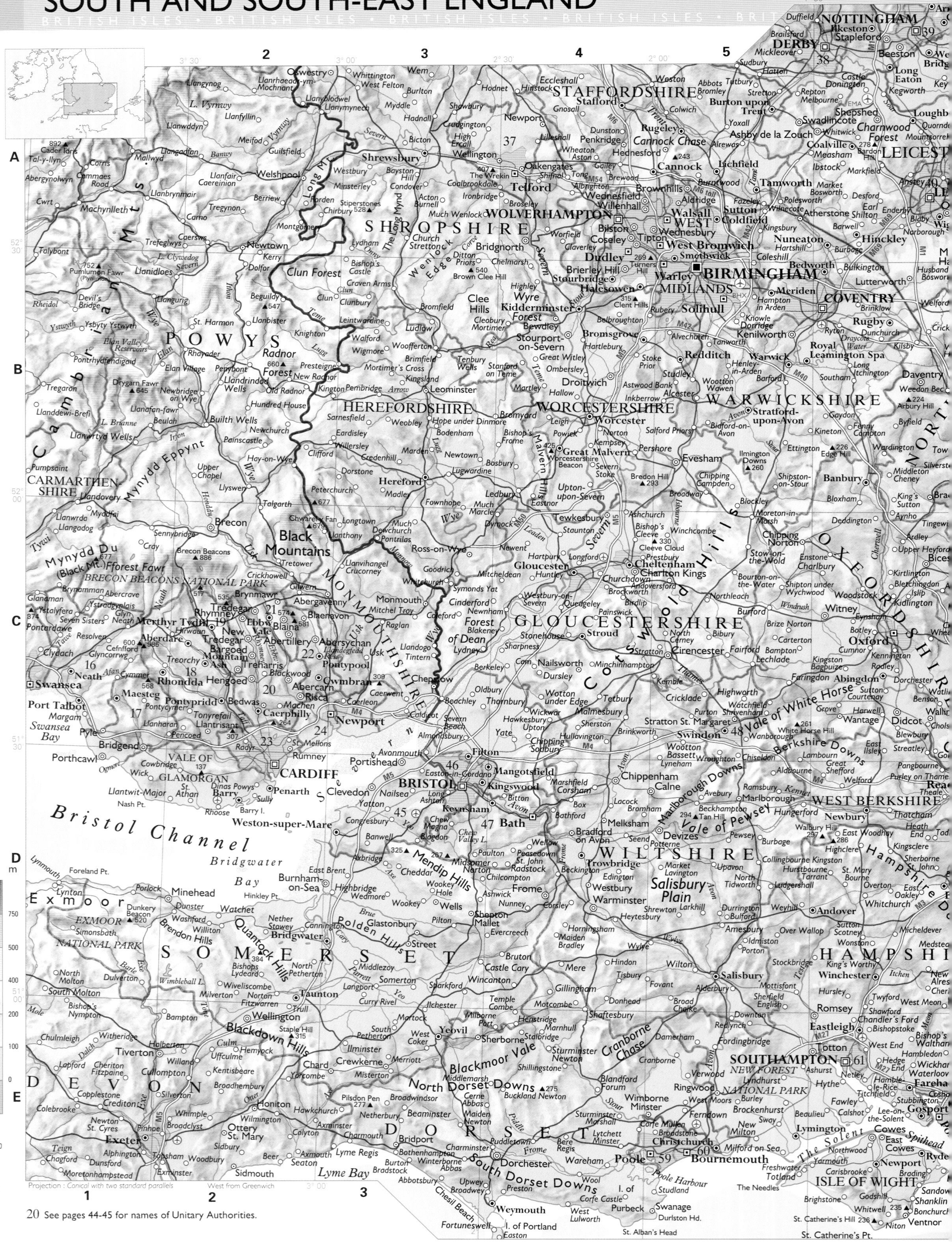

BRITISH ISLES • BRITISH ISLES • BRITISH ISLES • BRITISH ISLES • BRIT

6

West from Greenwich

ft m
2250 750
1500 500
1200 400
600 200
300 100
0
20 60
50 150
m ft

Projection : Conical with two standard parallels

20 See pages 44–45 for names of Unitary Authorities.

NOTTINGHAM
DERBY
LEICEST
COVENTRY
BIRMINGHAM
WEST MIDLANDS
WOLVERHAMPTON
STAFFORDSHIRE
SHROPSHIRE
Shrewsbury
Telford
POWYS
HEREFORDSHIRE
Hereford
WORCESTERSHIRE
Worcester
WARWICKSHIRE
Stratford-upon-Avon
GLOUCESTERSHIRE
Gloucester
Cheltenham
Cotswold Hills
OXFORDSHIRE
Oxford
MONMOUTHSHIRE
CARDIFF
Newport
BRISTOL
Bath
WILTSHIRE
Salisbury Plain
Salisbury
Swindon
Berkshire Downs
WEST BERKSHIRE
Newbury
Bristol Channel
Bridgwater Bay
Lyme Bay
EXMOOR NATIONAL PARK
Exmoor
SOMERSET
Taunton
Mendip Hills
DEVON
Exeter
DORSET
Dorchester
Weymouth
I. of Portland
Poole
BOURNEMOUTH
SOUTHAMPTON
HAMPSHIRE
Winchester
Eastleigh
NEW FOREST NATIONAL PARK
ISLE OF WIGHT
Newport
The Solent
CARMARTHEN SHIRE
Swansea
Port Talbot
Bridgend
VALE OF GLAMORGAN
Cardiff
Weston-super-Mare
Brecon Beacons National Park
Black Mountains
Abergavenny
Merthyr Tydfil
Blackdown Hills
Quantock Hills
Bridgwater
Glastonbury
Wells
Yeovil
Blackmoor Vale
North Dorset Downs
South Dorset Downs
Chesil Beach
Poole Harbour
Purbeck
Swanage

LINCOLNSHIRE

NORFOLK

NAT. PARK

BROADS

CAMBRIDGESHIRE

The Fens

Breckland

SUFFOLK

BEDFORDSHIRE

HERTFORDSHIRE

ESSEX

GREATER LONDON

LONDON

SURREY

WEST SUSSEX

EAST SUSSEX

KENT

North Downs

South Downs

The Weald

Thames Estuary

Strait of Dover

FRANCE

The Wash

East from Greenwich

1:1 000 000

0 5 10 20 30 40 50 km

5 0 5 10 15 20 25 30 35 miles

COPYRIGHT PHILIP'S

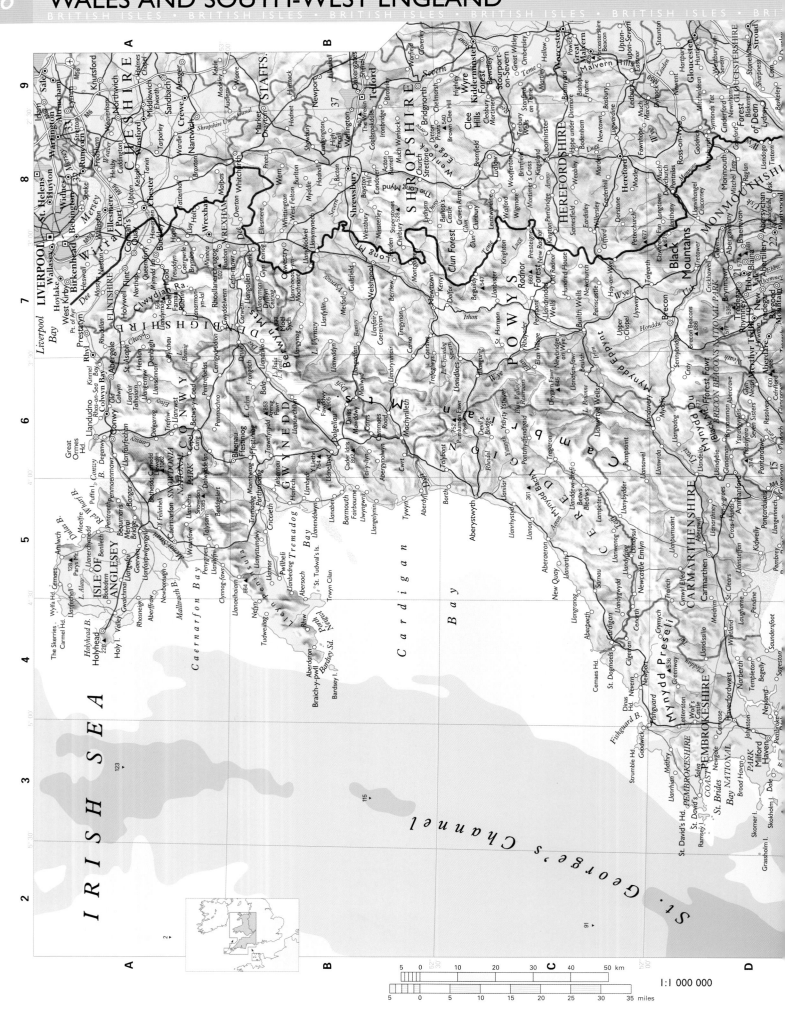

1:1 000 000

IS. OF SCILLY
on same scale

Isles of Scilly
Tresco   St. Martin's
Bryher   Hugh St. Mary's
Broad Sd. Town
St. Mary's Sd.
St. Agnes

CHANNEL
ISLANDS
on same scale

FRANCE

Passage de la Déroute

CHANNEL ISLANDS

Guernsey

Jersey

Alderney
St. Anne
C. de la Hague

St. Sampson
St. Peter Port
St. Martin
Torteval
Sark

Grosnez Pt.
St. Ouen's Bay
St. Brelade
Trinity   Rozel
St. Martin
St. Peter
St. Helier
Gorey
la Rocque Pt.

COPYRIGHT PHILIPS

Projection : Conical with two standard parallels

57 See pages 44–45 for names of Unitary Authorities.

West from Greenwich

SOMERSET
DORSET
DEVON
CORNWALL

Bristol Channel

Barnstaple or Bideford Bay

Exmoor
NATIONAL PARK

Dartmoor
DARTMOOR NATIONAL PARK

PLYMOUTH
TORBAY

7   7° 00'   **8**   6° 30'   **9**   **10**   5° 30'   **11**   **12**   **13**

A

Inishtrahull

ARGYLL
AND BUTE
Machrihanish Bay
Machrihanish
Earadale Pt.
Kintyre
446 Cnoc Moy
Southend
Johnston's Pt.
Sanda I.
Mull of Kintyre

Arran
Dippen
Pladda
Campbeltown

Heads of Ayr
Dunure
Ayr
Coylton
Ochiltree
Cumnock
Drongan
EAST
New Cumnock
Connel Park
700

Firth of Clyde

Ailsa Craig 334

Maybole
Dalrymple
Bellsbank
AYRSHIRE
Dalmellington

Turnberry
Kirkoswald
Crosshill
SOUTH
Dailly
Doon
Drumjohn
L. Doon

Girvan
AYRSHIRE
Barr
781
Carsphairn
796

Glengad Hd.
Culdaff
Gleneely
Inishowen Hd.
Giants Causeway
Benbane Hd.
The Skerries.
Ballintoy
Ballycastle B.
Fair Hd.
ven
Greencastle
Moville
Magilligan Pt.
Portstewart
Bushmills
Ballycastle
Ballyvoy
Runabay Hd.

Lendalfoot
Carrick
Stinchar
844 Merrick
710

Magilligan
Downhill
Portrush
Ballybogy
Rathlin I.
Knocklayd 517
Cushendun

Bennane Hd.
Pinwherry
Calmonel
Rhinns
of Kells
Glentrool Village
Clappershaws L.
New Galloway
Dalry

Lough Foyle
Carrowkeel
Bellarena
Macosquin
Coleraine
Derrykeighan
Armoy
Cushendall
Red B.

Ballantrae
Barrhill

North Channel

Beneraird 439

Eglinton
Ballykelly
Limavady
Crossgare
Ringsend
Ballymoney
Finvoy
Dunloy
Glenariff
Garron Pt.

Milleur Pt.
Corsewall Pt.

ahoe
Roe
Garvagh
Rasharkin
Clogh
Newtown Crommelin
554
Trostan
GLENARIFF NAT. PARK
436
Carnlough
Glenarm

Kirkcolm
Leswalt
L. Ryan

DUMFRIES &
GALLOWAY

ONDONDERRY
Kilrea
ANTRIM
Broughshane

123

Stranraer
Lochans
New Luce
Glenluce
Newton Stewart
Kirkcowan
Wigtown
Minnigaff
Creetown
Gatehouse of Fleet
Cairnsmore of Fleet

B

erin Mts.
683
Sawel Mt. 554
Draperstown
Tobermore
Bellaghy
Maghera
Inishrush
Ballymena
Agnews Hill 476
Larne

The Rhins
Portpatrick

Stoneykirk
Sandhead
The Machars
Wigtown B.
Kirkinner
Garlieston
Sorbie

nbridge
Rousky
Feeny
Dungiven
Swatragh
Moneymore
Ahoghill
Moorfields
Kells
Glenoe
I. Magee
Black Hd.
Whitehead
Lame Lough

269

Port Logan
Drummore
Luce Bay
Port William
Whauphill
Isle of Whithorn
Whithorn
Burrow Hd.

agh
Carrickmore
Cookstown
Coagh
Ballyronan
Randalstown
Antrim
Ballyclare
Ballynure
Eden
Greenisland
Carrickfergus

Mull of Galloway

23

inore
Sixmilecross
Pomeroy
Tullaghoge
Stewartstown
The Loup
Templepatrick
Dunmurry
Glengormley
Belfast Lough
Groomsport
Copeland I.
Donaghadee

HERN IRELAND
Lough Neagh
ter
BFS
Newtownabbey
Legoniel
BELFAST
Holywood
Dundonald
Bangor
Newtownards
Millisle

Pt. of Ayre

aghey
ONE
Donaghmore
Granville
Coalisland
Dungannon
Aghalee
Lisburn
Lagan
Drumbeg
Comber
Greyabbey
Ballywalter

Andreas
Bride
Sulby
Ramsey B.
Ramsey
Maughold

C

ugher
Ballygawley
Moy
Charlemont
Portadown
M1
Craigavon
Lurgan
Moira
Hillsborough
Carryduff
Saintfield
Killyleagh
Portavogie

Ballaugh
Kirk Michael
Snaefell 620
Maughold Hd.

etown
372
Emyvale
383
Slieve Beagh
Tedavnet
Aughnacloy
Caledon
Benburb
Armagh
Tandragee
Gilford
Banbridge
Dromore
Ballynahinch
Crossgar
Portaferry
Strangford
Ballyquintin Pt.
Killard Pt.

ISLE OF MAN
Peel
Glenmaye
483
South Barrule
St. John's
Foxdale
Laxey
Onchan
Douglas

Glaslough
Middletown
Keady
Markethill
ARMAGH
Loughbrickland
Katesbridge
DOWN
Clough
Downpatrick

MONAGHAN
Monaghan
Smithborough
Mountnorris
Rathfriland
Castlewellan
Ardglass

jes
Newbliss
Ballybay
Bessbrook
Newtown Hamilton
Poyntz Pass
Ballyroney
Kilcoo
Dundrum
Killough
17
St. John's Pt.

Bradda Hd.
Port Erin
Colby
Ballasalla
Castletown
Langness

125

Kilcross
577
Slieve Gullion
Cullyhanna
Newry
Mayobridge
Hilltown
Mourne Mts.
852
Slieve Donard
Newcastle
Dundrum B.

Calf of Man
Port St. Mary

D

AN
Drum
Rockcorry
Cootehill
Castleblaney
Crossmaglen
Meigh
Forkill
744
Annalong

Shercock
Carrickmacross
Cullaville
Kilcurry
Slieve Foye 590
Rostrevor
Lisnacree
Kilkeel

Stradone
Bailieborough
Louth
Warrenpoint
Greenore
Greencastle
Cranfield Pt.

Carrickford Lough

164

45

IRISH SEA

Virginia
L. Ramor
Mullagh
Kingscourt
Castletown
Dundalk
(Dún Dealgan)
Ballagan Pt.
Dromiskin
Dundalk Bay

castle
278
Carnbane East
Ceanannus Mor
(Kells)
Rathkenny
Castlebellingham
Annagassan
Dunany Pt.

Crossakiel
Nobber
Drumconrath
LOUTH
Clogherhead
Clogher Hd.
Termonfeckin

AND
MEATH
An Uaimh
(Navan)
Slane
Drogheda
(Droichead Atha)
Mornington
Laytown
Julianstown

Lene
aragh
Delvin
Athboy
Trim
Boyne
M1
Duleek
Ardcath
Balbriggan
Skerries

TH
Killucan
Ballivor
Dunshaughlin
Ratoath
Ballyboghil
Rush
Lambay I.

E

Downs
Royal Canal
Rathmolyon
Summerhill
Ashbourne
Dunboyne
Swords
Cloghran
Donabate
Malahide
Portmarnock

The Skerries
Carmel Hd.
Wylfa Hd.
Cemaes
Amlwch
Llanfechell
Llanerchymedd

Kinnegad
Clonard
Moyvally
Johnstown Bridge
Innfield
Kilcock
Maynooth
Leixlip
Lucan
Clonee
Finglas
Glasnevin
DUB
DUBLIN
Howth
Howth Hd.

Anglesey
Holyhead B.
Holyhead
L. Alaw
ISLE OF
ANGLESEY
220
Bodedern
128
Parys Mt.

Edenderry
Carbury
Donadea
Celbridge
Clondalkin
Dundrum
DUBLIN
(Baile Atha Cliath)
Blackrock
Dun Laoghaire (Dúnleary)

Holy I.
Valley
Gwalchmai
Llangefni

tbridge
Killane
Allenwood
Clane
Rathcoole
Tallaght

COPYRIGHT PHILIP'S

7   7° 00'   **8**   6° 30'   **9**   **10**   **11**   **12**   4° 30'   **13**

5   0   10   20   30   40   50 km

5   0   5   10   15   20   25   30   35 miles

1:1 000 000

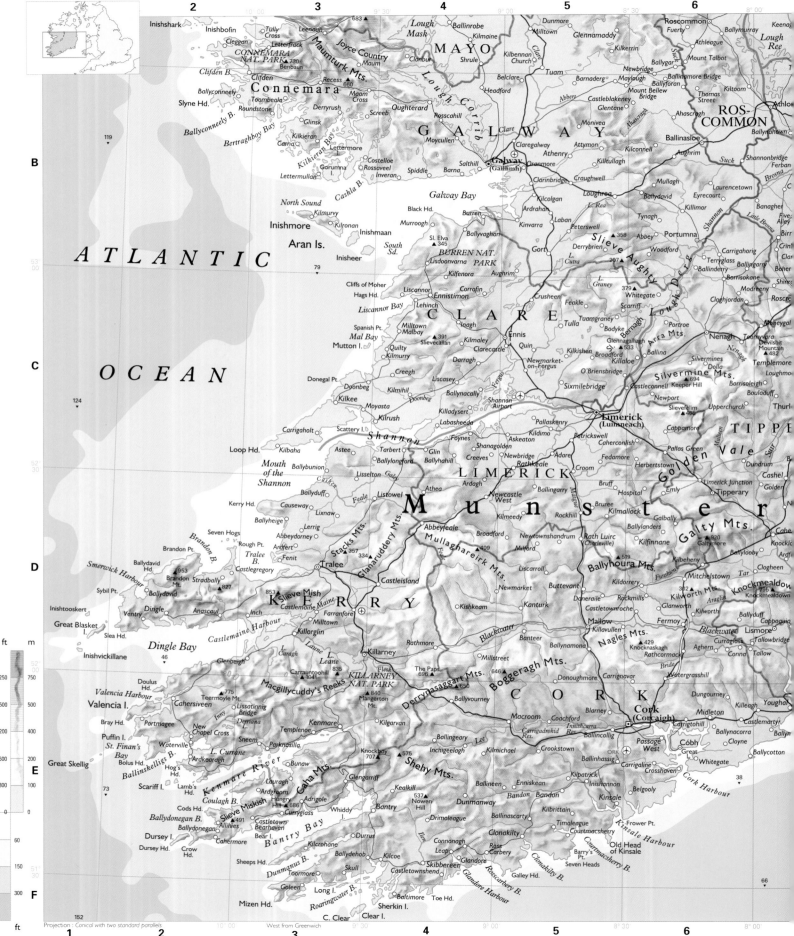

1:1 000 000

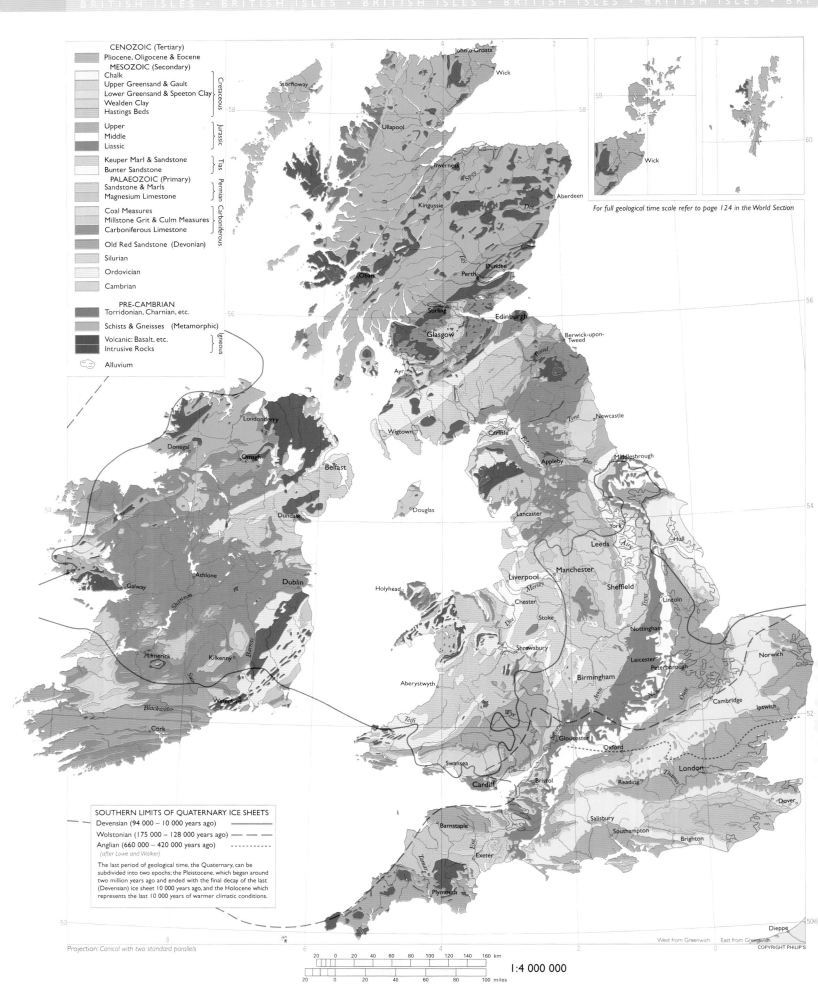

CENOZOIC (Tertiary)
Pliocene, Oligocene & Eocene

MESOZOIC (Secondary)
Chalk — Cretaceous
Upper Greensand & Gault
Lower Greensand & Speeton Clay
Wealden Clay
Hastings Beds

Upper — Jurassic
Middle
Liassic

Keuper Marl & Sandstone — Trias
Bunter Sandstone

PALAEOZOIC (Primary)
Sandstone & Marls — Permian
Magnesium Limestone

Coal Measures — Carboniferous
Millstone Grit & Culm Measures
Carboniferous Limestone

Old Red Sandstone (Devonian)
Silurian
Ordovician
Cambrian

PRE-CAMBRIAN
Torridonian, Charnian, etc.
Schists & Gneisses (Metamorphic)
Volcanic: Basalt, etc. — Igneous
Intrusive Rocks

Alluvium

For full geological time scale refer to page 124 in the World Section

SOUTHERN LIMITS OF QUATERNARY ICE SHEETS
Devensian (94 000 – 10 000 years ago) ———
Wolstonian (175 000 – 128 000 years ago) — — —
Anglian (660 000 – 420 000 years ago) ·········
(after Lowe and Walker)

The last period of geological time, the Quaternary, can be
subdivided into two epochs; the Pleistocene, which began around
two million years ago and ended with the final decay of the last
(Devensian) ice sheet 10 000 years ago, and the Holocene which
represents the last 10 000 years of warmer climatic conditions.

Projection: Conical with two standard parallels

20 0 20 40 60 80 100 120 140 160 km
20 0 20 40 60 80 100 miles

1:4 000 000

West from Greenwich | East from Greenwich
COPYRIGHT PHILIP'S

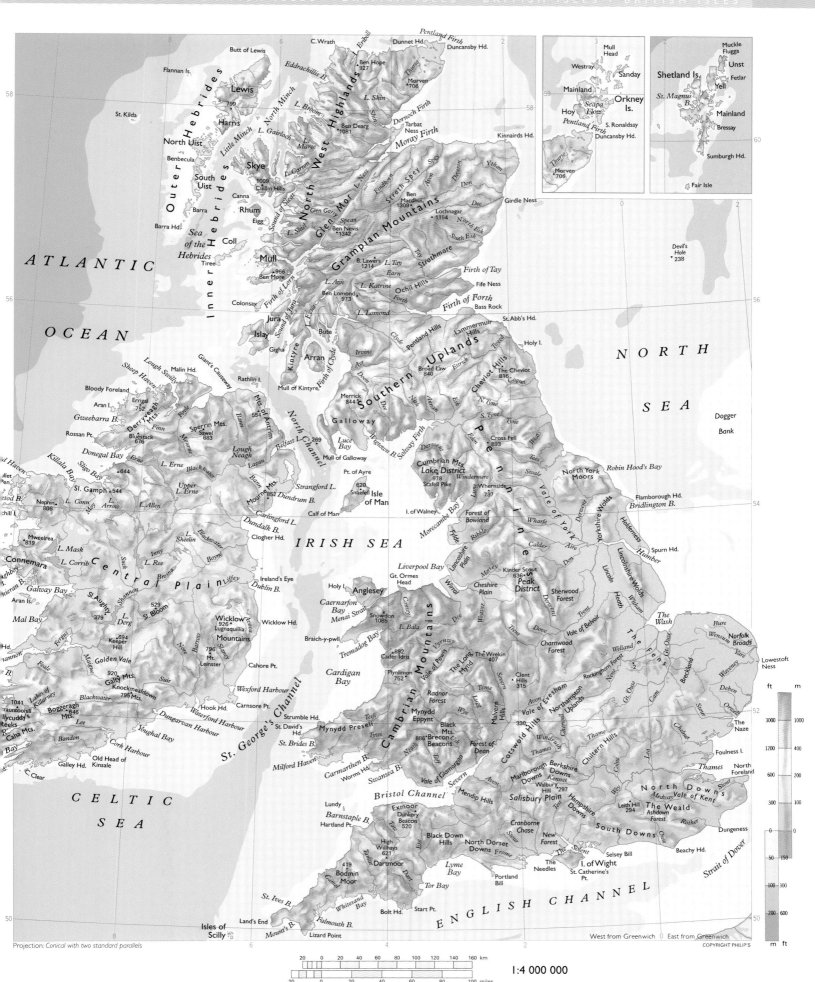

Projection: Conical with two standard parallels

West from Greenwich   0   East from Greenwich

COPYRIGHT PHILIP'S

20 0   20   40   60   80 100 120 140 160 km
20 0   20   40   60   80 100 miles

1:4 000 000

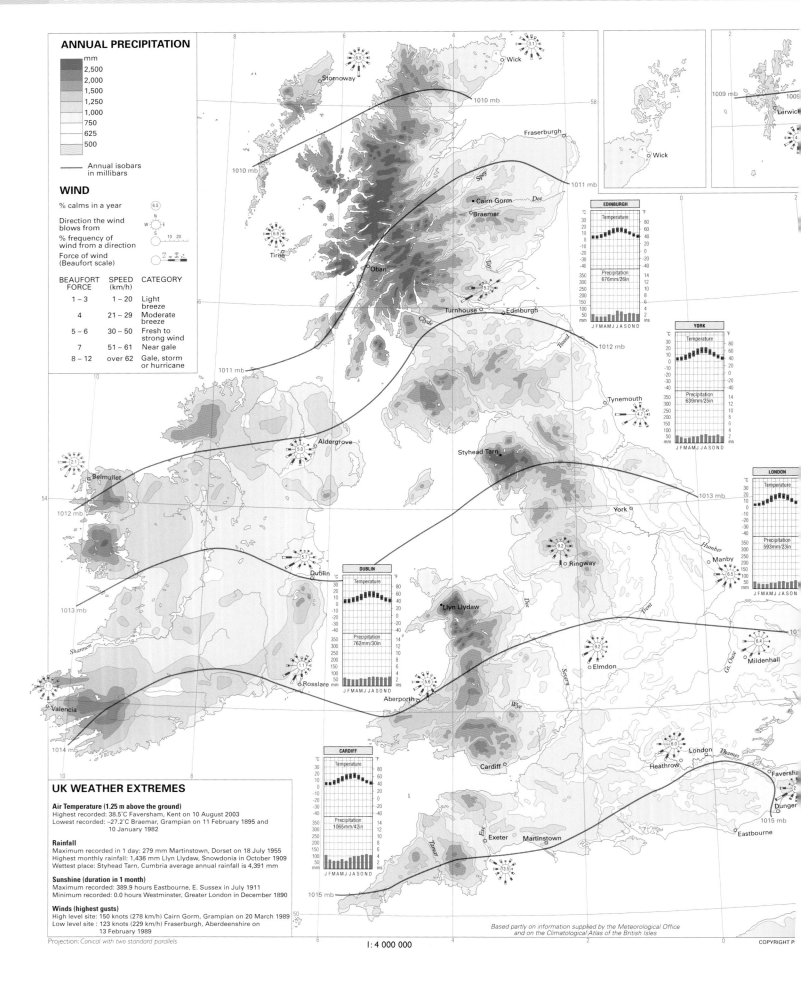

ANNUAL PRECIPITATION

mm
- 2,500
- 2,000
- 1,500
- 1,250
- 1,000
- 750
- 625
- 500

—— Annual isobars
in millibars

WIND

% calms in a year

Direction the wind
blows from

% frequency of
wind from a direction

Force of wind
(Beaufort scale)

BEAUFORT FORCE	SPEED (km/h)	CATEGORY
1 – 3	1 – 20	Light breeze
4	21 – 29	Moderate breeze
5 – 6	30 – 50	Fresh to strong wind
7	51 – 61	Near gale
8 – 12	over 62	Gale, storm or hurricane

UK WEATHER EXTREMES

Air Temperature (1.25 m above the ground)
Highest recorded: 38.5°C Faversham, Kent on 10 August 2003
Lowest recorded: –27.2°C Braemar, Grampian on 11 February 1895 and
10 January 1982

Rainfall
Maximum recorded in 1 day: 279 mm Martinstown, Dorset on 18 July 1955
Highest monthly rainfall: 1,436 mm Llyn Llydaw, Snowdonia in October 1909
Wettest place: Styhead Tarn, Cumbria average annual rainfall is 4,391 mm

Sunshine (duration in 1 month)
Maximum recorded: 389.9 hours Eastbourne, E. Sussex in July 1911
Minimum recorded: 0.0 hours Westminster, Greater London in December 1890

Winds (highest gusts)
High level site: 150 knots (278 km/h) Cairn Gorm, Grampian on 20 March 1989
Low level site: 123 knots (229 km/h) Fraserburgh, Aberdeenshire on
13 February 1989

Projection: Conical with two standard parallels

1 : 4 000 000

Based partly on information supplied by the Meteorological Office
and on the Climatological Atlas of the British Isles

COPYRIGHT P.

CLIMATE GRAPHS

Average monthly minimum temperature in degrees Celsius

Average monthly maximum temperature in degrees Celsius

Height of meteorological station above sea level in metres

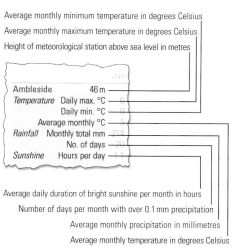

Ambleside	46 m	Jan
Temperature	Daily max. °C	6
	Daily min. °C	0
	Average monthly °C	3
Rainfall	Monthly total mm	214
	No. of days	20
Sunshine	Hours per day	1.1

Average daily duration of bright sunshine per month in hours

Number of days per month with over 0.1 mm precipitation

Average monthly precipitation in millimetres

Average monthly temperature in degrees Celsius

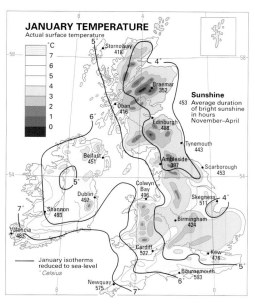

JANUARY TEMPERATURE
Actual surface temperature

°C
7
6
5
4
3
2
1
0

Sunshine
453 Average duration of bright sunshine in hours November–April

January isotherms reduced to sea-level
° Celsius

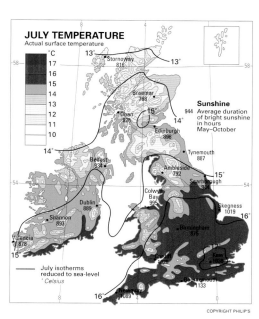

JULY TEMPERATURE
Actual surface temperature

°C
17
16
15
14
13
12
11
10

Sunshine
944 Average duration of bright sunshine in hours May–October

July isotherms reduced to sea-level
° Celsius

COPYRIGHT PHILIP'S

Ambleside 46 m		Jan	Feb	Mar	Apr	May	June	July	Aug	Sept	Oct	Nov	Dec	Year
Temperature	Daily max. °C	6	7	9	12	16	19	20	19	17	13	9	7	13
	Daily min. °C	0	0	2	4	6	9	11	11	9	6	3	1	5
	Average monthly °C	3	4	6	8	11	14	15	15	13	10	6	4	9
Rainfall	Monthly total mm	214	146	112	101	90	111	134	139	184	196	209	215	1,851
	No. of days	20	17	15	15	14	15	18	17	18	19	19	21	208
Sunshine	Hours per day	1.1	2	3.2	4.5	6	5.7	4.5	4.2	3.3	2.2	1.4	1	3.3

Belfast 4 m		Jan	Feb	Mar	Apr	May	June	July	Aug	Sept	Oct	Nov	Dec	Year
Temperature	Daily max. °C	6	7	9	12	15	18	18	18	16	13	9	7	12
	Daily min. °C	2	2	3	4	6	9	11	11	9	7	4	3	6
	Average monthly °C	4	4	6	8	11	13	15	15	13	10	7	5	9
Rainfall	Monthly total mm	80	52	50	48	52	68	94	77	80	83	72	90	845
	No. of days	20	17	16	16	15	16	19	17	18	19	19	21	213
Sunshine	Hours per day	1.5	2.3	3.4	5	6.3	6	4.4	4.4	3.6	2.6	1.8	1.1	3.5

Birkenhead 60 m		Jan	Feb	Mar	Apr	May	June	July	Aug	Sept	Oct	Nov	Dec	Year
Temperature	Daily max. °C	6	6	9	11	15	17	19	19	16	13	9	7	12
	Daily min. °C	2	2	3	5	8	11	13	13	11	8	5	3	7
	Average monthly °C	4	4	6	8	11	14	16	16	14	10	7	5	10
Rainfall	Monthly total mm	64	46	40	41	55	55	67	80	66	71	76	65	726
	No. of days	18	13	13	13	13	13	15	15	15	17	17	19	181
Sunshine	Hours per day	1.6	2.4	3.5	5.3	6.3	6.7	5.7	5.4	4.2	2.9	1.8	1.3	3.9

Birmingham 163 m		Jan	Feb	Mar	Apr	May	June	July	Aug	Sept	Oct	Nov	Dec	Year
Temperature	Daily max. °C	5	6	9	12	16	19	20	20	17	13	9	6	13
	Daily min. °C	2	2	3	5	7	10	12	12	10	7	5	3	7
	Average monthly °C	3	4	6	8	11	15	16	16	14	10	7	5	10
Rainfall	Monthly total mm	74	54	50	53	64	50	69	69	61	69	84	67	764
	No. of days	17	15	13	13	14	13	15	14	14	15	17	18	178
Sunshine	Hours per day	1.4	2.1	3.2	4.6	5.4	6	5.4	5.1	3.9	2.8	1.6	1.2	3.6

Cambridge 12 m		Jan	Feb	Mar	Apr	May	June	July	Aug	Sept	Oct	Nov	Dec	Year
Temperature	Daily max. °C	6	7	11	14	17	21	22	22	19	15	10	7	14
	Daily min. °C	1	1	2	4	7	10	12	12	10	6	4	2	6
	Average monthly °C	3	4	6	9	12	15	17	17	14	10	7	5	10
Rainfall	Monthly total mm	49	35	36	37	45	45	58	55	51	51	54	41	558
	No. of days	15	13	10	11	11	11	12	12	11	13	14	14	147
Sunshine	Hours per day	1.7	2.5	3.8	5.1	6.2	6.7	6	5.7	4.6	3.4	1.9	1.4	4.1

Craibstone 91 m		Jan	Feb	Mar	Apr	May	June	July	Aug	Sept	Oct	Nov	Dec	Year
Temperature	Daily max. °C	5	6	8	10	13	16	18	17	15	12	8	6	11
	Daily min. °C	0	0	2	3	5	8	10	10	8	6	3	1	5
	Average monthly °C	3	3	5	7	9	12	14	13	12	9	6	4	8
Rainfall	Monthly total mm	78	55	53	51	63	54	95	75	67	92	93	80	856
	No. of days	19	16	15	15	14	14	18	15	16	18	19	18	197
Sunshine	Hours per day	1.8	2.9	3.5	4.9	5.9	6.1	5.1	4.8	4.3	3..1	2	1.5	3.8

Durham 102 m		Jan	Feb	Mar	Apr	May	June	July	Aug	Sept	Oct	Nov	Dec	Year
Temperature	Daily max. °C	6	6	9	12	15	18	20	19	17	13	9	7	13
	Daily min. °C	0	0	1	3	6	9	11	10	9	6	3	2	5
	Average monthly °C	3	3	5	7	10	13	15	15	13	9	6	4	8
Rainfall	Monthly total mm	59	51	38	38	51	49	61	67	60	63	66	55	658
	No. of days	17	15	14	13	13	14	15	14	14	16	17	17	179
Sunshine	Hours per day	1.7	2.5	3.3	4.6	5.4	6	5.1	4.8	4.1	3	1.9	1.4	3.6

Lerwick 82 m		Jan	Feb	Mar	Apr	May	June	July	Aug	Sept	Oct	Nov	Dec	Year
Temperature	Daily max. °C	5	5	6	8	11	13	14	14	13	10	8	6	9
	Daily min. °C	1	1	2	3	5	7	10	10	8	6	4	3	5
	Average monthly °C	3	3	4	5	8	10	12	12	11	8	6	4	7
Rainfall	Monthly total mm	109	87	69	68	52	55	72	71	87	104	111	118	1,003
	No. of days	25	22	20	21	15	15	17	17	19	23	24	25	243
Sunshine	Hours per day	0.8	1.8	2.9	4.4	5.3	5.3	4	3.8	3.5	2.2	2.2	0.5	3

Plymouth 27 m		Jan	Feb	Mar	Apr	May	June	July	Aug	Sept	Oct	Nov	Dec	Year
Temperature	Daily max. °C	8	8	10	12	15	18	19	19	18	15	11	9	14
	Daily min. °C	4	4	5	6	8	11	13	13	12	9	7	5	8
	Average monthly °C	6	6	7	9	12	15	16	16	15	12	9	7	11
Rainfall	Monthly total mm	99	74	69	53	63	53	70	77	78	91	113	110	950
	No. of days	19	15	14	12	12	12	14	14	15	16	17	18	178
Sunshine	Hours per day	1.9	2.9	4.3	6.1	7.1	7.4	6.4	6.4	5.1	3.7	2.2	1.7	4.6

Renfrew 6 m		Jan	Feb	Mar	Apr	May	June	July	Aug	Sept	Oct	Nov	Dec	Year
Temperature	Daily max. °C	5	7	9	12	15	18	19	19	16	13	9	7	12
	Daily min. °C	1	1	2	4	6	9	11	11	9	6	4	2	6
	Average monthly °C	3	4	6	8	11	14	15	15	13	9	7	4	9
Rainfall	Monthly total mm	111	85	69	67	63	70	97	93	102	119	106	127	1,109
	No. of days	19	16	15	15	14	15	17	17	18	18	18	20	201
Sunshine	Hours per day	1.1	2.1	2.9	4.7	6	6.1	5.1	4.4	3.7	2.3	1.4	0.8	3.4

St Mary's 50 m		Jan	Feb	Mar	Apr	May	June	July	Aug	Sept	Oct	Nov	Dec	Year
Temperature	Daily max. °C	9	9	11	12	14	17	19	19	18	15	12	10	14
	Daily min. °C	6	6	7	7	9	12	13	14	13	11	9	7	9
	Average monthly °C	8	7	9	10	12	14	16	16	15	13	10	9	12
Rainfall	Monthly total mm	91	71	69	46	56	49	61	64	67	80	96	94	844
	No. of days	22	17	16	13	14	14	16	15	16	17	19	21	200
Sunshine	Hours per day	2	2.9	4.2	6.4	7.6	7.6	6.7	6.7	5.2	3.9	2.5	1.8	4.8

Southampton 20 m		Jan	Feb	Mar	Apr	May	June	July	Aug	Sept	Oct	Nov	Dec	Year
Temperature	Daily max. °C	7	8	11	14	17	20	22	22	19	15	11	8	15
	Daily min. °C	2	2	3	5	8	11	13	13	11	7	5	3	7
	Average monthly °C	5	5	7	10	13	16	17	17	15	11	8	6	11
Rainfall	Monthly total mm	83	56	52	45	56	49	60	69	70	86	94	84	804
	No. of days	17	13	13	12	12	12	13	13	14	14	16	17	166
Sunshine	Hours per day	1.8	2.6	4	5.7	6.7	7.2	6.5	6.4	4.9	3.6	2.2	1.6	4.5

Tiree 9 m		Jan	Feb	Mar	Apr	May	June	July	Aug	Sept	Oct	Nov	Dec	Year
Temperature	Daily Max. °C	7	7	9	10	13	15	16	16	15	12	9	8	12
	Daily Min. °C	4	3	4	5	7	10	11	11	10	8	6	5	7
	Average Monthly °C	5	5	6	8	10	12	14	14	13	10	8	6	9
Rainfall	Monthly Total mm	117	77	67	64	55	70	91	90	118	129	122	128	1,128
	No. of Days	23	19	17	17	15	16	20	18	20	23	22	24	234
Sunshine	Hours per Day	1.3	2.6	3.7	5.7	7.5	6.8	5.2	5.3	4.2	2.6	1.6	0.9	4

Valencia 9 m		Jan	Feb	Mar	Apr	May	June	July	Aug	Sept	Oct	Nov	Dec	Year
Temperature	Daily max. °C	9	9	11	13	15	17	18	18	17	14	12	10	14
	Daily min. °C	5	4	5	6	8	11	12	13	11	9	7	6	8
	Average monthly °C	7	7	8	9	11	14	15	15	14	12	9	9	11
Rainfall	Monthly total mm	165	107	103	75	86	81	107	95	122	140	151	168	1,400
	No. of days	20	15	14	13	13	13	15	15	16	17	18	21	190
Sunshine	Hours per day	1.6	2.5	3.5	5.2	6.5	5.9	4.7	4.9	3.8	2.8	2	1.3	3.7

WATER SUPPLY

Regions of reliably high rainfall (more than 1,250 mm in at least 70% of the years)

③ Major reservoirs (capacity over 20 million cubic metres, see list opposite for details)

→ Existing inter-regional transfers of water (by pipeline and river)

→ Proposed inter-regional transfers of water (by pipeline and river)

□ Proposed estuary storage site

▽ Proposed groundwater storage site

Principal sources of groundwater (porous and jointed aquifers)

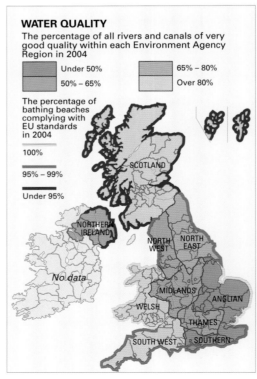

Drought orders in United Kingdom by Environment Agency Region 1976–2003

Anglian	20	South West	177
North East	92	Thames	13
North West	99	Welsh	65
Midlands	29	Scotland	2
Southern	114	N. Ireland	42

MAJOR RESERVOIRS (with capacity in million

England
1	Kielder Res.	198
2	Rutland Water	123
3	Haweswater	85
4	Grafham Water	59
5	Cow Green Res.	41
6	Thirlmere	41
7	Carsington Res.	36
8	Roadford Res.	35
9	Bewl Water Res.	31
10	Colliford Lake	29
11	Ladybower Res.	28
12	Hanningfield Res.	27
13	Abberton Res.	25
14	Draycote Water	23
15	Derwent Res.	22
16	Grimwith Res.	22
17	Wimbleball Lake	21
18	Chew Valley Lake	20
19	Balderhead Res.	20
20	Thames Valley (linked reservoirs)	
21	Lea Valley (linked reservoirs)	
22	Longendale (linked reservoirs)	

Wales
23	Elan Valley	99
24	Llyn Celyn	74
25	Llyn Brianne	62
26	Llyn Brenig	60
27	Llyn Vyrnwy	60
28	Llyn Clywedog	48
29	Llandegfedd Res.	22

Scotland
30	Loch Lomond	86
31	Loch Katrine	64
32	Megget Res.	64
33	Loch Ness	26
34	Blackwater Res.	25
35	Daer Res.	23
36	Carron Valley Res.	21

Ireland
37	Poulaphouca Res.	168
38	Inishcarra Res.	57
39	Carrigadrohid Res.	33

WATER SUPPLY IN THE UK

The pie graph represents the 16,076 million litres a day that were supplied by the public water authority and services companies in the UK in 2003.

Total water abstraction in England and Wales in 2003 was approximately 58,593 million litres a day.

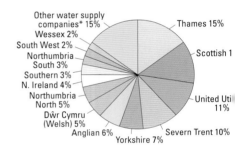

Other water supply companies* 15%
Wessex 2%
South West 2%
Northumbria South 3%
Southern 3%
N. Ireland 4%
Northumbria North 5%
Dŵr Cymru (Welsh) 5%
Anglian 6%
Yorkshire 7%
Severn Trent 10%
United Utilities 11%
Scottish 1
Thames 15%

*This is a group of 12 privately-owned companies who are not connected with the other water authorities

WATER ABSTRACTIONS

THAMES Environment Agency Region

1883 (16%) Water supply* in megalitres per day (with percentage of total abstraction from groundwater in brackets)

*Piped mains water, excluding water abstracted for agricultural and industrial use

SCOTLAND 2397 (7%)

N. IRELAND 710 (8%)

NORTH EAST 2256 (14%)

NORTH WEST 1602 (11%)

No data

MIDLANDS 2637 (36%)

WELSH 1505 (3%)

ANGLIAN 2153 (37%)

THAMES 4214 (35%)

SOUTH WEST 1249 (30%)

SOUTHERN 1303 (74%)

WATER QUALITY

The percentage of all rivers and canals of very good quality within each Environment Agency Region in 2004

Under 50%
50% – 65%
65% – 80%
Over 80%

The percentage of bathing beaches complying with EU standards in 2004

100%
95% – 99%
Under 95%

SCOTLAND

NORTHERN IRELAND

No data

NORTH WEST
NORTH EAST
MIDLANDS
WELSH
ANGLIAN
THAMES
SOUTH WEST
SOUTHERN

FLOOD RISK IN ENGLAND AND WALES

Areas at greatest risk from flooding (as designated by the Environment Agency in 2002)

Settlements with over 100 properties flooded in 2001

Ponteland
Skinningrove
Malton and Norton
Stockbridge
York
Barlby
Gowdall
Catcliffe
Mold
Ruthin
Hatton
Shrewsbury
Bewdley
Newport
Waltham Abbey
Wanstead
Woking
Uckfield
Portsmouth
Lewes

EU AIR QUALITY Emissions in thousand tonnes

	Sulphur dioxide			Nitrogen oxides		
	1975	1990	2002	1975	1990	2002
Austria	–	90	204	–	221	36
Belgium/Lux.	–	105	307	–	172	153
Denmark	418	183	200	182	270	25
Finland	–	260	211	–	290	85
France	3,329	1,200	1,434	1,608	1,487	596
Germany	3,325	5,633	1,479	2,532	3,033	608
Greece	–	–	318	–	338	509
Ireland	186	187	121	60	128	96
Italy	3,250	1,682	1,267	1,499	2,041	665
Netherlands	386	204	430	447	575	85
Portugal	178	286	293	104	216	295
Spain	–	2,205	1,929	–	1,247	1,968
Sweden	–	169	243	–	411	59
United Kingdom	5,310	3,754	1,587	2,365	2,731	1,003

FORESTRY

The percentage of the total area covered by woodland and forest

- Over 20%
- 15% – 20%
- 10% – 15%
- 5% – 10%
- Under 5%

△ Over 50% coniferous
◇ Over 50% broadleaves

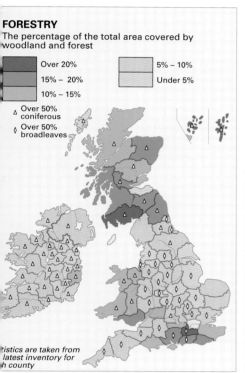

Statistics are taken from latest inventory for each county

NATURAL VEGETATION

The plant cover associated with a particular environment if it is unaffected by human activity

- Oak
- Beech and oak
- Ash and oak
- Birch and oakwood
- Scots pine
- Heath, moorland, water meadows, fen, bog and marsh

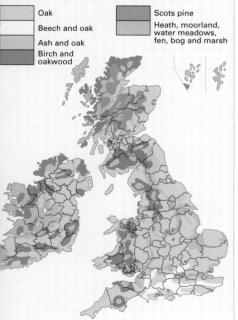

ACID RAIN

Average acidity of precipitation in the UK (pH scale)

- 4.29 and under (most acidic)
- 4.30 – 4.39
- 4.40 – 4.49
- 4.50 – 4.59
- 4.60 – 4.69
- 4.70 – 4.79
- 4.80 and over (least acidic)

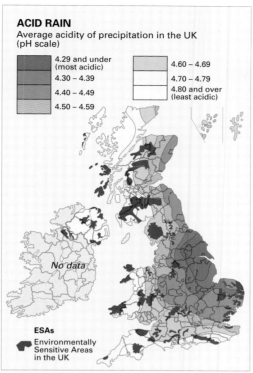

ESAs
Environmentally Sensitive Areas in the UK

GROUND LEVEL OZONE

The number of days each year with 8 hour periods with ozone levels exceeding 50 parts per billion

- More than 50
- 40 – 50
- 30 – 40
- 20 – 30
- Less than 20

Greenhouse Gas Emissions
- Carbon dioxide
- Methane
- Nitrous oxide

131 Total emissions in million tonnes of Carbon Equivalent (2003)

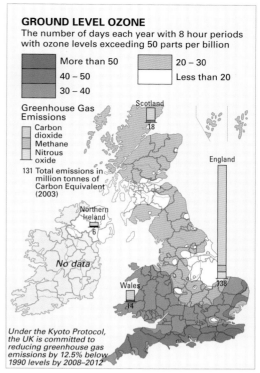

Under the Kyoto Protocol, the UK is committed to reducing greenhouse gas emissions by 12.5% below 1990 levels by 2008–2012

CONSERVATION

- National Parks
- Areas of Outstanding Natural Beauty
- National Scenic Areas
- Forest Parks, Regional Parks in Scotland and Special Protected Areas
- Green Belts (and the urban areas they surround)
- Heritage Coast (England and Wales)/Coastal Conservation Zones (Scotland)

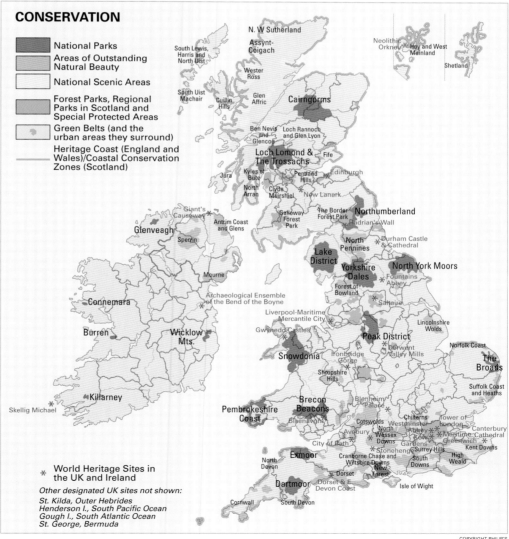

✳ World Heritage Sites in the UK and Ireland

Other designated UK sites not shown:
St. Kilda, Outer Hebrides
Henderson I., South Pacific Ocean
Gough I., South Atlantic Ocean
St. George, Bermuda

TYPES OF FARM

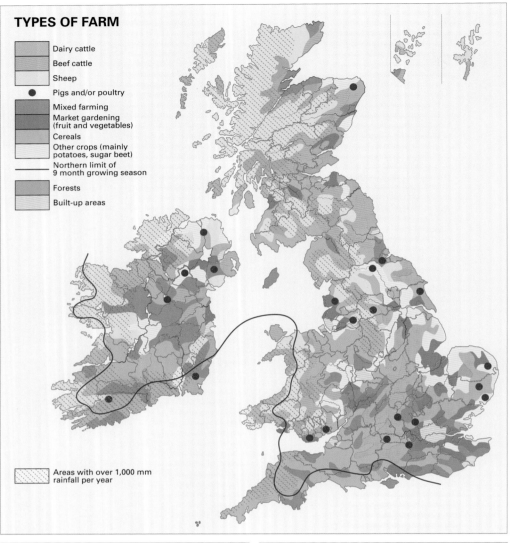

- Dairy cattle
- Beef cattle
- Sheep
- ● Pigs and/or poultry
- Mixed farming
- Market gardening (fruit and vegetables)
- Cereals
- Other crops (mainly potatoes, sugar beet)
- Northern limit of 9 month growing season
- Forests
- Built-up areas

Areas with over 1,000 mm rainfall per year

CEREAL FARMING
The percentage of the total farmland used for growing cereals in 2003

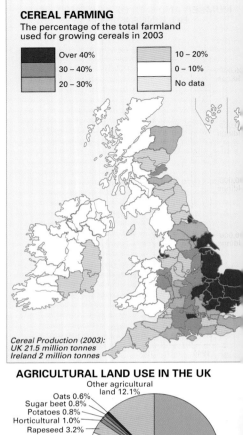

- Over 40%
- 30 – 40%
- 20 – 30%
- 10 – 20%
- 0 – 10%
- No data

Cereal Production (2003):
UK 21.5 million tonnes
Ireland 2 million tonnes

AGRICULTURAL LAND USE IN THE UK

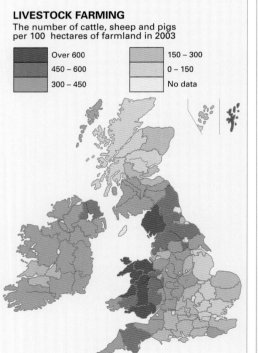

- Other agricultural land 12.1%
- Oats 0.6%
- Sugar beet 0.8%
- Potatoes 0.8%
- Horticultural 1.0%
- Rapeseed 3.2%
- Barley 5.8%
- Wheat 11.6%
- Rough grazing 25.2%
- Past 38.9

Total agricultural land area (2004): 17.2 million hectares

DAIRY FARMING
The number of dairy cows per 100 hectares of farmland in 2003

- Over 40
- 30 – 40
- 20 – 30
- 10 – 20
- 0 – 10
- No data

Milk Production (2003):
UK 15,056 million litres
Ireland 529 million litres

LIVESTOCK FARMING
The number of cattle, sheep and pigs per 100 hectares of farmland in 2003

- Over 600
- 450 – 600
- 300 – 450
- 150 – 300
- 0 – 150
- No data

FOOT-AND-MOUTH DISEASE
The number of confirmed cases of foot-and-mouth disease in 2001

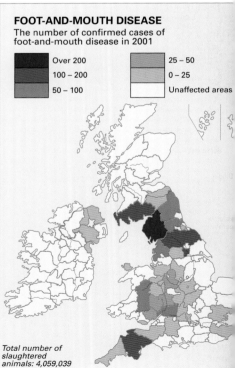

- Over 200
- 100 – 200
- 50 – 100
- 25 – 50
- 0 – 25
- Unaffected areas

Total number of
slaughtered
animals: 4,059,039

NUMBER AND SIZE OF AGRICULTURAL HOLDINGS IN THE UK

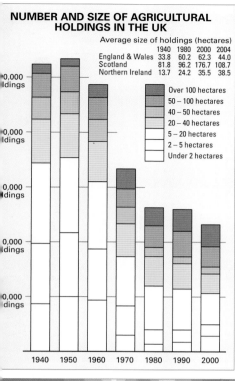

Average size of holdings (hectares)

	1940	1980	2000	2004
England & Wales	33.8	60.2	62.3	44.0
Scotland	81.8	96.2	176.7	108.7
Northern Ireland	13.7	24.2	35.5	38.5

- Over 100 hectares
- 50 – 100 hectares
- 40 – 50 hectares
- 20 – 40 hectares
- 5 – 20 hectares
- 2 – 5 hectares
- Under 2 hectares

LAND UNDER AGRICULTURE

The percentage of the total land area used for agriculture in 2003

- Over 80%
- 60 – 80%
- 40 – 60%
- 20 – 40%
- 0 – 20%
- No data

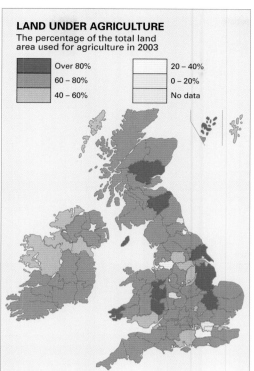

EMPLOYMENT IN AGRICULTURE

The percentage of the total workforce employed in agriculture in 2002

- Over 10%
- 2.5 – 10%
- 1 – 2.5%
- 0 – 1%

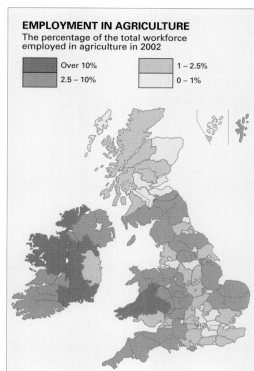

FISHING

Quantities of fish landed at major ports in 2003 (Ireland 2000)

('000 tonnes)
100
50
25
10
5

Type of fish landed
- Demersal (Deep-sea fish)
- Pelagic (Shallow-water fish)
- Shellfish

Fishing Regions
- IV   North Sea
- VIa   West Scotland
- VIIa   Irish Sea
- VIIb/h/j W. Ireland & Sole Bank
- VIId/e English Channel
- VIIf/g Bristol Ch. & S.E. Ireland
- Region boundary

Fish landed according to region of capture (2003)
- Demersal
- Pelagic
- Shellfish

Each symbol represents 10,000 tonnes caught

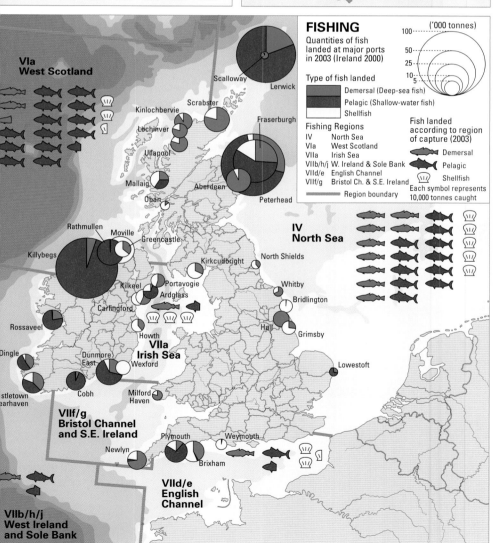

1000   500   200   100   50   m

CHANGES IN THE UK FISHING INDUSTRY

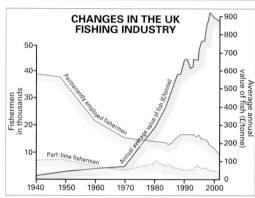

FORESTRY – WOODLAND COVER

- Northern Ireland
- Wales
- Scotland
- England

Woodland cover as % of total land area in the UK

Total area
- 2,500,000 hectares
- 2,000,000 hectares
- 1,500,000 hectares
- 1,000,000 hectares
- 500,000 hectares

4.7% 5.0% 5.8% 7.3% 9.0% 9.9% 11.7%
1905 1924 1947 1965 1980 1990 2004

FORESTRY – TIMBER CONSUMPTION

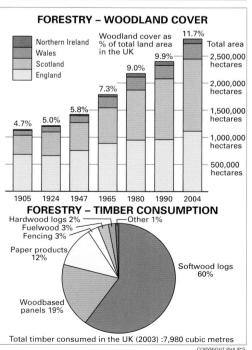

- Hardwood logs 2%
- Fuelwood 3%
- Fencing 3%
- Other 1%
- Paper products 12%
- Softwood logs 60%
- Woodbased panels 19%

Total timber consumed in the UK (2003) :7,980 cubic metres

EMPLOYMENT IN MANUFACTURING

The percentage of the workforce employed in manufacturing in 2003

- Over 25%
- 20 – 25%
- 15 – 20%
- 12.5 – 15%
- 10 – 12.5%
- Under 10%

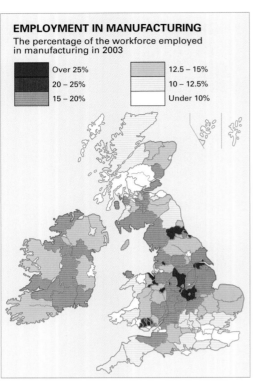

CHANGE IN MANUFACTURING EMPLOYMENT

The percentage change in the number of people employed in manufacturing by region 1991–2004*

- Over 20% gain
- 10 – 20% gain
- 0 – 10% gain
- 0 – 15% loss
- 15 – 25% loss
- Over 25% loss

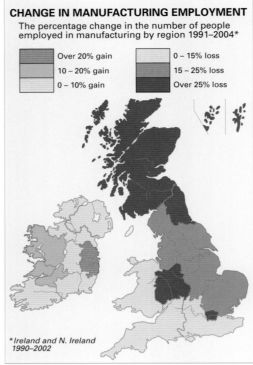

Ireland and N. Ireland 1990–2002

LOCATION OF MANUFACTURING INDUSTR

Heavy Industry
- ▲ Chemicals
- ■ Iron and steel
- ● Motor vehicles

Light Industry
- ◆ Electrical engineering
- ○ Science parks

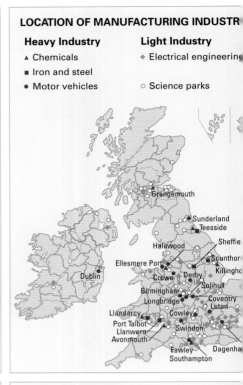

Grangemouth
Sunderland
Teesside
Sheffie
Halewood
Scunthor
Ellesmere Port
Killingho
Dublin
Crewe
Derby
Solihull
Birmingham
Coventry
Longbridge
Luton
Llandarcy
Cowley
Port Talbot
Swindon
Llanwern
Avonmouth
Fawley
Dagenha
Southampton

EMPLOYMENT IN SERVICES

The percentage of the workforce employed in the service industry in 2003

- Over 85%
- 80 – 85%
- 75 – 80%
- 70 – 75%
- Under 70%

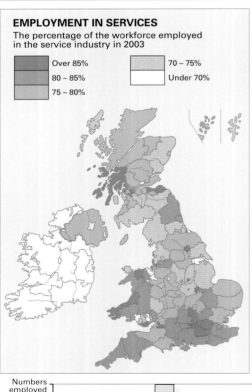

UNEMPLOYMENT

The percentage of the workforce unemployed in 2004

- Over 7%
- 6 – 7%
- 5 – 6%
- 4 – 5%
- 3 – 4%
- Under 3%

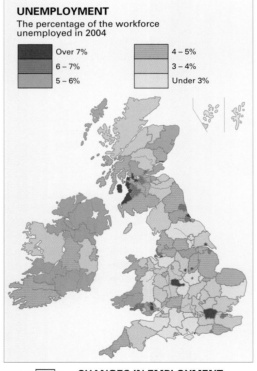

ASSISTED AREAS

The areas in which extra financial support from central government is focused to encourage economic growth

- Tier 1 with 40% aid limit
- Tier 2 with 30% aid limit

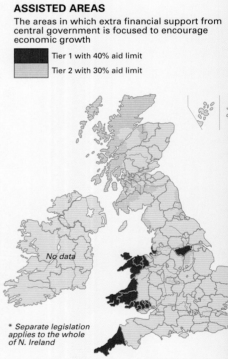

No data

Separate legislation applies to the whole of N. Ireland

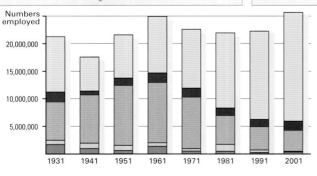

Numbers employed

20,000,000
15,000,000
10,000,000
5,000,000

1931 1941 1951 1961 1971 1981 1991 2001

CHANGES IN EMPLOYMENT IN THE UK

Employment by industry

- Services
- Transport
- Manufacturing
- Mining & energy supply
- Agriculture, forestry & fishing

MANUFACTURING OUTPUT IN THE UK

Total value 2003: £152.8 billion

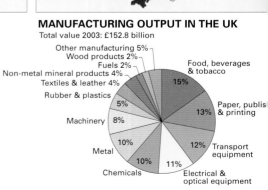

- Other manufacturing 5%
- Wood products 2%
- Fuels 2%
- Non-metal mineral products 4%
- Textiles & leather 4%
- Rubber & plastics 5%
- Machinery 8%
- Metal 10%
- Chemicals 10%
- Electrical & optical equipment 11%
- Transport equipment 12%
- Paper, publis & printing 13%
- Food, beverages & tobacco 15%

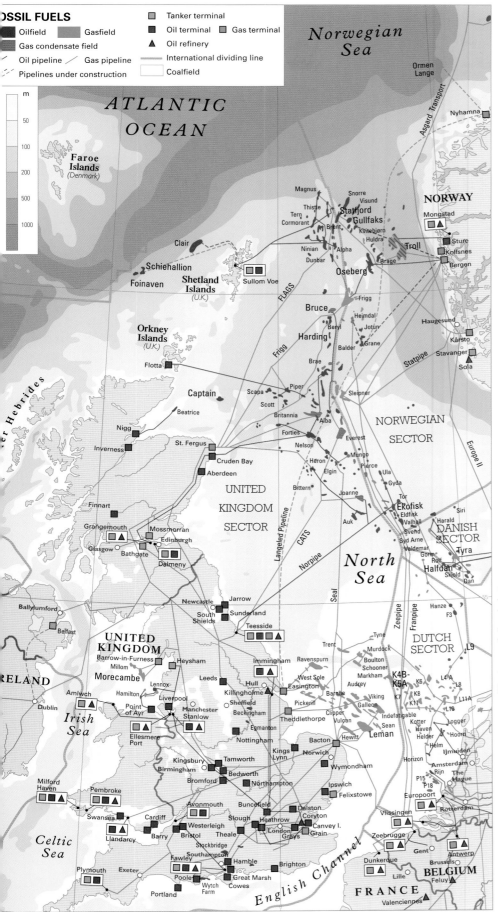

OSSIL FUELS

- ■ Oilfield
- ▨ Gasfield
- ▧ Gas condensate field
- ⟋ Oil pipeline
- ⟋ Gas pipeline
- ⟋ Pipelines under construction
- ▧ Tanker terminal
- ■ Oil terminal
- ▲ Oil refinery
- ▨ Gas terminal
- — International dividing line
- ☐ Coalfield

m
50
100
200
500
1000

ATLANTIC OCEAN

Norwegian Sea

Faroe Islands (Denmark)

NORWAY

North Sea

NORWEGIAN SECTOR

UNITED KINGDOM SECTOR

DANISH SECTOR

DUTCH SECTOR

UNITED KINGDOM

IRELAND

Irish Sea

Celtic Sea

English Channel

FRANCE

BELGIUM

ELECTRICITY GENERATION
Power Stations (with capacity) 2005

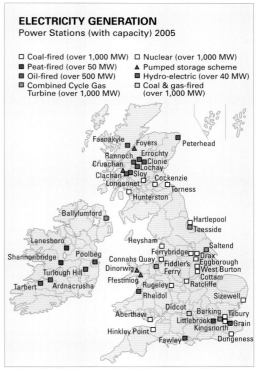

- ☐ Coal-fired (over 1,000 MW)
- ■ Peat-fired (over 50 MW)
- ◕ Oil-fired (over 500 MW)
- ☐ Combined Cycle Gas Turbine (over 1,000 MW)
- ☐ Nuclear (over 1,000 MW)
- ▲ Pumped storage scheme
- ▲ Hydro-electric (over 40 MW)
- ☐ Coal & gas-fired (over 1,000 MW)

ENERGY CONSUMPTION BY FUEL IN THE UK

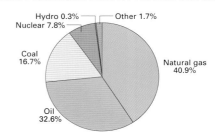

- Hydro 0.3%
- Other 1.7%
- Nuclear 7.8%
- Coal 16.7%
- Natural gas 40.9%
- Oil 32.6%

Total consumption in 2004: 234.9 million tonnes of oil equivalent

PRODUCTION OF PRIMARY FUELS IN THE UK

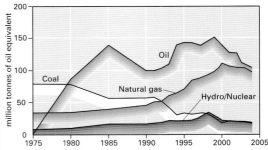

million tonnes of oil equivalent

Oil

Coal

Natural gas

Hydro/Nuclear

1975 1980 1985 1990 1995 2000 2005

RENEWABLE ENERGY PRODUCTION IN THE UK

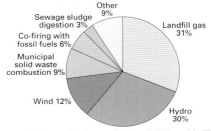

- Other 9%
- Sewage sludge digestion 3%
- Co-firing with fossil fuels 6%
- Municipal solid waste combustion 9%
- Wind 12%
- Landfill gas 31%
- Hydro 30%

Total generation of renewable energy in 2003 was 2.8 million tonnes of oil equivalent, 3.3% of total energy production in the UK

COPYRIGHT PHILIP'S

ROADS AND FERRIES

- M6 — Motorways
- — Main primary routes

⬡56 Average 24 hour flow of vehicles for major sections of motorway network. Figures are given in thousands for 2004

- - - - Principal car ferry routes
Esbjerg ⋯ Long-haul sea ferry destinations

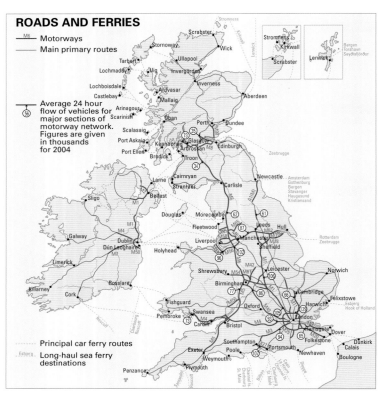

RAILWAYS

- — Electrified lines
- — Other main lines

Furthest distances from London reached within a journey time of

	3 hours	6 hours
1950	▲	●
2005	▲	●

Channel Tunnel
- - - - Channel Tunnel
—— High-speed rail link
⋯⋯ under construction

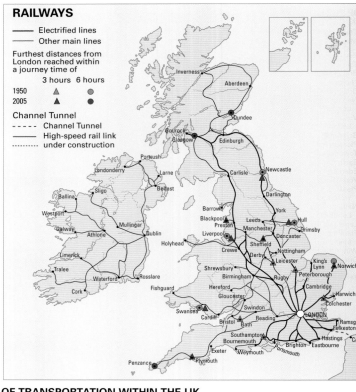

CHANNEL TUNNEL AND HIGH-SPEED LINKS IN EUROPE

Estimated journey times between London and other European cities

London – Berlin
London – Amsterdam
London – Paris
London – Brussels

	1990	Best time achievable using existing networks
	2002	Since opening of Channel Tunnel in 1994 and completion of high-speed links in Europe
	2007	Estimated journey times on completion of new link from London to Folkestone

Hours: 5 10 15 20

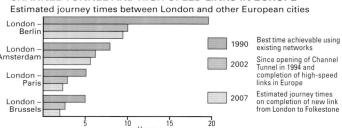

MEANS OF TRANSPORTATION WITHIN THE UK

'000 million tonne km 200 175 150 125 100 75 50 25 0

GOODS

0 100 200 300 400 500 600 700 '000 million passenger km

PASSENGERS

1975
1980
1985
1990
1995
2000

- Road
- Water
- Rail
- Pipelines
- Private Transport
- Public Transport
- Rail

Air transport accounted for 2,200 million passenger km in 1975, 4,000 million in 1985 and 7,600 million in 2000

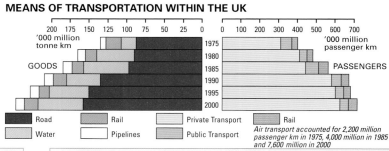

SEAPORTS

Goods traffic by port in thousand tonnes 2003

50,000
25,000
10,000
5,000

% imports — Foreign Traffic
% exports
% imports — Domestic Traffic
% exports

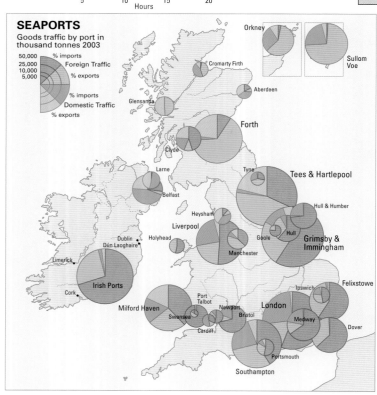

AIRPORTS

Passenger traffic in thousands (2004)

60,000
30,000

5,000
1,000

International Scheduled
International Chartered
Domestic Scheduled
Domestic Chartered

- Selected airports with over 100,000 passengers (2004)

* Comparable statistics for scheduled and chartered passengers in Ireland are not available

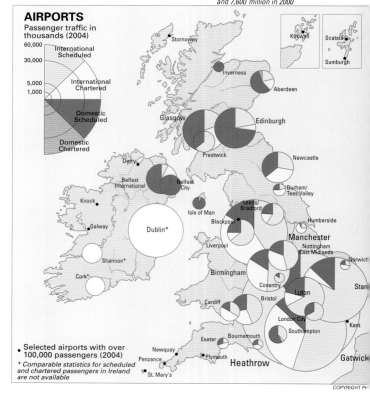

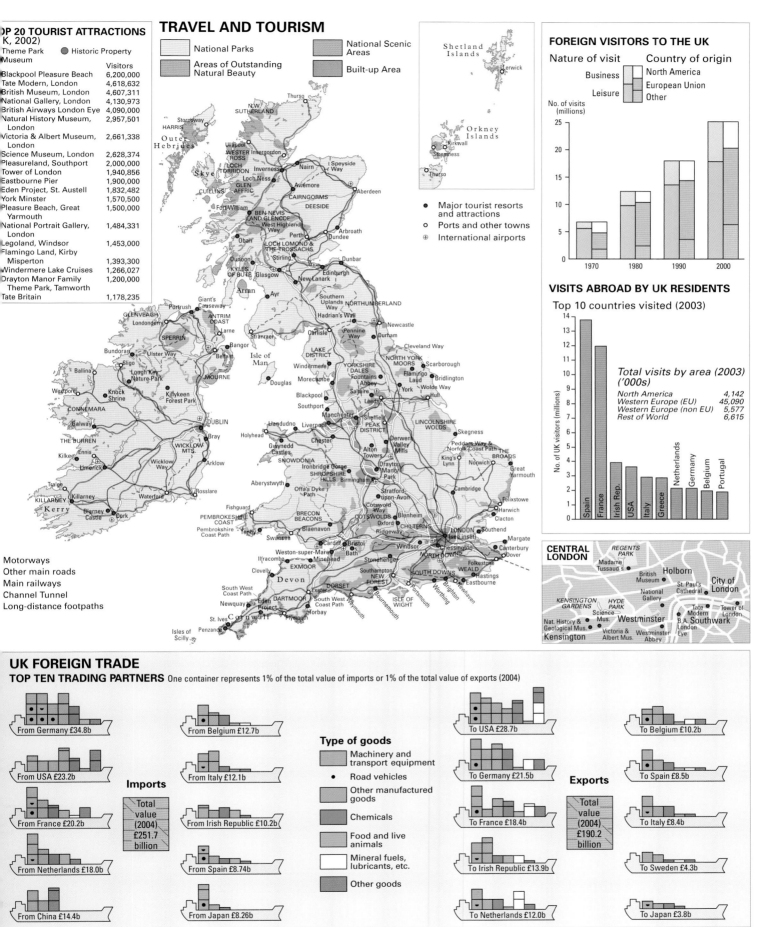

TOP 20 TOURIST ATTRACTIONS (UK, 2002)

Theme Park   ● Historic Property
Museum

	Visitors
Blackpool Pleasure Beach	6,200,000
Tate Modern, London	4,618,632
British Museum, London	4,607,311
National Gallery, London	4,130,973
British Airways London Eye	4,090,000
Natural History Museum, London	2,957,501
Victoria & Albert Museum, London	2,661,338
Science Museum, London	2,628,374
Pleasureland, Southport	2,000,000
Tower of London	1,940,856
Eastbourne Pier	1,900,000
Eden Project, St. Austell	1,832,482
York Minster	1,570,500
Pleasure Beach, Great Yarmouth	1,500,000
National Portrait Gallery, London	1,484,331
Legoland, Windsor	1,453,000
Flamingo Land, Kirby Misperton	1,393,300
Windermere Lake Cruises	1,266,027
Drayton Manor Family Theme Park, Tamworth	1,200,000
Tate Britain	1,178,235

TRAVEL AND TOURISM

National Parks
Areas of Outstanding Natural Beauty
National Scenic Areas
Built-up Area

● Major tourist resorts and attractions
○ Ports and other towns
⊕ International airports

Motorways
Other main roads
Main railways
Channel Tunnel
Long-distance footpaths

FOREIGN VISITORS TO THE UK

Nature of visit
Business
Leisure

Country of origin
North America
European Union
Other

No. of visits (millions)
1970 1980 1990 2000

VISITS ABROAD BY UK RESIDENTS

Top 10 countries visited (2003)

No. of UK visitors (millions)
Spain France Irish Rep. USA Italy Greece Netherlands Germany Belgium Portugal

Total visits by area (2003) ('000s)

North America	4,142
Western Europe (EU)	45,090
Western Europe (non EU)	5,577
Rest of World	6,615

CENTRAL LONDON

REGENTS PARK
Madame Tussaud's
British Museum
Holborn
St. Paul's Cathedral
City of London
KENSINGTON GARDENS
HYDE PARK
National Gallery
Science Mus.
Westminster
Tate Modern
Tower of London
B.A. London Eye
Southwark
Nat. History & Geological Mus.
Victoria & Albert Mus.
Westminster Abbey
Kensington

UK FOREIGN TRADE

TOP TEN TRADING PARTNERS One container represents 1% of the total value of imports or 1% of the total value of exports (2004)

Imports — Total value (2004) £251.7 billion

From Germany £34.8b
From USA £23.2b
From France £20.2b
From Netherlands £18.0b
From China £14.4b
From Belgium £12.7b
From Italy £12.1b
From Irish Republic £10.2b
From Spain £8.74b
From Japan £8.26b

Exports — Total value (2004) £190.2 billion

To USA £28.7b
To Germany £21.5b
To France £18.4b
To Irish Republic £13.9b
To Netherlands £12.0b
To Belgium £10.2b
To Spain £8.5b
To Italy £8.4b
To Sweden £4.3b
To Japan £3.8b

Type of goods
Machinery and transport equipment
● Road vehicles
Other manufactured goods
Chemicals
Food and live animals
Mineral fuels, lubricants, etc.
Other goods

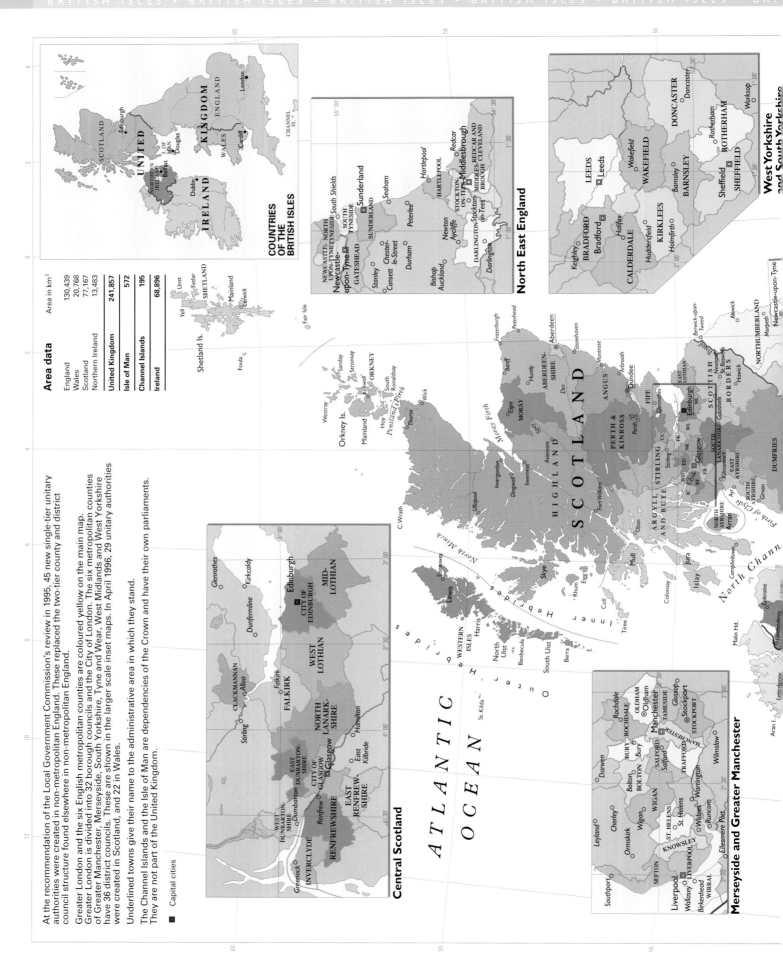

At the recommendation of the Local Government Commission's review in 1995, 45 new single-tier unitary authorities were created in non-metropolitan England. These replaced the two-tier county and district council structure found elsewhere in non-metropolitan England.

Greater London and the six English metropolitan counties are coloured yellow on the main map. Greater London is divided into 32 borough councils and the City of London. The six metropolitan counties of Greater Manchester, Merseyside, South Yorkshire, Tyne and Wear, West Midlands and West Yorkshire have 36 district councils. These are shown in the larger scale inset maps. In April 1996, 29 unitary authorities were created in Scotland, and 22 in Wales.

Underlined towns give their name to the administrative area in which they stand.

The Channel Islands and the Isle of Man are dependencies of the Crown and have their own parliaments. They are not part of the United Kingdom.

■ Capital cities

Area data

	Area in km²
England	130,439
Wales	20,768
Scotland	77,167
Northern Ireland	13,483
United Kingdom	**241,857**
Isle of Man	**572**
Channel Islands	**195**
Ireland	**68,896**

COUNTRIES OF THE BRITISH ISLES

North East England

West Yorkshire and South Yorkshire

Central Scotland

Merseyside and Greater Manchester

ATLANTIC OCEAN

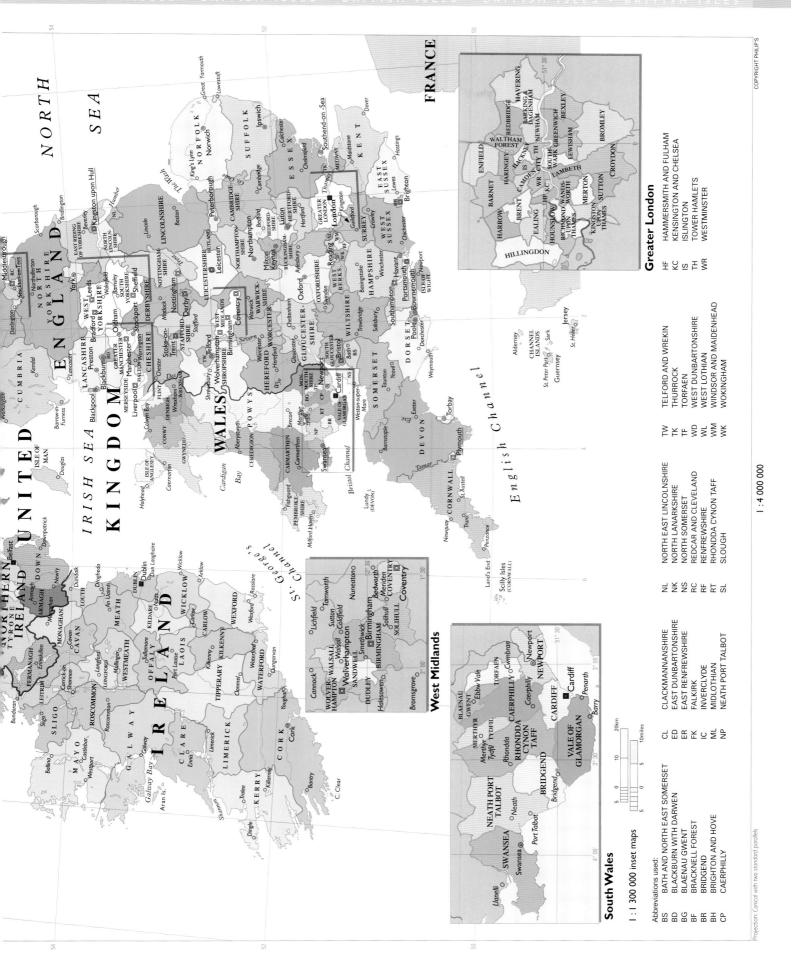

Greater London

HF	HAMMERSMITH AND FULHAM
KC	KENSINGTON AND CHELSEA
IS	ISLINGTON
TH	TOWER HAMLETS
WR	WESTMINSTER

1 : 4 000 000

TW	TELFORD AND WREKIN	NL	NORTH EAST LINCOLNSHIRE
TK	THURROCK	NK	NORTH LANARKSHIRE
TF	TORFAEN	NS	NORTH SOMERSET
WD	WEST DUNBARTONSHIRE	RC	REDCAR AND CLEVELAND
WL	WEST LOTHIAN	RF	RENFREWSHIRE
WM	WINDSOR AND MAIDENHEAD	RT	RHONDDA CYNON TAFF
WK	WOKINGHAM	SL	SLOUGH

West Midlands

South Wales
1 : 1 300 000 inset maps

Abbreviations used:

BS	BATH AND NORTH EAST SOMERSET
BD	BLACKBURN WITH DARWEN
BG	BLAENAU GWENT
BF	BRACKNELL FOREST
BR	BRIDGEND
BH	BRIGHTON AND HOVE
CP	CAERPHILLY

CL	CLACKMANNANSHIRE
ED	EAST DUNBARTONSHIRE
ER	EAST RENFREWSHIRE
FK	FALKIRK
IC	INVERCLYDE
ML	MIDLOTHIAN
NP	NEATH PORT TALBOT

Projection: Conical with two standard parallels

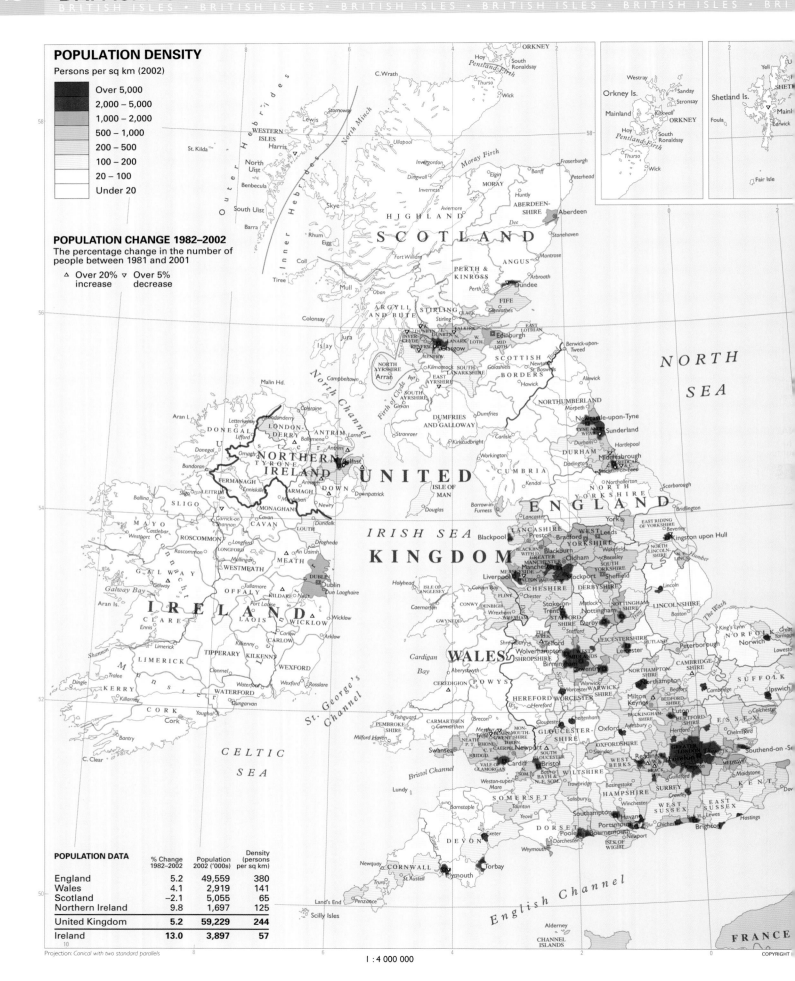

POPULATION DENSITY
Persons per sq km (2002)

- Over 5,000
- 2,000 – 5,000
- 1,000 – 2,000
- 500 – 1,000
- 200 – 500
- 100 – 200
- 20 – 100
- Under 20

POPULATION CHANGE 1982–2002
The percentage change in the number of people between 1981 and 2001

- △ Over 20% increase
- ▽ Over 5% decrease

POPULATION DATA	% Change 1982–2002	Population 2002 ('000s)	Density (persons per sq km)
England	5.2	49,559	380
Wales	4.1	2,919	141
Scotland	−2.1	5,055	65
Northern Ireland	9.8	1,697	125
United Kingdom	5.2	59,229	244
Ireland	13.0	3,897	57

Projection: Conical with two standard parallels

I : 4 000 000

COPYRIGHT

POPULATION DENSITY IN 1891

Persons per sq km

- Over 1,000
- 500 – 1,000
- 200 – 500
- 100 – 200
- 50 – 100
- 25 – 50
- Under 25

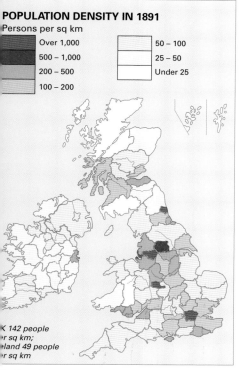

K 142 people
r sq km;
land 49 people
r sq km

ETHNIC GROUPS

Ethnic minorities as a % of total population in 2000–1

- Over 6%
- 4 – 6%
- 2 – 4%
- 0 – 2%

Ethnic minority groups

- Indian/ Pakistani/ Bangladeshi
- W. Indian/ African
- Other

77 000 Total number of ethnic minority people in each region

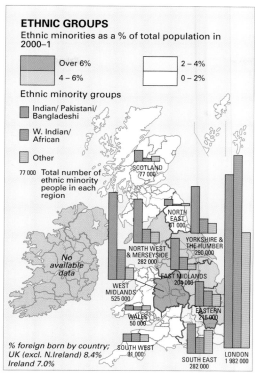

SCOTLAND 77 000

No available data

NORTH EAST 41 000

NORTH WEST & MERSEYSIDE 282 000

YORKSHIRE & THE HUMBER 290 000

EAST MIDLANDS 204 000

WEST MIDLANDS 525 000

WALES 50 000

EASTERN 216 000

SOUTH WEST 91 000

SOUTH EAST 282 000

LONDON 1 982 000

% foreign born by country; UK (excl. N.Ireland) 8.4% Ireland 7.0%

MIGRATION

The difference between the number moving in and the number moving away (per 1,000 inhabitants)*

- Over 10 moved in
- 5 – 10 moved in
- 0 – 5 moved in
- 0 – 5 moved away
- 5 – 10 moved away
- Over 10 moved away

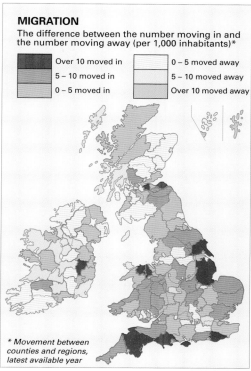

* Movement between counties and regions, latest available year

NATURAL POPULATION CHANGE

The difference between the number of births and the number of deaths per thousand inhabitants in 2001

- Over 7.5 more births
- 5 – 7.5 more births
- 2.5 – 5 more births
- 0 – 2.5 more births
- 0 – 2.5 more deaths
- Over 2.5 more deaths

1.1 more
hs than deaths;
and 6.0 more
hs than deaths

YOUNG PEOPLE

The percentage of the population under 15 years old in 2002

- Over 22.5%
- 20 – 22.5%
- 19 – 20%
- 18 – 19%
- Under 18%

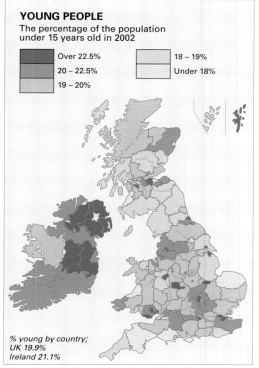

% young by country; UK 19.9% Ireland 21.1%

OLD PEOPLE

The percentage of the population over pensionable age* in 2002

- Over 22.5%
- 20 – 22.5%
- 17.5 – 20%
- 15 – 17.5%
- 12.5 – 15%
- Under 12.5%

*Pensionable age is 65 for males, 60 for females

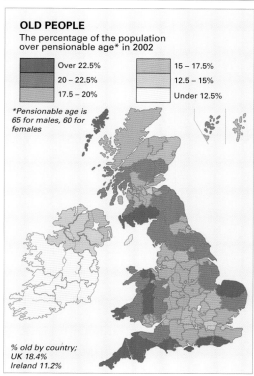

% old by country; UK 18.4% Ireland 11.2%

VITAL STATISTICS (1900–2000)

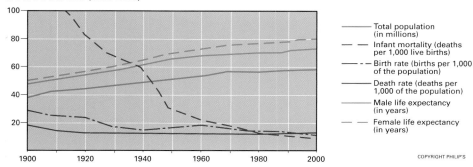

- Total population (in millions)
- Infant mortality (deaths per 1,000 live births)
- Birth rate (births per 1,000 of the population)
- Death rate (deaths per 1,000 of the population)
- Male life expectancy (in years)
- Female life expectancy (in years)

COPYRIGHT PHILIP'S

AGE STRUCTURE OF THE UK

1901   2004   Projected 2150

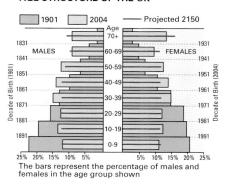

Age 70+, 60–69, 50–59, 40–49, 30–39, 20–29, 10–19, 0–9

MALES   FEMALES

Decade of Birth (1901): 1831, 1841, 1851, 1861, 1871, 1881, 1891
Decade of Birth (2004): 1931, 1941, 1951, 1961, 1971, 1981, 1991

25% 20% 15% 10% 5%   5% 10% 15% 20% 25%

The bars represent the percentage of males and females in the age group shown

HOME OWNERSHIP

The percentage of dwellings that were owner-occupied in 2003

Over 75%	65 – 70%
70 – 75%	Under 65%

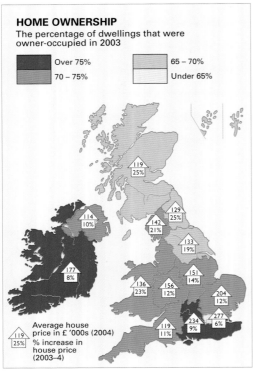

119
25%   Average house price in £ '000s (2004)

119
25%   % increase in house price (2003–4)

CAR OWNERSHIP

The number of new cars per thousand people in 2001*

Over 50	20 – 30
40 – 50	10 – 20
30 – 40	

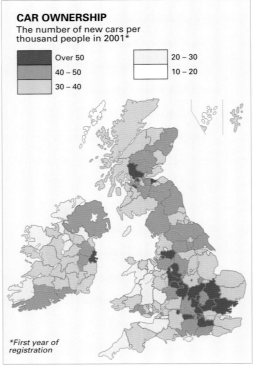

*First year of registration

INCOME

The average gross weekly earnings of males and females in full employment in 2004

Over £450	£375 – £400
£425 – £450	£350 – £375
£400 – £425	Under £350

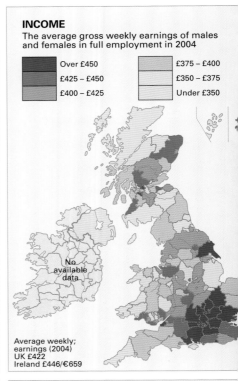

No available data

Average weekly; earnings (2004)
UK £422
Ireland £446/€659

HEALTH

The number of doctors per 100,000 people by region in 2002

Over 70	55 – 60
65 – 70	50 – 55
60 – 65	Under 50

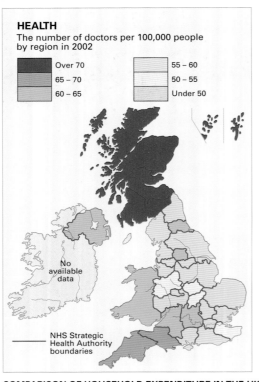

No available data

—— NHS Strategic Health Authority boundaries

EDUCATION

The percentage of pupils aged 16 staying on in full-time education in 2003–2004

Over 77.5%	70 – 72.5%
75 – 77.5%	67.5 – 70%
72.5 – 75%	Under 67.5%

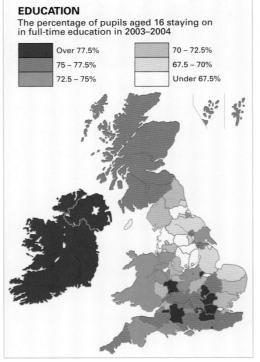

CRIME RATE

The number of recorded crimes per thousand people in 2003–4

Over 125	50 – 75
100 – 125	25 – 50
75 – 100	Under 25

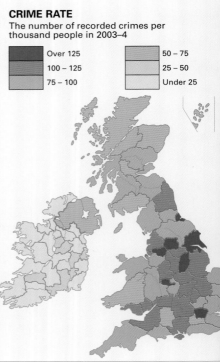

COMPARISON OF HOUSEHOLD EXPENDITURE IN THE UK

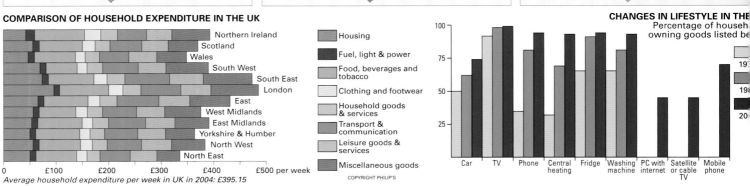

Northern Ireland
Scotland
Wales
South West
South East
London
East
West Midlands
East Midlands
Yorkshire & Humber
North West
North East

	Housing
	Fuel, light & power
	Food, beverages and tobacco
	Clothing and footwear
	Household goods & services
	Transport & communication
	Leisure goods & services
	Miscellaneous goods

0   £100   £200   £300   £400   £500 per week

Average household expenditure per week in UK in 2004: £395.15

COPYRIGHT PHILIP'S

CHANGES IN LIFESTYLE IN THE

Percentage of househ owning goods listed be

Car   TV   Phone   Central heating   Fridge   Washing machine   PC with internet   Satellite or cable TV   Mobile phone

19

19

20

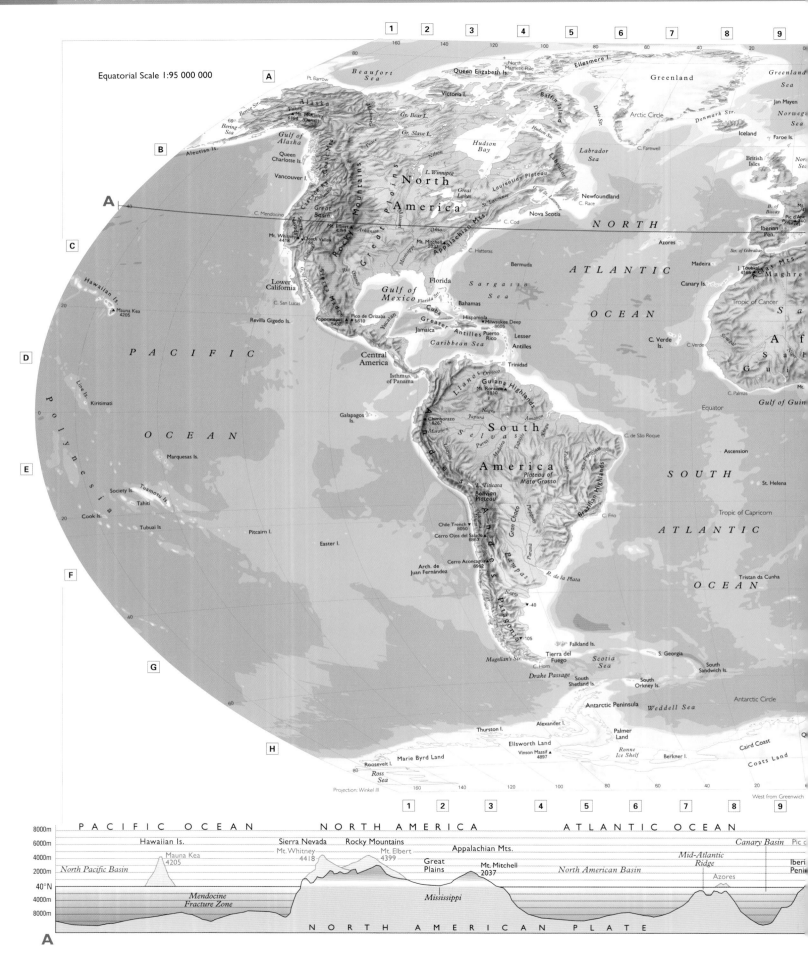

Equatorial Scale 1:95 000 000

Projection: Winkel III

West from Greenwich

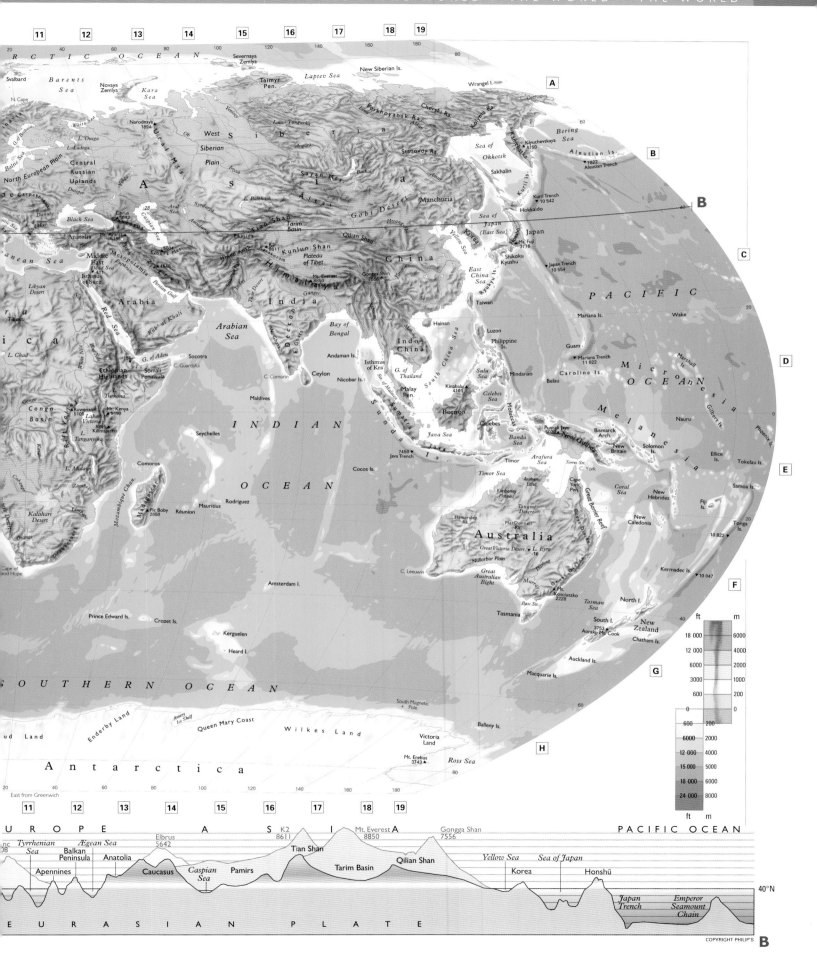

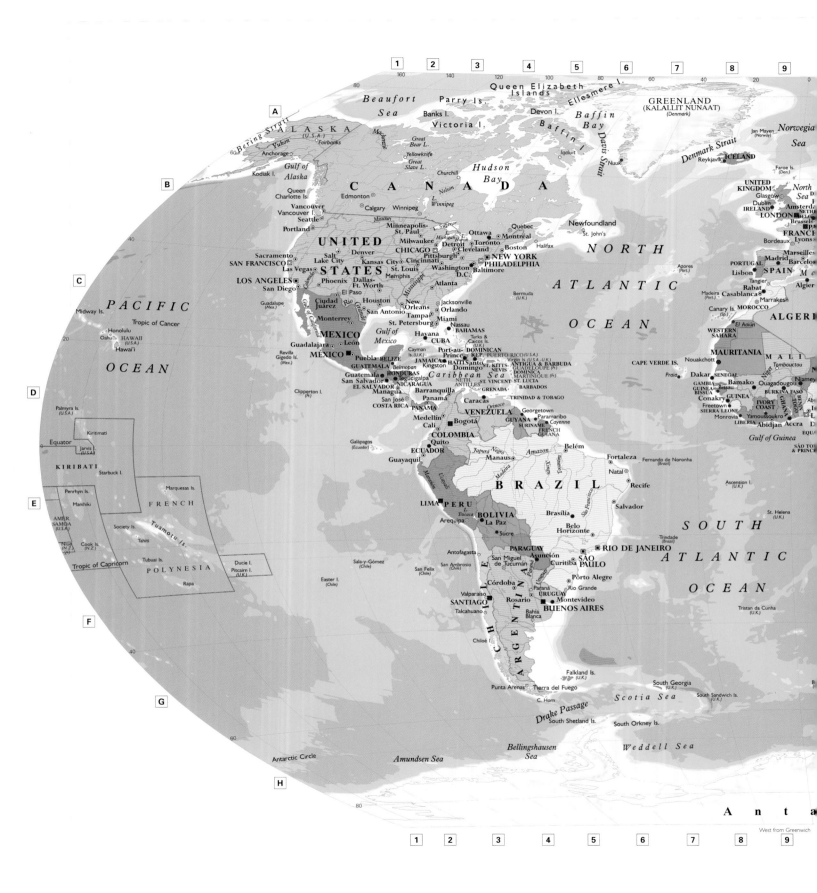

Projection: Winkel III

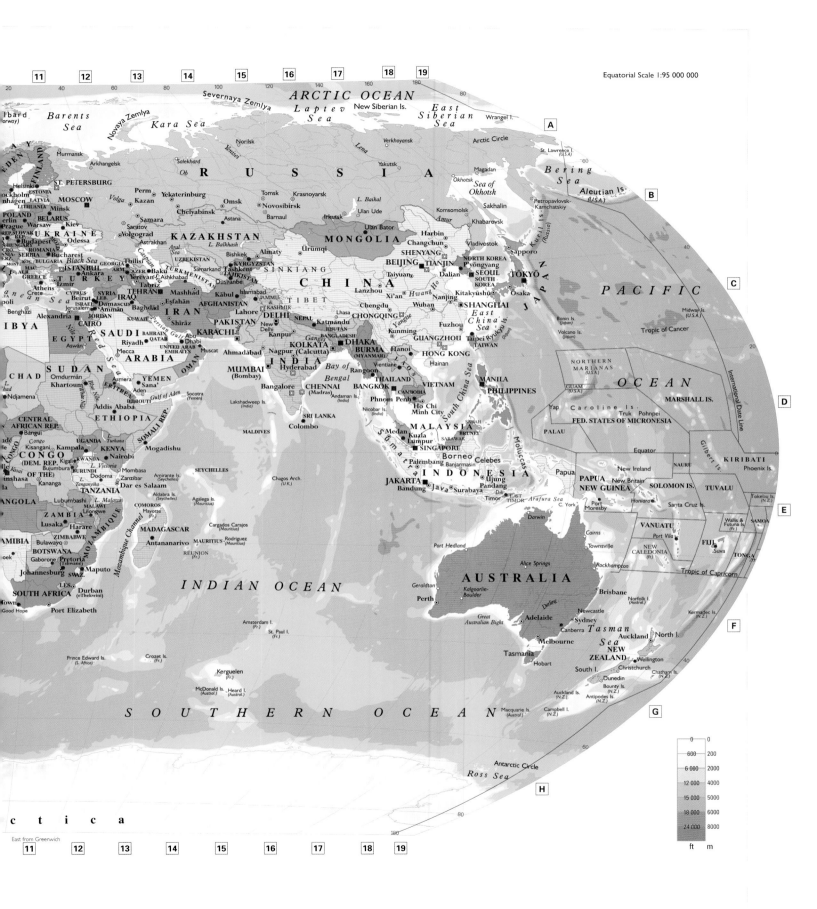

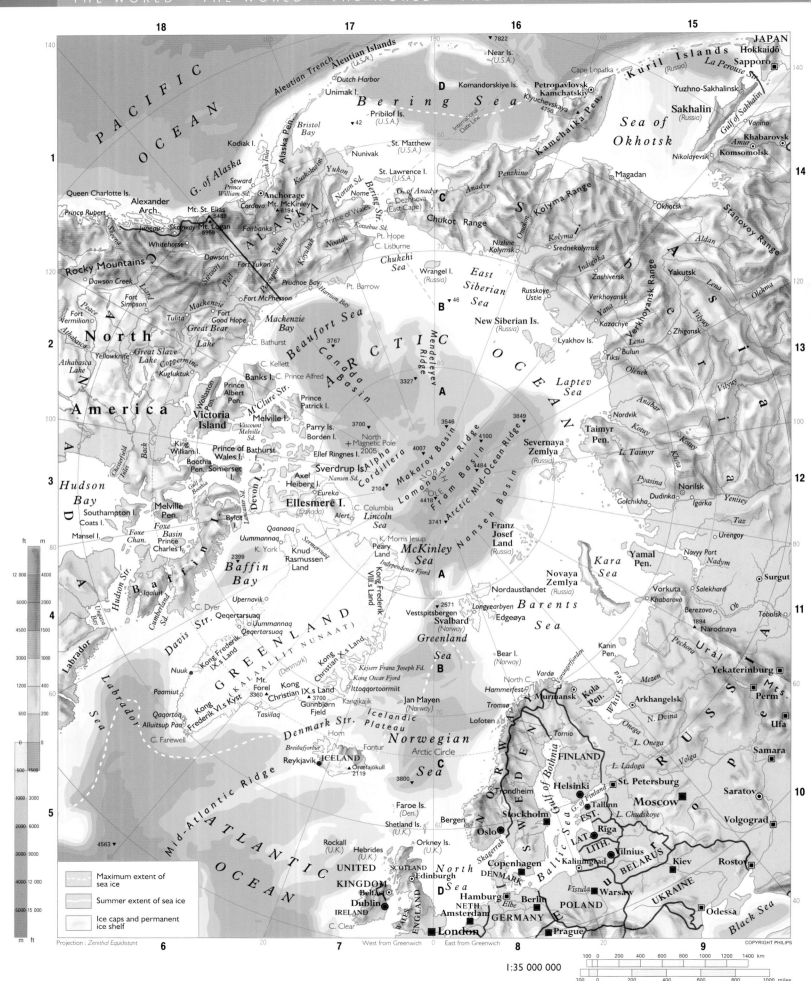

PACIFIC OCEAN

JAPAN
Hokkaidō
Sapporo

Aleutian Trench
Aleutian Islands (U.S.A.)
Kuril Islands (Russia)
La Perouse Str.
Yuzhno-Sakhalinsk
Near Is. ▼ 7822
Cape Lopatka

Dutch Harbor
Unimak I. ▼ 42
Bering Sea
Komandorskiye Is.
Petropavlovsk
Kamchatskiy
Klyuchevskaya 4750
Sea of Okhotsk
Sakhalin (Russia)
Gulf of Sakhalin
Vanino

Bristol Bay
Pribilof Is. (U.S.A.)
International Date Line
Kamchatka Pen.
Khabarovsk
Nikolayevsk
Komsomolsk

Kodiak I.
G. of Alaska
Nunivak
St. Matthew (U.S.A.)
Penzhino
Magadan
Amur

Seward
Prince William Sd.
Anchorage
Cordova Mt. McKinley ▲ 6194
Kuskokwim
Bering Str.
Nome
Norton Sd.
St. Lawrence I. (U.S.A.)
G. of Anadyr (East Cape)
Anadyr
Okhotsk
Stanovoy Range

Queen Charlotte Is.
Alexander Arch.
Mt. St. Elias ▲ 5489
Mt. Logan ▲ 5959
Fairbanks
ALASKA (U.S.A.)
Yukon
C. Prince of Wales
Dezhneva
Chukot Range
Nizhne Kolymsk
Kolyma Range
Srednekolymsk
Indigirka
Zashiversk
Yakutsk
Aldan
Lena

Prince Rupert
Skagway
Juneau
Whitehorse
Dawson
Fort Yukon
Porcupine
Pt. Hope
C. Lisburne
Chukchi Sea
Wrangel I. (Russia)
East Siberian Sea
Russkoye Ustie
Kolyma
Verkhoyansk
Yana
Kazachye
Zhigansk

Rocky Mountains
Dawson Creek
Stewart
Peel
Fort McPherson
Prudhoe Bay
Harrison Bay
Pt. Barrow
▼ 46
New Siberian Is. (Russia)
Lyakhov Is.
Tiksi
Bulun
Olenek

Fort Vermilion
Peace
Fort Simpson
Liard
Mackenzie
Fort Good Hope
Tulita
C. Bathurst
Beaufort Sea
▲ 3767
Canada Basin
Mendeleyev Ridge
Laptev Sea
Nordvik
Anabar

North America
Athabasca
Great Slave Lake
Yellowknife
Coppermine
Kugluktuk
Great Bear Lake
Mackenzie Bay
C. Kellett
ARCTIC
▲ 3327
OCEAN
Taimyr Pen.
Khatanga
L. Taimyr

Athabasca Lake
Banks I.
C. Prince Alfred
Makarov Basin
▲ 3546
▲ 3849
Severnaya Zemlya (Russia)
Pyasina
Norilsk

Victoria Island
Wollaston Pen.
Prince Albert Pen.
McClure Str.
Melville I.
Parry Is.
Prince Patrick I.
Borden I.
Lomonosov Ridge
Nansen Basin
4007
4100
4484
Golchikha
Dudinka
Igarka
Yenisey

Chesterfield Inlet
Back
King William I.
Viscount Melville Sd.
Prince of Bathurst I.
Ellef Ringnes I.
North Magnetic Pole 2005
Alpha Cordillera
2104
POLE
Fram Basin
4418
Arctic Mid-Ocean Ridge
Franz Josef Land (Russia)
Urengoy
Taz

Boothia Pen.
Somerset
Devon I.
Axel Heiberg I.
Sverdrup Is.
Nansen Sd.
Eureka
3741
Novaya Zemlya (Russia)
Kara Sea
Novyy Port
Nadym

Hudson Bay
Southampton I.
Coats I.
Melville Pen.
Foxe
Foxe Basin
Prince Charles I.
Bylot I.
Lancaster Sd.
Ellesmere I. (Sanada)
Alert
Lincoln Sea
C. Columbia
McKinley Sea
Nordaustlandet
Yamal Pen.
Vorkuta
Khabarovo
Surgut
Salekhard

Mansel I.
Hudson Str.
Iqaluit
Baffin Bay
2399
K. York
Qaanaaq
Uummannaq
Knud Rasmussen Land
Sermersuaq
Peary Land
K. Morris Jesup
Independence Fjord
Kong Frederik VIII.s Land
▲ 2571
Vestspitsbergen
Svalbard (Norway)
Longyearbyen
Edgeøya
Barents Sea
Berezovo
Narodnaya ▲ 1894
Tobolsk

Ungava Bay
Cumberland Sd.
C. Dyer
Qeqertarsuaq
Upernavik
Qeqertarsuaq
Uummannaq
Davis Str.
GREENLAND
Kong Frederik IX.s Land
(KALAALLIT NUNAAT)
(Denmark)
Kong Christian X.s Land
Greenland Sea
Bear I. (Norway)
Nordaustlandet
Novaya Zemlya
Kanin Pen.
Ural Mts.
Yekaterinburg
Perm

Labrador
Labrador Sea
Nuuk
Paamiut
Kong Frederik VI.s Kyst
Mt. Forel ▲ 3360
Kong Christian IX.s Land
Kejserr Franz Joseph Fd.
Kong Oscar Fjord
Ittoqqortoormiit
Kangikajik
Jan Mayen (Norway)
North C.
Hammerfest
Vardø
Varangerfjorden
Murmansk
Kola Pen.
White Sea
N. Dvina
Arkhangelsk
Mezen
Pechora
Ufa

Qaqortoq
Alluitsup Paa
C. Farewell
Tasiilaq
▲ 3700
Gunnbjørn Fjeld
Denmark Str.
Plateau
Icelandic Plateau
Tromsø
Lofoten
Murmansk
Onega
L. Onega
Samara

Reykjavik
Breiðafjörður
Horn
Fontur
ICELAND
Öræfajökull 2119
3800
Norwegian Sea
Arctic Circle
Trondheim
Bergen
FINLAND
Tornio
Gulf of Bothnia
L. Ladoga
Helsinki
St. Petersburg
Moscow
Volga
Saratov

Mid-Atlantic Ridge
4563 ▼
ATLANTIC OCEAN
Faroe Is. (Den.)
Shetland Is. (U.K.)
Rockall (U.K.)
Hebrides (U.K.)
Orkney Is. (U.K.)
North Sea
Oslo
SWEDEN
Stockholm
Tallinn
EST.
L. Chudskoye
Rīga
LAT.
Vilnius
LITH.
Kaliningrad
BELARUS
Kiev
Volgograd
Rostov

UNITED KINGDOM
SCOTLAND
Edinburgh
Belfast
Dublin
IRELAND
C. Clear
WALES
ENGLAND
London
Skagerrak
DENMARK
Copenhagen
Hamburg
NETH.
Amsterdam
Berlin
GERMANY
Prague
POLAND
Warsaw
Vistula
UKRAINE
Odessa
Black Sea
Baltic Sea

Maximum extent of sea ice
Summer extent of sea ice
Ice caps and permanent ice shelf

ft m
12 000 4000
6000 2000
4500 1500
3000 1000
1200 400
600 200
0 0
500 1500
1000 3000
2000 6000
3000 9000
4000 12 000
5000 15 000
m ft

Projection : Zenithal Equidistant
West from Greenwich
East from Greenwich
COPYRIGHT PHILIPS

1:35 000 000

100 0 200 400 600 800 1000 1200 1400 km
100 0 200 400 600 800 1000 miles

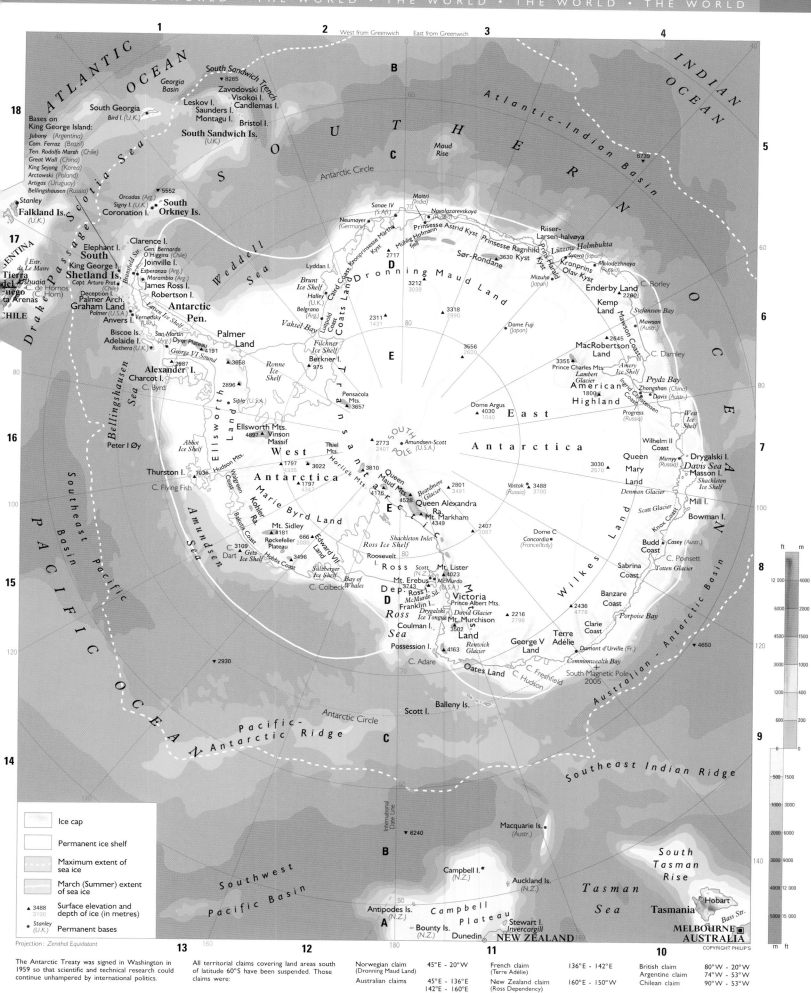

Bases on
King George Island:
Jubany (Argentina)
Com. Ferraz (Brazil)
Ten. Rodolfo Marsh (Chile)
Great Wall (China)
King Sejong (Korea)
Arctowski (Poland)
Artigas (Uruguay)
Bellingshausen (Russia)

Legend:

- Ice cap
- Permanent ice shelf
- Maximum extent of sea ice
- March (Summer) extent of sea ice
- ▲ 3488 / 3700 Surface elevation and depth of ice (in metres)
- • Stanley (U.K.) Permanent bases

Projection: Zenithal Equidistant

COPYRIGHT PHILIP'S

The Antarctic Treaty was signed in Washington in 1959 so that scientific and technical research could continue unhampered by international politics.

All territorial claims covering land areas south of latitude 60°S have been suspended. Those claims were:

Norwegian claim (Dronning Maud Land)	45°E – 20°W
Australian claims	45°E – 136°E / 142°E – 160°E
French claim (Terre Adélie)	136°E – 142°E
New Zealand claim (Ross Dependency)	160°E – 150°W
British claim	80°W – 20°W
Argentine claim	74°W – 53°W
Chilean claim	90°W – 53°W

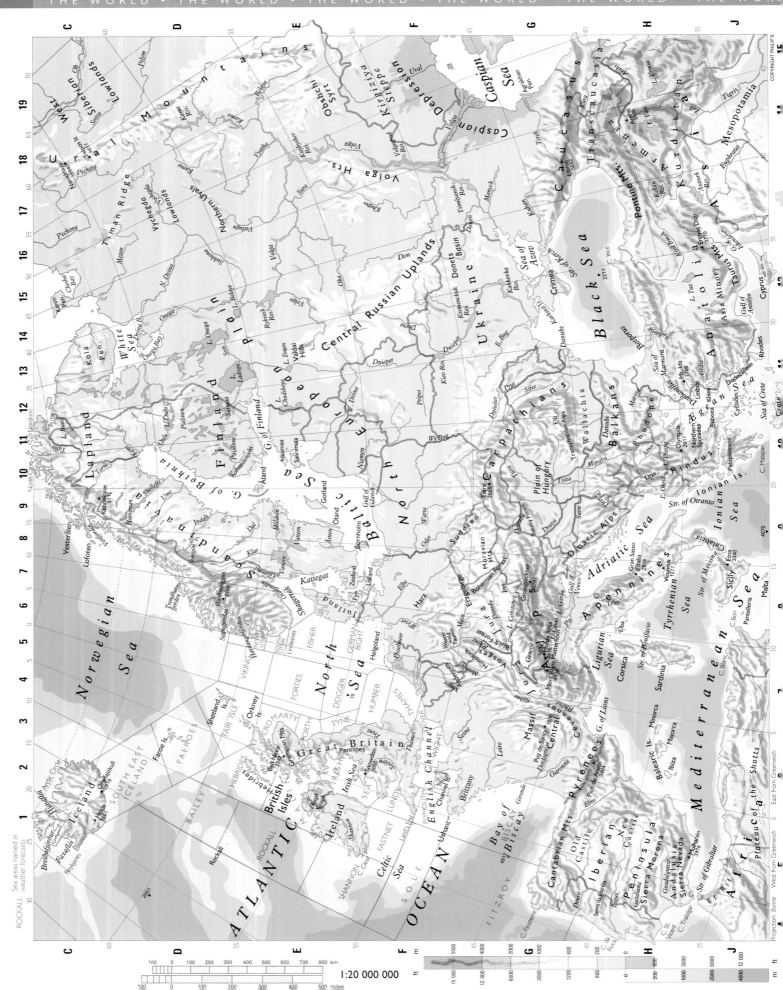

1:20 000 000

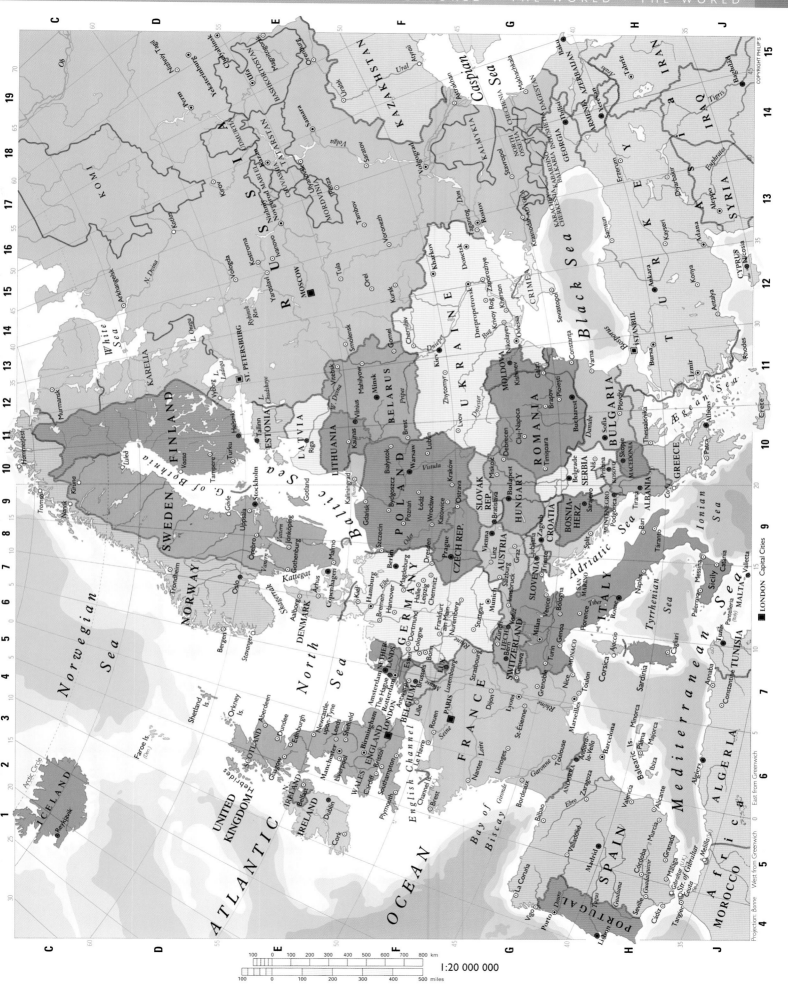

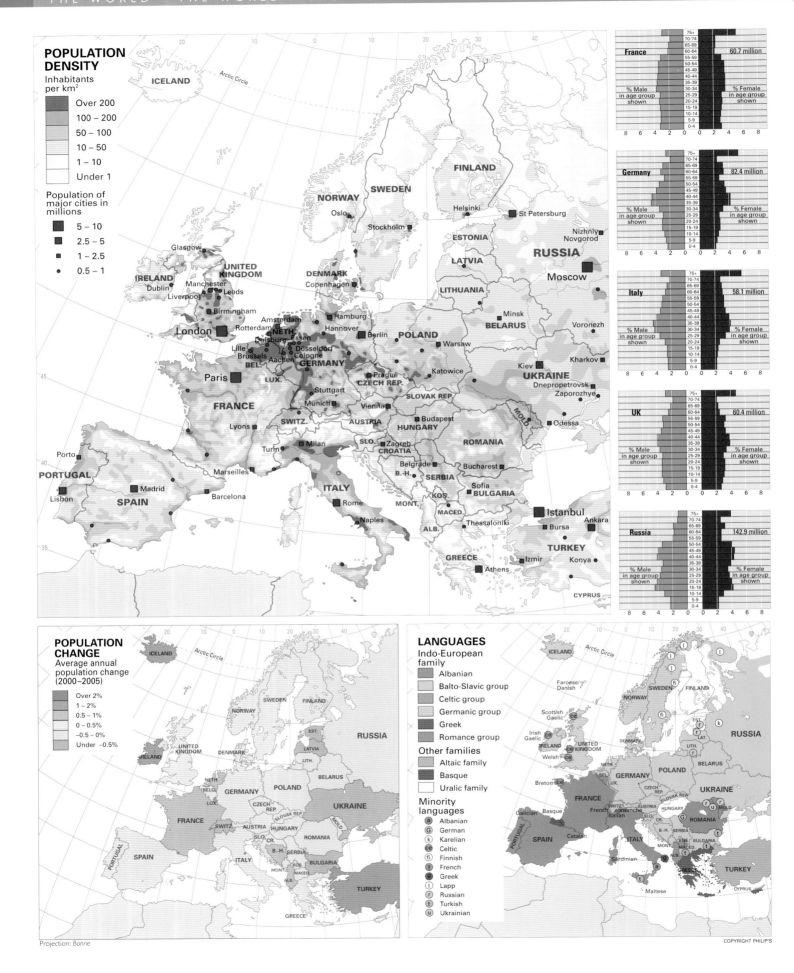

POPULATION DENSITY
Inhabitants per km²
- Over 200
- 100 – 200
- 50 – 100
- 10 – 50
- 1 – 10
- Under 1

Population of major cities in millions
- 5 – 10
- 2.5 – 5
- 1 – 2.5
- 0.5 – 1

Age/sex pyramids:
- France — 60.7 million
- Germany — 82.4 million
- Italy — 58.1 million
- UK — 60.4 million
- Russia — 142.9 million

(% Male in age group shown / % Female in age group shown)

POPULATION CHANGE
Average annual population change (2000–2005)
- Over 2%
- 1 – 2%
- 0.5 – 1%
- 0 – 0.5%
- -0.5 – 0%
- Under -0.5%

LANGUAGES
Indo-European family
- Albanian
- Balto-Slavic group
- Celtic group
- Germanic group
- Greek
- Romance group

Other families
- Altaic family
- Basque
- Uralic family

Minority languages
- (a) Albanian
- (G) German
- (k) Karelian
- (ce) Celtic
- (fi) Finnish
- (f) French
- (g) Greek
- (l) Lapp
- (r) Russian
- (t) Turkish
- (u) Ukrainian

Projection: Bonne

COPYRIGHT PHILIP'S

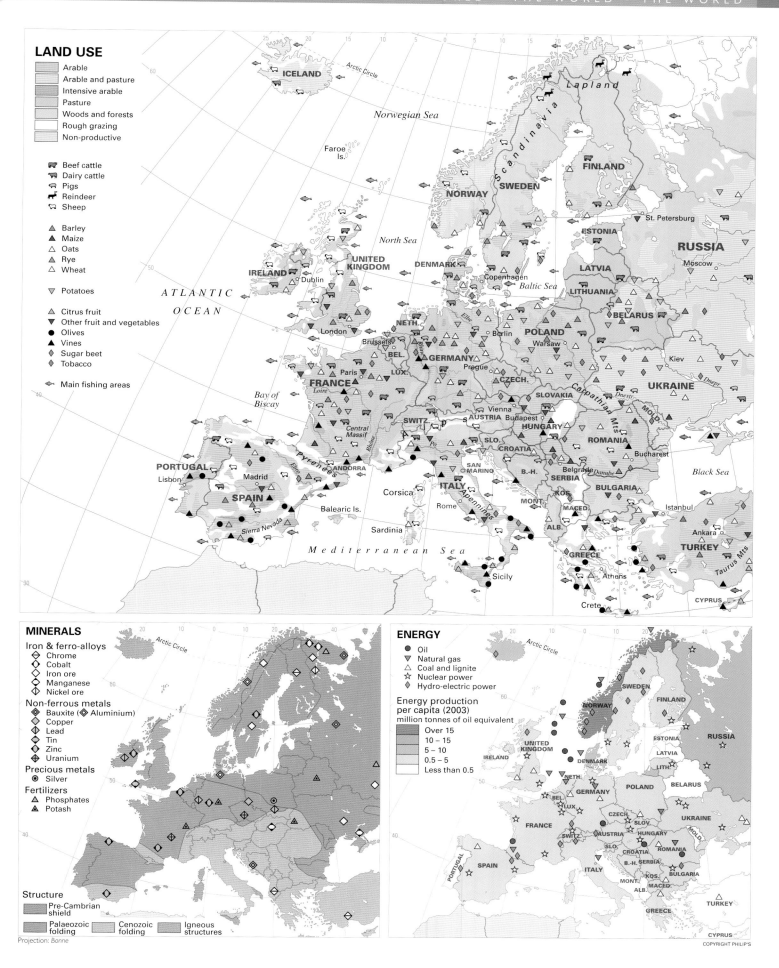

LAND USE

- Arable
- Arable and pasture
- Intensive arable
- Pasture
- Woods and forests
- Rough grazing
- Non-productive

- Beef cattle
- Dairy cattle
- Pigs
- Reindeer
- Sheep

- Barley
- Maize
- Oats
- Rye
- Wheat

- Potatoes

- Citrus fruit
- Other fruit and vegetables
- Olives
- Vines
- Sugar beet
- Tobacco

- Main fishing areas

ICELAND · Lapland · Norwegian Sea · Faroe Is. · FINLAND · SWEDEN · NORWAY · Scandinavia · St. Petersburg · ESTONIA · RUSSIA · North Sea · DENMARK · Copenhagen · Baltic Sea · LATVIA · Moscow · IRELAND · UNITED KINGDOM · Dublin · LITHUANIA · ATLANTIC OCEAN · BELARUS · London · NETH. · Berlin · POLAND · Kiev · Brussels · Elbe · Warsaw · BEL. · GERMANY · Prague · Dnepr · LUX. · Paris · Rhine · CZECH. · UKRAINE · FRANCE · Loire · Carpathian Mts · Bay of Biscay · SWITZ. · AUSTRIA · Vienna · Budapest · SLOVAKIA · Dnestr · MOLD · Central Massif · Rhône · SLO. · HUNGARY · ROMANIA · PORTUGAL · Pyrenees · ANDORRA · CROATIA · Bucharest · Lisbon · Madrid · SAN MARINO · B.-H. · SERBIA · Belgrade · Danube · Black Sea · SPAIN · Corsica · ITALY · Apennines · KOS · BULGARIA · Sierra Nevada · Balearic Is. · Rome · MONT · MACED · Istanbul · Sardinia · ALB. · TURKEY · Ankara · Mediterranean Sea · GREECE · Athens · Taurus Mts · Sicily · Crete · CYPRUS

MINERALS

Iron & ferro-alloys
- Chrome
- Cobalt
- Iron ore
- Manganese
- Nickel ore

Non-ferrous metals
- Bauxite (Aluminium)
- Copper
- Lead
- Tin
- Zinc
- Uranium

Precious metals
- Silver

Fertilizers
- Phosphates
- Potash

Structure
- Pre-Cambrian shield
- Palaeozoic folding
- Cenozoic folding
- Igneous structures

Arctic Circle

ENERGY

- Oil
- Natural gas
- Coal and lignite
- Nuclear power
- Hydro-electric power

Energy production per capita (2003)
million tonnes of oil equivalent
- Over 15
- 10 – 15
- 5 – 10
- 0.5 – 5
- Less than 0.5

Arctic Circle · SWEDEN · FINLAND · NORWAY · UNITED KINGDOM · IRELAND · ESTONIA · RUSSIA · DENMARK · LATVIA · LITH. · NETH. · GERMANY · POLAND · BELARUS · BEL. · LUX. · CZECH. · UKRAINE · FRANCE · SLOV. · HUNGARY · MOLD · SWITZ. · AUSTRIA · ROMANIA · SLO. · CROATIA · PORTUGAL · SPAIN · ITALY · B.-H. · SERBIA · BULGARIA · MONT. · KOS · MACED · ALB. · GREECE · TURKEY · CYPRUS

Projection: Bonne

COPYRIGHT PHILIP'S

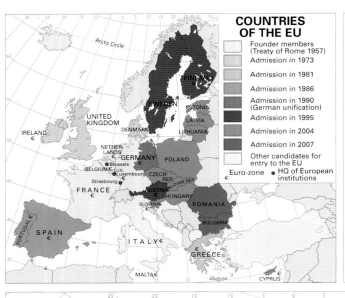

COUNTRIES OF THE EU

- Founder members (Treaty of Rome 1957)
- Admission in 1973
- Admission in 1981
- Admission in 1986
- Admission in 1990 (German unification)
- Admission in 1995
- Admission in 2004
- Admission in 2007
- Other candidates for entry to the EU

€ Euro-zone ● HQ of European institutions

EU COUNTRY COMPARISONS	Population (thousands)	Annual Income (US$ per capita)
Austria	8,185	31,300
Belgium	10,364	30,600
Cyprus	780	20,300
Czech Republic	10,241	16,800
Denmark	5,432	32,200
Estonia	1,333	14,300
Finland	5,223	29,000
France	60,656	28,700
Germany	82,431	28,700
Greece	10,668	21,300
Hungary	10,007	14,900
Ireland	4,016	31,900
Italy	58,103	27,700
Latvia	2,290	11,500
Lithuania	3,597	12,500
Luxembourg	469	58,900
Malta	399	18,200
Netherlands	16,407	29,500
Poland	38,635	12,000
Portugal	10,566	17,900
Slovakia	5,431	14,500
Slovenia	2,011	19,600
Spain	40,341	23,300
Sweden	9,002	28,400
United Kingdom	60,441	29,600
Total EU 2005 (25 countries)	**457,028**	**24,100**
Bulgaria (admitted in 2007)	7,450	9,000
Romania (admitted in 2007)	22,330	8,300

REGIONS OF THE EU

Austria (States)
1 Niederösterreich 2 Oberösterreich 3 Burgenland 4 Kärnten 5 Salzburg 6 Steiermark 7 Tirol 8 Wien 9 Vorarlberg

Belgium (Regions)
1 Bruxelles 2 Vlaanderen 3 Wallonie

Bulgaria (member state from 2007)

Cyprus (member state with no corresponding division)

Czech Republic (Kraj)
1 Jihovychod 2 Jihozapad 3 Moravskoslezsko 4 Praha 5 Severovychod 6 Severozapad 7 Stredni Cechy 8 Stredni Morava

Denmark (member state with no corresponding division)

Estonia (member state with no corresponding division)

Finland (Provinces)
1 Åland 2 Itä-Suomi 3 Väli-Suomi 4 Pohjois-Suomi 5 Uusimaa (Suuralue) 6 Etelä-Suomi

France (Regions)
1 Alsace 2 Aquitaine 3 Auvergne 4 Bourgogne 5 Bretagne 6 Centre 7 Champagne-Ardenne 8 Corse 9 Franche-Comté 10 Ile-de-France 11 Languedoc-Roussillon 12 Limousin 13 Loire (Pays de la) 14 Lorraine 15 Midi-Pyrénées 16 Nord-Pas-de-Calais 17 Normandie (Basse-) 18 Normandie (Haute-) 19 Picardie 20 Poitou-Charentes 21 Provence-Alpes-Côte d'Azur 22 Rhône-Alpes

Germany (Länder)
1 Baden-Württemberg 2 Niedersachsen 3 Bayern 4 Berlin 5 Brandenburg 6 Bremen 7 Hamburg 8 Hessen 9 Mecklenburg-Vorpommern 10 Nordrhein-Westfalen 11 Rheinland-Pfalz 12 Saarland 13 Sachsen 14 Sachsen-Anhalt 15 Schleswig-Holstein 16 Thüringen

Greece (Regions)
1 Anatoliki Makedonia kai Thraki 2 Kriti 3 Voreio Aigaio 4 Notio Aigaio 5 Epiros 6 Attiki 7 Sterea Ellas 8 Dytiki Ellas 9 Ionioi Nisoi 10 Dytiki Makedonia 11 Kentriki Makedonia 12 Peloponnese 13 Thessaly

Hungary (Megyék)
1 Del-Alfold 2 Del-Dunantul 3 Eszak-Alfold 4 Eszak-Magyarorszag 5 Kozep-Dunantul 6 Kozep-Magyarorszag 7 Nyugat-Dunantul

Ireland (Provinces)
1 Border, Midlands & Western 2 Southern & Eastern

Italy (Regions)
1 Abruzzo 2 Basilicata 3 Calàbria 4 Campània 5 Emília-Romagna 6 Friuli-Venézia Giulia 7 Lazio 8 Liguria 9 Lombardia 10 Marche 11 Molise 12 Umbria 13 Piemonte 14 Puglia 15 Sardegna 16 Sicilia 17 Toscana 18 Trentino-Alto Adige 19 Valle d'Aosta 20 Venéto

Latvia (member state with no corresponding division)

Lithuania (member state with no corresponding division)

Luxembourg (member state with no corresponding division)

Malta (member state with no corresponding division)

Netherlands (Regions)
1 Noord-Nederland 2 Oost-Nederland 3 West-Nederland 4 Zuid-Nederland

Poland (Voivodships)
1 Dolnośląskie 2 Kujawsko-Pomorskie 3 Łódzkie 4 Lubelskie 5 Lubuskie 6 Małopolskie 7 Mazowieckie 8 Opolskie 9 Podkarpackie 10 Podlaskie 11 Pomorskie 12 Śląskie 13 Swietokrzyskie 14 Warmińsko-Mazurski 15 Wielkopolskie 16 Zachodniopomorski

Portugal (Autonomous regions)
1 Alentejo 2 Algarve 3 Centro 4 Lisboa-Vale do Tejo 5 Norte

Romania (member state from 2007)

Slovak Republic (Kraj)
1 Bratislavsky Kraj 2 Stredne Slovensko 3 Vychodne Slovensko 4 Zapadne Slovensko

Slovenia (member state with no corresponding division)

Spain (Autonomous communities)
1 Andalucía 2 Aragon 3 Asturias 4 Islas Baleares 5 País Vasco 6 Islas Canarias 7 Cantabria 8 Castilla y Léon 9 Castilla-La Mancha 10 Cataluña 11 Extremadura 12 Galicia 13 Madrid 14 Murcia 15 Navarra 16 Rioja (La) 17 Valencia

Sweden (Regions)
1 Stockholm 2 Östra Mellansverige 3 Sydsverige 4 Västsverige 5 Norra Mellansverige 6 Mellersta Norrland 7 Övre Norrland 8 Småland med öarna

United Kingdom (Government Office Regions)
1 North East 2 North West 3 Yorkshire & the Humber 4 East Midlands 5 West Midlands 6 Eastern 7 London 8 South East 9 South West 10 Wales 11 Scotland 12 Northern Ireland

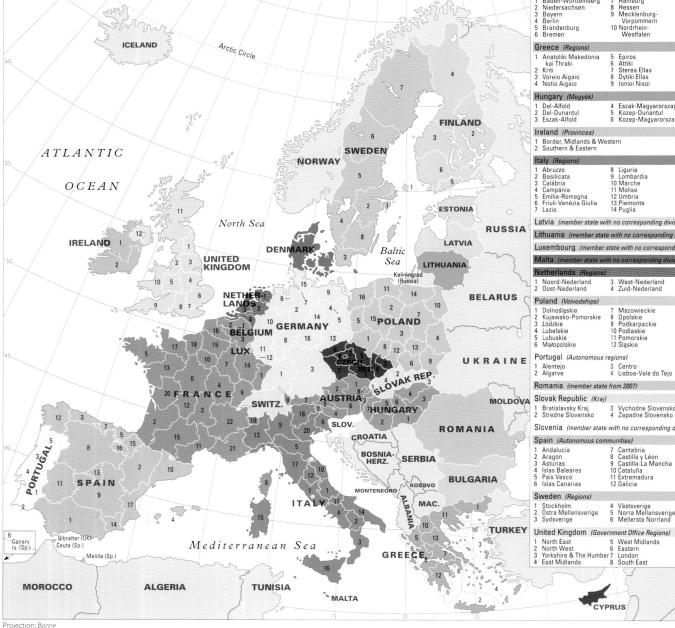

Projection: Bonne

COPYRIGHT P

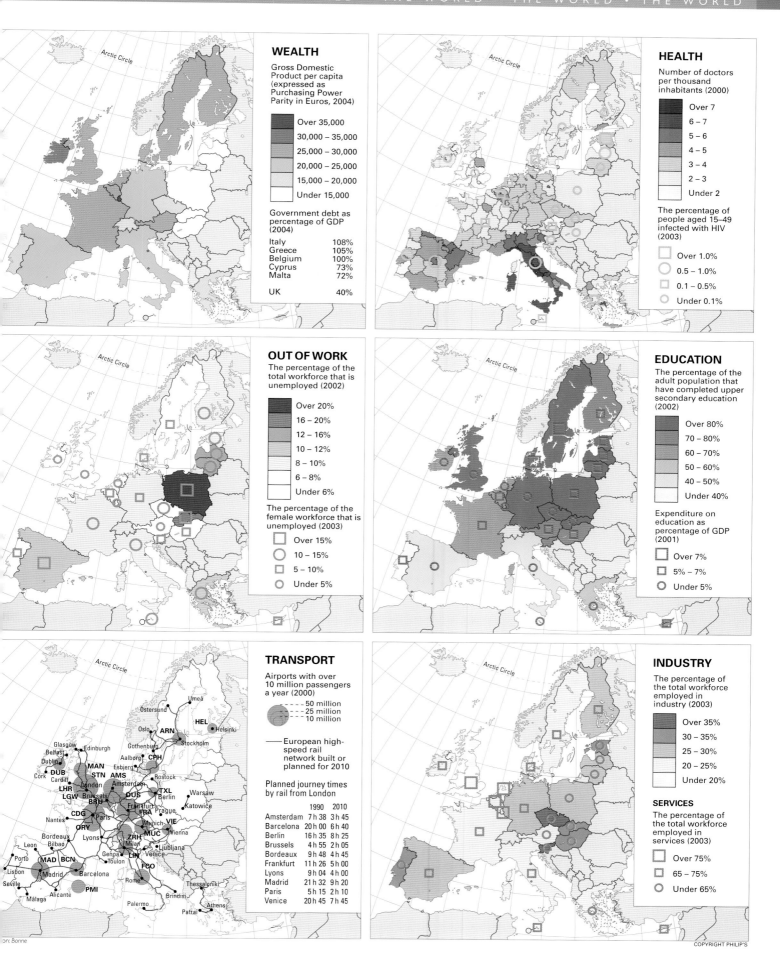

WEALTH

Gross Domestic
Product per capita
(expressed as
Purchasing Power
Parity in Euros, 2004)

- Over 35,000
- 30,000 – 35,000
- 25,000 – 30,000
- 20,000 – 25,000
- 15,000 – 20,000
- Under 15,000

Government debt as
percentage of GDP
(2004)

Italy	108%
Greece	105%
Belgium	100%
Cyprus	73%
Malta	72%
UK	40%

HEALTH

Number of doctors
per thousand
inhabitants (2000)

- Over 7
- 6 – 7
- 5 – 6
- 4 – 5
- 3 – 4
- 2 – 3
- Under 2

The percentage of
people aged 15–49
infected with HIV
(2003)

- Over 1.0%
- 0.5 – 1.0%
- 0.1 – 0.5%
- Under 0.1%

OUT OF WORK

The percentage of the
total workforce that is
unemployed (2002)

- Over 20%
- 16 – 20%
- 12 – 16%
- 10 – 12%
- 8 – 10%
- 6 – 8%
- Under 6%

The percentage of the
female workforce that is
unemployed (2003)

- Over 15%
- 10 – 15%
- 5 – 10%
- Under 5%

EDUCATION

The percentage of the
adult population that
have completed upper
secondary education
(2002)

- Over 80%
- 70 – 80%
- 60 – 70%
- 50 – 60%
- 40 – 50%
- Under 40%

Expenditure on
education as
percentage of GDP
(2001)

- Over 7%
- 5% – 7%
- Under 5%

TRANSPORT

Airports with over
10 million passengers
a year (2000)

- 50 million
- 25 million
- 10 million

— European high-
speed rail
network built or
planned for 2010

Planned journey times
by rail from London

	1990	2010
Amsterdam	7 h 38	3 h 45
Barcelona	20 h 00	6 h 40
Berlin	16 h 35	8 h 25
Brussels	4 h 55	2 h 05
Bordeaux	9 h 48	4 h 45
Frankfurt	11 h 26	5 h 00
Lyons	9 h 04	4 h 00
Madrid	21 h 32	9 h 20
Paris	5 h 15	2 h 10
Venice	20 h 45	7 h 45

Map labels: Umeå, Östersund, Oslo, ARN, HEL, Helsinki, Gothenburg, Stockholm, Glasgow, Edinburgh, Belfast, Dublin, Aalborg, CPH, Esbjerg, Rostock, Cork, DUB, Cardiff, MAN, STN, AMS, Amsterdam, London, LHR, LGW, DUS, TXL, Berlin, Warsaw, Brussels, BRU, FRA, Prague, Katowice, Nantes, CDG, Paris, Frankfurt, Munich, VIE, Vienna, ORY, Lyons, ZRH, MUC, Ljubljana, Bordeaux, Leon, Bilbao, Genoa, LIN, Milan, Venice, Porto, MAD, BCN, Toulon, FCO, Lisbon, Madrid, Barcelona, Rome, Thessaloniki, Seville, PMI, Málaga, Alicante, Brindisi, Palermo, Patrai, Athens

INDUSTRY

The percentage of
the total workforce
employed in
industry (2003)

- Over 35%
- 30 – 35%
- 25 – 30%
- 20 – 25%
- Under 20%

SERVICES

The percentage of
the total workforce
employed in
services (2003)

- Over 75%
- 65 – 75%
- Under 65%

on: Bonne

COPYRIGHT PHILIP'S

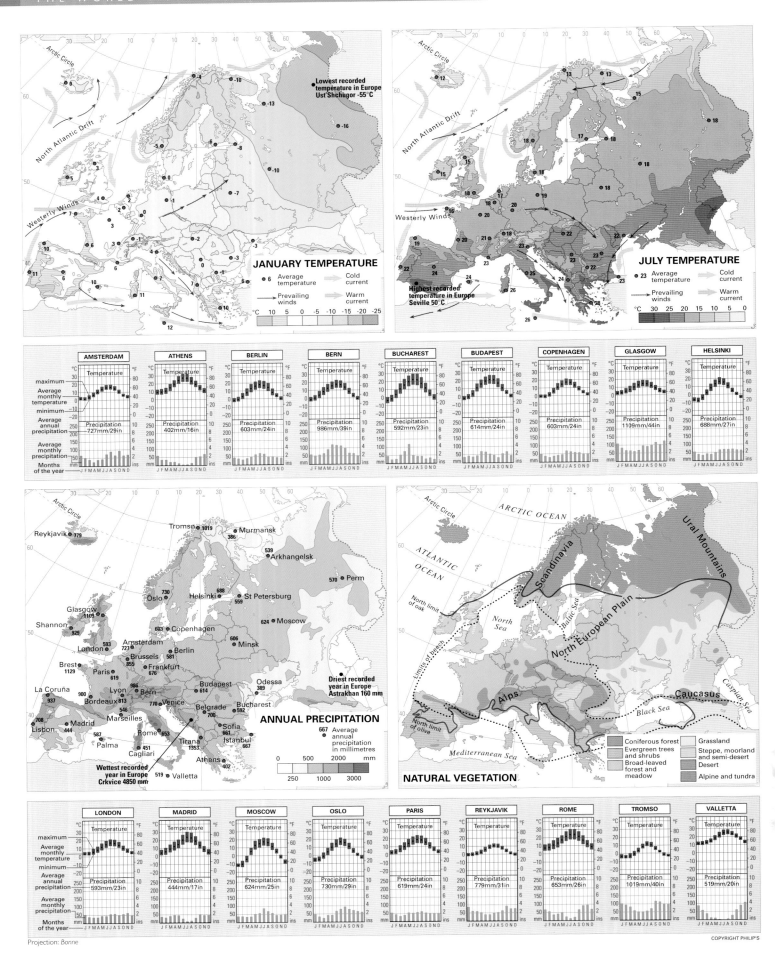

JANUARY TEMPERATURE

Lowest recorded temperature in Europe Ust'Shchugor -55°C

- 6 Average temperature
→ Prevailing winds
⇒ Cold current
⇒ Warm current

°C 10 5 0 -5 -10 -15 -20 -25

North Atlantic Drift

Westerly Winds

JULY TEMPERATURE

Highest recorded temperature in Europe Seville 50°C

- 23 Average temperature
→ Prevailing winds
⇒ Cold current
⇒ Warm current

°C 30 25 20 15 10 5 0

North Atlantic Drift

Westerly Winds

Climate graphs (top row)

AMSTERDAM	ATHENS	BERLIN	BERN	BUCHAREST	BUDAPEST	COPENHAGEN	GLASGOW	HELSINKI
Temperature	Temperature	Temperature	Temperature	Temperature	Temperature	Temperature	Temperature	Temperature
Precipitation 727mm/29in	Precipitation 402mm/16in	Precipitation 603mm/24in	Precipitation 986mm/39in	Precipitation 592mm/23in	Precipitation 614mm/24in	Precipitation 603mm/24in	Precipitation 1109mm/44in	Precipitation 688mm/27in

Legend (left of Amsterdam graph):
- maximum
- Average monthly temperature
- minimum
- Average annual precipitation
- Average monthly precipitation
- Months of the year — J F M A M J J A S O N D

ANNUAL PRECIPITATION

Reykjavik 779
Tromsø 1019 Murmansk 386
Arkhangelsk 539
Perm 570
Oslo 730 Helsinki 688 St Petersburg 559
Moscow 624
Glasgow 1109
Shannon 929
Minsk 606
London 593 Amsterdam 727 Berlin 581
Brest 1129 Brussels 855 Frankfurt 676
Paris 619
Odessa 389
Budapest 614
La Coruña 937 Lyon 986 Bern
Bordeaux 813 Venice 770
546
Madrid 708 Belgrade 700
Lisbon 444 Marseilles 661
Rome 653 Sofia 661
587 Tirana 1353 Istanbul 667
Palma 451
Cagliari
Athens 402
519 Valletta

Driest recorded year in Europe Astrakhan 160 mm

- 667 Average annual precipitation in millimetres

0 500 2000 mm
250 1000 3000

Wettest recorded year in Europe Crkvice 4850 mm

NATURAL VEGETATION

ARCTIC OCEAN
ATLANTIC OCEAN
Scandinavia
Ural Mountains
North limit of oak
North Sea
Baltic Sea
North European Plain
Limits of beech
Alps
Caucasus
Caspian Sea
North limit of olive
Black Sea
Mediterranean Sea

- Coniferous forest
- Evergreen trees and shrubs
- Broad-leaved forest and meadow
- Grassland
- Steppe, moorland and semi-desert
- Desert
- Alpine and tundra

Climate graphs (bottom row)

LONDON	MADRID	MOSCOW	OSLO	PARIS	REYKJAVIK	ROME	TROMSO	VALLETTA
Temperature	Temperature	Temperature	Temperature	Temperature	Temperature	Temperature	Temperature	Temperature
Precipitation 593mm/23in	Precipitation 444mm/17in	Precipitation 624mm/25in	Precipitation 730mm/29in	Precipitation 619mm/24in	Precipitation 779mm/31in	Precipitation 653mm/26in	Precipitation 1019mm/40in	Precipitation 519mm/20in

Legend (left of London graph):
- maximum
- Average monthly temperature
- minimum
- Average annual precipitation
- Average monthly precipitation
- Months of the year — J F M A M J J A S O N D

Projection: Bonne

COPYRIGHT PHILIP'S

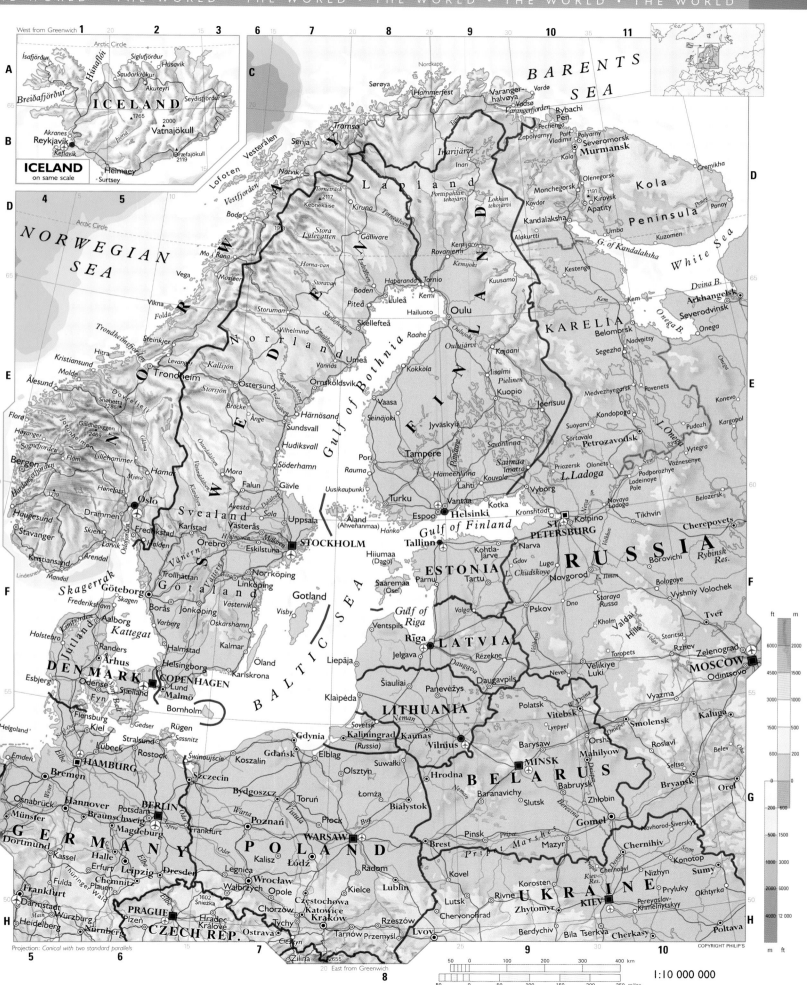

ATLANTIC OCEAN

NORWAY

Bergen
Osøyro
Stord
Bømlo
Haugesund
Kopervik
Åkrahamn
Sandnes
Bryne
Stavanger
Nærbø

Shetland Is.
Yell
Unst
Fetlar
Mainland
Lerwick
Foula
Fair Isle

Orkney Is.
Westray
Sanday
Stronsay
Mainland
Kirkwall
Hoy
South
Ronaldsay

C. Wrath
Pentland Firth
Thurso
Wick
Helmsdale

SCOTLAND
North West Highlands
Lairg
Golspie
Tain
Invergordon
Dingwall
Moray Firth
Buckie
Banff
Fraserburgh
Peterhead
Elgin
Nairn
Inverness
Huntly
Inverurie
Glen More
Aviemore
Spey
Grampian Mts.
Don
Aberdeen
Ben Nevis
Fort William
Dee
Ballater
Stonehaven
Oban
L. Awe
L. Lomond
Perth
Forfar
Arbroath
Montrose
Dundee
St. Andrews
Stirling
Glenrothes
Dunfermline
Kirkcaldy
Dunbar
Glasgow
Edinburgh
Berwick-upon-Tweed
Motherwell
Hamilton
East Kilbride
Irvine
Kilmarnock
Galashiels
Jedburgh
Hawick
Alnwick
Ayr
Southern Uplands
Cheviot Hills
Dumfries
Annan
Hexham
Newcastle-upon-Tyne
South Shields
Sunderland
Carlisle
Gateshead
Durham
Hartlepool
Darlington
Redcar
Middlesbrough
Stockton-on-Tees
Cumbrian Mts.
Scarborough
Whitehaven
Barrow-in-Furness
Lancaster
Bridlington
Harrogate
Keighley
York
Beverley
Kingston upon Hull
Blackpool
Burnley
Leeds
Bradford
Preston
Halifax
Huddersfield
Scunthorpe
Grimsby
Blackburn
Bolton
Doncaster
Barnsley
Rotherham
Lincoln
Louth
Oldham
Sheffield
Stockport
Mansfield
Manchester
Liverpool
Warrington
Skegness
Chester
Chesterfield
Boston
Crewe
The Wash
Stoke-on-Trent
Derby
Nottingham
Granthan
King's Lynn
Cromer
Stafford
Trent
Telford
Leicester
Norwich
Great Yarmouth
Shrewsbury
Nuneaton
Peterborough
Lowestoft
Welshpool
Wolverhampton
Coventry
Corby
BIRMINGHAM
Rugby
Northampton
Ely
Bury St. Edmunds
Ipswich
Redditch
Royal
Leamington Spa
Bedford
Cambridge
Worcester
Milton Keynes
Felixstowe
Hereford
Harwich
Colchester
Cheltenham
Oxford
Luton
Chelmsford
Gloucester
Hemel
Hempstead
Harlow
Cwmbran
Cotswold Hills
High Wycombe
Watford
Southend-on-Sea
Newport
Slough
LONDON
Swindon
Reading
Chatham
Margate
Cardiff
Bristol
Newbury
Maidstone
Canterbury
Dover
Bath
Basingstoke
Reigate
Guildford
Crawley
Ashford
Folkestone
Weston-super-Mare
Salisbury
Winchester
Fareham
Hastings
Havant
Brighton
Eastbourne
Worthing
Southampton
Portsmouth
Bournemouth
Poole
Isle of Wight
Newport
Weymouth

WALES
Cambrian Mts.
Snowdon
Anglesey
Holyhead
Bangor
Colwyn Bay
Wrexham
Pwllheli
Cardigan Bay
Aberystwyth
Cardigan
Fishguard
Haverfordwest
Milford Haven
Pembroke
Carmarthen
Llanelli
Swansea
Neath
Merthyr Tydfil
Rhondda
Port Talbot
Barry

I. of Man
Douglas

IRELAND
Dublin
Dun Laoghaire
Bray
Wicklow Mts.
Arklow
Wexford
Rosslare
Waterford
Dungarvan
Youghal
Cork
Cobh
Kinsale
Bandon
Limerick
Tralee
Killarney
Dingle
Valencia I.
Macgillycuddy's Reeks
Carrauntoohil
Bantry
C. Clear

NORTHERN IRELAND
Belfast
Londonderry
Coleraine
Ballymena
Larne
Antrim
Bangor
Lisburn
Lurgan
Portadown
Armagh
Newry
Omagh
Lough Neagh
Enniskillen
Lower L. Erne
Lifford
Buncrana
Letterkenny
Donegal
Bundoran
Sligo
Ballina
Castlebar
Westport
Achill I.
Connemara
Galway B.
Galway
Aran Is.
Ennis
Ballinasloe
Athlone
Mullingar
Longford
Roscommon
Lough Mask
Lough Corrib
Lough Ree
Lough Derg
Shannon
Listowel
Thurles
Tipperary
Clonmel
Carrick-on-Suir
Kilkenny
Carlow
Athy
Port Laoise
Tullamore
Ceanannus Mor
Cavan
Monaghan
Castleblaney
Dundalk
Drogheda
Boyne
Kells
Naas
Kildare

IRISH SEA
ST. GEORGE'S CHANNEL
NORTH CHANNEL
CELTIC SEA
NORTH SEA

Outer Hebrides
Lewis
Stornoway
Harris
North Uist
Benbecula
South Uist
Barra
St. Kilda
North Minch
Inner Hebrides
Sea of the Hebrides
Skye
Portree
Mallaig
Rhum
Eigg
Coll
Tiree
Tobermory
Mull
Colonsay
Jura
Islay
Arran
Campbeltown
Firth of Clyde
Malin Hd.
Mull of Galloway

FRANCE
Cherbourg
Le Havre
Rouen
Caen
Dieppe
Calais
Dunkerque
Boulogne-sur-Mer
Str. of Dover
C. Gris-Nez
Amiens
Abbeville
St. Quentin
Picardie

BELGIUM
Brugge
Gent
Brussel
Antwerpen
Lille
Tournai

NETHERLANDS
The Hague
Rotterdam
Hoek van Holland
Den Helder

Channel Is. (U.K.)
Guernsey
St. Peter Port
Jersey
St. Helier
Alderney
Sark

ENGLISH CHANNEL

Land's End
Isles of Scilly
Penzance
Falmouth
St. Austell
Truro
Newquay
Bude
Plymouth
Torbay
Exmouth
Exeter
Dartmoor
Exmoor
Barnstaple
Taunton
Yeovil
Bristol Channel

Projection: Conical with two standard parallels

1:5 000 000

East from Greenwich
West from Greenwich
COPYRIGHT PHILIP'S

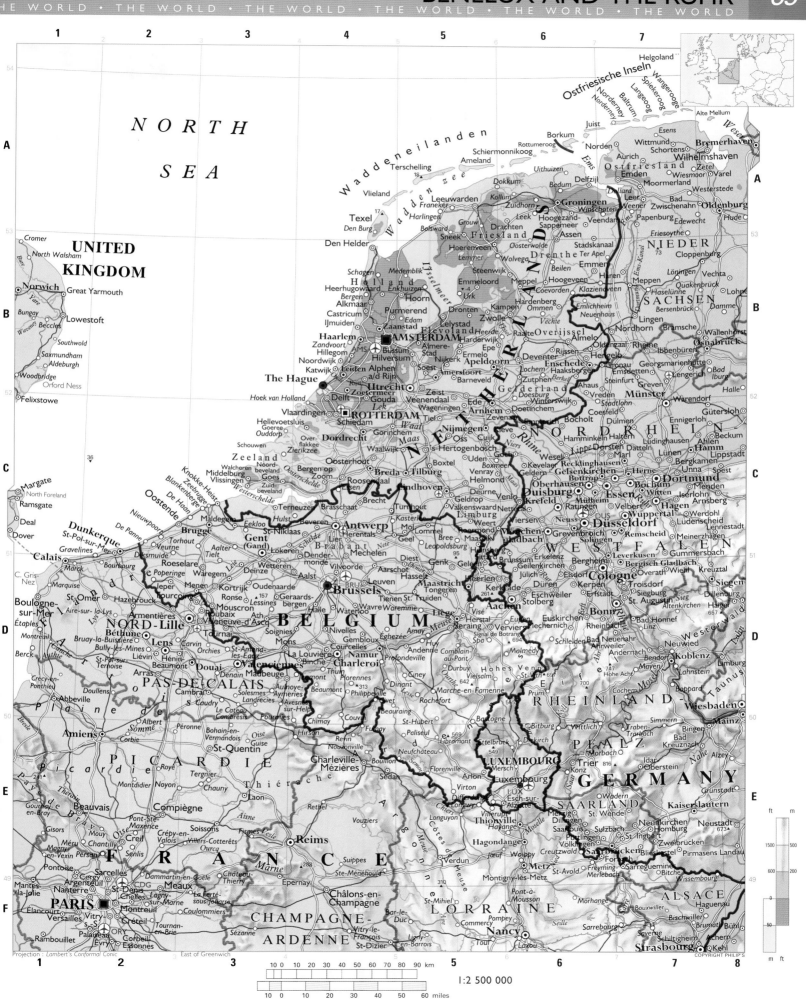

DENMARK

BALTIC SEA

NORTH SEA

UNITED KINGDOM

NETHERLANDS

AMSTERDAM
The Hague
ROTTERDAM

BELGIUM

BRUSSELS

LUXEMBOURG

GERMANY

HAMBURG
BREMEN
HANNOVER
BERLIN
Potsdam
Magdeburg
Leipzig
Dresden
Frankfurt
Cologne
Düsseldorf
Dortmund
Essen
Bonn
Stuttgart
Nuremberg
MUNICH
Augsburg

Hamburg
Lübeck
Rostock
Schwerin
Kiel

Brandenburg
Sachsen
Sachsen-Anhalt

Mecklenburg

Szczecin

PRAGUE
CZECH
Plzeň
České Budějovice

FRANCE

PARIS
Reims
Metz
Nancy
Strasbourg
Dijon
LYONS
Grenoble
MARSEILLES
Nice
MONACO
Monte-Carlo

SWITZERLAND
Bern
Zürich
Basel
Geneva
Lausanne
LIECHTENSTEIN
Vaduz

AUSTRIA
Innsbruck
Salzburg
Linz
Graz
Tirol
Steiermark
Kärnten

SLOVENIA
Ljubljana

ITALY
MILAN
Turin
Genoa
Venice
Verona
Padova
Bologna
Florence
SAN MARINO

ADRIATIC SEA

Mont Blanc

Projection: Conical with two standard parallels

1:5 000 000

COPYRIGHT PHILIP'S

East from Greenwich

FRANCE

Countries: UNITED KINGDOM, BELGIUM, LUXEMBOURG, GERMANY, SWITZERLAND, AUSTRIA, ITALY, FRANCE, ANDORRA, SPAIN

Regions: Normandie, Bretagne, Picardie, Lorraine, Alsace, Franche-Comté, Bourgogne, Nivernais, Bourbonnais, Auvergne, Massif Central, Provence, Côte d'Azur, Languedoc, Roussillon, Aquitaine, Gascogne, Guyenne, Béarn, Pyrénées, Île-de-France, Plaine de la Beauce, Plateau de Langres, Morvan

Seas and waters: English Channel, Bay of Biscay, Golfe de Gascogne, MEDITERRANEAN SEA, Golfe du Lion, Rhine, Rhône, Loire, Seine, Garonne, Dordogne, Saône, Marne, Moselle

Major cities: PARIS, MARSEILLES, LYONS, Bordeaux, Toulouse, Nantes, Nice, MONACO, Lille, Strasbourg, Nancy, Metz, Reims, Rouen, Le Havre, Caen, Rennes, Brest, Orléans, Tours, Le Mans, Angers, Dijon, Besançon, Grenoble, Clermont-Ferrand, Limoges, Poitiers, Angoulême, Montpellier, Nîmes, Avignon, Perpignan, Bayonne, Biarritz, Pau, Tarbes

Neighbouring cities: London, Southampton, Plymouth, Exeter, Bournemouth, Portsmouth, Brighton, Dover, Brussels, Charleroi, Namur, Liège, Maastricht, Aachen, Bonn, Frankfurt, Stuttgart, Karlsruhe, Mannheim, Heidelberg, Freiburg, Basel, Zürich, Bern, Geneva, Lausanne, Milan, Turin, Genoa, La Spezia, Parma, Bologna, Bilbao, San Sebastián, Pamplona, Logroño, Burgos, ANDORRA

Corsica — C. Corse, Bastia, Corte, Ajaccio, Bonifacio, Porto-Vecchio

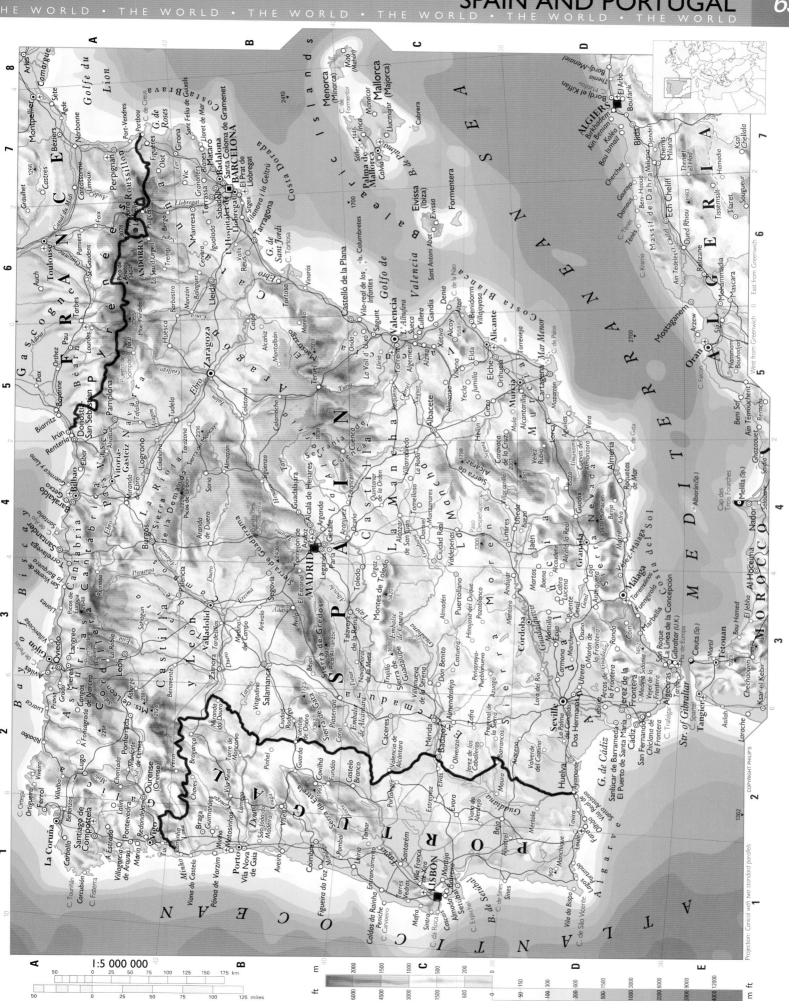

1:5 000 000

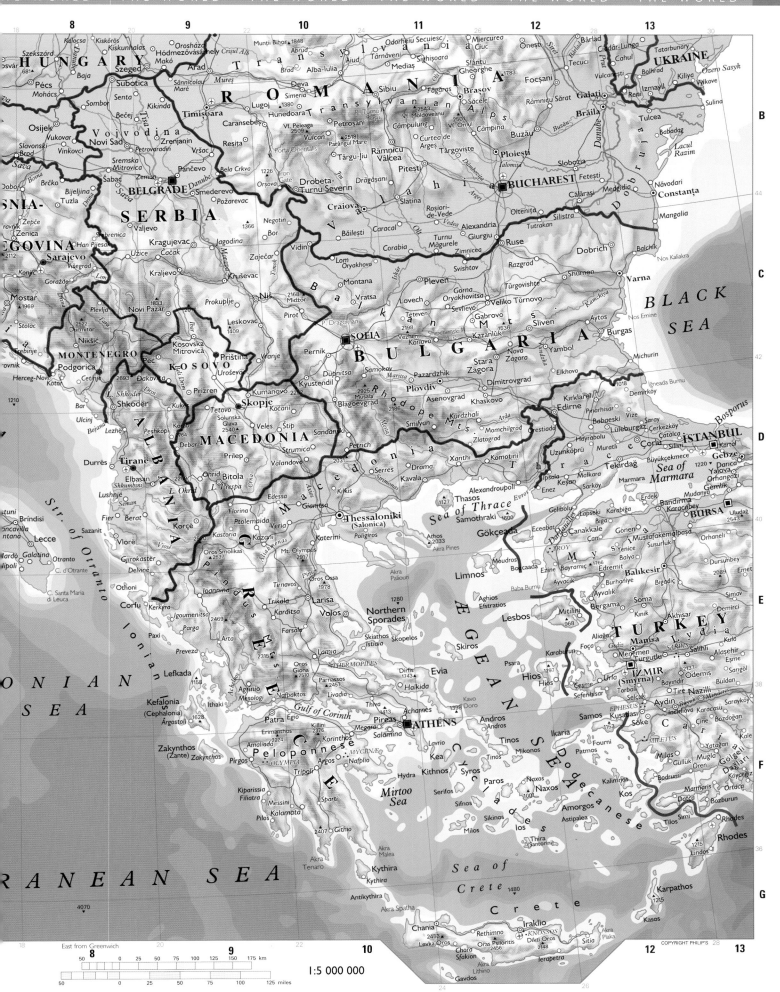

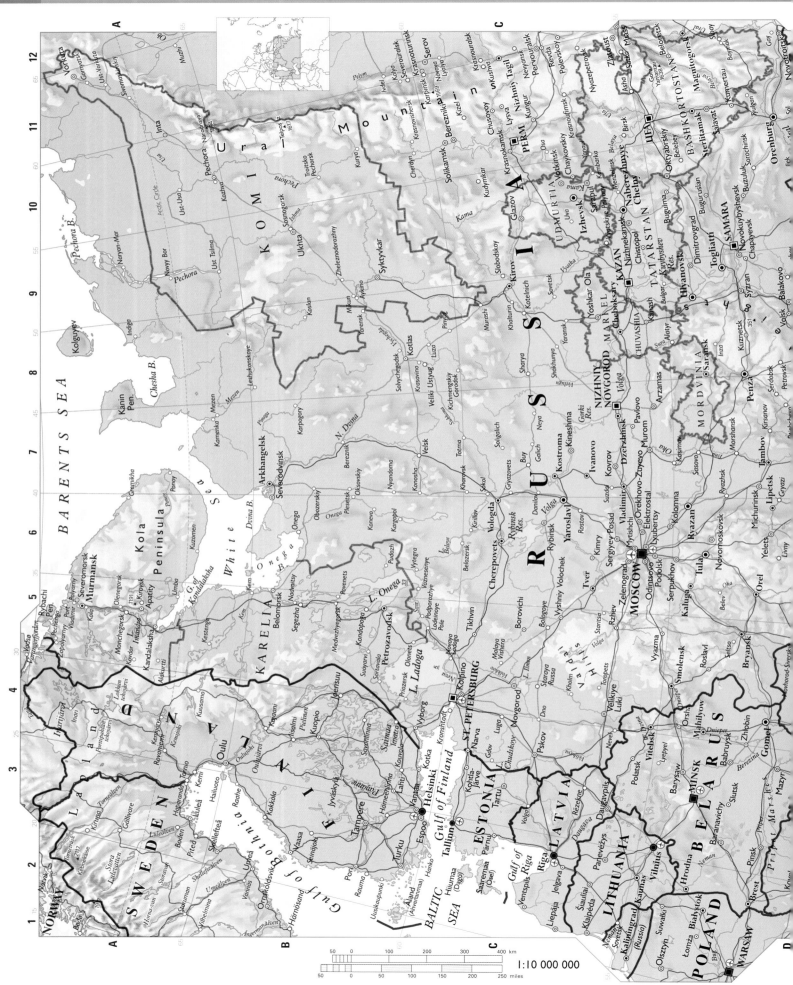

1:10 000 000

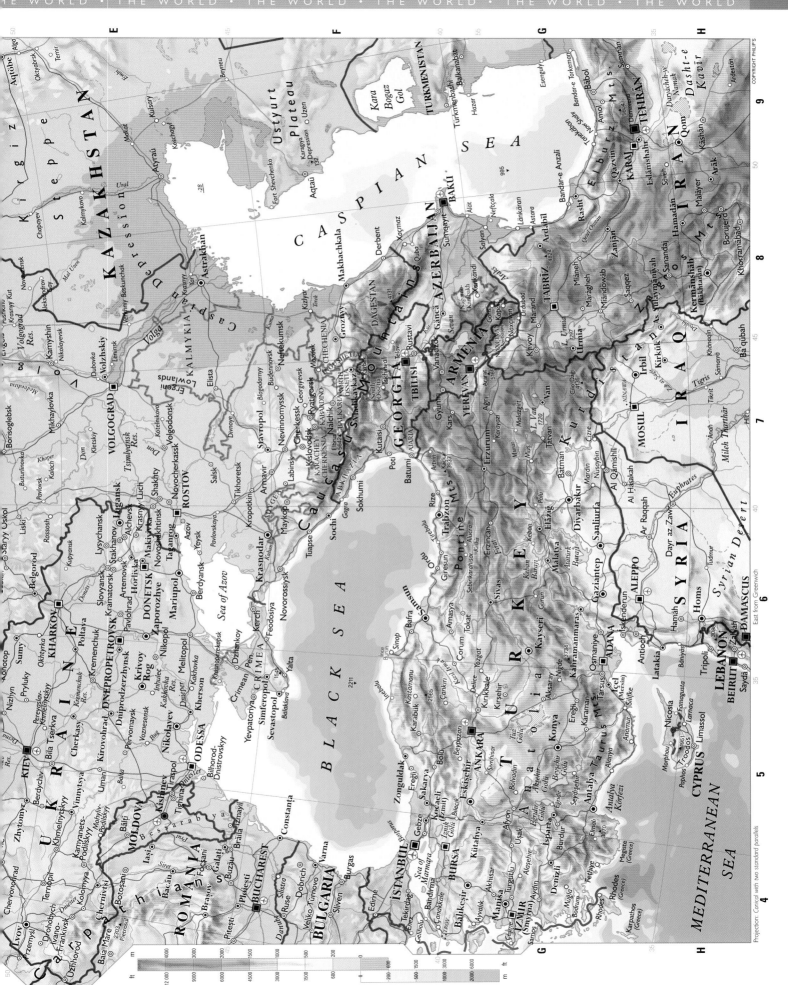

Projection: Conical with two standard parallels

East from Greenwich

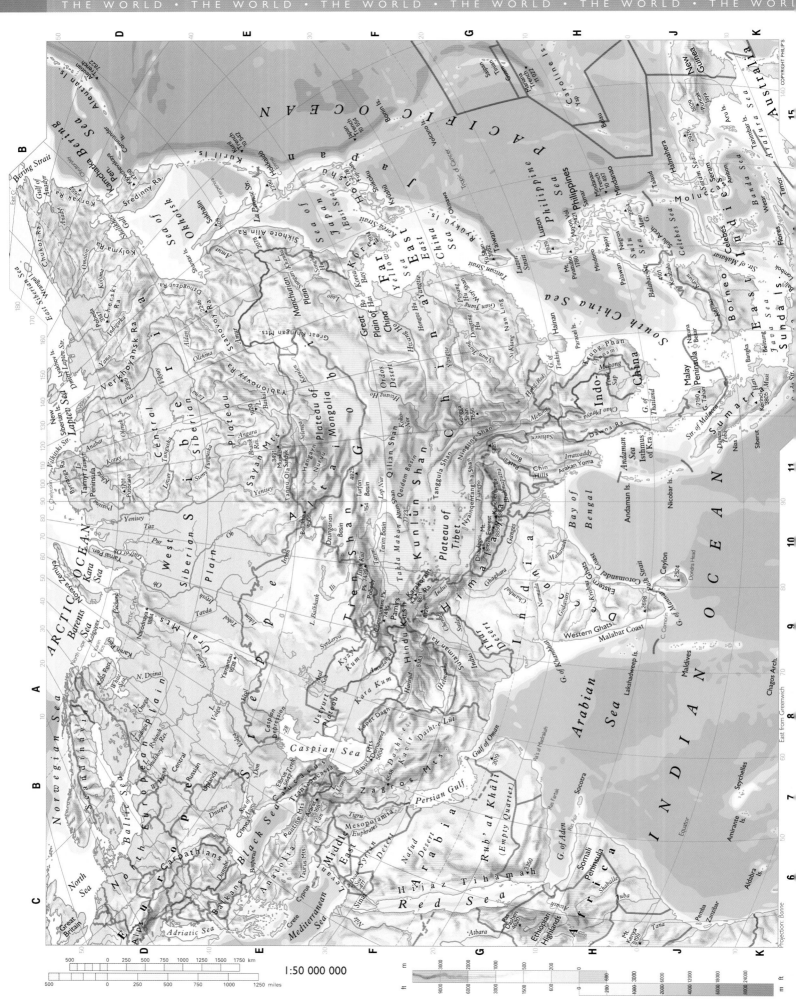

1:50 000 000

Projection: Bonne

RUSSIA
1 Adygea
2 Karachey-Cherkessia
3 Kabardino-Balkaria
4 North Ossetia
5 Ingushetia
6 Chechenia
7 Dagestan
8 Mordvinia
9 Chuvashia
10 Mari El
11 Tatarstan
12 Udmurtia

AZERBAIJAN
13 Naxçivan

GEORGIA
14 Ajaria
15 Abkhazia

Hanoi ● Capital Cities

500   0   250   500   750   1000   1250   1500 1750 km

500   0   250   500   750   1000   1250 miles

1:50 000 000

Projection: Bonne

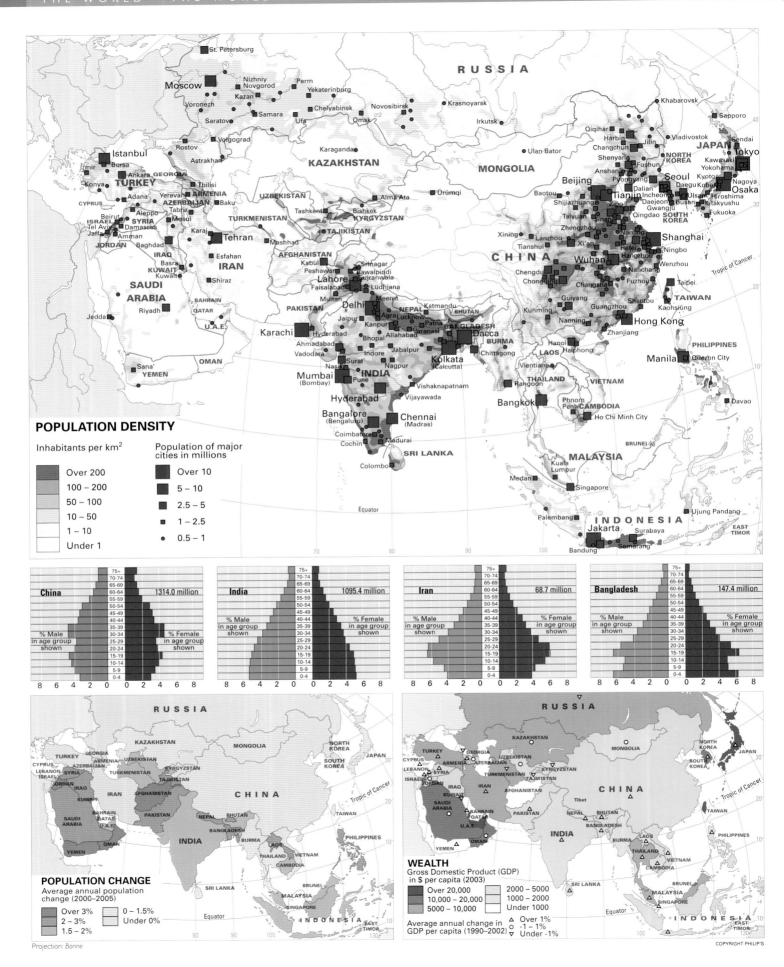

POPULATION DENSITY

Inhabitants per km²

- Over 200
- 100 – 200
- 50 – 100
- 10 – 50
- 1 – 10
- Under 1

Population of major cities in millions

- Over 10
- 5 – 10
- 2.5 – 5
- 1 – 2.5
- 0.5 – 1

Projection: Bonne

China 1314.0 million

India 1095.4 million

Iran 68.7 million

Bangladesh 147.4 million

% Male in age group shown / % Female in age group shown

Age groups: 75+, 70-74, 65-69, 60-64, 55-59, 50-54, 45-49, 40-44, 35-39, 30-34, 25-29, 20-24, 15-19, 10-14, 5-9, 0-4

Scale: 8 6 4 2 0 2 4 6 8

POPULATION CHANGE

Average annual population change (2000–2005)

- Over 3%
- 2 – 3%
- 1.5 – 2%
- 0 – 1.5%
- Under 0%

WEALTH

Gross Domestic Product (GDP) in $ per capita (2003)

- Over 20,000
- 10,000 – 20,000
- 5,000 – 10,000
- 2000 – 5000
- 1000 – 2000
- Under 1000

Average annual change in GDP per capita (1990–2002)

- △ Over 1%
- ○ -1 – 1%
- ▽ Under -1%

COPYRIGHT PHILIP'S

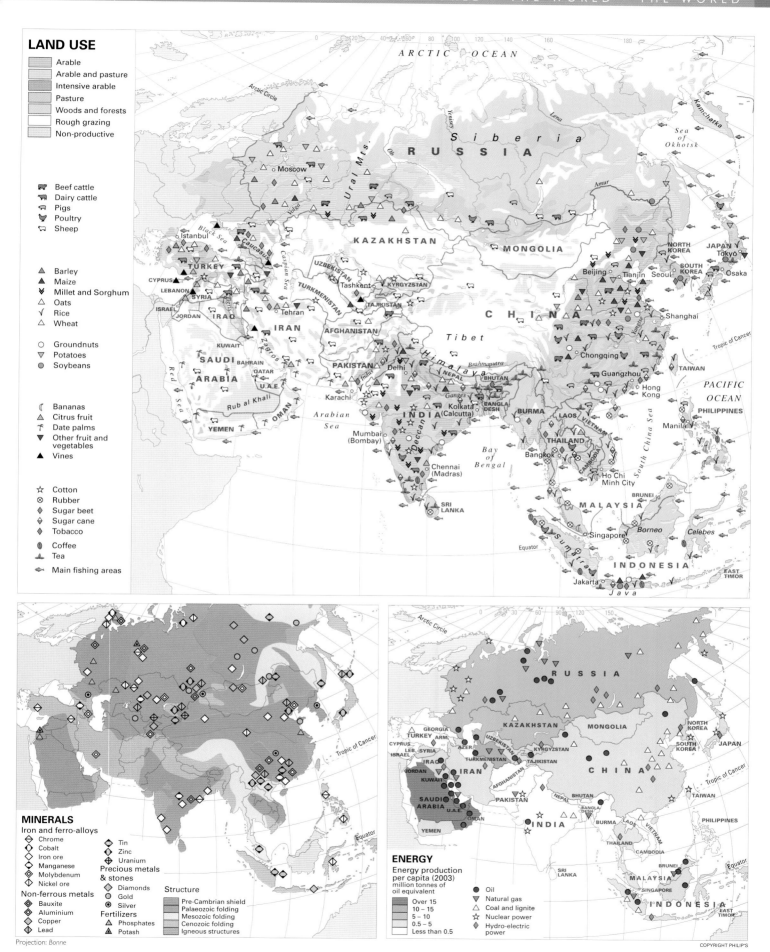

LAND USE

Arable
Arable and pasture
Intensive arable
Pasture
Woods and forests
Rough grazing
Non-productive

- Beef cattle
- Dairy cattle
- Pigs
- Poultry
- Sheep

- Barley
- Maize
- Millet and Sorghum
- Oats
- Rice
- Wheat

- Groundnuts
- Potatoes
- Soybeans

- Bananas
- Citrus fruit
- Date palms
- Other fruit and vegetables
- Vines

- Cotton
- Rubber
- Sugar beet
- Sugar cane
- Tobacco
- Coffee
- Tea
- Main fishing areas

MINERALS

Iron and ferro-alloys
- Chrome
- Cobalt
- Iron ore
- Manganese
- Molybdenum
- Nickel ore

Non-ferrous metals
- Bauxite
- Aluminium
- Copper
- Lead

- Tin
- Zinc
- Uranium

Precious metals & stones
- Diamonds
- Gold
- Silver

Fertilizers
- Phosphates
- Potash

Structure
- Pre-Cambrian shield
- Palaeozoic folding
- Mesozoic folding
- Cenozoic folding
- Igneous structures

ENERGY

Energy production per capita (2003) million tonnes of oil equivalent

- Over 15
- 10 – 15
- 5 – 10
- 0.5 – 5
- Less than 0.5

- Oil
- Natural gas
- Coal and lignite
- Nuclear power
- Hydro-electric power

Projection: *Bonne*

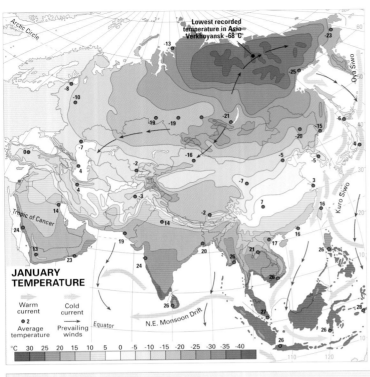

JANUARY TEMPERATURE

Lowest recorded temperature in Asia Verkhoyansk -68°C

Warm current

2 Average temperature

Cold current

Prevailing winds

N.E. Monsoon Drift

°C 30 25 20 15 10 5 0 -5 -10 -15 -20 -25 -30 -35 -40

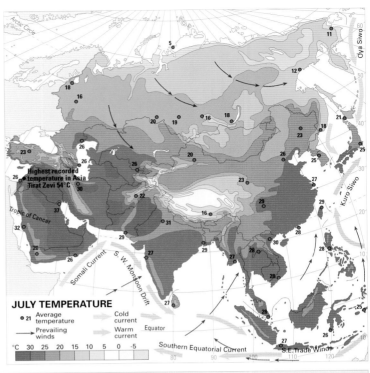

JULY TEMPERATURE

Highest recorded temperature in Asia Tirat Zevi 54°C

21 Average temperature

Cold current

Prevailing winds

Warm current

Somali Current · S. W. Monsoon Drift · Southern Equatorial Current · S.E. Trade Winds

°C 30 25 20 15 10 5 0 -5

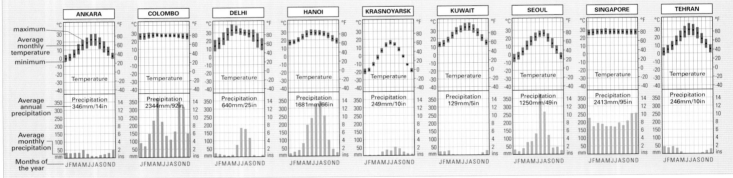

Climate graphs for ANKARA, COLOMBO, DELHI, HANOI, KRASNOYARSK, KUWAIT, SEOUL, SINGAPORE, TEHRAN

maximum / Average monthly temperature / minimum

Temperature

Average annual precipitation / Average monthly precipitation

Months of the year — J F M A M J J A S O N D

City	Average annual precipitation
ANKARA	346mm/14in
COLOMBO	2344mm/92in
DELHI	640mm/25in
HANOI	1681mm/66in
KRASNOYARSK	249mm/10in
KUWAIT	129mm/5in
SEOUL	1250mm/49in
SINGAPORE	2413mm/95in
TEHRAN	246mm/10in

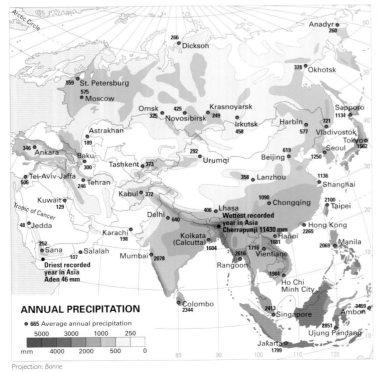

ANNUAL PRECIPITATION

Anadyr 260
Dickson 266
St. Petersburg 559
Moscow 575
Omsk 425
Novosibirsk 325
Krasnoyarsk 249
Okhotsk 378
Sapporo 1134
Harbin 577
Vladivostok 721
Irkutsk 458
Astrakhan 189
Ankara 346
Baku 300
Tashkent 373
Urumqi 292
Beijing 619
Seoul 1250
Tokyo 1562
Tel-Aviv-Jaffa 506
Tehran 246
Lanzhou 358
Shanghai 1136
Kabul 372
Chongqing 1090
Taipei 2100
Kuwait 129
Lhasa 406
Delhi 640
Hong Kong 2265
Jedda 48
Karachi 198
Kolkata (Calcutta) 1604
Hanoi 1681
Manila 2069
Sana 252
Salalah 107
Mumbai 2078
Rangoon 2616
Vientiane 1716
Ho Chi Minh City 1984
Colombo 2344
Singapore 2413
Ambon 3459
Ujung Pandang 2851
Jakarta 1799

Wettest recorded year in Asia Cherrapunji 11430 mm

Driest recorded year in Asia Aden 46 mm

665 Average annual precipitation

mm 5000 4000 3000 2000 1000 500 250 0

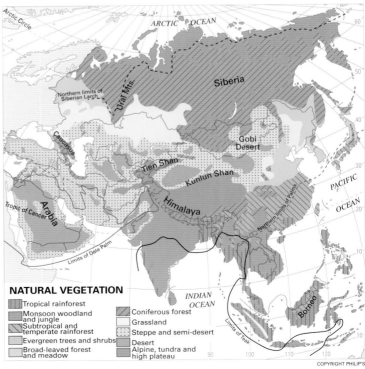

NATURAL VEGETATION

- Tropical rainforest
- Monsoon woodland and jungle
- Subtropical and temperate rainforest
- Evergreen trees and shrubs
- Broad-leaved forest and meadow
- Coniferous forest
- Grassland
- Steppe and semi-desert
- Desert
- Alpine, tundra and high plateau

ARCTIC OCEAN
Siberia
Ural Mts.
Northern limits of Siberian Larch
Gobi Desert
Caucasus
Tien Shan
Kunlun Shan
Himalaya
Arabia
Tropic of Cancer
INDIAN OCEAN
PACIFIC OCEAN
Borneo
Limits of Date Palm
Limits of Teak
Northern limits of Palms

Projection: *Bonne*

COPYRIGHT PHILIP'S

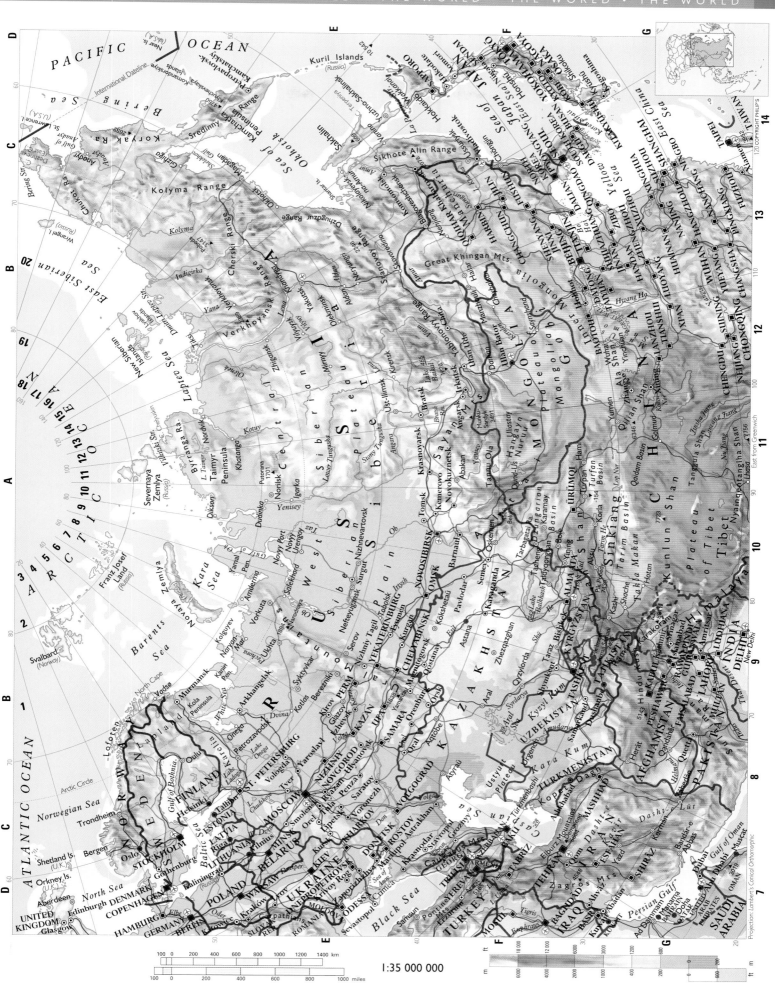

1:35 000 000

Projection: Lambert's Conical Orthomorphic

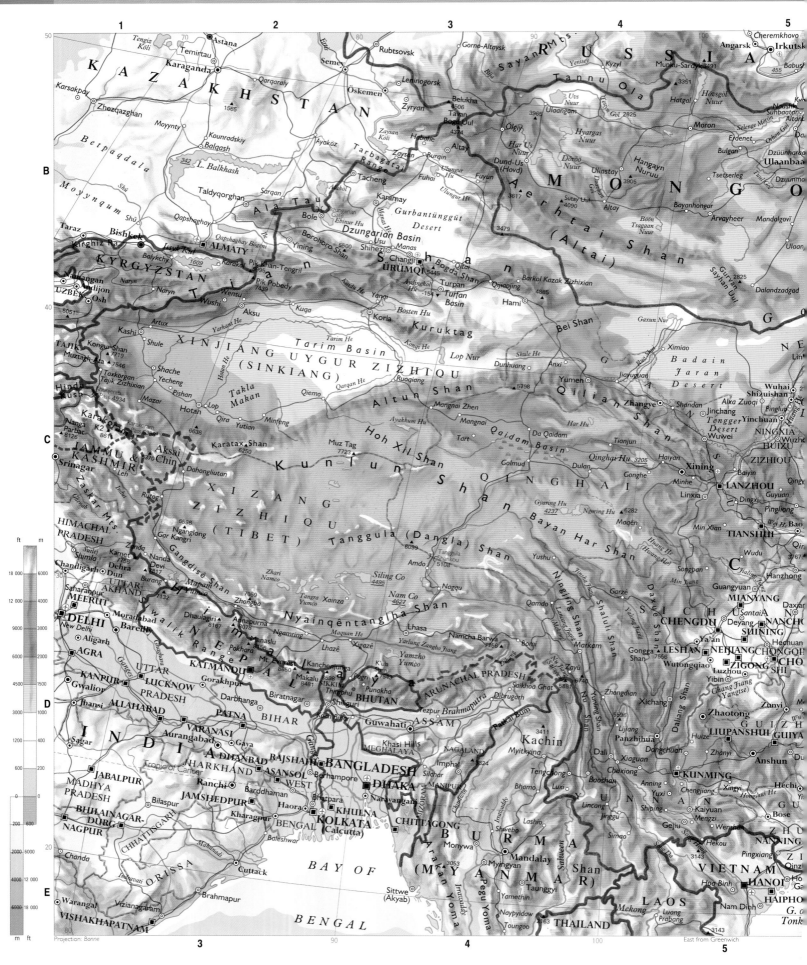

Projection: Bonne

East from Greenwich

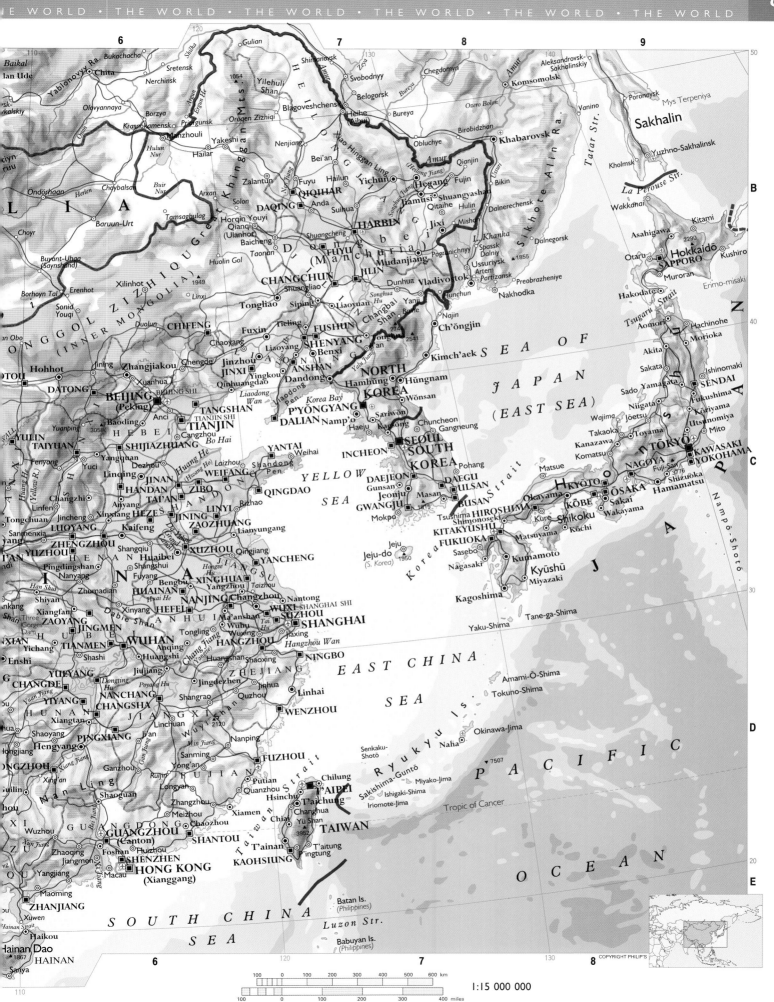

CHINA

RUSSIA

Sikhote Alin Ra.

Linkou
Jixi
Novokachalinsk
Kamen-Rybolov
L. Khanka
Suifenhe
Lipovcy
Manzovka
Ussuriysk
Spassk Dalniy
Gornyy
Yakovleyka
Arsenev
1855
Lazo
Margaritovo

Rakitnoye
Lesozavodsk
Kirovskiy
Ariadnoye
Plastun
Terney
Dalnegorsk
Kavalerovo

Hunchun
1498
Trudovoye
Artem
Vladivostok
Slavyanka
Nakhodka
Preobrazheniye
Khasan
Najin

Chŏngjin

NORTH
KOREA

Wakkanai
Rebun-Tō
Rishiri-Tō
Teshio
Otoineppu
Esashi
Ōmu
Mombetsu
Embetsu
Haboro
Nayoro
Engaru
Yūbetsu
Abashiri-Wan
Abashiri
Rausu-Dake
Rumoi
Shibetsu
Kitami
Shari
Nemu
Takikawa
Ishikari-Gawa
Asahigawa
2290
Daisetsu-Zan
2077
Hokkaidō
Kunas
Nakashibet
Kamui-Misaki
Otaru
SAPPORO
Ebetsu
Bibai
Iwamizawa
Obihiro
Poroshiri-Dake
2052
Kushiro
Honbetsu
Shibecha
Akkeshi
Iwanai
Shikotsu-Ko
Suttsu
Toya-Ko
Tomakomai
Setana
Uchiura-Wan
Muroran
Hiroo
Samani
Okushiri-Tō
Yakumo
Esashi
Matsumae
Shiragami-Misaki
Hakodate
Ohata
Mutsu
Tsugaru Strait
Shiriya-Zaki
Erimo-misaki

Esan-Misaki
Kanagi
Mutsu-Wan
Aomori
Goshogawara
Towada-Ko
Towada
Hachinohe
Henashi-Misaki
Hirosaki
Ōdate
Kuji
Noshiro
Iwate-San
2041
Morioka
Miyako
Oga-Hantō
Oga
Akita
Omagari
1914
Hanamaki
Kamaishi
Honjō
2230
Ichinoseki
Kesennuma
Sakata
1980
Furukawa
Ishinomaki
Tsuruoka
Yamagata
SENDAI
Sendai-Wan

SEA OF

JAPAN

(EAST SEA)

JAPAN

Sado
Ryōtsu
Niigata
Shibata
Fukushima
Sōma
Haranomachi
Aikawa
Niitsu
Higashijima-San
2024
Aizuwakamatsu
Kōriyama
Sanjo
Nagaoka
Sukagawa
Iwaki
Wajima
Suzu-Misaki
Tōkamachi
Tajima
Tanakura
Kitaibaraki
Nanao
Suzu-Wan
2578
Hitachi
Himi
Toyama
Nagano
Maebashi
Utsunomiya
Mito
Toyama-Wan
Takada
Kiryū
Oyama
Takaoka
Hodaka-Dake
3190
Takasaki
Tsuchiura
Kanazawa
Matsumoto
Kumagaya
Kawagoe
Komatsu
Takayama
Takasaki
3063
Kawaguchi
Funabashi
Fukui
2782
Ina
Kōfu
TOKYO
Chiba
Takefu
3192
Fuji-San
KAWASAKI
Ichihara
Iida
3776
Odawara
YOKOHAMA
Kyō-ga-Saki
Tsuruga
Gifu
Kiso-Gawa
Fuji
Numazu
Yokosuka
Tottori
Toyooka
Maizuru
Ōgaki
Ichinomiya
Shizuoka
Itō
Tateyama
Matsue
Yonago
Fukuchiyama
Ayabe
NAGOYA
Toyota
Okazaki
Ō-Shima
Izu-Shotō
Izumo
Tsuyama
Sanchi
KYŌTO
Ōtsu
Yokkaichi
Toyohashi
Nojima-Zaki
Ōda
Chūgoku-Sanchi
Himeji
Higashiōsaka
Hamamatsu
Iwata
Nii-Jima
Hamada
Okayama
KOBE
OSAKA
Matsusaka
Suruga-Wan
Miyake-Jima
Masuda
Fuchū
Amagasaki
Izumi-Sano
Irō-Zaki
HIROSHIMA
Fukuyama
Takamatsu
Naruto
Wakayama
Daiō-Misaki
Hagi
Iwakuni
Kure
Marugame
Awaji-Shima
1915
Owase
Yamaguchi
Ube
Tokuyama
Imabari
Ikeda
Tokushima
Tanabe
Shingū
Shimonoseki
Hōfu
Matsuyama
1955
Anan
Kushimoto
Iki
Nōgata
Fukuyama
Mugi
Shio-no-Misaki
KITAKYŪSHŪ
Kōchi
Muroto
FUKUOKA
Buzen
Beppu
Yawatahama
Muroto-Misaki
Karatsu
Saga
Kurume
Ōita
Uwajima
Tosa-Wan
Shikoku
Imari
Sasebo
Omuta
1787
Saiki
Nakamura
Sukumo
Ashizuri-Zaki
Nagasaki
Kumamoto
Nobeoka
Fukue-Shima
Yatsushiro
Hyūga
Gotō-Rettō
Isahaya
Amakusa-Shotō
Ushibuka
Kyūshū
Minamata
Miyazaki
Koshikijima-Rettō
Sendai
Miyakonojō
Kagoshima
Nichinan
Makurazaki
Kanoya
Ibusuki
Sata-Misaki

Honshū

Yeongdeok
SOUTH
KOREA
Pohang
ULSAN
Oki-Shotō
(Japan)
Ulleungdo
(S. Korea)
Tokdo
(Takeshima)
Tsushima
(Japan)

Korea Strait

PACIFIC OCEAN

Hachijō-Jima
Aoga-Shima
8412
9076

Nampo-Shoto

SEA OF JAPAN

Projection: Conical with two standard parallels
East from Greenwich
COPYRIGHT PHILIP'S
1:6 400 000

ft m
9000 3000
6000 2000
4500 1500
3000 1000
1200 400
600 200
0
600 200
6000 2000
12 000 4000
18 000 6000
24 000 8000
ft m

East from Greenwich

Projection: Bonne

1:20 000 000

| 100 | 0 | 100 | 200 | 300 | 400 | 500 | 600 | 700 | 800 km |

| 100 | 0 | 100 | 200 | 300 | 400 | 500 miles |

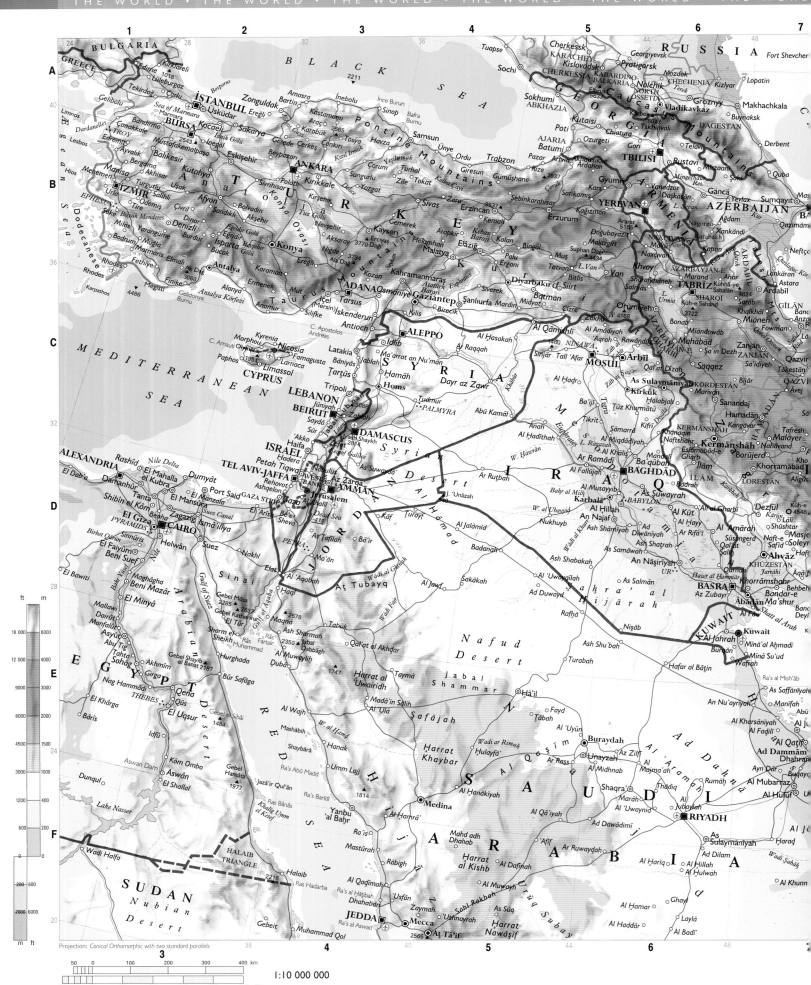

Projection: Conical Orthomorphic with two standard parallels

1:10 000 000

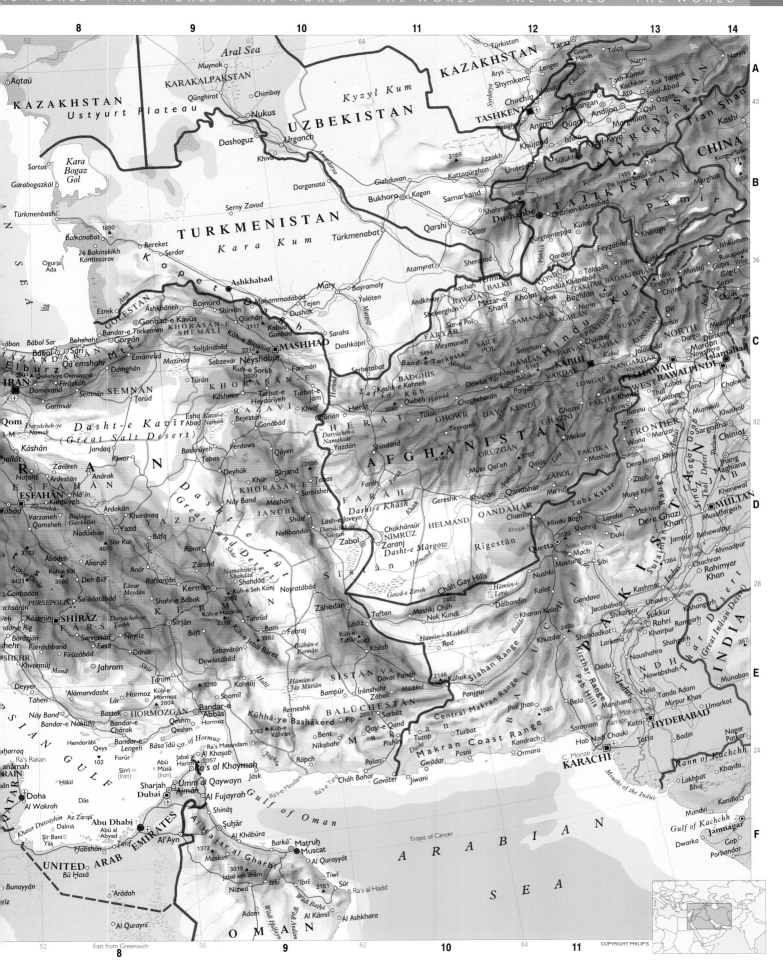

KAZAKHSTAN

UZBEKISTAN

KARAKALPAKSTAN

Aral Sea

Kyzyl Kum

KAZAKHSTAN

Ustyurt Plateau

Kara Bogaz Gol

TURKMENISTAN

Kara Kum

KYRGYZSTAN

TAJIKISTAN

Pamir

CHINA

TASHKENT

Dushanbe

Tian Shan

TURKMENISTAN

Ashkhabad

Hindu Kush

MASHHAD

KABUL

AFGHANISTAN

PESHAWAR

RAWALPINDI

Islamabad

IRAN

Herat

Dasht-e Kavir (Great Salt Desert)

Great Sand Desert

Qandahar

Quetta

PAKISTAN

MULTAN

ESFAHAN

Dasht-e Lut

Kerman

Zahedan

Rigestan

BALUCHESTAN

SHIRAZ

FARS

Makran Coast Range

HYDERABAD

INDIA

PERSIAN GULF

HORMOZGAN

Bandar-e Abbas

Gulf of Oman

KARACHI

Doha

Dubai

Abu Dhabi

UNITED ARAB EMIRATES

Muscat

OMAN

ARABIAN SEA

Tropic of Cancer

Gulf of Kachchh

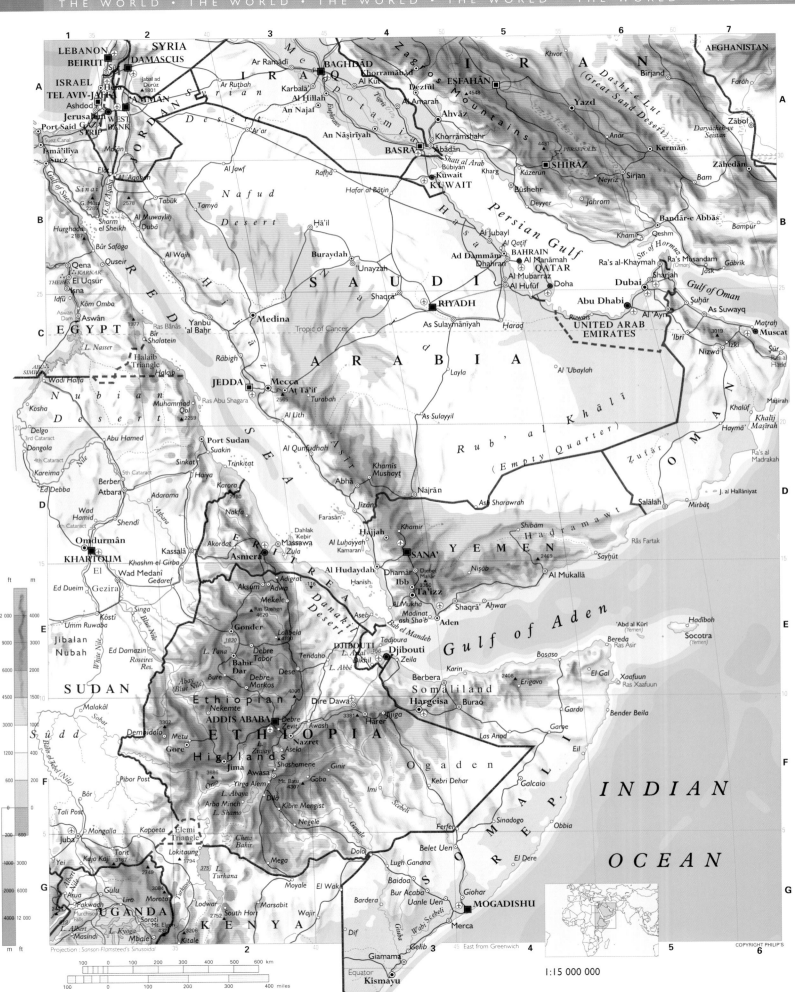

Projection : Sanson-Flamsteed's Sinusoidal

East from Greenwich

COPYRIGHT PHILIP'S

1:15 000 000

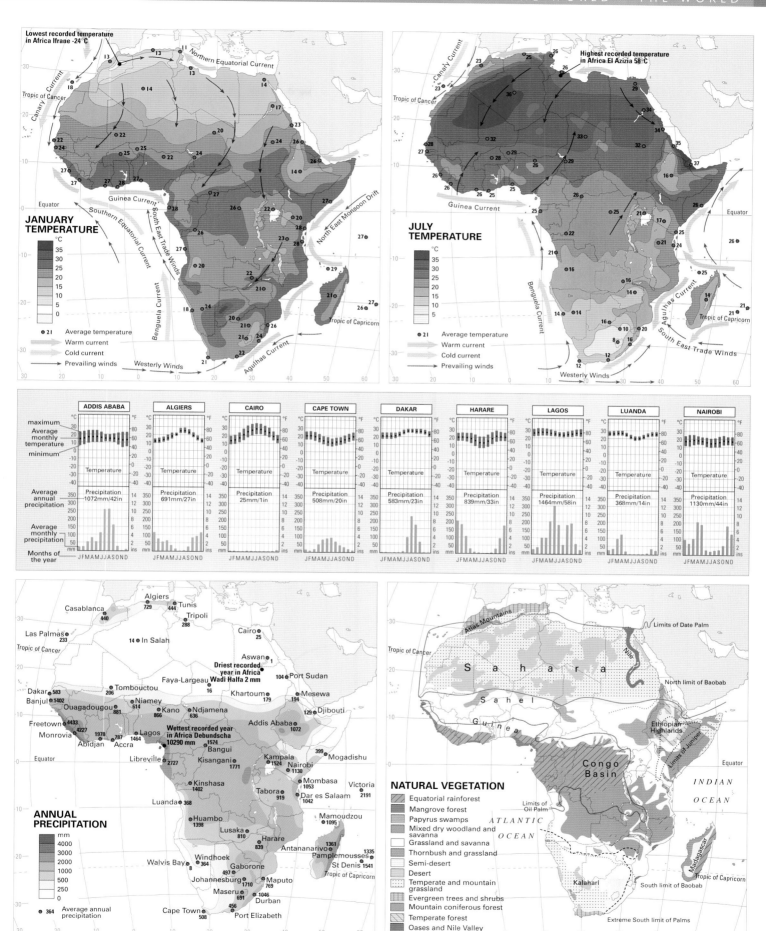

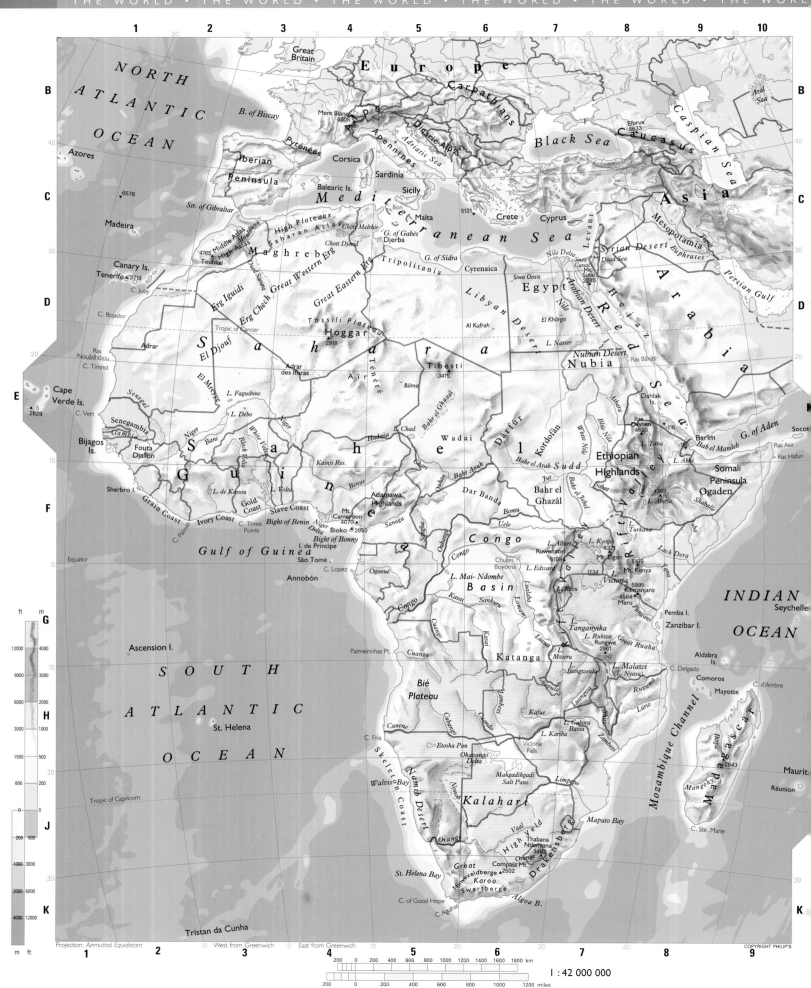

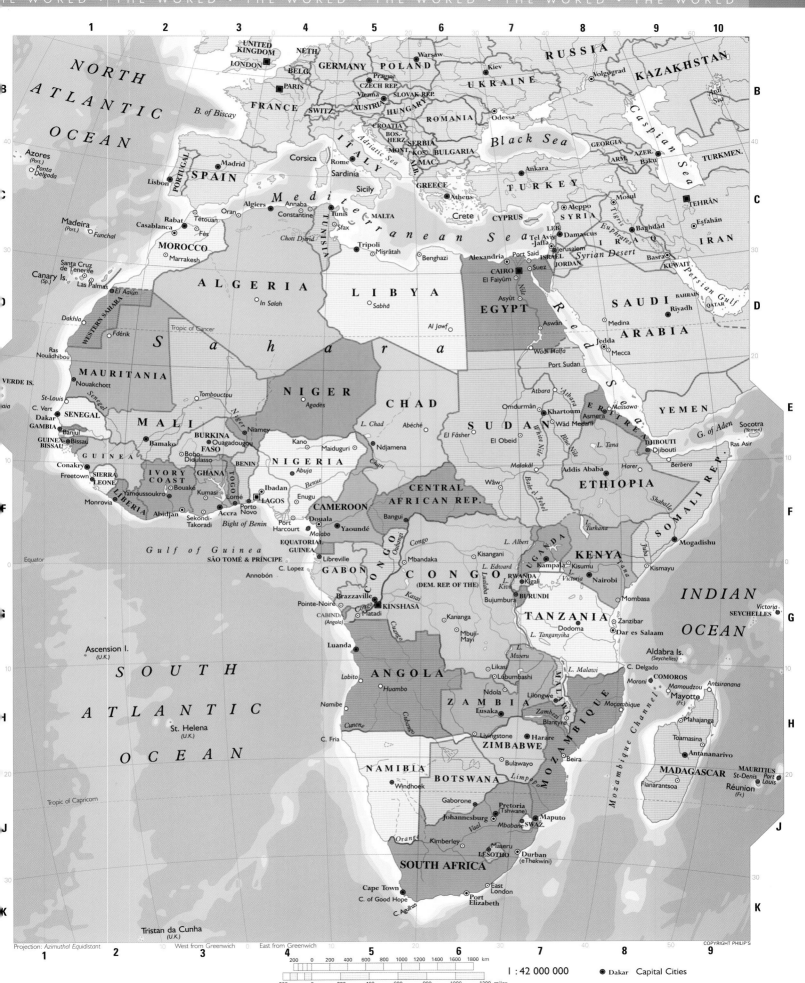

NORTH
ATLANTIC
OCEAN

SOUTH
ATLANTIC
OCEAN

RUSSIA

KAZAKHSTAN

Warsaw

UNITED
KINGDOM
LONDON
NETH.
GERMANY POLAND
BELG.
PARIS
FRANCE
Prague
CZECH REP.
SWITZ.
Vienna
AUSTRIA
SLOVAK REP.
HUNGARY
Kiev
UKRAINE
Volgograd
Odessa
ROMANIA
CROATIA
BOS.-
HERZ.
SERBIA
MONT.
KOS.
ITALY
Adriatic Sea
BULGARIA
MAC.
ALB.
GEORGIA
ARM.
AZER.
Baku
TURKMEN.
Aral
Sea

B. of Biscay

Corsica

Azores
(Port.)
Ponta
Delgada

Madrid
SPAIN

Lisbon
PORTUGAL

Rome
Sardinia

Sicily
Crete

GREECE
Athens

Ankara
TURKEY

Black Sea
Caspian
Sea

Mediterranean Sea

Madeira
(Port.)
Funchal

Casablanca
Rabat
Tétouan
Fès
Oran
Algiers
Annaba
Constantine
TUNISIA
Tunis
Sfax
MALTA

CYPRUS
Aleppo
SYRIA
Tel Aviv-
Jaffa
LEB.
Damascus
Jerusalem
ISRAEL
JORDAN
Mosul
Baghdad
IRAQ
Tigris
Euphrates
Esfahan
Tehran
IRAN

Santa Cruz
de Tenerife
Canary Is.
(Sp.)
Las Palmas

MOROCCO
Marrakesh

Tripoli
Misrātah

Benghazi

Alexandria
Port Said
CAIRO
Suez
El Faiyûm

Aswân

Medina
Riyadh
SAUDI
ARABIA
BAHRAIN
QATAR

KUWAIT
Basra
Persian Gulf

El Aaiún
WESTERN SAHARA
Tropic of Cancer

ALGERIA
In Salah

LIBYA
Sabhā

Chott Djerid

Al Jawf

EGYPT

Wâdi Halfa

Port Sudan
Jedda
Mecca

YEMEN

Dakhla

Fdérik

Ras
Nouâdhibou

Sahara

Nile
Red Sea

Atbara
'Atbara
Omdurmân
Khartoum
Wâd Medani

ERITREA
Massawa
Asmera

G. of Aden
Socotra
(Yemen)
Ras Asir

VERDE IS.

MAURITANIA
Nouakchott

Tombouctou

NIGER
Agadès

CHAD
Abéché

SUDAN
El Fâsher
El Obeid

L. Tana
DJIBOUTI
Djibouti
Berbera

St-Louis
C. Vert
Dakar
SENEGAL
GAMBIA
Banjul
GUINEA-
BISSAU
Bissau

Senegal

MALI
Bamako

Niger
Niamey
Kano
BURKINA
FASO
Bobo-
Dioulasso
Ouagadougou

L. Chad
Ndjamena
Maiduguri

NIGERIA
Abuja

Chari

CENTRAL
AFRICAN REP.
Bangui

Wâw
Malakâl
White Nile
Blue Nile
Bahr el Jebel

Addis Ababa
Harer
ETHIOPIA
Shabelle

L. Turkana

SOMALI REP.
Mogadishu

Conakry
Freetown
SIERRA
LEONE
GUINEA
IVORY
COAST
Yamoussoukro
Monrovia
LIBERIA
Abidjan
GHANA
Bouaké
Kumasi
Sekondi-
Takoradi
Accra
TOGO
BENIN
Lomé
Porto
Novo
Ibadan
LAGOS
Enugu
Benue
CAMEROON
Douala
Yaoundé
Port
Harcourt
Malabo
EQUATORIAL
GUINEA
Libreville
Ubangi
Congo
Mbandaka
Kisangani
L. Albert
L. Edward
L. Kivu
UGANDA
Kampala
RWANDA
Kigali
KENYA
Kisumu
L.
Victoria
Nairobi

Equator

Gulf of Guinea
Bight of Benin
SÃO TOMÉ & PRÍNCIPE
C. Lopez
Annobón

GABON
CONGO
CONGO
(DEM. REP. OF THE)
Brazzaville
Pointe-Noire
KINSHASA
Matadi
CABINDA
(Angola)
Kananga
Mbuji-
Mayi
Kasai
Lualaba
BURUNDI
Bujumbura
TANZANIA
Dodoma
Dar es Salaam
Zanzibar
L. Tanganyika
Mombasa
Kismayu

INDIAN
OCEAN

SEYCHELLES
Victoria

Ascension I.
(U.K.)

Luanda

ANGOLA
Huambo
Namibe
Lobito

Cuango
Cubango
Cunene
C. Fria

Likasi
Lubumbashi
Ndola
ZAMBIA
Lusaka
Zambezi
L. Mweru
L. Malawi
MALAWI
Lilongwe
Blantyre
Moçambique
C. Delgado
COMOROS
Moroni
Mamoudzou
Mayotte
(Fr.)
Antsiranana
Aldabra Is.
(Seychelles)

St. Helena
(U.K.)

Livingstone
Harare
ZIMBABWE
Bulawayo
Beira
MOZAMBIQUE
Mahajanga
Toamasina
Antananarivo
MADAGASCAR

MAURITIUS
St-Denis
Port
Louis
Réunion
(Fr.)

NAMIBIA
Windhoek
BOTSWANA
Gaborone
Limpopo
Mozambique Channel
Fianarantsoa

Tropic of Capricorn

Orange
Vaal
Kimberley
Johannesburg
Pretoria
(Tshwane)
Maputo
Mbabane
SWAZ.
Maseru
LESOTHO
Durban
(eThekwini)

SOUTH AFRICA
Cape Town
C. of Good Hope
C. Agulhas
East
London
Port
Elizabeth

Tristan da Cunha
(U.K.)

Projection: Azimuthal Equidistant
West from Greenwich
East from Greenwich
COPYRIGHT PHILIP'S

200   0   200   400   600   800 1000 1200 1400 1600 1800 km

1 : 42 000 000   • Dakar Capital Cities

200   0   200   400   600   800   1000   1200 miles

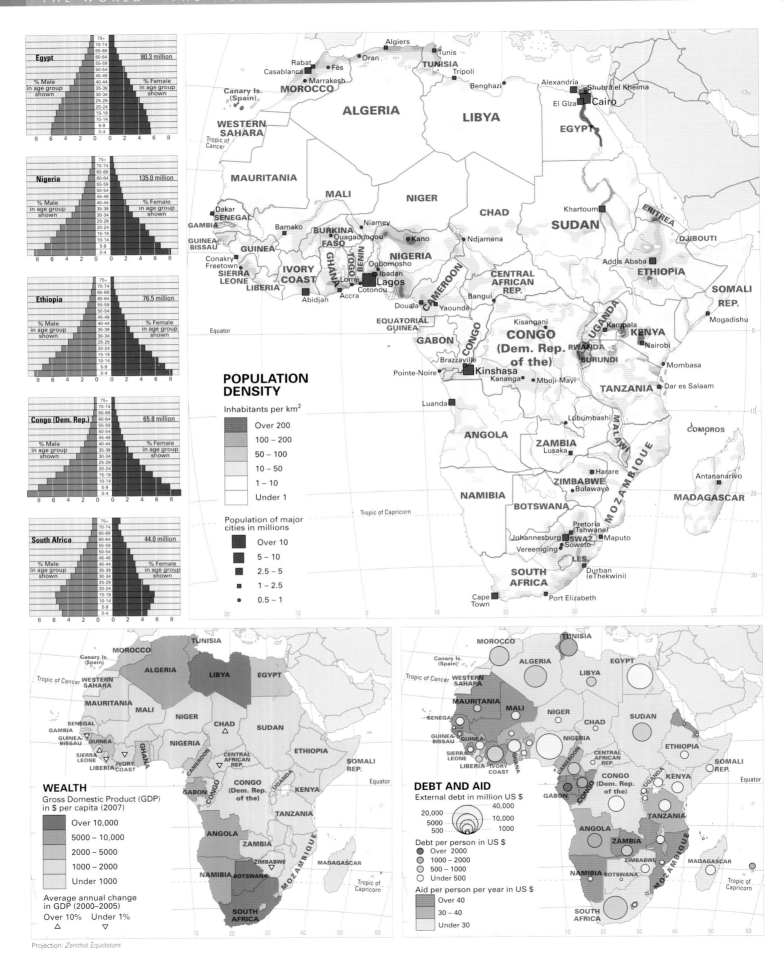

Egypt — 80.3 million
% Male in age group shown — % Female in age group shown

Nigeria — 135.0 million
% Male in age group shown — % Female in age group shown

Ethiopia — 76.5 million
% Male in age group shown — % Female in age group shown

Congo (Dem. Rep.) — 65.8 million
% Male in age group shown — % Female in age group shown

South Africa — 44.0 million
% Male in age group shown — % Female in age group shown

POPULATION DENSITY

Inhabitants per km²

- Over 200
- 100 – 200
- 50 – 100
- 10 – 50
- 1 – 10
- Under 1

Population of major cities in millions

- Over 10
- 5 – 10
- 2.5 – 5
- 1 – 2.5
- 0.5 – 1

WEALTH

Gross Domestic Product (GDP) in $ per capita (2007)

- Over 10,000
- 5000 – 10,000
- 2000 – 5000
- 1000 – 2000
- Under 1000

Average annual change in GDP (2000–2005)
Over 10% △   Under 1% ▽

DEBT AND AID

External debt in million US $
- 40,000
- 20,000
- 10,000
- 5000
- 1000

Debt per person in US $
- Over 2000
- 1000 – 2000
- 500 – 1000
- Under 500

Aid per person per year in US $
- Over 40
- 30 – 40
- Under 30

Projection: Zenithal Equidistant

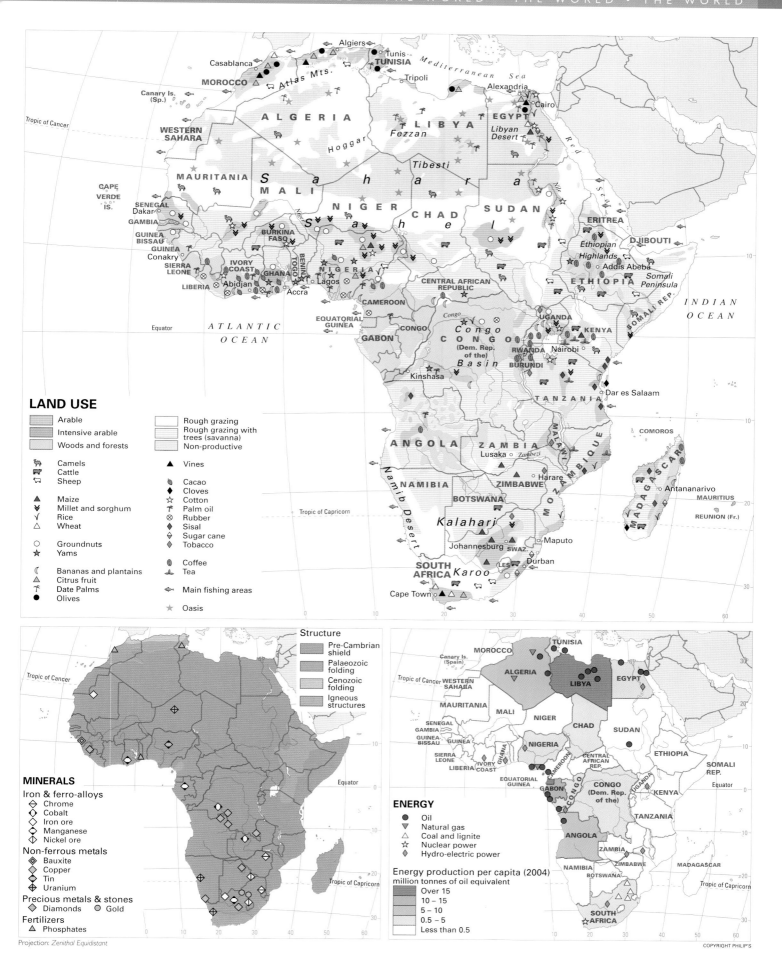

Algiers
Casablanca
Tunis
TUNISIA
MOROCCO
Tripoli
Alexandria
Atlas Mts.
Canary Is. (Sp.)
Mediterranean Sea
Cairo
EGYPT
Tropic of Cancer
WESTERN SAHARA
ALGERIA
LIBYA
Libyan Desert
Fezzan
Red Sea
Hoggar
Tibesti
MAURITANIA
MALI
NIGER
CHAD
SUDAN
ERITREA
DJIBOUTI
Nile
S a h a r a
CAPE VERDE IS.
SENEGAL
Dakar
GAMBIA
GUINEA BISSAU
GUINEA
Conakry
SIERRA LEONE
LIBERIA
IVORY COAST
GHANA
Abidjan
Accra
BURKINA FASO
BENIN
TOGO
NIGERIA
Lagos
S a h e l
CENTRAL AFRICAN REPUBLIC
CAMEROON
EQUATORIAL GUINEA
GABON
CONGO
Congo
CONGO (Dem. Rep. of the)
Basin
Kinshasa
Ethiopian Highlands
Addis Abeba
ETHIOPIA
Somali Peninsula
SOMALI REP.
UGANDA
KENYA
Nairobi
RWANDA
BURUNDI
TANZANIA
Dar es Salaam
INDIAN OCEAN
ATLANTIC OCEAN
Equator
ANGOLA
ZAMBIA
Lusaka
Zambezi
MALAWI
MOZAMBIQUE
COMOROS
NAMIBIA
ZIMBABWE
Harare
BOTSWANA
Kalahari
MADAGASCAR
Antananarivo
MAURITIUS
REUNION (Fr.)
Namib Desert
Tropic of Capricorn
Maputo
Johannesburg
SWAZ.
LES.
Durban
SOUTH AFRICA
Karoo
Cape Town

LAND USE

- Arable
- Intensive arable
- Woods and forests
- Rough grazing
- Rough grazing with trees (savanna)
- Non-productive

- Camels
- Cattle
- Sheep
- Maize
- Millet and sorghum
- Rice
- Wheat
- Groundnuts
- Yams
- Bananas and plantains
- Citrus fruit
- Date Palms
- Olives
- Vines
- Cacao
- Cloves
- Cotton
- Palm oil
- Rubber
- Sisal
- Sugar cane
- Tobacco
- Coffee
- Tea
- Main fishing areas
- Oasis

MINERALS

Iron & ferro-alloys
- Chrome
- Cobalt
- Iron ore
- Manganese
- Nickel ore

Non-ferrous metals
- Bauxite
- Copper
- Tin
- Uranium

Precious metals & stones
- Diamonds
- Gold

Fertilizers
- Phosphates

Structure
- Pre-Cambrian shield
- Palaeozoic folding
- Cenozoic folding
- Igneous structures

Tropic of Cancer
Equator
Tropic of Capricorn

ENERGY

- Oil
- Natural gas
- Coal and lignite
- Nuclear power
- Hydro-electric power

Energy production per capita (2004)
million tonnes of oil equivalent
- Over 15
- 10 – 15
- 5 – 10
- 0.5 – 5
- Less than 0.5

Canary Is. (Spain)
MOROCCO
TUNISIA
WESTERN SAHARA
ALGERIA
LIBYA
EGYPT
MAURITANIA
MALI
NIGER
CHAD
SUDAN
SENEGAL
GAMBIA
GUINEA-BISSAU
GUINEA
SIERRA LEONE
LIBERIA
IVORY COAST
GHANA
NIGERIA
CAMEROON
CENTRAL AFRICAN REP.
ETHIOPIA
SOMALI REP.
EQUATORIAL GUINEA
GABON
CONGO
CONGO (Dem. Rep. of the)
UGANDA
KENYA
TANZANIA
ANGOLA
ZAMBIA
ZIMBABWE
NAMIBIA
BOTSWANA
MADAGASCAR
SOUTH AFRICA
Tropic of Cancer
Equator
Tropic of Capricorn

Projection: Zenithal Equidistant

COPYRIGHT PHILIP'S

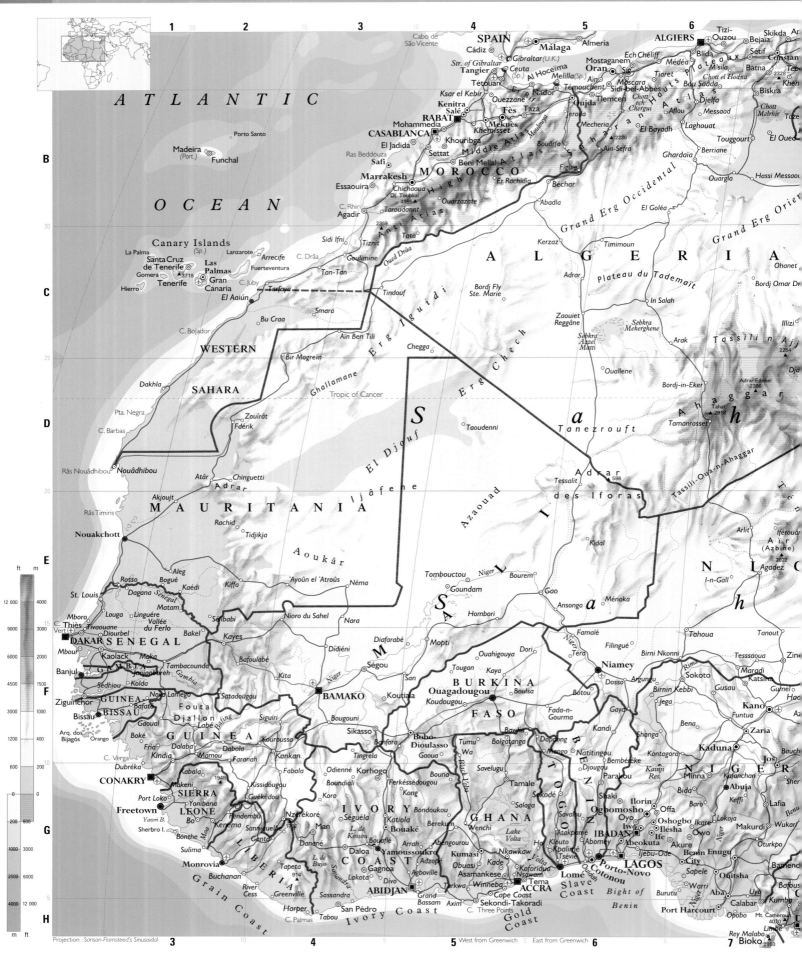

1:15 000 000

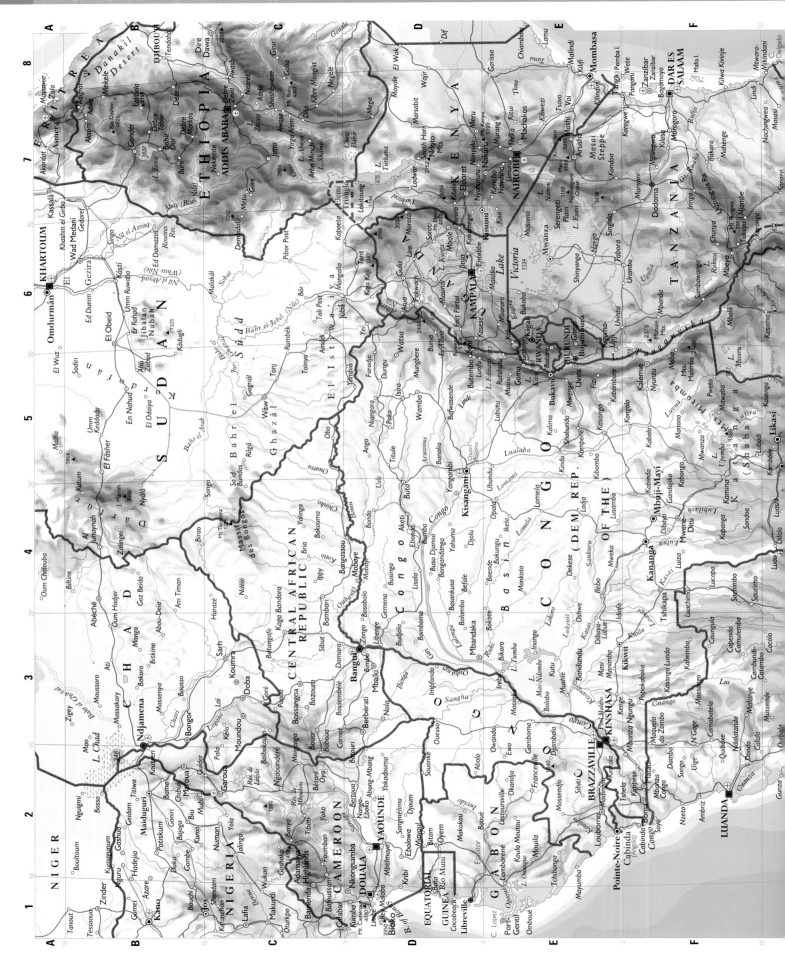

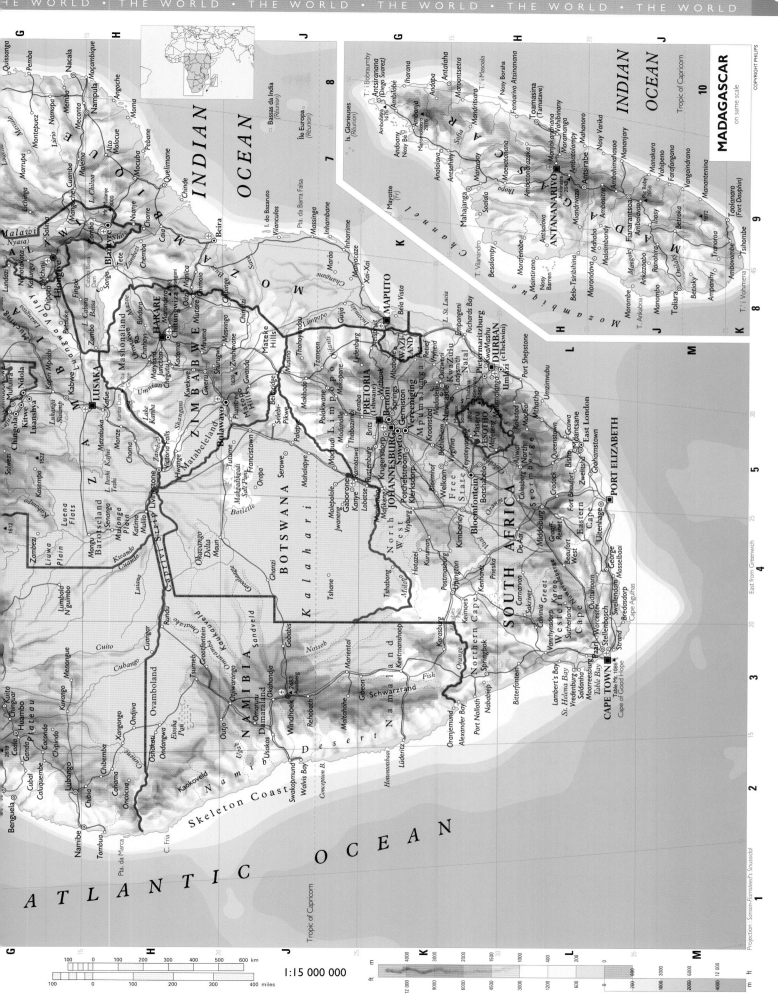

MADAGASCAR
on same scale

INDIAN OCEAN

INDIAN OCEAN

ATLANTIC OCEAN

Tropic of Capricorn

SOUTH AFRICA

NAMIBIA

BOTSWANA

ZIMBABWE

MOZAMBIQUE

Kalahari

Namib Desert

Skeleton Coast

1:15 000 000

COPYRIGHT PHILIPS

Projection : Sanson-Flamsteed's Sinusoidal

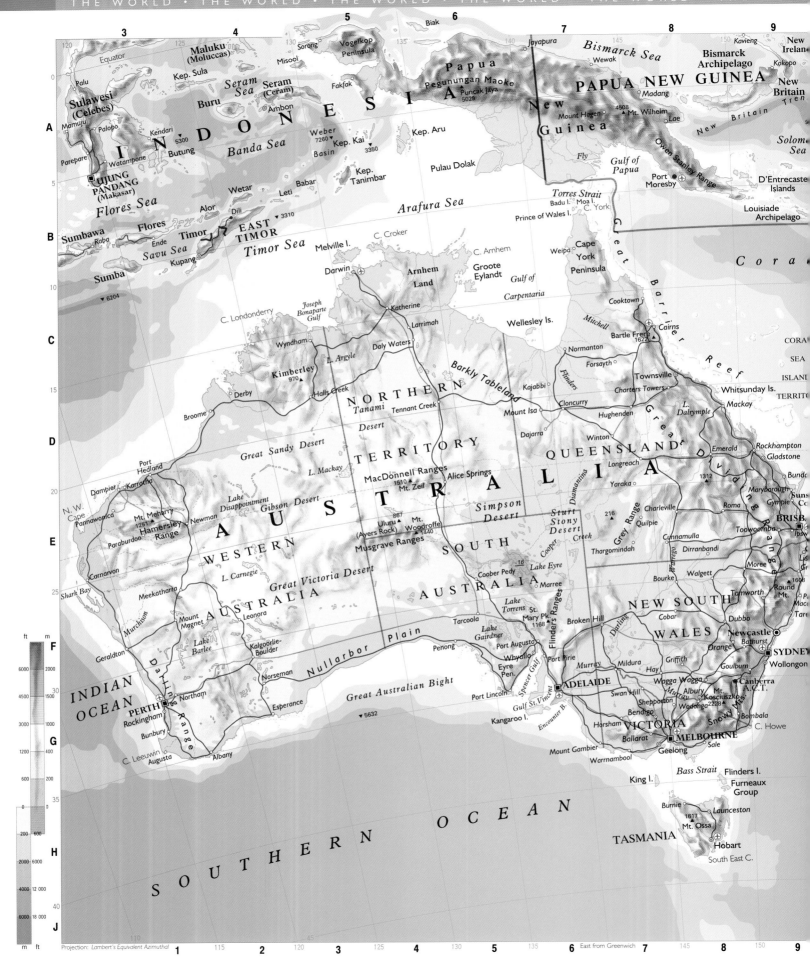

Projection: Lambert's Equivalent Azimuthal

East from Greenwich

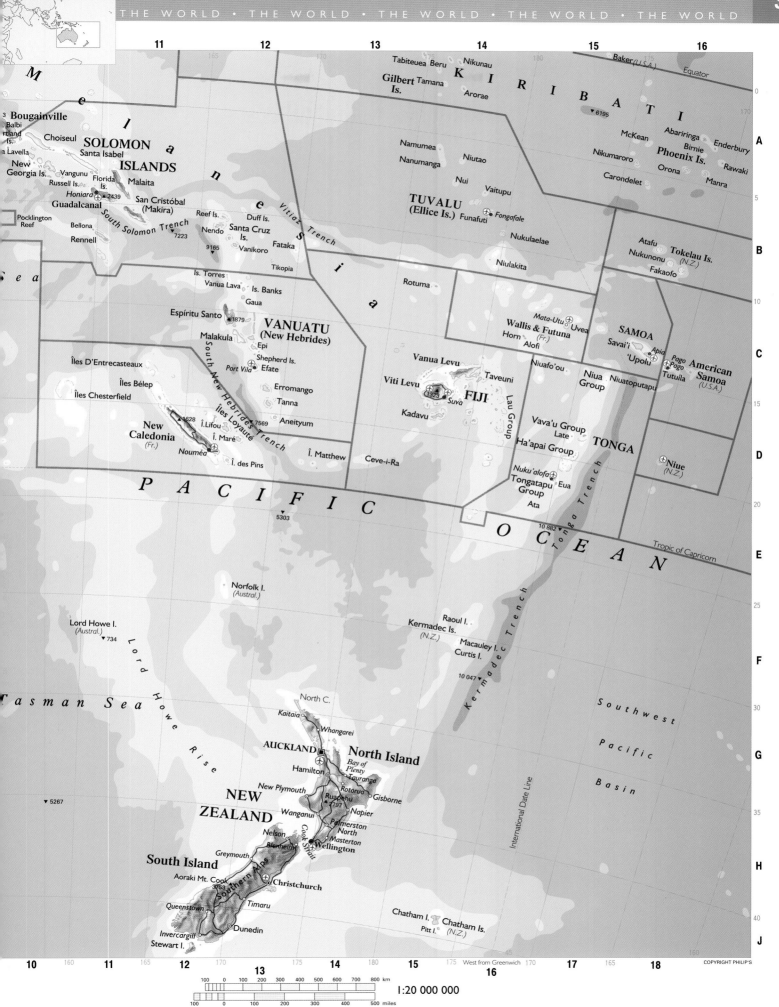

M e l a n e s i a

Bougainville
Balbi
rtland Is.
a Lavella
Choiseul
New
Georgia Is.
SOLOMON
Santa Isabel
ISLANDS
Vangunu Florida
Russell Is. Is.
Honiara 2439
Guadalcanal San Cristóbal
(Makira)
Pocklington Malaita
Reef
Bellona
Rennell
South Solomon Trench
7223

Tabiteuea Beru Nikunau
Gilbert Tamana
Is.
Arorae
K I R I B A T I
Baker (U.S.A.)
Equator
6195
McKean Abariringa Enderbury
Nikumaroro Birnie Rawaki
Orona Phoenix Is.
Carondelet Manra

Namumea
Nanumanga
Niutao
Nui
Vaitupu
TUVALU
(Ellice Is.) Funafuti Fongafale
Nukulaelae
Niulakita

Atafu Tokelau Is.
Nukunonu (N.Z.)
Fakaofo

Reef Is. Duff Is.
Nendo Santa Cruz
Vanikoro Is.
9165
Fataka
Tikopia
Is. Torres
Vanua Lava Is. Banks
Gaua
Espíritu Santo 1879
VANUATU
Malakula (New Hebrides)
Epi
Shepherd Is.
Port Vila Efate
Erromango
Tanna
Aneityum
7569

Vitiaz S Trench

M i c r o n e s i a

Rotuma

Mata-Utu Uvea
Wallis & Futuna
Horn (Fr.)
Alofi

Vanua Levu
Viti Levu Taveuni
1323 Suva FIJI
Kadavu

Niuafo'ou
Niua Niuatoputapu
Group
Vava'u Group
Late
Ha'apai Group TONGA
Nuku'alofa Eua
Tongatapu
Group
Ata

SAMOA
Savai'i
'Upolu Apia
Pago American
Pago Samoa
Tutuila (U.S.A.)

Niue
(N.Z.)

Îles D'Entrecasteaux
Îles Bélep
Îles Chesterfield
1628
New
Caledonia
(Fr.)
Nouméa
Î.Lifou
Îles Loyauté
Î. Maré
Î. des Pins
Î. Matthew
Ceve-i-Ra

P A C I F I C   O C E A N

Lau Group

Tonga Trench
10 882

Tropic of Capricorn

5303

Norfolk I.
(Austral.)

Lord Howe I.
(Austral.)
734

Raoul I.
Kermadec Is.
(N.Z.)
Macauley I.
Curtis I.
10 047

Kermadec Trench

S o u t h w e s t

P a c i f i c

B a s i n

Lord Howe Rise

Tasman Sea

5267

North C.
Kaitaia
Whangarei
AUCKLAND North Island
Hamilton Bay of
Plenty
New Plymouth Tauranga
Rotorua
NEW Ruapehu Gisborne
Wanganui 7797 Napier
ZEALAND Palmerston
Nelson North
Blenheim Masterton
Greymouth Cook Strait Wellington
South Island
Aoraki Mt. Cook
3753 Christchurch
Southern Alps
Queenstown
Timaru
Invercargill Dunedin
Stewart I.

International Date Line

Chatham I. Chatham Is.
Pitt I. (N.Z.)

100 0 100 200 300 400 500 600 700 800 km

100 0 100 200 300 400 500 miles

1:20 000 000

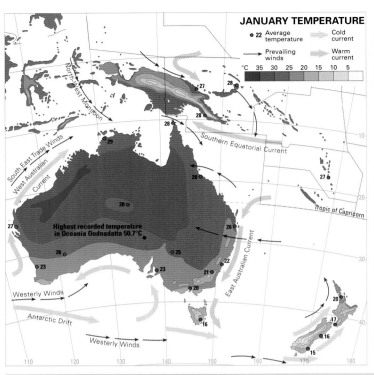

JANUARY TEMPERATURE

- 22 Average temperature
- → Prevailing winds
- ⇒ Cold current
- ⇒ Warm current

°C 35 30 25 20 15 10 5

Highest recorded temperature in Oceania Oodnadatta 50.7°C

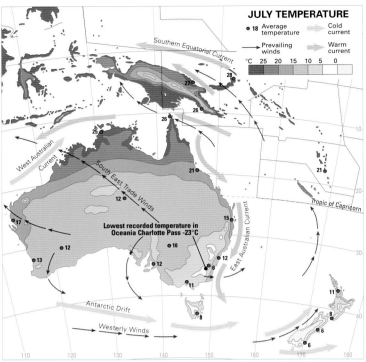

JULY TEMPERATURE

- 18 Average temperature
- → Prevailing winds
- ⇒ Cold current
- ⇒ Warm current

°C 25 20 15 10 5 0

Lowest recorded temperature in Oceania Charlotte Pass -23°C

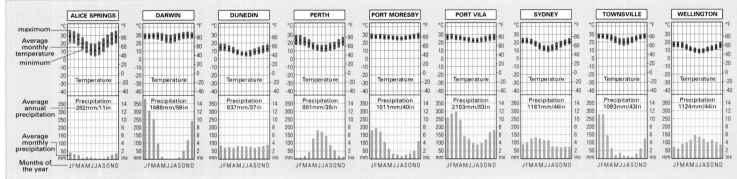

ALICE SPRINGS — Temperature — Precipitation 282mm/11in
DARWIN — Temperature — Precipitation 1488mm/59in
DUNEDIN — Temperature — Precipitation 937mm/37in
PERTH — Temperature — Precipitation 881mm/35in
PORT MORESBY — Temperature — Precipitation 1011mm/40in
PORT VILA — Temperature — Precipitation 2103mm/83in
SYDNEY — Temperature — Precipitation 1181mm/46in
TOWNSVILLE — Temperature — Precipitation 1093mm/43in
WELLINGTON — Temperature — Precipitation 1124mm/44in

maximum
Average monthly temperature
minimum
Average annual precipitation
Average monthly precipitation
Months of the year

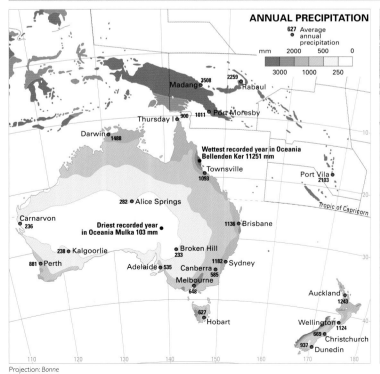

ANNUAL PRECIPITATION

- 627 Average annual precipitation

mm 2000 500 0
3000 1000 250

Wettest recorded year in Oceania Bellenden Ker 11251 mm

Driest recorded year in Oceania Mulka 103 mm

Madang 3508
Rabaul 2259
Port Moresby 1011
Thursday I. 900
Darwin 1488
Townsville 1093
Port Vila 2103
Alice Springs 282
Carnarvon 236
Brisbane 1136
Kalgoorlie 238
Broken Hill 233
Sydney 1182
Perth 881
Adelaide 535
Canberra 585
Melbourne 648
Auckland 1243
Hobart 627
Wellington 1124
Christchurch 669
Dunedin 937

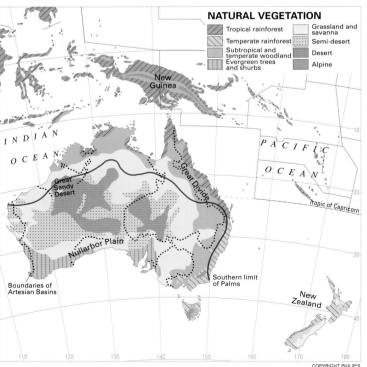

NATURAL VEGETATION

- Tropical rainforest
- Temperate rainforest
- Subtropical and temperate woodland
- Evergreen trees and shrubs
- Grassland and savanna
- Semi-desert
- Desert
- Alpine

New Guinea

INDIAN OCEAN

PACIFIC OCEAN

Great Sandy Desert

Nullarbor Plain

Great Divide

Southern limit of Palms

Boundaries of Artesian Basins

New Zealand

Projection: Bonne

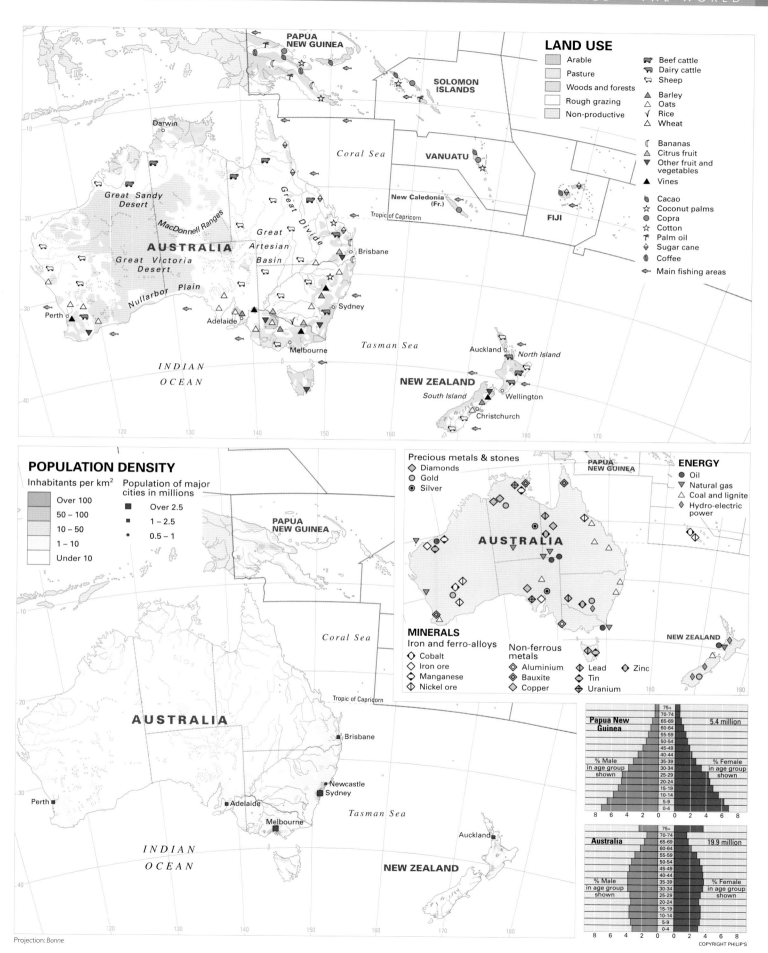

LAND USE

- Arable
- Pasture
- Woods and forests
- Rough grazing
- Non-productive

- Beef cattle
- Dairy cattle
- Sheep

- Barley
- Oats
- Rice
- Wheat

- Bananas
- Citrus fruit
- Other fruit and vegetables
- Vines

- Cacao
- Coconut palms
- Copra
- Cotton
- Palm oil
- Sugar cane
- Coffee

- Main fishing areas

PAPUA NEW GUINEA

SOLOMON ISLANDS

Darwin

Coral Sea

VANUATU

New Caledonia (Fr.)

Tropic of Capricorn

FIJI

Great Sandy Desert

MacDonnell Ranges

AUSTRALIA

Great Victoria Desert

Great Artesian Basin

Great Divide

Brisbane

Nullarbor Plain

Perth

Adelaide

Sydney

Melbourne

Tasman Sea

Auckland

North Island

NEW ZEALAND

INDIAN OCEAN

South Island

Wellington

Christchurch

POPULATION DENSITY

Inhabitants per km²
- Over 100
- 50 – 100
- 10 – 50
- 1 – 10
- Under 10

Population of major cities in millions
- Over 2.5
- 1 – 2.5
- 0.5 – 1

PAPUA NEW GUINEA

Coral Sea

Tropic of Capricorn

AUSTRALIA

Perth

Adelaide

Brisbane

Newcastle
Sydney

Melbourne

Tasman Sea

Auckland

INDIAN OCEAN

NEW ZEALAND

Precious metals & stones
- Diamonds
- Gold
- Silver

PAPUA NEW GUINEA

AUSTRALIA

NEW ZEALAND

MINERALS

Iron and ferro-alloys
- Cobalt
- Iron ore
- Manganese
- Nickel ore

Non-ferrous metals
- Aluminium
- Bauxite
- Copper
- Lead
- Tin
- Uranium
- Zinc

ENERGY
- Oil
- Natural gas
- Coal and lignite
- Hydro-electric power

Papua New Guinea		5.4 million
75+		
70-74		
65-69		
60-64		
55-59		
50-54		
45-49		
40-44		
% Male in age group shown	35-39	% Female in age group shown
	30-34	
	25-29	
	20-24	
	15-19	
	10-14	
	5-9	
	0-4	

8 6 4 2 0 0 2 4 6 8

Australia		19.9 million
75+		
70-74		
65-69		
60-64		
55-59		
50-54		
45-49		
40-44		
% Male in age group shown	35-39	% Female in age group shown
	30-34	
	25-29	
	20-24	
	15-19	
	10-14	
	5-9	
	0-4	

8 6 4 2 0 0 2 4 6 8

Projection: *Bonne*

COPYRIGHT PHILIP'S

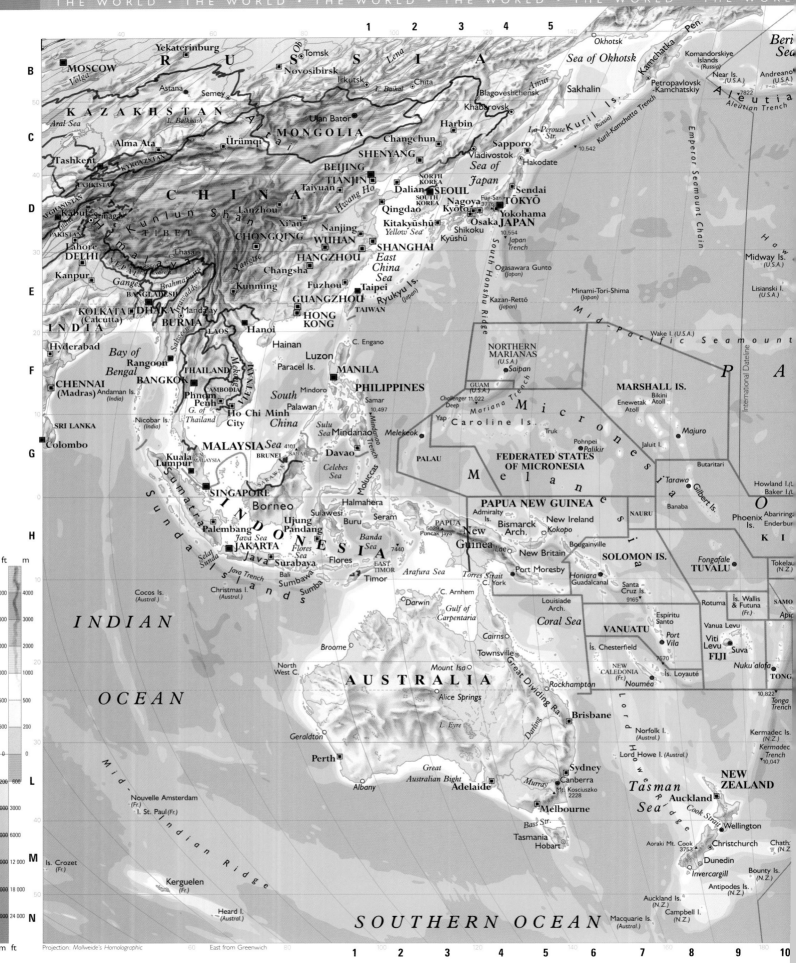

ft   m

12 000   4000

9000   3000

6000   2000

3000   1000

1500   500

600   200

0   0

200   600

1000   3000

2000   6000

4000   12 000

6000   18 000

8000   24 000

m   ft

Projection: Mollweide's Homolographic   East from Greenwich

ALASKA
(U.S.A.)
Anchorage
5959
Juneau

Bristol Bay

Gulf of Alaska

Prince of Wales I.
(U.S.A.) Prince Rupert
Queen Charlotte Is.
(Canada)

ROCKY

C A N A D A

Edmonton

L. Winnipeg

Newfoundland

Vancouver
Vancouver I.
Victoria
Seattle
Portland

Calgary

Regina

Winnipeg

L. Superior

Québec

St. Lawrence

St. John's

NORTH

Boise

Spokane

Minneapolis
Missouri

L. Huron
L. Michigan
Toronto
Detroit
L. Ontario
L. Erie

Montréal
Ottawa
Buffalo

Boston

Salt Lake
City

Denver

CHICAGO

Pittsburgh

Cincinnati

NEW YORK
PHILADELPHIA
Baltimore
Washington D.C.

ATLANTIC

C. Mendocino

6741

Sacramento

SAN FRANCISCO

4418

Colorado

UNITED STATES

Kansas City

St. Louis

Oklahoma City

Memphis

Atlanta

C. Hatteras

Bermuda
(U.K.)

LOS ANGELES
San Diego

Phoenix

Dallas

Houston

Jacksonville

Sargasso Sea

OCEAN

Guadalupe
(Mex.)

Ciudad
Juárez

Baja California

San Antonio

New
Orleans

Gulf of Mexico
Miami

BAHAMAS

West Indies

Tropic of Cancer

Gulf de California

Monterrey

Havana
CUBA

Honolulu

O'ahu
4205
HAWAI'I
(U.S.A.)
Hawai'i

C. San Lucas

Guadalajara

MEXICO
5610
Puebla

Mérida

7680

HAITI

8605

DOMINICAN REP.

Leeward
Is.

Is. de Revillagigedo
(Mex.)

Acapulco

BELIZE

Canal de Yucatán

JAMAICA

Kingston

PUERTO
RICO
(U.S.A.)

CIFIC

Johnston I.
(U.S.A.)

GUATEMALA
Guatemala
San Salvador
EL SALVADOR

HONDURAS

NICARAGUA
Managua

Caribbean Sea

BARBADOS
Windward Is.

orth West Christmas Ridge

Palmyra Is.
(U.S.A.)

Teraina

Tabuaeran
Kiritimati

I. Clipperton
(Fr.)

COSTA
RICA

Barranquilla

San José
Colón
PANAMA
Panamá

Maracaibo

Caracas
Orinoco

VENEZUELA

Jarvis I.
(U.S.A.)

Malden I.

Starbuck I.

I. del Coco
(Costa Rica)

Medellín

I. de Malpelo
(Colombia)

Cali

Bogotá

COLOMBIA

E A N

Equator

Galápagos
(Ecuador)

Quito
ECUADOR

BATI

Guayaquil

Iquitos

Amazonas

Tongareva

C. Paliñas

BRAZIL

Pukapuka
Manihiki

Vostok I.

Îs. Marquises

Caroline I.
(Millennium I.)
Flint I.

Trujillo

Suwarrow Is.

Îs. de la
Société

6369

PERU

6550

Îs. Tuamotu

Cook Is.
(N.Z.)

Papeete Tahiti

FRENCH POLYNESIA

Mururoa

Cuzco

LIMA

L. Titicaca

Nevada Ancohuma
6550

Rarotonga

Îs. Tubuaï

6866

Arequipa

La Paz
BOLIVIA

Tropic of Capricorn

Arica

Peru–

East Pacific Rise

Iquique
Chile

PARAGUAY

Henderson I.

Antofagasta

Pitcairn I.
(U.K.)

Rapa

San Félix
(Chile)

8050
Trench

San Ambrosio
(Chile)

Asunción

San Miguel
de Tucumán

Sala-y-Gómez
(Chile)

I. de Pascua
(Chile)

Porto
Alegre

Pacific-Antarctic Ridge

Arch. de
Juan Fernández
(Chile)

Valparaíso

Aconcagua
6962

Córdoba

Rosario

URUGUAY

SANTIAGO

BUENOS
AIRES

Montevideo

Río de la Plata

Chile Rise

Concepción

ARGENTINA

SOUTH

ATLANTIC

OCEAN

Patagonia

6212

Punta Arenas
Est. de Magallanes
Tierra del Fuego
C. de Hornos

Falkland Is.
(U.K.)

South Georgia
(U.K.)

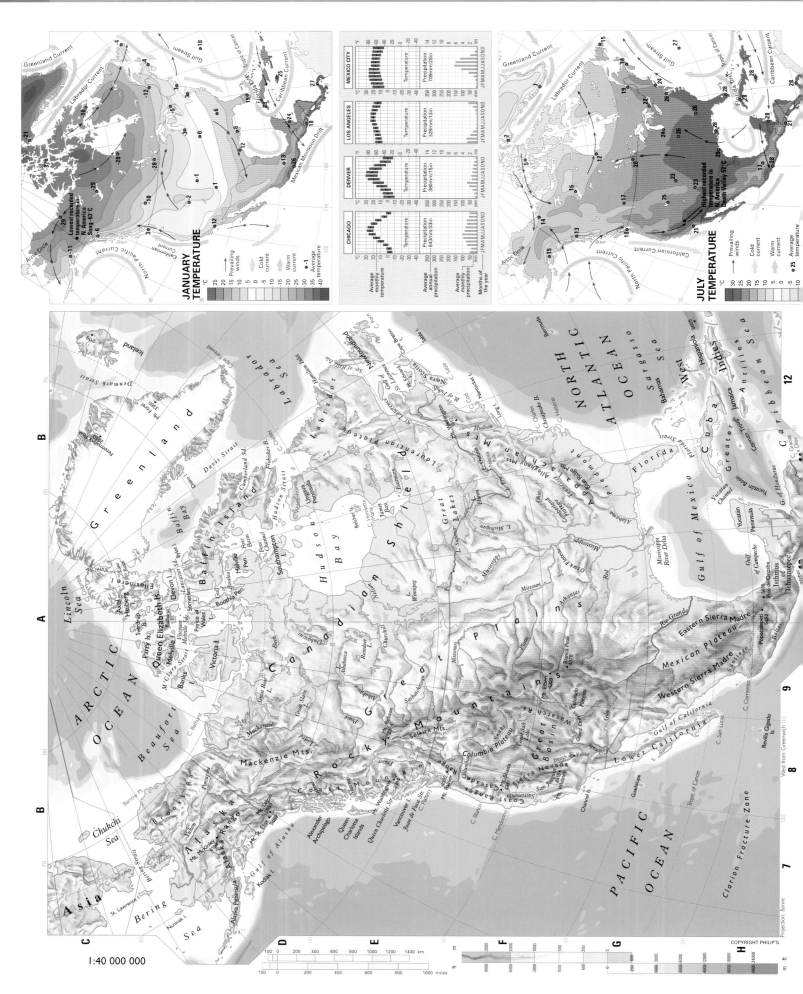

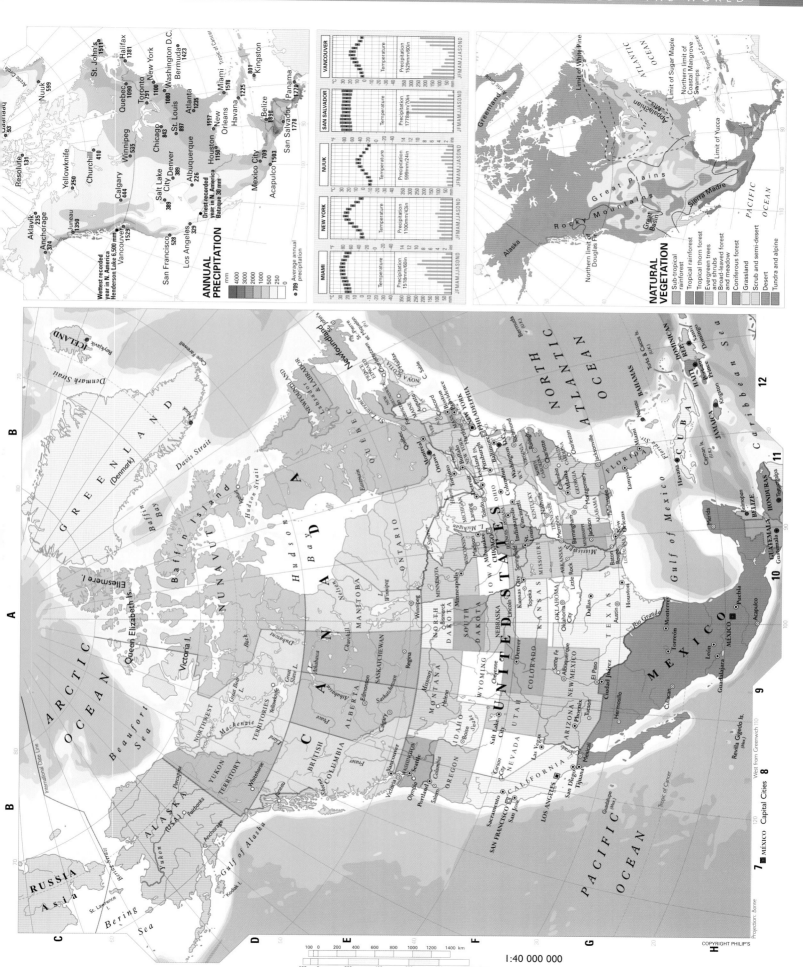

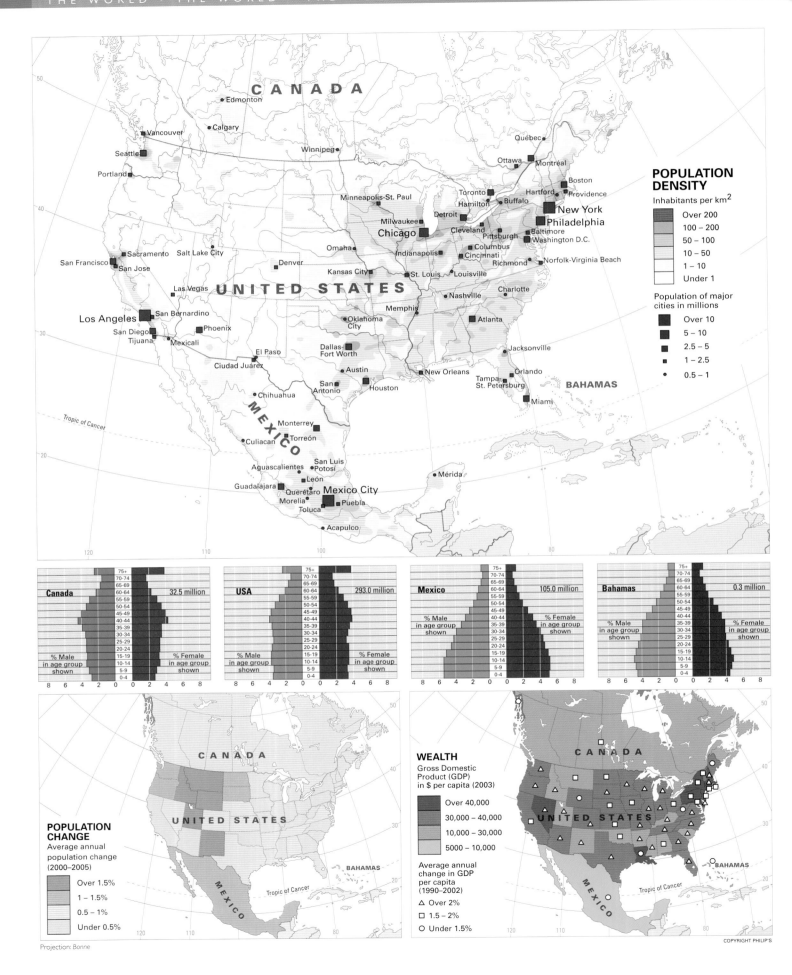

CANADA

Edmonton • Calgary

Vancouver
Seattle
Portland

Winnipeg

Québec
Ottawa Montréal
Boston
Toronto Hamilton Hartford Providence
Detroit Buffalo New York
Minneapolis-St. Paul Milwaukee Cleveland Philadelphia
Chicago Pittsburgh Baltimore
Columbus Washington D.C.
Omaha Indianapolis Cincinnati
Sacramento Salt Lake City Denver Kansas City St. Louis Louisville Richmond Norfolk-Virginia Beach
San Francisco San Jose
Las Vegas UNITED STATES Nashville Charlotte
Memphis
Los Angeles San Bernardino Oklahoma City Atlanta
San Diego Phoenix
Tijuana Mexicali Dallas-Fort Worth Jacksonville
El Paso Austin Orlando
Ciudad Juárez New Orleans Tampa-St. Petersburg BAHAMAS
Chihuahua San Antonio Houston Miami
MEXICO
Monterrey
Culiacan Torreón Mérida
San Luis Potosí
Aguascalientes León
Guadalajara Querétaro Mexico City
Morelia Puebla
Toluca
Acapulco

POPULATION DENSITY

Inhabitants per km²

	Over 200
	100 – 200
	50 – 100
	10 – 50
	1 – 10
	Under 1

Population of major cities in millions

■	Over 10
■	5 – 10
■	2.5 – 5
▪	1 – 2.5
•	0.5 – 1

Tropic of Cancer

Canada 32.5 million
% Male in age group shown
% Female in age group shown

USA 293.0 million
% Male in age group shown
% Female in age group shown

Mexico 105.0 million
% Male in age group shown
% Female in age group shown

Bahamas 0.3 million
% Male in age group shown
% Female in age group shown

Age groups: 75+, 70-74, 65-69, 60-64, 55-59, 50-54, 45-49, 40-44, 35-39, 30-34, 25-29, 20-24, 15-19, 10-14, 5-9, 0-4

CANADA

UNITED STATES

BAHAMAS

MEXICO

Tropic of Cancer

POPULATION CHANGE
Average annual population change (2000–2005)

	Over 1.5%
	1 – 1.5%
	0.5 – 1%
	Under 0.5%

CANADA

UNITED STATES

BAHAMAS

MEXICO

Tropic of Cancer

WEALTH
Gross Domestic Product (GDP) in $ per capita (2003)

	Over 40,000
	30,000 – 40,000
	10,000 – 30,000
	5000 – 10,000

Average annual change in GDP per capita (1990–2002)

△	Over 2%
□	1.5 – 2%
○	Under 1.5%

Projection: *Bonne*

COPYRIGHT PHILIP'S

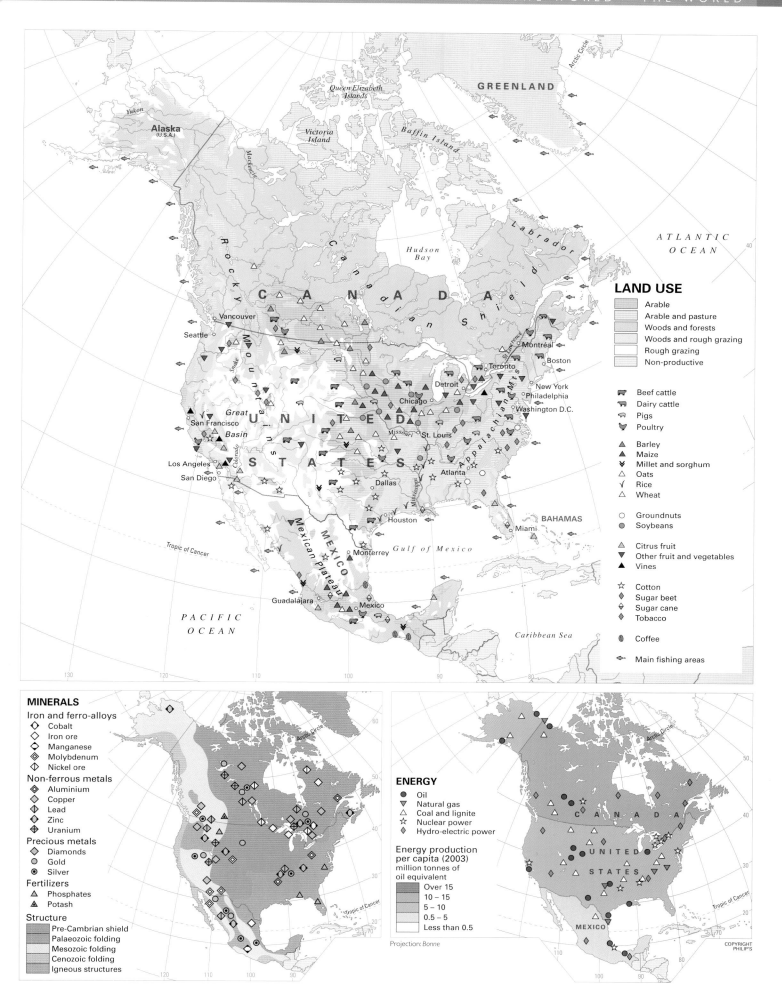

LAND USE

- Arable
- Arable and pasture
- Woods and forests
- Woods and rough grazing
- Rough grazing
- Non-productive

- Beef cattle
- Dairy cattle
- Pigs
- Poultry

- Barley
- Maize
- Millet and sorghum
- Oats
- Rice
- Wheat

- Groundnuts
- Soybeans

- Citrus fruit
- Other fruit and vegetables
- Vines

- Cotton
- Sugar beet
- Sugar cane
- Tobacco

- Coffee

- Main fishing areas

MINERALS

Iron and ferro-alloys
- Cobalt
- Iron ore
- Manganese
- Molybdenum
- Nickel ore

Non-ferrous metals
- Aluminium
- Copper
- Lead
- Zinc
- Uranium

Precious metals
- Diamonds
- Gold
- Silver

Fertilizers
- Phosphates
- Potash

Structure
- Pre-Cambrian shield
- Palaeozoic folding
- Mesozoic folding
- Cenozoic folding
- Igneous structures

ENERGY

- Oil
- Natural gas
- Coal and lignite
- Nuclear power
- Hydro-electric power

Energy production
per capita (2003)
million tonnes of
oil equivalent
- Over 15
- 10 – 15
- 5 – 10
- 0.5 – 5
- Less than 0.5

Projection: Bonne

COPYRIGHT
PHILIP'S

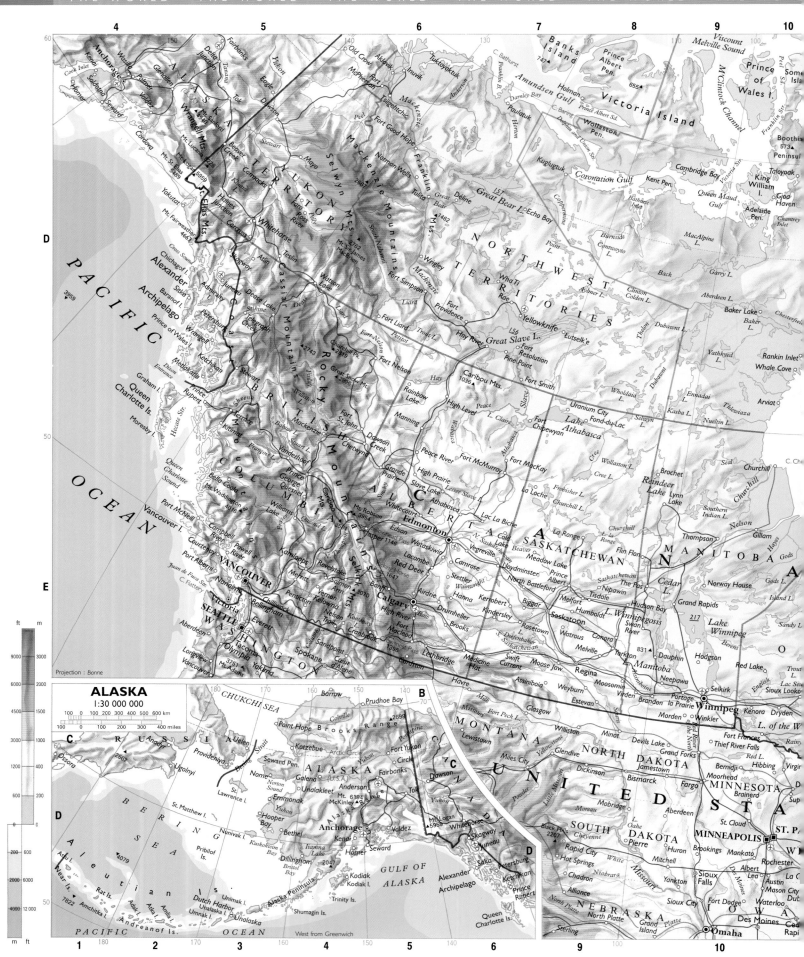

ALASKA
1:30 000 000

Projection : Bonne

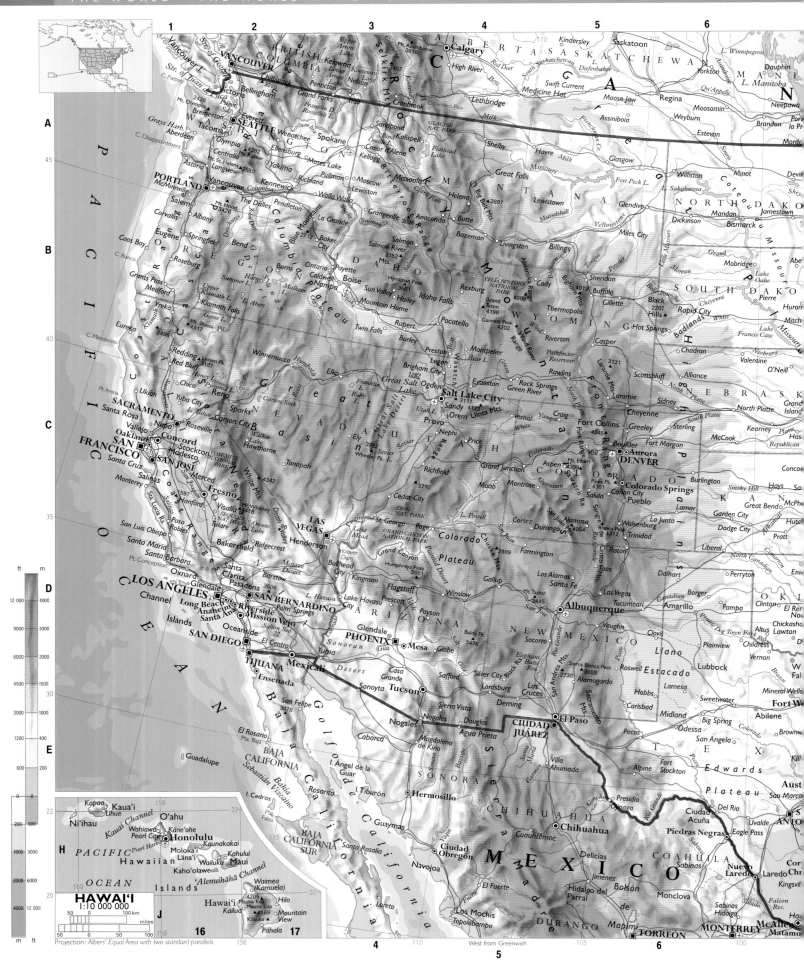

HAWAI'I
1:10 000 000

Projection: Albers' Equal Area with two standard parallels

1:12 000 000

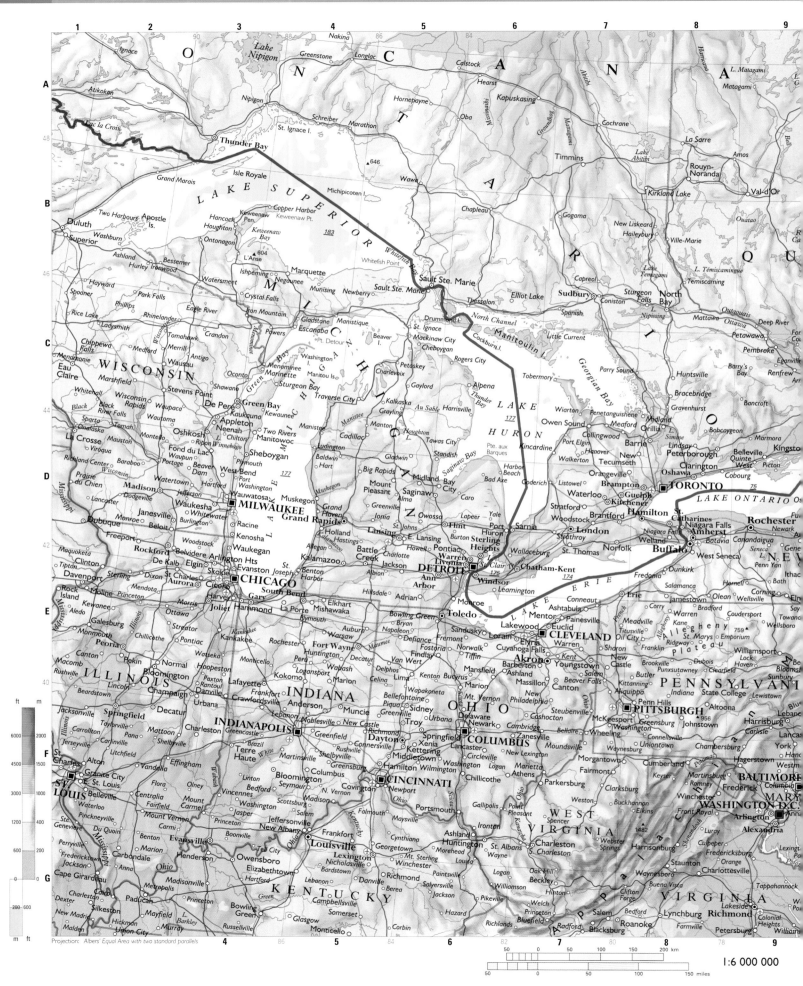

Projection: Albers' Equal Area with two standard parallels

1:6 000 000

TOURISM IN THE USA

Major tourist centres

Major concentration of hotels

Major National Parks

COPYRIGHT PHILIP'S

UNITED STATES

San Diego · Tijuana · Mexicali · Ensenada · Yuma · Phoenix · Tucson · Casa Grande · Douglas · Nogales · Gaborca · Nacozari de García · Nuevo Casas Grandes · CIUDAD JUÁREZ · El Paso · Deming · Las Cruces · Roswell · Carlsbad · Lubbock · Wichita Falls · Little Rock · Huntsville

Pta. Baja · I. Ángel de la Guarda · Tiburón · Hermosillo · Chihuahua · Cuauhtémoc · Ojinaga · Fort Stockton · Pecos · San Angelo · Abilene · Sherman · Fort Worth · DALLAS · Texarkana · Shreveport · Greenville · Monroe · Jackson · Meridian · Birmingham · Tuscaloosa · Montgomery

Bahía Sebastián Vizcaíno · Pt. Falsa · Santa Rosalía · Guaymas · Empalme · Ciudad Obregón · Navojoa · Huatabampo · Madera · Delicias · Ciudad Camargo · Jiménez · Villa Ahumada · Austin · Bryan · Waco · Brazos · Nacogdoches · Alexandria · Natchez · Hattiesburg · Mobile · Dothan · Pensacola

Los Mochis · Guasave · Guamúchil · El Fuerte · Hidalgo del Parral · San Pedro de las Colonias · Sabinas · Nueva Rosita · Piedras Negras · Eagle Pass · Del Rio · Ciudad Acuña · SAN ANTONIO · HOUSTON · Beaumont · Port Arthur · Lake Charles · Lafayette · Baton Rouge · NEW ORLEANS

Baja California · **Sierra Madre Occidental** · Culiacán · Gómez Palacio · TORREÓN · Saltillo · MONTERREY · Montemorelos · Linares · Victoria · Matagorda I. · Corpus Christi · Padre I. · Laguna Madre · Mississippi River Delta · C. San Blas

Mazatlán · Durango · El Salto · Sombrerete · Concepción del Oro · San Fernando · McAllen · Reynosa · Matamoros · Brownsville · **GULF OF MEXICO**

C. San Lázaro · La Paz · B. de La Paz · Cabo San Lucas · C. San Lucas · Rosario · Esculapa de Hidalgo · Presnillo · Zacatecas · Charcas · Matehuala · Ciudad Victoria · Tropic of Cancer

Islas Marías · Tepic · Tuxpan · Jerez · Aguascalientes · San Luis Potosí · Ciudad Mante · Ciudad Madero · Tampico · Yucatán Channel

GUADALAJARA · Puerto Vallarta · C. Corrientes · León · Guanajuato · Celaya · Querétaro · Ciudad Valles · Tamuín · Poza Rica · Papantla · Progreso · Tizimín · Cancún · Mérida · Motul · Cozumel I. · Cozumel

Ameca · L. de Chapala · Zamora · Irapuato · Pachuca · Tulancingo · Tuxpan · Magozal · C. Rojo · **Golfo de Campeche** · Valladolid · Peto · Ciudad Guzmán · Nevado de Colima 4240 · Colima · Morelia · MÉXICO · TOLUCA · Popocatépetl 5452 · Xalapa · Veracruz · Champotón · Campeche · Ticul · **Yucatán** · Felipe Carrillo Puerto

Manzanillo · Tecomán · Uruapan · Cuernavaca · PUEBLA · Pico de Orizaba 5610 · Orizaba · Córdoba · San Andrés Tuxtla · Ciudad del Carmen · Laguna de Términos · Chetumal · Corozal · Ambergris Cay

Lázaro Cárdenas · Balsas · Iguala · Tlapa · Tlaxcala 3397 · Minatitlán · Coatzacoalcos · Villahermosa · Escárcega · Belize City · Turneffe Is.

Acapulco 5448 · Chilpancingo · Chilapa · Oaxaca · **Istmo de Tehuantepec** · Palenque · Belmopan · BELIZE · Gulf of Honduras

Ometepec · TUXTLA GUTIÉRREZ · San Cristóbal de las Casas · Comitán · Puerto Barrios · Puerto Cortés · Tela · Trujillo

G. de Tehuantepec · Salina Cruz · Tonalá · Huixtla · Tapachula · Quezaltenango · GUATEMALA · Cobán · La Ceiba · San Pedro Sula · **HONDURAS** · Juticalpa · Comayagua · Santa Ana · Sonsonate · SAN SALVADOR · San Vicente · Tegucigalpa · Ocotal

EL SALVADOR · San Miguel · La Unión · G. de Fonseca · Choluteca · **NICARAGUA** · MANAGUA · León · Masaya · Pen. de Nicoya · Puntarenas · Grar Lage Nica

PACIFIC OCEAN

JAMAICA
1:3 000 000
10 0 10 20 30 40 50 km
10 0 10 20 30 miles

CARIBBEAN SEA

Montego Bay · Lucea · Negril · South Negril Pt. · Savanna-la-Mar · Falmouth · Wakefield · Cambridge · Maggotty · Black River · Great Pedro Bluff · Runaway Bay · St. Ann's Bay · Ocho Rios · The Cockpit Country · Mount Denham 985 · Dry Harbour Mountains · Don Figuero Mts. · Mandeville · Santa Cruz Mts. · May Pen · Alligator Pond · Galina Point · Port Maria · Moneague · Annotto Bay · Linstead · Spanish Town · Portmore · Kingston · Portland Bight · Portland Point · Blue Mountains 2256 Blue Mt. Pk. · John Crow Mts. · Port Antonio · Morant Point · Morant Bay · Port Morant

JAMAICA

Projection : Bonne

GUADELOUPE
Pte. de la Grande Vigie · Port-Louis · Petit-Canal · Grande-Terre · Le Moule · La Désirade · Pointe Allègre · Ste-Rose · Pointe-à-Pitre · Ste-Anne · Pointe des Châteaux · Pointe-Noire · Le Gosier · Îles de la Petite Terre · Basse-Terre · Bouillante · Capesterre-Belle-Eau · Soufrière 1467 · Basse-Terre · Trois-Rivières · St-Louis · Marie-Galante 204 · Capesterre-de-Marie-Galante · Îles des Saintes · Grand-Bourg · Pte. des Basses
GUADELOUPE (Fr.)

MARTINIQUE
Cap St-Martin · Basse-Pointe · Ste-Marie · Le Prêcheur · Montagne Pelée 1397 · La Trinité · St-Pierre · Presqu'île de la Caravelle · Le Robert · Schœlcher · Fort-de-France · Le Lamentin · Le François · Rivière-Salée · Le St-Esprit · St-Joseph · Rivière-Pilote · Le Marin · Pte. d'Enfer
MARTINIQUE (Fr.)

GUADELOUPE AND MARTINIQUE
1:2 000 000
10 0 10 20 30 40 km
10 0 10 20 30 miles

---

ft m 12 000 4000 · 9000 3000 · 6000 2000 · 4500 1500 · 3000 1000 · 1200 400 · 600 200 · 0 · 200 600 · 2000 6000 · 4000 12 000 · 6000 18 000
m ft

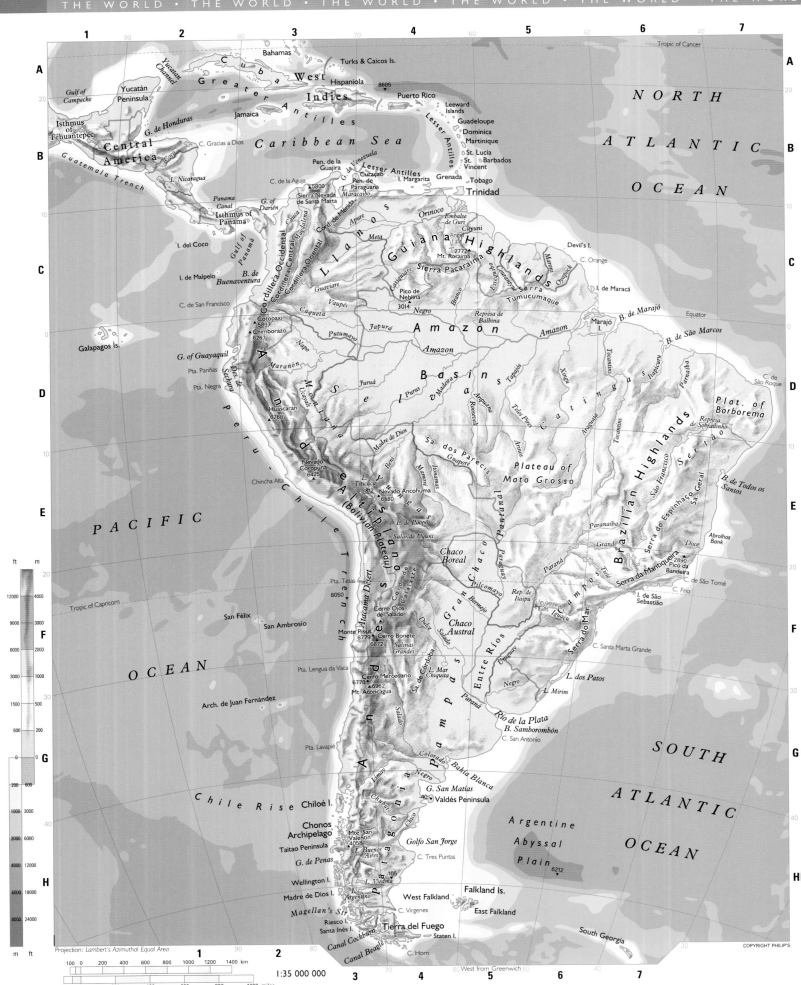

Tropic of Cancer

NORTH ATLANTIC OCEAN

Bahamas
Turks & Caicos Is.
Yucatán Channel
Cuba
West Indies
Greater Antilles
Gulf of Campeche
Yucatán Peninsula
Hispaniola
8605
Puerto Rico
Isthmus of Tehuantepec
G. de Honduras
C. Gracias a Dios
Jamaica
Leeward Islands
Guadeloupe
Dominica
Martinique
St. Lucia
St. Vincent
Barbados
Grenada
Tobago
Trinidad
Central America
Guatemala Trench
Caribbean Sea
Lesser Antilles
L. Nicaragua
Pen. de la Guajira
G. de Venezuela
Pen. de Paraguana
I. Margarita
Curaçao
C. de la Aguja
L. de Maracaibo
Panama Canal
G. of Darién
Sierra Nevada de Santa Marta
5800
Isthmus of Panama
I. del Coco
Gulf of Panamá
Cordillera Occidental
Cordillera Central
Cordillera Oriental
Cauca
Magdalena
Cord. de Mérida
Apure
Orinoco
Embalse de Guri
Cuyuni
Llanos
Meta
Guiana Highlands
Angel Falls
Mt. Roraima
2772
Devil's I.
C. Orange
I. de Malpelo
B. de Buenaventura
Guaviare
Casiquiare
Sierra Pacaraima
Branco
Serra Tumucumaque
C. de San Francisco
Cotopaxi
5897
Chimborazo
6267
Guaviare
Vaupés
Pico de Neblina
3014
Negro
Represa de Balbina
I. de Maracá
Galapagos Is.
G. of Guayaquil
Caquetá
Putumayo
Japurá
Amazon
Marajó I.
B. de Marajó
Equator
B. de São Marcos
C. de São Roque
Pta. Pariñas
Pta. Negra
Des. de Sechura
Napo
Marañón
Ucayali
Montaña
Juruá
Purus
Madeira
Amazon
Basins
Roosevelt
Aripuaná
Tapajós
Teles Pires
Xingu
Tocantins
Itapicuru
Parnaíba
Caatinga
Plat. de Borborema
Huascarán
6768
Madre de Dios
Beni
Mamoré
Guaporé
Sa. dos Parecis
Represa de Sobradinho
São Francisco
Sertão
Serra do Espinhaço
B. de Todos os Santos
Nevado Coropuna
6425
Chincha Alta
Titicaca
3812
Nevado Ancohuma
6550
Yungas
L. de Poopó
Salar de Uyuni
Plateau of Mato Grosso
Pantanal
Paraguay
Brazilian Highlands
Grande
Doce
Abrolhos Bank
Andes
Altiplano (Bolivian Plateau)
Chaco Boreal
Gran Chaco
Paraná
Paranaíba
Sa. Geral
Serra da Mantiqueira
Pico da Bandeira
2890
C. de São Tomé
Peru-Chile Trench
Pta. Tetas
8050
Atacama Desert
Cerro Ojos del Salado
Cord. de Calalaste
Bermejo
Pilcomayo
Chaco Austral
Rep. de Itaipú
Campos
Iguaçu
Iguaçu Falls
Serra do Mar
I. de São Sebastião
C. Frio
PACIFIC OCEAN
San Félix
San Ambrosio
Monte Pissis
6779
Cerro Bonete
6872
Dulce
Salado
Salinas Grandes
Entre Ríos
Uruguay
Negro
L. Mirim
C. Santa Marta Grande
Tropic of Capricorn
Cerro Mercedario
6770
Mt. Aconcagua
6962
Sa. de Córdoba
L. Mar Chiquita
Paraná
Pampas
L. dos Patos
Salado
Arch. de Juan Fernández
Río de la Plata
B. Samborombón
C. San Antonio
SOUTH ATLANTIC OCEAN
Colorado
Negro
Bahía Blanca
G. San Matías
Valdés Peninsula
Argentine Abyssal Plain
Chile Rise
Chiloé I.
Limay
Chubut
Patagonia
Chico
Negro
40
6212
Chonos Archipelago
Mte. San Valentín
4058
Golfo San Jorge
C. Tres Puntas
Taitao Peninsula
L. Buenos Aires
G. de Penas
Wellington I.
L. Viedma
-105
Falkland Is.
Madre de Dios I.
L. Argentino
West Falkland
Magellan's Str.
C. Virgenes
East Falkland
Riesco I.
Santa Inés I.
Tierra del Fuego
Staten I.
South Georgia
Canal Cockburn
Canal Beagle
C. Horn
West from Greenwich

ft m
12000 4000
9000 3000
6000 2000
3000 1000
1500 500
600 200
0 0
200 600
1000 3000
2000 6000
4000 12000
6000 18000
8000 24000
m ft

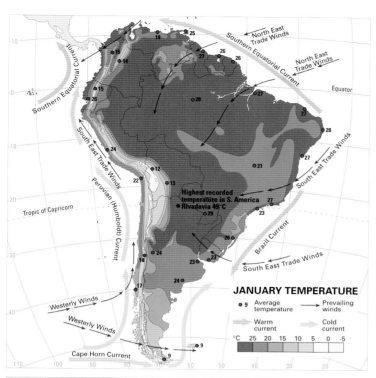

JANUARY TEMPERATURE

Highest recorded temperature in S. America Rivadavia 49°C

- 9 Average temperature
- → Prevailing winds
- Warm current
- Cold current

°C 25 20 15 10 5 0 -5

North East Trade Winds
Southern Equatorial Current
North East Trade Winds
Southern Equatorial Current
South East Trade Winds
South East Trade Winds
South East Trade Winds
Peruvian (Humboldt) Current
Brazil Current
Westerly Winds
Westerly Winds
Cape Horn Current
Equator
Tropic of Capricorn

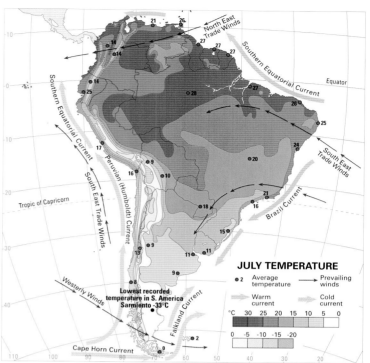

JULY TEMPERATURE

Lowest recorded temperature in S. America Sarmiento -33°C

- 9 Average temperature
- → Prevailing winds
- Warm current
- Cold current

°C 30 25 20 15 10 5 0
0 -5 -10 -15 -20

North East Trade Winds
Southern Equatorial Current
South East Trade Winds
Southern Equatorial Current
South East Trade Winds
Peruvian (Humboldt) Current
Brazil Current
Westerly Winds
Falkland Current
Cape Horn Current
Equator
Tropic of Capricorn

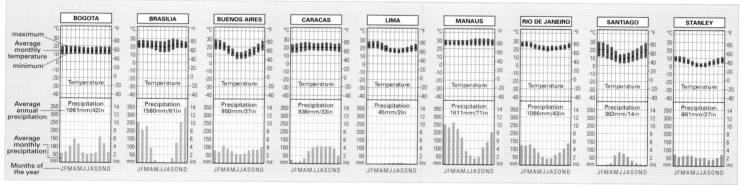

Climate graphs for: BOGOTA, BRASILIA, BUENOS AIRES, CARACAS, LIMA, MANAUS, RIO DE JANEIRO, SANTIAGO, STANLEY

- maximum
- Average monthly temperature
- minimum
- Average annual precipitation
- Average monthly precipitation
- Months of the year

City	Precipitation
BOGOTA	1061mm/42in
BRASILIA	1560mm/61in
BUENOS AIRES	950mm/37in
CARACAS	836mm/33in
LIMA	45mm/2in
MANAUS	1811mm/71in
RIO DE JANEIRO	1086mm/43in
SANTIAGO	363mm/14in
STANLEY	681mm/27in

JFMAMJJASOND

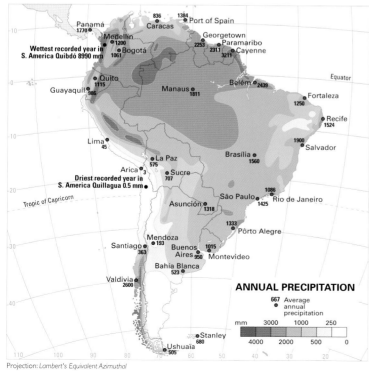

ANNUAL PRECIPITATION

Wettest recorded year in S. America Quibdó 8990 mm
Driest recorded year in S. America Quillagua 0.5 mm

Panamá 1770
Medellín 1200
Bogotá 1061
Caracas 836
Port of Spain 1384
Georgetown 2253
Paramaribo 2311
Cayenne 3211
Quito 1115
Guayaquil 986
Manaus 1811
Belém 2439
Fortaleza 1250
Recife 1524
Lima 45
La Paz 575
Arica 3
Sucre 707
Brasília 1560
Salvador 1900
São Paulo 1425
Rio de Janeiro 1086
Asunción 1318
Pôrto Alegre 1333
Mendoza 193
Santiago 363
Buenos Aires 950
Montevideo 1015
Bahía Blanca 523
Valdivia 2600
Stanley 680
Ushuaïa 505

- 667 Average annual precipitation

mm 3000 1000 250
4000 2000 500 0

Equator
Tropic of Capricorn

NATURAL VEGETATION

Guiana Highlands
Amazon Basin
South limit of wild rubber
Andes
Atacama Desert
South limit of Quebracho
Brazilian Highlands
Pampas
Patagonia
PACIFIC OCEAN
ATLANTIC OCEAN

Equator
Tropic of Capricorn

- Tropical rainforest
- Tropical thorn forest
- Temperate rainforest
- Evergreen trees and shrubs
- Grassland and savanna
- Semi-desert
- Desert
- Alpine and high plateau

Projection: *Lambert's Equivalent Azimuthal*

COPYRIGHT PHILIP'S

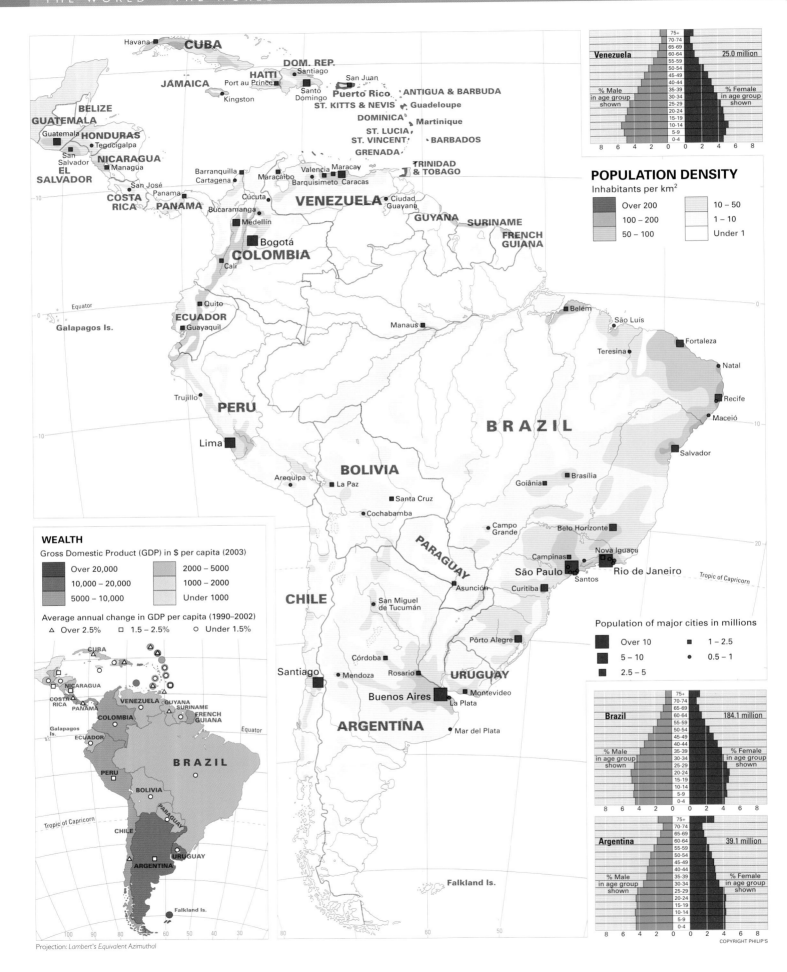

Venezuela 25.0 million

% Male in age group shown — % Female in age group shown

75+ 70-74 65-69 60-64 55-59 50-54 45-49 40-44 35-39 30-34 25-29 20-24 15-19 10-14 5-9 0-4

8 6 4 2 0 0 2 4 6 8

POPULATION DENSITY
Inhabitants per km²

Over 200	10 – 50
100 – 200	1 – 10
50 – 100	Under 1

WEALTH
Gross Domestic Product (GDP) in $ per capita (2003)

Over 20,000	2000 – 5000
10,000 – 20,000	1000 – 2000
5000 – 10,000	Under 1000

Average annual change in GDP per capita (1990–2002)

△ Over 2.5%   □ 1.5 – 2.5%   ○ Under 1.5%

Population of major cities in millions

■ Over 10	■ 1 – 2.5
■ 5 – 10	● 0.5 – 1
■ 2.5 – 5	

Brazil 184.1 million

% Male in age group shown — % Female in age group shown

75+ 70-74 65-69 60-64 55-59 50-54 45-49 40-44 35-39 30-34 25-29 20-24 15-19 10-14 5-9 0-4

8 6 4 2 0 0 2 4 6 8

Argentina 39.1 million

% Male in age group shown — % Female in age group shown

75+ 70-74 65-69 60-64 55-59 50-54 45-49 40-44 35-39 30-34 25-29 20-24 15-19 10-14 5-9 0-4

8 6 4 2 0 0 2 4 6 8

Projection: *Lambert's Equivalent Azimuthal*

COPYRIGHT PHILIP'S

LAND USE

- Arable
- Intensive arable
- Pasture
- Woods and forests
- Rough grazing
- Non-productive
- Main fishing areas

- Beef cattle
- Dairy cattle
- Pigs
- Poultry
- Sheep

- Maize
- Millet and sorghum
- Rice
- Wheat

- Groundnuts
- Potatoes
- Soybeans

- Bananas
- Citrus fruit
- Other fruit and vegetables
- Vines

- Cacao
- Coconut palms
- Cotton
- Sugar cane
- Tobacco

- Coffee
- Tea

MINERALS

Iron and ferro-alloys
- Chrome
- Cobalt
- Iron ore
- Manganese
- Molybdenum
- Nickel ore

Non-ferrous metals
- Aluminium
- Bauxite
- Copper
- Lead
- Tin

Precious metals & stones
- Diamonds
- Gold
- Silver

Fertilizers
- Phosphates

Structure
- Pre-Cambrian shield
- Palaeozoic folding
- Mesozoic folding
- Cenozoic folding
- Igneous structures

ENERGY
- Oil
- Natural gas
- Coal and lignite
- Nuclear power
- Hydro-electric power

Energy production per capita (2003)
million tonnes of oil equivalent
- Over 15
- 10 – 15
- 5 – 10
- 0.5 – 5
- Less than 0.5

Projection: *Lambert's Equivalent Azimuthal*

COPYRIGHT PHILIP'S

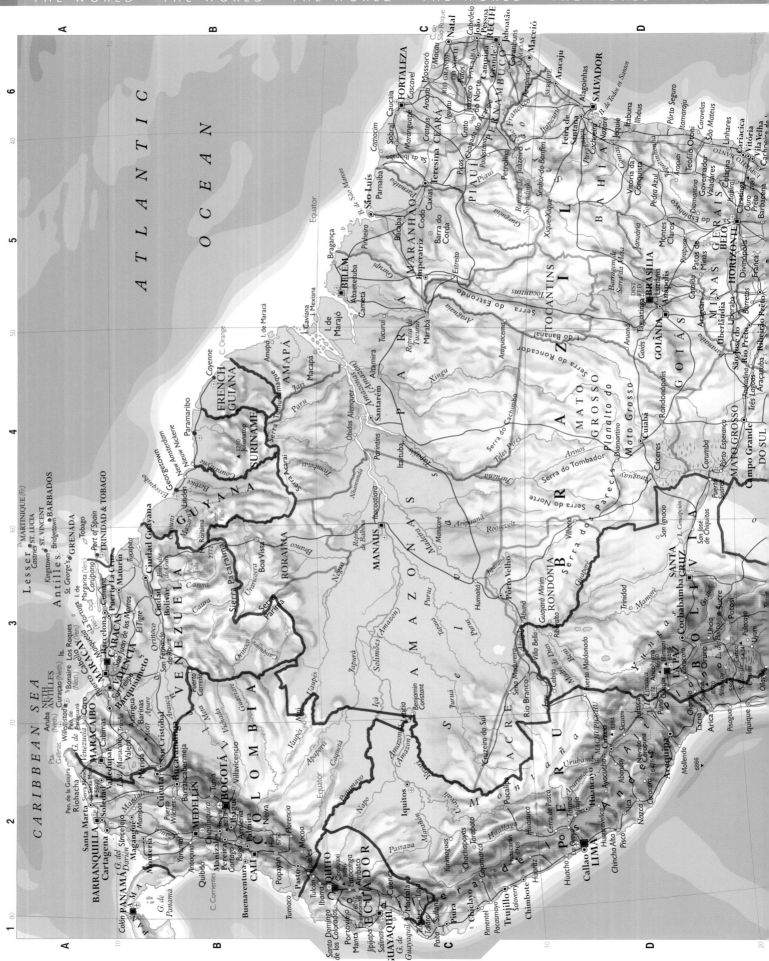

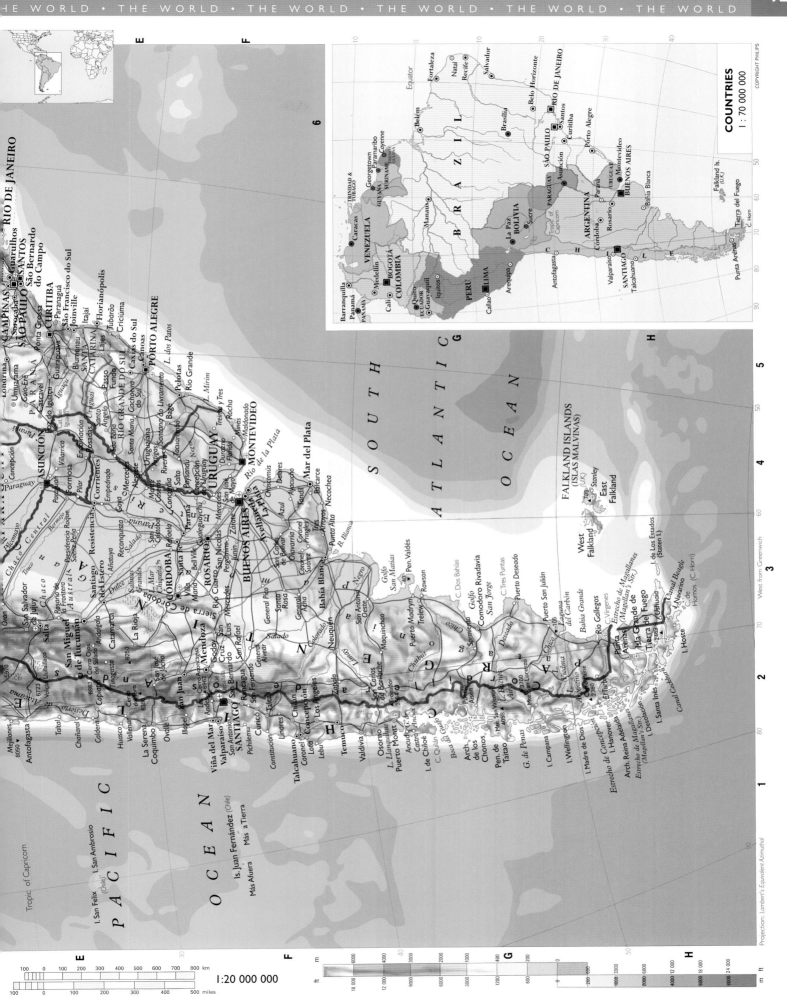

RIO DE JANEIRO

CAMPINAS
Guarulhos
SÃO PAULO
Santos
São Bernardo do Campo
Soracaba
CURITIBA
Ponta Grossa
Paranaguá
São Francisco do Sul
Joinville
Itajaí
Blumenau
Florianópolis
Tubarão
Criciúma
Lajes
PORTO ALEGRE
Caxias do Sul
Canoas
L. dos Patos
Pelotas
Rio Grande
L. Mirim

SANTA CATARINA
RIO GRANDE DO SUL

ASUNCIÓN
PARANA
Concepción
Paraguay
Villarrica
Pilar
Formosa
Resistencia
CORRIENTES
Goya
URUGUAY
MONTEVIDEO
Río de la Plata
Mar del Plata

SOUTH

ATLANTIC

OCEAN

FALKLAND ISLANDS
(ISLAS MALVINAS)
(UK)
Stanley
East Falkland
West Falkland

CÓRDOBA
ROSARIO
BUENOS AIRES
Bahía Blanca

Mendoza
San Juan
San Luis
San Rafael

SANTIAGO
Valparaíso
Viña del Mar

Concepción
Talcahuano
Temuco
Valdivia
Osorno
Puerto Montt
I. de Chiloé

A R G E N T I N A

Neuquén
San Carlos de Bariloche
Puerto Madryn
Trelew
Rawson
Comodoro Rivadavia
Puerto Deseado
Puerto San Julián
Río Gallegos
Punta Arenas
Tierra del Fuego
Ushuaia
C. Horn

PACIFIC

OCEAN

Tropic of Capricorn

I. San Félix (Chile)
I. San Ambrosio
Is. Juan Fernández (Chile)
Más a Tierra
Más Afuera

Antofagasta

Projection: Lambert's Equivalent Azimuthal

E   F   G   H

1:20 000 000

100 0 100 200 300 400 500 600 700 800 km
100 0 100 200 300 400 500 miles

COUNTRIES
1:70 000 000

BRAZIL

VENEZUELA
COLOMBIA
ECUADOR
PERU
BOLIVIA
PARAGUAY
ARGENTINA
CHILE
URUGUAY

Caracas
BOGOTÁ
Quito
Guayaquil
LIMA
La Paz
Sucre
Arequipa
ASUNCIÓN
SANTIAGO
Valparaíso
Córdoba
Rosario
BUENOS AIRES
MONTEVIDEO
Bahía Blanca
Punta Arenas
Tierra del Fuego
C. Horn
Falkland Is. (UK)

Panamá
Barranquilla
Medellín
Cali
Iquitos
Manaus
Belém
Fortaleza
Natal
Recife
Salvador
Belo Horizonte
Brasília
RIO DE JANEIRO
SÃO PAULO
Santos
Curitiba
Pôrto Alegre

Georgetown
Paramaribo
Cayenne
TRINIDAD & TOBAGO
GUYANA
SURINAM
FRENCH GUIANA

Equator
Tropic of Capricorn

COPYRIGHT PHILIP'S

m ft
6000 18 000
4000 12 000
3000 9000
2000 6000
1000 3000
400 1200
200 600
0 0
200 600
1000 3000
3000 9000
4000 12 000
6000 18 000
8000 24 000
ft m

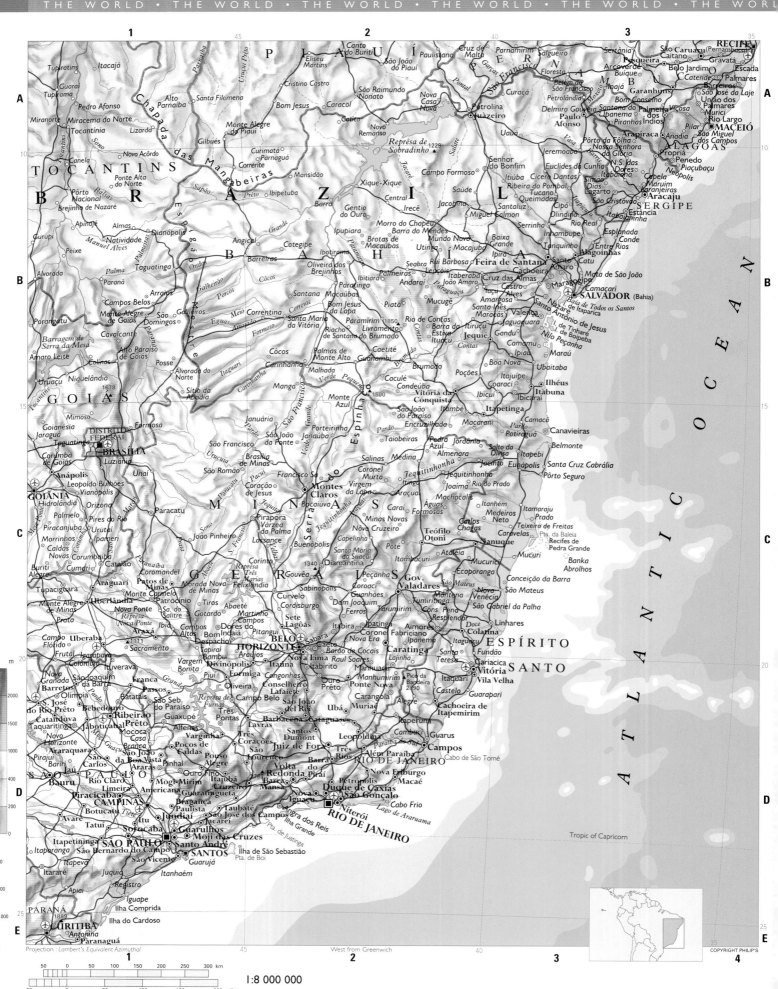

Projection : Lambert's Equivalent Azimuthal

West from Greenwich

COPYRIGHT PHILIP'S

1:8 000 000

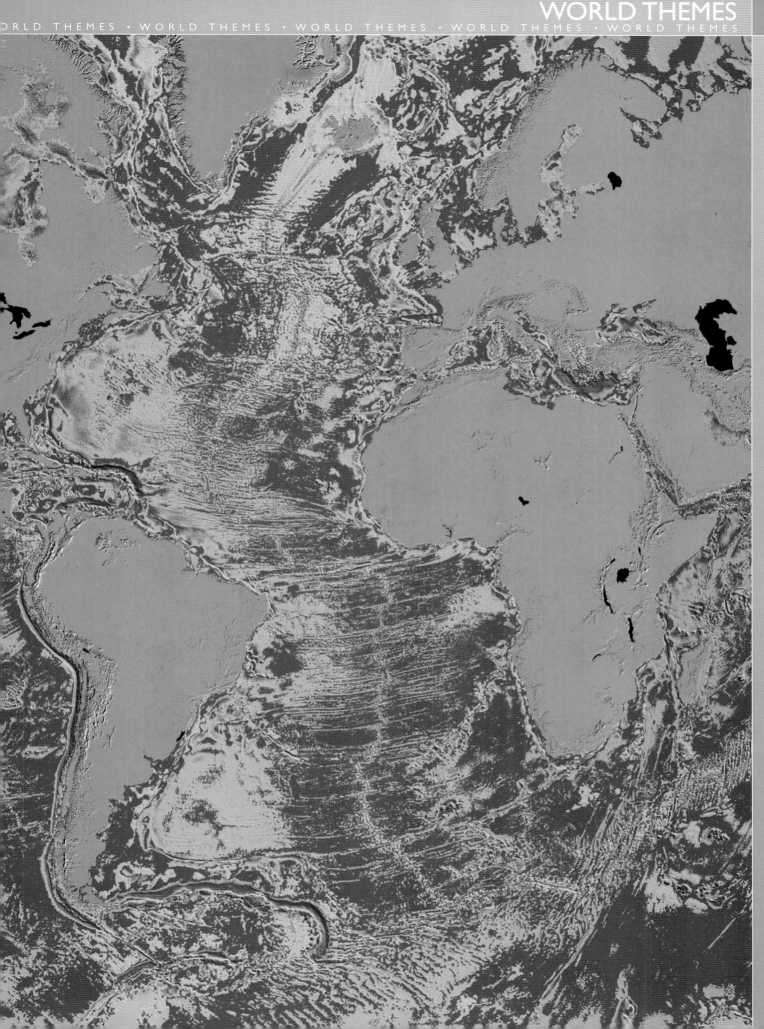

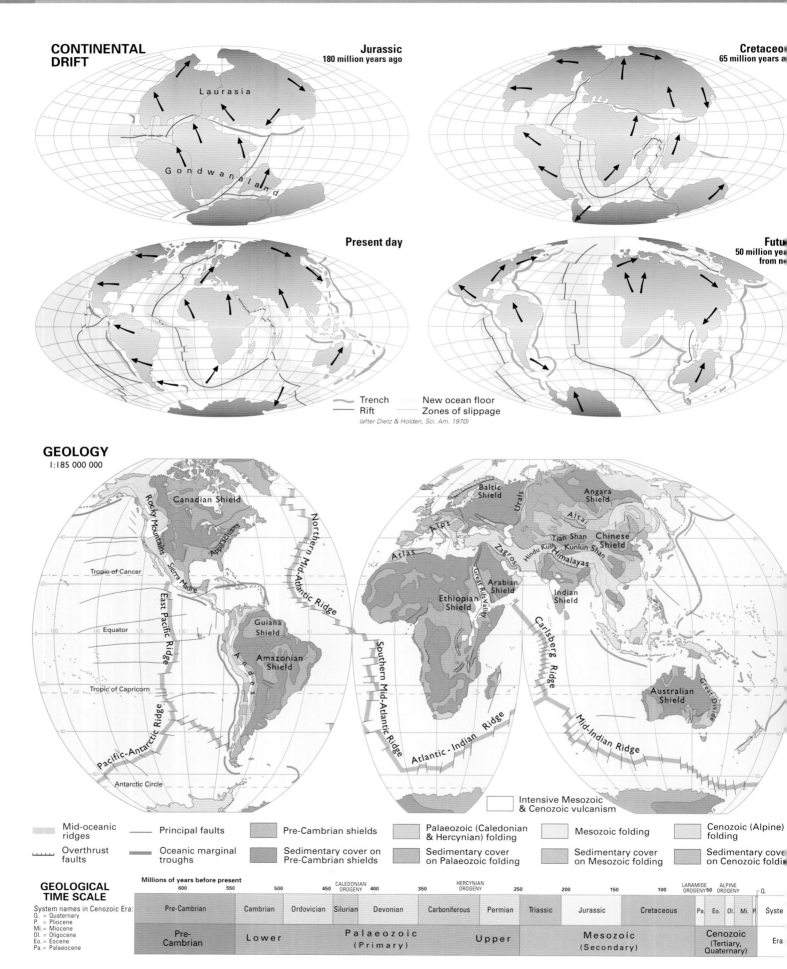

CONTINENTAL DRIFT

Jurassic
180 million years ago

Laurasia

Gondwanaland

Cretaceou
65 million years a

Present day

Futu
50 million yea
from n

Trench — New ocean floor
Rift — Zones of slippage
(after Dietz & Holden, Sci. Am. 1970)

GEOLOGY
1:185 000 000

Canadian Shield
Rocky Mountains
Appalachians
Northern Mid-Atlantic Ridge
Sierra Madre
Tropic of Cancer
East Pacific Ridge
Equator
Guiana Shield
Amazonian Shield
Andes
Tropic of Capricorn
Pacific-Antarctic Ridge
Antarctic Circle

Baltic Shield
Urals
Angara Shield
Altai
Alps
Tian Shan
Chinese Shield
Atlas
Zagros
Hindu Kush
Kunlun Shan
Himalayas
Great Rift Valley
Arabian Shield
Indian Shield
Ethiopian Shield
Carlsberg Ridge
Southern Mid-Atlantic Ridge
Atlantic - Indian Ridge
Mid-Indian Ridge
Australian Shield
Great Divide

Intensive Mesozoic & Cenozoic vulcanism

Mid-oceanic ridges — Principal faults — Pre-Cambrian shields — Palaeozoic (Caledonian & Hercynian) folding — Mesozoic folding — Cenozoic (Alpine) folding

Overthrust faults — Oceanic marginal troughs — Sedimentary cover on Pre-Cambrian shields — Sedimentary cover on Palaeozoic folding — Sedimentary cover on Mesozoic folding — Sedimentary cove on Cenozoic foldi

GEOLOGICAL TIME SCALE

System names in Cenozoic Era:
Q. = Quaternary
P. = Pliocene
Mi. = Miocene
Ol. = Oligocene
Eo. = Eocene
Pa. = Palaeocene

Millions of years before present

600	550	500	450 CALEDONIAN OROGENY 400	350	HERCYNIAN OROGENY	250	200	150	100	LARAMIDE OROGENY 50 ALPINE OROGENY	Q.

Pre-Cambrian	Cambrian	Ordovician	Silurian	Devonian	Carboniferous	Permian	Triassic	Jurassic	Cretaceous	Pa.	Eo.	Ol.	Mi. P.	Syste

Pre-Cambrian	Lower	Palaeozoic (Primary)		Upper	Mesozoic (Secondary)		Cenozoic (Tertiary, Quaternary)	Era

VOLCANOES AND PLATE TECTONICS

1:185 000 000

'Ring of Fire'

Constructive boundary (plates moving apart)

Destructive boundary (plates colliding)

Conservative boundary (plates sliding past each other)

Direction of movement along plate boundaries 7.2 (cm/year)

Submarine volcanoes

Geysers

Land volcanoes active since 1700

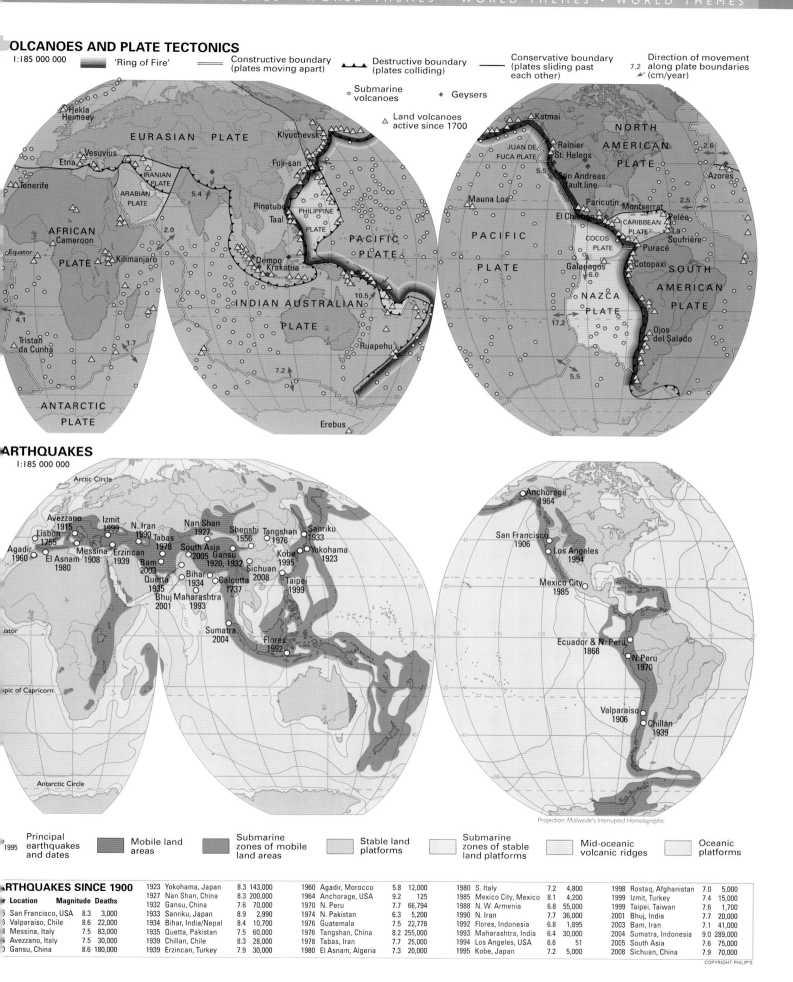

EARTHQUAKES

1:185 000 000

Projection: Mollweide's Interrupted Homolographic

1995 Principal earthquakes and dates

Mobile land areas

Submarine zones of mobile land areas

Stable land platforms

Submarine zones of stable land platforms

Mid-oceanic volcanic ridges

Oceanic platforms

EARTHQUAKES SINCE 1900

Location	Magnitude	Deaths											
San Francisco, USA	8.3	3,000	1923 Yokohama, Japan	8.3	143,000	1960 Agadir, Morocco	5.8	12,000	1980 S. Italy	7.2	4,800	1998 Rostaq, Afghanistan	7.0	5,000
Valparaiso, Chile	8.6	22,000	1927 Nan Shan, China	8.3	200,000	1964 Anchorage, USA	9.2	125	1985 Mexico City, Mexico	8.1	4,200	1999 Izmit, Turkey	7.4	15,000
Messina, Italy	7.5	83,000	1932 Gansu, China	7.6	70,000	1970 N. Peru	7.7	66,794	1988 N. W. Armenia	6.8	55,000	1999 Taipei, Taiwan	7.6	1,700
Avezzano, Italy	7.5	30,000	1933 Sanriku, Japan	8.9	2,990	1974 N. Pakistan	6.3	5,200	1990 N. Iran	7.7	36,000	2001 Bhuj, India	7.7	20,000
Gansu, China	8.6	180,000	1934 Bihar, India/Nepal	8.4	10,700	1976 Guatemala	7.5	22,778	1992 Flores, Indonesia	6.8	1,895	2003 Bam, Iran	7.1	41,000
			1935 Quetta, Pakistan	7.5	60,000	1976 Tangshan, China	8.2	255,000	1993 Maharashtra, India	6.4	30,000	2004 Sumatra, Indonesia	9.0	289,000
			1939 Chillán, Chile	8.3	28,000	1978 Tabas, Iran	7.7	25,000	1994 Los Angeles, USA	6.6	51	2005 South Asia	7.6	75,000
			1939 Erzincan, Turkey	7.9	30,000	1980 El Asnam, Algeria	7.3	20,000	1995 Kobe, Japan	7.2	5,000	2008 Sichuan, China	7.9	70,000

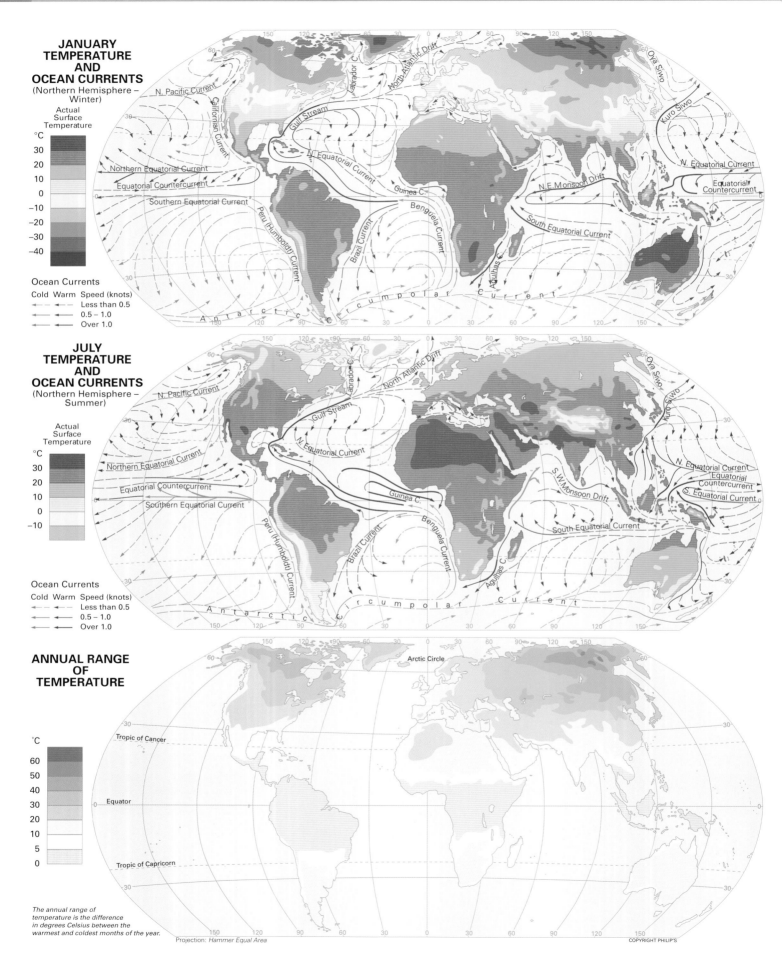

JANUARY TEMPERATURE AND OCEAN CURRENTS
(Northern Hemisphere – Winter)

Actual Surface Temperature

°C
30
20
10
0
−10
−20
−30
−40

Ocean Currents
Cold Warm Speed (knots)
Less than 0.5
0.5 – 1.0
Over 1.0

JULY TEMPERATURE AND OCEAN CURRENTS
(Northern Hemisphere – Summer)

Actual Surface Temperature

°C
30
20
10
0
−10

Ocean Currents
Cold Warm Speed (knots)
Less than 0.5
0.5 – 1.0
Over 1.0

ANNUAL RANGE OF TEMPERATURE

°C
60
50
40
30
20
10
5
0

The annual range of temperature is the difference in degrees Celsius between the warmest and coldest months of the year.

Projection: Hammer Equal Area

COPYRIGHT PHILIP'S

1 : 190 000 000

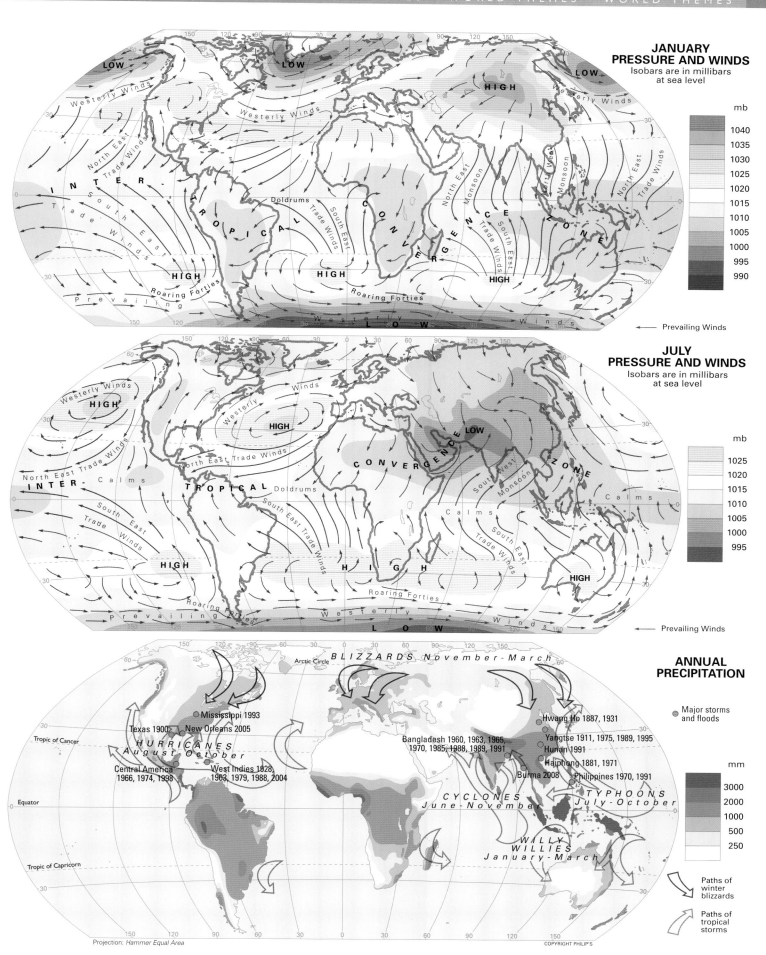

JANUARY PRESSURE AND WINDS
Isobars are in millibars at sea level

mb
| 1040 |
| 1035 |
| 1030 |
| 1025 |
| 1020 |
| 1015 |
| 1010 |
| 1005 |
| 1000 |
| 995 |
| 990 |

⟵ Prevailing Winds

JULY PRESSURE AND WINDS
Isobars are in millibars at sea level

mb
| 1025 |
| 1020 |
| 1015 |
| 1010 |
| 1005 |
| 1000 |
| 995 |

⟵ Prevailing Winds

ANNUAL PRECIPITATION

● Major storms and floods

mm
| 3000 |
| 2000 |
| 1000 |
| 500 |
| 250 |

Paths of winter blizzards

Paths of tropical storms

Mississippi 1993
Texas 1900
New Orleans 2005
HURRICANES
August–October
Central America 1966, 1974, 1998
West Indies 1928, 1963, 1979, 1988, 2004
BLIZZARDS November–March
Hwang Ho 1887, 1931
Yangtse 1911, 1975, 1989, 1995
Hunan 1991
Bangladesh 1960, 1963, 1965, 1970, 1985, 1988, 1989, 1991
Haiphong 1881, 1971
Burma 2008
Philippines 1970, 1991
CYCLONES June–November
TYPHOONS July–October
WILLY WILLIES January–March

Arctic Circle
Tropic of Cancer
Equator
Tropic of Capricorn

Projection: Hammer Equal Area

COPYRIGHT PHILIP'S

CLIMATE REGIONS *(after Köppen)*

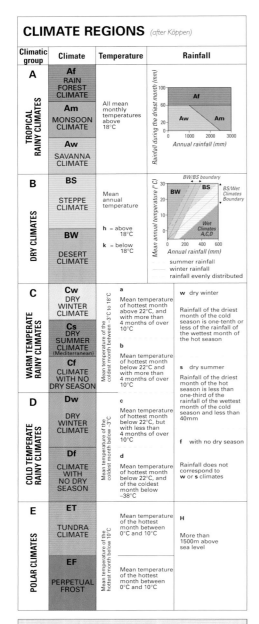

Climatic group	Climate	Temperature	Rainfall
A TROPICAL RAINY CLIMATES	**Af** RAIN FOREST CLIMATE / **Am** MONSOON CLIMATE / **Aw** SAVANNA CLIMATE	All mean monthly temperatures above 18°C	*Rainfall during the driest month (mm)* chart: Af, Aw, Am vs Annual rainfall (mm)
B DRY CLIMATES	**BS** STEPPE CLIMATE / **BW** DESERT CLIMATE	Mean annual temperature / h = above 18°C / k = below 18°C	chart: BW, BS, Wet Climates A,C,D; summer rainfall / winter rainfall / rainfall evenly distributed
C WARM TEMPERATE RAINY CLIMATES	**Cw** DRY WINTER CLIMATE / **Cs** DRY SUMMER CLIMATE (Mediterranean) / **Cf** CLIMATE WITH NO DRY SEASON	Mean temperature of the coldest month between –3°C to 18°C	**a** Mean temperature of hottest month above 22°C, and with more than 4 months of over 10°C **b** Mean temperature of hottest month below 22°C and with more than 4 months of over 10°C **w** dry winter — Rainfall of the driest month of the cold season is one-tenth or less of the rainfall of the wettest month of the hot season **s** dry summer — Rainfall of the driest month of the hot season is less than one-third of the rainfall of the wettest month of the cold season and less than 40mm **f** with no dry season
D COLD TEMPERATE RAINY CLIMATES	**Dw** DRY WINTER CLIMATE / **Df** CLIMATE WITH NO DRY SEASON	Mean temperature of the coldest month below –3°C	**c** Mean temperature of hottest month below 22°C, but with less than 4 months of over 10°C **d** Mean temperature of hottest month below 22°C, and of the coldest month below –38°C Rainfall does not correspond to **w** or **s** climates
E POLAR CLIMATES	**ET** TUNDRA CLIMATE / **EF** PERPETUAL FROST	Mean temperature of the hottest month below 10°C	**H** More than 1500m above sea level / Mean temperature of the hottest month between 0°C and 10°C

CLIMATE RECORDS

Highest recorded temperature: Al Aziziyah, Libya, 58°C, 13 September 1922.

Lowest recorded temperature (outside poles): Verkhoyansk, Siberia, –68°C, 6 February 1933. Verkhoyansk also registered the greatest annual range of temperature: –70°C to 37°C.

Highest barometric pressure: Agata, Siberia, 1,083.8 mb at altitude 262 m, 31 December 1968.

Lowest barometric pressure: Typhoon Tip, 480 km west of Guam, Pacific Ocean, 870 mb, 12 October 1979.

Driest place: Quillagua, N. Chile, 0.5 mm, 1964–2001.

Wettest place (12 months): Cherrapunji, Meghalaya, N.E. India, August 1860 to August 1861. Cherrapunji also holds the record for rainfall in one month: 2930 mm, July 1861.

Highest recorded wind speed: Mt Washington, New Hampshire, USA, 371 km/h, 12 April 1934. This is three times as strong as hurricane force on the Beaufort Scale.

Windiest place: Commonwealth Bay, George V Coast, Antarctica, where gales frequently reach over 320 km/h.

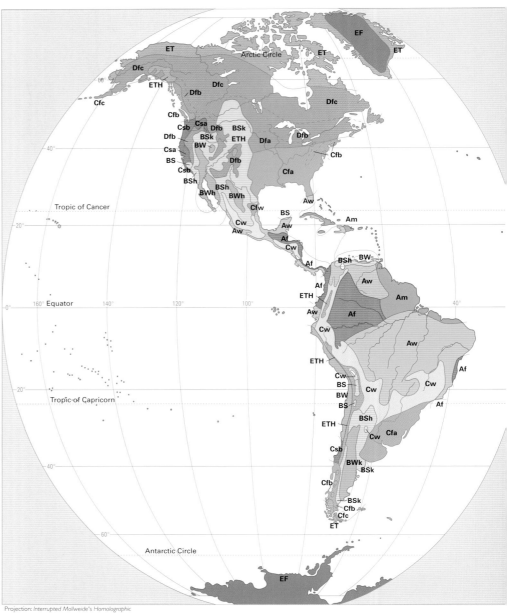

Projection: Interrupted Mollweide's Homolographic

THE MONSOON

In early March, which normally marks the end of the subcontinent's cool season and the start of the hot season, winds blow outwards from the mainland. But as the overhead sun and the ITCZ move northwards, the land is intensely heated, and a low-pressure system develops. The south-east trade winds, which are drawn across the Equator, change direction and are sucked into the interior to become south-westerly winds, bringing heavy rain. By November, the overhead sun and the ITCZ have again moved southwards and the wind directions are again reversed. Cool winds blow from the Asian interior to the sea, losing any moisture on the Himalayas before descending to the coast.

Monthly rainfall

mm	
400	→ wind direction
200	
100	━ ITCZ
50	(intertro
25	converg zone)

March – Start of the hot, dry season, the ITCZ is over the southern Indian Ocean.

July – The rainy season, the ITCZ has migrated northwards; winds blow onshore.

November – The ITCZ has returned s the offshore winds are cool and dry.

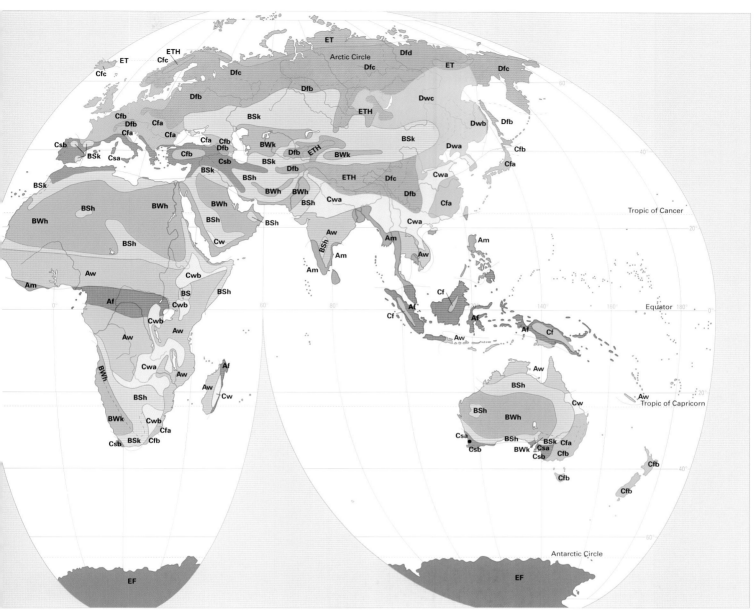

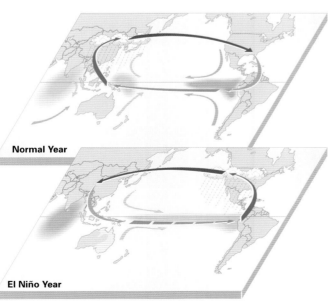

Normal Year

El Niño Year

EL NIÑO

In a normal year, south-easterly trade winds drive surface waters westwards off the coast of South America, drawing cold, nutrient-rich water up from below. In an El Niño year (which occurs every 2–7 years), warm water from the west Pacific suppresses up-welling in the east, depriving the region of nutrients. The water is warmed by as much as 7°C, disturbing the tropical atmospheric circulation. During an intense El Niño, the south-east trade winds change direction and become equatorial westerlies, resulting in climatic extremes in many regions of the world, such as drought in parts of Australia and India, and heavy rainfall in south-eastern USA. An intense El Niño occurred in 1997–8, with resultant freak weather conditions across the entire Pacific region.

WINDCHILL FACTOR

In sub-zero weather, even moderate winds significantly reduce effective temperatures. The chart below shows the windchill effect across a range of speeds.

	Wind speed (km/h)				
	16	32	48	64	80
0°C	−8	−14	−17	−19	−20
−5°C	−14	−21	−25	−27	−28
−10°C	−20	−28	−33	−35	−36
−15°C	−26	−36	−40	−43	−44
−20°C	−32	−42	−48	−51	−52
−25°C	−38	−49	−56	−59	−60
−30°C	−44	−57	−63	−66	−68
−35°C	−51	−64	−72	−74	−76
−40°C	−57	−71	−78	−82	−84
−45°C	−63	−78	−86	−90	−92
−50°C	−69	−85	−94	−98	−100

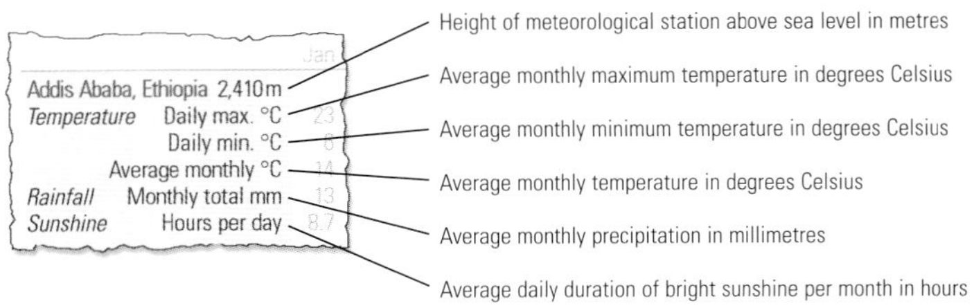
Jan
Addis Ababa, Ethiopia 2,410 m
Temperature Daily max. °C 23
Daily min. °C 6
Average monthly °C 14
Rainfall Monthly total mm 13
Sunshine Hours per day 8.7
Height of meteorological station above sea level in metres
Average monthly maximum temperature in degrees Celsius
Average monthly minimum temperature in degrees Celsius
Average monthly temperature in degrees Celsius
Average monthly precipitation in millimetres
Average daily duration of bright sunshine per month in hours

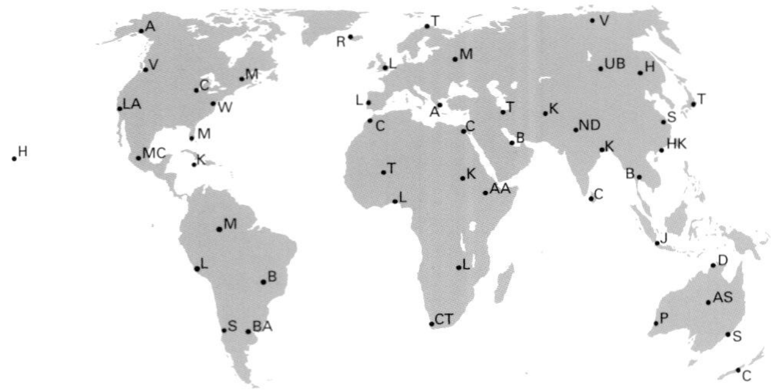

		Jan	Feb	Mar	Apr	May	June	July	Aug	Sept	Oct	Nov	Dec	Year
Addis Ababa, Ethiopia	2,410 m													
Temperature	Daily max. °C	23	24	25	24	25	23	20	20	21	22	23	22	23
	Daily min. °C	6	7	9	10	9	10	11	11	10	7	5	5	8
	Average monthly °C	14	15	17	17	17	16	16	15	15	15	14	14	15
Rainfall	Monthly total mm	13	35	67	91	81	117	247	255	167	29	8	5	1,115
Sunshine	Hours per day	8.7	8.2	7.6	8.1	6.5	4.8	2.8	3.2	5.2	7.6	6.7	7	6.4
Alice Springs, Australia	580 m													
Temperature	Daily max. °C	35	35	32	27	23	19	19	23	27	31	33	35	28
	Daily min. °C	21	20	17	12	8	5	4	6	10	15	18	20	13
	Average monthly °C	28	27	25	20	15	12	12	14	18	23	25	27	21
Rainfall	Monthly total mm	44	33	27	10	15	13	7	8	7	18	29	38	249
Sunshine	Hours per day	10.3	10.4	9.3	9.2	8	8	8.9	9.8	10	9.7	10.1	10	9.5
Anchorage, USA	183 m													
Temperature	Daily max. °C	−7	−3	0	7	13	18	19	17	13	6	−2	−6	−6
	Daily min. °C	−15	−12	−9	−2	4	8	10	9	5	−2	−9	−14	−2
	Average monthly °C	−11	−7	−4	3	9	13	15	13	9	2	−5	−10	−4
Rainfall	Monthly total mm	20	18	13	11	13	25	47	64	64	47	28	24	374
Sunshine	Hours per day	2.4	4.1	6.6	8.3	8.3	9.2	8.5	6	4.4	3.1	2.6	1.6	5.4
Athens, Greece	107 m													
Temperature	Daily max. °C	13	14	16	20	25	30	33	33	29	24	19	15	23
	Daily min. °C	6	7	8	11	16	20	23	23	19	15	12	8	14
	Average monthly °C	10	10	12	16	20	25	28	28	24	20	15	11	18
Rainfall	Monthly total mm	62	37	37	23	23	14	6	7	15	51	56	71	402
Sunshine	Hours per day	3.9	5.2	5.8	7.7	8.9	10.7	11.9	11.5	9.4	6.8	4.8	3.8	7.3
Bahrain City, Bahrain	2 m													
Temperature	Daily max. °C	20	21	25	29	33	36	37	38	36	32	27	22	30
	Daily min. °C	14	15	18	22	25	29	31	32	29	25	22	16	23
	Average monthly °C	17	18	21	25	29	32	34	35	32	29	25	19	26
Rainfall	Monthly total mm	18	12	10	9	2	0	0	0	0	0.4	3	16	70
Sunshine	Hours per day	5.9	6.9	7.9	8.8	10.6	13.2	12.1	12	12	10.3	7.7	6.4	9.5
Bangkok, Thailand	10 m													
Temperature	Daily max. °C	32	33	34	35	34	33	32	32	32	31	31	31	33
	Daily min. °C	20	23	24	26	25	25	25	24	24	24	23	20	24
	Average monthly °C	26	28	29	30	30	29	28	28	28	28	27	26	28
Rainfall	Monthly total mm	9	30	36	82	165	153	168	183	310	239	55	8	1,438
Sunshine	Hours per day	8.2	8	8	10	7.5	6.1	4.7	5.2	5.2	6.1	7.3	7.8	7
Brasilia, Brazil	910 m													
Temperature	Daily max. °C	28	28	28	28	27	27	27	29	30	29	28	27	28
	Daily min. °C	18	18	18	17	15	13	13	14	16	18	18	18	16
	Average monthly °C	23	23	23	22	21	20	20	21	23	24	23	22	22
Rainfall	Monthly total mm	252	204	227	93	17	3	6	3	30	127	255	343	1,560
Sunshine	Hours per day	5.8	5.7	6	7.4	8.7	9.3	9.6	9.8	7.9	6.5	4.8	4.4	7.2
Buenos Aires, Argentina	25 m													
Temperature	Daily max. °C	30	29	26	22	18	14	14	16	18	21	25	28	22
	Daily min. °C	17	17	16	12	9	5	6	6	8	10	14	16	11
	Average monthly °C	23	23	21	17	13	10	10	11	13	15	19	22	16
Rainfall	Monthly total mm	79	71	109	89	76	61	56	61	79	86	84	99	950
Sunshine	Hours per day	9.2	8.5	7.5	6.8	4.9	3.5	3.8	5.2	6	6.8	8.1	8.5	6.6
Cairo, Egypt	75 m													
Temperature	Daily max. °C	19	21	24	28	32	35	35	35	33	30	26	21	28
	Daily min. °C	9	9	12	14	18	20	22	22	20	18	14	10	16
	Average monthly °C	14	15	18	21	25	28	29	28	26	24	20	16	22
Rainfall	Monthly total mm	4	4	3	1	2	1	0	0	1	1	3	7	27
Sunshine	Hours per day	6.9	8.4	8.7	9.7	10.5	11.9	11.7	11.3	10.4	9.4	8.3	6.4	9.5
Cape Town, South Africa	44 m													
Temperature	Daily max. °C	26	26	25	23	20	18	17	18	19	21	24	25	22
	Daily min. °C	15	15	14	11	9	7	7	7	8	10	13	15	11
	Average monthly °C	21	20	20	17	14	13	12	12	14	16	18	20	16
Rainfall	Monthly total mm	12	19	17	42	67	98	68	76	36	45	12	13	505
Sunshine	Hours per day	11.4	10.2	9.4	7.7	6.1	5.7	6.4	6.6	7.6	8.6	10.2	10.9	8.4
Casablanca, Morocco	59 m													
Temperature	Daily max. °C	17	18	20	21	22	24	26	26	26	24	21	18	22
	Daily min. °C	8	9	11	12	15	18	19	20	18	15	12	10	14
	Average monthly °C	13	13	15	16	18	21	23	23	22	20	17	14	18
Rainfall	Monthly total mm	78	61	54	37	20	3	0	1	6	28	58	94	440
Sunshine	Hours per day	5.2	6.3	7.3	9	9.4	9.7	10.2	9.7	9.1	7.4	5.9	5.3	7.9

		Jan	Feb	Mar	Apr	May	June	July	Aug	Sept	Oct	Nov	Dec	Year
Chicago, USA	186 m													
Temperature	Daily max. °C	1	2	6	14	21	26	29	28	24	17	8	2	15
	Daily min. °C	−7	−6	−2	5	11	16	20	19	14	8	0	−5	−6
	Average monthly °C	−3	−2	2	9	16	21	24	23	19	13	4	−2	4
Rainfall	Monthly total mm	47	41	70	77	96	103	86	80	69	71	56	48	844
Sunshine	Hours per day	4	5	6.6	6.9	8.9	10.2	10	9.2	8.2	6.9	4.5	3.7	7
Christchurch, New Zealand	5 m													
Temperature	Daily max. °C	21	21	19	17	13	11	10	11	14	17	19	21	16
	Daily min. °C	12	12	10	7	4	2	1	3	5	7	8	11	7
	Average monthly °C	16	16	15	12	9	6	6	7	9	12	13	16	11
Rainfall	Monthly total mm	56	46	43	46	76	69	61	58	51	51	51	61	669
Sunshine	Hours per day	7	6.5	5.6	4.7	4.3	3.9	4.1	4.7	5.6	6.1	6.9	6.3	5.5
Colombo, Sri Lanka	10 m													
Temperature	Daily max. °C	30	31	31	31	30	30	29	29	30	29	29	30	30
	Daily min. °C	22	22	23	24	25	25	25	25	25	24	23	22	24
	Average monthly °C	26	26	27	28	28	27	27	27	27	27	26	26	27
Rainfall	Monthly total mm	101	66	118	230	394	220	140	102	174	348	333	142	2,368
Sunshine	Hours per day	7.9	9	8.1	7.2	6.4	5.4	6.1	6.3	6.2	6.5	6.4	7.8	6.9
Darwin, Australia	30 m													
Temperature	Daily max. °C	32	32	33	33	33	31	31	32	33	34	34	33	33
	Daily min. °C	25	25	25	24	23	21	19	21	23	25	26	26	24
	Average monthly °C	29	29	29	29	28	26	25	26	28	29	30	29	28
Rainfall	Monthly total mm	405	309	279	77	8	2	0	1	15	48	108	214	1,466
Sunshine	Hours per day	5.8	5.8	6.6	9.8	9.3	10	9.9	10.4	10.1	9.4	9.6	6.8	8.6
Harbin, China	175 m													
Temperature	Daily max. °C	−14	−9	0	12	21	26	29	27	20	12	−1	−11	9
	Daily min. °C	−26	−23	−12	−1	7	14	18	16	8	0	−12	−22	−3
	Average monthly °C	−20	−16	−6	6	14	20	23	22	14	6	−7	−17	3
Rainfall	Monthly total mm	4	6	17	23	44	92	167	119	52	36	12	5	577
Sunshine	Hours per day	6.4	7.8	8	7.8	8.3	8.6	8.6	8.2	7.2	6.9	6.1	5.7	7.5
Hong Kong, China	35 m													
Temperature	Daily max. °C	18	18	20	24	28	30	31	31	30	27	24	20	25
	Daily min. °C	13	13	16	19	23	26	26	26	25	23	19	15	20
	Average monthly °C	16	15	18	22	25	28	28	28	27	25	21	17	23
Rainfall	Monthly total mm	30	60	70	133	332	479	286	415	364	33	46	17	2,265
Sunshine	Hours per day	4.7	3.5	3.1	3.8	5	5.4	6.8	6.5	6.6	7	6.2	5.5	5.3
Honolulu, Hawaii	5 m													
Temperature	Daily max. °C	26	26	26	27	28	29	29	29	30	29	28	26	28
	Daily min. °C	19	19	19	20	21	22	23	23	23	22	21	20	21
	Average monthly °C	23	22	23	23	24	26	26	26	26	26	24	23	24
Rainfall	Monthly total mm	96	84	73	33	25	8	11	23	25	47	55	76	556
Sunshine	Hours per day	7.3	7.7	8.3	8.6	8.8	9.1	9.4	9.3	9.2	8.3	7.5	6.2	8.3
Jakarta, Indonesia	10 m													
Temperature	Daily max. °C	29	29	30	31	31	31	31	31	31	31	30	29	30
	Daily min. °C	23	23	23	24	24	23	23	23	23	23	23	23	23
	Average monthly °C	26	26	27	27	27	27	27	27	27	27	27	26	27
Rainfall	Monthly total mm	300	300	211	147	114	97	64	43	66	112	142	203	1,799
Sunshine	Hours per day	6.1	6.5	7.7	8.5	8.4	8.5	9.1	9.5	9.6	9	7.7	7.1	8.1
Kabul, Afghanistan	1,791 m													
Temperature	Daily max. °C	2	4	12	19	26	31	33	33	30	22	17	8	20
	Daily min. °C	−8	−6	1	6	11	13	16	15	11	6	1	−3	5
	Average monthly °C	−3	−1	6	13	18	22	25	24	20	14	9	3	12
Rainfall	Monthly total mm	28	61	72	117	33	1	7	1	0	1	37	14	372
Sunshine	Hours per day	5.9	6	5.7	6.8	10.1	11.5	11.4	11.2	9.8	9.4	7.8	6.1	8.5
Khartoum, Sudan	380 m													
Temperature	Daily max. °C	32	33	37	40	42	41	38	36	38	39	35	32	37
	Daily min. °C	16	17	20	23	26	27	26	25	25	25	21	17	22
	Average monthly °C	24	25	28	32	34	34	32	30	32	32	28	25	30
Rainfall	Monthly total mm	0	0	0	1	7	5	56	80	28	2	0	0	179
Sunshine	Hours per day	10.6	11.2	10.4	10.8	10.4	10.1	8.6	8.6	9.6	10.3	10.8	10.6	10.2
Kingston, Jamaica	35 m													
Temperature	Daily max. °C	30	30	30	31	31	32	32	32	32	31	31	31	31
	Daily min. °C	20	20	20	21	22	24	23	23	23	23	22	21	22
	Average monthly °C	25	25	25	26	26	28	28	28	27	27	26	26	26
Rainfall	Monthly total mm	23	15	23	31	102	89	38	91	99	180	74	36	801
Sunshine	Hours per day	8.3	8.8	8.7	8.7	8.3	7.8	8.5	8.5	7.6	7.3	8.3	7.7	8.2

		Jan	Feb	Mar	Apr	May	June	July	Aug	Sept	Oct	Nov	Dec	Year
Kolkata (Calcutta), India 5m														
Temperature	Daily max. °C	27	29	34	36	35	34	32	32	32	32	29	26	31
	Daily min. °C	13	15	21	24	25	26	26	26	26	23	18	13	21
	Average monthly °C	20	22	27	30	30	30	29	29	29	28	23	20	26
Rainfall	Monthly total mm	10	30	34	44	140	297	325	332	253	114	20	5	1,604
Sunshine	Hours per day	8.6	8.7	8.9	9	8.7	5.4	4.1	4.1	5.1	6.5	8.3	8.4	7.1
Lagos, Nigeria 40m														
Temperature	Daily max. °C	32	33	33	32	31	29	28	28	29	30	31	32	31
	Daily min. °C	22	23	23	23	23	22	22	21	22	22	23	22	22
	Average monthly °C	27	28	28	28	27	26	25	24	25	26	27	27	26
Rainfall	Monthly total mm	28	41	99	99	203	300	180	56	180	190	63	25	1,464
Sunshine	Hours per day	5.9	6.8	6.3	6.1	5.6	3.8	2.8	3.3	3	5.1	6.6	6.5	5.2
Lima, Peru 120m														
Temperature	Daily max. °C	28	29	29	27	24	20	20	19	20	22	24	26	24
	Daily min. °C	19	20	19	17	16	15	14	14	14	15	16	17	16
	Average monthly °C	24	24	24	22	20	17	17	16	17	18	20	21	20
Rainfall	Monthly total mm	1	1	1	1	5	5	8	8	8	3	3	1	45
Sunshine	Hours per day	6.3	6.8	6.9	6.7	4	1.4	1.1	1	1.1	2.5	4.1	5	3.9
Lisbon, Portugal 77m														
Temperature	Daily max. °C	14	15	17	20	21	25	27	28	26	22	17	15	21
	Daily min. °C	8	8	10	12	13	15	17	17	17	14	11	9	13
	Average monthly °C	11	12	14	16	17	20	22	23	21	18	14	12	17
Rainfall	Monthly total mm	111	76	109	54	44	16	3	4	33	62	93	103	708
Sunshine	Hours per day	4.7	5.9	6	8.3	9.1	10.6	11.4	10.7	8.4	6.7	5.2	4.6	7.7
London (Kew), UK 5m														
Temperature	Daily max. °C	6	7	10	13	17	20	22	21	19	14	10	7	14
	Daily min. °C	2	2	3	6	8	12	14	13	11	8	5	4	7
	Average monthly °C	4	5	7	9	12	16	18	17	15	11	8	5	11
Rainfall	Monthly total mm	54	40	37	37	46	45	57	59	49	57	64	48	593
Sunshine	Hours per day	1.7	2.3	3.5	5.7	6.7	7	6.6	6	5	3.3	1.9	1.4	4.3
Los Angeles, USA 30m														
Temperature	Daily max. °C	18	18	18	19	20	22	24	24	24	23	22	19	21
	Daily min. °C	7	8	9	11	13	15	17	17	16	14	11	9	12
	Average monthly °C	12	13	14	15	17	18	21	21	20	18	16	14	17
Rainfall	Monthly total mm	69	74	46	28	3	3	0	0	5	10	28	61	327
Sunshine	Hours per day	6.9	8.2	8.9	8.8	9.5	10.3	11.7	11	10.1	8.6	8.2	7.6	9.2
Lusaka, Zambia 1,154m														
Temperature	Daily max. °C	26	26	26	27	25	23	23	26	29	31	29	27	27
	Daily min. °C	17	17	16	15	12	10	9	11	15	18	18	17	15
	Average monthly °C	22	22	21	21	18	17	16	19	22	25	23	22	21
Rainfall	Monthly total mm	224	173	90	19	3	1	0	1	1	17	85	196	810
Sunshine	Hours per day	5.1	5.4	6.9	8.9	9	9	9.1	9.6	9.5	9	7	5.5	7.8
Manaus, Brazil 45m														
Temperature	Daily max. °C	31	31	31	31	31	31	32	33	34	34	33	32	32
	Daily min. °C	24	24	24	24	24	24	24	24	24	25	25	24	24
	Average monthly °C	28	28	28	27	28	28	28	29	29	29	29	28	28
Rainfall	Monthly total mm	278	278	300	287	193	99	61	41	62	112	165	220	2,096
Sunshine	Hours per day	3.9	4	3.6	3.9	5.4	6.9	7.9	8.2	7.5	6.6	5.9	4.9	5.7
Mexico City, Mexico 2,309m														
Temperature	Daily max. °C	21	23	26	27	26	25	23	24	23	22	21	21	24
	Daily min. °C	5	6	7	9	10	11	11	11	11	9	6	5	8
	Average monthly °C	13	15	16	18	18	18	17	17	17	16	14	13	16
Rainfall	Monthly total mm	8	4	9	23	57	111	160	149	119	46	16	7	709
Sunshine	Hours per day	7.3	8.1	8.5	8.1	7.8	7	6.2	6.4	5.6	6.3	7	7.3	7.1
Miami, USA 2m														
Temperature	Daily max. °C	24	25	27	28	30	31	32	32	31	29	27	25	28
	Daily min. °C	14	15	16	19	21	23	24	24	24	22	18	15	20
	Average monthly °C	19	20	21	23	25	27	28	28	27	25	22	20	24
Rainfall	Monthly total mm	51	48	58	99	163	188	170	178	241	208	71	43	1,518
Sunshine	Hours per day	7.7	8.3	8.7	9.4	8.9	8.5	8.7	8.4	7.1	6.5	7.5	7.1	8.1
Montreal, Canada 57m														
Temperature	Daily max. °C	−6	−4	2	11	18	23	26	25	20	14	5	−3	11
	Daily min. °C	−13	−11	−5	2	9	14	17	16	11	6	0	−9	3
	Average monthly °C	−9	−8	−2	6	13	19	22	20	16	10	3	−6	7
Rainfall	Monthly total mm	87	76	86	83	81	91	98	87	96	84	89	89	1,047
Sunshine	Hours per day	2.8	3.4	4.5	5.2	6.7	7.7	8.2	7.7	5.6	4.3	2.4	2.2	5.1
Moscow, Russia 156m														
Temperature	Daily max. °C	−6	−4	1	9	18	22	24	22	17	10	1	−5	9
	Daily min. °C	−14	−16	−11	−1	5	9	12	9	4	−2	−6	−12	−2
	Average monthly °C	−10	−10	−5	4	12	15	18	16	10	4	−2	−8	4
Rainfall	Monthly total mm	31	28	33	35	52	67	74	74	58	51	36	36	575
Sunshine	Hours per day	1	1.9	3.7	5.2	7.8	8.3	8.4	7.1	4.4	2.4	1	0.6	4.4
New Delhi, India 220m														
Temperature	Daily max. °C	21	24	29	36	41	39	35	34	34	34	28	23	32
	Daily min. °C	6	10	14	20	26	28	27	26	24	17	11	7	18
	Average monthly °C	14	17	22	28	33	34	31	30	29	26	20	15	25
Rainfall	Monthly total mm	25	21	13	8	13	77	178	184	123	10	2	11	665
Sunshine	Hours per day	7.7	8.2	8.2	8.7	9.2	7.9	6	6.3	6.9	9.4	8.7	8.3	8

		Jan	Feb	Mar	Apr	May	June	July	Aug	Sept	Oct	Nov	Dec	Year
Perth, Australia 60m														
Temperature	Daily max. °C	29	30	27	25	21	18	17	18	19	21	25	27	23
	Daily min. °C	17	18	16	14	12	10	9	9	10	11	14	16	13
	Average monthly °C	23	24	22	19	16	14	13	13	15	16	19	22	18
Rainfall	Monthly total mm	8	13	22	44	128	189	177	145	84	58	19	13	900
Sunshine	Hours per day	10.4	9.8	8.8	7.5	5.7	4.8	5.4	6	7.2	8.1	9.6	10.4	7.8
Reykjavik, Iceland 18m														
Temperature	Daily max. °C	2	3	5	6	10	13	15	14	12	8	5	4	8
	Daily min. °C	−3	−3	−1	1	4	7	9	8	6	3	0	−2	3
	Average monthly °C	0	0	2	4	7	10	12	11	9	5	3	1	5
Rainfall	Monthly total mm	89	64	62	56	42	42	50	56	67	94	78	79	779
Sunshine	Hours per day	0.8	2	3.6	4.5	5.9	6.1	5.8	5.4	3.5	2.3	1.1	0.3	3.7
Santiago, Chile 520m														
Temperature	Daily max. °C	30	29	27	24	19	15	15	17	19	22	26	29	23
	Daily min. °C	12	11	10	7	5	3	3	4	6	7	9	11	7
	Average monthly °C	21	20	18	15	12	9	9	10	12	15	17	20	15
Rainfall	Monthly total mm	3	3	5	13	64	84	76	56	31	15	8	5	363
Sunshine	Hours per day	10.8	8.9	8.5	5.5	3.6	3.3	3.3	3.6	4.8	6.1	8.7	10.1	6.4
Shanghai, China 5m														
Temperature	Daily max. °C	8	8	13	19	24	28	32	32	27	23	17	10	20
	Daily min. °C	−1	0	4	9	14	19	23	23	19	13	7	2	11
	Average monthly °C	3	4	8	14	19	23	27	27	23	18	12	6	15
Rainfall	Monthly total mm	48	59	84	94	94	180	147	142	130	71	51	36	1,136
Sunshine	Hours per day	4	3.7	4.4	4.8	5.4	4.7	6.9	7.5	5.3	5.6	4.7	4.5	5.1
Sydney, Australia 40m														
Temperature	Daily max. °C	26	26	25	22	19	17	17	18	20	22	24	25	22
	Daily min. °C	18	19	17	14	11	9	8	9	11	13	16	17	14
	Average monthly °C	22	22	21	18	15	13	12	13	16	18	20	21	18
Rainfall	Monthly total mm	89	101	127	135	127	117	117	76	74	71	74	74	1,182
Sunshine	Hours per day	7.5	7	6.4	6.1	5.7	5.3	6.1	7	7.3	7.5	7.5	7.5	6.8
Tehran, Iran 1,191m														
Temperature	Daily max. °C	9	11	16	21	29	30	37	36	29	24	16	11	22
	Daily min. °C	−1	1	4	10	16	20	23	23	18	12	6	1	11
	Average monthly °C	4	6	10	15	22	25	30	29	23	18	11	6	17
Rainfall	Monthly total mm	37	23	36	31	14	2	1	1	1	5	29	27	207
Sunshine	Hours per day	5.9	6.7	7.5	7.4	8.6	11.6	11.2	11	10.1	7.6	6.9	6.3	8.4
Timbuktu, Mali 269m														
Temperature	Daily max. °C	31	35	38	41	43	42	38	35	38	40	37	31	37
	Daily min. °C	13	16	18	22	26	27	25	24	24	23	18	14	21
	Average monthly °C	22	25	28	31	34	34	32	30	31	31	28	23	29
Rainfall	Monthly total mm	0	0	0	1	4	20	54	93	31	3	0	0	206
Sunshine	Hours per day	9.1	9.6	9.6	9.7	9.8	9.4	9.6	9	9.3	9.5	9.5	8.9	9.4
Tokyo, Japan 5m														
Temperature	Daily max. °C	9	9	12	18	22	25	29	30	27	20	16	11	19
	Daily min. °C	−1	−1	3	4	13	17	22	23	19	13	7	1	10
	Average monthly °C	4	4	8	11	18	21	25	26	23	17	11	6	14
Rainfall	Monthly total mm	48	73	101	135	131	182	146	147	217	220	101	61	1,562
Sunshine	Hours per day	6	5.9	5.7	6	6.2	5	5.8	6.6	4.5	4.4	4.8	5.4	5.5
Tromsø, Norway 100m														
Temperature	Daily max. °C	−2	−2	0	3	7	12	16	14	10	5	2	0	5
	Daily min. °C	−6	−6	−5	−2	1	6	9	8	5	1	−2	−4	0
	Average monthly °C	−4	−4	−3	0	4	9	13	11	7	3	0	−2	3
Rainfall	Monthly total mm	96	79	91	65	61	59	56	80	109	115	88	95	994
Sunshine	Hours per day	0.1	1.6	2.9	6.1	5.7	6.9	7.9	4.8	3.5	1.7	0.3	0	3.5
Ulan Bator, Mongolia 1,305m														
Temperature	Daily max. °C	−19	−13	−4	7	13	21	22	21	14	6	−6	−16	4
	Daily min. °C	−32	−29	−22	−8	−2	7	11	8	2	−8	−20	−28	−11
	Average monthly °C	−26	−21	−13	−1	6	14	16	14	8	−1	−13	−22	−4
Rainfall	Monthly total mm	1	1	2	5	10	28	76	51	23	5	5	2	209
Sunshine	Hours per day	6.4	7.8	8	7.8	8.3	8.6	8.6	8.2	7.2	6.9	6.1	5.7	7.5
Vancouver, Canada 5m														
Temperature	Daily max. °C	6	7	10	14	17	20	23	22	19	14	9	7	14
	Daily min. °C	0	1	3	5	8	11	13	12	10	7	3	2	6
	Average monthly °C	3	4	6	9	13	16	18	17	14	10	6	4	10
Rainfall	Monthly total mm	214	161	151	90	69	65	39	44	83	172	198	243	1,529
Sunshine	Hours per day	1.6	3	3.8	5.9	7.5	7.4	9.5	8.2	6	3.7	2	1.4	5
Verkhoyansk, Russia 137m														
Temperature	Daily max. °C	−47	−40	−20	−1	11	21	24	21	12	−8	−33	−42	−8
	Daily min. °C	−51	−48	−40	−25	−7	4	6	1	−6	−20	−39	−50	−23
	Average monthly °C	−49	−44	−30	−13	2	12	15	11	3	−14	−36	−46	−16
Rainfall	Monthly total mm	7	5	5	4	5	25	33	30	13	11	10	7	155
Sunshine	Hours per day	0	2.6	6.9	9.6	9.7	10	9.7	7.5	4.1	2.4	0.6	0	5.4
Washington, USA 22m														
Temperature	Daily max. °C	7	8	12	19	25	29	31	30	26	20	14	8	19
	Daily min. °C	−1	−1	2	8	13	18	21	20	16	10	4	−1	9
	Average monthly °C	3	3	7	13	19	24	26	25	21	15	9	4	14
Rainfall	Monthly total mm	84	68	96	85	103	88	108	120	100	78	75	75	1,080
Sunshine	Hours per day	4.4	5.7	6.7	7.4	8.2	8.8	8.6	8.2	7.5	6.5	5.3	4.5	6.8

Tropical Rain Forest
Tall broadleaved evergreen forest, trees 30–50m high with climbers and epiphytes forming continuous canopies. Associated with wet climate 2–3000mm precipitation per year and high temperatures 24–28°C. High diversity of species, typically 100 per ha including lianas, bamboo, palms, rubber, mahogany. Mangrove swamps form in coastal areas.

Subtropical and Temperate Rain Forest
Precipitation which is less than in the Tropical Rain Forest falls in the long wet season interspersed with a season of reduced rainfall and lower temperatures. As a result there are fewer species, a thinner canopy, fewer lianas and denser ground level foliage. Vegetation consists of evergreen oak, laurel, bamboo, magnolia and tree ferns.

Monsoon Woodland and Open Jungle
Mostly deciduous trees because of the long dry season and lower temperatu Trees can reach 30m but are sparser than in the rain forests; there is l competition for light and thick jungle vegetation grows at lower levels. H species diversity including lianas, bamboo, teak, sandalwood, sal and bany

Diagram shows the highly stratified nature of the tropical rain forest. Crowns of trees form numerous layers at different heights and the dense shade limits undergrowth.

Temperate Deciduous and Coniferous Forest
A transition zone between broadleaves and conifers. Broadleaves are better suited to the warmer, damper and flatter locations.

Northern Coniferous Forest (Taiga)
Forming a large continuous belt across Northern America and Eurasia with a uniformity in tree species. Characteristically trees are tall, conical with short branches and wax-covered needle-shaped leaves to retain moisture. Cold climate with prolonged harsh winters and cool summers where average temperatures for more than six months of the year are under 0°C. Undergrowth is sparse with mosses and lichens. Tree species include pine, fir, spruce, larch, tamarisk.

Mountainous Forest, mainly Coniferous
Mild winters, high humidity and high levels of rainfall throughout the year provide habitat for dense needle-leaf evergreen forests and the largest trees in the world, up to 100m, including the Douglas fir, redwood and giant sequoia.

High Plateau Steppe and Tundra
Similar to arctic tundra with frozen ground for the majority of the year. Very sparse ground coverage of low, shallow-rooted herbs, small shrubs, mosses, lichens and heather interspersed with bare soil.

Arctic Tundra
Average temperatures are 0°C, precipitation is mainly snowfall and the ground remains frozen for 10 months of the year. Vegetation flourishes when the shallow surface layer melts in the long summer days. Underlying permafrost remains frozen and surface water cannot drain away, making conditions marshy. Consisting of sedges, snow lichen, arctic meadow grass, cotton grasses and dwarf willow.

Polar and Mountainous Ice Desert
Areas of bare rock and ice with patches of rock-strewn lithosols, low in organic matter and low water content. In sheltered patches only a few mosses, lichens and low shrubs can grow, including woolly moss and purple saxifrage.

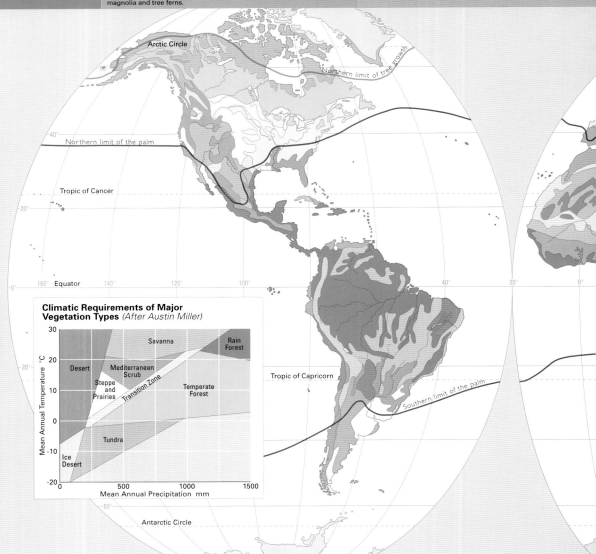

Climatic Requirements of Major Vegetation Types *(After Austin Miller)*

(x-axis: Mean Annual Precipitation mm, 0 to 1500; y-axis: Mean Annual Temperature °C, -20 to 30)

Regions labelled: Desert, Savanna, Rain Forest, Mediterranean Scrub, Steppe and Prairies, Transition Zone, Temperate Forest, Tundra, Ice Desert

SOIL REGIONS
1:220 000 000

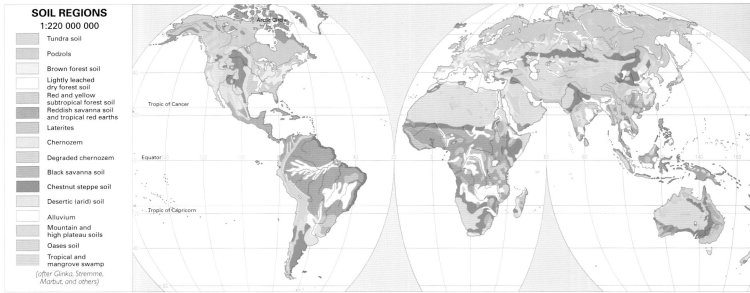

- Tundra soil
- Podzols
- Brown forest soil
- Lightly leached dry forest soil
- Red and yellow subtropical forest soil
- Reddish savanna soil and tropical red earths
- Laterites
- Chernozem
- Degraded chernozem
- Black savanna soil
- Chestnut steppe soil
- Desertic (arid) soil
- Alluvium
- Mountain and high plateau soils
- Oases soil
- Tropical and mangrove swamp

(after Glinka, Stremme, Marbut, and others)

Projection: Interrupted Mollweide's Homolographic

btropical and Temperate Woodland, Scrub and Bush
t clearings with woody shrubs and tall grasses. Trees are fire-resistant and
er deciduous or xerophytic because of long dry periods. Species include
alyptus, acacia, mimosa and euphorbia.

Tropical Savanna with Low Trees and Bush
Tall, coarse grass with enough precipitation to support a scattering of short
deciduous trees and thorn scrub. Vegetation consisting of elephant grass,
acacia, palms and baobob is limited by aridity, grazing animals and periodic
fires; trees have developed thick, woody bark, small leaves or thorns.

Tropical Savanna and Grassland
Areas with a hot climate and long dry season. Extensive areas of tall grasses
often reaching 3.5m with scattered fire and drought resistant bushes, low trees
and thickets of elephant grass. Shrubs include acacia, baobab and palms.

NATURAL VEGETATION
(after Austin Miller)

1:116 000 000

Dry Semi-desert with Shrub and Grass
Xerophytic shrubs with thin grass cover and
few trees, limited by a long dry season and
short, hot, rainy period. Sagebrush, bunch
grass and acacia shrubs are common.

Desert Shrub
Scattered xerophytic plants able to withstand
daytime extremes in temperature and long
periods of drought. There is a large diversity
of desert flora such as cacti, yucca, tamarisk,
hard grass and artemisia.

Desert
Precipitation less than 250mm per year;
vegetation is very sparse, mainly bare rock,
sand dunes and salt flats. Vegetation
comprises a few xerophytic shrubs and
ephemeral flowers.

Dry Steppe and Shrub
Semi-arid with cold, dry winters and hot
summers. Bare soil with sparsely
distributed short grasses and scattered
shrubs and short trees. Species include acacia,
artemisia, saksaul and tamarisk.

Temperate Grasslands, Prairie and Steppe
Continuous, tall, dense and deep-rooted
swards of ancient grasslands, considered to
be natural climax vegetation as determined
by soil and climate. Average precipitation
250–750mm with a long dry season, limiting
growth of trees and shrubs. Includes Stipa
grass, buffalo grass, blue stems and loco
weed.

Mediterranean Hardwood Forest and Scrub
Areas with hot and arid summers. Sparse
evergreen trees are short and twisted
with thick bark, interspersed with areas of
scrub land. Trees have waxy leaves or thorns
and deep root systems to resist drought.
Many of the hardwood forests have been
cleared by man, resulting in extensive scrub
formation – maquis and chaparral. Species
found are evergreen oak, stone pine, cork,
olive and myrtle.

Temperate Deciduous Forest and Meadow
Areas of relatively high, well-distributed
rainfall and temperatures favourable for forest
growth. The tall broadleaved trees form a
canopy in the summer, but shed their leaves
in the winter. The undergrowth is sparse and
poorly developed, but in the spring, herbs
and flowers develop quickly. Diverse species
with up to 20 per ha, including oak, beech,
birch, maple, ash, elm, chestnut and
hornbeam. Many of these forests have been
cleared for urbanization and farming.

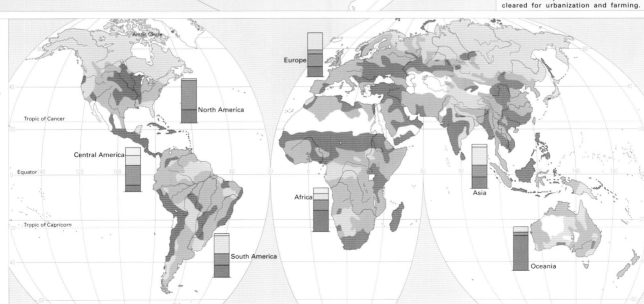

OIL DEGRADATION
1:220 000 000

reas of Concern
- Areas of serious concern
- Areas of some concern
- Stable terrain
- Non-vegetated land

auses of soil egradation by region)
- Grazing practices
- Other agricultural practices
- Industrialization
- Deforestation
- Fuelwood collection

(after Wageningen 1990)

COPYRIGHT PHILIP'S

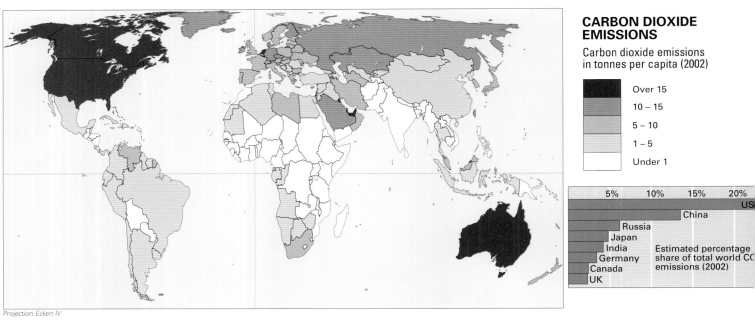

Projection: *Eckert IV*

CARBON DIOXIDE EMISSIONS

Carbon dioxide emissions in tonnes per capita (2002)

■	Over 15
■	10 – 15
■	5 – 10
■	1 – 5
□	Under 1

5%   10%   15%   20%

US
China
Russia
Japan
India
Germany
Canada
UK

Estimated percentage share of total world CO emissions (2002)

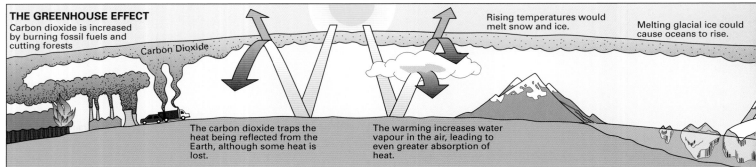

THE GREENHOUSE EFFECT

Carbon dioxide is increased by burning fossil fuels and cutting forests

Carbon Dioxide

The carbon dioxide traps the heat being reflected from the Earth, although some heat is lost.

The warming increases water vapour in the air, leading to even greater absorption of heat.

Rising temperatures would melt snow and ice.

Melting glacial ice could cause oceans to rise.

THINNING OZONE LAYER

Total atmospheric ozone concentration in the southern and northern hemispheres (Dobson Units, 2000)

In 1985, scientists working in Antarctica discovered a thinning of the ozone layer, commonly known as an 'ozone hole'. This caused immediate alarm because the ozone layer absorbs most of the Sun's dangerous ultraviolet radiation, which is believed to cause an increase in skin cancer, cataracts and damage to the immune system. Since 1985, ozone depletion has increased and, by 2003, the ozone hole over the South Pole was estimated to be larger than North America. The false-colour images, left, show the total atmospheric ozone concentration in the southern hemisphere (in September 2000) and the northern hemisphere (in March 2000) with the ozone hole clearly identifiable at the centre. The data is from the Tiros Ozone Vertical Sounder, an instrument on the American TIROS weather satellite. The colours represent the ozone concentration in Dobson Units (DU). Scientists agree that ozone depletion is caused by CFCs, a group of manufactured chemicals used in air-conditioning systems and refrigerators. In a 1987 treaty most industrial nations agreed to phase out CFCs and a complete ban on most CFCs was agreed after the end of 1995. However, scientists believe that the chemicals will remain in the atmosphere for 50 to 100 years. As a result, ozone depletion will continue for many years.

Northern Hemisphere   **Southern Hemisphere**

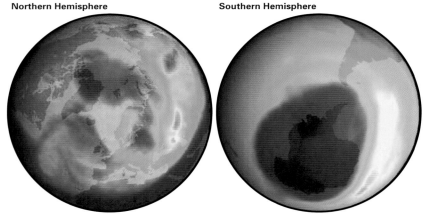

PROJECTED CHANGE IN GLOBAL WARMING

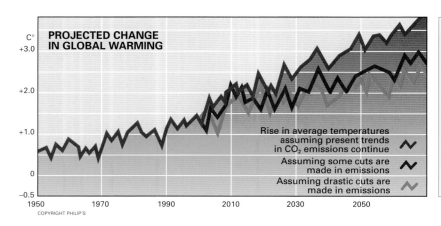

Rise in average temperatures assuming present trends in CO₂ emissions continue

Assuming some cuts are made in emissions

Assuming drastic cuts are made in emissions

C°
+3.0
+2.0
+1.0
0
−0.5

1950   1970   1990   2010   2030   2050

COPYRIGHT PHILIP'S

POSSIBLE EFFECT OF SEA LEVEL RISE IN FLORIDA

Sea levels have risen worldwide by about 2 cm since 1900. If CO₂ emissions continue at the same rate, the sea level is expected to rise by 7.4 m by 2200. The map shows the dramatic effects that such a rise could have on the southern part of Florida in the USA.

☐ Submerged land area if sea level rises 7.4 m

Daytona Beach
ORLANDO
C. Canaveral
TAMPA
Palm Bay
St. Petersburg
Sarasota
West Palm Beach
Charlotte Harbor
Fort Lauderdale
MIAMI
Florida Bay
Florida Keys
Straits

PREDICTED CHANGE IN TEMPERATURE

The difference between actual annual average surface air temperature, 1960–90, and predicted annual average surface air temperature, 2070–2100. This map shows the predicted increase, assuming a 'medium growth' of the global economy and assuming that no measures to combat the emission of greenhouse gases are taken.

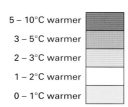

- 5 – 10°C warmer
- 3 – 5°C warmer
- 2 – 3°C warmer
- 1 – 2°C warmer
- 0 – 1°C warmer

Source: The Hadley Centre of Climate Prediction and Research, The Met. Office.

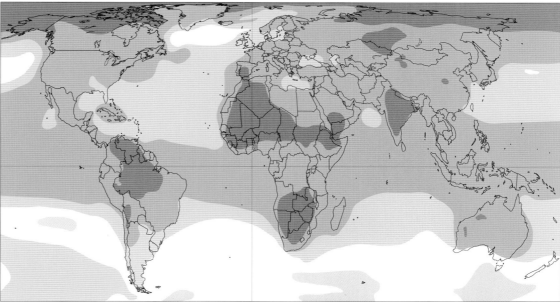

PREDICTED CHANGE IN PRECIPITATION

The difference between actual annual average precipitation, 1960–90, and predicted annual average precipitation, 2070–2100. It should be noted that these predicted annual mean changes mask quite significant seasonal detail.

- Over 2 mm more rain per day
- 1 – 2 mm more rain per day
- 0.5 – 1 mm more rain per day
- 0.2 – 0.5 mm more rain per day
- no change
- 0.2 – 0.5 mm less rain per day
- 0.5 – 1 mm less rain per day
- 1 – 2 mm less rain per day
- Over 2 mm less rain per day

DESERTIFICATION AND DEFORESTATION

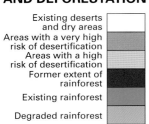

- Existing deserts and dry areas
- Areas with a very high risk of desertification
- Areas with a high risk of desertification
- Former extent of rainforest
- Existing rainforest
- Degraded rainforest

■ Major famines since 1900 (with dates)

Deforestation 1990–2000

	Annual deforestation (thous. hectares)	Annual deforestation rate (%)
Brazil	2,309	0.4
Indonesia	1,312	1.2
Mexico	631	1.1
Congo (Dem. Rep.)	532	0.4
Burma (Myanmar)	517	1.4
Nigeria	398	2.6
Peru	269	1.4

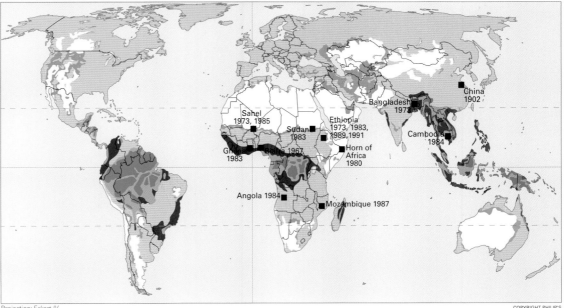

Projection: *Eckert IV*

COPYRIGHT PHILIP'S

AGRICULTURAL PRODUCTION

Staple Crops

Wheat

China 15.5% | India 11.7% | USA 11.4% | Russia 6.1% | France 5.5%

World total (2003): 556,349,000 tonnes

Rice

China 28.2% | India 22.4% | Indonesia 8.8% | Bangladesh 6.5% | Vietnam 5.9%

World total (2003): 589,126,000 tonnes

Cassava

Nigeria 17.7% | Brazil 11.7% | Indonesia 9.8% | Thailand 9.7% | D. R. Congo 7.9%

World total (2003): 189,100,000 tonnes

Barley

Russia 12.7% | Canada 8.7% | Germany 7.6% | France 6.9% | Spain 6.1% | Australia 6.0%

World total (2003): 141,503,000 tonnes

Maize

USA 40.3% | China 17.9% | Brazil 7.5% | Mexico 3.1%

World total (2003): 638,043,000 tonnes

Potatoes

China 21.5% | Russia 11.8% | India 7.5% | USA 6.7% | Ukraine 6.0%

World total (2003): 310,810,000 tonnes

Soybeans

USA 34.8% | Brazil 27.2% | Argentina 18.4% | China 8.7%

World total (2003): 189,234,000 tonnes

Millet

India 35.9% | Nigeria 20.5% | Niger 8.4% | China 6.5% | Burkina F. 4.1%

World total (2003): 29,806,000 tonnes

Animal Products

Milk

USA 14.9% | India 7.4% | Russia 6.3% | Germany 5.4% | France 4.8%

World total (2003): 526,915,000 tonnes

Eggs

China 43.2% | USA 8.5% | India 4.6% | Russia 3.4%

World total (2003): 60,469,000 tonnes

Chicken

USA 22.8% | China 14.6% | Brazil 11.9% | Mexico 3.3%

World total (2003): 65,015,000 tonnes

Beef and Veal

USA 20.2% | Brazil 12.8% | China 10.6% | Argentina 4.8% | Australia 3.5%

World total (2003): 58,922,000 tonnes

Pigmeat

China 46.7% | USA 9.2% | Germany 4.3%

World total (2003): 98,507,000 tonnes

Sugars

Sugar Cane

Brazil 28.9% | India 21.7% | China 6.9% | Thailand 4.8% | Pakistan 3.9%

World total (2003): 1,333,253,000 tonnes

Sugar Beet

France 12.5% | USA 11.9% | Germany 11.3% | Russia 8.3% | Ukraine 5.2% | Poland 4.7%

World total (2003): 233,487,000 tonnes

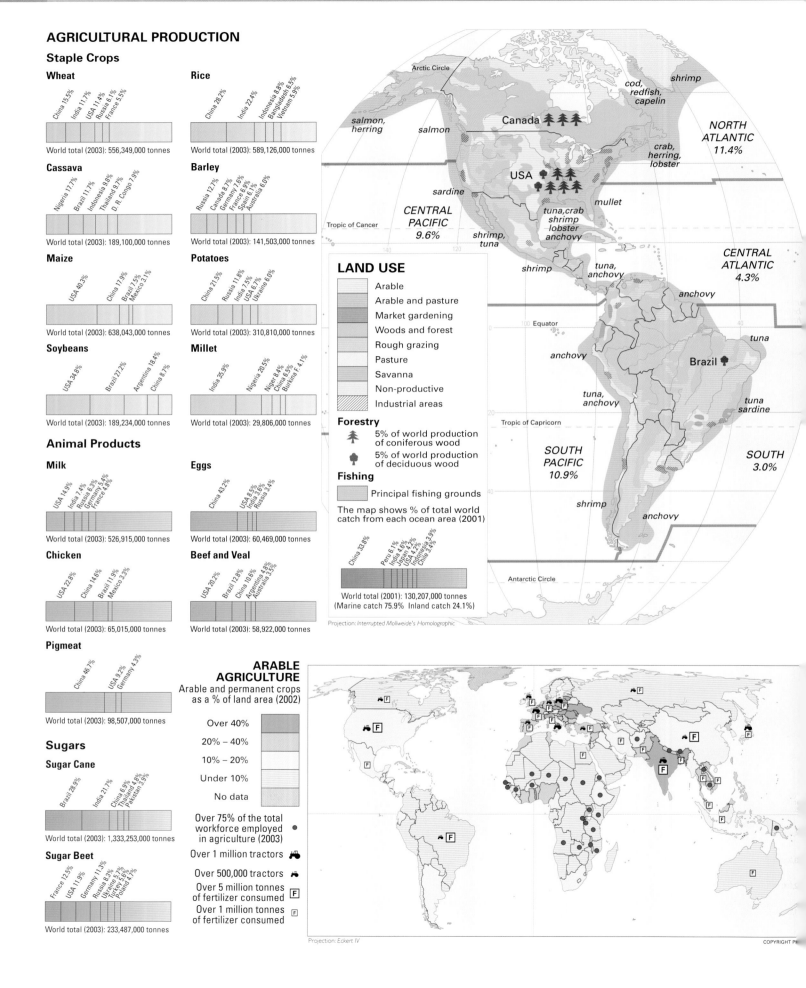

LAND USE

- Arable
- Arable and pasture
- Market gardening
- Woods and forest
- Rough grazing
- Pasture
- Savanna
- Non-productive
- Industrial areas

Forestry

🌲 5% of world production of coniferous wood

🌳 5% of world production of deciduous wood

Fishing

Principal fishing grounds

The map shows % of total world catch from each ocean area (2001)

China 33.9% | Peru 6.1% | India 4.6% | Japan 4.2% | USA 4.2% | Indonesia 3.9% | Chile 3%

World total (2001): 130,207,000 tonnes
(Marine catch 75.9% Inland catch 24.1%)

Projection: Interrupted Mollweide's Homolographic

Arctic Circle
cod, redfish, capelin — shrimp
salmon, herring — salmon
Canada
USA
sardine
mullet
Tropic of Cancer
CENTRAL PACIFIC 9.6%
tuna, crab shrimp lobster anchovy
shrimp, tuna
crab, herring, lobster
NORTH ATLANTIC 11.4%
CENTRAL ATLANTIC 4.3%
shrimp
tuna, anchovy
Equator
anchovy
anchovy
Brazil
tuna, anchovy
tuna, anchovy
tuna
tuna sardine
Tropic of Capricorn
SOUTH PACIFIC 10.9%
SOUTH 3.0%
shrimp
anchovy
Antarctic Circle

ARABLE AGRICULTURE

Arable and permanent crops as a % of land area (2002)

- Over 40%
- 20% – 40%
- 10% – 20%
- Under 10%
- No data

● Over 75% of the total workforce employed in agriculture (2003)

🚜 Over 1 million tractors

🚜 Over 500,000 tractors

F Over 5 million tonnes of fertilizer consumed

F Over 1 million tonnes of fertilizer consumed

Projection: Eckert IV

COPYRIGHT P

LAND USE, FORESTRY AND FISHING

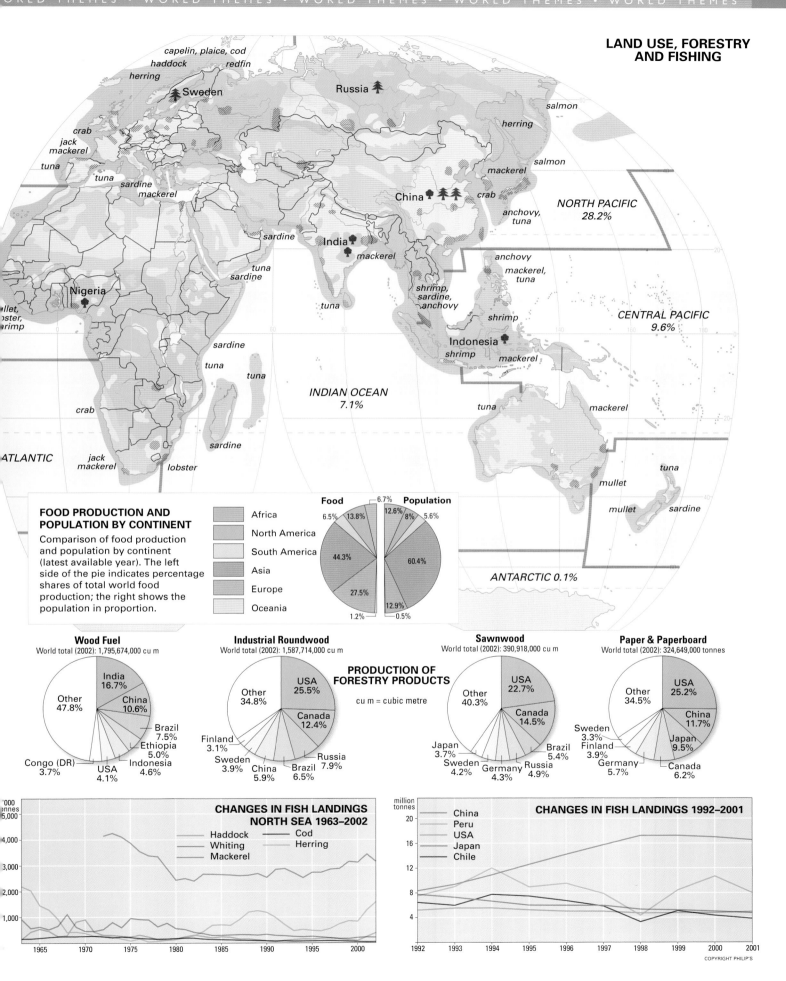

capelin, plaice, cod
haddock   redfin
herring

Sweden

Russia

salmon

herring

crab
jack
mackerel

salmon

tuna

mackerel

tuna

sardine
mackerel

China

crab

NORTH PACIFIC
28.2%

anchovy,
tuna

India

mackerel

anchovy
mackerel,
tuna

Nigeria

sardine

tuna
sardine

shrimp,
sardine,
anchovy

shrimp

CENTRAL PACIFIC
9.6%

llet,
oster,
rimp

tuna

Indonesia
shrimp

mackerel

sardine

tuna

tuna

INDIAN OCEAN
7.1%

tuna

mackerel

crab

jack
mackerel   lobster

sardine

ATLANTIC

tuna

mullet

mullet   sardine

FOOD PRODUCTION AND POPULATION BY CONTINENT

Comparison of food production and population by continent (latest available year). The left side of the pie indicates percentage shares of total world food production; the right shows the population in proportion.

Africa
North America
South America
Asia
Europe
Oceania

Food   **Population**

6.7%
6.5% 13.8%   12.6% 8% 5.6%

44.3%   60.4%

27.5%

12.9%
1.2%   0.5%

ANTARCTIC 0.1%

PRODUCTION OF FORESTRY PRODUCTS

cu m = cubic metre

Wood Fuel
World total (2002): 1,795,674,000 cu m

India 16.7%
Other 47.8%
China 10.6%
Brazil 7.5%
Ethiopia 5.0%
Congo (DR) 3.7%
USA 4.1%
Indonesia 4.6%

Industrial Roundwood
World total (2002): 1,587,714,000 cu m

USA 25.5%
Other 34.8%
Canada 12.4%
Finland 3.1%
Sweden 3.9%
China 5.9%
Brazil 6.5%
Russia 7.9%

Sawnwood
World total (2002): 390,918,000 cu m

USA 22.7%
Other 40.3%
Canada 14.5%
Japan 3.7%
Sweden 4.2%
Germany 4.3%
Russia 4.9%
Brazil 5.4%

Paper & Paperboard
World total (2002): 324,649,000 tonnes

USA 25.2%
Other 34.5%
China 11.7%
Sweden 3.3%
Finland 3.9%
Germany 5.7%
Japan 9.5%
Canada 6.2%

CHANGES IN FISH LANDINGS NORTH SEA 1963–2002

'000 tonnes

5,000
4,000
3,000
2,000
1,000

Haddock   Cod
Whiting   Herring
Mackerel

1965 1970 1975 1980 1985 1990 1995 2000

CHANGES IN FISH LANDINGS 1992–2001

million tonnes

20
16
12
8
4

China
Peru
USA
Japan
Chile

1992 1993 1994 1995 1996 1997 1998 1999 2000 2001

COPYRIGHT PHILIP'S

ENERGY PRODUCTION BY REGION
Each square represents 1% of world energy production (2002)

North America
Europe
Eastern Europe & Eurasia
Middle East
Japan
Africa
Asia
South America
Australasia

ENERGY CONSUMPTION BY REGION
Each square represents 1% of world energy consumption (2002)

North America
Europe
Eastern Europe & Eurasia
Middle East
Asia
Africa
South America
Japa
Australa

ENERGY BALANCE
Difference between energy production and consumption in millions of tonnes of oil equivalent (MtOe) 2004

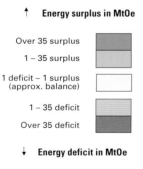

↑ Energy surplus in MtOe

Over 35 surplus
1 – 35 surplus
1 deficit – 1 surplus (approx. balance)
1 – 35 deficit
Over 35 deficit

↓ Energy deficit in MtOe

Fossil fuel production
	Principal	Secondary
Oilfields	●	●
Gasfields	▽	▽
Coalfields	△	△

Projection: Ec

OIL RESERVES
World oil reserves by region and country, thousand million tonnes (2003)

Al:	Algeria
Au:	Australia
Br:	Brazil
Cn:	China
In:	Indonesia
Iq:	Iraq
Ka:	Kazakhstan
Li:	Libya
Ma:	Malaysia

Ni:	Nigeria
Po:	Poland
Ru:	Russia
SA:	Saudi Arabia
S Af:	South Africa
Tm:	Turkmenistan
UAE:	United Arab Emirates
Uk:	Ukraine
USA:	United States of America
Ve:	Venezuela

Middle East, UAE, Kuwait, Iraq, Iran, Saudi Arabia, South America, Ve, Africa, Ni, Li, E. Europe & Eurasia, Ru, North America, USA, Asia & Oceania, Cn, Western Europe

Saudi Arabia 12.8%, Russia 11.4%, USA 9.2%, Iran 5.1%, Mexico 4.6%, China 4.1%, Norway 4.1%, Venezuela 4.1%

Oil production

World total (2003): 3,697,000,000 tonnes

GAS RESERVES
World natural gas reserves by region and country, thousand million tonnes of oil equivalent (2003)

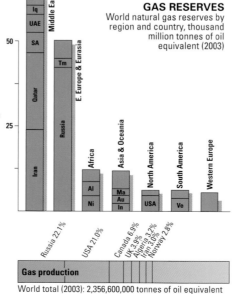

Middle East, Iq, UAE, SA, Qatar, Iran, E. Europe & Eurasia, Tm, Russia, Africa, Al, Ni, Asia & Oceania, Ma, Au, In, North America, USA, South America, Ve, Western Europe

Russia 22.1%, USA 21.0%, Canada 6.9%, UK 3.9%, Algeria 3.2%, Iran 3.0%, Norway 2.8%

Gas production

World total (2003): 2,356,600,000 tonnes of oil equivalent

COAL RESERVES
World coal reserves by region and country, thousand million tonnes (2003, including lignite)

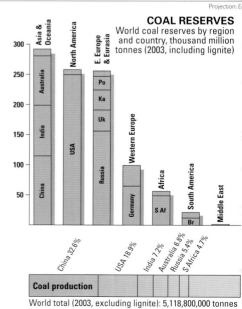

Asia & Oceania, Australia, India, China, North America, USA, E. Europe & Eurasia, Po, Ka, Uk, Russia, Western Europe, Germany, Africa, S Af, South America, Br, Middle East

China 32.6%, USA 18.9%, India 7.2%, Australia 6.8%, Russia 5.4%, S Africa 4.7%

Coal production

World total (2003, excluding lignite): 5,118,800,000 tonnes

ELECTRICITY GENERATION
Percentage of electricity generated
by source (2004)

- Over 75% from thermal
- 50 – 75% from thermal
- Over 75% from hydro
- 50 – 75% from hydro
- Over 50% from nuclear
- No dominant source
- No data
- elected geothermal plants ○
- elected hydroelectric plants ◆

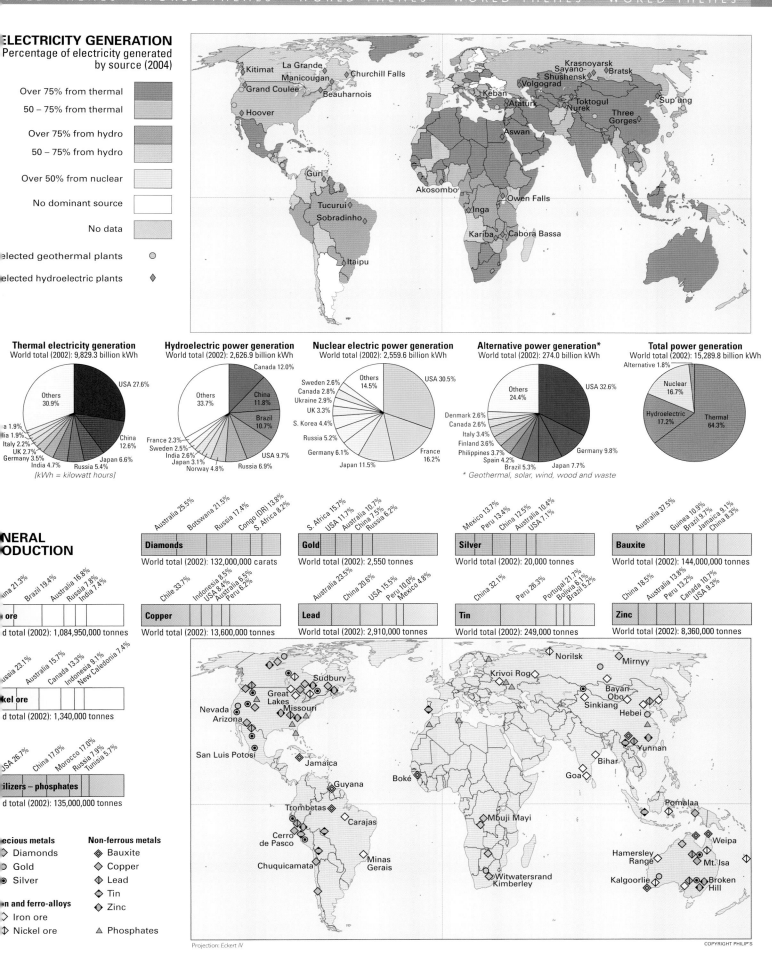

Thermal electricity generation
World total (2002): 9,829.3 billion kWh

- USA 27.6%
- Others 30.9%
- China 12.6%
- a 1.9%
- ia 1.9%
- Italy 2.2%
- UK 2.7%
- Germany 3.5%
- India 4.7%
- Russia 5.4%
- Japan 6.6%

[kWh = kilowatt hours]

Hydroelectric power generation
World total (2002): 2,626.9 billion kWh

- Canada 12.0%
- China 11.8%
- Brazil 10.7%
- Others 33.7%
- France 2.3%
- Sweden 2.5%
- India 2.6%
- Japan 3.1%
- Norway 4.8%
- Russia 6.9%
- USA 9.7%

Nuclear electric power generation
World total (2002): 2,559.6 billion kWh

- USA 30.5%
- Others 14.5%
- Sweden 2.6%
- Canada 2.8%
- Ukraine 2.9%
- UK 3.3%
- S. Korea 4.4%
- Russia 5.2%
- Germany 6.1%
- Japan 11.5%
- France 16.2%

Alternative power generation*
World total (2002): 274.0 billion kWh

- USA 32.6%
- Others 24.4%
- Denmark 2.6%
- Canada 2.6%
- Italy 3.4%
- Finland 3.6%
- Philippines 3.7%
- Spain 4.2%
- Brazil 5.3%
- Japan 7.7%
- Germany 9.8%
- France 16.2%

* Geothermal, solar, wind, wood and waste

Total power generation
World total (2002): 15,289.8 billion kWh

- Alternative 1.8%
- Nuclear 16.7%
- Hydroelectric 17.2%
- Thermal 64.3%

NERAL ODUCTION

Diamonds
World total (2002): 132,000,000 carats

| Australia 25.5% | Botswana 21.5% | Russia 17.4% | Congo (DR) 13.8% | S. Africa 8.2% |

Gold
World total (2002): 2,550 tonnes

| S. Africa 15.7% | USA 11.7% | Australia 10.7% | China 7.5% | Russia 6.2% |

Silver
World total (2002): 20,000 tonnes

| Mexico 13.7% | Peru 13.4% | China 12.5% | Australia 10.4% | USA 7.1% |

Bauxite
World total (2002): 144,000,000 tonnes

| Australia 37.5% | Guinea 10.9% | Brazil 9.7% | Jamaica 9.1% | China 8.3% |

Copper
World total (2002): 13,600,000 tonnes

| Chile 33.7% | Indonesia 8.5% | USA 8.4% | Australia 6.5% | Peru 6.2% |

Lead
World total (2002): 2,910,000 tonnes

| Australia 23.5% | China 20.6% | USA 15.5% | Peru 10.0% | Mexico 4.8% |

Tin
World total (2002): 249,000 tonnes

| China 32.1% | Peru 26.3% | Portugal 21.7% | Bolivia 6.1% | Brazil 5.2% |

Zinc
World total (2002): 8,360,000 tonnes

| China 18.5% | Australia 13.8% | Peru 13.2% | Canada 10.7% | USA 9.3% |

ore
d total (2002): 1,084,950,000 tonnes

| ina 21.3% | Brazil 19.4% | Australia 16.8% | Russia 7.8% | India 7.4% |

kel ore
d total (2002): 1,340,000 tonnes

| ssia 23.1% | Australia 15.7% | Canada 13.3% | Indonesia 9.1% | New Caledonia 7.4% |

ilizers – phosphates
d total (2002): 135,000,000 tonnes

| USA 26.7% | China 17.0% | Morocco 17.0% | Russia 7.9% | Tunisia 5.7% |

ecious metals
- ◇ Diamonds
- ○ Gold
- ● Silver

n and ferro-alloys
- ◇ Iron ore
- ◇ Nickel ore

Non-ferrous metals
- ◈ Bauxite
- ◇ Copper
- ◈ Lead
- ◇ Tin
- ◇ Zinc
- △ Phosphates

Projection: *Eckert IV*

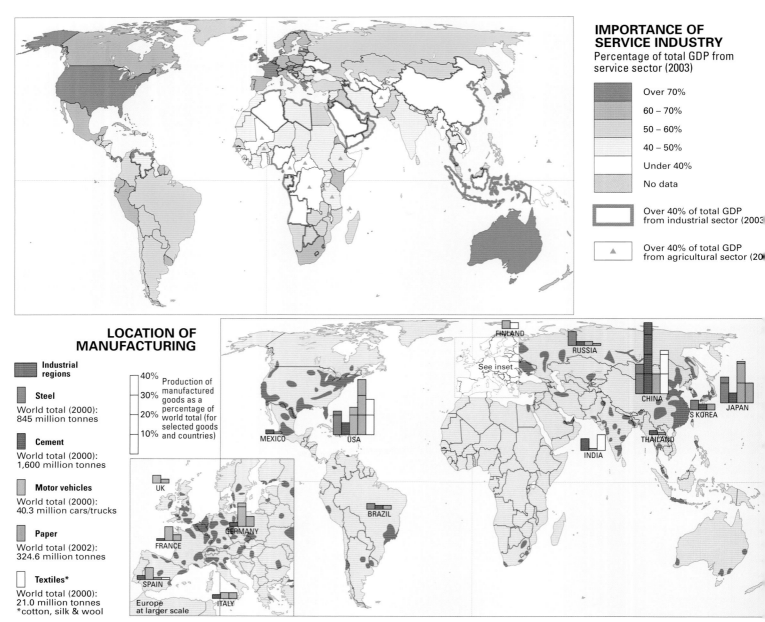

IMPORTANCE OF SERVICE INDUSTRY

Percentage of total GDP from service sector (2003)

- Over 70%
- 60 – 70%
- 50 – 60%
- 40 – 50%
- Under 40%
- No data

- Over 40% of total GDP from industrial sector (2003

- ▲ Over 40% of total GDP from agricultural sector (20

LOCATION OF MANUFACTURING

- **Industrial regions**

- **Steel**
World total (2000): 845 million tonnes

- **Cement**
World total (2000): 1,600 million tonnes

- **Motor vehicles**
World total (2000): 40.3 million cars/trucks

- **Paper**
World total (2002): 324.6 million tonnes

- **Textiles***
World total (2000): 21.0 million tonnes
*cotton, silk & wool

40% – 10% Production of manufactured goods as a percentage of world total (for selected goods and countries)

FINLAND · RUSSIA · See inset · CHINA · JAPAN · S KOREA · THAILAND · INDIA · MEXICO · USA · BRAZIL

UK · GERMANY · FRANCE · SPAIN · ITALY · Europe at larger scale

EMPLOYMENT BY ECONOMIC ACTIVITY Selected countries (2002)

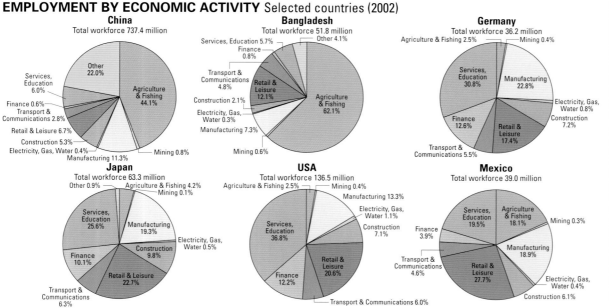

China — Total workforce 737.4 million
- Other 22.0%
- Agriculture & Fishing 44.1%
- Services, Education 6.0%
- Finance 0.6%
- Transport & Communications 2.8%
- Retail & Leisure 6.7%
- Construction 5.3%
- Electricity, Gas, Water 0.4%
- Manufacturing 11.3%
- Mining 0.8%

Bangladesh — Total workforce 51.8 million
- Services, Education 5.7%
- Other 4.1%
- Finance 0.8%
- Transport & Communications 4.8%
- Retail & Leisure 12.1%
- Construction 2.1%
- Agriculture & Fishing 62.1%
- Electricity, Gas, Water 0.3%
- Manufacturing 7.3%
- Mining 0.6%

Germany — Total workforce 36.2 million
- Agriculture & Fishing 2.5%
- Mining 0.4%
- Services, Education 30.8%
- Manufacturing 22.8%
- Electricity, Gas, Water 0.8%
- Construction 7.2%
- Finance 12.6%
- Retail & Leisure 17.4%
- Transport & Communications 5.5%

Japan — Total workforce 63.3 million
- Other 0.9%
- Agriculture & Fishing 4.2%
- Mining 0.1%
- Services, Education 25.6%
- Manufacturing 19.3%
- Electricity, Gas, Water 0.5%
- Construction 9.8%
- Finance 10.1%
- Retail & Leisure 22.7%
- Transport & Communications 6.3%

USA — Total workforce 136.5 million
- Agriculture & Fishing 2.5%
- Mining 0.4%
- Manufacturing 13.3%
- Electricity, Gas, Water 1.1%
- Construction 7.1%
- Services, Education 36.8%
- Retail & Leisure 20.6%
- Finance 12.2%
- Transport & Communications 6.0%

Mexico — Total workforce 39.0 million
- Services, Education 19.5%
- Agriculture & Fishing 18.1%
- Mining 0.3%
- Finance 3.9%
- Manufacturing 18.9%
- Transport & Communications 4.6%
- Retail & Leisure 27.7%
- Electricity, Gas, Water 0.4%
- Construction 6.1%

RESEARCH & DEVELOPMEN

Scientists and engineers in R&D (per million people) 1990–2003

Country	Total
Finland	7,43
Iceland	6,59
Sweden	5,17
Japan	5,08
Denmark	4,82
USA	4,52
Norway	4,44
Singapore	4,35
Luxembourg	3,75
Switzerland	3,59
Canada	3,48
Australia	3,44
Russia	3,41
Germany	3,22
Belgium	3,18
France	3,13
South Korea	2,97
Netherlands	2,82
UK	2,69
New Zealand	2,59

WORLD TRADE

Percentage share of total world exports by value (2003)

- Over 5%
- 2.5 – 5%
- 1 – 2.5%
- 0.25 – 1%
- 0.1 – 0.25%
- Under 0.1%
- No data

The members of 'G8', the inner circle of OECD, account for more than half the total. The majority of nations contribute less than one quarter of 1% to the worldwide total of exports; EU countries account for 35%; the Pacific Rim nations over 50%.

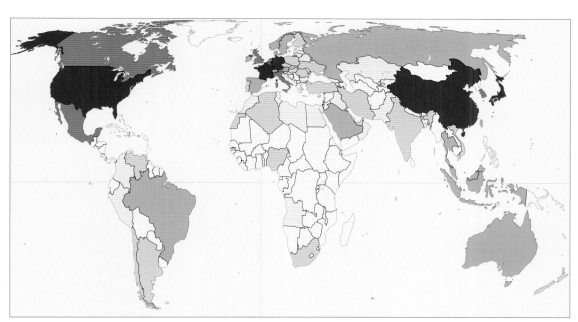

MAJOR EXPORTS Leading manufactured items and their exporters

Motor Vehicles
World total (2004): US$ 265,898 million

Germany 19%, Japan 15%, USA 9%, Canada 8%, France 7%, Spain 5%, Belgium 5%, UK 4%, Mexico 4%, Korea 3%, Italy 3%, China 2%, Sweden 2%, Other 13%

Telecommunications Gear
World total (2004): US$ 405,989 million

China 26%, S. Korea 9%, Japan 9%, USA 7%, Germany 7%, Mexico 5%, UK 3%, Malaysia 3%, France 3%, Singapore 3%, Sweden 3%, Hungary 3%, Other 17%

Petrol Products
World total (2004): US$ 496,092 million

Russia 15%, Norway 8%, Venezuela 6%, UK 6%, Canada 5%, Mexico 5%, Algeria 4%, Netherlands 4%, Singapore 3%, USA 3%, Other 41%

Computers
World total (2004): US$ 236,396 million

China 26%, USA 10%, Neth. 8%, Germany 7%, Singapore 7%, Malaysia 5%, Mexico 5%, Korea 4%, Ireland 4%, UK 4%, Japan 4%, Other 15%

Electrical Components
World total (2004): US$ 838,552 million

China 13%, USA 11%, Japan 10%, Germany 9%, Singapore 7%, S. Korea 4%, Malaysia 4%, France 3%, Mexico 3%, Other 36%

Pharmaceuticals
World total (2004): US$ 311,399 million

Germany 11%, Belgium 10%, USA 8%, Switzerland 7%, France 7%, UK 7%, Ireland 6%, Italy 4%, Neth. 3%, Sweden 2%, Other 37%

MULTINATIONAL CORPORATIONS (MNCs)

Country of origin of world's top 200 MNCs (top 200 are ranked by revenue, 2002)

USA 86, Japan 32, Germany 18, France 16, UK 13, Neth. 7.5, Switz. 6, Italy 5, S. Korea 4, Spain 4, China 3, Others 5.5

Top ten MNCs by revenue (million US$), 2002

Wal-Mart	Supermarket chain	219,812	USA
Exxon Mobil	Petroleum	191,581	USA
General Motors	Motor vehicles	177,260	USA
BP	Petroleum	174,218	UK
Ford Motor	Motor vehicles	162,412	USA
Enron*	Energy	138,718	USA
DaimlerChrysler	Motor vehicles	136,897	Germany
Royal Dutch/Shell	Petroleum	135,211	Neth/UK
General Electric	Energy and finance	125,913	USA
Toyota Motor	Motor vehicles	120,814	Japan

* Enron ceased trading in 2002

INTERNET AND TELECOMMUNICATIONS

Percentage of total population using the Internet (2003)

World total 604.1 million Internet users

- Over 50%
- 10 – 50%
- 5 – 10%
- 1 – 5%
- Under 1%
- No data

Telecommunications

Trade in office machines and telecom equipment, percentage of world total (2002)

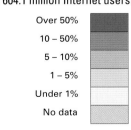

IMPORT EXPORT
40%
30%
20%
10%

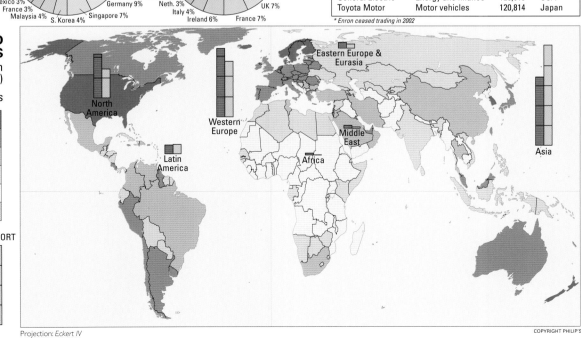

Projection: *Eckert IV*

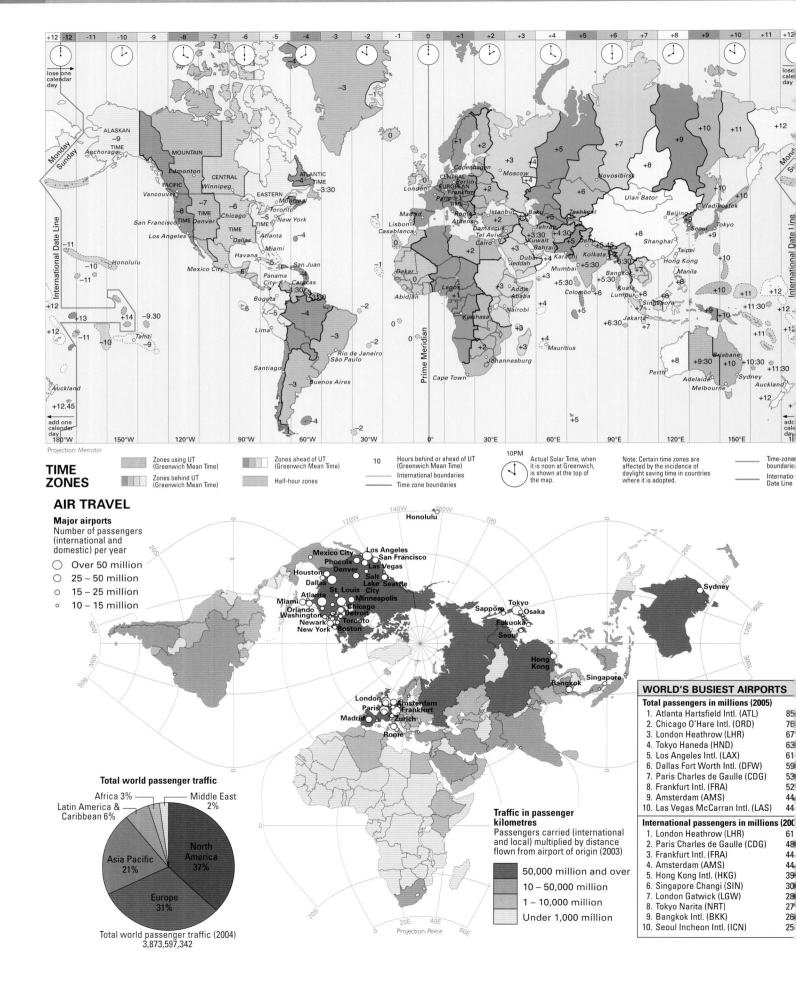

TIME ZONES

Projection: Mercator

Zones using UT (Greenwich Mean Time)
Zones behind UT (Greenwich Mean Time)
Zones ahead of UT (Greenwich Mean Time)
Half-hour zones

10 Hours behind or ahead of UT (Greenwich Mean Time)
International boundaries
Time zone boundaries

10PM Actual Solar Time, when it is noon at Greenwich, is shown at the top of the map.

Note: Certain time zones are affected by the incidence of daylight saving time in countries where it is adopted.

Time-zone boundaries
International Date Line

AIR TRAVEL

Major airports
Number of passengers (international and domestic) per year

○ Over 50 million
○ 25 – 50 million
○ 15 – 25 million
○ 10 – 15 million

Projection: Peirce

Traffic in passenger kilometres
Passengers carried (international and local) multiplied by distance flown from airport of origin (2003)

■ 50,000 million and over
■ 10 – 50,000 million
■ 1 – 10,000 million
□ Under 1,000 million

Total world passenger traffic

Africa 3%
Middle East 2%
Latin America & Caribbean 6%
North America 37%
Asia Pacific 21%
Europe 31%

Total world passenger traffic (2004)
3,873,597,342

WORLD'S BUSIEST AIRPORTS

Total passengers in millions (2005)

1. Atlanta Hartsfield Intl. (ATL)	85
2. Chicago O'Hare Intl. (ORD)	76
3. London Heathrow (LHR)	67
4. Tokyo Haneda (HND)	63
5. Los Angeles Intl. (LAX)	61
6. Dallas Fort Worth Intl. (DFW)	59
7. Paris Charles de Gaulle (CDG)	53
8. Frankfurt Intl. (FRA)	52
9. Amsterdam (AMS)	44
10. Las Vegas McCarran Intl. (LAS)	44

International passengers in millions (200)

1. London Heathrow (LHR)	61
2. Paris Charles de Gaulle (CDG)	48
3. Frankfurt Intl. (FRA)	44
4. Amsterdam (AMS)	44
5. Hong Kong Intl. (HKG)	39
6. Singapore Changi (SIN)	30
7. London Gatwick (LGW)	28
8. Tokyo Narita (NRT)	27
9. Bangkok Intl. (BKK)	26
10. Seoul Incheon Intl. (ICN)	25

UNESCO WORLD HERITAGE SITES 2005

Total sites = 812 (628 cultural, 160 natural and 24 mixed)

Region	Cultural sites	Natural sites	Mixed sites
Africa	31	32	2
Arab States	56	4	1
Asia & Pacific	112	43	9
Europe & North America	352	48	9
Latin America & Caribbean	77	33	3

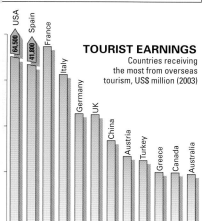

TOURIST EARNINGS

Countries receiving the most from overseas tourism, US$ million (2003)

USA 64,500
Spain 41,800
France

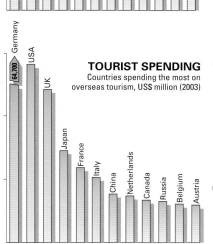

TOURIST SPENDING

Countries spending the most on overseas tourism, US$ million (2003)

Germany 64,700

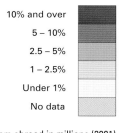

IMPORTANCE OF TOURISM

Tourism receipts as a percentage of Gross National Income (2002)

- 10% and over
- 5 – 10%
- 2.5 – 5%
- 1 – 2.5%
- Under 1%
- No data

Arrivals from abroad in millions (2001)

France	75.6
Spain	49.5
USA	45.5
Italy	39.0
China	33.2

(UK = 23.4 million)

Europe at larger scale

Destinations

- ■ Cultural & historical centres
- □ Coastal resorts
- □ Ski resorts
- ■ Centres of entertainment
- ■ Places of pilgrimage
- ■ Places of great natural beauty

□ Other tourist destinations

Movement of tourists

- More than 10 million
- 5 – 10 million
- 3 – 5 million
- Less than 3 million

TOURIST DESTINATIONS

Projection: *Peirce*

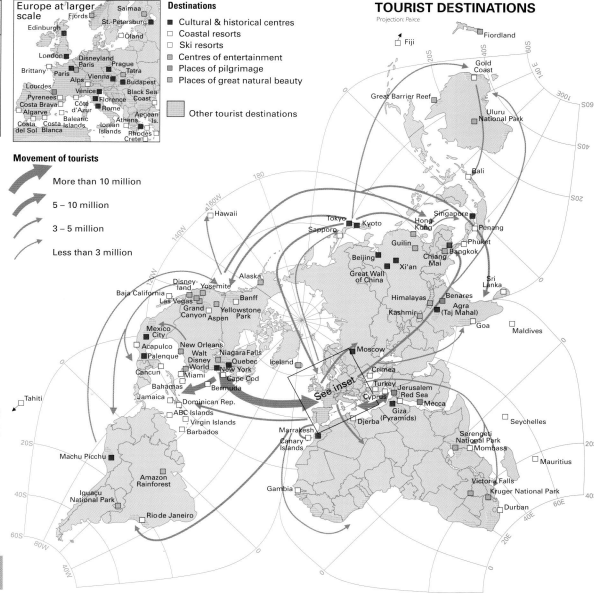

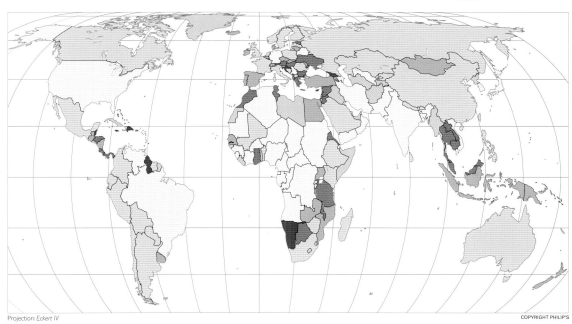

Projection: *Eckert IV*

COPYRIGHT PHILIP'S

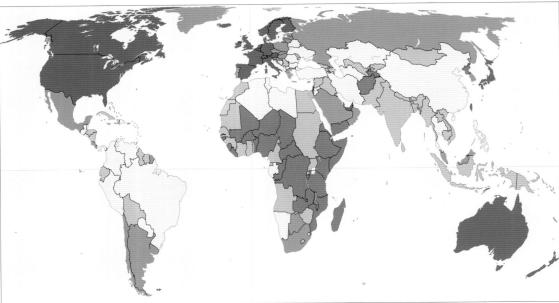

WEALTH

Gross Domestic Product per capita PPP (2003)

Annual value of goods and services divided by the population, using purchasing power parity (PPP) which gives real prices instead of variable exchange rates.

 Over 250% world average

 100 – 250% world average

World average: US$ 8,200

50 – 100% world average

15 – 50% world average

Under 15% world average

No data

Highest GDP (US$)		Lowest GDP (US$)	
Lux'bourg	55,100	East Timor	500
USA	37,800	Sierra Leone	500
Norway	37,700	Somalia	500
San Marino	34,600	Burundi	600
Switzerland	32,800	Congo (D.Rep.)	600

(UK = US$ 27,700)

WATER SUPPLY

Percentage of total population with access to safe drinking water (2000)

Over 90%

75 – 90%

60 – 75%

45 – 60%

30 – 45%

Under 30%

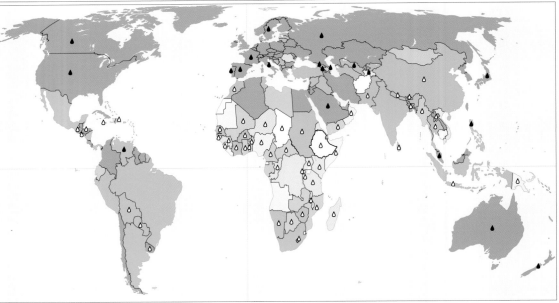

Least amount of safe drinking water

Afghanistan	13%	Cambodia	30%
Ethiopia	24%	Mauritania	37%
Chad	27%	Angola	38%
Sierra Leone	28%	Oman	39%

Daily consumption per capita

△ Under 80 litres ▲ Over 320 litres

80 litres a day is considered necessary for a reasonable quality of life

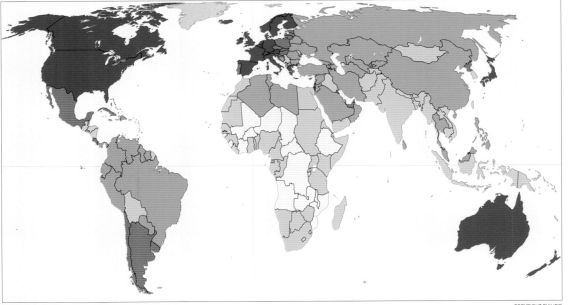

HUMAN DEVELOPMENT INDEX (HDI)

HDI (calculated by the UNDP) gives a value to countries using indicators of life expectancy, education and standards of living in 2002. Higher values show more developed countries.

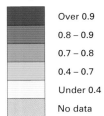

Over 0.9

0.8 – 0.9

0.7 – 0.8

0.4 – 0.7

Under 0.4

No data

Highest values		Lowest values	
Norway	0.952	Sierra Leone	0.273
Australia	0.946	Niger	0.292
Sweden	0.946	Burkina Faso	0.302
Canada	0.943	Mali	0.326
Netherlands	0.942	Burundi	0.339

(UK = 0.936)

HEALTH CARE

Number of qualified doctors
per 100,000 people (2003)

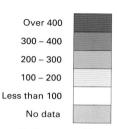

- Over 400
- 300 – 400
- 200 – 300
- 100 – 200
- Less than 100
- No data

Countries with the most and least
doctors per 100,000 people

Most doctors		Least doctors	
Italy	607	Burundi	1
Cuba	596	Mozambique	2
Georgia	463	Rwanda	2
Belarus	450	Chad	3
Greece	438	Ethiopia	3

(UK = 164 doctors)

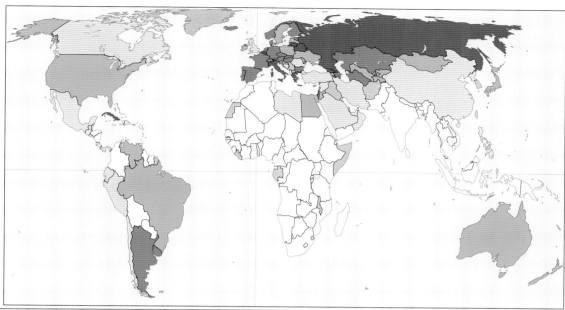

ILLITERACY AND EDUCATION

Percentage of adult population
unable to read or write (2003)

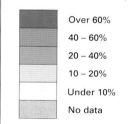

- Over 60%
- 40 – 60%
- 20 – 40%
- 10 – 20%
- Under 10%
- No data

Countries with the highest
and lowest illiteracy rates

Highest (%)		Lowest (%)	
Niger	82	Australia	0
Burkina Faso	73	Denmark	0
Sierra Leone	69	Finland	0
Guinea	64	Liechtenstein	0
Afghanistan	44	Luxembourg	0

(UK = 1%)

GENDER DEVELOPMENT INDEX (GDI)

GDI shows economic and social differences
between men and women by using
various UNDP indicators (2002). Countries
with higher values of GDI have more
equality between men and women.

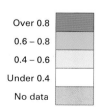

- Over 0.8
- 0.6 – 0.8
- 0.4 – 0.6
- Under 0.4
- No data

Highest values		Lowest values	
Norway	0.955	Niger	0.278
Sweden	0.946	Burkina Faso	0.291
Australia	0.945	Mali	0.309
Canada	0.941	Guinea-Bissau	0.329
Netherlands	0.938	Burundi	0.337

(UK = 0.934)

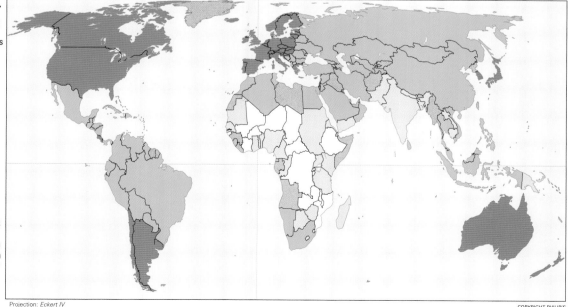

Projection: *Eckert IV*

COPYRIGHT PHILIP'S

AGE DISTRIBUTION PYRAMIDS (2005)

The bars represent the percentage of the total population (males plus females) in each age group. Developed countries such as New Zealand have populations spread evenly across age groups and usually a growing percentage of elderly people. Developing countries such as Kenya have the great majority of their people in the younger age groups, about to enter their most fertile years.

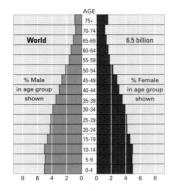

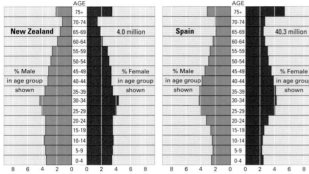

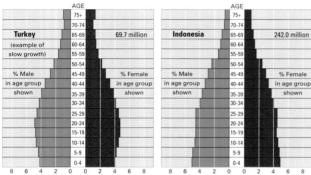

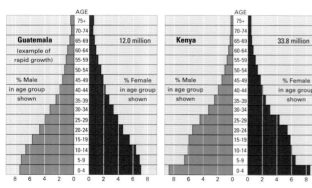

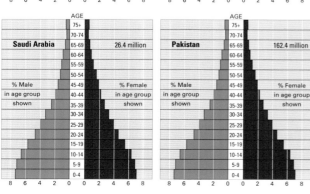

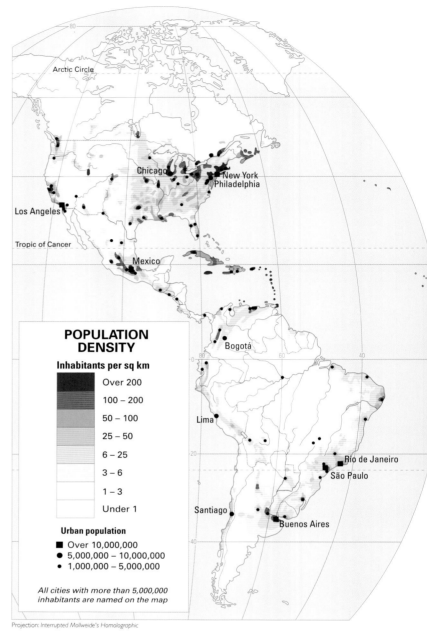

POPULATION DENSITY

Inhabitants per sq km

- Over 200
- 100 – 200
- 50 – 100
- 25 – 50
- 6 – 25
- 3 – 6
- 1 – 3
- Under 1

Urban population
- ■ Over 10,000,000
- ● 5,000,000 – 10,000,000
- • 1,000,000 – 5,000,000

All cities with more than 5,000,000 inhabitants are named on the map

Projection: *Interrupted Mollweide's Homolographic*

POPULATION CHANGE 1930–2020
Population totals are in millions

Figures in italics represent the percentage average annual increase for the period shown

	1930	1930– 1960	1960	1960– 1990	1990	1990– 2020	2020
World	2,013	*1.4%*	3,019	*1.9%*	5,292	*1.4%*	8,062
Africa	155	*2.0%*	281	*2.9%*	648	*2.7%*	1,441
North America	135	*1.3%*	199	*1.1%*	276	*0.6%*	327
Latin America*	129	*1.8%*	218	*2.4%*	448	*1.6%*	719
Asia	1,073	*1.5%*	1,669	*2.1%*	3,108	*1.4%*	4,680
Europe	355	*0.6%*	425	*0.6%*	498	*0.1%*	514
Oceania	10	*1.4%*	16	*1.8%*	27	*1.1%*	37
CIS	176	*0.7%*	214	*1.0%*	288	*0.6%*	343

* South America plus Central America, Mexico and the West Indies
Commonwealth of Independent States, formerly the USSR

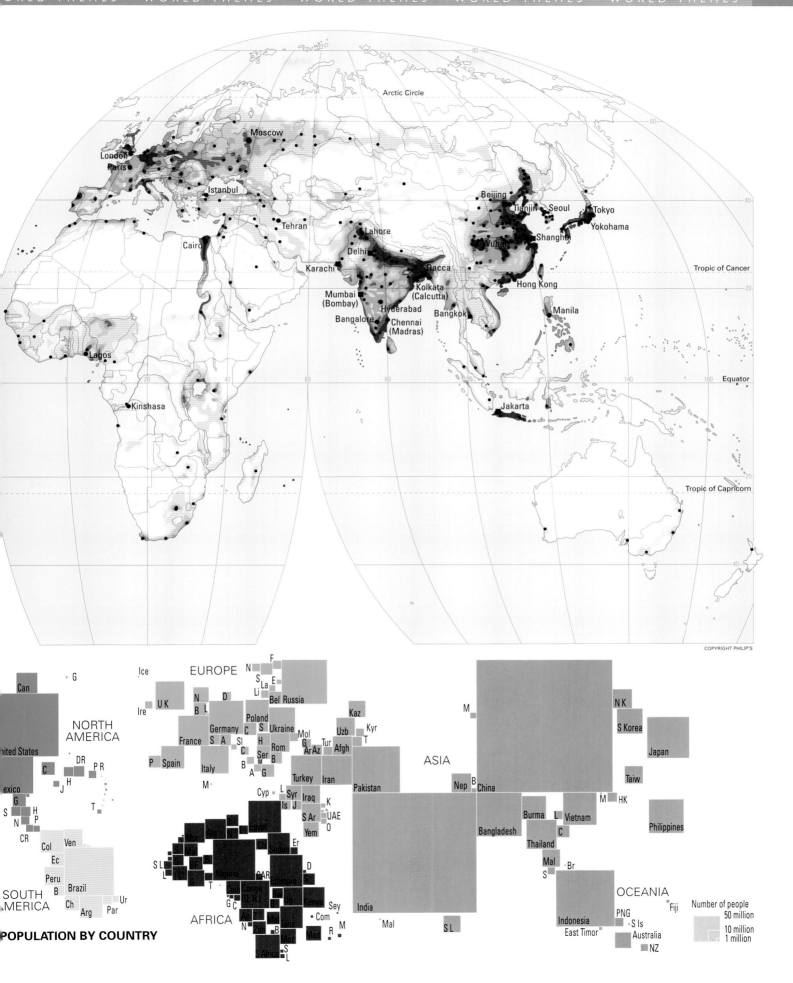

POPULATION BY COUNTRY

POPULATION DENSITY

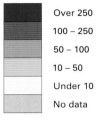

Density of people per square kilometre (2004)

- Over 250
- 100 – 250
- 50 – 100
- 10 – 50
- Under 10
- No data

Most and least densely populated countries

Most		Least	
Singapore	6,283	W. Sahara	1.0
Malta	1,256	Mongolia	1.8
Maldives	1,131	Namibia	2.4
Bahrain	1,019	Australia	2.6
Bangladesh	982	Botswana	2.6

(UK = 246.2 people per square km)

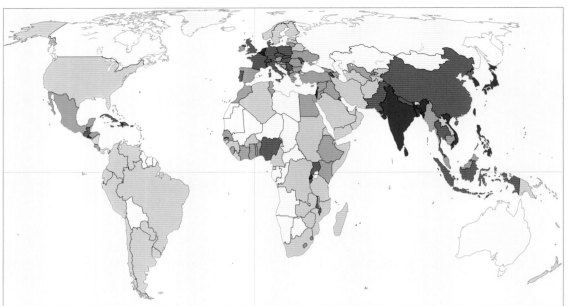

POPULATION CHANGE

Expected change in total population (2000–2010)

- Over 40% gain
- 20 – 40% gain
- 10 – 20% gain
- 0 – 10% gain
- Loss or no change
- No data

Greatest population gains and losses

Greatest gains (%)		Greatest losses (%)	
Afghanistan	44.4	Bulgaria	– 8.6
Kuwait	41.2	Trinidad & Tob.	– 7.4
Yemen	41.0	Latvia	– 6.7
Uganda	39.8	Estonia	– 6.4
Oman	39.1	Ukraine	– 6.1

(UK = 3% gain)

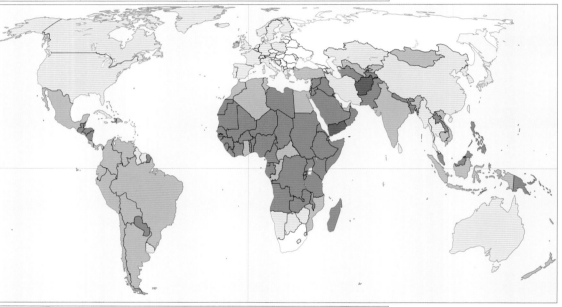

URBAN POPULATION

People living in urban areas as a percentage of total population (2002)

- Over 80%
- 60 – 80%
- 40 – 60%
- 20 – 40%
- Under 20%
- No data

Countries that are the most and least urbanized (%)

Most urbanized		Least urbanized	
Singapore	100	Bhutan	8.2
Belgium	97.2	Burundi	9.6
Kuwait	96.2	Uganda	12.2
Iceland	92.7	Papua N. G.	13.2
Uruguay	92.4	Nepal	14.6

(UK = 89.0%)

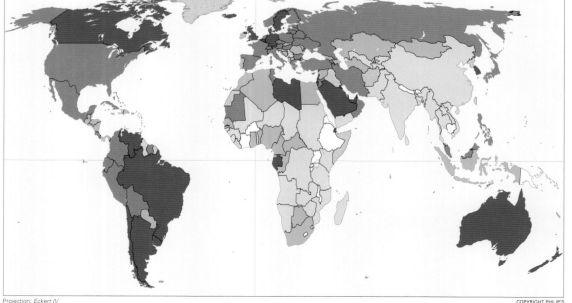

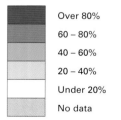

Projection: *Eckert IV*

COPYRIGHT PHILIP'S

CHILD MORTALITY

Deaths of children under 1 year old per 1,000 live births (2004)

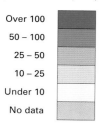

- Over 100
- 50 – 100
- 25 – 50
- 10 – 25
- Under 10
- No data

Countries with the highest and lowest child mortality

Highest		Lowest	
Angola	193	Singapore	2
Afghanistan	166	Sweden	3
Sierra Leone	145	Japan	3
Mozambique	137	Iceland	3
Liberia	131	Finland	4

(UK = 5 deaths)

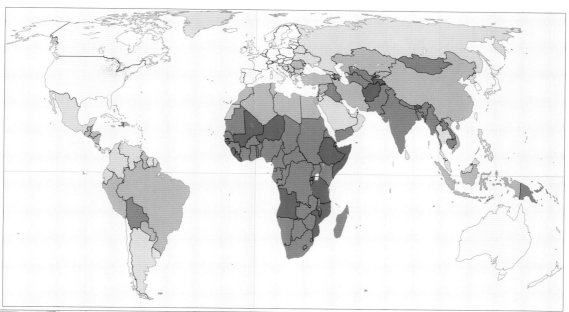

LIFE EXPECTANCY

Life expectancy at birth in years (2004)

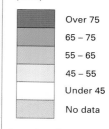

- Over 75
- 65 – 75
- 55 – 65
- 45 – 55
- Under 45
- No data

Countries with the longest and shortest life expectancy at birth in years

Longest		Shortest	
Andorra	83.5	Botswana	30.8
San Marino	81.5	Zambia	35.2
Singapore	81.5	Angola	36.8
Japan	81.0	Lesotho	36.8
Switzerland	80.3	Mozambique	37.1

(UK = 78.3 years)

FAMILY SIZE

Children born per woman (2004)

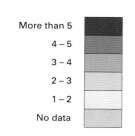

- More than 5
- 4 – 5
- 3 – 4
- 2 – 3
- 1 – 2
- No data

Countries with the largest and smallest family size

Largest		Smallest	
Somalia	6.9	Singapore	1.0
Niger	6.8	Lithuania	1.2
Afghanistan	6.8	Czech Rep.	1.2
Yemen	6.8	Slovenia	1.2
Uganda	6.6	Latvia	1.3

(UK = 1.7 children)

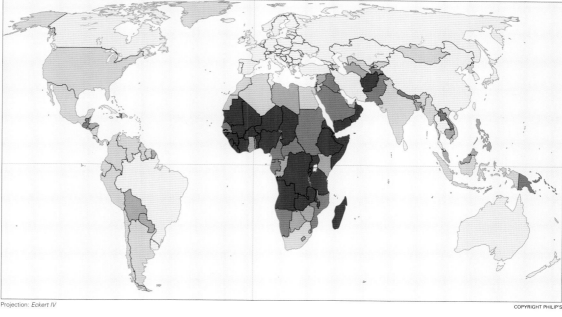

Projection: *Eckert IV*

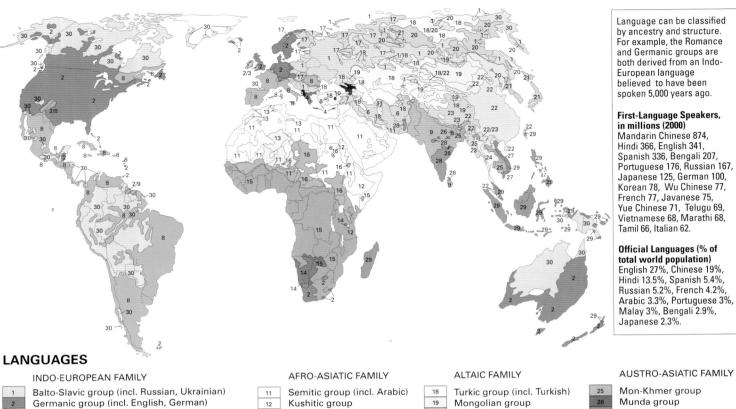

Language can be classified by ancestry and structure. For example, the Romance and Germanic groups are both derived from an Indo-European language believed to have been spoken 5,000 years ago.

First-Language Speakers, in millions (2000)
Mandarin Chinese 874, Hindi 366, English 341, Spanish 336, Bengali 207, Portuguese 176, Russian 167, Japanese 125, German 100, Korean 78, Wu Chinese 77, French 77, Javanese 75, Yue Chinese 71, Telugu 69, Vietnamese 68, Marathi 68, Tamil 66, Italian 62.

Official Languages (% of total world population)
English 27%, Chinese 19%, Hindi 13.5%, Spanish 5.4%, Russian 5.2%, French 4.2%, Arabic 3.3%, Portuguese 3%, Malay 3%, Bengali 2.9%, Japanese 2.3%.

LANGUAGES

INDO-EUROPEAN FAMILY
1. Balto-Slavic group (incl. Russian, Ukrainian)
2. Germanic group (incl. English, German)
3. Celtic group
4. Greek
5. Albanian
6. Iranian group
7. Armenian
8. Romance group (incl. Spanish, Portuguese, French, Italian)
9. Indo-Aryan group (incl. Hindi, Bengali, Urdu, Punjabi, Marathi)
10. CAUCASIAN FAMILY

AFRO-ASIATIC FAMILY
11. Semitic group (incl. Arabic)
12. Kushitic group
13. Berber group

14. KHOISAN FAMILY

15. NIGER-CONGO FAMILY

16. NILO-SAHARAN FAMILY

17. URALIC FAMILY

ALTAIC FAMILY
18. Turkic group (incl. Turkish)
19. Mongolian group
20. Tungus-Manchu group
21. Japanese and Korean

SINO-TIBETAN FAMILY
22. Sinitic (Chinese) languages (incl. Mandarin, Wu, Yue)
23. Tibetic-Burmic languages

24. TAI FAMILY

AUSTRO-ASIATIC FAMILY
25. Mon-Khmer group
26. Munda group
27. Vietnamese

28. DRAVIDIAN FAMILY (incl. Telugu, Tamil)

29. AUSTRONESIAN FAMILY (incl. Malay-Indonesian, Javanese)

30. OTHER LANGUAGES

RELIGIONS

- Roman Catholicism
- Orthodox and other Eastern Churches
- Protestantism
- Sunni Islam
- Shiite Islam
- Buddhism
- Hinduism
- Confucianism
- Judaism
- Shintoism
- Tribal Religions

Religious Adherents, in millions (2004)

Christian	2,107	Non-religious and Atheist	1,054
Roman Catholic	1,106		
Protestants	370	Hindu	851
Orthodox	218	Chinese trad.	402
Others	413	Buddhist	375
Islam	1,283	Ethnic religions	253
Sunni	1,065	Sikhs	25
Shi'ite	205	Judaism	15
Others	13	Spiritism	13

UNITED NATIONS

Created in 1945 to promote peace and co-operation and based in New York, the United Nations is the world's largest international organization, with an annual budget of US$1.3 billion (2002). Each member of the General Assembly has one vote, while the five permanent members of the 15-nation Security Council – China, France, Russia, UK and USA – hold a veto. The Secretariat is the UN's principal administrative arm. The 54 members of the Economic and Social Council are responsible for economic, social, cultural, educational, health and related matters. The UN has 16 specialized agencies – based in Canada, France, Switzerland and Italy, as well as the USA – which help members in fields such as education (UNESCO), agriculture (FAO), medicine (WHO) and finance (IFC). By the end of 1994, all the original 11 trust territories of the Trusteeship Council had become independent.

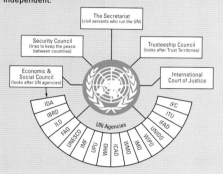

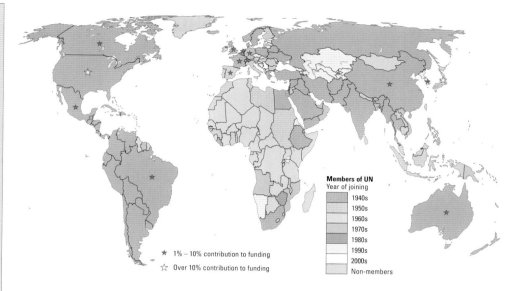

Members of UN
Year of joining
- 1940s
- 1950s
- 1960s
- 1970s
- 1980s
- 1990s
- 2000s
- Non-members

★ 1% – 10% contribution to funding
☆ Over 10% contribution to funding

MEMBERSHIP OF THE UN In 1945 there were 51 members; by the end of 2006 membership had increased to 192 following the admission of East Timor, Switzerland and Montenegro. There are 2 independent states which are not members of the UN – Taiwan and the Vatican City. All the successor states of the former USSR had joined by the end of 1992. The official languages of the UN are Chinese, English, French, Russian, Spanish and Arabic.

FUNDING The UN regular budget for 2005 was US$1.8 billion. Contributions are assessed by the members' ability to pay, with the maximum 22% of the total (USA's share), the minimum 0.01%. The European Union pays over 37% of the budget.

PEACEKEEPING The UN has been involved in 54 peace-keeping operations worldwide since 1948.

INTERNATIONAL ORGANIZATIONS

ACP African-Caribbean-Pacific (formed in 1963). Members have economic ties with the EU.
APEC Asia-Pacific Economic Co-operation (formed in 1989). It aims to enhance economic growth and prosperity for the region and to strengthen the Asia-Pacific community. APEC is the only intergovernmental grouping in the world operating on the basis of non-binding commitments, open dialogue, and equal respect for the views of all participants. There are 21 member economies.
ARAB LEAGUE (formed in 1945). The League's aim is to promote economic, social, political and military co-operation. There are 22 member nations.
ASEAN Association of South-east Asian Nations (formed in 1967). Cambodia joined in 1999.
AU The African Union replaced the Organization of African Unity (formed in 1963) in 2002. Its 53 members represent over 94% of Africa's population. Arabic, French, Portuguese and English are recognized as working languages.
COLOMBO PLAN (formed in 1951). Its 25 members aim to promote economic and social development in Asia and the Pacific.
COMMONWEALTH The Commonwealth of Nations evolved from the British Empire. Pakistan was suspended in 1999, and Zimbabwe in 2002. In response to its continued suspension, Zimbabwe left the Commonwealth in December 2003. It now comprises 16 Queen's realms, 31 republics and 6 indigenous monarchies, giving a total of 53 member states.
EU European Union (evolved from the European Community in 1993). Cyprus, the Czech Republic, Estonia, Hungary, Latvia, Lithuania, Malta, Poland, the Slovak Republic and Slovenia joined the EU in May 2004. Bulgaria and Romania joined in January 2007. The other 15 members of the EU are Austria, Belgium, Denmark, Finland, France, Germany, Greece, Ireland, Italy, Luxembourg, Netherlands, Portugal, Spain, Sweden and the UK – together they aim to integrate economies, co-ordinate social developments and bring about political union.
LAIA Latin American Integration Association (1980). Its aim is to promote freer regional trade.
NATO North Atlantic Treaty Organization (formed in 1949). It continues after 1991 despite the winding up of the Warsaw Pact. Bulgaria, Estonia, Latvia, Lithuania, Romania, the Slovak Republic and Slovenia became members in 2004.
OAS Organization of American States (formed in 1948). It aims to promote social and economic co-operation between developed countries of North America and developing nations of Latin America.

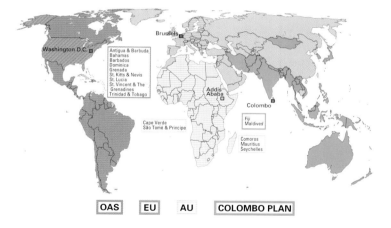

| OAS | EU | AU | COLOMBO PLAN |

OECD Organization for Economic Co-operation and Development (formed in 1961). It comprises 30 major free-market economies. Poland, Hungary and South Korea joined in 1996, and the Slovak Republic in 2000. 'G8' is its 'inner group' of leading industrial nations, comprising Canada, France, Germany, Italy, Japan, Russia, UK and USA.
OPEC Organization of Petroleum Exporting Countries (formed in 1960). It controls about three-quarters of the world's oil supply. Gabon left the organization in 1996.

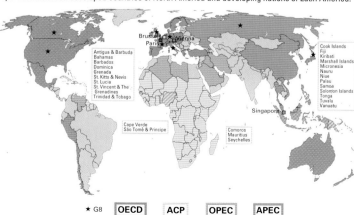

★ G8 | OECD | ACP | OPEC | APEC |

| NATO | LAIA | ARAB LEAGUE | COMMONWEALTH | ASEAN |

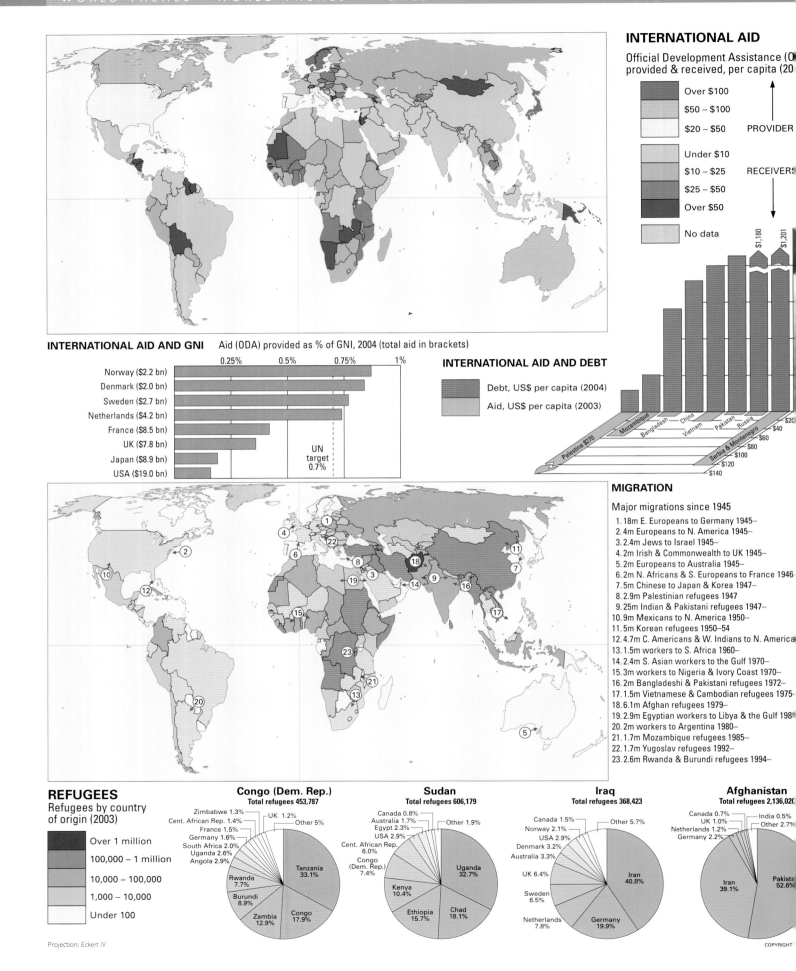

INTERNATIONAL AID

Official Development Assistance (O
provided & received, per capita (20

Over $100	
$50 – $100	PROVIDER
$20 – $50	
Under $10	
$10 – $25	RECEIVERS
$25 – $50	
Over $50	
No data	

$1,180 $1,201

INTERNATIONAL AID AND GNI

Aid (ODA) provided as % of GNI, 2004 (total aid in brackets)

Norway ($2.2 bn)
Denmark ($2.0 bn)
Sweden ($2.7 bn)
Netherlands ($4.2 bn)
France ($8.5 bn)
UK ($7.8 bn)
Japan ($8.9 bn)
USA ($19.0 bn)

0.25% 0.5% 0.75% 1%

UN target 0.7%

INTERNATIONAL AID AND DEBT

Debt, US$ per capita (2004)
Aid, US$ per capita (2003)

Palestine $270
Mozambique
Bangladesh
China
Vietnam
Pakistan
Russia
Serbia & Montenegro

$20 $40 $60 $80 $100 $120 $140

MIGRATION

Major migrations since 1945

1. 18m E. Europeans to Germany 1945–
2. 4m Europeans to N. America 1945–
3. 2.4m Jews to Israel 1945–
4. 2m Irish & Commonwealth to UK 1945–
5. 2m Europeans to Australia 1945–
6. 2m N. Africans & S. Europeans to France 1946–
7. 5m Chinese to Japan & Korea 1947–
8. 2.9m Palestinian refugees 1947
9. 25m Indian & Pakistani refugees 1947–
10. 9m Mexicans to N. America 1950–
11. 5m Korean refugees 1950–54
12. 4.7m C. Americans & W. Indians to N. America
13. 1.5m workers to S. Africa 1960–
14. 2.4m S. Asian workers to the Gulf 1970–
15. 3m workers to Nigeria & Ivory Coast 1970–
16. 2m Bangladeshi & Pakistani refugees 1972–
17. 1.5m Vietnamese & Cambodian refugees 1975–
18. 6.1m Afghan refugees 1979–
19. 2.9m Egyptian workers to Libya & the Gulf 198
20. 2m workers to Argentina 1980–
21. 1.7m Mozambique refugees 1985–
22. 1.7m Yugoslav refugees 1992–
23. 2.6m Rwanda & Burundi refugees 1994–

REFUGEES

Refugees by country of origin (2003)

Over 1 million	
100,000 – 1 million	
10,000 – 100,000	
1,000 – 10,000	
Under 100	

Congo (Dem. Rep.)
Total refugees 453,787

Zimbabwe 1.3%
Cent. African Rep. 1.4%
UK 1.2%
France 1.5%
Germany 1.6%
South Africa 2.0%
Uganda 2.6%
Angola 2.9%
Other 5%
Tanzania 33.1%
Rwanda 7.7%
Burundi 8.9%
Zambia 12.9%
Congo 17.9%

Sudan
Total refugees 606,179

Canada 0.8%
Australia 1.7%
Egypt 2.3%
USA 2.9%
Cent. African Rep. 6.0%
Congo (Dem. Rep.) 7.4%
Other 1.9%
Uganda 32.7%
Kenya 10.4%
Ethiopia 15.7%
Chad 18.1%

Iraq
Total refugees 368,423

Canada 1.5%
Norway 2.1%
USA 2.9%
Denmark 3.2%
Australia 3.3%
Other 5.7%
Iran 40.8%
UK 6.4%
Sweden 6.5%
Netherlands 7.8%
Germany 19.9%

Afghanistan
Total refugees 2,136,020

Canada 0.7%
UK 1.0%
Netherlands 1.2%
Germany 2.2%
India 0.5%
Other 2.7%
Iran 39.1%
Pakistan 52.6%

CONFLICTS

Armed conflict since 1994

Countries in the top half of the Human Developement Index (HDI)

Countries in the bottom half of the HDI

No data

Countries with at least one armed conflict between 1994 and mid-2005

MAJOR WARS SINCE 1900	
War	Total deaths
Second World War (1939–45)	55,000,000
First World War (1914–18)	8,500,000
Korean War (1950–53)	4,000,000
Congolese Civil War (1998–)	3,800,000
Vietnam War (1965–73)	3,000,000
Sudanese Civil War (1983–2000)	2,000,000

HIV/AIDS

Percentage of adults (15 – 49 years) living with HIV/AIDS (2003)

15 – 40%

5 – 15%

0.5 – 5%

0.1 – 0.5%

Under 0.1%

No data

Total number of adults and children living with HIV/AIDS by region (2004)

Human Immunodeficiency Virus (HIV) is passed from one person to another and attacks the body's defence against illness. It develops into the Acquired Immunodeficiency Syndrome (AIDS) when a particularly severe illness, such as cancer, takes hold. The pandemic started just over 20 years ago and, by 2005, 40.3 millon people were living with HIV or AIDS.

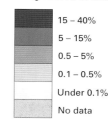

DRUGS

Countries producing illegal drugs

Cannabis

Poppy

Coca leaves

Cocaine

Amphetamines

Major routes of drug trafficking

Opium

Coca leaves

Cocaine

Heroin

Hashish and marijuana

Amphetamines (usually used within producing countries)

Conflicts relating to drug trafficking

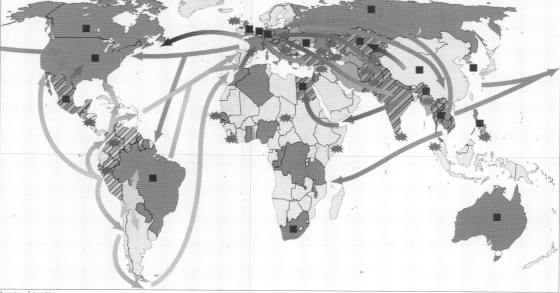

Projection: Eckert IV

COUNTRY	POPULATION							LAND & AGRICULTURE				TRADE, TOURISM & ENERGY					
	Total population (millions)	Population density (persons per km²)	Life expectancy (years)	Average annual population change (%)	Birth rate (births per thousand people)	Death rate (deaths per thousand people)	Urban population (% of total)	Land area (thousand km²)	Arable & permanent crops (% of land area)	Permanent pasture (% of land area)	Forest (% of land area)	Imports (US$ per capita)	Exports (US$ per capita)	Tourism receipts (US$ per capita)	Energy produced (tonnes of oil equiv. per capita)	Energy consumed (tonnes of oil equiv. per capita)	CO emiss. per c. (me tonn
	2005	2005	2005	2005	2005	2005	2005		2002	2002	2000	2004	2004	2003	2002	2002	200
Afghanistan	29.9	46	43	4.8	47	21	24	652	12	46	2	126	15	–	0.01	0.02	0.0
Albania	3.6	124	77	0.5	15	5	45	29	26	19	36	577	153	145	0.39	0.69	1.
Algeria	32.5	14	73	1.2	17	5	60	2,382	3	13	1	469	990	5	4.91	1.00	2.6
Angola	11.8	9	37	–0.1	45	26	37	1,247	3	43	56	415	1,081	6	4.41	0.29	1.1
Argentina	39.5	14	76	1.0	17	8	91	2,780	13	52	13	558	855	53	2.23	1.58	3.3
Armenia	3.0	100	72	–0.3	12	8	64	30	20	30	12	433	283	24	0.35	1.34	2.9
Australia	20.1	3	80	0.9	12	7	93	7,741	6	52	21	4,881	4,323	513	13.32	7.03	19
Austria	8.2	98	79	0.1	9	10	66	84	18	23	47	12,341	12,524	1,716	1.57	4.25	8.9
Azerbaijan	7.9	91	63	0.6	20	10	50	87	23	31	13	458	401	7.3	2.78	1.92	4.3
Bahamas	0.3	21	66	0.7	18	9	90	14	1	0.2	84	5,433	2,120	2,840	0	3.88	11.2
Bahrain	0.7	700	74	1.5	18	4	90	0.7	9	6	0	8,386	11,721	–	15.29	14.88	30.8
Bangladesh	144.3	1,002	62	2.1	30	8	25	144	65	5	10	70	52	0.4	0.07	0.10	0.2
Barbados	0.3	696	72	0.3	13	9	53	0.4	40	5	5	3,463	687	2,527	0.27	1.88	5.8
Belarus	10.3	50	69	–0.1	11	14	72	208	28	15	45	1,317	1,114	26	0.21	2.80	7.4
Belgium	10.4	335	79	0.2	10	10	97	31	25	21	22	22,596	24,587	782	1.20	6.63	13.6
Belize	0.3	13	67	2.3	29	6	49	23	4	2	59	1,933	1,338	520	0.07	1.14	3.0
Benin	7.6	67	51	2.8	42	14	46	113	25	5	24	123	95	11	0.01	0.09	0.2
Bhutan	2.2	47	54	2.1	34	13	9	47	4	9	64	89	70	3.6	0.24	0.21	0.2
Bolivia	8.9	8	66	1.5	24	8	64	1,099	3	31	49	179	223	13	0.92	0.44	1.2
Bosnia-Herzegovina	4.4	86	73	0.4	12	8	45	51	21	20	45	1,182	386	53	1.37	1.64	3.5
Botswana	1.6	3	34	0.0	23	29	52	582	1	45	22	1,409	1,838	223	0.38	0.81	2.
Brazil	186.1	22	72	1.1	17	6	84	8,514	8	23	63	328	510	13	0.91	1.17	1.9
Brunei	0.4	67	75	1.9	19	3	78	6	3	1	84	13,000	19,250	–	52.12	5.75	14.9
Bulgaria	7.5	68	72	–0.9	10	14	71	111	32	16	33	1,631	1,218	221	1.42	2.84	6
Burkina Faso	13.5	49	44	2.5	44	19	19	274	16	22	26	64	31	1.5	0	0.03	0.0
Burma (Myanmar)	47.0	69	56	0.4	18	12	31	677	16	1	52	37	45	1.2	0.21	0.10	0
Burundi	7.8	279	43	2.2	40	17	11	28	52	38	4	18	4,082	0.1	0.01	0.03	0.0
Cambodia	13.6	75	59	1.8	27	9	20	181	22	8	53	230	170	29	0	0.02	0.0
Cameroon	17.0	36	48	1.9	35	15	53	475	15	4	51	116	144	2.1	0.29	0.13	0.3
Canada	32.8	3	80	0.9	11	7	81	9,971	5	3	27	7,808	9,622	323	14.00	10.05	19.0
Cape Verde Is.	0.4	100	71	0.7	25	7	58	4	1	1	21	968	153	213	0	0.15	0.3
Central African Rep.	4.2	7	41	1.5	35	20	44	623	3	5	37	32	41	0.7	0.01	0.04	0.0
Chad	9.7	8	48	3.0	46	16	26	1,284	3	36	10	52	38	2.6	0	0.01	0.0
Chile	16.0	21	77	1.0	16	6	88	757	3	17	21	1,408	1,825	54	0.49	1.67	3
China	1,306.3	136	72	0.6	13	7	41	9,597	17	43	18	423	446	13	0.81	0.83	2.7
Colombia	43.0	38	72	1.5	21	6	77	1,139	4	40	48	357	360	19	1.79	0.72	1.1
Comoros	0.7	350	62	2.9	38	8	36	2	66	8	4	126	40	30	0	0.05	0.1
Congo	3.0	9	49	1.3	28	15	54	342	1	29	65	12	37	0.3	4.41	0.14	0.8
Congo (Dem. Rep.)	60.1	25	49	3.0	44	14	33	2,345	3	7	60	259	394	1.9	0.05	0.04	0.0
Costa Rica	4.0	78	77	1.5	19	4	62	51	10	46	39	1,961	1,546	323	0.48	0.96	1
Croatia	4.5	79	74	0.0	10	11	60	57	28	28	32	3,711	1,743	1,417	1.01	2.09	5.0
Cuba	11.3	103	77	0.3	12	7	76	111	34	26	21	469	186	163	0.30	1.05	3.0
Cyprus	0.8	89	78	0.5	13	8	70	9	13	0.4	13	7,091	1,429	2,519	0	3.59	10.2
Czech Republic	10.2	129	76	–0.1	9	11	75	79	43	13	34	6,685	6,521	349	2.65	3.87	10.9
Denmark	5.4	126	78	0.3	11	11	86	43	54	9	11	11,750	13,530	975	5.44	3.85	10.9
Djibouti	0.5	22	43	2.1	40	19	85	23	0	57	0	1,330	310	8	0	1.27	2
Dominican Republic	9.0	184	67	1.3	23	7	60	49	33	44	28	899	605	346	0.02	0.75	2.2
East Timor	1.0	67	66	2.1	27	6	8	15	–	–	–	167	8	–	–	–	
Ecuador	13.4	47	76	1.2	23	4	63	284	11	18	38	571	564	30	1.80	0.69	1.8
Egypt	77.5	77	71	1.8	23	5	42	1,001	3	0.0	0	248	142	59	0.89	0.77	1.8
El Salvador	6.7	319	71	1.8	27	6	60	21	43	38	6	891	485	34	0.14	0.45	0
Equatorial Guinea	0.5	18	56	2.4	36	12	50	28	8	4	62	2,334	5,542	28	23.55	2.51	8.0
Eritrea	4.7	39	52	2.5	39	14	21	118	4	58	16	132	1,371	16	0	0.05	0.1
Estonia	1.3	29	72	–0.7	10	13	70	45	15	2	49	5,629	4,385	519	0	3.33	13.8
Ethiopia	73.1	65	49	2.4	39	15	16	1,104	10	18	5	29	8	1	0.01	0.26	0.0
Fiji	0.9	50	70	1.4	23	6	53	18	16	10	45	928	677	388	0.17	0.53	1.7
Finland	5.2	15	78	0.2	11	10	61	338	7	0	72	8,687	11,738	364	2.04	5.91	10.4
France	60.7	111	77	0.4	12	9	77	552	36	18	28	6,914	6,903	610	2.12	4.55	6
Gabon	1.4	5	56	2.5	36	12	85	268	2	18	85	875	2,650	12	9.86	0.68	3.5
Gambia, The	1.6	145	55	2.9	40	12	26	11	26	46	48	113	72	18	0	0.07	0
Gaza Strip (OPT)*	1.4	4,667	72	3.8	40	4	–	0.4	–	–	–	1,357	146	2.9	–	–	
Georgia	4.7	67	76	–0.4	10	9	52	70	15	28	43	384	193	31	0.32	1.01	0.7
Germany	82.4	231	79	0.0	8	11	89	357	34	14	31	8,698	10,841	279	1.60	4.33	10.2
Ghana	21.9	92	56	1.3	24	11	46	239	28	37	28	169	137	19	0.10	0.17	0.2
Greece	10.7	81	79	0.2	10	10	61	132	30	36	28	5,073	1,449	1,000	0.96	3.25	9

WEALTH						SOCIAL INDICATORS										COUNTRY
GNI (million US$)	GNI per capita (PPP US$)	Average annual growth in GDP per capita (%)	Agriculture (% of GDP)	Industry (% of GDP)	Services (% of GDP)	Human Develop. Index (HDI) value	Food intake (calories per capita per day)	Population per doctor	Adults living with HIV/AIDS (% 15–49 year olds)	Gender Develop. Index (GDI) value	Illiteracy rate (% adults)	Motor vehicles per thousand people	Internet usage per thousand people	Aid donated (−)/received (US$ per capita)	Military spending (% of GDP)	
2004	2004	1990–2002	2004	2004	2004	2002	2003	2003	2003	2002	2003	2002	2003	2002	2004	
5,543	–	–	60	20	20	–	1,539.0	–	0.1	–	64	0.6	1	63	2.6	Afghanistan
6,641	5,070	6.0	46.2	25.4	28.4	0.781	2,847.8	730	0.1	0.778	13	70.5	10	90	1.5	Albania
3,676	6,260	0.3	10.3	57.4	32.3	0.704	3,021.5	1,176	0.1	0.688	30	88.2	16	6	3.2	Algeria
4,441	2,030	−0.1	8	67	25	0.381	2,082.7	20,000	3.9	–	58	18.4	3	35	10.6	Angola
2,338	12,460	1.7	10.6	35.9	53.5	0.853	2,992.1	329	0.7	0.841	3	197.7	112	256	1.3	Argentina
3,424	4,270	1.7	22.9	36.1	41.1	0.754	2,267.7	348	0.1	0.752	1	–	37	57	6.5	Armenia
1,173	29,200	2.6	3.4	28.2	68.4	0.946	3,053.6	405	0.1	0.945	0	623.8	567	−45	2.7	Australia
2,147	31,790	1.9	2.3	30.8	66.9	0.934	3,673.3	310	0.3	0.924	2	586	462	−63	0.9	Austria
7,828	3,830	0.2	14.1	45.7	40.2	0.746	2,574.8	279	0.1	–	3	57.9	37	18	2.6	Azerbaijan
4,684	16,140	0.1	3	7	90	0.815	2,754.9	613	3.0	0.825	4	342	192	33	–	Bahamas
8,834	18,070	1.5	0.7	41	58.4	0.843	–	592	0.3	0.832	11	325.3	246	214	6.3	Bahrain
1,230	1,980	3.1	21.2	27.1	51.7	0.509	2,205.0	4,348	0.1	0.499	57	1.5	2	11	1.8	Bangladesh
2,507	15,060	1.6	6	16	78	0.888	3,091.1	730	1.5	–	3	268.2	112	30	–	Barbados
0,856	6,900	0.2	11	36.4	52.6	0.790	3,000.3	222	0.3	0.789	1	155.8	141	19	1.4	Belarus
2,837	31,360	1.8	1.3	25.7	73	0.942	3,583.8	239	0.2	0.938	2	523.1	386	−104	1.3	Belgium
1,115	6,510	1.7	17.7	15	67.3	0.737	2,868.6	980	2.4	0.718	6	161	109	230	2.0	Belize
3,667	1,120	2.1	36.3	14.3	49.4	0.421	2,547.9	10,000	1.9	0.406	59	2.3	10	47	2.4	Benin
677	660	3.6	45	10	45	0.536	–	20,000	0.1	–	58	–	15	33	1.8	Bhutan
8,656	2,590	1.1	13	28	59	0.681	2,235.2	1,316	0.1	0.674	13	55.6	32	68	1.6	Bolivia
7,841	7,430	18.0	14.2	30.8	55	0.781	2,893.6	690	0.1	–	–	–	26	163	4.5	Bosnia-Herzegovina
7,490	8,920	2.5	4	44	52	0.589	2,151.4	3,448	37.3	0.581	20	73.7	35	46	3.9	Botswana
2,096	8,020	1.3	10.1	38.6	51.3	0.775	3,049.5	485	0.7	0.768	14	111.9	82	163	1.8	Brazil
–	–	−0.5	5	45	50	0.867	2,855.3	1,010	0.1	0.768	8	629.7	102	11	5.1	Brunei
1,326	7,870	−2.1	11.5	30.1	58.4	0.796	2,847.9	291	0.1	0.795	1	313.5	206	40	2.6	Bulgaria
4,436	1,220	1.6	39.5	19.3	41.3	0.302	2,461.9	25,000	4.2	0.291	73	4	4	36	1.3	Burkina Faso
–	–	5.7	56.6	8.8	34.5	0.551	2,937.1	3,333	1.2	–	17	5.7	1	3	2.1	Burma (Myanmar)
669	660	−3.9	48.1	19	32.9	0.339	1,648.6	100,000	6.0	0.337	48	2.5	2	15	6.0	Burundi
4,430	2,180	4.1	35	30	35	0.568	2,045.8	6,250	2.6	0.557	30	0.9	2	41	3.0	Cambodia
3,138	2,090	−0.1	43.7	20.1	36.2	0.501	2,273.2	14,286	6.9	0.491	21	11	4	78	1.6	Cameroon
5,629	30,660	2.2	2.3	26.4	71.3	0.943	3,589.3	535	0.3	0.941	3	581.6	513	−4	1.1	Canada
852	5,650	3.4	12.1	21.9	66	0.717	3,243.2	5,882	0.1	0.709	23	39.8	36	340	1.5	Cape Verde Is.
1,226	1,110	−0.2	55	20	25	0.361	1,980.4	25,000	13.5	0.345	49	3.1	1	20	1.0	Central African Rep.
2,277	1,420	−0.5	22.6	35.6	41.7	0.379	2,113.5	33,333	4.8	0.368	52	0.9	2	25	2.1	Chad
8,407	10,500	4.4	6.3	38.2	55.5	0.839	2,863.2	870	0.3	0.830	4	135	272	3	3.8	Chile
76,846	5,530	8.6	13.8	52.9	33.3	0.745	2,951.0	610	0.1	0.741	14	10.2	63	2	4.3	China
0,626	6,820	0.4	13.4	32.1	54.5	0.773	2,584.6	1,064	0.7	0.770	7	28.4	53	7	3.4	Colombia
328	1,840	−1.4	40	4	56	0.530	1,753.9	14,286	0.1	0.510	43	–	4	14	3.0	Comoros
2,974	750	−1.6	7.4	52	40.6	0.494	2,161.7	4,000	4.9	0.488	16	14.9	4	53	2.8	Congo
6,416	680	−8.1	55	11	34	0.365	1,599.1	14,286	4.2	0.355	34	–	1	3	1.5	Congo (Dem. Rep.)
8,969	9,530	2.7	8.5	29.7	61.8	0.834	2,875.5	625	0.6	0.823	4	136.6	193	3	0.4	Costa Rica
9,700	11,670	2.1	8.2	30.1	61.7	0.830	2,779.0	420	0.1	0.827	1	312.6	232	15	2.4	Croatia
–	–	3.5	6.6	25.5	67.9	0.809	3,151.8	168	0.1	–	3	0.9	11	6	1.8	Cuba
3,633	22,330	3.2	7.35	20.2	72.45	0.883	3,254.6	372	0.1	0.875	2	516.2	294	62	3.8	Cyprus
3,155	18,400	1.4	3.4	39.3	57.3	0.868	3,171.3	292	0.1	0.865	0	394.8	308	11	2.0	Czech Republic
9,422	31,550	2.1	2.2	25.5	72.3	0.932	3,439.3	273	0.2	0.931	0	430.6	513	−302	1.5	Denmark
739	2,270	−3.8	3.5	15.8	80.7	0.454	2,219.7	7,692	2.9	–	32	2.7	7	72	4.4	Djibouti
8,443	6,750	4.2	18	24	58	0.738	2,347.1	526	1.7	0.728	15	99.7	64	27	1.1	Dominican Republic
506	430	–	25.4	17.2	57.4	–	2,805.8	–	–	–	52	–	–	2200	–	East Timor
8,783	3,690	0.0	8.7	30.5	60.9	0.735	2,754.0	690	0.3	0.721	7	47.1	46	9	2.2	Ecuador
0,129	4,120	2.5	17.2	33	49.8	0.653	3,338.0	459	0.1	0.634	42	35.4	39	16	3.4	Egypt
5,613	4,980	2.3	9.2	31.1	59.7	0.720	2,583.8	794	0.7	0.709	20	63.5	84	38	1.1	El Salvador
437	7,400	20.8	3	95.7	1.3	0.703	–	4,000	3.4	0.691	14	–	4	68	2.5	Equatorial Guinea
806	1,050	1.5	12.4	25.9	61.7	0.439	1,512.8	20,000	2.7	0.431	41	–	7	18	13.4	Eritrea
9,435	13,190	2.3	4.1	28.9	67	0.853	3,002.2	319	1.0	0.852	1	359.4	444	83	2.0	Estonia
7,747	810	2.3	47	12.4	40.6	0.359	1,857.3	33,333	4.4	0.346	27	1.7	1	5	4.6	Ethiopia
2,281	5,770	1.8	16.6	22.4	61	0.758	2,893.6	2,941	0.1	0.747	7	126.1	61	45	2.2	Fiji
1,024	29,560	2.5	3.3	30.2	66.5	0.935	3,100.4	322	0.1	0.933	0	485.7	534	−73	2.0	Finland
58,731	29,320	1.6	2.7	24.3	73	0.932	3,653.9	303	0.4	0.929	1	590.4	366	−89	2.6	France
5,415	5,600	−0.2	7.4	46.7	45.9	0.648	2,636.8	–	8.1	–	37	16.4	26	236	2.0	Gabon
414	1,900	0.0	26.8	14.5	58.7	0.452	2,272.7	25,000	1.2	0.446	60	4	19	30	0.3	Gambia, The
3,771	1,110	−4.9	9	28	63	–	2,179.8	–	–	–	–	–	40	615	–	Gaza Strip (OPT)*
4,683	2,930	−3.9	20.5	22.6	56.9	0.739	2,354.3	216	0.1	–	1	62.1	31	32	0.6	Georgia
38,974	27,950	1.3	1	31	68	0.925	3,495.6	275	0.1	0.921	1	580.5	473	−68	1.5	Germany
8,090	2,280	1.8	34.3	24.2	41.4	0.568	2,667.2	11,111	3.1	0.564	25	10.5	8	332	0.6	Ghana
3,917	22,000	2.2	7	22	71	0.902	3,721.1	228	0.2	0.894	2	414.4	150	509	4.3	Greece

COUNTRY	POPULATION							LAND & AGRICULTURE				TRADE, TOURISM & ENERGY					
	Total population (millions)	Population density (persons per km²)	Life expectancy (years)	Average annual population change (%)	Birth rate (births per thousand people)	Death rate (deaths per thousand people)	Urban population (% of total)	Land area (thousand km²)	Arable & permanent crops (% of land area)	Permanent pasture (% of land area)	Forest (% of land area)	Imports (US$ per capita)	Exports (US$ per capita)	Tourism receipts (US$ per capita)	Energy produced (tonnes of oil equiv. per capita)	Energy consumed (tonnes of oil equiv. per capita)	CO_2 emissi per ca (met tonne
	2005	2005	2005	2005	2005	2005	2005	2002	2002	2002	2000	2004	2004	2003	2002	2002	200
Guatemala	12.0	110	65	2.6	34	7	47	109	18	24	26	648	243	52	0.12	0.30	0.8
Guinea	9.5	39	50	2.4	42	15	37	246	6	43	28	68	75	0	0.01	0.06	0.1
Guinea-Bissau	1.4	39	47	2.0	38	17	36	36	20	39	78	74	39	1.4	0	0.09	0.2
Guyana	0.8	4	66	0.3	19	8	39	215	3	6	86	813	713	49	0	0.83	2.2
Haiti	8.1	289	53	2.3	37	12	39	28	39	18	3	134	42	12	0.01	0.09	0.2
Honduras	7.2	64	66	2.2	31	7	46	112	13	13	48	463	202	47	0.08	0.37	0.8
Hungary	10.0	108	72	−0.3	10	13	66	93	52	12	20	5,868	5,462	344	1.02	2.63	5.9
Iceland	0.3	3	80	0.9	14	7	93	103	0	23	0	11,023	9,673	1,063	8.20	11.59	10.4
India	1,080.3	329	64	1.4	22	8	29	3,287	57	4	22	83	64	3.3	0.24	0.33	0.9
Indonesia	242.0	126	70	1.5	21	6	48	1,905	19	6	58	186	289	17	0.86	0.47	1.4
Iran	68.0	41	70	0.9	17	6	68	1,648	10	27	5	460	570	26	3.79	2.12	5.
Iraq	26.1	60	69	2.7	33	5	67	438	14	9	2	379	387	–	4.35	1.14	2.7
Ireland	4.0	57	78	1.2	15	8	60	70	16	48	10	15,163	25,950	969	0.27	3.92	10.2
Israel	6.3	300	79	1.2	18	6	92	21	20	7	6	5,848	5,462	324	0	3.20	10.5
Italy	58.1	193	80	0.1	9	10	68	301	38	15	34	5,668	5,790	537	0.54	3.29	8.1
Ivory Coast	17.3	54	49	2.1	36	15	46	322	22	41	–	194	296	4.9	0.16	0.15	0.3
Jamaica	2.7	245	76	0.7	17	5	52	11	26	21	30	1,342	622	502	0.02	1.39	4.2
Japan	127.4	337	81	0.1	9	9	66	378	13	1	64	3,154	4,229	70	0.84	4.31	9.4
Jordan	5.8	63	78	2.3	22	3	79	89	4	8	1	1,310	552	141	0.05	1.00	2.9
Kazakhstan	15.2	6	67	0.3	16	9	56	2,725	8	69	5	860	1,215	37	6.39	3.46	9.7
Kenya	33.8	58	48	2.6	40	15	42	580	9	37	30	124	77	10	0.03	0.12	0.2
Korea, North	22.9	189	71	0.9	16	7	62	121	23	0.4	68	92	52	–	1.14	1.20	3.1
Korea, South	48.6	496	76	0.4	10	6	80	99	19	1	63	4,407	5,156	108	0.64	4.32	9.8
Kuwait	2.3	128	77	3.4	22	3	96	18	1	8	0	4,835	11,922	51	49.91	10.35	23.1
Kyrgyzstan	5.1	26	68	1.3	22	7	34	200	7	49	5	152	127	9.4	0.59	1.13	0.9
Laos	6.2	26	55	2.4	36	12	22	237	4	4	54	93	59	14	0.14	0.16	0.1
Latvia	2.3	35	71	−0.7	9	13	66	65	30	10	47	2,596	1,552	97	0.34	2.08	3.
Lebanon	3.8	380	73	1.3	19	6	88	10	31	2	4	2,148	469	267	0.02	1.49	4.3
Lesotho	2.0	67	37	0.1	27	25	18	30	11	67	0	365	242	10	0.04	0.08	0.1
Liberia	2.9	26	48	2.7	44	18	48	111	6	21	36	1,742	372	–	0	0.04	0.1
Libya	5.8	3	77	2.3	27	3	87	1,760	1	8	0	1,246	3,216	14	13.89	2.98	8.9
Lithuania	3.6	55	74	−0.3	9	11	67	65	46	8	31	3,061	2,467	177	1.24	3.12	5.5
Luxembourg	0.5	167	79	1.3	12	8	92	3	–	–	–	32,600	26,800	5,586	0.09	8.48	24.2
Macedonia (FYROM)	2.0	80	74	0.3	12	9	60	26	24	25	36	1,339	815	29	0.82	1.31	4.1
Madagascar	18.0	31	57	3.0	42	11	27	587	6	41	20	64	48	4.2	0.01	0.04	0.1
Malawi	12.7	108	37	2.1	44	23	17	118	26	20	28	41	40	2.6	0.02	0.05	0.0
Malaysia	24.0	73	72	1.8	23	5	65	330	23	1	59	4,138	5,146	246	3.69	2.48	5.8
Mali	11.4	9	45	2.8	47	19	34	1,240	4	25	11	81	80	9.1	0.01	0.03	0.0
Malta	0.4	127	79	0.4	10	8	92	0.3	31	0	0	8,518	6,563	1,740	0	2.31	7.4
Mauritania	3.1	3	53	2.9	42	13	64	1,026	0	38	0	277	175	3.5	0	0.42	1.1
Mauritius	1.2	600	72	0.8	16	7	44	2	53	4	8	1,871	1,677	581	0.02	1.18	3.0
Mexico	106.2	54	75	1.2	21	5	76	1,958	14	42	29	1,797	1,718	89	2.28	1.58	3.9
Micronesia, Fed. States	0.1	100	70	−0.1	25	5	30	0.7	51	16	0	1,490	220	170	–	–	–
Moldova	4.5	132	65	0.2	15	13	46	34	65	12	10	407	229	13	0.02	0.93	2.4
Mongolia	2.8	2	65	1.5	22	7	57	1,567	1	83	7	357	305	51	0.54	0.75	3.1
Morocco	32.7	73	71	1.6	22	6	59	447	21	47	7	478	298	87	0.01	0.36	1.
Mozambique	19.4	24	40	1.5	36	21	38	802	6	56	39	50	36	5.1	0.12	0.13	0.0
Namibia	2.0	2	44	0.7	25	18	34	824	1	46	10	737	678	167	0.14	0.61	1.1
Nepal	27.7	196	60	2.2	32	9	16	147	23	12	27	51	21	7.2	0.02	0.06	0.1
Netherlands	16.4	390	79	0.5	11	9	67	42	28	29	11	15,409	17,872	564	3.98	6.01	16.0
New Zealand	4.0	15	79	1.0	14	8	86	271	13	52	30	4,943	4,963	994	4.51	5.49	9.9
Nicaragua	5.5	43	70	1.9	25	4	58	130	18	40	27	367	136	28	0.04	0.29	0.7
Niger	12.2	10	42	2.6	48	21	23	1,267	4	9	1	33	23	2.3	0.01	0.04	0.
Nigeria	128.8	140	47	2.4	41	17	48	924	36	43	15	133	264	2	0.94	0.17	0.7
Norway	4.6	14	79	0.4	12	9	81	324	3	1	29	9,991	16,661	552	57.43	10.83	9.9
Oman	3.0	14	73	3.3	37	4	79	310	0	5	0	2,124	4,380	73	21.41	3.11	8.6
Pakistan	162.4	202	63	2.0	31	8	35	796	29	6	3	86	93	0.7	0.18	0.29	0.6
Panama	3.1	40	72	1.3	20	7	58	76	9	21	39	2,311	1,838	189	0.21	1.72	4.1
Papua New Guinea	5.5	12	65	2.3	30	7	13	463	2	0.2	68	246	443	0.9	0.59	0.21	0.4
Paraguay	6.3	15	75	2.5	30	5	59	407	8	55	59	529	466	10	1.97	1.59	0.6
Peru	27.9	22	70	1.4	21	6	75	1,285	3	21	51	344	441	33	0.37	0.52	
Philippines	87.9	293	70	1.8	26	5	63	300	36	5	19		0.09	0.37	0.13	0.34	0.
Poland	38.6	123	74	0.0	11	10	62	323	47	14	31	2,114	1,968	105	1.97	2.17	7.4
Portugal	10.6	115	78	0.4	11	10	56	89	29	16	40	4,915	3,555	654	0.23	2.57	6.1
Qatar	0.9	82	74	2.6	16	5	92	11	2	5	0	6,833	16,667	–	85.75	15.28	45.7

	WEALTH					SOCIAL INDICATORS										COUNTRY
GNI million US$	GNI per capita (PPP US$)	Average annual growth in GDP per capita (%)	Agriculture (% of GDP)	Industry (% of GDP)	Services (% of GDP)	Human Develop. Index (HDI) value	Food intake (calories per capita per day)	Population per doctor	Adults living with HIV/AIDS (% 15–49 year olds)	Gender Develop. Index (GDI) value	Illiteracy rate (% adults)	Motor vehicles per thousand people	Internet usage per thousand people	Aid donated (–) /received (US$ per capita)	Military spending (% of GDP)	
2004	2004	1990–2002	2004	2004	2004	2002	2003	2003	2003	2002	2003	2002	2003	2002	2004	
26,945	4,140	1.3	22.7	19.5	57.9	0.649	2,219.1	917	1.1	0.635	29	61.8	33	17	0.8	Guatemala
3,681	2,130	1.7	25	38.2	36.8	0.425	2,408.9	7,692	3.2	–	64	2.4	5	39	1.7	Guinea
250	690	–2.2	62	12	26	0.350	2,024.2	5,882	10.0	0.329	58	–	15	82	3.1	Guinea-Bissau
765	4,110	4.1	38.3	19.9	41.8	0.719	2,691.7	3,846	2.5	0.715	1	100.8	142	361	0.9	Guyana
3,380	1,680	–3.0	30	20	50	0.463	2,086.2	4,000	5.6	0.458	47	19.3	18	16	0.9	Haiti
7,321	2,710	0.3	12.7	32.1	55.3	0.672	2,355.8	1,149	1.8	0.662	24	11.7	25	82	1.4	Honduras
3,315	15,620	2.4	3.3	31.4	65.3	0.848	3,483.2	282	0.1	0.847	1	305.2	232	25	1.8	Hungary
1,199	32,360	2.1	11.2	9.6	79.2	0.941	3,249.3	284	0.2	0.938	0	639.7	648	–	–	Iceland
4,580	3,100	4.0	23.6	28.4	48	0.595	2,459.0	1,961	0.8	0.572	40	12.9	17	3	2.5	India
8,007	3,460	2.1	14.6	45	40.4	0.692	2,903.9	6,250	0.1	0.685	11	27.6	38	12	3.0	Indonesia
3,984	7,550	2.2	11.2	40.9	48.7	0.732	3,084.9	–	0.1	0.713	21	25.8	72	6	3.3	Iran
–	–	–	13.6	58.6	27.8	–	2,197.0	–	0.1	–	60	47.2	1	32	–	Iraq
7,761	33,170	6.8	5	46	49	0.936	3,656.4	418	0.1	0.929	2	422.8	317	–71	0.9	Ireland
8,124	23,510	1.8	2.8	37.7	59.5	0.908	3,666.1	267	0.1	0.906	5	295.5	301	107	8.7	Israel
03,562	27,860	1.5	2.3	28.8	68.9	0.920	3,670.6	165	0.4	0.914	1	641.1	337	–17	1.8	Italy
3,263	1,390	–0.1	27.8	19.4	52.8	0.399	2,630.6	11,111	7.0	0.379	49	6.6	14	58	1.2	Ivory Coast
7,738	3,630	–0.1	6.1	32.7	61.3	0.764	2,684.7	1,176	1.2	0.762	12	74.8	228	6	0.4	Jamaica
49,910	30,040	1.0	1.3	24.7	74.1	0.938	2,760.9	495	0.1	0.932	1	566.8	483	–55	1.0	Japan
1,629	4,640	0.9	2.4	26	71.5	0.750	2,673.5	488	0.1	0.734	9	98.1	81	99	14.6	Jordan
3,780	6,980	–0.7	7.4	37.8	54.8	0.766	2,676.5	290	0.1	0.761	2	86.8	16	40	0.9	Kazakhstan
4,987	1,050	–0.6	19.3	18.5	62.4	0.488	2,090.1	7,143	6.7	0.486	15	16.7	13	14	1.3	Kenya
–	–	–	30.2	33.8	36	0.888	2,141.7	556	–	–	1	–	–	–	–	Korea, North
3,036	20,400	4.7	3.2	40.4	56.3	–	3,058.0	–	0.1	0.882	2	293.2	610	–4	2.8	Korea, South
3,052	19,510	–1.7	0.4	60.5	39.1	0.838	3,010.0	625	0.12	0.827	16	399.9	228	–4	5.3	Kuwait
2,050	1,840	–3.2	38.5	22.8	38.7	0.701	2,999.1	368	0.1	...	3	37.2	38	10	1.4	Kyrgyzstan
2,239	1,850	3.8	49.5	27.5	23	0.534	2,311.7	1,639	0.1	0.528	47	–	3	40	0.5	Laos
2,570	11,850	0.2	4.4	24.8	70.8	0.823	2,938.0	344	0.4	0.823	1	314.7	404	42	1.2	Latvia
2,668	5,380	3.1	12	21	67	0.758	3,195.9	365	0.1	0.755	13	416.5	117	230	3.1	Lebanon
1,336	3,210	2.4	15.2	43.9	40.9	0.493	2,638.3	14,286	28.9	0.483	15	–	10	22	2.3	Lesotho
391	130	–	76.9	5.4	17.7	–	1,899.8	781	5.9	–	42	9.7	0	28	0.2	Liberia
5,257	4,490	–	8.7	45.7	45.6	0.794	3,319.8	833	0.2	–	17	140.1	29	3	3.9	Libya
9,727	12,610	–0.3	6.1	33.4	60.5	0.842	3,324.5	248	0.1	0.841	1	375.7	202	63	1.9	Lithuania
5,302	61,220	3.7	0.5	16.3	83.1	0.933	3,701.0	394	0.2	0.926	0	746.9	370	–294	0.9	Luxembourg
4,855	6,480	–0.7	11.2	26	62.8	0.793	2,654.6	457	0.1	–	–	166.5	49	119	6.0	Macedonia (FYROM)
5,181	830	–0.9	29.3	16.7	54	0.469	2,004.6	11,111	1.7	0.462	31	4.9	4	20	1.2	Madagascar
1,922	620	1.1	54.8	19.2	26	0.388	2,154.6	–	14.2	0.374	37	6.9	3	45	0.7	Malawi
7,132	9,630	3.6	7.2	33.6	59.1	0.793	2,881.1	1,471	0.4	0.786	11	18.8	344	7	2.0	Malaysia
4,335	980	1.7	45	17	38	0.326	2,173.9	25,000	1.9	0.309	54	4.1	2	50	0.4	Mali
4,913	18,720	3.6	3	23	74	0.875	3,586.9	344	0.1	0.866	7	713.2	303	63	0.7	Malta
1,210	2,050	1.6	25	29	46	0.465	2,772.0	7,143	0.6	0.456	58	11.2	4	73	1.7	Mauritania
5,730	4,090	4.0	7.6	30	62.4	0.785	2,954.8	1,176	0.1	0.775	14	113.1	123	35	0.2	Mauritius
3,080	9,590	1.4	4	27.2	68.9	0.802	3,144.7	641	0.3	0.792	8	185.2	118	11	0.9	Mexico
252	590	–1.8	50	4	46	–	–	–	–	–	11	–	6	–	–	Micronesia, Fed. States
2,563	1,930	–6.9	22.4	24.8	52.8	0.681	2,806.0	369	0.2	0.678	1	64.3	80	23	0.4	Moldova
1,484	2,020	0.2	20.6	21.5	58	0.668	2,249.1	360	0.1	0.664	1	18	58	119	2.2	Mongolia
6,518	4,100	0.8	21.2	35.8	43	0.620	3,051.8	2,041	0.1	0.604	48	56.9	33	18	5.0	Morocco
4,710	1,160	4.5	21.1	32.1	46.9	0.354	2,078.9	50,000	12.2	0.339	52	8.7	3	34	2.2	Mozambique
4,813	6,960	0.9	11.3	30.8	57.9	0.607	2,277.5	3,448	21.3	0.602	16	38	34	80	3.1	Namibia
6,538	1,470	2.3	40	20	40	0.504	2,453.1	20,000	0.5	0.484	55	5.5	3	16	1.5	Nepal
5,148	31,220	2.2	2.4	24.5	73.1	0.942	3,362.3	305	0.2	0.938	1	438.6	522	–202	1.6	Netherlands
2,465	22,130	2.1	4.6	27.4	68	0.926	3,219.2	457	0.1	0.924	1	632.3	526	–25	1.0	New Zealand
4,452	3,300	1.5	20.7	24.7	54.6	0.667	2,298.0	1,613	0.2	0.66	32	36.5	17	138	0.7	Nicaragua
2,836	830	–0.8	39	17	44	0.292	2,130.4	33,333	1.2	0.278	82	8.9	1	30	1.1	Niger
3,983	930	–0.3	36.3	30.5	33.3	0.466	2,725.5	3,704	5.4	0.458	32	0.6	6	2	0.8	Nigeria
8,398	38,550	3.0	2.2	36.3	61.6	0.956	3,484.2	272	0.1	0.955	0	523.8	346	–304	1.9	Norway
0,508	13,250	0.9	3.1	41.1	55.8	0.770	–	730	0.1	0.747	24	191.6	71	26	11.4	Oman
0,663	2,160	1.1	22.6	24.1	53.3	0.497	2,418.8	1,471	0.1	0.471	54	11.1	10	5	4.9	Pakistan
3,468	6,870	2.5	7.2	13	79.8	0.791	2,271.7	826	0.9	0.785	7	96.3	62	66	1.1	Panama
3,262	2,300	0.5	34.5	34.7	30.8	0.542	2,175.0	16,667	0.6	0.536	34	20.6	14	74	1.4	Papua New Guinea
6,752	4,870	–0.5	25.3	24.9	49.8	0.751	2,565.3	2,041	0.5	0.736	6	66	20	14	0.9	Paraguay
5,043	5,370	2.2	8	27	65	0.752	2,570.9	971	0.5	0.736	9	50.1	104	33	1.4	Peru
6,930	4,890	1.1	14.8	31.9	53.2	0.753	2,379.3	870	0.1	0.751	4	34.3	44	14	1.0	Philippines
2,398	12,640	4.2	2.9	31.3	65.9	0.850	3,374.5	455	0.1	0.848	1	325.1	232	26	1.7	Poland
9,790	19,250	2.5	5.9	30.2	63.9	0.897	3,740.9	314	0.5	0.894	7	734.1	194	–26	2.3	Portugal
–	–	–	0.3	58.2	41.5	0.833	–	455	0.1	–	17	517.3	113	8	10.0	Qatar

COUNTRY	POPULATION							LAND & AGRICULTURE				TRADE, TOURISM & ENERGY					
	Total population (millions)	Population density (persons per km^2)	Life expectancy (years)	Average annual population change (%)	Birth rate (births per thousand people)	Death rate (deaths per thousand people)	Urban population (% of total)	Land area (thousand km^2)	Arable & permanent crops (% of land area)	Permanent pasture (% of land area)	Forest (% of land area)	Imports (US$ per capita)	Exports (US$ per capita)	Tourism receipts (US$ per capita)	Energy produced (tonnes of oil equiv. per capita)	Energy consumed (tonnes of oil equiv. per capita)	CO$_2$ emissi per ca (met tonne
	2005	2005	2005	2005	2005	2005	2005		2002	2002	2000	2004	2004	2003	2002	2002	200
Romania	22.3	94	71	−0.1	11	12	55	238	43	21	28	1,275	1,056	20	1.34	1.91	4.4
Russia	143.4	8	67	−0.4	10	15	73	17,075	7	5	50	648	1,133	31	7.94	4.78	11.2
Rwanda	8.4	323	47	2.4	41	16	22	26	55	19	12	31	8	3.7	0.01	0.04	0.1
St Lucia	0.2	200	74	1.3	20	5	31	0.5	30	3	15	1,335	330	1,410	0	0.63	2.3
Saudi Arabia	26.4	13	75	2.3	30	3	89	2,150	2	79	1	1,372	4,280	130	19.50	4.98	13.5
Senegal	11.7	60	57	2.5	35	11	51	197	13	29	32	182	117	16	0	0.15	0.4
Serbia & Montenegro[†]	10.8	106	75	0.0	12	10	52	102	37	18	2.8	883	300	14	1.06	1.60	4.7
Sierra Leone	5.9	82	73	2.2	43	21	40	72	8	31	67	45	8	10	0	0.06	0.1
Singapore	4.4	4,400	82	1.6	9	4	100	0.7	3	0	3	35,273	32,364	909	0	9.35	27.8
Slovak Republic	5.4	110	75	0.2	11	9	58	49	32	18	42	5,494	5,415	160	1.42	3.89	7.
Slovenia	2.0	100	76	0.0	9	10	51	20	10	15	55	8,035	7,485	671	1.81	3.78	8.3
Solomon Is.	0.5	18	73	2.7	31	4	17	29	3	1	91	134	148	4	0	0.13	0.3
Somalia	8.6	13	48	3.4	46	17	36	638	2	69	12	40	9	–	0	0.03	0.0
South Africa	44.3	36	43	−0.3	18	21	58	1,221	13	69	7	890	947	96	3.22	2.66	9.1
Spain	40.3	80	80	0.2	10	10	77	498	38	23	29	5,509	4,280	1,037	0.81	3.64	8.2
Sri Lanka	20.1	305	73	0.8	16	6	21	66	29	7	30	361	264	21	0.04	0.24	0.6
Sudan	40.2	16	59	2.6	36	9	41	2,506	7	49	26	87	84	2.9	0.29	0.10	0.2
Suriname	0.4	2	69	0.3	18	7	77	163	0	0	90	1,510	1,238	10	2.39	2.41	3.9
Swaziland	1.1	65	36	0.3	28	25	24	17	11	71	30	1,036	818	24	0.12	0.32	1.2
Sweden	9.0	20	80	0.2	10	10	83	450	7	1	66	10,886	13,522	589	3.83	6.18	6.2
Switzerland	7.5	183	80	0.5	10	8	68	41	11	27	30	16,147	17,427	1,243	2.12	4.24	
Syria	18.4	99	70	2.3	28	5	50	185	29	45	3	274	331	77	2.03	1.19	2.9
Taiwan	22.9	636	77	0.6	13	6	77	36	23	–	58	7,223	7,445	130	0.52	4.52	12.
Tajikistan	7.2	50	65	2.2	33	8	24	143	7	23	3	181	157	0.3	0.54	0.82	1.0
Tanzania	36.8	39	45	1.8	38	17	38	945	6	40	44	54	34	12	0.02	0.05	0.
Thailand	64.2	125	72	0.9	16	7	33	513	38	2	29	1,259	1,369	122	0.53	1.18	3.1
Togo	5.4	95	53	2.1	33	12	36	57	49	19	9	153	123	2.4	0	0.08	0.2
Trinidad & Tobago	1.0	200	69	−0.7	13	9	76	5	24	2	50	4,650	6,671	242	21.21	11.40	24.9
Tunisia	10.0	61	75	1.0	16	5	64	164	32	31	3	1,152	993	158	0.63	0.85	2.1
Turkey	69.7	89	72	1.1	17	6	67	775	37	17	13	1,356	997	189	0.34	1.12	2.8
Turkmenistan	5.0	10	61	1.8	30	9	46	488	4	65	8	570	800	–	12.17	3.01	8.8
Uganda	27.3	116	52	3.3	47	13	12	241	37	26	21	48	23	6.9	0.02	0.03	0.0
Ukraine	47.0	78	67	−0.6	10	16	67	604	55	13	17	669	700	20	1.86	3.43	7.1
United Arab Emirates	2.6	31	75	1.5	19	4	86	84	3	4	4	17,562	26,723	554	64.99	21.18	44.1
United Kingdom	60.4	247	78	0.3	11	10	89	242	24	46	11	7,275	5,748	377	4.50	3.97	9.5
USA	295.7	31	78	0.9	14	8	81	9,629	19	26	25	4,992	2,689	218	6.04	8.33	19.9
Uruguay	3.4	19	76	0.5	14	9	93	175	8	77	7	609	647	102	0.67	1.11	1.6
Uzbekistan	26.9	60	64	1.7	26	8	36	447	12	54	5	105	138	1.8	2.32	2.01	4.4
Venezuela	25.4	28	74	1.4	19	5	88	912	4	21	56	590	1,411	13	8.27	2.90	5.4
Vietnam	83.5	253	71	1.0	17	6	27	332	27	2	30	315	284	1	0.41	0.26	0.7
West Bank (OPT)*	2.4	400	73	3.1	32	4	–	6	–	–	–	625	85	1.7	–	–	
Western Sahara	0.3	1	–	2.2	–	–	94	266	0	19	0	–	–	–	0	0.32	1.0.
Yemen	20.7	39	62	3.5	43	9	26	528	3	30	1	180	216	6.7	1.16	0.19	0.
Zambia	11.3	15	38	2.1	41	20	37	753	7	40	42	134	137	13	0.21	0.25	0.2
Zimbabwe	12.2	31	37	0.5	30	25	36	394	9	44	49	131	115	3.6	0.32	0.41	0.8

NOTES

SERBIA & MONTENEGRO[†]
Serbia & Montenegro became separate states in June 2006. Kosovo separated from Serbia in February 2008.

OPT*
Occupied Palestinian Territory.

PER CAPITA
An amount divided by the total population of a country or the amount per person.

PPP
Purchasing Power Parity (PPP) is a method used to enable real comparisons to be made between countries when measuring wealth. The UN International Comparison Programme gives estimates of the PPP for each country, so it can be used as an indicator of real price levels for goods and services rather than using currency exchange rates (see GNI and GNI per capita).

POPULATION TOTAL
These are estimates of the mid-year total in 2005.

POPULATION DENSITY
The total population divided by the land area (both are recorded in the table above).

LIFE EXPECTANCY
The average age that a child born today is expected to live to, if mortality levels of today last throughout its lifetime.

AVERAGE ANNUAL CHANGE
These are estimates of the percentage growth or decline of a country's population as a yearly average.

BIRTH/DEATH RATES
These are 2005 estimates from the CIA World Factbook.

URBAN POPULATION
The urban population shows the percentage of the total population living in towns and cities (each country will differ with regard to the size or type of town that is defined as an urban area).

LAND AREA
This is the total land area of a country, less the area of major lakes and rivers, in square kilometres.

ARABLE AND PERMANENT CROPS
These figures give a percentage of the total land area that is used for crops and fruit (including temporary fallow land or meadows).

PERMANENT PASTURE
This is the percentage of land area that has permanent forage crops for cattle or horses, cultivated or wild. Some land may be classified both as permanent pasture or as forest (see Forest), especially areas of scrub or savanna.

FOREST
Natural/planted trees including cleared land that will be reforested in the near future as a percentage of the land area.

IMPORTS AND EXPORTS
The total value of goods imported into a country and exported to other countries, given in US dollars ($) per capita.

TOURISM RECEIPTS
The amount of income generated from tourism in US dollars per capita.

PRODUCTION AND CONSUMPTIO OF ENERGY
The total amount of commercial energ produced or consumed in a country pe capita (see note). It is expressed in met tonnes of oil equivalent (an energy uni giving the heating value derived from one tonne of oil).

CARBON DIOXIDE EMISSIONS
The amount of carbon dioxide that ea country produces per capita.

WEALTH · SOCIAL INDICATORS · COUNTRY

GNI (million US$)	GNI per capita (PPP US$)	Average annual growth in GDP per capita (%)	Agriculture (% of GDP)	Industry (% of GDP)	Services (% of GDP)	Human Develop. Index (HDI) value	Food intake (calories per capita per day)	Population per doctor	Adults living with HIV/AIDS (% 15–49 year olds)	Gender Develop. Index (GDI) value	Illiteracy rate (% adults)	Motor vehicles per thousand people	Internet usage per thousand people	Aid donated (–)/received (US$ per capita)	Military spending (% of GDP)	Country
2004	2004	1990–2002	2004	2004	2004	2002	2003	2003	2003	2002	2003	2002	2003	2002	2004	
63,910	8,190	0.1	13.1	33.7	53.2	0.778	3,454.6	529	0.1	0.775	2	166.2	184	17	2.5	Romania
37,335	9,620	–2.4	4.9	33.9	61.2	0.795	3,071.8	238	0.9	0.794	1	185.1	41	7	–	Russia
1,875	1,300	0.3	41.1	21.2	37.7	0.431	2,084.2	50,000	5.1	0.423	30	3.5	3	47	3.2	Rwanda
706	5,560	0.2	7	20	73	0.777	2,988.2	1,724	–	–	33	172.1	82	259	–	St Lucia
42,180	14,010	–0.6	4.2	67.2	28.6	0.768	2,844.5	654	0.1	0.739	21	372.2	67	–64	10.0	Saudi Arabia
6,967	1,720	1.2	15.9	21.4	62.7	0.437	2,279.5	10,000	0.8	0.429	60	28.3	22	33	1.5	Senegal
21,715	1,910	–	15.5	27.6	56.8	–	2,678.4	–	0.2	–	7	171.8	79	185	–	Serbia & Montenegro†
1,113	790	–5.9	49	30	21	0.273	1,936.0	11,111	7.0	–	69	7.9	2	17	1.7	Sierra Leone
104,994	26,590	3.8	0	32.6	67.4	0.902	–	714	0.2	0.884	7	134.9	509	0.3	4.9	Singapore
34,907	14,370	2.1	3.5	30.1	66.4	0.842	2,888.9	307	0.1	0.84	–	278.1	256	21	1.9	Slovak Republic
29,555	20,730	4.2	3	36	60	0.895	3,001.4	457	0.1	0.892	1	478.9	376	31	1.7	Slovenia
260	1,760	–2.4	42	11	47	0.624	2,264.9	7,692	–	–	–	–	5	56	–	Solomon Is.
–	–	–	65	10	25	–	1,628.0	–	1.0	–	62	1.4	9	7	0.9	Somalia
165,326	10,960	0.0	3.6	31.2	65.2	0.666	2,956.1	4,000	21.5	0.661	14	145.4	68	11	1.5	South Africa
875,817	25,070	2.3	3.5	28.5	68	0.922	3,370.6	304	0.5	0.916	2	545.9	239	–33	1.2	Spain
19,618	4,000	3.4	19.1	26.2	54.7	0.740	2,385.3	2,326	0.1	0.738	8	34	12	29	2.6	Sri Lanka
18,152	1,870	3.1	38.7	20.3	41	0.505	2,227.8	6,250	2.6	0.485	39	3.3	9	4	3.0	Sudan
997	1,990	0.5	13	22	65	0.780	2,652.1	2,000	1.2	–	7	203.5	42	108	0.7	Suriname
1,859	4,970	0.1	16.1	43.4	40.5	0.519	2,322.0	6,667	38.8	0.505	18	87.3	26	87	1.4	Swaziland
321,401	29,770	2.0	2	29	69	0.946	3,185.4	348	0.1	0.946	1	542.7	573	–189	1.7	Sweden
356,052	35,370	0.4	1.5	34	64.5	0.936	3,526.2	286	0.5	0.932	1	562.5	351	–147	1.0	Switzerland
21,125	3,550	1.8	25	31	44	0.710	3,038.0	704	0.1	0.689	23	32	13	11	5.9	Syria
–	–	–	1.7	30.9	67.4	–	–	–	–	–	14	–	–	–	2.6	Taiwan
1,779	1,150	–8.1	23.7	24.3	52	0.671	1,827.6	472	0.1	0.668	1	22	1	9	3.9	Tajikistan
1,560	660	0.7	43.2	17.2	39.6	0.407	1,974.9	25,000	8.8	0.401	22	3.8	7	33	0.2	Tanzania
158,703	8,020	2.9	9	44.3	46.7	0.768	2,467.3	3,333	1.5	0.766	4	126.1	111	2	1.8	Thailand
1,868	1,690	–0.7	39.5	20.4	40.1	0.495	2,345.4	16,667	4.1	0.477	39	16.2	42	14	1.9	Togo
11,360	11,180	2.9	2.7	47	50.3	0.801	2,732.4	1,333	3.2	0.795	2	219.8	106	22	0.6	Trinidad & Tobago
26,301	7,310	3.1	13.8	31.8	54.4	0.745	3,237.8	1,429	0.1	0.734	26	86.7	64	38	1.5	Tunisia
268,741	7,680	1.3	11.7	29.8	58.5	0.751	3,357.0	813	0.1	0.746	13	89.3	85	4	5.3	Turkey
6,615	6,910	–3.2	28.5	42.7	28.8	0.752	2,741.6	333	0.1	0.748	2	–	2	3	3.4	Turkmenistan
6,911	1,520	3.9	35.8	20.8	43.6	0.493	2,409.6	20,000	4.1	0.487	30	5.5	5	53	2.2	Uganda
60,297	6,250	–6.0	18	45.1	36.9	0.777	3,053.6	334	2	0.773	1	107.8	19	13	1.4	Ukraine
98,673	21,000	0.0	4	58.5	37.5	0.824	3,224.7	565	0.2	–	22	441.8	275	2	3.1	United Arab Emirates
2,016,393	31,460	2.4	1	26.3	72.7	0.936	3,412.2	610	0.1	0.934	1	497.9	423	–75	2.4	United Kingdom
12,150,931	39,710	2.0	0.9	19.7	79.4	0.939	3,774.1	358	0.6	0.936	3	800	551	–24	3.3	USA
13,414	9,070	1.4	7.9	27.4	64.8	0.833	2,828.0	258	0.3	0.829	2	217.3	119	7	2.0	Uruguay
11,860	1,860	–0.9	38	26.3	35.7	0.709	2,240.6	341	0.1	0.705	1	–	19	3	2.0	Uzbekistan
104,958	5,760	–1.0	0.1	46.5	53.4	0.778	2,336.3	500	0.5	0.77	7	100.2	60	3	1.5	Venezuela
45,082	2,700	5.9	21.8	40.1	38.1	0.691	2,566.2	1,852	0.4	0.689	6	0.7	43	34	2.5	Vietnam
3,771	1,110	–4.9	9	28	63	–	2,179.8	–	–	–	–	–	40	870	–	West Bank (OPT)*
–	–	–	–	–	40	–	–	–	–	–	–	–	–	–	–	Western Sahara
1,218	820	2.5	15.5	44.7	39.7	0.482	2,038.3	4,545	0.1	0.436	50	50.1	5	23	7.8	Yemen
4,748	890	–1.2	14.9	28.9	56.1	0.389	1,927.4	14,286	16.5	0.375	19	0.8	6	62	1.8	Zambia
6,165	2,180	–0.8	18.1	24.3	57.7	0.491	1,942.6	16,667	33.7	0.482	9	50.7	43	14	4.3	Zimbabwe

NI
oss National Income: this used to referred to as GNP (Gross National duct) and is a good indication of ountry's wealth. It is the income in dollars from goods and services in ountry for one year, including income m overseas.

I PER CAPITA
e GNI (see above) divided by the al population by using the PPP method e note).

ERAGE ANNUAL GROWTH IN GDP
e growth or decline of the Gross mestic Product per capita (decline wn as a negative [–] number), as an rage over the 12 years from 1990 to 2. The GDP is the value of all goods services made in a country in one r, but unlike GNI (see above) it does include income gained from abroad.

AGRICULTURE, INDUSTRY AND SERVICES
The percentage contributions that each of these three sectors makes to a country's GDP (see note).

HUMAN DEVELOPMENT INDEX (HDI)
Produced by the UN Development Programme using indicators of life expectancy, knowledge and standards of living to give a value between 0 and 1 for each country. A high value shows a higher human development.

FOOD INTAKE
The amount of food (measured in calories) supplied, divided by the total population. Belgium and Luxembourg are shown as one country.

POPULATION PER DOCTOR
The total population divided by the number of qualified doctors.

ADULTS LIVING WITH HIV/AIDS
The percentage of all adults (aged 15–49) who have the Human Immunodeficiency Virus or the Acquired Immunodeficiency Syndrome. The total number of adults and children with HIV/AIDS in 2002 was 42 million.

GENDER DEVELOPMENT INDEX (GDI)
Like the HDI (see note), the GDI uses the same UNDP indicators but gives a value between 0 and 1 to measure the social and economic differences between men and women. The higher the value, the more equality exists between men and women.

ILLITERACY
The percentage of all adult men and women (over 15 years) who cannot read or write simple sentences.

MOTOR VEHICLES AND INTERNET USAGE
These are good indicators of a country's development wealth. They are shown in total numbers per 1,000 people.

AID DONATED AND RECEIVED
Aid defined here is Official Development Assistance (ODA) in US dollars per capita. The OECD Development Assistance Committee uses donations from donor countries and redistributes the money in the form of grants or loans to developing countries on their list of aid recipients. Donations are shown in the table with a negative (–) number. The money is given for economic development and welfare and not for military purposes.

MILITARY SPENDING
Government spending on the military or defence as a percentage of GDP.

Each topic list is divided into continents and within a continent the items are listed in order of size. The bottom part of many of the lists is selective in order to give examples from as many different countries as possible. The figures are rounded as appropriate.

World, Continents, Oceans

	km²	miles²	%
The World	509,450,000	196,672,000	–
Land	149,450,000	57,688,000	29.3
Water	360,000,000	138,984,000	70.7
Asia	44,500,000	17,177,000	29.8
Africa	30,302,000	11,697,000	20.3
North America	24,241,000	9,357,000	16.2
South America	17,793,000	6,868,000	11.9
Antarctica	14,100,000	5,443,000	9.4
Europe	9,957,000	3,843,000	6.7
Australia & Oceania	8,557,000	3,303,000	5.7
Pacific Ocean	155,557,000	60,061,000	46.4
Atlantic Ocean	76,762,000	29,638,000	22.9
Indian Ocean	68,556,000	26,470,000	20.4
Southern Ocean	20,327,000	7,848,000	6.1
Arctic Ocean	14,056,000	5,427,000	4.2

Ocean Depths

Atlantic Ocean	m	ft
Puerto Rico (Milwaukee) Deep	8,605	28,232
Cayman Trench	7,680	25,197
Gulf of Mexico	5,203	17,070
Mediterranean Sea	5,121	16,801
Black Sea	2,211	7,254
North Sea	660	2,165
Indian Ocean	**m**	**ft**
Java Trench	7,450	24,442
Red Sea	2,635	8,454
Pacific Ocean	**m**	**ft**
Mariana Trench	11,022	36,161
Tonga Trench	10,882	35,702
Japan Trench	10,554	34,626
Kuril Trench	10,542	34,587
Arctic Ocean	**m**	**ft**
Molloy Deep	5,608	18,399

Mountains

Europe		m	ft
Elbrus	*Russia*	5,642	18,510
Mont Blanc	*France/Italy*	4,807	15,771
Monte Rosa	*Italy/Switzerland*	4,634	15,203
Dom	Switzerland	4,545	14,911
Liskamm	*Switzerland*	4,527	14,852
Weisshorn	*Switzerland*	4,505	14,780
Taschorn	Switzerland	4,490	14,730
Matterhorn/Cervino	*Italy/Switzerland*	4,478	14,691
Mont Maudit	*France/Italy*	4,465	14,649
Dent Blanche	*Switzerland*	4,356	14,291
Nadelhorn	*Switzerland*	4,327	14,196
Grandes Jorasses	*France/Italy*	4,208	13,806
Jungfrau	*Switzerland*	4,158	13,642
Grossglockner	*Austria*	3,797	12,457
Mulhacén	*Spain*	3,478	11,411
Zugspitze	*Germany*	2,962	9,718
Olympus	*Greece*	2,917	9,570
Triglav	*Slovenia*	2,863	9,393
Gerlachovsky	*Slovak Republic*	2,655	8,711
Galdhøpiggen	*Norway*	2,469	8,100
Kebnekaise	*Sweden*	2,117	6,946
Ben Nevis	*UK*	1,342	4,403
Asia		**m**	**ft**
Everest	*China/Nepal*	8,850	29,035
K2 (Godwin Austen)	*China/Kashmir*	8,611	28,251
Kanchenjunga	*India/Nepal*	8,598	28,208
Lhotse	*China/Nepal*	8,516	27,939
Makalu	*China/Nepal*	8,481	27,824
Cho Oyu	*China/Nepal*	8,201	26,906
Dhaulagiri	*Nepal*	8,167	26,795
Manaslu	*Nepal*	8,156	26,758
Nanga Parbat	*Kashmir*	8,126	26,660
Annapurna	*Nepal*	8,078	26,502
Gasherbrum	*China/Kashmir*	8,068	26,469
Xixabangma	*China*	8,012	26,286
Kangbachen	*India/Nepal*	7,902	25,925
Trivor	*Pakistan*	7,720	25,328
Pik Kommunizma	*Tajikistan*	7,495	24,590
Demavend	*Iran*	5,604	18,386
Ararat	*Turkey*	5,165	16,945
Gunong Kinabalu	*Malaysia (Borneo)*	4,101	13,455
Fuji-San	*Japan*	3,776	12,388
Africa		**m**	**ft**
Kilimanjaro	*Tanzania*	5,895	19,340
Mt Kenya	*Kenya*	5,199	17,057
Ruwenzori	*Uganda/Congo (D.R.)*	5,109	16,762
Ras Dashen	*Ethiopia*	4,620	15,157
Meru	*Tanzania*	4,565	14,977
Karisimbi	*Rwanda/Congo (D.R.)*	4,507	14,787
Mt Elgon	*Kenya/Uganda*	4,321	14,176
Batu	*Ethiopia*	4,307	14,130
Toubkal	*Morocco*	4,165	13,665
Mt Cameroun	*Cameroon*	4,070	13,353
Oceania		**m**	**ft**
Puncak Jaya	*Indonesia*	5,029	16,499
Puncak Trikora	*Indonesia*	4,730	15,518
Puncak Mandala	*Indonesia*	4,702	15,427
Mt Wilhelm	*Papua New Guinea*	4,508	14,790
Mauna Kea	*USA (Hawaii)*	4,205	13,796
Mauna Loa	*USA (Hawaii)*	4,169	13,678
Aoraki Mt Cook	*New Zealand*	3,753	12,313
Mt Kosciuszko	*Australia*	2,228	7,309
North America		**m**	**ft**
Mt McKinley (Denali)	*USA (Alaska)*	6,194	20,321
Mt Logan	*Canada*	5,959	19,551
Pico de Orizaba	*Mexico*	5,610	18,405
Mt St Elias	*USA/Canada*	5,489	18,008
Popocatépetl	*Mexico*	5,452	17,887
Mt Foraker	*USA (Alaska)*	5,304	17,401
Iztaccihuatl	*Mexico*	5,286	17,342
Lucania	*Canada*	5,226	17,146
Mt Steele	*Canada*	5,073	16,644
Mt Bona	*USA (Alaska)*	5,005	16,420
Mt Whitney	*USA*	4,418	14,495
Tajumulco	*Guatemala*	4,220	13,845
Chirripó Grande	*Costa Rica*	3,837	12,589
Pico Duarte	*Dominican Rep.*	3,175	10,417
South America		**m**	**ft**
Aconcagua	*Argentina*	6,962	22,841
Bonete	*Argentina*	6,872	22,546
Ojos del Salado	*Argentina/Chile*	6,863	22,516
Pissis	*Argentina*	6,779	22,241
Mercedario	*Argentina/Chile*	6,770	22,211
Huascarán	*Peru*	6,768	22,204
Llullaillaco	*Argentina/Chile*	6,723	22,057
Nudo de Cachi	*Argentina*	6,720	22,047
Yerupaja	*Peru*	6,632	21,758
Sajama	*Bolivia*	6,520	21,391
Chimborazo	*Ecuador*	6,267	20,561
Pico Cristóbal Colón	*Colombia*	5,800	19,029
Pico Bolivar	*Venezuela*	5,007	16,427
Antarctica		**m**	**ft**
Vinson Massif		4,897	16,066
Mt Kirkpatrick		4,528	14,855

Rivers

Europe		km	miles
Volga	*Caspian Sea*	3,700	2,300
Danube	*Black Sea*	2,850	1,770
Ural	*Caspian Sea*	2,535	1,575
Dnieper	*Black Sea*	2,285	1,420
Kama	*Volga*	2,030	1,260
Don	*Volga*	1,990	1,240
Petchora	*Arctic Ocean*	1,790	1,110
Oka	*Volga*	1,480	920
Dniester	*Black Sea*	1,400	870
Vyatka	*Kama*	1,370	850
Rhine	*North Sea*	1,320	820
N. Dvina	*Arctic Ocean*	1,290	800
Elbe	*North Sea*	1,145	710
Asia		**km**	**miles**
Yangtze	*Pacific Ocean*	6,380	3,960
Yenisey–Angara	*Arctic Ocean*	5,550	3,445
Huang He	*Pacific Ocean*	5,464	3,395
Ob–Irtysh	*Arctic Ocean*	5,410	3,360
Mekong	*Pacific Ocean*	4,500	2,795
Amur	*Pacific Ocean*	4,442	2,760
Lena	*Arctic Ocean*	4,402	2,735
Irtysh	*Ob*	4,250	2,640
Yenisey	*Arctic Ocean*	4,090	2,540
Ob	*Arctic Ocean*	3,680	2,285
Indus	*Indian Ocean*	3,100	1,925
Brahmaputra	*Indian Ocean*	2,900	1,800
Syrdarya	*Aral Sea*	2,860	1,775
Salween	*Indian Ocean*	2,800	1,740
Euphrates	*Indian Ocean*	2,700	1,675
Amudarya	*Aral Sea*	2,540	1,575
Africa		**km**	**miles**
Nile	*Mediterranean*	6,670	4,140
Congo	*Atlantic Ocean*	4,670	2,900
Niger	*Atlantic Ocean*	4,180	2,595
Zambezi	*Indian Ocean*	3,540	2,200
Oubangi/Uele	*Congo (Dem. Rep.)*	2,250	1,400
Kasai	*Congo (Dem. Rep.)*	1,950	1,210
Shaballe	*Indian Ocean*	1,930	1,200
Orange	*Atlantic Ocean*	1,860	1,155
Cubango	*Okavango Delta*	1,800	1,120
Limpopo	*Indian Ocean*	1,770	1,100
Senegal	*Atlantic Ocean*	1,640	1,020
Australia		**km**	**miles**
Murray–Darling	*Southern Ocean*	3,750	2,330
Darling	*Murray*	3,070	1,905
Murray	*Southern Ocean*	2,575	1,600
Murrumbidgee	*Murray*	1,690	1,050
North America		**km**	**miles**
Mississippi–Missouri	*Gulf of Mexico*	5,971	3,710
Mackenzie	*Arctic Ocean*	4,240	2,630
Missouri	*Mississippi*	4,088	2,540
Mississippi	*Gulf of Mexico*	3,782	2,350
Yukon	*Pacific Ocean*	3,185	1,980
Rio Grande	*Gulf of Mexico*	3,030	1,880
Arkansas	*Mississippi*	2,340	1,450
Colorado	*Pacific Ocean*	2,330	1,445
Red	*Mississippi*	2,040	1,270
Columbia	*Pacific Ocean*	1,950	1,210
Saskatchewan	*Lake Winnipeg*	1,940	1,205
South America		**km**	**miles**
Amazon	*Atlantic Ocean*	6,450	4,010
Paraná–Plate	*Atlantic Ocean*	4,500	2,800
Purus	*Amazon*	3,350	2,080
Madeira	*Amazon*	3,200	1,990
São Francisco	*Atlantic Ocean*	2,900	1,800
Paraná	*Plate*	2,800	1,740
Tocantins	*Atlantic Ocean*	2,750	1,710
Orinoco	*Atlantic Ocean*	2,740	1,700
Paraguay	*Paraná*	2,550	1,580
Pilcomayo	*Paraná*	2,500	1,550
Araguaia	*Tocantins*	2,250	1,400

Lakes

Europe		km²	miles²
Lake Ladoga	*Russia*	17,700	6,800
Lake Onega	*Russia*	9,700	3,700
Saimaa system	*Finland*	8,000	3,100
Vänern	*Sweden*	5,500	2,100
Asia		**km²**	**miles²**
Caspian Sea	*Asia*	371,000	143,000
Lake Baikal	*Russia*	30,500	11,780
Aral Sea	*Kazakhstan/Uzbekistan*	28,687	11,086
Tonlé Sap	*Cambodia*	20,000	7,700
Lake Balqash	*Kazakhstan*	18,500	7,100
Africa		**km²**	**miles²**
Lake Victoria	*East Africa*	68,000	26,000
Lake Tanganyika	*Central Africa*	33,000	13,000
Lake Malawi/Nyasa	*East Africa*	29,600	11,430
Lake Chad	*Central Africa*	25,000	9,700
Lake Turkana	*Ethiopia/Kenya*	8,500	3,290
Lake Volta	*Ghana*	8,480	3,270
Australia		**km²**	**miles²**
Lake Eyre	*Australia*	8,900	3,400
Lake Torrens	*Australia*	5,800	2,200
Lake Gairdner	*Australia*	4,800	1,900
North America		**km²**	**miles²**
Lake Superior	*Canada/USA*	82,350	31,800
Lake Huron	*Canada/USA*	59,600	23,010
Lake Michigan	*USA*	58,000	22,400
Great Bear Lake	*Canada*	31,800	12,280
Great Slave Lake	*Canada*	28,500	11,000
Lake Erie	*Canada/USA*	25,700	9,900
Lake Winnipeg	*Canada*	24,400	9,400
Lake Ontario	*Canada/USA*	19,500	7,500
Lake Nicaragua	*Nicaragua*	8,200	3,200
South America		**km²**	**miles²**
Lake Titicaca	*Bolivia/Peru*	8,300	3,200
Lake Poopo	*Bolivia*	2,800	1,100

Islands

Europe		km²	miles²
Great Britain	*UK*	229,880	88,700
Iceland	*Atlantic Ocean*	103,000	39,800
Ireland	*Ireland/UK*	84,400	32,600
Novaya Zemlya (N.)	*Russia*	48,200	18,600
Sicily	*Italy*	25,500	9,800
Corsica	*France*	8,700	3,400
Asia		**km²**	**miles²**
Borneo	*South-east Asia*	744,360	287,400
Sumatra	*Indonesia*	473,600	182,860
Honshu	*Japan*	230,500	88,980
Celebes	*Indonesia*	189,000	73,000
Java	*Indonesia*	126,700	48,900
Luzon	*Philippines*	104,700	40,400
Hokkaido	*Japan*	78,400	30,300
Africa		**km²**	**miles²**
Madagascar	*Indian Ocean*	587,040	226,660
Socotra	*Indian Ocean*	3,600	1,400
Réunion	*Indian Ocean*	2,500	965
Oceania		**km²**	**miles²**
New Guinea	*Indonesia/Papua NG*	821,030	317,000
New Zealand (S.)	*Pacific Ocean*	150,500	58,100
New Zealand (N.)	*Pacific Ocean*	114,700	44,300
Tasmania	*Australia*	67,800	26,200
Hawaii	*Pacific Ocean*	10,450	4,000
North America		**km²**	**miles²**
Greenland	*Atlantic Ocean*	2,175,600	839,800
Baffin Is.	*Canada*	508,000	196,100
Victoria Is.	*Canada*	212,200	81,900
Ellesmere Is.	*Canada*	212,000	81,800
Cuba	*Caribbean Sea*	110,860	42,800
Hispaniola	*Dominican Rep./Haiti*	76,200	29,400
Jamaica	*Caribbean Sea*	11,400	4,400
Puerto Rico	*Atlantic Ocean*	8,900	3,400
South America		**km²**	**miles²**
Tierra del Fuego	*Argentina/Chile*	47,000	18,100
Falkland Is. (E.)	*Atlantic Ocean*	6,800	2,600

How to use the Index

The index contains the names of all the principal places and features shown on the maps. Each name is followed by an additional entry in italics giving the country or region within which it is located. The alphabetical order of names composed of two or more words is governed primarily by the first word and then by the second. This is an example of the rule:

Abbeville *France* 50°6N 1°49E **68** A4
Abbey Town *U.K.* 54°51N 3°17W **22** C2
Abbot Ice Shelf *Antarctica* 73°0S 92°0W **55** D16
Abbots Bromley *U.K.* 52°50N 1°52W **23** G5

Physical features composed of a proper name (Erie) and a description (Lake) are positioned alphabetically by the proper name. The description is positioned after the proper name and is usually abbreviated:

Erie, L. *N. Amer.* 42°15N 81°0W **112** D7

Where a description forms part of a settlement or administrative name, however, it is always written in full and put in its true alphabetical position:

Mount Isa *Australia* 20°42S 139°26E **98** E6

Names beginning with M' and Mc are indexed as if they were spelled Mac. Names beginning St. are alphabetized under Saint, but Santa and San are spelled in full and are alphabetized accordingly. If the same place name occurs two or more times in the index and all are in the same country, each is followed by the name of the administrative subdivision in which it is located.

The geographical co-ordinates that follow each name in the index give the latitude and longitude of each place. The first co-ordinate indicates latitude – the distance north or south of the Equator. The second co-ordinate indicates longitude – the distance east or west of the Greenwich Meridian. Both latitude and longitude are measured in degrees and minutes (there are 60 minutes in a degree).

The latitude is followed by N(orth) or S(outh) and the longitude by E(ast) or W(est).

The number in bold type that follows the geographical co-ordinates refers to the number of the map page where that feature or place will be found. This is usually the largest scale at which the place or feature appears.

The letter and figure that are immediately after the page number give the grid square on the map page, within which the feature is situated. The letter represents the latitude and the figure the longitude. A lower-case letter immediately after the page number refers to an inset map on that page.

In some cases the feature itself may fall within the specified square, while the name is outside. This is usually the case only with features that are larger than a grid square.

Rivers are indexed to their mouths or confluences, and carry the symbol → after their names. The following symbols are also used in the index: ■ country, ⊠ overseas territory or dependency, □ first-order administrative area, △ national park, ✈ (LHR) principal airport (and location identifier).

Abbreviations used in the Index

Afghan. – Afghanistan
Ala. – Alabama
Alta. – Alberta
Amer. – America(n)
Arch. – Archipelago
Ariz. – Arizona
Ark. – Arkansas
Atl. Oc. – Atlantic Ocean
B. – Baie, Bahía, Bay, Bucht, Bugt
B.C. – British Columbia
Bangla. – Bangladesh
C. – Cabo, Cap, Cape, Coast
C.A.R. – Central African Republic
Calif. – California
Cent. – Central
Chan. – Channel
Colo. – Colorado
Conn. – Connecticut
Cord. – Cordillera
Cr. – Creek
D.C. – District of Columbia
Del. – Delaware
Dom. Rep. – Dominican Republic
E. – East
El Salv. – El Salvador
Eq. Guin. – Equatorial Guinea
Fla. – Florida
Falk. Is. – Falkland Is.
G. – Golfe, Golfo, Gulf
Ga. – Georgia
Hd. – Head
Hts. – Heights
I.(s). – Île, Ilha, Insel, Isla, Island, Isle(s)
Ill. – Illinois
Ind. – Indiana
Ind. Oc. – Indian Ocean
Ivory C. – Ivory Coast
Kans. – Kansas
Ky. – Kentucky
L. – Lac, Lacul, Lago, Lagoa, Lake, Limni, Loch, Lough
La. – Louisiana
Lux. – Luxembourg
Madag. – Madagascar
Man. – Manitoba
Mass. – Massachusetts
Md. – Maryland
Me. – Maine
Mich. – Michigan
Minn. – Minnesota
Miss. – Mississippi
Mo. – Missouri
Mont. – Montana
Mozam. – Mozambique
Mt.(s) – Mont, Monte, Monti, Montaña, Mountain
N. – Nord, Norte, North, Northern,
N.B. – New Brunswick
N.C. – North Carolina
N. Cal. – New Caledonia
N. Dak. – North Dakota
N.H. – New Hampshire
N.J. – New Jersey
N. Mex. – New Mexico
N.S. – Nova Scotia
N.S.W. – New South Wales
N.W.T. – North West Territory
N.Y. – New York
N.Z. – New Zealand
Nat. Park – National Park
Nebr. – Nebraska
Neths. – Netherlands
Nev. – Nevada
Nfld. – Newfoundland and Labrador
Nic. – Nicaragua
Okla. – Oklahoma
Ont. – Ontario
Oreg. – Oregon
P.E.I. – Prince Edward Island
Pa. – Pennsylvania
Pac. Oc. – Pacific Ocean
Papua N.G. – Papua New Guinea
Pen. – Peninsula, Péninsule
Phil. – Philippines
Pk. – Peak
Plat. – Plateau
Prov. – Province, Provincial
Pt. – Point
Pta. – Ponta, Punta
Pte. – Pointe
Qué. – Québec
Queens. – Queensland
R. – Rio, River
R.I. – Rhode Island
Ra.(s) – Range(s)
Reg. – Region
Rep. – Republic
Res. – Reserve, Reservoir
S. – San, South
Si. Arabia – Saudi Arabia
S.C. – South Carolina
S. Dak. – South Dakota
Sa. – Serra, Sierra
Sask. – Saskatchewan
Scot. – Scotland
Sd. – Sound
Sib. – Siberia
St. – Saint, Sankt, Sint
Str. – Strait, Stretto
Switz. – Switzerland
Tas. – Tasmania
Tenn. – Tennessee
Tex. – Texas
Trin. & Tob.. – Trinidad & Tobago
U.A.E. – United Arab Emirates
U.K. – United Kingdom
U.S.A. – United States of America
Va. – Virginia
Vic. – Victoria
Vol. – Volcano
Vt. – Vermont
W. – West
W. Va. – West Virginia
Wash. – Washington
Wis. – Wisconsin

A

Aachen *Germany* 50°45N 6°6E **66** C4
Aalborg *Denmark* 57°2N 9°54E **63** F5
Aalst *Belgium* 50°56N 4°2E **65** D4
Aarau *Switz.* 47°23N 8°4E **66** E5
Aare → *Switz.* 47°33N 8°14E **66** E5
Aba *Nigeria* 5°10N 7°19E **94** G7
Abaco I. *Bahamas* 26°25N 77°10W **115** B9
Ābādān *Iran* 30°22N 48°20E **86** D7
Abaetetuba *Brazil* 1°40S 48°50W **120** C5
Abakan *Russia* 53°40N 91°10E **79** D11
Abancay *Peru* 13°35S 72°55W **120** D2
Abariringa *Kiribati* 2°50S 171°40W **99** A16
Abaya, L. *Ethiopia* 6°30N 37°50E **88** F2
Abbé, L. *Ethiopia* 11°8N 41°47E **88** E3
Abbeville *France* 50°6N 1°49E **68** A4
Abbey Town *U.K.* 54°51N 3°17W **22** C2
Abbot Ice Shelf *Antarctica* 73°0S 92°0W **55** D16
Abbots Bromley *U.K.* 52°50N 1°52W **23** G5
Abbotsbury *U.K.* 50°40N 2°37W **24** E3
Abéché *Chad* 13°50N 20°35E **95** F10
Abeokuta *Nigeria* 7°3N 3°19E **94** G6
Aberaeron *U.K.* 52°15N 4°15W **26** C5
Aberchirder *U.K.* 57°34N 2°37W **19** G12
Aberdare *U.K.* 51°43N 3°27W **26** D7
Aberdeen *U.K.* 57°9N 2°5W **19** H13
Aberdeen *S. Dak., U.S.A.* 45°28N 98°29W **110** A7
Aberdeen *Wash., U.S.A.* 46°59N 123°50W **110** A2
Aberdeenshire □ *U.K.* 57°17N 2°36W **19** H12
Aberdyfi *U.K.* 52°33N 4°3W **26** B5
Aberfeldy *U.K.* 56°37N 3°51W **21** A8
Aberfoyle *U.K.* 56°11N 4°23W **20** B7
Abergavenny *U.K.* 51°49N 3°1W **26** D7
Abergele *U.K.* 53°17N 3°35W **26** A6
Aberporth *U.K.* 52°8N 4°33W **26** C4
Abersoch *U.K.* 52°49N 4°30W **26** B5
Abersychan *U.K.* 51°44N 3°3W **26** D7
Abert, L. *U.S.A.* 42°38N 120°14W **110** B2
Abertillery *U.K.* 51°44N 3°8W **26** D7
Aberystwyth *U.K.* 52°25N 4°5W **26** C5
Abhā *Si. Arabia* 18°0N 42°34E **88** D3
Abidjan *Ivory C.* 5°26N 3°58W **94** G5
Abilene *U.S.A.* 32°28N 99°43W **110** D7
Abingdon *U.K.* 51°40N 1°17W **24** C6
Abitibi, L. *Canada* 48°40N 79°40W **109** E12
Abkhazia □ *Georgia* 43°12N 41°5E **73** F7
Abomey *Benin* 7°10N 2°5E **94** G6
Aboyne *U.K.* 57°4N 2°47W **19** H12
Absaroka Range *U.S.A.* 44°45N 109°50W **110** B5
Abu Dhabi *U.A.E.* 24°28N 54°22E **87** E8
Abu Hamed *Sudan* 19°32N 33°13E **95** E12
Abuja *Nigeria* 9°5N 7°32E **94** G7
Abunã *Brazil* 9°40S 65°20W **120** C3
Abunã → *Brazil* 9°41S 65°20W **120** C3
Acaponeta *Mexico* 22°30N 105°22W **114** C3
Acapulco *Mexico* 16°51N 99°55W **114** D5
Acarai, Serra *Brazil* 1°50N 57°50W **120** B4
Acarigua *Venezuela* 9°33N 69°12W **120** B3
Accomac *U.S.A.* 37°43N 75°40W **113** G10
Accra *Ghana* 5°35N 0°6W **94** G5
Accrington *U.K.* 53°45N 2°22W **23** E4
Aceh □ *Indonesia* 4°15N 97°30E **83** C1
Acharnes *Greece* 38°5N 23°44E **71** E10
Acheloos → *Greece* 38°19N 21°7E **71** E9
Achill Hd. *Ireland* 53°58N 10°15W **28** D1
Achill I. *Ireland* 53°58N 10°1W **28** D1
Acklins I. *Bahamas* 22°30N 74°0W **115** C10
Acle *U.K.* 52°39N 1°33E **25** A12
Aconcagua, Cerro *Argentina* 32°39S 70°0W **121** F3
Acre □ *Brazil* 9°1S 71°0W **120** C2
Acre → *Brazil* 8°45S 67°22W **120** C3
Acton Burnell *U.K.* 52°37N 2°41W **23** G3
Ad Dammām *Si. Arabia* 26°20N 50°5E **86** E7
Ad Dīwānīyah *Iraq* 32°0N 45°0E **86** D6
Adair, C. *Canada* 71°30N 71°34W **109** B12
Adak I. *U.S.A.* 51°45N 176°45W **108** D2
Adamawa Highlands *Cameroon* 7°20N 12°20E **95** G7
Adam's Bridge *Sri Lanka* 9°15N 79°40E **84** Q11
Adana *Turkey* 37°0N 35°16E **73** G6
Adare, C. *Antarctica* 71°0S 171°0E **55** D11
Addis Ababa *Ethiopia* 9°2N 38°42E **88** F2
Adelaide *Australia* 34°52S 138°30E **98** G6
Adelaide I. *Antarctica* 67°15S 68°30W **55** C17
Adelaide Pen. *Canada* 68°15N 97°30W **108** C10
Adélie, Terre *Antarctica* 68°0S 140°0E **55** C10
Aden *Yemen* 12°45N 45°0E **88** E4
Aden, G. of *Asia* 12°30N 47°30E **88** E4
Adige → *Italy* 45°9N 12°20E **70** B5
Adigrat *Ethiopia* 14°20N 39°26E **88** E2
Adirondack Mts. *U.S.A.* 44°0N 74°0W **113** D10
Adjuntas *Puerto Rico* 18°10N 66°43W **115** d
Admiralty Is. *Papua N. G.* 2°0S 147°0E **102** H6
Adour → *France* 43°32N 1°32W **68** E3
Adrar *Mauritania* 20°30N 7°30E **94** D3
Adrar des Iforas *Africa* 19°40N 1°40E **94** C5
Adrian *U.S.A.* 41°54N 84°2W **112** E5
Adriatic Sea *Medit. S.* 43°0N 16°0E **70** C6
Adwa *Ethiopia* 14°15N 38°52E **88** E2
Adwick le Street *U.K.* 53°34N 1°10W **23** E6
Adygea □ *Russia* 45°0N 40°0E **73** F7
Ægean Sea *Medit. S.* 38°30N 25°0E **71** E11
Aerhtai Shan *Mongolia* 46°40N 92°45E **80** B4
Afghanistan ■ *Asia* 33°0N 65°0E **87** C11
Africa 10°0N 20°0E **90** E6
Afyon *Turkey* 38°45N 30°33E **73** G5
Agadez *Niger* 16°58N 7°59E **94** E7
Agadir *Morocco* 30°28N 9°55W **94** B4
Agartala *India* 23°50N 91°23E **85** H17
Agen *France* 44°12N 0°38E **68** D4
Agra *India* 27°17N 77°58E **84** F10
Ağri *Turkey* 39°44N 43°3E **73** G7
Agrigento *Italy* 37°19N 13°34E **70** F5
Agua Prieta *Mexico* 31°18N 109°34W **114** A3
Aguadilla *Puerto Rico* 18°26N 67°10W **115** d
Aguascalientes *Mexico* 21°53N 102°18W **114** C4
Aguila, Punta *Puerto Rico* 17°57N 67°13W **115** d
Aguja, C. de la *Colombia* 11°18N 74°12W **116** B3
Agujereada, Pta. *Puerto Rico* 18°30N 67°8W **115** d
Agulhas, C. *S. Africa* 34°52S 20°0E **97** L4
Ahaggar *Algeria* 23°0N 6°30E **94** D76
Ahmadabad *India* 23°0N 72°40E **84** H8
Ahmadnagar *India* 19°7N 74°46E **84** K9
Ahmadpur *Pakistan* 29°12N 71°10E **84** E7
Ahvāz *Iran* 31°20N 48°40E **86** D7
Ahvenanmaa *Finland* 60°15N 20°0E **63** E8
Aḥwar *Yemen* 13°30N 46°40E **88** E4
Aihui *China* 50°10N 127°30E **81** A7
Ailsa Craig *U.K.* 55°15N 5°6W **20** D5
Aimorés *Brazil* 19°30S 41°4W **122** C2
Aïn Témouchent *Algeria* 35°16N 1°8W **94** A5
Ainsdale *U.K.* 53°37N 3°2W **23** E2
Aïr *Niger* 18°30N 8°0E **94** E7
Air Force I. *Canada* 67°58N 74°5W **109** C12
Aird, The *U.K.* 57°25N 4°33W **19** H8
Airdrie *Canada* 51°18N 114°2W **108** D8
Airdrie *U.K.* 55°52N 3°57W **21** C8
Aire → *U.K.* 53°43N 0°55W **23** E7
Aisgill *U.K.* 54°23N 2°21W **22** D4
Aisne → *France* 49°26N 2°50E **68** B5
Aix-en-Provence *France* 43°32N 5°27E **68** E6
Aix-les-Bains *France* 45°41N 5°53E **68** D6
Aizawl *India* 23°40N 92°44E **85** H18
Aizuwakamatsu *Japan* 37°30N 139°56E **82** E6
Ajaccio *France* 41°55N 8°40E **68** F8
Ajanta Ra. *India* 20°28N 75°50E **84** J9
Ajaria □ *Georgia* 41°30N 42°0E **73** F7
Ajdābiyā *Libya* 30°54N 20°4E **95** B10
'Ajmān *U.A.E.* 25°25N 55°30E **87** E8
Ajmer *India* 26°28N 74°37E **84** F9
Aketi *Dem. Rep. of the Congo* 2°38N 23°47E **96** D4
Akhisar *Turkey* 38°56N 27°48E **73** G4
Akimiski I. *Canada* 52°50N 81°30W **109** D11
Akita *Japan* 39°45N 140°7E **82** D7
'Akko *Israel* 32°55N 35°4E **86** C3
Aklavik *Canada* 68°12N 135°0W **108** C6
Akola *India* 20°42N 77°2E **84** J10
Akpatok I. *Canada* 60°25N 68°8W **109** C13
Akranes *Iceland* 64°19N 22°5W **63** B1
Akron *U.S.A.* 41°5N 81°31W **112** E7
Aksai Chin *China* 35°15N 79°55E **84** B11
Aksaray *Turkey* 38°25N 34°2E **73** G5
Akşehir Gölü *Turkey* 38°30N 31°25E **73** G5
Aksu *China* 41°5N 80°10E **80** B3
Aksum *Ethiopia* 14°5N 38°40E **88** E2
Akure *Nigeria* 7°15N 5°5E **94** G7
Akureyri *Iceland* 65°40N 18°6W **63** A2
Al 'Amārah *Iraq* 31°55N 47°15E **86** D6
Al 'Aqabah *Jordan* 29°31N 35°0E **86** D3
Al 'Aramah *Si. Arabia* 25°30N 46°0E **86** E6
Al 'Ayn *U.A.E.* 24°15N 55°45E **87** E8
Al Fallūjah *Iraq* 33°20N 43°55E **86** C5
Al Fāw *Iraq* 30°0N 48°30E **86** D7
Al Ḥadīthah *Iraq* 34°0N 41°13E **86** C5
Al Ḥillah *Iraq* 32°30N 44°25E **86** C6
Al Hoceïma *Morocco* 35°8N 3°58W **94** A5
Al Ḥudaydah *Yemen* 14°50N 43°0E **88** E3
Al Hufūf *Si. Arabia* 25°25N 49°45E **86** E7
Al Jahrah *Kuwait* 29°25N 47°40E **86** D6
Al Jawf *Libya* 24°10N 23°24E **95** D10
Al Jawf *Si. Arabia* 29°55N 39°40E **86** D4
Al Jubayl *Si. Arabia* 27°0N 49°50E **86** E7
Al Khalīl *West Bank* 31°32N 35°6E **86** D3
Al Khums *Libya* 32°40N 14°17E **95** B8
Al Kufrah *Libya* 24°17N 23°15E **95** D10
Al Kūt *Iraq* 32°30N 46°0E **86** C6
Al Manāmah *Bahrain* 26°10N 50°30E **87** E7
Al Mubarraz *Si. Arabia* 25°30N 49°40E **86** E7
Al Mukallā *Yemen* 14°33N 49°2E **88** E4
Al Musayyib *Iraq* 32°49N 44°20E **86** C6
Al Qāmishlī *Syria* 37°2N 41°14E **86** B5
Al Qaţīf *Si. Arabia* 26°35N 50°0E **86** E7
Al Qunfudhah *Si. Arabia* 19°3N 41°4E **88** D3
Alabama □ *U.S.A.* 33°0N 87°0W **111** D9
Alabama → *U.S.A.* 31°8N 87°57W **111** D9
Alagoas □ *Brazil* 9°0S 36°0W **122** A3
Alagoinhas *Brazil* 12°7S 38°20W **122** B3
Alai Range *Asia* 39°45N 72°0E **87** B13
Alamogordo *U.S.A.* 32°54N 105°57W **110** D5
Alamosa *U.S.A.* 37°28N 105°52W **110** C5
Åland = Ahvenanmaa *Finland* 60°15N 20°0E **63** E8
Alanya *Turkey* 36°38N 32°0E **73** G5
Alaşehir *Turkey* 38°23N 28°30E **73** G4
Alaska □ *U.S.A.* 64°0N 154°0W **108** C5
Alaska, G. of *Pac. Oc.* 58°0N 145°0W **108** D5
Alaska Peninsula *U.S.A.* 56°0N 159°0W **108** D4
Alaska Range *U.S.A.* 62°50N 151°0W **108** C4
Alba-Iulia *Romania* 46°8N 23°39E **67** E12
Albacete *Spain* 39°0N 1°50W **69** C5
Albanel, L. *Canada* 50°55N 73°12W **109** D12
Albania ■ *Europe* 41°0N 20°0E **71** D9
Albany *Australia* 35°1S 117°58E **98** H2
Albany *Ga., U.S.A.* 31°35N 84°10W **111** D10
Albany *N.Y., U.S.A.* 42°39N 73°45W **113** D11
Albany *Oreg., U.S.A.* 44°38N 123°6W **110** B2
Albany → *Canada* 52°17N 81°31W **109** D11
Albemarle Sd. *U.S.A.* 36°5N 76°0W **111** C11
Albert, L. *Africa* 1°30N 31°0E **96** D6
Albert Lea *U.S.A.* 43°39N 93°22W **111** B8
Albert Nile → *Uganda* 3°36N 32°2E **96** D6
Alberta □ *Canada* 54°40N 115°0W **108** D8
Albertville *France* 45°40N 6°22E **68** D7
Albi *France* 43°56N 2°9E **68** E5
Albion *U.S.A.* 42°15N 84°45W **112** D5
Albrighton *U.K.* 52°38N 2°16W **23** G4
Albuquerque *U.S.A.* 35°5N 106°39W **110** C5
Albury *Australia* 36°3S 146°56E **98** H8
Alcalá de Henares *Spain* 40°28N 3°22W **69** B4
Alcester *U.K.* 52°14N 1°52W **24** B5
Alchevsk *Ukraine* 48°30N 38°45E **73** E6
Alcoy *Spain* 38°43N 0°30W **69** C5
Aldabra Is. *Seychelles* 9°22S 46°28E **91** G8
Aldan *Russia* 58°40N 125°30E **79** D14

Aldan → Russia 63°28N 129°35E 79 C14
Aldborough U.K. 54°5N 1°22W 22 D6
Aldbourne U.K. 51°29N 1°37W 24 D5
Aldbrough U.K. 53°49N 0°6W 23 E8
Aldeburgh U.K. 52°10N 1°37E 25 B12
Alderbury U.K. 51°3N 1°44W 24 D5
Alderley Edge U.K. 53°18N 2°13W 23 F4
Alderney U.K. 49°42N 2°11W 27 H9
Aldershot U.K. 51°15N 0°44W 25 D7
Aledo U.S.A. 41°12N 90°45W 112 E2
Alegrete Brazil 29°40S 56°0W 121 E4
Além Paraíba Brazil 21°52S 42°41W 122 D2
Alençon France 48°27N 0°4E 68 B4
Alenquer Brazil 1°56S 54°46W 120 C4
'Alenuihāhā Channel
   U.S.A. 20°30N 156°0W 110 H17
Aleppo Syria 36°10N 37°15E 86 B4
Alert Canada 83°2N 60°0W 109 A13
Alès France 44°9N 4°5E 68 D6
Alessándria Italy 44°54N 8°37E 70 B3
Ålesund Norway 62°28N 6°12E 63 E5
Aleutian Is. Pac. Oc. 52°0N 175°0W 102 B10
Aleutian Trench Pac. Oc. 48°0N 180°0E 102 C10
Alexander Arch. U.S.A. 56°0N 136°0W 108 D6
Alexander I. Antarctica 69°0S 70°0W 55 C17
Alexandria Egypt 31°13N 29°58E 95 B11
Alexandria 55°59N 4°35W 20 C6
Alexandria La., U.S.A. 31°18N 92°27W 111 D8
Alexandria Va., U.S.A. 38°49N 77°5W 112 F9
Alford Aberds., U.K. 57°14N 2°41W 19 H12
Alford Lincs., U.K. 53°15N 0°10E 23 F9
Alfreton U.K. 53°6N 1°24W 23 F6
Alfriston U.K. 50°48N 0°10E 25 E9
Algarve Portugal 36°58N 8°20W 69 D1
Algeciras Spain 36°9N 5°28W 69 D3
Algeria ■ Africa 28°30N 2°0E 94 C6
Algiers Algeria 36°42N 3°8E 94 A6
Algoa B. S. Africa 33°50S 25°45E 90 K6
Alicante Spain 38°23N 0°30W 69 C5
Alice Springs Australia 23°40S 133°50E 98 E5
Aligarh India 27°55N 78°10E 84 F11
Alipur Duar India 26°30N 89°35E 85 F16
Aliquippa U.S.A. 40°37N 80°15W 112 E7
Aliwal North S. Africa 30°45S 26°45E 97 L5
Alkmaar Neths. 52°37N 4°45E 65 B4
Allahabad India 25°25N 81°58E 85 G12
Allegan U.S.A. 42°32N 85°51W 112 D5
Allegheny → U.S.A. 40°27N 80°1W 112 E8
Allegheny Mts. U.S.A. 38°15N 80°10W 111 C11
Allègre, Pte. Guadeloupe 16°22N 61°46W 114 b
Allen → U.K. 54°58N 2°18W 22 C4
Allen, Bog of Ireland 53°15N 7°0W 31 B9
Allen, L. Ireland 54°8N 8°4W 28 C5
Allendale Town U.K. 54°53N 2°14W 22 C4
Allenheads U.K. 54°49N 2°12W 22 C4
Allentown U.S.A. 40°37N 75°29W 113 E10
Alleppey India 9°30N 76°28E 84 Q10
Alleynes B. Barbados 13°13N 59°39W 115 g
Alliance U.S.A. 42°6N 102°52W 110 B6
Allier → France 46°57N 3°4E 68 C5
Alligator Pond Jamaica 17°52N 77°34W 114 a
Alloa U.K. 56°7N 3°47W 21 B8
Allonby U.K. 54°46N 3°26W 22 C2
Alma U.S.A. 43°23N 84°39W 112 D5
Alma Ata Kazakhstan 43°15N 76°57E 79 E9
Almada Portugal 38°41N 9°8W 69 C1
Almelo Neths. 52°22N 6°42E 65 B6
Almería Spain 36°52N 2°27W 69 D4
Almondsbury U.K. 51°32N 2°34W 24 C3
Aln → U.K. 55°24N 1°37W 22 B5
Alness U.K. 57°41N 4°16W 19 H8
Alnmouth U.K. 55°24N 1°37W 22 B5
Alnwick U.K. 55°24N 1°42W 22 B5
Alor Indonesia 8°15S 124°30E 83 D4
Alor Setar Malaysia 6°7N 100°22E 83 C2
Alpena U.S.A. 45°4N 83°27W 112 C6
Alpes Maritimes Europe 44°10N 7°10E 68 D7
Alphington U.K. 50°42N 3°31W 27 F6
Alpine U.S.A. 30°22N 103°40W 110 D6
Alps Europe 46°30N 9°30E 66 E5
Alrewas U.K. 52°44N 1°44W 23 G5
Alsace □ France 48°15N 7°25E 68 B7
Alsager U.K. 53°6N 2°18W 23 F4
Alston U.K. 54°49N 2°25W 22 C4
Altaimira Brazil 3°12S 52°10W 120 C4
Altamura Italy 40°49N 16°33E 70 D7
Altanbulag Mongolia 50°16N 106°30E 80 A5
Altarnun U.K. 50°35N 4°32W 27 F4
Altay China 47°48N 88°10E 80 B3
Altiplano Bolivia 17°0S 68°0W 120 D3
Alton U.K. 51°9N 0°59W 25 D7
Alton U.S.A. 38°53N 90°11W 112 F2
Altoona U.S.A. 40°31N 78°24W 112 E8
Altrincham U.K. 53°24N 2°21W 23 F4
Altun Shan China 38°30N 88°0E 80 C3
Altus U.S.A. 34°38N 99°20W 110 D7
Alucra Turkey 40°22N 38°47E 73 B6
Alvechurch U.K. 52°21N 1°57W 24 B5
Alwar India 27°38N 76°34E 84 F10
Alwinton U.K. 55°21N 2°7W 22 B4
Alxa Zuoqi China 38°50N 105°40E 80 C5
Alyth U.K. 56°38N 3°13W 19 J11
Amadjuak L. Canada 65°0N 71°8W 109 C12
Amagasaki Japan 34°42N 135°23E 82 F4
Amapá Brazil 2°5N 50°50W 120 B4
Amapá □ Brazil 1°40N 52°0W 120 B4
Amarillo U.S.A. 35°13N 101°50W 110 C6
Amasya Turkey 40°40N 35°50E 73 B6
Amazon = Amazonas →
   S. Amer. 0°5S 50°0W 120 C4
Amazonas □ Brazil 5°0S 65°0W 120 C3
Amazonas → S. Amer. 0°5S 50°0W 120 C4
Ambala India 30°23N 76°56E 84 D10
Ambato Ecuador 1°5S 78°42W 120 C2
Ambergris Cay Belize 18°0N 87°55W 114 D7
Ambikapur India 23°15N 83°15E 85 H12
Ambilobé Madag. 13°10S 49°3E 97 G9
Amble U.K. 55°20N 1°36W 22 B5

Ambleside U.K. 54°26N 2°58W 22 D3
Ambon Indonesia 3°43S 128°12E 83 D4
Amchitka I. U.S.A. 51°32N 179°0E 108 D1
Amderma Russia 69°45N 61°30E 79 C8
Ameca Mexico 20°33N 104°2W 114 C4
American Highland Antarctica 73°0S 75°0E 55 D6
American Samoa ☑
   Pac. Oc. 14°20S 170°40W 99 C16
Americana Brazil 22°45S 47°20W 122 D1
Amersfoort Neths. 52°9N 5°23E 65 B5
Amersham U.K. 51°40N 0°36W 25 C7
Ames U.S.A. 42°2N 93°37W 111 B8
Amesbury U.K. 51°10N 1°46W 24 D5
Amherst Canada 45°48N 64°8W 109 E13
Amiens France 49°54N 2°16E 68 B5
Amirante Is. Seychelles 6°0S 53°0E 74 J7
Amla I. U.S.A. 52°4N 173°30W 108 D2
Amlwch U.K. 53°24N 4°20W 26 A5
'Ammān Jordan 31°57N 35°52E 86 D3
Ammanford U.K. 51°48N 3°59W 26 D6
Amos Canada 48°35N 78°5W 109 E12
Ampleforth U.K. 54°13N 1°6W 22 D6
Ampthill U.K. 52°2N 0°30W 25 B8
Amravati India 20°55N 77°45E 84 J10
Amreli India 21°35N 71°17E 84 J7
Amritsar India 31°35N 74°57E 84 D9
Amroha India 28°53N 78°30E 84 E11
Amsterdam Neths. 52°23N 4°54E 65 B4
Amsterdam U.S.A. 42°56N 74°11W 113 D10
Amsterdam ✈ (AMS) Neths. 52°18N 4°45E 65 B4
Amsterdam I. Ind. Oc. 38°30S 77°30E 53 F13
Amudarya → Uzbekistan 43°58N 59°34E 87 A9
Amund Ringnes I. Canada 78°20N 96°25W 109 B10
Amundsen Gulf Canada 71°0N 124°0W 108 B7
Amundsen Sea Antarctica 72°0S 115°0W 55 D15
Amuntai Indonesia 2°28S 115°25E 83 D3
Amur → Russia 52°56N 141°10E 79 D16
An Najaf Iraq 32°3N 44°15E 86 C6
An Uaimh Ireland 53°39N 6°41W 29 D8
Anaconda U.S.A. 46°8N 112°57W 110 A4
Anadyr Russia 64°35N 177°20E 79 C19
Anadyr, G. of Russia 64°0N 180°0E 79 C20
Anaheim U.S.A. 33°50N 117°55W 110 D3
Anambas, Kepulauan
   Indonesia 3°20N 106°30E 83 C2
Anamur Turkey 36°8N 32°58E 73 G5
Anantapur India 14°39N 77°42E 84 M10
Anápolis Brazil 16°15S 48°50W 122 C1
Anār Iran 30°55N 55°13E 87 D8
Anatolia Turkey 39°0N 30°0E 73 G5
Añatuya Argentina 28°20S 62°50W 121 E3
Ancaster U.K. 52°59N 0°32W 23 F7
Ancholme → U.K. 53°40N 0°32W 23 E7
Anchorage U.S.A. 61°13N 149°54W 108 C5
Anci China 39°20N 116°40E 81 C6
Ancohuma Bolivia 16°0S 68°50W 120 D3
Ancona Italy 43°38N 13°30E 70 C5
Ancrum U.K. 55°31N 2°35W 21 C10
Ancud Chile 42°0S 73°50W 121 G2
Ancud, G. de Chile 42°0S 73°0W 121 G2
Anda China 46°24N 125°19E 81 B7
Andalgalá Argentina 27°40S 66°30W 121 E3
Andalucía □ Spain 37°35N 5°0W 69 D3
Andalusia U.S.A. 31°18N 86°29W 111 D9
Andaman Is. Ind. Oc. 12°30N 92°45E 83 B1
Anderson Alaska, U.S.A. 64°25N 149°15W 108 C5
Anderson Ind., U.S.A. 40°10N 85°41W 112 E5
Anderson S.C., U.S.A. 34°31N 82°39W 111 D10
Anderson → Canada 69°42N 129°0W 108 C7
Andes, Cord. de los S. Amer. 20°0S 68°0W 121 E3
Andhra Pradesh □ India 18°0N 79°0E 84 L11
Andijon Uzbekistan 41°10N 72°15E 87 A13
Andorra ■ Europe 42°30N 1°30E 68 E4
Andorra La Vella Andorra 42°31N 1°32E 68 E4
Andover U.K. 51°12N 1°29W 24 D6
Andradina Brazil 20°54S 51°23W 120 E4
Andreanof Is. U.S.A. 51°30N 176°0W 108 D2
Ándria Italy 41°13N 16°17E 70 D7
Andros Greece 37°50N 24°57E 71 F11
Andros I. Bahamas 24°30N 78°0W 115 C9
Anegada B. Virgin Is. 18°45N 64°20W 115 e
Aneityum Vanuatu 20°12S 169°45E 99 E12
Angara → Russia 58°5N 94°20E 79 D11
Angarsk Russia 52°30N 104°0E 79 D12
Ånge Sweden 62°31N 15°35E 63 E7
Angel Falls Venezuela 5°57N 62°30W 120 B3
Angeles Phil. 15°9N 120°33E 83 B4
Ångermanälven → Sweden 64°0N 17°20E 63 E7
Angers France 47°30N 0°35W 68 C3
Anglesey U.K. 53°17N 4°20W 64 E4
Anglesey □ U.K. 53°16N 4°18W 26 A5
Angoche Mozam. 16°8S 39°55E 97 H7
Angola ■ Africa 12°0S 18°0E 97 G3
Angoulême France 45°39N 0°10E 68 D4
Angoumois France 45°50N 0°25E 68 D3
Angra dos Reis Brazil 23°0S 44°10W 122 D2
Angren Uzbekistan 41°1N 70°12E 87 A12
Anguilla ☑ W. Indies 18°14N 63°5W 115 D12
Angus □ U.K. 56°46N 2°56W 19 J11
Angus, Braes of U.K. 56°51N 3°10W 19 J11
Anhui □ China 32°0N 117°0E 81 C6
Anjou France 47°20N 0°15W 68 C3
Ankang China 32°40N 109°1E 81 C5
Ankara Turkey 39°57N 32°54E 73 G5
Ann, C. U.S.A. 42°38N 70°35W 113 D12
Ann Arbor U.S.A. 42°17N 83°45W 112 D6
Annaba Algeria 36°50N 7°46E 94 A7
Annalee → Ireland 54°2N 7°24W 28 C7
Annan U.K. 54°59N 3°16W 21 D9
Annan → U.K. 54°58N 3°16W 21 D9
Annandale U.K. 55°10N 3°25W 21 D9
Annapolis U.S.A. 38°59N 76°30W 112 F9
Annapurna Nepal 28°34N 83°50E 85 E14
Annfield Plain U.K. 54°52N 1°44W 22 C5
Anning China 24°55N 102°26E 80 D5
Anniston U.S.A. 33°39N 85°50W 111 D9
Annobón Atl. Oc. 1°25S 5°36E 90 G4

Annotto B. Jamaica 18°17N 76°45W 114 a
Anqing China 30°30N 117°3E 81 C6
Anshan China 41°5N 122°58E 81 B7
Anshun China 26°18N 105°57E 80 D5
Anstey U.K. 52°41N 1°12W 23 G6
Anstruther U.K. 56°14N 2°41W 21 B10
Antalaha Madag. 14°57S 50°20E 97 G10
Antalya Turkey 36°52N 30°45E 73 G5
Antalya Körfezi Turkey 36°15N 31°30E 73 G5
Antananarivo Madag. 18°55S 47°31E 97 H9
Antarctic Pen. Antarctica 67°0S 60°0W 55 C18
Antarctica 90°0S 0°0 55 E3
Anti Atlas Morocco 30°0N 8°30W 94 C4
Antibes France 43°34N 7°6E 68 E7
Anticosti, Î. d' Canada 49°30N 63°0W 109 E13
Antigo U.S.A. 45°9N 89°9W 112 C3
Antigonish Canada 45°38N 61°58W 109 E13
Antigua & Barbuda ■
   W. Indies 17°20N 61°48W 115 D12
Antioch Turkey 36°14N 36°10E 73 G6
Antioquia Colombia 6°40N 75°55W 120 B2
Antipodes Is. Pac. Oc. 49°45S 178°40E 102 M9
Antofagasta Chile 23°50S 70°30W 121 E2
Antrim U.K. 54°43N 6°14W 29 B9
Antrim □ U.K. 54°56N 6°25W 29 B9
Antrim, Mts. of U.K. 55°3N 6°14W 29 A9
Antsirabe Madag. 19°55S 47°2E 97 H9
Antsiranana Madag. 12°25S 49°20E 97 G9
Antwerp Belgium 51°13N 4°25E 65 C4
Anuradhapura Sri Lanka 8°22N 80°28E 84 Q12
Anvers = Antwerp Belgium 51°13N 4°25E 65 C4
Anxi China 40°30N 95°43E 80 B4
Anyang China 36°5N 114°21E 81 C6
Ánzio Italy 41°27N 12°37E 70 D5
Aomori Japan 40°45N 140°45E 82 C7
Aoraki Mount Cook N.Z. 43°36S 170°9E 99 J13
Aosta Italy 45°45N 7°20E 70 B2
Aozou Strip Chad 22°0N 19°0E 95 D9
Apalachee B. U.S.A. 30°0N 84°0W 111 D10
Apaporis → Colombia 1°23S 69°25W 120 C3
Apatity Russia 67°34N 33°22E 72 A5
Apeldoorn Neths. 52°13N 5°57E 65 B5
Apia Samoa 13°50S 171°50W 99 C16
Apostle Is. U.S.A. 47°0N 90°40W 112 B2
Appalachian Mts. U.S.A. 38°0N 80°0W 112 G7
Appennini Italy 44°30N 10°0E 70 B4
Appleby-in-Westmorland
   U.K. 54°35N 2°29W 22 C4
Applecross Forest U.K. 57°27N 5°40W 18 H6
Appledore Devon, U.K. 51°3N 4°13W 27 E5
Appledore Kent, U.K. 51°1N 0°47E 25 D10
Appleton U.S.A. 44°16N 88°25W 112 C3
Apure → Venezuela 7°37N 66°25W 120 B3
Apurímac → Peru 12°17S 73°56W 120 D2
Aqaba, G. of Red Sea 29°0N 34°40E 86 D3
Aqtaü Kazakhstan 43°39N 51°12E 73 F9
Aqtöbe Kazakhstan 50°17N 57°10E 73 D10
Aquitain, Bassin France 44°0N 0°30W 68 D3
Ar Ramādī Iraq 33°25N 43°20E 86 C5
'Ara Iraq 25°35N 84°32E 85 G14
'Arab, Bahr el → Sudan 9°0N 29°30E 95 G11
Arab, Shatt al → Asia 29°57N 48°34E 86 D7
Arabia Asia 25°0N 45°0E 74 F6
Arabian Desert Egypt 27°30N 32°30E 95 C12
Arabian Gulf = Persian Gulf
   Asia 27°0N 50°0E 87 E7
Arabian Sea Ind. Oc. 16°0N 65°0E 74 G8
Aracaju Brazil 10°55S 37°4W 122 B3
Aracati Brazil 4°30S 37°44W 120 C6
Araçatuba Brazil 21°10S 50°30W 120 E4
Araçuaí Brazil 16°52S 42°4W 122 C2
Arad Romania 46°10N 21°20E 67 E11
Arafura Sea E. Indies 9°0S 135°0E 83 D5
Aragón □ Spain 41°25N 0°40W 69 B5
Araguacema Brazil 8°50S 49°20W 120 C5
Araguaia → Brazil 5°21S 48°41W 120 C5
Araguari Brazil 18°38S 48°11W 122 C1
Arāk Iran 34°0N 49°40E 86 C7
Arakan Coast Burma 19°0N 94°0E 85 K19
Arakan Yoma Burma 20°0N 94°40E 85 K19
Aral Kazakhstan 46°41N 61°45E 79 E8
Aral Sea Asia 44°30N 60°0E 79 E8
Aran I. Ireland 55°0N 8°30W 28 B4
Aran Is. Ireland 53°6N 9°38W 30 B3
Aransas Pass U.S.A. 27°55N 97°9W 111 E7
Arapiraca Brazil 9°45S 36°39W 122 A3
Araraquara Brazil 21°50S 48°0W 122 D1
Araras Brazil 22°22S 47°23W 122 D1
Ararat Turkey 39°50N 44°15E 73 G7
Araripe, Chapada do Brazil 7°20S 40°0W 120 C5
Aras, Rūd-e → Asia 40°5N 48°29E 86 A7
Arauca → Venezuela 7°24N 66°35W 120 B3
Araxá Brazil 19°35S 46°55W 122 C1
Arbroath U.K. 56°34N 2°35W 21 A11
Arcachon France 44°40N 1°10W 68 D3
Arctic Bay Canada 73°1N 85°7W 109 B11
Arctic Ocean Arctic 78°0N 160°0W 54 B18
Ardabīl Iran 38°15N 48°18E 86 B7
Ardee Ireland 53°52N 6°33W 29 D8
Ardennes Belgium 49°50N 5°5E 65 D5
Arderin Ireland 53°2N 7°39W 31 B7
Ardgour U.K. 56°45N 5°25W 18 J7
Ardingly U.K. 51°3N 0°4W 25 D8
Ardivachar Pt. U.K. 57°23N 7°26W 18 H3
Ardmore U.S.A. 34°10N 97°8W 111 D7
Ardnamurchan U.K. 56°43N 6°14W 18 J5
Ardnamurchan, Pt. of U.K. 56°43N 6°14W 18 J5
Ardnave Pt. U.K. 55°53N 6°20W 20 C3
Ardrossan U.K. 55°39N 4°49W 20 C6
Ards Pen. U.K. 54°33N 5°34W 29 B10
Arecibo Puerto Rico 18°29N 66°43W 115 d
Arena, Pt. U.S.A. 38°57N 123°44W 110 C2
Arendal Norway 58°28N 8°46E 63 F5
Arequipa Peru 16°20S 71°30W 120 D2
Arezzo Italy 43°25N 11°53E 70 C4
Argentan France 48°45N 0°1W 68 B3
Argentina ■ S. Amer. 35°0S 66°0W 121 F3
Argentino, L. Argentina 50°10S 73°0W 121 H2
Argostoli Greece 38°11N 20°29E 71 E9

Argyle, L. Australia 16°20S 128°40E 98 D4
Argyll U.K. 56°10N 5°20W 20 B5
Argyll & Bute □ U.K. 56°13N 5°28W 20 B4
Århus Denmark 56°8N 10°11E 63 F6
Ariana Tunisia 36°52N 10°12E 95 A8
Arica Chile 18°32S 70°20W 120 D2
Arinos → Brazil 10°25S 58°20W 120 D4
Aripuanã → Brazil 5°7S 60°25W 120 C3
Arisaig U.K. 56°55N 5°51W 18 J6
Arizona □ U.S.A. 34°0N 112°0W 110 D4
Arkaig, L. U.K. 56°59N 5°10W 18 J7
Arkansas □ U.S.A. 35°0N 92°30W 111 D8
Arkansas → U.S.A. 33°47N 91°4W 111 D8
Arkansas City U.S.A. 37°4N 97°2W 111 C7
Arkhangelsk Russia 64°38N 40°36E 72 B7
Arklow Ireland 52°48N 6°10W 31 C10
Arkle → U.K. 54°24N 1°56W 22 D5
Arklow Ireland 52°48N 6°10W 31 C10
Arles France 43°41N 4°40E 68 E6
Arlington U.S.A. 38°53N 77°7W 112 F9
Arlon Belgium 49°42N 5°49E 65 E5
Armagh U.K. 54°21N 6°39W 29 C8
Armagh □ U.K. 54°18N 6°37W 29 C8
Armavir Russia 45°2N 41°7E 73 E7
Armenia Colombia 4°35N 75°45W 120 B2
Armenia ■ Asia 40°20N 45°0E 73 F7
Arnaud → Canada 59°59N 69°46W 109 D13
Arnhem Neths. 51°58N 5°55E 65 C5
Arnhem, C. Australia 12°20S 137°30E 98 C6
Arnhem Land Australia 13°10S 134°30E 98 C5
Arno → Italy 43°41N 10°17E 70 C4
Arnold U.K. 53°1N 1°7W 23 F6
Arnprior Canada 45°26N 76°21W 112 C9
Arnside U.K. 54°12N 2°49W 22 D3
Arra Mts. Ireland 52°50N 8°22W 30 C6
Arran U.K. 55°34N 5°12W 20 C5
Arras France 50°17N 2°46E 68 A5
Arrecife Canary Is. 28°57N 13°37W 94 C3
Arrow, L. Ireland 54°3N 8°19W 28 C5
Artemovsk Ukraine 48°35N 38°0E 73 E6
Artigas Uruguay 30°20S 56°30W 121 F4
Artois France 50°20N 2°30E 68 A5
Artux China 39°40N 76°10E 80 C2
Artvin Turkey 41°14N 41°44E 73 F7
Aru, Kepulauan Indonesia 6°0S 134°30E 83 D5
Arua Uganda 3°1N 30°58E 96 D6
Aruanã Brazil 14°54S 51°10W 120 D4
Aruba ☑ W. Indies 12°30N 70°0W 115 E11
Arunachal Pradesh □ India 28°0N 95°0E 85 F19
Arundel U.K. 50°51N 0°33W 25 E7
Arusha Tanzania 3°20S 36°40E 96 E7
Aruwimi →
   Dem. Rep. of the Congo 1°13N 23°36E 96 D4
Arvayheer Mongolia 46°15N 102°48E 80 B5
Arviat Canada 61°6N 93°59W 108 C10
Arxan China 47°11N 119°57E 81 B6
Arzamas Russia 55°27N 43°55E 72 C7
As Sulaymānīyah Iraq 35°35N 45°29E 86 C6
As Sulaymānīyah Si. Arabia 24°9N 47°18E 86 E6
As Suwayq Oman 23°51N 57°26E 88 C6
Aş Şuwayrah Iraq 32°55N 45°0E 86 C6
Asahigawa Japan 43°46N 142°22E 82 B8
Asamankese Ghana 5°50N 0°40W 94 G5
Asansol India 23°40N 87°1E 85 H15
Asbestos Canada 45°47N 71°58W 113 C12
Asbury Park U.S.A. 40°13N 74°1W 113 E10
Ascension I. Atl. Oc. 7°57S 14°23W 52 E9
Áscoli Piceno Italy 42°51N 13°34E 70 C5
Ascot U.K. 51°25N 0°40W 25 D7
Aseb Eritrea 13°0N 42°40E 88 E3
Asenovgrad Bulgaria 42°1N 24°51E 71 C11
Asfordby U.K. 52°47N 0°57W 23 G7
Ash Kent, U.K. 51°16N 1°17E 25 D11
Ash Surrey, U.K. 51°15N 0°43W 25 D7
Ashbourne U.K. 53°2N 1°43W 23 F5
Ashburton U.K. 50°30N 3°46W 27 F6
Ashby de la Zouch U.K. 52°46N 1°29W 23 G6
Ashchurch U.K. 52°0N 2°5W 24 C4
Ashdown Forest U.K. 51°3N 0°5E 25 D9
Asheville U.S.A. 35°36N 82°33W 111 C10
Ashford Derby, U.K. 53°14N 1°42W 23 F5
Ashford Kent, U.K. 51°8N 0°53E 25 D10
Ashington U.K. 55°11N 1°33W 22 B5
Ashkhabad Turkmenistan 38°0N 57°50E 87 B9
Ashland Ky., U.S.A. 38°28N 82°38W 112 F6
Ashland Ohio, U.S.A. 40°52N 82°19W 112 E6
Ashland Wis., U.S.A. 46°35N 90°53W 112 B2
Ashqelon Israel 31°42N 34°35E 86 D3
Ashtabula U.S.A. 41°52N 80°47W 112 E7
Ashton-in-Makerfield U.K. 53°30N 2°40W 23 F4
Ashton under Lyne U.K. 53°29N 2°6W 23 F4
Ashuanipi, L. Canada 52°45N 66°15W 109 D13
Ashwater U.K. 50°43N 4°19W 27 F5
Ashwick U.K. 51°13N 2°31W 24 D3
Asia 45°0N 75°0E 74 E9
Asinara Italy 41°4N 8°16E 70 D3
'Asīr □ Si. Arabia 18°40N 42°30E 88 D3
Asir, Ras Somali Rep. 11°55N 51°10E 88 E5
Askrigg U.K. 54°19N 2°6W 22 D4
Aslackby U.K. 52°53N 0°24E 23 G8
Asmera Eritrea 15°19N 38°55E 88 D2
Aspatria U.K. 54°47N 3°19W 22 C2
Aspen U.S.A. 39°11N 106°49W 110 C5
Assal, L. Djibouti 11°40N 42°26E 88 E3
Assam □ India 26°0N 93°0E 85 G18
Assen Neths. 53°0N 6°35E 65 A6
Assiniboia Canada 49°40N 105°59W 108 E9
Assiniboine → Canada 49°53N 97°8W 108 E10
Assisi Italy 43°4N 12°37E 70 C5
Assynt U.K. 58°12N 5°12W 18 F7
Assynt, L. U.K. 58°10N 5°3W 18 F7
Astana Kazakhstan 51°10N 71°30E 79 D9
Asti Italy 44°54N 8°12E 70 B3
Astipálea Greece 36°32N 26°22E 71 F12
Astoria U.S.A. 46°11N 123°50W 110 A2
Astrakhan Russia 46°25N 48°5E 73 E8
Asturias □ Spain 43°15N 6°0W 69 A3
Astwood Bank U.K. 52°15N 1°56W 24 B5

Asunción Paraguay 25°10S 57°30W 121 E4
Aswân Egypt 24°4N 32°57E 95 D12
Aswan Dam Egypt 23°54N 32°54E 95 D12
Asyût Egypt 27°11N 31°4E 95 C12
Aţ Ţā'if Si. Arabia 21°5N 40°27E 88 C3
Atacama, Desierto de Chile 24°0S 69°20W 121 E3
Atatürk Baraji Turkey 37°28N 38°30E 73 G6
Atbara Sudan 17°42N 33°59E 95 E12
Atbara → Sudan 17°40N 33°56E 95 E12
Atchafalaya B. U.S.A. 29°25N 91°25W 111 E8
Athabasca Canada 54°45N 113°20W 108 D8
Athabasca → Canada 58°40N 110°50W 108 D8
Athabasca, L. Canada 59°15N 109°15W 108 D9
Athboy Ireland 53°37N 6°56W 29 D8
Athenry Ireland 53°18N 8°44W 30 B5
Athens Greece 37°58N 23°43E 71 F10
Athens Ga., U.S.A. 33°57N 83°23W 111 D10
Athens Ohio, U.S.A. 39°20N 82°6W 112 F6
Atherstone U.K. 52°35N 1°33W 23 G5
Atherton U.K. 53°32N 2°30W 23 E4
Athlone Ireland 53°25N 7°56W 30 B7
Atholl, Forest of U.K. 56°51N 3°50W 19 J10
Athos Greece 40°9N 24°22E 71 D11
Athy Ireland 53°0N 7°0W 31 B8
Atikokan Canada 48°45N 91°37W 112 A2
Atka I. U.S.A. 52°7N 174°30W 108 D2
Atlanta U.S.A. 33°45N 84°23W 111 D10
Atlantic City U.S.A. 39°21N 74°27W 113 F10
Atlantic Ocean 0°0 20°0W 52 E9
Atlin Canada 59°31N 133°41W 108 D6
Attawapiskat Canada 52°56N 82°24W 109 D11
Attawapiskat → Canada 52°57N 82°18W 109 D11
Attleborough U.K. 52°32N 1°1E 25 A11
Attu I. U.S.A. 52°55N 172°55E 108 D1
Atyraū Kazakhstan 47°5N 52°0E 73 E9
Au Sable → U.S.A. 44°25N 83°20W 112 C6
Aube → France 48°34N 3°43E 68 B5
Auburn Ind., U.S.A. 41°22N 85°4W 112 E5
Auburn N.Y., U.S.A. 42°56N 76°34W 112 D9
Aubusson France 45°57N 2°11E 68 D5
Auch France 43°39N 0°36E 68 E4
Auchterarder U.K. 56°18N 3°41W 21 B8
Auchtermuchty U.K. 56°18N 3°13W 21 B9
Auckland N.Z. 36°52S 174°46E 99 H13
Auckland Is. Pac. Oc. 50°40S 166°5E 102 N8
Aude → France 43°13N 3°14E 68 E5
Audlem U.K. 52°59N 2°30W 23 G4
Aughnacloy U.K. 54°25N 6°59W 29 C8
Augsburg Germany 48°25N 10°52E 66 D6
Augusta Australia 34°19S 115°9E 98 G2
Augusta U.S.A. 33°28N 81°58W 111 D10
Aunis France 46°5N 0°50W 68 C3
Aurangabad Bihar, India 24°45N 84°18E 85 G14
Aurangabad Maharashtra,
   India 19°50N 75°23E 84 K9
Aurillac France 44°55N 2°26E 68 D5
Aurora Colo., U.S.A. 39°43N 104°49W 110 C6
Aurora Ill., U.S.A. 41°45N 88°19W 112 E3
Austin U.S.A. 30°17N 97°45W 110 D7
Austral Seamount Chain
   Pac. Oc. 24°0S 150°0W 103 K13
Australia ■ Oceania 23°0S 135°0E 98 E3
Australian Capital Territory □
   Australia 35°30S 149°0E 98 H8
Austria ■ Europe 47°0N 14°0E 66 E8
Autun France 46°58N 4°17E 68 C6
Auvergne □ France 45°20N 3°15E 68 D5
Auvergne, Mts. d' France 45°20N 2°55E 68 D5
Auxerre France 47°48N 3°32E 68 C5
Availon France 47°30N 3°53E 68 C5
Avaré Brazil 23°4S 48°58W 122 D1
Avebury U.K. 51°26N 1°50W 24 D5
Avellaneda Argentina 34°40S 58°22W 121 F4
Avellino Italy 40°54N 14°47E 70 D6
Aversa Italy 40°58N 14°12E 70 D6
Aveton Gifford U.K. 50°18N 3°50W 27 G6
Aviemore U.K. 57°12N 3°50W 19 H10
Avignon France 43°57N 4°50E 68 E6
Ávila Spain 40°39N 4°43W 69 B3
Avilés Spain 43°35N 5°57W 69 A3
Avoca → Ireland 52°48N 6°10W 31 C10
Avon → Bristol, U.K. 51°29N 2°41W 24 D3
Avon → Dorset, U.K. 50°44N 1°46W 24 E5
Avon → Warks., U.K. 52°0N 2°8W 24 B5
Avonmouth U.K. 51°30N 2°42W 24 C3
Avranches France 48°40N 1°20W 68 B3
Awasa Ethiopia 7°2N 38°28E 88 F2
Awash Ethiopia 9°1N 40°10E 88 F3
Awbārī, Idehan Libya 27°10N 11°30E 95 C8
Awe, L. U.K. 56°17N 5°16W 20 B5
Axbridge U.K. 51°17N 2°49W 24 D3
Axe → U.K. 50°42N 3°4W 27 F8
Axe Edge U.K. 53°14N 1°57W 23 F5
Axel Heiberg I. Canada 80°0N 90°0W 109 B11
Axholme, Isle of U.K. 53°32N 0°50W 23 E7
Axios → Greece 40°57N 22°35E 71 D10
Axminster U.K. 50°46N 3°0W 27 F7
Axmouth U.K. 50°42N 3°3W 27 F7
Ayacucho Argentina 37°5S 58°20W 121 F4
Ayacucho Peru 13°0S 74°0W 120 D2
Aydın Turkey 37°51N 27°51E 73 G4
Aydingkol Hu China 42°40N 89°15E 80 B3
Ayers Rock = Uluru Australia 25°23S 131°5E 98 F5
Aylesbury U.K. 51°49N 0°49W 25 C7
Aylesford U.K. 51°18N 0°30E 25 D9
Aylmer, L. Canada 64°5N 108°30W 108 C8
Aylsham U.K. 52°48N 1°15E 25 A11
Aynho U.K. 52°0N 1°15W 24 C6
Ayr U.K. 55°28N 4°38W 20 D6
Ayr → U.K. 55°28N 4°38W 20 D6
Aysgarth U.K. 54°18N 2°1W 22 D5
Ayton Borders, U.K. 55°51N 2°6W 21 C11
Ayton N. Yorks., U.K. 54°15N 0°28W 22 D8
Ayvalık Turkey 39°20N 26°46E 73 G4
Az Zarqā Jordan 32°5N 36°4E 86 C4
Az Zāwiyah Libya 32°52N 12°56E 95 B8
Azad Kashmir □ Pakistan 33°50N 73°50E 84 B8
Azamgarh India 26°5N 83°13E 85 F13

Azare Nigeria 11°55N 10°10E 94 F8
Azerbaijan ■ Asia 40°20N 48°0E 73 F8
Azores Atl. Oc. 38°0N 27°0W 91 C1
Azov Russia 47°3N 39°25E 73 E6
Azov, Sea of Europe 46°0N 36°30E 73 E6
Azuero, Pen. de Panama 7°30N 80°30W 115 F8
Azul Argentina 36°42S 59°43W 121 F4

B

Bab el Mandeb Red Sea 12°35N 43°25E 88 E3
Bābā, Koh-i- Afghan. 34°30N 67°0E 84 B5
Babine L. Canada 54°48N 126°0W 108 D7
Bābol Iran 36°40N 52°50E 87 B8
Babruysk Belarus 53°10N 29°15E 67 B15
Babuyan Chan. Phil. 18°40N 121°30E 83 B4
Babylon Iraq 32°34N 44°22E 86 C6
Bac Lieu Vietnam 9°17N 105°43E 83 C2
Bacabal Brazil 4°15S 44°45W 120 C5
Bacău Romania 46°35N 26°55E 67 E14
Back → Canada 65°10N 104°0W 108 C9
Bacolod Phil. 10°40N 122°57E 83 B4
Bacton U.K. 52°52N 1°27E 25 A11
Bacup U.K. 53°42N 2°11W 23 E4
Bad Axe U.S.A. 43°48N 83°0W 112 D6
Badagara India 11°35N 75°40E 84 P9
Badajoz Spain 38°50N 6°59W 69 C2
Badakhshān □ Afghan. 36°30N 71°0E 87 B12
Badalona Spain 41°26N 2°15E 69 B7
Baden-Württemberg □
  Germany 48°20N 8°40E 66 D5
Badenoch U.K. 56°59N 4°15W 19 J9
Bādghīs □ Afghan. 35°0N 63°0E 87 C10
Badlands U.S.A. 43°55N 102°30W 110 B6
Baffin B. N. Amer. 72°0N 64°0W 109 B13
Baffin I. Canada 68°0N 75°0W 109 C12
Bafoulabé Mali 13°50N 10°55W 94 F3
Bafra Turkey 41°34N 35°54E 73 F6
Bagamoyo Tanzania 6°28S 38°55E 96 F7
Bagé Brazil 31°20S 54°15W 121 F4
Baggy Pt. U.K. 51°8N 4°16W 27 E5
Baghdād Iraq 33°20N 44°23E 86 C6
Baghlān Afghan. 32°12N 68°46E 87 B12
Bagshot U.K. 51°22N 0°41W 25 D7
Baguio Phil. 16°26N 120°34E 83 B4
Bahamas ■ N. Amer. 24°0N 75°0W 115 C10
Baharampur India 24°2N 88°27E 85 G16
Bahawalpur Pakistan 29°24N 71°40E 84 E7
Bahía = Salvador Brazil 13°0S 38°30W 122 D6
Bahía □ Brazil 12°0S 42°0W 122 B2
Bahía Blanca Argentina 38°35S 62°13W 121 F3
Bahir Dar Ethiopia 11°37N 37°10E 88 E2
Bahraich India 27°38N 81°37E 85 F12
Bahrain ■ Asia 26°0N 50°35E 87 E7
Baia Mare Romania 47°40N 23°35E 67 E12
Baicheng China 45°38N 122°42E 81 B7
Baidoa Somali Rep. 3°8N 43°30E 88 G3
Baie-Comeau Canada 49°12N 68°10W 109 E13
Baie-St-Paul Canada 47°28N 70°32W 113 B12
Baie Verte Canada 49°55N 56°12W 109 E14
Ba'iji Iraq 35°0N 43°30E 86 C5
Baikal, L. Russia 53°0N 108°0E 79 D12
Baildon U.K. 53°51N 1°46W 23 E5
Bain → U.K. 53°6N 0°12W 23 F8
Bainbridge U.K. 54°18N 2°6W 22 D4
Baiyin China 36°45N 104°14E 80 C5
Baja, Pta. Mexico 29°58N 115°49W 114 B1
Baja California Mexico 31°10N 115°12W 114 A1
Baker, L. Canada 64°0N 96°0W 108 C10
Baker City U.S.A. 44°47N 117°50W 110 B3
Baker I. Pac. Oc. 0°10N 176°35W 99 A15
Baker Lake Canada 64°20N 96°3W 108 C10
Bakers Dozen Is. Canada 56°45N 78°45W 109 D12
Bakersfield U.S.A. 35°23N 119°1W 110 C3
Bakewell U.K. 53°13N 1°40W 23 F5
Baku Azerbaijan 40°29N 49°56E 73 F8
Bala U.K. 52°54N 3°36W 26 B6
Bala, L. U.K. 52°53N 3°37W 26 B6
Balabac Str. E. Indies 7°53N 117°5E 83 C3
Balaghat Ra. India 18°50N 76°30E 84 K10
Balaklava Ukraine 44°30N 33°30E 73 F5
Balakovo Russia 52°4N 47°55E 72 D8
Balashov Russia 51°30N 43°10E 73 D7
Balaton Hungary 46°50N 17°40E 67 E9
Balbi, Mt. Papua N. G. 5°55S 154°58E 99 B10
Balbina, Reprêsa de Brazil 2°0S 59°30W 120 C4
Balbriggan Ireland 53°37N 6°11W 29 D9
Balcarce Argentina 38°0S 58°10W 121 F4
Balderton U.K. 53°3N 0°47W 23 F7
Baldock U.K. 52°0N 0°11W 25 C8
Baldoyle Ireland 53°24N 6°8W 31 B10
Baldwin U.S.A. 43°54N 85°51W 112 D5
Baldy Peak U.S.A. 33°54N 109°34W 110 D5
Balearic Is. Spain 39°30N 3°0E 69 C7
Baleine → Canada 58°15N 67°40W 109 D13
Baleshare U.K. 57°31N 7°22W 18 G3
Baleshwar India 21°35N 87°3E 85 J15
Bali Indonesia 8°20S 115°0E 83 D3
Balıkeşir Turkey 39°39N 27°53E 73 G4
Balikpapan Indonesia 1°10S 116°55E 83 D3
Balkan Mts. Bulgaria 43°15N 23°0E 71 C10
Balkanabat Turkmenistan 39°30N 54°22E 87 B7
Balkhash, L. Kazakhstan 46°0N 74°50E 79 E9
Ballachulish U.K. 56°41N 5°8W 18 J7
Ballaghaderreen Ireland 53°55N 8°34W 28 D4
Ballantrae U.K. 55°6N 4°59W 20 D6
Ballarat Australia 37°33S 143°50E 98 H7
Ballater U.K. 57°3N 3°3W 19 H11
Balleny Is. Antarctica 66°30S 163°0E 55 C11
Ballina Ireland 54°7N 9°9W 28 C3
Ballinasloe Ireland 53°20N 8°13W 30 B6
Ballinrobe Ireland 53°38N 9°13W 28 D3
Ballinskelligs B. Ireland 51°48N 10°13W 30 E2
Ballybunion Ireland 52°31N 9°40W 30 D3
Ballycastle U.K. 55°12N 6°15W 29 A9
Ballyclare U.K. 54°46N 6°0W 29 B10
Ballyhaunis Ireland 53°46N 8°46W 28 D4

Ballyhoura Mts. Ireland 52°18N 8°33W 30 D5
Ballymena U.K. 54°52N 6°17W 29 B9
Ballymoney U.K. 55°5N 6°31W 29 A8
Ballymote Ireland 54°5N 8°31W 28 C4
Ballynahinch U.K. 54°24N 5°54W 29 C10
Ballyquintin Pt. U.K. 54°20N 5°30W 29 C11
Ballyshannon Ireland 54°30N 8°11W 28 B5
Balmoral Forest U.K. 57°0N 3°15W 19 J11
Balrampur India 27°30N 82°20E 85 F13
Balsas → Mexico 17°55N 102°10W 114 D4
Baltic Sea Europe 57°0N 19°0E 63 F7
Baltimore Ireland 51°29N 9°22W 30 F4
Baltimore U.S.A. 39°17N 76°36W 112 F9
Baluchistan □ Pakistan 27°30N 65°0E 84 F4
Bam Iran 29°7N 58°14E 87 D9
Bamako Mali 12°34N 7°55W 94 F4
Bambari C.A.R. 5°40N 20°35E 96 C4
Bamberg Germany 49°54N 10°54E 66 D6
Bamburgh U.K. 55°37N 1°43W 22 A5
Bamenda Cameroon 5°57N 10°11E 96 C2
Bamford U.K. 53°22N 1°41W 23 F5
Bāmīān □ Afghan. 35°0N 67°0E 87 C11
Bampton Devon, U.K. 50°59N 3°29W 27 F7
Bampton Oxon., U.K. 51°44N 1°32W 24 C5
Banaba Kiribati 0°45S 169°50E 102 H8
Bananal, I. do Brazil 11°30S 50°30W 120 D4
Banbridge U.K. 54°22N 6°16W 29 C9
Banbury U.K. 52°4N 1°20W 24 B6
Banchory U.K. 57°3N 2°29W 19 H13
Bancroft Canada 45°3N 77°51W 112 C9
Banda India 25°30N 80°26E 84 G12
Banda, Kepulauan Indonesia 4°37S 129°50E 83 D4
Banda Aceh Indonesia 5°35N 95°20E 83 C1
Banda Sea Indonesia 6°0S 130°0E 83 D5
Bandar-e Abbās Iran 27°15N 56°15E 87 E9
Bandar-e Anzali Iran 37°30N 49°30E 86 B7
Bandar-e Ma'shur Iran 30°35N 49°10E 86 D7
Bandar-e Torkeman Iran 37°0N 54°10E 87 B8
Bandar Lampung Indonesia 5°20S 105°10E 83 D2
Bandar Seri Begawan Brunei 4°52N 115°0E 83 C3
Bandeira, Pico da Brazil 20°26S 41°47W 122 D2
Bandırma Turkey 40°20N 28°0E 73 F4
Bandon Ireland 51°44N 8°44W 30 E5
Bandon → Ireland 51°43N 8°37W 30 E5
Bandundu
  Dem. Rep. of the Congo 3°15S 17°22E 96 E3
Bandung Indonesia 6°54S 107°36E 83 D2
Banes Cuba 21°0N 75°42W 115 C10
Banff Canada 51°10N 115°34W 108 D8
Banff U.K. 57°40N 2°33W 19 G12
Bangalore India 12°59N 77°40E 84 N10
Bangassou C.A.R. 4°55N 23°7E 96 D4
Banggai, Kepulauan Indonesia 1°40S 123°30E 83 D4
Bangka Indonesia 2°0S 105°50E 83 D2
Bangkok Thailand 13°45N 100°35E 83 B2
Bangladesh ■ Asia 24°0N 90°0E 85 H17
Bangor Down, U.K. 54°40N 5°40W 29 B10
Bangor Gwynedd, U.K. 53°14N 4°8W 26 A5
Bangui C.A.R. 4°23N 18°35E 96 D3
Bangweulu, L. Zambia 11°0S 30°0E 96 G6
Banham U.K. 52°27N 1°2E 25 B11
Bani Dom. Rep. 18°16N 70°22W 115 D10
Banja Luka Bos.-H. 44°49N 17°11E 70 B7
Banjarmasin Indonesia 3°20S 114°35E 83 D3
Banjul Gambia 13°28N 16°40W 94 F2
Bankend U.K. 55°1N 3°33W 21 D8
Banks I. Canada 73°15N 121°30W 108 B7
Banks Is. Vanuatu 13°50S 167°30E 99 C12
Bann → U.K. 55°8N 6°41W 29 A8
Bannockburn U.K. 56°5N 3°55W 21 B8
Bannu Pakistan 33°0N 70°18E 84 C7
Banská Bystrica Slovak Rep. 48°46N 19°14E 67 D10
Bantry Ireland 51°41N 9°27W 30 E4
Bantry B. Ireland 51°37N 9°44W 30 E3
Banwell U.K. 51°19N 2°52W 24 D3
Banyak, Kepulauan Indonesia 2°10N 97°10E 83 C1
Banyuwangi Indonesia 8°13S 114°21E 83 D3
Baoding China 38°50N 115°28E 81 C6
Baoji China 34°20N 107°5E 80 C5
Baoshan China 25°10N 99°5E 80 D4
Baotou China 40°32N 110°2E 81 B6
Ba'qūbah Iraq 33°45N 44°50E 86 C6
Bar Harbor U.S.A. 44°23N 68°13W 113 C13
Bar-le-Duc France 48°47N 5°10E 68 B6
Baraboo U.S.A. 43°28N 89°45W 112 D3
Baracoa Cuba 20°20N 74°30W 115 C10
Barahona Dom. Rep. 18°13N 71°7W 115 D10
Barail Range India 25°15N 93°20E 85 G18
Barakaldo Spain 43°18N 2°59W 69 A4
Baranavichy Belarus 53°10N 26°0E 67 B14
Baranof I. U.S.A. 57°0N 135°0W 108 D6
Barbacena Brazil 21°15S 43°56W 122 D2
Barbados ■ W. Indies 13°10N 59°30W 115 g
Barberton U.S.A. 41°1N 81°39W 112 E7
Barcelona Spain 41°22N 2°10E 69 B7
Barcelona Venezuela 10°10N 64°40W 120 A3
Barceloneta Puerto Rico 18°27N 66°32W 115 d
Barddhaman India 23°14N 87°39E 85 H15
Bardīyah Libya 31°45N 25°5E 95 B10
Bardney U.K. 53°13N 0°19W 23 F8
Bardsey I. U.K. 52°45N 4°47W 26 B4
Bardstown U.S.A. 37°49N 85°28W 112 G5
Bareilly India 28°22N 79°27E 84 E11
Barford U.K. 52°16N 1°35W 24 B5
Bargoed U.K. 51°42N 3°15W 26 D7
Barham U.K. 51°12N 1°11E 25 D11
Barhi India 24°15N 85°25E 85 G14
Bari Italy 41°8N 16°51E 70 D7
Bari Doab Pakistan 30°20N 73°0E 84 D8
Barīm Yemen 12°39N 43°25E 90 E8
Barinas Venezuela 8°36N 70°15W 120 B2
Baring, C. Canada 70°0N 117°30W 108 C8
Barisal Bangla. 22°45N 90°20E 85 H17
Barisal □ Bangla. 22°45N 90°20E 85 H17
Barking and Dagenham □
  U.K. 51°32N 0°10E 25 C9
Barkly Tableland Australia 17°50S 136°40E 98 D6

Barlborough U.K. 53°17N 1°17W 23 F6
Barlby U.K. 53°48N 1°2W 23 E6
Barlee, L. Australia 29°15S 119°30E 98 F2
Barletta Italy 41°19N 16°17E 70 D7
Barmby Moor U.K. 53°56N 0°49W 23 E7
Barmer India 25°45N 71°20E 84 G7
Barmoor Castle U.K. 55°39N 1°59W 22 A5
Barmouth U.K. 52°44N 4°4W 26 B5
Barnard Castle U.K. 54°33N 1°55W 22 C5
Barnaul Russia 53°20N 83°40E 79 D10
Barnet □ U.K. 51°38N 0°9W 25 C8
Barnetby le Wold U.K. 53°34N 0°24W 23 E8
Barnoldswick U.K. 53°55N 2°11W 23 E4
Barnsley U.K. 53°34N 1°27W 23 E6
Barnstaple U.K. 51°5N 4°4W 27 E5
Barotseland Zambia 15°0S 24°0E 97 H4
Barques, Pt. Aux U.S.A. 44°4N 82°58W 112 C6
Barquísimeto Venezuela 10°4N 69°19W 120 A3
Barra Brazil 11°5S 43°10W 122 B2
Barra U.K. 57°0N 7°29W 18 J2
Barra, Sd. of U.K. 57°4N 7°25W 18 H1
Barra do Corda Brazil 5°30S 45°10W 120 C5
Barra do Piraí Brazil 22°30S 43°50W 122 D2
Barra Mansa Brazil 22°35S 44°12W 122 D2
Barrancabermeja Colombia 7°0N 73°50W 120 B2
Barranquilla Colombia 11°0N 74°50W 120 A2
Barreiras Brazil 12°8S 45°0W 122 B2
Barreiro Portugal 38°39N 9°5W 69 C1
Barreiros Brazil 8°49S 35°12W 122 A3
Barretos Brazil 20°30S 48°35W 122 D1
Barrhead U.K. 55°48N 4°23W 20 C7
Barrie Canada 44°24N 79°40W 109 E12
Barrow U.S.A. 71°18N 156°47W 108 A4
Barrow → Ireland 52°25N 6°58W 31 D9
Barrow-in-Furness U.K. 54°7N 3°14W 22 D2
Barrow upon Humber U.K. 53°41N 0°23W 23 E8
Barrowford U.K. 53°51N 2°14W 23 E4
Barry U.K. 51°24N 3°16W 27 E7
Barry's Bay Canada 45°29N 77°41W 112 C9
Barstow U.S.A. 34°54N 117°1W 110 D3
Bartlesville U.S.A. 36°45N 95°59W 111 C7
Barton U.K. 54°29N 1°38W 22 D5
Barton upon Humber U.K. 53°41N 0°25W 23 E8
Barú, Volcan Panama 8°55N 82°35W 115 F8
Barwell U.K. 52°35N 1°21W 23 G6
Barysaw Belarus 54°17N 28°28E 67 A15
Bashkortostan □ Russia 54°0N 57°0E 72 D10
Basilan Phil. 6°35N 122°0E 83 C4
Basildon U.K. 51°34N 0°28E 25 C9
Basingstoke U.K. 51°15N 1°5W 24 D6
Baskatong, Rés. Canada 46°46N 75°50W 113 B10
Basle Switz. 47°35N 7°35E 66 E4
Basque Provinces = País Vasco □
  Spain 42°50N 2°45W 69 A4
Basra Iraq 30°30N 47°50E 86 D6
Bass Rock U.K. 56°5N 2°38W 21 B10
Bass Str. Australia 39°15S 146°30E 98 H8
Bassas da India Ind. Oc. 22°0S 39°0E 97 J7
Basse-Pointe Martinique 14°52N 61°8W 114 c
Basse-Terre Guadeloupe 16°0N 61°44W 114 b
Bassein Burma 16°45N 94°30E 85 L19
Bassenthwaite L. U.K. 54°40N 3°14W 22 C2
Basses, Pte. des Guadeloupe 15°52N 61°17W 114 b
Basseterre St. Kitts & Nevis 17°17N 62°43W 115 D12
Basti India 26°52N 82°55E 85 F13
Bastia France 42°40N 9°30E 68 E8
Baston U.K. 52°43N 0°21W 23 G8
Bata Eq. Guin. 1°57N 9°50E 96 D1
Batabanó, G. de Cuba 22°30N 82°30W 115 C8
Batangas Phil. 13°35N 121°10E 83 B4
Batatais Brazil 20°54S 47°37W 122 D1
Batavia U.S.A. 43°0N 78°11W 112 D8
Batdambang Cambodia 13°7N 103°12E 83 B2
Bath U.K. 51°23N 2°22W 24 D4
Bath Maine, U.S.A. 43°55N 69°49W 113 D13
Bath N.Y., U.S.A. 42°20N 77°19W 112 D9
Bathford U.K. 51°24N 2°18W 24 D4
Bathgate U.K. 55°54N 3°39W 21 C8
Bathsheba Barbados 13°13N 59°32W 115 g
Bathurst Australia 33°25S 149°31E 98 G8
Bathurst Canada 47°37N 65°43W 109 E13
Bathurst, C. Canada 70°34N 128°0W 108 B7
Bathurst Inlet Canada 66°50N 108°1W 108 C9
Batley U.K. 53°43N 1°38W 23 E5
Batman Turkey 37°55N 41°5E 73 G7
Batna Algeria 35°34N 6°15E 94 A7
Baton Rouge U.S.A. 30°27N 91°11W 111 D8
Batticaloa Sri Lanka 7°43N 81°45E 84 R12
Battle U.K. 50°55N 0°30E 25 E9
Battle Creek U.S.A. 42°19N 85°11W 112 D5
Batu, Kepulauan Indonesia 0°30S 98°25E 83 D1
Batu Pahat Malaysia 1°50N 102°56E 83 D2
Batumi Georgia 41°39N 41°44E 73 F7
Bauld, C. Canada 51°38N 55°26W 109 D14
Bauru Brazil 22°10S 49°0W 122 D1
Bavaria = Bayern □ Germany 48°50N 12°0E 66 D6
Bawdsey U.K. 52°1N 1°27E 25 B11
Bawtry U.K. 53°26N 1°2W 23 F6
Bay City U.S.A. 43°36N 83°54W 112 D6
Bayamo Cuba 20°20N 76°40W 115 C9
Bayamón Puerto Rico 18°24N 66°9W 115 d
Bayan Har Shan China 34°0N 98°0E 80 C4
Bayanhongor Mongolia 46°8N 102°43E 80 B5
Bayern □ Germany 48°50N 12°0E 66 D6
Bayeux France 49°17N 0°42W 68 B3
Bayonne France 43°30N 1°28W 68 E3
Beachley U.K. 51°37N 2°39W 24 C3
Beachy Hd. U.K. 50°44N 0°15E 25 E9
Beacon U.S.A. 41°30N 73°58W 113 E11
Beaconsfield U.K. 51°36N 0°38W 25 C7
Beadnell U.K. 55°33N 1°38W 22 A5
Beagle, Canal S. Amer. 55°0S 68°30W 121 H3
Beaminster U.K. 50°48N 2°44W 24 E3
Bear → U.S.A. 41°30N 112°8W 110 B4
Bear I. Arctic 74°30N 19°0E 54 B8

Bear I. Ireland 51°38N 9°50W 30 E3
Bear I. U.S.A. 41°59N 111°21W 110 B4
Beardmore Glacier Antarctica 84°30S 170°0E 55 E11
Beardstown U.S.A. 40°1N 90°26W 112 E2
Béarn France 43°20N 0°30W 68 E3
Bearsden U.K. 55°55N 4°21W 20 C7
Bearsted U.K. 51°16N 0°35E 25 D10
Beatrice U.S.A. 40°16N 96°45W 111 B7
Beattock U.K. 55°20N 3°28W 21 D9
Beauce, Plaine de la France 48°10N 1°45E 68 B4
Beaufort Sea Arctic 72°0N 140°0W 54 B1
Beaufort West S. Africa 32°18S 22°36E 97 L4
Beauharnois Canada 45°20N 73°52W 113 C11
Beaulieu U.K. 50°48N 1°27W 24 E6
Beauly U.K. 57°30N 4°28W 19 H9
Beauly → U.K. 57°29N 4°27W 19 H9
Beauly Firth U.K. 57°30N 4°20W 19 H9
Beaumaris U.K. 53°16N 4°6W 26 A5
Beaumont U.S.A. 30°5N 94°6W 111 D8
Beaune France 47°2N 4°50E 68 C6
Beauvais France 49°25N 2°8E 68 B5
Beaver → U.S.A. 55°26N 107°45W 108 D9
Beaver Creek Canada 63°0N 141°0W 108 C5
Beaver Dam U.S.A. 43°28N 88°50W 112 D3
Beaver Falls U.S.A. 40°46N 80°20W 112 E7
Beawar India 26°3N 74°18E 84 F9
Bebedouro Brazil 21°0S 48°25W 122 D1
Bebington U.K. 53°22N 3°0W 23 F3
Beccles U.K. 52°27N 1°35E 25 B12
Béchar Algeria 31°38N 2°18W 94 B5
Beckermet U.K. 54°27N 3°30W 22 D1
Beckfoot U.K. 54°50N 3°24W 22 C2
Beckingham U.K. 53°24N 0°50W 23 F7
Beckley U.S.A. 37°47N 81°11W 112 G7
Bedale U.K. 54°18N 1°36W 22 D5
Beddgelert U.K. 53°1N 4°6W 26 A5
Bedford U.K. 52°8N 0°28W 25 B8
Bedford Ind., U.S.A. 38°52N 86°29W 112 F4
Bedford Va., U.S.A. 37°20N 79°31W 112 G8
Bedford Level U.K. 52°32N 0°7W 25 A8
Bedfordshire □ U.K. 52°4N 0°28W 25 B8
Bedlington U.K. 55°8N 1°35W 22 B5
Bedworth U.K. 52°29N 1°28W 24 B6
Beef I. Br. Virgin Is. 18°26N 64°30W 115 e
Beeford U.K. 53°58N 0°17W 23 E8
Beer U.K. 50°41N 3°6W 27 F7
Be'er Sheva Israel 31°15N 34°48E 86 D3
Beeston U.K. 52°56N 1°14W 23 G6
Bei Jiang → China 23°2N 112°58E 81 D6
Bei'an China 48°10N 126°20E 81 B7
Beighton U.K. 53°21N 1°20W 23 F6
Beihai China 21°28N 109°6E 81 D5
Beijing China 39°53N 116°21E 81 C6
Beira Mozam. 19°50S 34°52E 97 H6
Beirut Lebanon 33°53N 35°31E 86 C3
Beitbridge Zimbabwe 22°12S 30°0E 97 J6
Beith U.K. 55°45N 4°38W 20 C6
Béja Tunisia 36°43N 9°12E 95 A7
Bejaïa Algeria 36°42N 5°2E 94 A7
Békéscsaba Hungary 46°40N 21°5E 67 E11
Bela Pakistan 26°12N 66°20E 84 F5
Belarus ■ Europe 53°30N 27°0E 72 D4
Belau = Palau ■ Palau 7°30N 134°30E 83 C5
Belbroughton U.K. 52°24N 2°7W 24 B4
Belcher Chan. Canada 77°15N 95°0W 109 B10
Belcher Is. Canada 56°15N 78°45W 109 D12
Belém Brazil 1°20S 48°30W 120 C5
Belep, Îs. N. Cal. 19°45S 163°40E 99 D11
Belet Uen Somali Rep. 4°30N 45°5E 88 G4
Belfast U.K. 54°37N 5°56W 29 B10
Belfast L. U.K. 54°40N 5°50W 29 B10
Belford U.K. 55°36N 1°49W 22 A5
Belgaum India 15°55N 74°35E 84 M9
Belgium ■ Europe 50°30N 5°0E 65 D4
Belgorod Russia 50°35N 36°35E 73 D6
Belgrade Serbia 44°50N 20°37E 71 B9
Belitung Indonesia 3°10S 107°50E 83 D2
Belize ■ Cent. Amer. 17°0N 88°30W 114 D7
Belize City Belize 17°25N 88°10W 114 D7
Bell Peninsula Canada 63°50N 82°0W 109 C11
Bell Ville Argentina 32°40S 62°40W 121 F3
Bella Coola Canada 52°25N 126°40W 108 D7
Bellaire U.S.A. 40°1N 80°45W 112 E7
Bellary India 15°10N 76°56E 84 M10
Belle Fourche → U.S.A. 44°26N 102°18W 110 B6
Belle-Île France 47°20N 3°10W 68 C2
Belle Isle Canada 51°57N 55°25W 109 D14
Belle Isle, Str. of Canada 51°30N 56°30W 109 D14
Bellefontaine U.S.A. 40°22N 83°46W 112 E6
Belleplaine Barbados 13°15N 59°34W 115 g
Belleville Canada 44°10N 77°23W 109 E12
Belleville U.S.A. 38°31N 89°59W 112 F3
Bellingham U.K. 55°9N 2°16W 22 B4
Bellingham U.S.A. 48°46N 122°29W 110 A2
Bellingshausen Sea Antarctica 66°0S 80°0W 55 C17
Bellinzona Switz. 46°11N 9°1E 66 E5
Belmonte Brazil 16°0S 39°0W 122 C3
Belmopan Belize 17°18N 88°30W 114 D7
Belmullet Ireland 54°14N 9°58W 28 C2
Belo Horizonte Brazil 19°55S 43°56W 122 C2
Belo Jardim Brazil 8°20S 36°26W 122 A3
Beloit U.S.A. 42°31N 89°2W 112 D3
Belomorsk Russia 64°35N 34°54E 72 B5
Beloretsk Russia 53°58N 58°24E 72 D10
Beloye, L. Russia 60°10N 37°35E 72 B6
Belper U.K. 53°2N 1°29W 23 F6
Belsay U.K. 55°6N 1°51W 22 B5
Belton N. Lincs., U.K. 53°33N 0°48W 23 E7
Belton Norfolk, U.K. 52°35N 1°40E 25 A12
Beltsy Moldova 47°48N 27°58E 67 E14
Belturbet Ireland 54°6N 7°26W 28 C7
Belukha Russia 49°50N 86°50E 79 E10
Belvidere U.S.A. 42°15N 88°50W 112 D3
Bembridge U.K. 50°41N 1°5W 24 E6
Bemidji U.S.A. 47°28N 94°53W 111 A8
Ben Cruachan U.K. 56°26N 5°8W 20 B5

Ben Dearg U.K. 57°47N 4°56W 19 G8
Ben Hope U.K. 58°25N 4°36W 19 F8
Ben Lawers U.K. 56°32N 4°14W 20 A7
Ben Lomond U.K. 56°11N 4°38W 20 A6
Ben Macdhui U.K. 57°4N 3°40W 19 H10
Ben Mhor U.K. 57°15N 7°18W 18 H3
Ben More Argyll & Bute, U.K. 56°26N 6°1W 20 B3
Ben More Stirling, U.K. 56°23N 4°32W 20 B6
Ben More Assynt U.K. 58°8N 4°52W 19 F8
Ben Nevis U.K. 56°48N 5°1W 18 J7
Ben Vorlich U.K. 56°21N 4°14W 20 B7
Ben Wyvis U.K. 57°40N 4°35W 19 G8
Benares = Varanasi India 25°22N 83°0E 85 G13
Benbecula U.K. 57°26N 7°21W 18 H3
Bend U.S.A. 44°4N 121°19W 110 B2
Benderloch U.K. 56°30N 5°22W 20 A5
Bendigo Australia 36°40S 144°15E 98 H7
Benevento Italy 41°8N 14°45E 70 D6
Bengal, Bay of Ind. Oc. 15°0N 90°0E 85 M17
Bengbu China 32°58N 117°20E 81 C6
Benghazi Libya 32°11N 20°3E 95 B10
Bengkulu Indonesia 3°50S 102°12E 83 D2
Benguela Angola 12°37S 13°25E 97 G2
Beni → Bolivia 10°23S 65°24W 120 D3
Beni Mellal Morocco 32°21N 6°21W 94 B4
Beni Suef Egypt 29°5N 31°6E 95 C12
Benidorm Spain 38°33N 0°9W 69 C5
Benin ■ Africa 10°0N 2°0E 94 G6
Benin, Bight of W. Afr. 5°0N 3°0E 94 H6
Benin City Nigeria 6°20N 5°31E 94 G7
Benington U.K. 53°0N 0°5E 23 F9
Benjamin Constant Brazil 4°40S 70°15W 120 C2
Benoni S. Africa 26°11S 28°18E 97 K5
Benson U.K. 51°37N 1°6W 24 C6
Bentley Hants., U.K. 51°12N 0°52W 25 D7
Bentley S. Yorks., U.K. 53°33N 1°8W 23 E6
Benton U.S.A. 38°0N 88°55W 112 G3
Benton Harbor U.S.A. 42°6N 86°27W 112 D4
Benue → Nigeria 7°48N 6°46E 94 G7
Benxi China 41°20N 123°48E 81 B7
Beppu Japan 33°15N 131°30E 82 G2
Berber Sudan 18°0N 34°0E 95 E12
Berbera Somali Rep. 10°30N 45°2E 88 E4
Berbérati C.A.R. 4°15N 15°40E 96 D3
Berbice → Guyana 6°20N 57°32W 120 B4
Berdyansk Ukraine 46°45N 36°50E 73 E6
Berdychiv Ukraine 49°57N 28°30E 73 E4
Bere Alston U.K. 50°29N 4°13W 27 G5
Bere Regis U.K. 50°45N 2°14W 24 E4
Berea U.S.A. 37°34N 84°17W 112 G5
Berens → Canada 52°25N 97°2W 108 D10
Berezina → Belarus 52°33N 30°14E 72 D5
Bereznik Russia 62°51N 42°40E 72 B7
Berezniki Russia 59°24N 56°46E 72 C10
Bérgamo Italy 45°41N 9°43E 70 B3
Bergen Norway 60°20N 5°20E 63 E5
Bergen op Zoom Neths. 51°28N 4°18E 65 C4
Bergerac France 44°51N 0°30E 68 D4
Bergisch Gladbach Germany 50°59N 7°8E 65 D7
Bering Sea Pac. Oc. 58°0N 171°0W 102 D1
Bering Strait Pac. Oc. 65°30N 169°0W 108 C3
Berkeley U.K. 51°41N 2°27W 24 C4
Berkhamsted U.K. 51°45N 0°33W 25 C7
Berkner I. Antarctica 79°30S 50°0W 55 D18
Berkshire Downs U.K. 51°33N 1°29W 24 C6
Berlin Germany 52°31N 13°23E 66 B7
Berlin U.S.A. 44°28N 71°11W 113 C12
Bermejo → Argentina 26°51S 58°23W 121 E4
Bermuda ☑ Atl. Oc. 32°45N 65°0W 52 C6
Bern Switz. 46°57N 7°28E 66 E4
Berneray U.K. 57°43N 7°11W 18 G3
Berry France 46°50N 2°0E 68 C5
Berry Hd. U.K. 50°24N 3°29W 27 G7
Bertraghboy B. Ireland 53°22N 9°54W 30 B3
Berwick U.S.A. 41°3N 76°14W 112 E9
Berwick-upon-Tweed U.K. 55°46N 2°0W 22 A5
Berwyn Mts. U.K. 52°54N 3°26W 26 B7
Besançon France 47°15N 6°2E 68 C7
Bessarabiya Moldova 47°0N 28°10E 67 E15
Bessemer U.S.A. 46°29N 90°3W 112 B2
Bethel U.S.A. 60°48N 161°45W 108 C3
Bethesda U.K. 53°10N 4°9W 26 A5
Bethlehem S. Africa 28°14S 28°18E 97 K5
Bethlehem U.S.A. 40°37N 75°23W 113 E10
Béthune France 50°30N 2°38E 68 A5
Bettiah India 26°48N 84°33E 85 F14
Betul India 21°58N 77°59E 84 J10
Betws-y-Coed U.K. 53°5N 3°48W 26 A6
Beverley U.K. 53°51N 0°26W 23 E8
Bewdley U.K. 52°23N 2°19W 24 B4
Bexhill U.K. 50°51N 0°29E 25 E9
Bexley □ U.K. 51°27N 0°9E 25 C9
Beyneu Kazakhstan 45°18N 55°9E 73 E10
Beypazarı Turkey 40°10N 31°56E 73 F5
Beyşehir Gölü Turkey 37°41N 31°33E 73 G5
Béziers France 43°20N 3°12E 68 E5
Bhagalpur India 25°10N 87°0E 85 G15
Bhaktapur Nepal 27°38N 85°24E 85 F14
Bhanrer Ra. India 23°40N 79°45E 84 H11
Bharatpur India 27°15N 77°30E 84 F10
Bharuch India 21°47N 73°0E 84 J8
Bhatinda India 30°15N 74°57E 84 D9
Bhatpara India 22°50N 88°25E 85 H16
Bhavnagar India 21°45N 72°10E 84 J8
Bhilainagar-Durg India 21°13N 81°26E 85 J12
Bhilwara India 25°25N 74°38E 84 G9
Bhima → India 16°25N 77°17E 84 L10
Bhiwandi India 19°20N 73°0E 84 K8
Bhiwani India 28°50N 76°9E 84 E10
Bhopal India 23°20N 77°30E 84 H10
Bhubaneshwar India 20°15N 85°50E 85 J14
Bhuj India 23°15N 69°49E 84 H6
Bhusawal India 21°3N 75°46E 84 J9
Bhutan ■ Asia 27°25N 90°30E 85 F17
Biała Podlaska Poland 52°4N 23°6E 67 B12
Białystok Poland 53°10N 23°10E 67 B12
Biarritz France 43°29N 1°33W 68 E3
Bibury U.K. 51°45N 1°49W 24 C5
Bicester U.K. 51°54N 1°9W 24 C6

Bicton　　　　　　　　　　　　　　　　　　　　　　　　　　　　　Burnham-on-Crouch

Bicton U.K. 52°44N 2°48W 23 G3
Bida Nigeria 9°3N 5°58E 94 G7
Biddeford U.S.A. 43°30N 70°28W 113 D12
Biddenden U.K. 51°7N 0°40E 25 D10
Biddulph U.K. 53°7N 2°10W 23 F4
Bideford U.K. 51°1N 4°13W 27 E5
Bideford Bay U.K. 51°5N 4°20W 27 E5
Bidford-on-Avon U.K. 52°11N 1°50W 24 B5
Bié Plateau Angola 12°0S 16°0E 97 G3
Biel Switz. 47°8N 7°14E 66 E4
Bielefeld Germany 52°1N 8°33E 66 B5
Biella Italy 45°34N 8°3E 70 B3
Bielsko-Biała Poland 49°50N 19°2E 67 D10
Bien Hoa Vietnam 10°57N 106°49E 83 B2
Bienville, L. Canada 55°5N 72°40W 109 D12
Big Belt Mts. U.S.A. 46°30N 111°25W 110 A4
Big Rapids U.S.A. 43°42N 85°29W 112 D5
Big Sioux → U.S.A. 42°29N 96°27W 111 B7
Big Spring U.S.A. 32°15N 101°28W 110 D6
Big Trout L. Canada 53°40N 90°0W 109 D11
Bigbury U.K. 50°18N 3°53W 27 G6
Bigbury B. U.K. 50°16N 3°54W 27 G6
Biggar Canada 52°4N 108°0W 108 D9
Biggar U.K. 55°38N 3°32W 21 C8
Biggleswade U.K. 52°5N 0°14W 25 B8
Bighorn → U.S.A. 46°10N 107°28W 110 A5
Bighorn Mts. U.S.A. 44°25N 107°0W 110 B5
Bihar India 25°5N 85°40E 85 G14
Bihar □ India 25°0N 86°0E 85 G15
Bijagós, Arquipélago dos
Guinea-Biss. 11°15N 16°10W 94 F2
Bijapur India 16°50N 75°55E 84 L9
Bikaner India 28°2N 73°18E 84 E8
Bikini Atoll Marshall Is. 12°0N 167°30E 102 F8
Bila Tserkva Ukraine 49°45N 30°10E 67 D16
Bilaspur India 22°2N 82°15E 85 H13
Bilbao Spain 43°16N 2°56W 69 A4
Bilecik Turkey 40°5N 30°5E 73 F5
Bilhorod-Dnistrovskyy
Ukraine 46°11N 30°23E 73 E5
Billericay U.K. 51°38N 0°26E 25 C9
Billesdon U.K. 52°38N 0°54W 23 G7
Billingham U.K. 54°36N 1°17W 22 C6
Billinghay U.K. 53°5N 0°15W 23 F8
Billings U.S.A. 45°47N 108°30W 110 A5
Billingshurst U.K. 51°2N 0°27W 25 D8
Bilma Niger 18°50N 13°30E 95 E8
Biloxi U.S.A. 30°24N 88°53W 111 D9
Bilston U.K. 52°34N 2°4W 23 G4
Bimini Is. Bahamas 25°42N 79°25W 115 B9
Binbrook U.K. 53°26N 0°10W 23 E8
Bingham U.K. 52°57N 0°58W 23 G7
Binghamton U.S.A. 42°6N 75°55W 113 D10
Bingley U.K. 53°51N 1°50W 23 E5
Bioko Eq. Guin. 3°30N 8°40E 96 D1
Biratnagar Nepal 26°27N 87°17E 85 F15
Birchington U.K. 51°22N 1°19E 25 D11
Birdlip U.K. 51°50N 2°5W 24 C4
Birkdale U.K. 53°38N 3°1W 23 E2
Birkenhead U.K. 53°23N 3°2W 23 F2
Birmingham U.K. 52°29N 1°52W 23 H5
Birmingham U.S.A. 33°31N 86°48W 111 D9
Birmingham Int. ✈ (BHX)
U.K. 52°32N 1°45W 23 H5
Birnin Kebbi Nigeria 12°32N 4°12E 94 F6
Birr Ireland 53°6N 7°54W 30 B7
Birtley Northumberland, U.K. 55°6N 2°12W 22 B4
Birtley Tyne & Wear, U.K. 54°54N 1°34W 22 C5
Biscay, B. of Atl. Oc. 45°0N 2°0W 68 D1
Bishkek Kyrgyzstan 42°54N 74°46E 79 E9
Bishop Auckland U.K. 54°39N 1°40W 22 C5
Bishop's Castle U.K. 52°30N 2°59W 23 H3
Bishop's Cleeve U.K. 51°57N 2°3W 24 C4
Bishop's Frome U.K. 52°8N 2°29W 24 B4
Bishop's Nympton U.K. 51°0N 3°47W 27 F6
Bishop's Stortford U.K. 51°52N 0°10E 25 C9
Bishop's Waltham U.K. 50°57N 1°11W 24 E6
Bishopsteignton U.K. 50°33N 3°33W 27 F6
Bishopstoke U.K. 50°58N 1°19W 24 E6
Biskra Algeria 34°50N 5°44E 94 B7
Bismarck U.S.A. 46°48N 100°47W 110 A6
Bismarck Arch. Papua N. G. 2°30S 150°0E 98 A9
Bissau Guinea-Biss. 11°45N 15°45W 94 F2
Bitola Macedonia 41°1N 21°20E 71 D9
Bitterfontein S. Africa 31°1S 18°32E 97 L3
Bitterroot Range U.S.A. 46°0N 114°20W 110 A4
Bitton U.K. 51°25N 2°27W 24 D4
Biu Nigeria 10°40N 12°3E 95 F8
Biwa-Ko Japan 35°15N 136°10E 82 F5
Bizerte Tunisia 37°15N 9°50E 95 A7
Blaby U.K. 52°35N 1°10W 23 G6
Black Combe U.K. 54°16N 3°20W 22 D2
Black Esk → U.K. 55°12N 3°11W 21 D9
Black Forest = Schwarzwald
Germany 48°30N 8°20E 66 D5
Black Hd. Ireland 53°9N 9°16W 30 B4
Black Hd. U.K. 50°0N 5°7W 27 H3
Black Hills U.S.A. 44°0N 103°45W 110 B6
Black Isle U.K. 57°35N 4°16W 19 G9
Black Mts. U.K. 51°55N 3°7W 26 D7
Black Range U.S.A. 33°15N 107°50W 110 D5
Black River Jamaica 18°0N 77°50W 114 a
Black River Falls U.S.A. 44°18N 90°51W 112 C2
Black Rock Barbados 13°7N 59°37W 115 g
Black Sea Eurasia 43°30N 35°0E 73 F6
Blackburn U.K. 53°45N 2°29W 23 E4
Blackdown Hills U.K. 50°57N 3°15W 24 E2
Blackmoor Vale U.K. 50°54N 2°28W 24 E4
Blackpool U.K. 53°49N 3°3W 23 E2
Blackrock Ireland 53°18N 6°11W 31 B10
Blacksburg U.S.A. 37°14N 80°25W 112 G7
Blacksod B. Ireland 54°6N 10°0W 28 C1
Blackwater → Meath, Ireland 53°39N 6°41W 29 D8
Blackwater → Waterford,
Ireland 52°4N 7°52W 30 D7
Blackwater → Armagh, U.K. 54°31N 6°35W 29 C8
Blackwater → Essex, U.K. 51°44N 0°53E 25 C10
Blaenau Ffestiniog U.K. 53°0N 3°56W 26 B6

Blaenavon U.K. 51°46N 3°5W 26 D7
Blagdon U.K. 51°20N 2°43W 24 D3
Blagoevgrad Bulgaria 42°2N 23°5E 71 C10
Blagoveshchensk Russia 50°20N 127°30E 79 D14
Blair Atholl U.K. 56°46N 3°50W 19 J10
Blairgowrie U.K. 56°35N 3°21W 21 A9
Blakeney Gloucs., U.K. 51°46N 2°28W 24 C4
Blakeney Norfolk, U.K. 52°58N 1°1E 25 A11
Blanc, Mont Europe 45°48N 6°50E 68 D7
Blanca, B. Argentina 39°10S 61°30W 121 F3
Blanca Peak U.S.A. 37°35N 105°29W 110 C5
Blanco, C. U.S.A. 42°51N 124°34W 110 B2
Blandford Forum U.K. 50°51N 2°9W 24 E4
Blanquilla Venezuela 11°51N 64°37W 115 E12
Blantyre Malawi 15°45S 35°0E 97 H6
Blarney Ireland 51°56N 8°33W 30 E5
Blaydon U.K. 54°58N 1°42W 22 C5
Blean U.K. 51°18N 1°3E 25 D11
Bleasdale Moors U.K. 53°55N 2°35W 23 E3
Blenheim N.Z. 41°38S 173°57E 99 J13
Bletchingdon U.K. 51°51N 1°15W 24 C6
Bletchley U.K. 51°59N 0°44W 25 C7
Blida Algeria 36°30N 2°49E 94 A6
Blisworth U.K. 52°10N 0°56W 25 B7
Blitar Indonesia 8°5S 112°11E 83 D3
Blockley U.K. 52°1N 1°44W 24 B5
Bloemfontein S. Africa 29°6S 26°7E 97 K5
Blofield U.K. 52°38N 1°26E 25 A11
Blois France 47°35N 1°20E 68 C4
Bloody Foreland Ireland 55°10N 8°17W 28 A5
Bloomington Ill., U.S.A. 40°28N 89°0W 112 E3
Bloomington Ind., U.S.A. 39°10N 86°32W 112 F4
Bloomsburg U.S.A. 41°0N 76°27W 112 E9
Bloxham U.K. 52°1N 1°21W 24 B6
Blue Mountain Pk. Jamaica 18°3N 76°36W 114 a
Blue Mts. Jamaica 18°3N 76°36W 114 a
Blue Mts. Oreg., U.S.A. 45°0N 118°20W 110 A3
Blue Mts. Pa., U.S.A. 40°30N 76°30W 112 E9
Blue Nile → Sudan 15°38N 32°31E 95 E12
Blue Ridge Mts. U.S.A. 36°30N 80°15W 111 C10
Blue Stack Mts. Ireland 54°42N 8°12W 28 B5
Bluefield U.S.A. 37°15N 81°17W 112 G7
Bluefields Nic. 12°20N 83°50W 115 E8
Blumenau Brazil 27°0S 49°0W 121 E5
Blundeston U.K. 52°31N 1°42E 25 A12
Blyth Northumberland, U.K. 55°8N 1°31W 22 B5
Blyth Notts., U.K. 53°22N 1°3W 23 F6
Blyth → U.K. 55°8N 1°33W 22 B5
Blyth Bridge U.K. 55°42N 3°22W 21 C9
Blyton U.K. 53°27N 0°42W 23 F7
Bo S. Leone 7°55N 11°50W 94 G3
Bo Hai China 39°0N 119°0E 81 C6
Boa Vista Brazil 2°48N 60°30W 120 B3
Bobcaygeon Canada 44°33N 78°33W 112 C8
Bobo-Dioulasso Burkina Faso 11°8N 4°13W 94 F5
Bóbr → Poland 52°4N 15°4E 66 B8
Bochum Germany 51°28N 7°13E 66 C4
Boddam U.K. 59°56N 1°17W 18 C15
Boden Sweden 65°50N 21°42E 63 D8
Bodiam U.K. 51°0N 0°34E 25 D10
Bodinnick U.K. 50°20N 4°38W 27 G4
Bodmin U.K. 50°28N 4°43W 27 G4
Bodmin Moor U.K. 50°33N 4°36W 27 F4
Bodø Norway 67°17N 14°24E 63 D6
Bodrog → Hungary 48°11N 21°22E 67 D11
Bodrum Turkey 37°3N 27°30E 73 G4
Bogalusa U.S.A. 30°47N 89°52W 111 D9
Bogda Shan China 43°35N 89°40E 80 B3
Boggeragh Mts. Ireland 52°2N 8°55W 30 D5
Bognor Regis U.K. 50°47N 0°40W 25 E7
Bogor Indonesia 6°36S 106°48E 83 D2
Bogotá Colombia 4°34N 74°0W 120 B2
Bogra Bangla. 24°51N 89°22E 85 G16
Böhmerwald Germany 49°8N 13°14E 66 D7
Bohol Sea Phil. 9°0N 124°0E 83 C4
Boise U.S.A. 43°37N 116°13W 110 B3
Boké Guinea 10°56N 14°17W 94 F3
Bole China 45°11N 81°37E 80 B3
Bolivia ■ S. Amer. 17°6S 64°0W 120 D3
Bollington U.K. 53°18N 2°6W 23 F4
Bolney U.K. 50°59N 0°12W 25 E8
Bologna Italy 44°29N 11°20E 70 B4
Bologoye Russia 57°55N 34°5E 72 C5
Bolsena, L. di Italy 42°36N 11°56E 70 C4
Bolsover U.K. 53°14N 1°16W 23 F6
Bolt Head U.K. 50°12N 3°48W 27 G6
Bolt Tail U.K. 50°14N 3°52W 27 G6
Bolton U.K. 53°35N 2°26W 23 E4
Bolton Abbey U.K. 53°59N 1°53W 23 E5
Bolton by Bowland U.K. 53°56N 2°20W 23 E4
Bolton le Sands U.K. 54°6N 2°48W 22 D3
Bolu Turkey 40°45N 31°35E 73 F5
Bolvadin Turkey 38°45N 31°4E 73 G5
Bolzano Italy 46°31N 11°22E 70 A4
Bom Despacho Brazil 19°43S 45°15W 122 C1
Bom Jesus da Lapa Brazil 13°15S 43°25W 122 B2
Bombala Australia 36°56S 149°15E 98 H8
Bombay = Mumbai India 18°56N 72°50E 84 K8
Bomu → C.A.R. 4°40N 22°30E 96 D4
Bon, C. Tunisia 37°1N 11°2E 90 C5
Bonaire Neth. Ant. 12°10N 68°15W 115 E11
Bonar Bridge U.K. 57°54N 4°20W 19 G9
Bonavista Canada 48°40N 53°5W 109 E14
Bonchester Bridge U.K. 55°24N 2°39W 21 D10
Bonchurch U.K. 50°37N 1°11W 24 E6
Bo'ness U.K. 56°1N 3°37W 21 B8
Bongor Chad 10°35N 15°20E 95 F9
Bongos, Massif des C.A.R. 8°40N 22°25E 96 C4
Bonifacio France 41°24N 9°10E 68 F8
Bonn Germany 50°46N 7°6E 66 C4
Bonny, Bight of Africa 3°30N 9°20E 96 D1
Bonnyrigg U.K. 55°53N 3°6W 21 C9
Boonville U.S.A. 38°3N 87°16W 112 F4
Boothia, Gulf of Canada 71°0N 90°0W 109 B11
Boothia Pen. Canada 71°0N 94°0W 108 B10
Bootle Cumb., U.K. 54°18N 3°22W 22 D2
Bootle Mersey., U.K. 53°28N 3°1W 23 F2

Borås Sweden 57°43N 12°56E 63 F6
Borborema, Planalto da Brazil 7°0S 37°0W 116 D7
Bordeaux France 44°50N 0°36W 68 D3
Borden I. Canada 78°30N 111°30W 109 B8
Borden Pen. Canada 73°0N 83°0W 109 B11
Bordon U.K. 51°8N 0°52W 25 D7
Borehamwood U.K. 51°40N 0°15W 25 C8
Boreland U.K. 55°13N 3°17W 21 D9
Borger U.S.A. 35°39N 101°24W 110 C6
Borhoyn Tal Mongolia 43°50N 111°58E 81 B6
Borisoglebsk Russia 51°27N 42°5E 73 D7
Borkou Chad 18°15N 18°50E 95 E9
Borneo E. Indies 1°0N 115°0E 83 C3
Bornholm Denmark 55°10N 15°0E 63 F7
Borohoro Shan China 44°6N 83°10E 80 B3
Boroughbridge U.K. 54°6N 1°24W 22 D6
Borovichi Russia 58°25N 33°55E 72 C5
Borrowdale U.K. 54°31N 3°10W 22 C2
Borth U.K. 52°29N 4°2W 26 C5
Borūjerd Iran 33°55N 48°50E 86 C7
Brechin U.K. 56°44N 2°39W 19 J12
Bosaso Somali Rep. 11°12N 49°18E 88 E4
Bosbury U.K. 52°5N 2°26W 24 B4
Boscastle U.K. 50°41N 4°42W 27 F4
Boscobelle Barbados 13°17N 59°35W 115 g
Bose China 23°53N 106°35E 80 D5
Bosham U.K. 50°49N 0°51W 25 E7
Bosnia-Herzegovina ■ Europe 44°0N 18°0E 70 B7
Bosporus Turkey 41°5N 29°3E 73 F4
Bossangoa C.A.R. 6°35N 17°30E 96 C3
Bosten Hu China 41°55N 87°40E 80 B3
Boston U.K. 52°59N 0°2W 23 G8
Boston U.S.A. 42°22N 71°3W 113 D12
Bothel U.K. 54°45N 3°15W 22 C2
Bothnia, G. of Europe 62°0N 20°0E 63 E8
Botletle → Botswana 20°10S 23°15E 97 J4
Botoşani Romania 47°42N 26°41E 67 E14
Botswana ■ Africa 22°0S 24°0E 97 J4
Bottesford U.K. 52°57N 0°47W 23 G7
Bottrop Germany 51°31N 6°58E 65 C6
Botucatu Brazil 22°55S 48°30W 122 D1
Bou Saâda Algeria 35°11N 4°9E 94 A6
Bouaké Ivory C. 7°40N 5°2W 94 G4
Bouar C.A.R. 6°0N 15°40E 96 C3
Bouârfa Morocco 32°32N 1°58W 94 B5
Bougainville I. Papua N. G. 6°0S 155°0E 99 B10
Bouillante Guadeloupe 16°8N 61°46W 114 b
Boulder U.S.A. 40°1N 105°17W 110 B5
Boulogne-sur-Mer France 50°42N 1°36E 68 A4
Bounty Is. Pac. Oc. 48°0S 178°30E 102 M9
Bourbonnais France 46°28N 3°0E 68 C5
Bourg-en-Bresse France 46°13N 5°12E 68 C6
Bourges France 47°9N 2°25E 68 C5
Bourgogne □ France 47°0N 4°50E 68 C6
Bourke Australia 30°8S 145°55E 98 G8
Bourne U.K. 52°47N 0°22W 23 G8
Bournemouth U.K. 50°43N 1°52W 24 E5
Bourton-on-the-Water U.K. 51°52N 1°45W 24 C5
Bouvet I. Antarctica 54°26S 3°24E 52 G10
Bovey Tracey U.K. 50°36N 3°41W 27 F6
Bow → Canada 49°57N 111°41W 108 D8
Bowes U.K. 54°32N 1°59W 22 C5
Bowland, Forest of U.K. 54°0N 2°30W 23 E3
Bowling Green Ky., U.S.A. 36°59N 86°27W 112 G4
Bowling Green Ohio, U.S.A. 41°23N 83°39W 112 E6
Bowmore U.K. 55°45N 6°17W 20 C3
Bowness-on-Solway U.K. 54°57N 3°12W 22 C2
Bowness-on-Windermere
U.K. 54°22N 2°55W 22 D3
Box U.K. 51°25N 2°15W 24 D4
Box Hill U.K. 51°15N 0°16W 25 D8
Boyle Ireland 53°59N 8°18W 28 D5
Boyne → Ireland 53°43N 6°15W 29 D9
Boyoma, Chutes
Dem. Rep. of the Congo 0°35N 25°23E 90 F6
Bozeat U.K. 52°14N 0°40W 25 B7
Bozeman U.S.A. 45°41N 111°2W 110 A4
Bozoum C.A.R. 6°25N 16°35E 96 C3
Brabant □ Belgium 50°46N 4°30E 65 D4
Brač Croatia 43°20N 16°40E 70 C7
Bracadale, L. U.K. 57°20N 6°30W 18 H4
Bracebridge Canada 45°2N 79°19W 112 C8
Bracebridge Heath U.K. 53°12N 0°32W 23 F7
Bräcke Sweden 62°45N 15°26E 63 E7
Brackley U.K. 52°2N 1°8W 24 B6
Bracknell U.K. 51°25N 0°43W 25 D7
Bradford U.K. 53°47N 1°45W 23 E5
Bradford U.S.A. 41°58N 78°38W 112 E8
Bradford on Avon U.K. 51°21N 2°14W 24 D4
Brading U.K. 50°41N 1°8W 24 E6
Bradwell-on-Sea U.K. 51°43N 0°56E 25 C10
Bradworthy U.K. 50°53N 4°24W 27 F5
Braemar U.K. 57°2N 3°26W 19 H11
Braga Portugal 41°35N 8°25W 69 B1
Bragança Brazil 1°0S 47°2W 120 C5
Bragança Paulista Brazil 22°55S 46°32W 122 D1
Brahmanbaria Bangla. 23°58N 91°15E 85 H17
Brahmani → India 20°39N 86°46E 85 J15
Brahmapur India 19°15N 84°54E 85 K14
Brahmaputra → Asia 23°40N 90°35E 85 H16
Braich-y-pwll U.K. 52°47N 4°46W 26 B4
Brăila Romania 45°19N 27°59E 67 F14
Brailsford U.K. 52°58N 1°35W 23 G5
Brainerd U.S.A. 46°22N 94°12W 111 A8
Braintree U.K. 51°53N 0°34E 25 C10
Bramford U.K. 52°4N 1°7E 25 B11
Brampton Canada 43°45N 79°45W 112 D8
Brampton Cambs., U.K. 52°20N 0°14W 25 B8
Brampton Cumb., U.K. 54°57N 2°44W 22 C3
Brancaster U.K. 52°58N 0°38E 25 A10
Branco → Brazil 1°20S 61°50W 120 C3
Brandenburg Germany 52°25N 12°33E 66 B7
Brandenburg □ Germany 52°50N 13°0E 66 B7
Branderburgh U.K. 57°43N 3°17W 19 G11
Brandon Canada 49°50N 99°57W 108 E10
Brandon Durham, U.K. 54°46N 1°37W 22 C5
Brandon Suffolk, U.K. 52°27N 0°38E 25 B9
Brandon B. Ireland 52°17N 10°8W 30 D2
Brandon Mt. Ireland 52°15N 10°15W 30 D2

Branston U.K. 53°12N 0°27W 23 F8
Brantford Canada 43°10N 80°15W 112 D7
Bras d'Or L. Canada 45°50N 60°50W 113 C17
Brasília Brazil 15°47S 47°55W 122 C1
Brașov Romania 45°38N 25°35E 67 F13
Bratislava Slovak Rep. 48°10N 17°7E 67 D9
Bratsk Russia 56°10N 101°30E 79 D12
Brattleboro U.S.A. 42°51N 72°34W 113 D11
Braunschweig Germany 52°15N 10°31E 66 B6
Braunton U.K. 51°7N 4°10W 27 E5
Bray Ireland 53°13N 6°7W 31 B10
Bray U.K. 51°30N 0°41W 25 D7
Brazil U.S.A. 39°32N 87°8W 112 F4
Brazil ■ S. Amer. 12°0S 50°0W 120 D4
Brazilian Highlands Brazil 18°0S 46°30W 116 E6
Brazos → U.S.A. 28°53N 95°23W 111 E7
Brazzaville Congo 4°9S 15°12E 96 E3
Breadalbane U.K. 56°30N 4°15W 20 A7
Breage U.K. 50°6N 5°20W 27 G3
Breamish → U.K. 55°35N 2°2W 22 A4
Brechin U.K. 56°44N 2°39W 19 J12
Breckland U.K. 52°30N 0°40E 25 B10
Brecon U.K. 51°57N 3°23W 26 D7
Brecon Beacons U.K. 51°53N 3°26W 26 D7
Brecon Beacons △ U.K. 51°50N 3°30W 26 D6
Breda Neths. 51°35N 4°45E 65 C4
Brede U.K. 50°56N 0°36E 25 E10
Bredon Hill U.K. 52°3N 2°2W 24 B4
Bregenz Austria 47°30N 9°45E 66 E5
Breiðafjörður Iceland 65°15N 23°15W 63 A1
Bremen Germany 53°4N 8°47E 66 B5
Bremerhaven Germany 53°33N 8°36E 66 B5
Bremerton U.S.A. 47°34N 122°37W 110 A2
Brendon Hills U.K. 51°6N 3°25W 24 D2
Brennerpass Austria 47°2N 11°30E 66 E6
Brent □ U.K. 51°33N 0°16W 25 C8
Brentwood U.K. 51°37N 0°19E 25 C9
Bréscia Italy 45°33N 10°15E 70 B4
Bressay U.K. 60°9N 1°6W 18 B15
Brest Belarus 52°10N 23°40E 67 B12
Brest France 48°24N 4°31W 68 B1
Bretagne □ France 48°10N 3°0W 68 B2
Breton Sd. U.S.A. 29°35N 89°15W 111 E9
Brewer U.S.A. 44°48N 68°46W 113 C13
Brewood U.K. 52°41N 2°9W 23 G4
Briançon France 44°54N 6°39E 68 D7
Bridestowe U.K. 50°41N 4°7W 27 F5
Bridge U.K. 51°15N 1°8E 25 D11
Bridgefield Barbados 13°9N 59°36W 115 g
Bridgend U.K. 51°30N 3°34W 27 D6
Bridgeport U.S.A. 41°11N 73°12W 113 E11
Bridgeton U.S.A. 39°26N 75°14W 113 F10
Bridgetown Barbados 13°6N 59°37W 115 g
Bridgewater Canada 44°25N 64°31W 109 E13
Bridgnorth U.K. 52°32N 2°25W 23 G4
Bridgwater U.K. 51°8N 2°59W 24 D3
Bridgwater B. U.K. 51°15N 3°15W 24 D2
Bridlington U.K. 54°5N 0°12W 22 D8
Bridlington B. U.K. 54°4N 0°10W 23 D8
Bridport U.K. 50°44N 2°45W 24 E3
Brierfield U.K. 53°49N 2°14W 23 E4
Brierley Hill U.K. 52°29N 2°6W 23 H4
Brigg U.K. 53°34N 0°28W 23 E8
Brigham City U.S.A. 41°31N 112°1W 110 B4
Brighouse U.K. 53°42N 1°46W 23 E5
Brighstone U.K. 50°38N 1°24W 24 E6
Brightlingsea U.K. 51°49N 1°2E 25 C11
Brighton U.K. 50°49N 0°7W 25 E8
Brigstock U.K. 52°27N 0°36W 25 B7
Brill U.K. 51°49N 1°1W 24 C6
Brimfield U.K. 52°18N 2°41W 24 B3
Brinklow U.K. 52°25N 1°22W 24 B6
Brinkworth U.K. 51°33N 1°59W 24 C5
Brisbane Australia 27°25S 153°2E 98 F9
Bristol U.K. 51°26N 2°35W 24 D3
Bristol B. U.S.A. 58°0N 160°0W 108 D4
Bristol Channel U.K. 51°18N 4°30W 27 E5
Briston U.K. 52°51N 1°4E 25 A11
British Columbia □ Canada 55°0N 125°15W 108 D7
British Virgin Is. ☑ W. Indies 18°30N 64°30W 115 e
Brittany = Bretagne □ France 48°10N 3°0W 68 B2
Brive-la-Gaillarde France 45°10N 1°32E 68 D4
Brixham U.K. 50°23N 3°31W 27 G6
Brixworth U.K. 52°20N 0°54W 25 B7
Brize Norton U.K. 51°46N 1°34W 24 C5
Brno Czech Rep. 49°10N 16°35E 67 D9
Broad B. U.K. 58°14N 6°18W 18 F5
Broad Chalke U.K. 51°2N 1°56W 24 D5
Broad Haven Ireland 54°20N 9°55W 28 C2
Broad Law U.K. 55°30N 3°21W 21 C9
Broad Sd. U.K. 49°55N 6°21W 27 H1
Broadclyst U.K. 50°46N 3°27W 27 F7
Broadhembury U.K. 50°49N 3°18W 27 F7
Broadstairs U.K. 51°21N 1°27E 25 D11
Broadway U.K. 52°2N 1°50W 24 B5
Broadwindsor U.K. 50°48N 2°47W 24 E3
Brochet Canada 57°53N 101°40W 108 D9
Brock I. Canada 77°52N 114°19W 109 B8
Brocken Germany 51°47N 10°37E 66 C6
Brockenhurst U.K. 50°49N 1°34W 24 E5
Brockville Canada 44°35N 75°41W 113 C10
Brockworth U.K. 51°51N 2°9W 24 C4
Brodeur Pen. Canada 72°30N 88°10W 109 B11
Brodick U.K. 55°35N 5°9W 20 D5
Broken Hill Australia 31°58S 141°29E 98 G7
Bromfield U.K. 52°24N 2°45W 23 H3
Bromham U.K. 51°23N 2°1W 24 D4
Bromley □ U.K. 51°24N 0°2E 25 D9
Brompton U.K. 54°21N 1°25W 22 D6
Bromsgrove U.K. 52°21N 2°2W 24 B4
Bromyard U.K. 52°11N 2°30W 24 B3
Brookings U.S.A. 44°19N 96°48W 111 B7
Brooks Canada 50°35N 111°55W 108 D8
Brooks Range U.S.A. 68°0N 152°0W 108 C5
Broom, L. U.K. 57°55N 5°15W 18 G7
Broome Australia 18°0S 122°15E 98 D3
Broomhill U.K. 55°18N 1°36W 22 B5

Brora U.K. 58°0N 3°52W 19 F10
Brora → U.K. 58°0N 3°51W 19 F10
Broseley U.K. 52°37N 2°29W 23 G4
Brosna → Ireland 53°14N 7°58W 30 B7
Brothertoft U.K. 53°0N 0°7W 23 F8
Brotton U.K. 54°35N 0°56W 22 C7
Brough Cumb., U.K. 54°32N 2°18W 22 C4
Brough E. Riding, U.K. 53°44N 0°36W 23 E7
Brough Hd. U.K. 59°8N 3°20W 19 D11
Broughton Borders, U.K. 55°37N 3°24W 21 C9
Broughton N. Lincs., U.K. 53°34N 0°34W 23 E7
Broughton Northants., U.K. 52°22N 0°46W 25 B7
Broughton-in-Furness U.K. 54°17N 3°13W 22 D2
Broughty Ferry U.K. 56°29N 2°51W 21 B10
Brown Willy U.K. 50°35N 4°37W 27 F4
Brownhills U.K. 52°39N 1°54W 23 G5
Brownsville U.S.A. 25°54N 97°30W 111 E7
Brownwood U.S.A. 31°43N 98°59W 110 D7
Broxburn U.K. 55°56N 3°28W 21 C9
Bruay-la-Buissière France 50°29N 2°33E 68 A5
Bruce, Mt. Australia 22°37S 118°8E 98 E2
Bruce L. U.K. 51°3N 2°59W 24 D3
Brugge Belgium 51°13N 3°13E 65 C3
Brumado Brazil 14°14S 41°40W 122 B2
Brunei ■ Asia 4°50N 115°0E 83 C3
Brunswick Ga., U.S.A. 31°10N 81°30W 111 D10
Brunswick Maine, U.S.A. 43°55N 69°58W 113 D13
Brunton U.K. 55°2N 2°6W 22 B4
Brussels Belgium 50°51N 4°21E 65 D4
Bruton U.K. 51°7N 2°27W 24 D4
Bryan Ohio, U.S.A. 41°28N 84°33W 112 E5
Bryan Tex., U.S.A. 30°40N 96°22W 111 D7
Bryansk Russia 53°13N 34°25E 72 D4
Bryher U.K. 49°57N 6°22W 27 H1
Brynamman U.K. 51°49N 3°51W 26 D6
Brynmawr U.K. 51°48N 3°10W 26 D7
Bucaramanga Colombia 7°0N 73°0W 120 B2
Buchan U.K. 57°32N 2°21W 19 G13
Buchan Ness U.K. 57°29N 1°46W 19 G14
Buchanan Liberia 5°57N 10°2W 94 G3
Bucharest Romania 44°27N 26°10E 67 F14
Buckden U.K. 52°18N 0°14W 25 B8
Buckfastleigh U.K. 50°28N 3°48W 27 G6
Buckhannon U.S.A. 39°0N 80°8W 112 F7
Buckhaven U.K. 56°11N 3°3W 21 B9
Buckie U.K. 57°41N 2°58W 19 G12
Buckingham Canada 45°37N 75°24W 113 C10
Buckingham U.K. 51°59N 0°57W 25 C7
Buckinghamshire □ U.K. 51°53N 0°55W 25 C7
Buckland Brewer U.K. 50°58N 4°15W 27 F5
Buckland Newton U.K. 50°50N 2°26W 24 E4
Buckley U.K. 53°10N 3°5W 26 A7
Budapest Hungary 47°29N 19°3E 67 E10
Bude U.K. 50°49N 4°34W 27 F4
Bude B. U.K. 50°49N 4°35W 27 F4
Budle B. U.K. 55°37N 1°45W 22 A5
Budleigh Salterton U.K. 50°37N 3°19W 27 F7
Buena Vista U.S.A. 37°44N 79°21W 112 G8
Buenaventura Colombia 3°53N 77°4W 120 B2
Buenos Aires Argentina 34°36S 58°22W 121 F4
Buenos Aires, L. Argentina 46°35S 72°30W 121 G2
Buffalo N.Y., U.S.A. 42°53N 78°53W 112 D8
Buffalo Wyo., U.S.A. 44°21N 106°42W 110 B5
Bug → Poland 52°31N 21°5E 67 B11
Bug → Ukraine 46°59N 31°58E 73 E5
Bugle U.K. 50°24N 4°47W 27 G4
Bugulma Russia 54°33N 52°48E 72 D9
Buguruslan Russia 53°39N 52°26E 72 D9
Builth Wells U.K. 52°9N 3°25W 26 C7
Buir Nur Mongolia 47°50N 117°42E 81 B6
Bujumbura Burundi 3°16S 29°18E 96 E5
Bukavu Dem. Rep. of the Congo 2°20S 28°52E 96 E5
Bukhoro Uzbekistan 39°48N 64°25E 87 B11
Bukittinggi Indonesia 0°20S 100°20E 83 D2
Bulawayo Zimbabwe 20°7S 28°32E 97 J5
Bulford U.K. 51°11N 1°45W 24 D5
Bulgan Mongolia 48°45N 103°34E 80 B5
Bulgaria ■ Europe 42°35N 25°30E 71 C11
Bullhead City U.S.A. 35°8N 114°32W 110 C4
Bunbury Australia 33°20S 115°35E 98 G2
Bunclody Ireland 52°39N 6°40W 31 C9
Buncrana Ireland 55°8N 7°27W 28 A7
Bundaberg Australia 24°54S 152°22E 98 E9
Bundi India 25°30N 75°35E 84 G9
Bundoran Ireland 54°28N 8°16W 28 C5
Bungay U.K. 52°27N 1°28E 25 B11
Buntingford U.K. 51°56N 0°0 25 C9
Bunwell U.K. 52°30N 1°9E 25 A11
Buon Ma Thuot Vietnam 12°40N 108°3E 83 B2
Bur Acaba Somali Rep. 3°12N 44°20E 88 G3
Bûr Safâga Egypt 26°43N 33°57E 95 C12
Burao Somali Rep. 9°32N 45°32E 88 F4
Buraydah Si. Arabia 26°20N 43°59E 86 E5
Burbage Derby., U.K. 53°15N 1°55W 23 F5
Burbage Leics., U.K. 52°32N 1°21W 23 G6
Burbage Wilts., U.K. 51°21N 1°39W 24 D5
Burdur Turkey 37°45N 30°17E 73 G5
Bure → U.K. 52°38N 1°43E 25 A12
Burford U.K. 51°49N 1°38W 24 C5
Burgas Bulgaria 42°33N 27°29E 71 C12
Burgess Hill U.K. 50°58N 0°6W 25 E8
Burgh le Marsh U.K. 53°9N 0°15E 23 F9
Burghead U.K. 57°43N 3°30W 19 G11
Burgos Spain 42°21N 3°41W 69 A4
Burgundy = Bourgogne □
France 47°0N 4°50E 68 C6
Burhanpur India 21°18N 76°14E 84 J10
Burkina Faso ■ Africa 12°0N 1°0W 94 F5
Burley Hants., U.K. 50°49N 1°43W 24 E5
Burley N. Yorks., U.K. 53°54N 1°45W 23 E5
Burley U.S.A. 42°32N 113°48W 110 B4
Burlington Colo., U.S.A. 39°18N 102°16W 110 C6
Burlington Iowa, U.S.A. 40°49N 91°14W 111 B8
Burlington Vt., U.S.A. 44°29N 73°12W 113 C11
Burlington Wis., U.S.A. 42°41N 88°17W 112 D3
Burma ■ Asia 21°0N 96°30E 85 J20
Burnham Market U.K. 52°57N 0°44E 25 A10
Burnham-on-Crouch U.K. 51°38N 0°49E 25 C10

Burnham-on-Sea *U.K.* 51°14N 3°0W **24** D2
Burnie *Australia* 41°4S 145°56E **98** J8
Burnley *U.K.* 53°47N 2°14W **23** E4
Burnmouth *U.K.* 55°50N 2°4W **21** C11
Burns *U.S.A.* 43°35N 119°3W **110** B3
Burnside → *Canada* 66°51N 108°4W **108** C9
Burntisland *U.K.* 56°4N 3°13W **21** B9
Burqin *China* 47°43N 87°0E **80** B3
Burray *U.K.* 58°51N 2°54W **19** E12
Burren △ *Ireland* 53°1N 8°58W **30** B4
Burrow Hd. *U.K.* 54°41N 4°24W **20** E7
Burry Port *U.K.* 51°41N 4°15W **26** D5
Bursa *Turkey* 40°15N 29°5E **73** F4
Burstwick *U.K.* 53°44N 0°8W **23** E8
Burton *U.K.* 54°11N 2°43W **22** D3
Burton Agnes *U.K.* 54°4N 0°18W **22** D8
Burton Bradstock *U.K.* 50°42N 2°43W **24** E3
Burton Fleming *U.K.* 54°8N 0°20W **22** D8
Burton Latimer *U.K.* 52°22N 0°41W **25** B7
Burton upon Stather *U.K.* 53°39N 0°41W **23** E7
Burton upon Trent *U.K.* 52°48N 1°38W **23** G5
Buru *Indonesia* 3°30S 126°30E **83** D4
Burundi ■ *Africa* 3°15S 30°0E **96** E5
Burwash *U.K.* 50°59N 0°23E **25** E9
Burwell *U.K.* 52°17N 0°20E **25** B9
Burwick *U.K.* 58°45N 2°58W **19** E12
Bury *U.K.* 53°35N 2°17W **23** E4
Bury St. Edmunds *U.K.* 52°15N 0°43E **25** B10
Busan *S. Korea* 35°5N 129°0E **81** C7
Būshehr *Iran* 28°55N 50°55E **87** D7
Bushey *U.K.* 51°38N 0°22W **25** C8
Busto Arsizio *Italy* 45°37N 8°51E **70** B3
Buta *Dem. Rep. of the Congo* 2°50N 24°53E **96** D4
Butare *Rwanda* 2°31S 29°52E **96** E5
Butaritari *Kiribati* 3°30N 174°0E **102** G9
Bute *U.K.* 55°48N 5°2W **20** C5
Bute, Kyles of *U.K.* 55°55N 5°10W **20** C5
Butembo *Dem. Rep. of the Congo* 0°9N 29°18E **96** D5
Butha Qi *China* 48°0N 122°32E **81** B7
Butler *U.S.A.* 40°52N 79°54W **112** E8
Buton *Indonesia* 5°0S 122°45E **83** D4
Butte *U.S.A.* 46°0N 112°32W **110** A4
Buttermere *U.K.* 54°32N 3°16W **22** C2
Butterworth *Malaysia* 5°24N 100°23E **83** C2
Buttevant *Ireland* 52°14N 8°40W **30** D5
Butuan *Phil.* 8°57N 125°33E **83** C4
Buxton *U.K.* 53°16N 1°54W **23** F5
Buyant-Uhaa *Mongolia* 44°55N 110°11E **81** B6
Buzău *Romania* 45°10N 26°50E **67** F14
Buzuluk *Russia* 52°48N 52°12E **72** D9
Bydgoszcz *Poland* 53°10N 18°0E **67** B9
Byfield *U.K.* 52°10N 1°14W **24** B6
Bylot I. *Canada* 73°13N 78°34W **109** B12
Byrranga Ra. *Russia* 75°0N 100°0E **79** B12
Bytom *Poland* 50°25N 18°54E **67** C10

C

Ca Mau *Vietnam* 9°7N 105°8E **83** C2
Cabanatuan *Phil.* 15°30N 120°58E **83** B4
Cabedelo *Brazil* 7°0S 34°50W **120** C6
Cabimas *Venezuela* 10°23N 71°25W **120** A2
Cabinda *Angola* 5°33S 12°11E **96** F2
Cabinda □ *Angola* 5°0S 12°30E **96** F2
Cabo Frio *Brazil* 22°51S 42°3W **122** D2
Cabo San Lucas *Mexico* 22°53N 109°54W **114** C3
Cabonga, Réservoir *Canada* 47°20N 76°40W **109** E12
Cabora Bassa Dam *Mozam.* 15°20S 32°50E **97** H6
Cabot Str. *Canada* 47°15N 59°40W **109** E14
Čačak *Serbia* 43°54N 20°20E **71** C9
Cáceres *Brazil* 16°5S 57°40W **120** D4
Cáceres *Spain* 39°26N 6°23W **69** C2
Cachimbo, Serra do *Brazil* 9°30S 55°30W **120** C4
Cachoeira *Brazil* 12°30S 39°0W **122** B3
Cachoeira do Sul *Brazil* 30°3S 52°53W **121** F4
Cachoeiro de Itapemirim *Brazil* 20°51S 41°7W **122** D2
Cader Idris *U.K.* 52°42N 3°53W **26** B6
Cadillac *U.S.A.* 44°15N 85°24W **112** C5
Cádiz *Spain* 36°30N 6°20W **69** D2
Cádiz, G. de *Spain* 36°40N 7°0W **69** D2
Caen *France* 49°10N 0°22W **68** B3
Caenby Corner *U.K.* 53°24N 0°33W **23** F7
Caernarfon *U.K.* 53°8N 4°16W **26** A5
Caernarfon B. *U.K.* 53°4N 4°40W **26** A4
Caerphilly *U.K.* 51°35N 3°13W **27** D7
Caersws *U.K.* 52°31N 3°26W **26** B7
Caeté *Brazil* 19°55S 43°40W **122** C2
Caetité *Brazil* 13°50S 42°32W **122** B2
Cagayan de Oro *Phil.* 8°30N 124°40E **83** C4
Cágliari *Italy* 39°13N 9°7E **70** E3
Caguas *Puerto Rico* 18°14N 66°2W **115** d
Caha Mts. *Ireland* 51°45N 9°40W **30** E3
Caher *Ireland* 52°22N 7°56W **30** D7
Cahersiveen *Ireland* 51°56N 10°14W **30** E2
Cahore Pt. *Ireland* 52°33N 6°12W **31** C10
Cahors *France* 44°27N 1°27E **68** D4
Cairn Gorm *U.K.* 57°7N 3°39W **19** H10
Cairngorm Mts. *U.K.* 57°6N 3°42W **19** H10
Cairngorms △ *U.K.* 57°10N 3°50W **19** H10
Cairnryan *U.K.* 54°59N 5°1W **20** E5
Cairns *Australia* 16°57S 145°45E **98** D8
Cairnsmore of Fleet *U.K.* 54°59N 4°20W **20** E7
Cairo *Egypt* 30°2N 31°13E **95** B12
Cairo *U.S.A.* 37°0N 89°11W **112** G3
Caister-on-Sea *U.K.* 52°40N 1°43E **25** A12
Caistor *U.K.* 53°30N 0°18W **23** F8
Caithness *U.K.* 58°25N 3°35W **19** F10
Caithness, Ord of *U.K.* 58°8N 3°36W **19** F10
Caja de Muertos, I. *Puerto Rico* 17°54N 66°32W **115** d
Cajamarca *Peru* 7°5S 78°28W **120** C2
Calabar *Nigeria* 4°57N 8°20E **94** H7
Calábria □ *Italy* 39°0N 16°30E **70** E7
Calais *France* 50°57N 1°56E **68** A4
Calais *U.S.A.* 45°11N 67°17W **113** C14
Calama *Chile* 22°30S 68°55W **121** E3
Calamian Group *Phil.* 11°50N 119°55E **83** B3
Calanscio, Sarīr *Libya* 27°30N 21°30E **95** C10
Calapan *Phil.* 13°25N 121°7E **83** B4
Calbayog *Phil.* 12°4N 124°38E **83** B4
Calcutta = Kolkata *India* 22°34N 88°21E **85** H16
Caldbeck *U.K.* 54°45N 3°3W **22** C2
Calder → *U.K.* 53°44N 1°22W **23** E6
Calder Bridge *U.K.* 54°27N 3°29W **22** D2
Caldera *Chile* 27°5S 70°55W **121** E2
Caldew → *U.K.* 54°54N 2°56W **22** C3
Caldwell *U.S.A.* 43°40N 116°41W **110** B3
Caledonian Canal *U.K.* 57°29N 4°15W **19** H9
Calgary *Canada* 51°0N 114°10W **108** D8
Cali *Colombia* 3°25N 76°35W **120** B2
Calicut *India* 11°15N 75°43E **84** P9
California □ *U.S.A.* 37°30N 119°30W **110** C2
California, G. de *Mexico* 27°0N 111°0W **114** B2
Callan *Ireland* 52°32N 7°24W **31** C8
Callander *U.K.* 56°15N 4°13W **20** B7
Callao *Peru* 12°3S 77°8W **120** D2
Calne *U.K.* 51°26N 2°0W **24** D5
Calshot *U.K.* 50°48N 1°19W **24** E6
Calstock *U.K.* 50°30N 4°13W **27** F5
Caltanissetta *Italy* 37°29N 14°4E **70** F6
Calvi *France* 42°34N 8°45E **68** E8
Calvinia *S. Africa* 31°28S 19°45E **97** L3
Cam → *U.K.* 52°21N 0°16E **25** B9
Cam Ranh *Vietnam* 11°54N 109°12E **83** B2
Camagüey *Cuba* 21°20N 77°55W **115** C9
Camargue *France* 43°34N 4°34E **68** E6
Camberley *U.K.* 51°20N 0°44W **25** D7
Cambo *U.K.* 55°10N 1°57W **22** B5
Cambodia ■ *Asia* 12°15N 105°0E **83** B2
Camborne *U.K.* 50°12N 5°19W **27** G3
Cambrai *France* 50°11N 3°14E **68** A5
Cambrian Mts. *U.K.* 52°3N 3°57W **26** C6
Cambridge *Jamaica* 18°18N 77°54W **114** a
Cambridge *U.K.* 52°12N 0°8E **25** B9
Cambridge *Mass., U.S.A.* 42°23N 71°7W **113** D12
Cambridge *Md., U.S.A.* 38°34N 76°5W **113** F9
Cambridge *Ohio, U.S.A.* 40°2N 81°35W **112** E7
Cambridge Bay *Canada* 69°10N 105°0W **108** C9
Cambridgeshire □ *U.K.* 52°25N 0°7W **25** B8
Camden *Ark., U.S.A.* 33°35N 92°50W **111** D8
Camden *N.J., U.S.A.* 39°55N 75°7W **113** F10
Camden □ *U.K.* 51°32N 0°8W **25** C8
Camel → *U.K.* 50°31N 4°51W **27** F4
Camelford *U.K.* 50°37N 4°42W **27** F4
Cameroon ■ *Africa* 6°0N 12°30E **96** C2
Cameroun, Mt. *Cameroon* 4°13N 9°10E **96** D1
Cametá *Brazil* 2°12S 49°30W **120** C5
Camocim *Brazil* 2°55S 40°50W **120** C5
Campana, I. *Chile* 48°20S 75°20W **121** G2
Campánia □ *Italy* 41°0N 14°30E **70** D6
Campbell I. *Pac. Oc.* 52°30S 169°0E **102** N8
Campbell River *Canada* 50°5N 125°20W **108** D7
Campbellsville *U.S.A.* 37°21N 85°20W **112** G5
Campbellton *Canada* 47°57N 66°43W **109** E13
Campbeltown *U.K.* 55°26N 5°36W **20** D4
Campeche *Mexico* 19°51N 90°32W **114** D6
Campeche, Golfo de *Mexico* 19°30N 93°0W **114** D6
Campina Grande *Brazil* 7°20S 35°47W **120** C6
Campinas *Brazil* 22°50S 47°0W **122** D1
Campo Belo *Brazil* 20°52S 45°16W **122** D1
Campo Grande *Brazil* 20°25S 54°40W **120** E4
Campobasso *Italy* 41°34N 14°39E **70** D6
Campos *Brazil* 21°50S 41°20W **122** D2
Campos Belos *Brazil* 13°10S 47°3W **122** B1
Camrose *Canada* 53°0N 112°50W **108** D8
Can Tho *Vietnam* 10°2N 105°46E **83** B2
Canada ■ *N. Amer.* 60°0N 100°0W **108** D10
Canadian → *U.S.A.* 35°28N 95°3W **111** C7
Canadian Shield *Canada* 53°0N 75°0W **104** C9
Çanakkale *Turkey* 40°8N 26°24E **73** F4
Canandaigua *U.S.A.* 42°54N 77°17W **112** D9
Cananea *Mexico* 31°0N 110°18W **114** A2
Canaries *St. Lucia* 13°55N 61°4W **115** f
Canary Is. *Atl. Oc.* 28°30N 16°0W **94** C2
Canaveral, C. *U.S.A.* 28°27N 80°32W **111** E10
Canavieiras *Brazil* 15°39S 39°0W **122** C3
Canberra *Australia* 35°15S 149°8E **98** H8
Cancún *Mexico* 21°8N 86°44W **114** C7
Cangzhou *China* 38°19N 116°52E **81** C6
Caniapiscau → *Canada* 56°40N 69°30W **109** D13
Caniapiscau, L. de *Canada* 54°10N 69°55W **109** D13
Çankırı *Turkey* 40°40N 33°37E **73** F5
Canna *U.K.* 57°3N 6°33W **18** H4
Canna, Sd. of *U.K.* 57°1N 6°30W **18** H5
Cannanore *India* 11°53N 75°27E **84** P9
Cannes *France* 43°32N 7°1E **68** E7
Cannington *U.K.* 51°9N 3°4W **24** D2
Cannock *U.K.* 52°41N 2°1W **23** G4
Cannock Chase *U.K.* 52°44N 2°4W **23** G4
Canoas *Brazil* 29°56S 51°11W **121** E4
Cañon City *U.S.A.* 38°27N 105°14W **110** C5
Canonbie *U.K.* 55°5N 2°58W **21** D10
Canora *Canada* 51°40N 102°30W **108** D9
Canso *Canada* 45°20N 61°0W **113** C17
Cantabria □ *Spain* 43°10N 4°0W **69** A4
Cantábrica, Cordillera *Spain* 43°0N 5°10W **69** A3
Canterbury *U.K.* 51°16N 1°6E **25** D11
Canton = Guangzhou *China* 23°6N 113°13E **81** D6
Canton *Ill., U.S.A.* 40°33N 90°2W **112** E2
Canton *N.Y., U.S.A.* 44°36N 75°10W **113** C10
Canton *Ohio, U.S.A.* 40°48N 81°23W **112** E7
Canvey *U.K.* 51°31N 0°37E **25** C10
Cap-de-la-Madeleine *Canada* 46°22N 72°31W **113** B11
Cap-Haïtien *Haiti* 19°40N 72°20W **115** D10
Cap Pt. *St. Lucia* 14°7N 60°57W **115** f
Cape Breton I. *Canada* 46°0N 60°30W **113** C17
Cape Charles *U.S.A.* 37°16N 76°1W **113** G10
Cape Coast *Ghana* 5°5N 1°15W **94** G5
Cape Coral *U.S.A.* 26°33N 81°57W **111** E10
Cape Dorset *Canada* 64°14N 76°32W **109** C12
Cape Fear → *U.S.A.* 33°53N 78°1W **111** D11
Cape Girardeau *U.S.A.* 37°19N 89°32W **112** G3
Cape May *U.S.A.* 38°56N 74°56W **113** F10
Cape Town *S. Africa* 33°55S 18°22E **97** L3
Cape Verde Is. ■ *Atl. Oc.* 16°0N 24°0W **91** E1
Cape York Peninsula *Australia* 12°0S 142°30E **98** C7
Capela *Brazil* 10°30S 37°0W **122** B3
Capesterre-Belle-Eau *Guadeloupe* 16°4N 61°36W **114** b
Capesterre-de-Marie-Galante *Guadeloupe* 15°53N 61°14W **114** b
Capreol *Canada* 46°43N 80°56W **112** B7
Capri *Italy* 40°33N 14°14E **70** D6
Caprivi Strip *Namibia* 18°0S 23°0E **97** H4
Caquetá → *Colombia* 1°15S 69°15W **120** C3
Caracas *Venezuela* 10°30N 66°55W **120** A3
Caracol *Brazil* 9°15S 43°22W **122** A2
Carangola *Brazil* 20°44S 42°5W **122** D2
Caratasca, L. *Honduras* 15°20N 83°40W **115** D8
Caratinga *Brazil* 19°50S 42°10W **122** C2
Caravelas *Brazil* 17°45S 39°15W **122** C3
Caravelle, Presqu'île de la *Martinique* 14°46N 60°48W **114** c
Carbón, L. del *Argentina* 49°35S 68°21W **121** G3
Carbondale *Ill., U.S.A.* 37°44N 89°13W **112** G3
Carbondale *Pa., U.S.A.* 41°35N 75°30W **113** E10
Carbonear *Canada* 47°42N 53°13W **109** E14
Carcassonne *France* 43°13N 2°20E **68** E5
Carcross *Canada* 60°13N 134°45W **108** C6
Cardamon Hills *India* 9°30N 77°15E **84** Q10
Cárdenas *Cuba* 23°0N 81°30W **115** C8
Cardiff *U.K.* 51°29N 3°10W **27** E7
Cardigan *U.K.* 52°5N 4°40W **26** C4
Cardigan B. *U.K.* 52°30N 4°30W **26** B4
Cardington *U.K.* 52°6N 0°25W **25** B8
Cardston *Canada* 49°15N 113°20W **108** E8
Cariacica *Brazil* 20°16S 40°25W **122** D2
Caribbean Sea *W. Indies* 15°0N 75°0W **115** E10
Cariboo Mts. *Canada* 53°0N 121°0W **108** D7
Caribou *U.S.A.* 46°52N 68°1W **113** B13
Caribou Mts. *Canada* 59°12N 115°40W **108** D8
Carinhanha *Brazil* 14°15S 44°46W **122** B2
Carinhanha → *Brazil* 14°20S 43°47W **122** B2
Carinthia = Kärnten □ *Austria* 46°52N 13°30E **66** E8
Carisbrooke *U.K.* 50°41N 1°19W **24** E6
Cark *U.K.* 54°11N 2°58W **22** D3
Carleton Place *Canada* 45°8N 76°9W **113** C9
Carleton Rode *U.K.* 52°30N 1°7E **25** A11
Carlingford L. *U.K.* 54°3N 6°9W **29** C9
Carlinville *U.S.A.* 39°17N 89°53W **112** F3
Carlisle *U.K.* 54°54N 2°56W **22** C3
Carlisle *U.S.A.* 40°12N 77°12W **112** E9
Carlisle B. *Barbados* 13°5N 59°37W **115** g
Carlops *U.K.* 55°47N 3°20W **21** C9
Carlow *Ireland* 52°50N 6°56W **31** C9
Carlow □ *Ireland* 52°43N 6°50W **31** C9
Carlsbad *U.S.A.* 32°25N 104°14W **110** D6
Carlton *U.K.* 52°59N 1°5W **23** G6
Carlton Colville *U.K.* 52°27N 1°43E **25** B12
Carlton Miniott *U.K.* 54°12N 1°22W **22** D6
Carluke *U.K.* 55°45N 3°50W **21** C8
Carmacks *Canada* 62°5N 136°16W **108** C6
Carmarthen *U.K.* 51°52N 4°19W **26** D5
Carmarthen B. *U.K.* 51°40N 4°30W **26** D4
Carmarthenshire □ *U.K.* 51°55N 4°13W **26** D5
Carmaux *France* 44°3N 2°10E **68** D5
Carmi *U.S.A.* 38°5N 88°10W **112** F3
Carn Ban *U.K.* 57°7N 4°15W **19** H9
Carn Eige *U.K.* 57°17N 5°8W **18** H7
Carnarvon *Australia* 24°51S 113°42E **98** E1
Carnarvon *S. Africa* 30°56S 22°8E **97** L4
Carndonagh *Ireland* 55°16N 7°15W **29** A7
Carnegie, L. *Australia* 26°5S 122°30E **98** F3
Carnforth *U.K.* 54°7N 2°45W **22** D3
Carno *U.K.* 52°34N 3°30W **26** B6
Carnoustie *U.K.* 56°30N 2°42W **21** A10
Carnsore Pt. *Ireland* 52°10N 6°22W **31** D10
Caro *U.S.A.* 43°29N 83°24W **112** D6
Carolina *Puerto Rico* 18°23N 65°58W **115** d
Caroline I. *Kiribati* 9°58S 150°13W **103** H12
Caroline Is. *Micronesia* 8°0N 150°0E **102** G7
Carondelet *Kiribati* 5°33S 173°50E **99** B16
Caroni → *Venezuela* 8°21N 62°43W **120** B3
Carpathians *Europe* 49°30N 21°0E **67** D11
Carpentaria, G. of *Australia* 14°0S 139°0E **98** C6
Carpentras *France* 44°3N 5°2E **68** D6
Carpi *Italy* 44°47N 10°53E **70** B4
Carrara *Italy* 44°5N 10°6E **70** B4
Carrauntoohill *Ireland* 52°0N 9°45W **30** E3
Carrick-on-Shannon *Ireland* 53°57N 8°5W **28** D5
Carrick-on-Suir *Ireland* 52°21N 7°24W **31** D8
Carrickfergus *U.K.* 54°43N 5°49W **29** B10
Carrickmacross *Ireland* 53°59N 6°43W **29** D8
Carrollton *U.S.A.* 39°18N 90°24W **112** F2
Carron → *U.K.* 57°53N 4°22W **19** G9
Carron, L. *U.K.* 57°22N 5°35W **18** H6
Carson City *U.S.A.* 39°10N 119°46W **110** C3
Carson Sink *U.S.A.* 39°50N 118°25W **110** C3
Cartagena *Colombia* 10°25N 75°33W **120** A2
Cartagena *Spain* 37°38N 0°59W **69** D5
Cartago *Colombia* 4°45N 75°55W **120** B2
Carthage *Tunisia* 36°52N 10°20E **95** A8
Cartmel *U.K.* 54°12N 2°57W **22** D3
Cartwright *Canada* 53°41N 56°58W **109** D14
Caruaru *Brazil* 8°15S 35°55W **122** A3
Carúpano *Venezuela* 10°39N 63°15W **120** A3
Casa Grande *U.S.A.* 32°53N 111°45W **110** D4
Casablanca *Morocco* 33°36N 7°36W **94** B4
Cascade Ra. *U.S.A.* 47°0N 121°30W **110** A2
Cascavel *Ceará, Brazil* 4°7S 38°14W **120** C6
Cascavel *Paraná, Brazil* 24°57S 53°28W **121** E4
Caserta *Italy* 41°4N 14°20E **70** D6
Cashel *Ireland* 52°30N 7°53W **30** C7
Casiquiare → *Venezuela* 2°1N 67°7W **120** B3
Casper *U.S.A.* 42°51N 106°19W **110** B5
Caspian Depression *Eurasia* 47°0N 48°0E **73** E8
Caspian Sea *Eurasia* 43°0N 50°0E **73** F9
Cassiar Mts. *Canada* 59°30N 130°30W **108** D6
Castellammare di Stábia *Italy* 40°42N 14°29E **70** D6
Castelló de la Plana *Spain* 39°58N 0°3W **69** C5
Castelsarrasin *France* 44°2N 1°7E **68** E4
Castilla-La Mancha □ *Spain* 39°30N 3°30W **69** C4
Castilla y Leon □ *Spain* 42°0N 5°0W **69** B3
Castle Acre *U.K.* 52°42N 0°42E **25** A10
Castle Cary *U.K.* 51°6N 2°31W **24** D3
Castle Donington *U.K.* 52°51N 1°20W **23** G6
Castle Douglas *U.K.* 54°56N 3°56W **21** E8
Castlebar *Ireland* 53°52N 9°18W **28** D3
Castlebay *U.K.* 56°57N 7°31W **18** J2
Castleblaney *Ireland* 54°7N 6°44W **29** C8
Castlederg *U.K.* 54°42N 7°35W **28** B6
Castleford *U.K.* 53°43N 1°21W **23** E6
Castlemaine Harbour *Ireland* 52°8N 9°50W **30** D3
Castlepollard *Ireland* 53°41N 7°19W **28** D7
Castlerea *Ireland* 53°46N 8°29W **28** D5
Castleside *U.K.* 54°50N 1°52W **22** C5
Castleton *Derby, U.K.* 53°22N 1°46W **23** F5
Castleton *N. Yorks., U.K.* 54°28N 0°57W **22** D7
Castletown *I. of Man* 54°5N 4°38W **29** C12
Castletown Bearhaven *Ireland* 51°39N 9°55W **30** E3
Castres *France* 43°37N 2°13E **68** E5
Castries *St. Lucia* 14°2N 60°58W **115** f
Castro *Chile* 42°30S 73°50W **121** G2
Castro Alves *Brazil* 12°46S 39°33W **122** B3
Cat I. *Bahamas* 24°30N 75°30W **115** C9
Cataguases *Brazil* 21°23S 42°39W **122** D2
Catalão *Brazil* 18°10S 47°57W **122** C1
Cataluña □ *Spain* 41°40N 1°15E **69** B6
Catamarca *Argentina* 28°30S 65°50W **121** E3
Catanduanes □ *Phil.* 13°50N 124°20E **83** B4
Catanduva *Brazil* 21°5S 48°58W **122** D1
Catánia *Italy* 37°30N 15°6E **70** F6
Catanzaro *Italy* 38°54N 16°35E **70** E7
Catcleugh *U.K.* 55°20N 2°24W **22** B4
Caterham *U.K.* 51°15N 0°4W **25** D8
Catoche, C. *Mexico* 21°35N 87°5W **114** C7
Caton *U.K.* 54°5N 2°42W **22** D3
Catsfield *U.K.* 50°54N 0°28E **25** E9
Catskill *U.S.A.* 42°14N 73°52W **113** D11
Catskill Mts. *U.S.A.* 42°10N 74°25W **113** D10
Catterick *U.K.* 54°23N 1°37W **22** D5
Catterick Camp *U.K.* 54°22N 1°42W **22** D5
Catton *U.K.* 54°55N 2°15W **22** C4
Cauca → *Colombia* 8°54N 74°28W **120** B2
Caucaia *Brazil* 3°40S 38°35W **120** C6
Caucasus Mountains *Eurasia* 42°50N 44°0E **73** F7
Caulkerbush *U.K.* 54°54N 3°41W **21** E9
Caura → *Venezuela* 7°38N 64°53W **120** B3
Cauvery → *India* 11°9N 78°52E **84** P11
Cavan *Ireland* 54°0N 7°22W **28** D7
Cavan □ *Ireland* 54°1N 7°16W **29** C7
Caviana, I. *Brazil* 0°10N 50°10W **120** B4
Cawood *U.K.* 53°50N 1°8W **23** E6
Cawston *U.K.* 52°47N 1°9E **25** A11
Caxias *Brazil* 4°55S 43°20W **120** C5
Caxias do Sul *Brazil* 29°10S 51°10W **121** E4
Cayenne *Fr. Guiana* 5°5N 52°18W **120** B4
Cayey *Puerto Rico* 18°7N 66°10W **115** d
Cayman Is. ☑ *W. Indies* 19°40N 80°30W **115** D8
Cayuga L. *U.S.A.* 42°41N 76°41W **112** D9
Ceanannus Mor *Ireland* 53°44N 6°53W **29** D8
Ceará □ *Brazil* 5°0S 40°0W **120** C6
Cebu *Phil.* 10°18N 123°54E **83** B4
Cedar City *U.S.A.* 37°41N 113°4W **110** C4
Cedar L. *Canada* 53°10N 100°0W **108** D10
Cedar Rapids *U.S.A.* 41°59N 91°40W **111** B81
Cefalù *Italy* 38°2N 14°1E **70** E6
Cegléd *Hungary* 47°11N 19°47E **67** E10
Celaya *Mexico* 20°31N 100°37W **114** C4
Celebes Sea *Indonesia* 3°0N 123°0E **83** C4
Celina *U.S.A.* 40°33N 84°35W **112** E5
Cellar Hd. *U.K.* 58°25N 6°11W **18** F5
Celtic Sea *Atl. Oc.* 50°9N 9°34W **64** F2
Cemaes *U.K.* 53°24N 4°27W **26** A5
Central, Cordillera *Colombia* 5°0N 75°0W **116** C3
Central, Cordillera *Puerto Rico* 18°8N 66°35W **115** d
Central African Rep. ■ *Africa* 7°0N 20°0E **96** C4
Central Makran Range *Pakistan* 26°30N 64°15E **84** F4
Central Russian Uplands *Europe* 54°0N 36°0E **56** E13
Central Siberian Plateau *Russia* 65°0N 105°0E **74** B12
Centralia *Ill., U.S.A.* 38°32N 89°8W **112** F3
Centralia *Wash., U.S.A.* 46°43N 122°58W **110** A2
Cephalonia = Kefalonia *Greece* 38°15N 20°30E **71** E9
Ceredigion □ *U.K.* 52°16N 4°15W **26** C5
Cerignola *Italy* 41°17N 15°53E **70** D6
Cerne Abbas *U.K.* 50°49N 2°29W **24** E4
Cerrigydrudion *U.K.* 53°1N 3°35W **26** A6
Cesena *Italy* 44°8N 12°15E **70** B5
České Budějovice *Czech Rep.* 48°55N 14°25E **66** D8
Çeşme *Turkey* 38°20N 26°23E **73** G4
Ceuta *N. Afr.* 35°52N 5°18W **69** E3
Ceve-i-Ra *Fiji* 21°46S 174°31E **99** E13
Cévennes *France* 44°10N 3°50E **68** D5
Chacewater *U.K.* 50°15N 5°11W **27** G3
Chachapoyas *Peru* 6°15S 77°50W **120** C2
Chaco Austral *S. Amer.* 27°0S 61°30W **121** E3
Chaco Boreal *S. Amer.* 22°0S 60°0W **121** E4
Chaco Central *S. Amer.* 24°0S 61°0W **121** E3
Chad ■ *Africa* 15°0N 17°15E **95** F8
Chad, L. *Chad* 13°30N 14°30E **95** F8
Chadron *U.S.A.* 42°50N 103°0W **110** B6
Chagford *U.K.* 50°40N 3°50W **27** F6
Chaghcharān *Afghan.* 34°31N 65°15E **87** C11
Chagos Arch. ☑ *Ind. Oc.* 6°0S 72°0E **75** J9
Chāh Gay Hills *Afghan.* 29°30N 64°0E **87** D10
Chakradharpur *India* 22°45N 85°40E **85** H14
Chaleur B. *Canada* 47°55N 65°30W **113** B15
Chalisgaon *India* 20°30N 75°10E **84** J9
Challenger Deep *Pac. Oc.* 11°30N 142°0E **102** F6
Chalon-sur-Saône *France* 46°48N 4°50E **68** C6
Châlons-en-Champagne *France* 48°58N 4°20E **68** B6
Chambal → *India* 26°29N 79°15E **84** F11
Chambersburg *U.S.A.* 39°56N 77°40W **112** F9
Chambéry *France* 45°34N 5°55E **68** D6
Chamonix-Mont Blanc *France* 45°55N 6°51E **68** D7
Champagne *France* 48°40N 4°20E **68** B6
Champaign *U.S.A.* 40°7N 88°15W **112** E3
Champlain, L. *U.S.A.* 44°40N 73°20W **113** C11
Chañaral *Chile* 26°23S 70°40W **121** E2
Chancery Lane *Barbados* 13°3N 59°30W **115** g
Chandigarh *India* 30°43N 76°47E **84** D10
Chandler's Ford *U.K.* 50°59N 1°22W **24** E6
Chandpur *Bangla.* 23°8N 90°45E **85** H17
Chandrapur *India* 19°57N 79°25E **84** K11
Changbai Shan *China* 42°20N 129°0E **81** B7
Changchun *China* 43°57N 125°17E **81** B7
Changde *China* 29°4N 111°35E **81** D6
Changhua *Taiwan* 24°2N 120°30E **81** D7
Changji *China* 44°1N 87°19E **80** B3
Changsha *China* 28°12N 113°0E **81** D6
Changzhi *China* 36°10N 113°6E **81** C6
Changzhou *China* 31°47N 119°58E **81** C6
Chania *Greece* 35°30N 24°4E **71** G11
Channel Is. *U.K.* 49°19N 2°24W **27** J9
Channel Is. *U.S.A.* 33°40N 119°15W **110** D2
Channel-Port aux Basques *Canada* 47°30N 59°9W **109** E14
Chantrey Inlet *Canada* 67°48N 96°20W **108** C10
Chaoyang *China* 41°35N 120°22E **81** B7
Chaozhou *China* 23°42N 116°32E **81** D6
Chapala, L. de *Mexico* 20°15N 103°0W **114** C4
Chapayevsk *Russia* 53°0N 49°40E **72** D8
Chapel en le Frith *U.K.* 53°20N 1°54W **23** F5
Chapel St. Leonards *U.K.* 53°13N 0°20E **23** F9
Chapleau *Canada* 47°50N 83°24W **109** E11
Charaña *Bolivia* 17°30S 69°25W **120** D3
Chard *U.K.* 50°52N 2°58W **24** E3
Chari → *Chad* 12°58N 14°31E **95** F8
Chārīkār *Afghan.* 35°0N 69°10E **87** C12
Charing *U.K.* 51°12N 0°49E **25** D10
Charlbury *U.K.* 51°53N 1°28W **24** C6
Charleroi *Belgium* 50°24N 4°27E **65** D4
Charles, C. *U.S.A.* 37°7N 75°58W **113** G10
Charles City *U.S.A.* 43°4N 92°41W **111** B81
Charleston *Ill., U.S.A.* 39°30N 88°10W **112** F3
Charleston *Mo., U.S.A.* 36°55N 89°21W **112** G3
Charleston *S.C., U.S.A.* 32°46N 79°56W **111** D11
Charleston *W. Va., U.S.A.* 38°21N 81°38W **112** F7
Charlestown *Ireland* 53°58N 8°48W **28** D4
Charlestown of Aberlour *U.K.* 57°28N 3°14W **19** H11
Charleville *Australia* 26°24S 146°15E **98** F8
Charleville-Mézières *France* 49°44N 4°40E **68** B6
Charlevoix *U.S.A.* 45°19N 85°16W **112** C5
Charlotte *Mich., U.S.A.* 42°34N 84°50W **112** D5
Charlotte *N.C., U.S.A.* 35°13N 80°50W **111** C10
Charlotte Amalie *U.S. Virgin Is.* 18°21N 64°56W **115** e
Charlotte Harbor *U.S.A.* 26°57N 82°4W **111** E10
Charlottesville *U.S.A.* 38°2N 78°30W **112** F8
Charlottetown *Canada* 46°14N 63°8W **113** B16
Charlton I. *Canada* 52°0N 79°20W **109** D12
Charlton Kings *U.K.* 51°53N 2°3W **24** C4
Charlwood *U.K.* 51°9N 0°13W **25** D8
Charminster *U.K.* 50°44N 2°28W **24** E4
Charmouth *U.K.* 50°44N 2°54W **24** E3
Charnwood Forest *U.K.* 52°44N 1°17W **23** G6
Charolles *France* 46°27N 4°16E **68** C6
Charters Towers *Australia* 20°5S 146°13E **98** E8
Chartham *U.K.* 51°14N 1°1E **25** D11
Chartres *France* 48°29N 1°30E **68** B4
Chascomús *Argentina* 35°30S 58°0W **121** F4
Châteaubriant *France* 47°43N 1°23W **68** C3
Châteaulin *France* 48°11N 4°8W **68** B1
Châteauroux *France* 46°50N 1°40E **68** C4
Châteaux, Pte. des *Guadeloupe* 16°15N 61°10W **114** b
Châtellerault *France* 46°50N 0°30E **68** C4
Chatham *Canada* 47°2N 65°28W **109** E13
Chatham *U.K.* 51°22N 0°32E **25** D10
Chatham Is. *Pac. Oc.* 44°0S 176°40W **99** J15
Chatham-Kent *Canada* 42°24N 82°11W **112** D6
Chattanooga *U.S.A.* 35°3N 85°19W **111** C9
Chatteris *U.K.* 52°28N 0°2E **25** B9
Chatton *U.K.* 55°35N 2°0W **22** A5
Chaumont *France* 48°7N 5°8E **68** B6
Chaykovskiy *Russia* 56°47N 54°9E **72** C9
Cheadle *Gt. Man., U.K.* 53°23N 2°12W **23** F4
Cheadle *Staffs., U.K.* 52°59N 1°58W **23** G5
Cheb *Czech Rep.* 50°9N 12°28E **66** C7
Cheboksary *Russia* 56°8N 47°12E **72** C8
Cheboygan *U.S.A.* 45°39N 84°29W **112** C5
Chech, Erg *Africa* 25°0N 2°15W **94** D5
Chechenia □ *Russia* 43°30N 45°29E **73** F8
Chedabucto B. *Canada* 45°25N 61°8W **113** C17
Cheddar *U.K.* 51°17N 2°46W **24** D3
Cheddleton *U.K.* 53°4N 2°2W **23** F4
Cheduba I. *Burma* 18°45N 93°40E **85** K18
Chegutu *Zimbabwe* 18°10S 30°14E **97** H6
Chełm *Poland* 51°8N 23°30E **67** C12
Chelmer → *U.K.* 51°44N 0°30E **25** C10
Chelmsford *U.K.* 51°44N 0°29E **25** C9
Cheltenham *U.K.* 51°54N 2°4W **24** C4
Chelyabinsk *Russia* 55°10N 61°24E **79** D8
Chelyuskin, C. *Russia* 77°30N 103°0E **79** B12
Chemnitz *Germany* 50°51N 12°54E **66** C7
Chenab → *Pakistan* 30°23N 71°2E **84** D7
Chengde *China* 40°59N 117°58E **81** B6
Chengdu *China* 30°38N 104°2E **80** C5
Chengjiang *China* 24°39N 103°0E **80** D5
Chennai *India* 13°8N 80°19E **84** N12
Chepstow *U.K.* 51°38N 2°41W **26** D8
Cher → *France* 47°21N 0°29E **68** C4
Cherbourg *France* 49°39N 1°40W **68** B3
Cherepovets *Russia* 59°5N 37°55E **72** C6
Chergui, Chott ech *Algeria* 34°21N 0°25E **94** B6
Cheriton *U.K.* 51°3N 1°8W **24** D6
Cheriton Fitzpaine *U.K.* 50°51N 3°35W **27** F6
Cherkasy *Ukraine* 49°27N 32°4E **73** E5
Cherkessk *Russia* 44°15N 42°5E **73** F7
Chernihiv *Ukraine* 51°28N 31°20E **72** D5
Chernivtsi *Ukraine* 48°15N 25°52E **67** D13

Chernobyl   Crummock Water

Chernobyl Ukraine 51°20N 30°15E 67 C16
Cherokee U.S.A. 42°45N 95°33W 111 B7
Cherrapunji India 25°17N 91°47E 85 G17
Cherski Ra. Russia 65°0N 143°0E 79 C16
Chertsey U.K. 51°23N 0°30W 25 D7
Chervonohrad Ukraine 50°25N 24°10E 73 D3
Cherwell → U.K. 51°44N 1°14W 24 C6
Chesapeake B. U.S.A. 38°0N 76°10W 112 F9
Chesha B. Russia 67°20N 47°0E 72 A8
Chesham U.K. 51°43N 0°36W 25 C7
Cheshire □ U.K. 53°14N 2°30W 23 F4
Cheshunt U.K. 51°43N 0°1W 25 C8
Chesil Beach U.K. 50°37N 2°33W 24 E3
Chester U.K. 53°12N 2°53W 23 F3
Chester U.S.A. 39°51N 75°22W 113 F10
Chester-le-Street U.K. 54°51N 1°34W 22 C5
Chesterfield U.K. 53°15N 1°25W 23 F6
Chesterfield, Is. N. Cal. 19°52S 158°15E 99 D10
Chesterfield Inlet Canada 63°30N 90°45W 108 C10
Chesuncook L. U.S.A. 46°0N 69°21W 113 B13
Chetumal Mexico 18°30N 88°20W 114 D7
Chetwynd Canada 55°45N 121°36W 108 D7
Cheviot, The U.K. 55°29N 2°9W 22 B4
Cheviot Hills U.K. 55°20N 2°30W 22 B3
Chew Bahir Ethiopia 4°40N 36°50E 88 G2
Chew Magna U.K. 51°22N 2°37W 24 D3
Cheyenne U.S.A. 41°8N 104°49W 110 B6
Cheyenne → U.S.A. 44°41N 101°18W 110 B6
Chhapra India 25°48N 84°44E 85 G14
Chhattisgarh □ India 22°0N 82°0E 85 J12
Chi → Thailand 15°11N 104°43E 83 B2
Chiai Taiwan 23°29N 120°25E 81 D7
Chiang Mai Thailand 18°47N 98°59E 83 B1
Chiávari Italy 44°19N 9°19E 70 B3
Chiba Japan 35°30N 140°7E 82 F7
Chibougamau Canada 49°56N 74°24W 109 E12
Chibougamau, L. Canada 49°50N 74°20W 113 A10
Chic-Chocs, Mts. Canada 48°55N 66°0W 113 A14
Chicago U.S.A. 41°52N 87°38W 112 E4
Chichagof I. U.S.A. 57°30N 135°30W 108 D6
Chichester U.K. 50°50N 0°47W 25 E7
Chickasha U.S.A. 35°3N 97°58W 110 C7
Chiclayo Peru 6°42S 79°50W 120 C2
Chico U.S.A. 39°44N 121°50W 110 C2
Chico → Chubut, Argentina 44°0S 67°0W 121 G3
Chico → Santa Cruz, Argentina 50°0S 68°30W 121 G3
Chicopee U.S.A. 42°9N 72°37W 113 D11
Chicoutimi Canada 48°28N 71°5W 113 A12
Chiddingfold U.K. 51°7N 0°37W 25 D7
Chidley, C. Canada 60°23N 64°26W 109 C13
Chieti Italy 42°21N 14°10E 70 C6
Chifeng China 42°18N 118°58E 81 B6
Chihuahua Mexico 28°38N 106°5W 114 B3
Chilapa Mexico 17°36N 99°10W 114 D5
Chilaw Sri Lanka 7°30N 79°50E 84 R11
Childress U.S.A. 34°25N 100°13W 110 D6
Chile ■ S. Amer. 35°0S 72°0W 121 F2
Chile Rise Pac. Oc. 38°0S 92°0W 103 L18
Chilham U.K. 51°15N 0°59E 25 D10
Chililabombwe Zambia 12°18S 27°43E 97 G5
Chilka L. India 19°40N 85°25E 85 K14
Chillán Chile 36°40S 72°10W 121 F2
Chillicothe Ill., U.S.A. 40°55N 89°29W 112 E3
Chillicothe Ohio, U.S.A. 39°20N 82°59W 112 F6
Chilliwack Canada 49°10N 121°54W 108 E7
Chiloé, I. de Chile 42°30S 73°50W 121 G2
Chilpancingo Mexico 17°33N 99°30W 114 D5
Chiltern Hills U.K. 51°40N 0°53W 25 C7
Chilton U.S.A. 44°2N 88°10W 112 C3
Chilung Taiwan 25°3N 121°45E 81 D7
Chilwa, L. Malawi 15°15S 35°40E 97 H7
Chimborazo Ecuador 1°29S 78°55W 120 C2
Chimbote Peru 9°0S 78°35W 120 C2
Chimkent Kazakhstan 42°18N 69°36E 87 A12
Chin □ Burma 22°0N 93°0E 85 J18
Chin Hills Burma 22°30N 93°30E 85 H18
China ■ Asia 30°0N 110°0E 81 C6
China, Great Plain of Asia 35°0N 115°0E 74 E13
Chinandega Nic. 12°35N 87°12W 114 E7
Chincha Alta Peru 13°25S 76°7W 120 D2
Chindwin → Burma 21°26N 95°15E 85 J19
Chingola Zambia 12°31S 27°53E 97 G5
Chinhoyi Zimbabwe 17°20S 30°8E 97 H6
Chiniot Pakistan 31°45N 73°0E 84 D8
Chinon France 47°10N 0°15E 68 C4
Chióggia Italy 45°13N 12°17E 70 B5
Chios Greece 38°27N 26°9E 71 E12
Chipata Zambia 13°38S 32°28E 97 G6
Chipman Canada 46°6N 65°53W 113 B15
Chippenham U.K. 51°27N 2°6W 24 D4
Chippewa Falls U.S.A. 44°56N 91°24W 112 C2
Chipping Campden U.K. 52°3N 1°45W 24 B5
Chipping Norton U.K. 51°56N 1°32W 24 C5
Chipping Ongar U.K. 51°42N 0°15E 25 C9
Chipping Sodbury U.K. 51°33N 2°23W 24 C4
Chiquinquira Colombia 5°37N 73°50W 120 B2
Chirbury U.K. 52°35N 3°4W 23 G2
Chirchiq Uzbekistan 41°29N 69°35E 87 A12
Chiredzi Zimbabwe 21°0S 31°38E 97 J6
Chirnside U.K. 55°48N 2°12W 21 C11
Chisasibi Canada 53°50N 79°0W 109 D12
Chiseldon U.K. 51°31N 1°44W 24 C5
Chistopol Russia 55°25N 50°38E 72 C9
Chita Russia 52°0N 113°35E 79 D13
Chitral Pakistan 35°50N 71°56E 84 B7
Chittagong Bangla. 22°19N 91°48E 85 H17
Chittagong □ Bangla. 24°5N 91°0E 85 G17
Chitungwiza Zimbabwe 18°0S 31°6E 97 H6
Choiseul St. Lucia 13°47N 61°3W 115 f
Choiseul Solomon Is. 7°0S 156°40E 99 B10
Cholet France 47°4N 0°52W 68 C3
Chollerton U.K. 55°4N 2°7W 22 B4
Cholsey U.K. 51°35N 1°8W 24 C6
Choluteca Honduras 13°20N 87°14W 114 E7
Chon Buri Thailand 13°21N 101°1E 83 B2
Ch'ŏngjin N. Korea 41°47N 129°50E 81 B7
Chongqing China 29°35N 106°25E 80 D5
Chongqing Shi □ China 30°0N 108°0E 80 C5

Chonos, Arch. de los Chile 45°0S 75°0W 121 G2
Chorley U.K. 53°39N 2°38W 23 E4
Chorzów Poland 50°18N 18°57E 67 C10
Choybalsan Mongolia 48°4N 114°30E 81 B6
Christchurch N.Z. 43°33S 172°47E 99 J13
Christchurch U.K. 50°44N 1°47W 24 E5
Christmas I. Ind. Oc. 10°30S 105°40E 83 E2
Chubut → Argentina 43°20S 65°5W 121 G3
Chudleigh U.K. 50°36N 3°36W 27 F6
Chudskoye, L. Russia 58°13N 27°30E 72 C4
Chukchi Sea Russia 68°0N 175°0W 54 B17
Chukot Ra. Russia 68°0N 175°0E 79 C19
Chulmleigh U.K. 50°54N 3°51W 27 F6
Chuncheon S. Korea 37°58N 127°44E 81 C7
Chuquicamata Chile 22°15S 69°0W 121 E3
Chur Switz. 46°52N 9°32E 66 E5
Church Stretton U.K. 52°32N 2°48W 23 G3
Churchdown U.K. 51°52N 2°10W 24 C4
Churchill Canada 58°47N 94°11W 108 D10
Churchill → Man., Canada 58°47N 94°12W 108 D10
Churchill → Nfld. & L., Canada 53°19N 60°10W 109 D13
Churchill, C. Canada 58°46N 93°12W 108 D10
Churchill Falls Canada 53°36N 64°19W 109 D13
Churchill L. Canada 55°55N 108°20W 108 D9
Churchill Pk. Canada 58°10N 125°10W 108 D7
Churu India 28°20N 74°50E 84 E9
Chuska Mts. U.S.A. 36°15N 108°50W 110 C5
Chusovoy Russia 58°22N 57°50E 72 C4
Chuuk Micronesia 7°25N 151°46E 102 G7
Chuvashia □ Russia 55°30N 47°0E 72 C8
Cicero U.S.A. 41°51N 87°44W 112 E4
Ciechanów Poland 52°52N 20°38E 67 B11
Ciego de Ávila Cuba 21°50N 78°50W 115 C9
Cienfuegos Cuba 22°10N 80°30W 115 C8
Cilo Dağı Turkey 37°28N 43°55E 73 G7
Cimarron → U.S.A. 36°10N 96°16W 111 C7
Cincinnati U.S.A. 39°9N 84°27W 112 F5
Cinderford U.K. 51°49N 2°30W 24 C3
Cinto, Mte. France 42°24N 8°54E 68 E8
Circle U.S.A. 65°50N 144°4W 108 C5
Circleville U.S.A. 39°36N 82°57W 112 F6
Cirebon Indonesia 6°45S 108°32E 83 D2
Cirencester U.K. 51°43N 1°57W 24 C5
Ciudad Acuña Mexico 29°18N 100°55W 114 B4
Ciudad Bolívar Venezuela 8°5N 63°36W 120 B3
Ciudad del Carmen Mexico 18°38N 91°50W 114 D6
Ciudad Guayana Venezuela 8°0N 62°30W 120 B3
Ciudad Guzmán Mexico 19°41N 103°29W 114 D4
Ciudad Juárez Mexico 31°44N 106°29W 114 A3
Ciudad Madero Mexico 22°19N 97°50W 114 C5
Ciudad Mante Mexico 22°44N 98°59W 114 C5
Ciudad Obregón Mexico 27°29N 109°56W 114 B3
Ciudad Real Spain 38°59N 3°55W 69 C4
Ciudad Valles Mexico 21°59N 99°1W 114 C5
Ciudad Victoria Mexico 23°44N 99°8W 114 C5
Civitavécchia Italy 42°6N 11°48E 70 C4
Cizre Turkey 37°19N 42°10E 73 G7
Clackmannan U.K. 56°7N 3°45W 21 B8
Clacton-on-Sea U.K. 51°47N 1°11E 25 C11
Claire, L. Canada 58°35N 112°5W 108 D8
Clara Ireland 53°21N 7°37W 28 E6
Clare U.K. 52°4N 0°34E 25 B10
Clare → Ireland 52°45N 9°0W 30 C4
Clare □ Ireland 52°20N 9°2W 28 E3
Clare I. Ireland 53°49N 10°0W 28 D1
Claremont U.S.A. 43°23N 72°20W 113 D11
Clark Fork → U.S.A. 48°9N 116°15W 110 A3
Clarksburg U.S.A. 39°17N 80°30W 112 F7
Clarksdale U.S.A. 34°12N 90°35W 111 D8
Clarksville U.S.A. 36°32N 87°21W 111 C9
Claverley U.K. 52°32N 2°18W 23 G4
Clay Cross U.K. 53°10N 1°25W 23 F6
Claydon U.K. 52°7N 1°8E 25 B11
Clear, C. Ireland 51°25N 9°32W 30 F3
Clear I. Ireland 51°26N 9°30W 30 F4
Clearfield U.S.A. 41°2N 78°27W 112 E8
Clearwater U.S.A. 27°59N 82°48W 111 E10
Cleator Moor U.K. 54°32N 3°30W 22 C2
Clee Hills U.K. 52°26N 2°35W 23 H3
Cleethorpes U.K. 53°33N 0°3W 23 E8
Cleeve Cloud U.K. 51°56N 2°0W 24 C5
Clent Hills U.K. 52°25N 2°4W 24 B4
Cleobury Mortimer U.K. 52°22N 2°28W 23 H4
Clermont-Ferrand France 45°46N 3°4E 68 D5
Clevedon U.K. 51°26N 2°52W 24 D3
Cleveland Miss., U.S.A. 33°45N 90°43W 111 D8
Cleveland Ohio, U.S.A. 41°29N 81°41W 112 E7
Cleveland Hills U.K. 54°25N 1°11W 22 D6
Clew B. Ireland 53°50N 9°49W 28 D2
Cley U.K. 52°57N 1°2E 25 A11
Clifden Ireland 53°29N 10°1W 28 E1
Cliffe U.K. 51°28N 0°31E 25 D10
Clifford U.K. 52°7N 3°6W 24 B2
Clinton Iowa, U.S.A. 41°51N 90°12W 112 E2
Clinton Okla., U.S.A. 35°31N 98°58W 110 C7
Clinton Colden L. Canada 63°58N 107°27W 108 C9
Clipston U.K. 52°27N 0°58W 25 B7
Clitheroe U.K. 53°53N 2°22W 23 E4
Clogher Hd. Ireland 53°48N 6°14W 29 D9
Cloghran Ireland 53°27N 6°14W 31 B10
Clonakilty Ireland 51°37N 8°53W 30 E5
Clonakilty B. Ireland 51°35N 8°51W 30 E5
Cloncurry → Australia 18°37S 140°40E 98 E7
Clondalkin Ireland 53°19N 6°25W 31 B10
Clones Ireland 54°11N 7°15W 29 C7
Clonmel Ireland 52°21N 7°42W 31 D7
Clontarf Ireland 53°22N 6°11W 31 B10
Cloughton U.K. 54°20N 0°26W 22 D8
Clovelly U.K. 51°0N 4°25W 27 F5
Clovis U.S.A. 34°24N 103°12W 110 D6
Clowne U.K. 53°16N 1°17W 23 F6
Cluj-Napoca Romania 46°47N 23°38E 67 E12
Clun Forest U.K. 52°27N 3°7W 23 H2
Clunbury U.K. 52°25N 2°55W 23 H3
Clwyd → U.K. 53°19N 3°31W 26 A6
Clyde → U.K. 55°55N 4°30W 20 C6

Clyde, Firth of U.K. 55°22N 5°1W 20 D5
Clyde River Canada 70°30N 68°30W 109 B13
Clydebank U.K. 55°54N 4°23W 20 C7
Clydesdale U.K. 55°43N 3°51W 21 C8
Coalbrookdale U.K. 52°39N 2°30W 23 G4
Coalisland U.K. 54°33N 6°42W 29 B8
Coalville U.K. 52°44N 1°23W 23 G6
Coamo Puerto Rico 18°5N 66°22W 115 d
Coast Mts. Canada 55°0N 129°20W 108 D7
Coast Ranges U.S.A. 39°0N 123°0W 110 B2
Coatbridge U.K. 55°52N 4°6W 20 C7
Coaticook Canada 45°10N 71°46W 113 C12
Coats I. Canada 62°30N 83°0W 109 C11
Coats Land Antarctica 77°0S 25°0W 55 D1
Coatzacoalcos Mexico 18°7N 94°25W 114 D6
Cobán Guatemala 15°30N 90°21W 114 D6
Cobar Australia 31°27S 145°48E 98 G8
Cóbh Ireland 51°51N 8°17W 30 E6
Cobija Bolivia 11°0S 68°50W 120 D3
Cobourg Canada 43°58N 78°10W 112 D8
Cochabamba Bolivia 17°26S 66°10W 120 D3
Cochin India 9°58N 76°20E 84 Q10
Cochrane Canada 49°0N 81°0W 109 E11
Cockburn, Canal Chile 54°30S 72°0W 121 H2
Cockburn I. Canada 45°55N 83°22W 112 C6
Cockburn Town Bahamas 24°2N 74°31W 115 C10
Cockerham U.K. 53°58N 2°49W 23 E4
Cockermouth U.K. 54°40N 3°22W 22 C2
Cockfield U.K. 52°8N 0°48E 25 B10
Cockpit Country, The Jamaica 18°15N 77°45W 114 a
Coco → Cent. Amer. 15°0N 83°8W 115 E8
Coco, I. del Pac. Oc. 5°25N 87°55W 103 G19
Cocos Is. Ind. Oc. 12°10S 96°55E 83 E1
Cod, C. U.S.A. 42°5N 70°10W 113 D12
Coddenham U.K. 52°9N 1°8E 25 B11
Codó Brazil 4°30S 43°55W 120 C5
Cody U.S.A. 44°32N 109°3W 110 B5
Coeur d'Alene U.S.A. 47°41N 116°46W 110 A3
Coggeshall U.K. 51°52N 0°42E 25 C10
Cognac France 45°41N 0°20W 68 D3
Coigach U.K. 57°59N 5°14W 18 G7
Coigach, Rubha U.K. 58°6N 5°26W 18 F7
Coimbatore India 11°2N 76°59E 84 P10
Coimbra Portugal 40°15N 8°27W 69 B1
Colatina Brazil 19°32S 40°37W 122 C2
Colchester U.K. 51°54N 0°55E 25 C10
Cold Fell U.K. 54°53N 2°36W 22 C3
Coldstream U.K. 55°39N 2°15W 21 C11
Colebrook U.S.A. 44°54N 71°30W 113 C12
Colebrooke U.K. 50°47N 3°44W 27 F6
Coleford U.K. 51°47N 2°36W 24 C3
Coleraine U.K. 55°8N 6°41W 29 A8
Coleshill U.K. 52°30N 1°41W 23 G5
Colgrave Sd. U.K. 60°36N 0°58W 18 A16
Colima Mexico 19°14N 103°43W 114 D4
Colima, Nevado de Mexico 19°33N 103°38W 114 D4
Coll U.K. 56°39N 6°34W 20 J4
Collier Law U.K. 54°47N 1°59W 22 C5
Collingbourne Kingston U.K. 51°18N 1°40W 24 D5
Collingham U.K. 53°8N 0°46W 23 F7
Collingwood Canada 44°29N 80°13W 112 C7
Collooney Ireland 54°11N 8°29W 28 C5
Colmar France 48°5N 7°20E 68 B7
Colne U.K. 53°51N 2°9W 23 E4
Colne → Bucks., U.K. 51°27N 0°32W 25 D7
Colne → Essex, U.K. 51°51N 0°58E 25 C10
Cologne Germany 50°56N 6°57E 66 C4
Colombia ■ S. Amer. 3°45N 73°0W 120 B2
Colombo Sri Lanka 6°56N 79°58E 84 R11
Colonsay U.K. 56°5N 6°12W 20 B3
Colorado □ U.S.A. 39°30N 105°30W 110 C5
Colorado → Argentina 39°50S 62°8W 121 F3
Colorado → N. Amer. 31°45N 114°40W 110 D4
Colorado → U.S.A. 28°36N 95°59W 111 E7
Colorado Plateau U.S.A. 37°0N 111°0W 110 C4
Colorado Springs U.S.A. 38°50N 104°49W 110 C6
Colsterworth U.K. 52°49N 0°37W 23 G7
Coltishall U.K. 52°44N 1°21E 25 A11
Columbia Mo., U.S.A. 38°57N 92°20W 111 C8
Columbia S.C., U.S.A. 34°0N 81°2W 111 D10
Columbia Tenn., U.S.A. 35°37N 87°2W 111 C9
Columbia → N. Amer. 46°15N 124°5W 110 A2
Columbia, District of □ U.S.A. 38°55N 77°0W 112 F9
Columbia Plateau U.S.A. 44°0N 117°30W 110 B3
Columbus Ga., U.S.A. 32°28N 84°59W 111 D10
Columbus Ind., U.S.A. 39°13N 85°55W 112 F5
Columbus Miss., U.S.A. 33°30N 88°25W 111 D9
Columbus Nebr., U.S.A. 41°26N 97°22W 111 B7
Columbus Ohio, U.S.A. 39°58N 83°0W 112 F6
Colville → U.S.A. 70°25N 150°30W 108 A4
Colwell U.K. 55°5N 2°4W 22 B4
Colwich U.K. 52°48N 1°58W 23 G5
Colwyn Bay U.K. 53°18N 3°44W 26 A6
Colyton U.K. 50°44N 3°5W 27 F7
Comayagua Honduras 14°25N 87°37W 114 E7
Combe Martin U.K. 51°12N 4°3W 27 E5
Comber U.K. 54°33N 5°45W 29 B10
Comeragh Mts. Ireland 52°18N 7°34W 31 D7
Comilla Bangla. 23°28N 91°10E 85 H17
Comitán Mexico 16°15N 92°8W 114 D6
Committee B. Canada 68°30N 86°30W 109 C11
Communism Pk. Tajikistan 39°0N 72°2E 87 B13
Como Italy 45°47N 9°5E 70 B3
Como, Lago di Italy 46°0N 9°11E 70 B3
Comodoro Rivadavia Argentina 45°50S 67°40W 121 G3
Comorin, C. India 8°3N 77°40E 84 Q10
Comoros ■ Ind. Oc. 12°10S 44°15E 91 H8
Compass Mt. S. Africa 31°45S 24°32E 90 K6
Compiègne France 49°24N 2°50E 68 B5
Conakry Guinea 9°29N 13°49W 94 G3
Conceição da Barra Brazil 18°35S 39°45W 122 C3
Conceição Chile 36°50S 73°0W 121 F2
Concepción Paraguay 23°22S 57°26W 121 E4
Concepción, Est. de Chile 50°30S 74°55W 121 H2
Concepción del Oro Mexico 24°38N 101°25W 114 C4

Concepción del Uruguay Argentina 32°35S 58°20W 121 F4
Conception, Pt. U.S.A. 34°27N 120°28W 110 D2
Conchos → Mexico 29°35N 104°25W 114 B4
Concord U.S.A. 43°12N 71°32W 113 D12
Concordia Argentina 31°20S 58°2W 121 F4
Concordia U.S.A. 39°34N 97°40W 110 C7
Condeúba Brazil 14°52S 42°0W 122 B2
Condover U.K. 52°39N 2°44W 23 G3
Congleton U.K. 53°10N 2°13W 23 F4
Congo ■ Africa 1°0S 16°0E 96 E3
Congo → Africa 6°4S 12°24E 96 F2
Congo, Dem. Rep. of the ■ Africa 3°0S 23°0E 96 E4
Congo Basin Africa 0°10S 24°30E 96 E4
Congresbury U.K. 51°22N 2°48W 24 D3
Coningsby U.K. 53°7N 0°10W 23 F8
Conisbrough U.K. 53°29N 1°14W 23 F6
Coniston Canada 46°29N 80°51W 112 B7
Coniston U.K. 54°22N 3°5W 22 D2
Coniston Water U.K. 54°20N 3°5W 22 D2
Conn, L. Ireland 54°3N 9°15W 28 C3
Connacht □ Ireland 53°43N 9°12W 28 D3
Connah's Quay U.K. 53°13N 3°4W 26 A7
Conneaut U.S.A. 41°57N 80°34W 112 E7
Connecticut □ U.S.A. 41°30N 72°45W 113 E11
Connecticut → U.S.A. 41°16N 72°20W 113 E11
Connellsville U.S.A. 40°1N 79°35W 112 E8
Connemara Ireland 53°29N 9°45W 28 D2
Connemara △ Ireland 53°32N 9°52W 28 D2
Connersville U.S.A. 39°39N 85°8W 112 F5
Conselheiro Lafaiete Brazil 20°40S 43°48W 122 D2
Consett U.K. 54°51N 1°50W 22 C5
Constance, L. Europe 47°35N 9°25E 66 E5
Constanţa Romania 44°14N 28°38E 67 F15
Constantine Algeria 36°25N 6°42E 94 A7
Constitución Chile 35°20S 72°30W 121 F2
Contas → Brazil 14°17S 39°1W 122 B3
Contwoyto L. Canada 65°42N 110°50W 108 C8
Conway Ark., U.S.A. 35°5N 92°26W 111 C8
Conway N.H., U.S.A. 43°59N 71°7W 113 D12
Conwy U.K. 53°17N 3°50W 26 A6
Conwy □ U.K. 53°10N 3°44W 26 A6
Conwy → U.K. 53°17N 3°50W 26 A6
Coober Pedy Australia 29°1S 134°43E 98 F6
Cook Inlet U.S.A. 60°0N 152°0W 108 D4
Cook Is. Pac. Oc. 17°0S 160°0W 103 J12
Cook Strait N.Z. 41°15S 174°29E 99 J13
Cookstown U.K. 54°39N 6°45W 29 B8
Cooktown Australia 15°30S 145°16E 98 D8
Coondapoor India 13°42N 74°40E 84 N9
Coos Bay U.S.A. 43°22N 124°13W 110 B2
Cootehill Ireland 54°4N 7°5W 29 C7
Copenhagen Denmark 55°40N 12°26E 63 F6
Copiapó Chile 27°30S 70°20W 121 E2
Copper Harbor U.S.A. 47°28N 87°53W 112 B4
Coppermine → Canada 67°49N 116°4W 108 C8
Coquet → U.K. 55°20N 1°32W 22 B5
Coquet I. U.K. 55°20N 1°36W 22 B5
Coquimbo Chile 30°0S 71°20W 121 E2
Coracora Peru 15°5S 73°45W 120 D2
Coral Harbour Canada 64°8N 83°10W 109 C11
Coral Sea Pac. Oc. 15°0S 150°0E 98 C9
Corbin U.S.A. 36°57N 84°6W 112 G5
Corbridge U.K. 54°58N 2°0W 22 C5
Corby U.K. 52°30N 0°41W 25 A7
Corby Glen U.K. 52°49N 0°30W 23 G7
Cordele U.S.A. 31°58N 83°47W 111 D10
Córdoba Argentina 31°20S 64°10W 121 F3
Córdoba Mexico 18°53N 96°56W 114 D5
Córdoba Spain 37°50N 4°50W 69 D3
Córdoba, Sierra de Argentina 31°10S 64°25W 121 F3
Cordova U.S.A. 60°33N 145°45W 108 C5
Corfe Castle U.K. 50°38N 2°3W 24 E4
Corfe Mullen U.K. 50°46N 2°1W 24 E4
Corfu Greece 39°38N 19°50E 71 E8
Corinth Greece 37°56N 22°55E 71 F10
Corinth U.S.A. 34°56N 88°31W 111 D9
Corinth, G. of Greece 38°16N 22°30E 71 E10
Corinto Brazil 18°20S 44°30W 122 C2
Cork Ireland 51°54N 8°29W 30 E6
Cork □ Ireland 51°57N 8°40W 30 E6
Cork Harbour Ireland 51°47N 8°16W 30 E6
Corner Brook Canada 48°57N 57°58W 109 E14
Corning U.S.A. 42°9N 77°3W 112 D9
Cornwall Canada 45°2N 74°44W 113 C10
Cornwall □ U.K. 50°26N 4°40W 27 G4
Cornwall, C. U.K. 50°8N 5°43W 27 G2
Cornwall I. Canada 77°37N 94°38W 109 B10
Cornwallis I. Canada 75°8N 95°0W 109 B10
Coro Venezuela 11°25N 69°41W 120 A3
Corocoro Bolivia 17°15S 68°28W 120 D3
Coromandel Coast India 12°30N 81°0E 84 N12
Coronation Gulf Canada 68°25N 110°0W 108 B8
Coronel Chile 37°0S 73°10W 121 F2
Coronel Fabriciano Brazil 19°31S 42°38W 122 C2
Coronel Pringles Argentina 38°0S 61°30W 121 F3
Coronel Suárez Argentina 37°30S 61°52W 121 F3
Coropuna, Nevado Peru 15°30S 72°41W 120 D2
Corpus Christi U.S.A. 27°47N 97°24W 110 E7
Corraun Pen. Ireland 53°54N 9°54W 28 D2
Corrib, L. Ireland 53°27N 9°16W 28 D3
Corrientes Argentina 27°30S 58°45W 121 E4
Corrientes, C. Colombia 5°30N 77°34W 120 B2
Corrientes, C. Mexico 20°25N 105°42W 114 C3
Corringham U.K. 53°25N 0°41W 23 F7
Corry U.S.A. 41°55N 79°39W 112 E8
Corse, C. France 43°1N 9°25E 68 E8
Corsham U.K. 51°27N 2°10W 24 D4
Corsica □ France 42°0N 9°0E 68 F8
Corsicana U.S.A. 32°6N 96°28W 111 D7
Corsley U.K. 51°13N 2°14W 24 D4
Corte France 42°19N 9°11E 68 E8
Cortez U.S.A. 37°21N 108°35W 110 C5
Cortland U.S.A. 42°36N 76°11W 113 D9
Corton U.K. 52°31N 1°45E 25 A12
Çorum Turkey 40°30N 34°57E 73 F5
Corumbá Brazil 19°0S 57°30W 120 D4
Corunna = La Coruña Spain 43°20N 8°25W 69 A1

Corvallis U.S.A. 44°34N 123°16W 110 B2
Corve → U.K. 52°22N 2°43W 23 H3
Coseley U.K. 52°33N 2°5W 23 G4
Cosenza Italy 39°18N 16°15E 70 E7
Cosham U.K. 50°51N 1°2W 24 E6
Coshocton U.S.A. 40°16N 81°51W 112 E7
Costa Blanca Spain 38°25N 0°10W 69 C5
Costa Brava Spain 41°30N 3°0E 69 B7
Costa del Sol Spain 36°30N 4°30W 69 D3
Costa Dorada Spain 41°12N 1°15E 69 B6
Costa Rica ■ Cent. Amer. 10°0N 84°0W 115 F8
Costessey U.K. 52°40N 1°13E 25 A11
Cotabato Phil. 7°14N 124°15E 83 C6
Côte d' Azur France 43°25N 7°10E 68 E7
Côte-d'Ivoire = Ivory Coast ■ Africa 7°30N 5°0W 94 G4
Coteau du Missouri U.S.A. 47°0N 100°0W 110 A6
Cotentin France 49°15N 1°30W 68 B3
Cotherstone U.K. 54°35N 1°59W 22 C5
Cotonou Benin 6°20N 2°25E 94 G6
Cotopaxi Ecuador 0°40S 78°30W 120 C2
Cotswold Hills U.K. 51°42N 2°10W 24 C4
Cottbus Germany 51°45N 14°20E 66 C8
Cottenham U.K. 52°18N 0°9E 25 B9
Coudersport U.S.A. 41°46N 78°1W 112 E8
Council Bluffs U.S.A. 41°16N 95°52W 111 B7
Courantyne → S. Amer. 5°55N 57°5W 120 B4
Courtenay Canada 49°45N 125°0W 108 E7
Cove U.K. 56°0N 4°51W 20 B6
Coventry U.K. 52°25N 1°28W 24 B6
Cover → U.K. 54°17N 1°47W 22 D5
Coverack U.K. 50°1N 5°7W 27 G3
Covington U.S.A. 39°5N 84°30W 112 F5
Cowal U.K. 56°5N 5°8W 20 B5
Cowbridge U.K. 51°27N 3°27W 27 E7
Cowdenbeath U.K. 56°7N 3°21W 21 B9
Cowes U.K. 50°45N 1°18W 24 E6
Cowfold U.K. 50°59N 0°16W 25 E8
Cowpen U.K. 55°8N 1°32W 22 B5
Cox's Bazar Bangla. 21°26N 91°59E 85 J17
Cozumel, Isla Mexico 20°30N 86°40W 114 C7
Crab Hill Barbados 13°19N 59°38W 115 g
Cradock S. Africa 32°8S 25°36E 97 L5
Craig U.S.A. 40°31N 107°33W 110 B5
Craigavon U.K. 54°27N 6°23W 29 C9
Crail U.K. 56°16N 2°37W 21 B10
Craiova Romania 44°21N 23°48E 67 F12
Cramlington U.K. 55°6N 1°34W 22 B5
Cranborne U.K. 50°55N 1°54W 24 E5
Cranborne Chase U.K. 50°56N 2°6W 24 E4
Cranbrook Canada 49°30N 115°46W 108 E8
Cranbrook U.K. 51°6N 0°34E 25 D10
Crandon U.S.A. 45°34N 88°54W 112 C3
Crane, The Barbados 13°6N 59°27W 115 g
Cranleigh U.K. 51°8N 0°28W 25 D8
Cranwell U.K. 53°3N 0°27W 23 F8
Crateús Brazil 5°10S 40°39W 120 C5
Crato Brazil 7°10S 39°25W 120 C6
Craven Arms U.K. 52°26N 2°50W 23 H3
Crawfordsville U.S.A. 40°2N 86°54W 112 E4
Crawley U.K. 51°7N 0°11W 25 D8
Credenhill U.K. 52°5N 2°48W 24 B3
Crediton U.K. 50°47N 3°40W 27 F6
Cree → Canada 58°57N 105°47W 108 D9
Cree → U.K. 54°55N 4°25W 20 E4
Cree L. Canada 57°30N 106°30W 108 D9
Cremona Italy 45°7N 10°2E 70 B4
Cres Croatia 44°58N 14°25E 70 B6
Crest Greece 35°15N 25°0E 71 G11
Créteil France 48°47N 2°27E 68 B5
Creuse → France 47°0N 0°34E 68 C4
Crewe U.K. 53°6N 2°26W 23 F4
Crewkerne U.K. 50°53N 2°48W 24 E3
Crianlarich U.K. 56°24N 4°37W 20 B6
Criccieth U.K. 52°55N 4°13W 26 B5
Crick U.K. 52°22N 1°8W 24 B6
Crickhowell U.K. 51°52N 3°8W 26 D7
Cricklade U.K. 51°38N 1°50W 24 C5
Crieff U.K. 56°22N 3°50W 21 B8
Criffell U.K. 54°56N 3°39W 21 E8
Crimea □ Ukraine 45°30N 33°10E 73 E5
Crimean Pen. Ukraine 45°0N 34°0E 73 F5
Crişul Alb → Romania 46°42N 21°17E 67 E11
Crişul Negru → Romania 46°42N 21°16E 67 E11
Croagh Patrick Ireland 53°46N 9°40W 28 D2
Croatia ■ Europe 45°20N 16°0E 70 B7
Croglin U.K. 54°50N 2°39W 22 C4
Crohy Hd. Ireland 54°55N 8°26W 28 B5
Croker, C. Australia 10°58S 132°35E 98 C5
Cromarty U.K. 57°40N 4°2W 19 G9
Cromarty Firth U.K. 57°40N 4°15W 19 G9
Cromdale, Hills of U.K. 57°20N 3°28W 19 H11
Cromer U.K. 52°56N 1°17E 25 A11
Crondall U.K. 51°14N 0°51W 25 D7
Crook U.K. 54°43N 1°45W 22 C5
Crooked I. Bahamas 22°50N 74°10W 115 C10
Crooklands U.K. 54°16N 2°42W 22 D3
Crosby Cumb., U.K. 54°45N 3°25W 22 C2
Crosby Mersey., U.K. 53°30N 3°3W 23 F2
Crosby Ravensworth U.K. 54°33N 2°35W 22 C3
Cross Fell U.K. 54°43N 2°28W 22 C4
Cross Sound U.S.A. 58°0N 135°0W 108 D6
Crosshaven Ireland 51°47N 8°17W 30 E6
Crossmaglen U.K. 54°5N 6°36W 29 C8
Crotone Italy 39°5N 17°8E 70 E7
Crouch → U.K. 51°37N 0°53E 25 C10
Crow Hd. Ireland 51°35N 10°9W 30 E2
Crow Sound U.K. 49°56N 6°16W 27 H1
Crowborough U.K. 51°3N 0°11E 25 D9
Crowland U.K. 52°41N 0°10W 23 G8
Crowle U.K. 53°36N 0°49W 23 E7
Crowsnest Pass Canada 49°40N 114°40W 108 E8
Croyde U.K. 51°7N 4°14W 27 E5
Croydon □ U.K. 51°22N 0°5W 25 D8
Crozet, Is. Ind. Oc. 46°27S 52°0E 53 G12
Cruden Bay U.K. 57°25N 1°52W 19 H14
Crudgington U.K. 52°46N 2°32W 23 G3
Crummock Water U.K. 54°33N 3°18W 22 C2

Cruz Bay

East Bengal

Cruz Bay *U.S. Virgin Is.* 18°20N 64°48W **115 e**
Cruz das Almas *Brazil* 12°0S 39°6W **122 B3**
Cruzeiro *Brazil* 22°33S 45°0W **122 D1**
Cruzeiro do Sul *Brazil* 7°35S 72°35W **120 C2**
Crystal Falls *U.S.A.* 46°5N 88°20W **112 B3**
Cuando → *Angola* 17°30S 23°15E **97 H4**
Cuango
  Dem. Rep. of the Congo 3°14S 17°22E **96 E3**
Cuanza → *Angola* 9°21S 13°9E **96 F2**
Cuauhtémoc *Mexico* 28°25N 106°52W **114 B3**
Cuba ■ *W. Indies* 22°0N 79°0W **115 C9**
Cubango → *Africa* 18°50S 22°25E **97 H4**
Cuckfield *U.K.* 51°1N 0°8W **25 D8**
Cúcuta *Colombia* 7°54N 72°31W **120 B2**
Cuddalore *India* 11°46N 79°45E **84 P11**
Cuenca *Ecuador* 2°50S 79°9W **120 C2**
Cuenca *Spain* 40°5N 2°10W **69 B4**
Cuernavaca *Mexico* 18°55N 99°15W **114 D5**
Cuiabá *Brazil* 15°30S 56°0W **120 D4**
Cuillin Hills *U.K.* 57°13N 6°15W **18 H5**
Cuillin Sd. *U.K.* 57°4N 6°20W **18 H5**
Cuito → *Angola* 18°1S 20°48E **97 H4**
Culebra *Puerto Rico* 18°19N 65°18W **115 d**
Culiacán *Mexico* 24°50N 107°23W **114 C3**
Cullen *U.K.* 57°42N 2°49W **19 G12**
Cullompton *U.K.* 50°51N 3°24W **27 F7**
Culm → *U.K.* 50°46N 3°31W **27 F6**
Culpeper *U.S.A.* 38°30N 78°0W **112 F9**
Cumaná *Venezuela* 10°30N 64°5W **120 A3**
Cumberland *U.S.A.* 39°39N 78°46E **84 P11**
Cumberland → *U.S.A.* 37°9N 88°25W **111 C9**
Cumberland Pen. *Canada* 67°0N 64°0W **109 C13**
Cumberland Plateau *U.S.A.* 36°0N 85°0W **111 C10**
Cumberland Sd. *Canada* 65°30N 66°0W **109 C13**
Cumbernauld *U.K.* 55°57N 3°58W **21 C8**
Cumbrae Is. *U.K.* 55°46N 4°54W **20 C6**
Cumbria □ *U.K.* 54°42N 2°52W **22 C3**
Cumbrian Mts. *U.K.* 54°30N 3°0W **22 D2**
Cummertrees *U.K.* 54°59N 3°20W **21 D9**
Cumnock *U.K.* 55°28N 4°17W **20 D7**
Cumnor *U.K.* 51°44N 1°19W **24 C6**
Cumwhinton *U.K.* 54°52N 2°50W **22 C3**
Cunene → *Angola* 17°20S 11°50E **97 H2**
Cúneo *Italy* 44°23N 7°32E **70 D2**
Cunnamulla *Australia* 28°2S 145°38E **98 F8**
Cunninghame *U.K.* 55°38N 4°35W **20 C6**
Cupar *U.K.* 56°19N 3°1W **21 B9**
Curaçao *Neth. Ant.* 12°10N 69°0W **115 E11**
Curicó *Chile* 34°55S 71°20W **121 F2**
Curitiba *Brazil* 25°20S 49°10W **122 E1**
Curlew Mts. *Ireland* 54°0N 8°20W **28 D5**
Curry Rivel *U.K.* 51°1N 2°52W **24 D3**
Curvelo *Brazil* 18°45S 44°27W **122 C2**
Cuttack *India* 20°25N 85°57E **85 J14**
Cuxhaven *Germany* 53°51N 8°41E **66 B5**
Cuyahoga Falls *U.S.A.* 41°8N 81°29W **112 E7**
Cuyuni → *Guyana* 6°23N 58°41W **120 B4**
Cuzco *Peru* 13°32S 72°0W **120 D2**
Cwmbran *U.K.* 51°39N 3°2W **26 D7**
Cyclades *Greece* 37°0N 24°30E **71 F11**
Cynthiana *U.S.A.* 38°23N 84°18W **112 F5**
Cyprus ■ *Asia* 35°0N 33°0E **86 C2**
Cyrenaica *Libya* 27°0N 23°0E **95 C10**
Czech Rep. ■ *Europe* 50°0N 15°0E **66 D8**
Częstochowa *Poland* 50°49N 19°7E **67 C10**

D

Da Lat *Vietnam* 11°56N 108°25E **83 B2**
Da Nang *Vietnam* 16°4N 108°13E **83 A2**
Da Qaidam *China* 37°50N 95°15E **80 C4**
Daba Shan *China* 32°0N 109°0E **81 C5**
Dabie Shan *China* 31°20N 115°20E **81 C6**
Dadra & Nagar Haveli □ *India* 20°5N 73°0E **84 J8**
Dadu *Pakistan* 26°45N 67°45E **84 F5**
Daegu *S. Korea* 35°50N 128°37E **81 C7**
Daejeon *S. Korea* 36°20N 127°28E **81 C7**
Dagestan □ *Russia* 42°30N 47°0E **73 F8**
Dagupan *Phil.* 16°3N 120°20E **83 B4**
Dahod *India* 22°50N 74°15E **84 H9**
Dahonglituan *China* 35°45N 79°20E **80 C2**
Daingean *Ireland* 53°18N 7°17W **31 B8**
Dajarra *Australia* 21°42S 139°30E **98 E6**
Dakar *Senegal* 14°34N 17°29W **94 F2**
Dakhla *W. Sahara* 23°50N 15°53W **94 D2**
Dakhla, El Wâhât el- *Egypt* 25°30N 28°50E **95 C11**
Dalandzadgad *Mongolia* 43°27N 104°30E **80 B5**
Dalbeattie *U.K.* 54°56N 3°50W **21 E8**
Dalhart *U.S.A.* 36°4N 102°31W **110 C6**
Dalhousie *Canada* 48°5N 66°26W **113 A14**
Dali *China* 25°40N 100°10E **80 D5**
Dalian *China* 38°50N 121°40E **81 C7**
Daliang Shan *China* 28°0N 102°45E **80 D5**
Dalkeith *U.K.* 55°54N 3°4W **21 C9**
Dalkey *Ireland* 53°16N 6°6W **31 B10**
Dallas *U.S.A.* 32°47N 96°48W **111 D7**
Dalles, The *U.S.A.* 45°36N 121°10W **110 A2**
Dalmatia *Croatia* 43°20N 17°0E **70 C7**
Dalmellington *U.K.* 55°19N 4°23W **20 D6**
Daloa *Ivory C.* 7°0N 6°30W **94 G4**
Dalry *U.K.* 55°42N 4°43W **20 C6**
Dalrymple, L. *Australia* 20°40S 147°0E **98 E8**
Dalton *Dumf. & Gall., U.K.* 55°4N 3°24W **21 D9**
Dalton *N. Yorks., U.K.* 54°28N 1°32W **22 D5**
Dalton-in-Furness *U.K.* 54°10N 3°11W **22 D2**
Daly Waters *Australia* 16°15S 133°24E **98 D5**
Daman *India* 20°25N 72°57E **84 J8**
Damanhûr *Egypt* 31°0N 30°30E **95 B12**
Damaraland *Namibia* 20°0S 15°0E **97 H2**
Damascus *Syria* 33°30N 36°18E **86 C4**
Damävand, Qolleh-ye *Iran* 35°56N 52°10E **87 C8**
Damerham *U.K.* 50°56N 1°51W **24 E5**
Dampier *Australia* 20°41S 116°42E **98 E2**
Danakil Desert *Ethiopia* 12°45N 41°0E **88 E3**
Danbury *U.S.A.* 41°24N 73°28W **113 E11**
Dandong *China* 40°10N 124°20E **81 B7**
Danube → *Europe* 45°20N 29°40E **67 F15**
Danville *Ill., U.S.A.* 40°8N 87°37W **112 E4**

Danville *Ky., U.S.A.* 37°39N 84°46W **112 G5**
Danville *Va., U.S.A.* 36°36N 79°23W **111 C11**
Dar Banda *Africa* 8°0N 23°0E **90 F6**
Dar es Salaam *Tanzania* 6°50S 39°12E **96 F7**
Darbhanga *India* 26°15N 85°55E **85 F14**
Dardanelles *Turkey* 40°17N 26°32E **71 D12**
Darent → *U.K.* 51°28N 0°14E **25 D9**
Dârfûr *Sudan* 13°40N 24°0E **95 F10**
Darhan *Mongolia* 49°37N 106°21E **80 B5**
Darién, G. del *Colombia* 9°0N 77°0W **120 B2**
Darjiling *India* 27°3N 88°18E **85 F16**
Darling → *Australia* 34°4S 141°54E **98 G7**
Darling Ra. *Australia* 32°30S 116°20E **98 G2**
Darlington *U.K.* 54°32N 1°33W **22 C5**
Darmstadt *Germany* 49°51N 8°39E **66 D5**
Darnah *Libya* 32°45N 22°45E **95 B10**
Darnley, C. *Antarctica* 68°0S 69°0E **55 C6**
Darnley B. *Canada* 69°30N 123°30W **108 C7**
Dart → *U.K.* 50°24N 3°39W **27 G6**
Dartford *U.K.* 51°26N 0°13E **25 D9**
Dartington *U.K.* 50°27N 3°43W **27 G6**
Dartmoor *U.K.* 50°38N 3°57W **27 F6**
Dartmoor △ *U.K.* 50°37N 3°59W **27 F6**
Dartmouth *Canada* 44°40N 63°30W **113 C16**
Dartmouth *U.K.* 50°21N 3°36W **27 G6**
Darton *U.K.* 53°35N 1°31W **23 E5**
Darwen *U.K.* 53°42N 2°29W **23 E4**
Darwin *Australia* 12°25S 130°51E **98 C5**
Dashen, Ras *Ethiopia* 13°8N 38°26E **88 E2**
Dashoguz *Turkmenistan* 41°49N 59°58E **87 A9**
Dasht → *Pakistan* 25°10N 61°40E **84 G2**
Datong *China* 40°6N 113°18E **81 B6**
Daxian *China* 31°15N 107°23E **80 C5**
Daxue Shan *China* 30°30N 101°30E **80 C5**
Dayr az Zawr *Syria* 35°20N 40°5E **86 C5**
Dayton *U.S.A.* 39°45N 84°12W **112 F5**
Daytona Beach *U.S.A.* 29°13N 81°1W **111 E10**
De Aar *S. Africa* 30°39S 24°0E **97 L4**
De Pere *U.S.A.* 44°27N 88°4W **112 C3**
Dead Sea *Asia* 31°30N 35°30E **86 D3**
Deal *U.K.* 51°13N 1°25E **25 D11**
Dean, Forest of *U.K.* 51°45N 2°33W **24 C3**
Dease → *Canada* 59°56N 128°32W **108 D7**
Dease Lake *Canada* 58°25N 130°6W **108 D6**
Death Valley *U.S.A.* 36°15N 116°50W **110 C3**
Deben → *U.K.* 52°0N 1°25E **25 C11**
Debenham *U.K.* 52°14N 1°12E **25 B11**
Debre Markos *Ethiopia* 10°20N 37°40E **88 E2**
Debre Tabor *Ethiopia* 11°50N 38°26E **88 E2**
Debrecen *Hungary* 47°33N 21°42E **67 E11**
Decatur *Ala., U.S.A.* 34°36N 86°59W **111 D9**
Decatur *Ill., U.S.A.* 39°51N 88°57W **112 F3**
Decatur *Ind., U.S.A.* 40°50N 84°56W **112 E5**
Deccan *India* 18°0N 79°0E **84 L11**
Deddington *U.K.* 51°59N 1°18W **24 C6**
Dee → *Aberds., U.K.* 57°9N 2°5W **19 H13**
Dee → *Dumf. & Gall., U.K.* 54°51N 4°3W **20 E7**
Dee → *Wales, U.K.* 53°22N 3°17W **26 A7**
Deeping Fen *U.K.* 52°45N 0°15W **23 G8**
Deeping St. Nicholas *U.K.* 52°44N 0°12W **23 G8**
Deer Lake *Canada* 49°11N 57°27W **109 E14**
Defiance *U.S.A.* 41°17N 84°22W **112 E5**
Dehra Dun *India* 30°20N 78°4E **84 D11**
DeKalb *U.S.A.* 41°56N 88°46W **112 E3**
Del Rio *U.S.A.* 29°22N 100°54W **110 E6**
Delabole *U.K.* 50°37N 4°46W **27 F4**
Delaware *U.S.A.* 40°18N 83°4W **112 E6**
Delaware □ *U.S.A.* 39°0N 75°20W **113 F10**
Delaware → *U.S.A.* 39°15N 75°20W **113 F10**
Delaware B. *U.S.A.* 39°0N 75°10W **111 C12**
Delft *Neths.* 52°1N 4°22E **65 B4**
Delfzijl *Neths.* 53°20N 6°55E **65 A6**
Delgado, C. *Mozam.* 10°45S 40°40E **96 G8**
Delhi *India* 28°39N 77°13E **84 E10**
Delice *Turkey* 39°54N 34°2E **73 G5**
Delicias *Mexico* 28°13N 105°28W **114 B3**
Déline *Canada* 65°11N 123°25W **108 C7**
Delphos *U.S.A.* 40°51N 84°21W **112 E5**
Delta Junction *U.S.A.* 64°2N 145°44W **108 C5**
Demanda, Sierra de la *Spain* 42°15N 3°0W **69 A4**
Demavend *Iran* 32°16N 107°46W **110 D5**
Demopolis *U.S.A.* 32°31N 87°50W **111 D9**
Den Helder *Neths.* 52°57N 4°45E **65 B4**
Denbigh *U.K.* 53°12N 3°25W **26 A7**
Denbighshire □ *U.K.* 53°8N 3°22W **26 A7**
Denby Dale *U.K.* 53°34N 1°40W **23 E5**
Denham, Mt. *Jamaica* 18°13N 77°32W **114 a**
Denia *Spain* 38°49N 0°8E **69 C6**
Denizli *Turkey* 37°42N 29°2E **73 G4**
Denmark ■ *Europe* 55°45N 10°0E **63 F6**
Denmark Str. *Atl. Oc.* 66°0N 30°0W **54 C6**
Dennery *St. Lucia* 13°55N 60°54W **115 f**
Denny *U.K.* 56°1N 3°55W **21 B8**
Denpasar *Indonesia* 8°39S 115°13E **83 D3**
Dent *U.K.* 54°17N 2°27W **22 D4**
Denton *Gt. Man., U.K.* 53°27N 2°9W **23 E4**
Denton *Lincs., U.K.* 52°53N 0°43W **23 G7**
Denton *Tex., U.S.A.* 33°13N 97°8W **111 D7**
D'Entrecasteaux Is. *Papua N.G.* 9°0S 151°0E **98 B9**
Denver *U.S.A.* 39°42N 104°59W **110 C5**
Deoghar *India* 24°30N 86°42E **85 G15**

Deolali *India* 19°58N 73°50E **84 K8**
Deosai Mts. *Pakistan* 35°40N 75°0E **84 B9**
Dera Ghazi Khan *Pakistan* 30°5N 70°43E **84 D7**
Dera Ismail Khan *Pakistan* 31°50N 70°50E **84 D7**
Derbent *Russia* 42°5N 48°15E **73 F8**
Derby *Australia* 17°18S 123°38E **98 D3**
Derby *U.K.* 52°56N 1°28W **23 G6**
Derbyshire □ *U.K.* 53°11N 1°38W **23 F5**
Dereham *U.K.* 52°41N 0°57E **25 A10**
Derg → *U.K.* 54°44N 7°26W **28 B7**
Derg, L. *Ireland* 53°0N 8°20W **30 C6**
Deridder *U.S.A.* 30°51N 93°17W **111 D8**
Derry = Londonderry *U.K.* 55°0N 7°20W **28 A7**
Derrynasaggart Mts. *Ireland* 51°58N 9°15W **30 E4**
Derryveagh Mts. *Ireland* 54°56N 8°11W **28 B5**
Derwent → *Derby., U.K.* 52°57N 1°28W **23 G6**
Derwent → *N. Yorks., U.K.* 53°45N 0°58W **23 E7**
Derwent → *Tyne & W., U.K.* 54°58N 1°41W **22 C5**
Derwent Water *U.K.* 54°35N 3°9W **22 C2**
Des Moines *U.S.A.* 41°35N 93°37W **111 B8**
Des Moines → *U.S.A.* 40°23N 91°25W **111 B81**
Desborough *U.K.* 52°27N 0°49W **25 B7**
Deschutes → *U.S.A.* 45°38N 120°55W **110 A2**
Dese *Ethiopia* 11°5N 39°40E **88 E2**
Deseado → *Argentina* 47°45S 65°54W **121 G3**
Desford *U.K.* 52°37N 1°17W **23 G6**
Desolación, I. *Chile* 53°0S 74°0W **121 H2**
Dessau *Germany* 51°51N 12°14E **66 C7**
Detour, Pt. *U.S.A.* 45°40N 86°40W **112 C4**
Detroit *U.S.A.* 42°19N 83°12W **112 D6**
Deutsche Bucht *Germany* 54°15N 8°0E **66 A5**
Deventer *Neths.* 52°15N 6°10E **65 B6**
Deveron → *U.K.* 57°41N 2°32W **19 G12**
Devils Lake *U.S.A.* 48°7N 98°52W **110 A7**
Devizes *U.K.* 51°22N 1°58W **24 D5**
Devon □ *U.K.* 50°50N 3°40W **27 F6**
Devon I. *Canada* 75°10N 85°0W **109 B11**
Devonport *U.K.* 50°22N 4°11W **27 G5**
Dewey *Puerto Rico* 18°18N 65°18W **115 d**
Dewsbury *U.K.* 53°42N 1°37W **23 E5**
Dexter *U.S.A.* 36°48N 89°57W **112 G3**
Deyang *China* 31°3N 104°27E **80 C5**
Dezfūl *Iran* 32°20N 48°30E **86 C7**
Dezhneva, Mys. *Russia* 66°5N 169°40W **79 C20**
Dezhou *China* 37°26N 116°18E **81 C6**
Dhahran *Si. Arabia* 26°10N 50°7E **87 E7**
Dhaka *Bangla.* 23°43N 90°26E **85 H17**
Dhaka □ *Bangla.* 24°25N 90°25E **85 G17**
Dhamār *Yemen* 14°30N 44°20E **88 E3**
Dhamtari *India* 20°42N 81°35E **85 J12**
Dhanbad *India* 23°50N 86°30E **85 H15**
Dharwad *India* 15°30N 75°4E **84 M9**
Dhaulagiri *Nepal* 28°39N 83°28E **85 E13**
Dhenkanal *India* 20°45N 85°35E **85 J14**
Dhuburi *India* 26°2N 89°59E **85 F16**
Dhule *India* 20°58N 74°50E **84 J9**
Diamantina *Brazil* 18°17S 43°40W **122 C2**
Diamantina → *Australia* 26°45S 139°10E **98 F6**
Diamantino *Brazil* 14°30S 56°30W **120 D4**
Dibrugarh *India* 27°29N 94°55E **85 F19**
Dickinson *U.S.A.* 46°53N 102°47W **110 A6**
Didcot *U.K.* 51°36N 1°14W **24 C6**
Diefenbaker, L. *Canada* 51°0N 106°55W **108 D9**
Dieppe *France* 49°54N 1°4E **68 B4**
Digby *Canada* 44°38N 65°50W **109 E13**
Digne-les-Bains *France* 44°5N 6°12E **68 D7**
Dijon *France* 47°20N 5°3E **68 C6**
Dikson *Russia* 73°40N 80°5E **79 B10**
Dili *E. Timor* 8°39S 125°34E **83 D4**
Dillingham *U.S.A.* 59°3N 158°28W **108 D4**
Dimitrovgrad *Bulgaria* 42°5N 25°35E **71 C11**
Dimitrovgrad *Russia* 54°14N 49°39E **72 D8**
Dinajpur *Bangla.* 25°33N 88°43E **85 G16**
Dinan *France* 48°28N 2°2W **68 B2**
Dinant *Belgium* 50°16N 4°55E **65 D4**
Dinaric Alps *Croatia* 44°0N 16°30E **70 C7**
Dingle *Ireland* 52°9N 10°17W **30 D2**
Dingle B. *Ireland* 52°3N 10°20W **30 D2**
Dingwall *U.K.* 57°36N 4°26W **19 G9**
Dipolog *Phil.* 8°36N 123°20E **83 C4**
Dire Dawa *Ethiopia* 9°35N 41°45E **88 F3**
Dirranbandi *Australia* 28°33S 148°17E **98 F8**
Disappointment, C. *U.S.A.* 46°18N 124°5W **110 A2**
Disappointment, L. *Australia* 23°20S 122°40E **98 E3**
Diss *U.K.* 52°23N 1°7E **25 B11**
Distington *U.K.* 54°36N 3°32W **22 C1**
District of Columbia □ *U.S.A.* 38°55N 77°0W **112 F9**
Distrito Federal □ *Brazil* 15°45S 47°45W **122 C1**
Ditchingham *U.K.* 52°28N 1°28E **25 B11**
Ditchling Beacon *U.K.* 50°54N 0°6W **25 E8**
Dittisham *U.K.* 50°22N 3°37W **27 G6**
Ditton Priors *U.K.* 52°30N 2°34W **23 H3**
Diu *India* 20°45N 70°58E **84 J7**
Divinópolis *Brazil* 20°10S 44°54W **122 D2**
Dixon *U.S.A.* 41°50N 89°29W **112 E3**
Dixon Entrance *U.S.A.* 54°30N 132°0W **108 D6**
Diyarbakır *Turkey* 37°55N 40°18E **73 G7**
Dizzard Pt. *U.K.* 50°44N 4°40W **27 F4**
Djerba, Î. de *Tunisia* 33°50N 10°48E **95 B86**
Djerid, Chott *Tunisia* 33°42N 8°30E **94 B7**
Djibouti *Djibouti* 11°30N 43°5E **88 E3**
Djibouti ■ *Africa* 12°0N 43°0E **88 E3**
Djourab, Erg du *Chad* 16°40N 18°50E **95 E9**
Dmitri Laptev Str. *Russia* 73°0N 140°0E **79 B15**
Dnepropetrovsk *Ukraine* 48°30N 35°0E **73 E6**
Dnieper → *Ukraine* 46°30N 32°18E **73 E5**
Dniester → *Europe* 46°18N 30°17E **67 E16**
Dniprodzerzhynsk *Ukraine* 48°32N 34°37E **73 E5**
Doba *Chad* 8°40N 16°50E **95 G9**
Doberai, Jazirah *Indonesia* 1°25S 133°0E **83 D5**
Dobrich *Bulgaria* 43°37N 27°49E **71 C12**
Dobruja *Europe* 44°30N 28°15E **67 F15**
Docking *U.K.* 52°54N 0°38E **25 A10**
Doddington *Cambs., U.K.* 52°30N 0°3E **25 B9**
Doddington *Northumberland, U.K.* 55°33N 1°54W **22 A5**
Dodecanese *Greece* 36°35N 27°0E **71 F12**
Dodge City *U.S.A.* 37°45N 100°1W **110 C6**

Dodman Pt. *U.K.* 50°13N 4°48W **27 G4**
Dodoma *Tanzania* 6°8S 35°45E **96 F7**
Doha *Qatar* 25°15N 51°35E **87 E7**
Dolbeau-Mistassini *Canada* 48°53N 72°14W **109 E12**
Dole *France* 47°7N 5°31E **68 C6**
Dolgarrog *U.K.* 53°11N 3°50W **26 A6**
Dolgellau *U.K.* 52°45N 3°53W **26 B6**
Dolo *Ethiopia* 4°11N 42°3E **88 G3**
Dolomites *Italy* 46°23N 11°51E **70 A4**
Dolores *Argentina* 36°20S 57°40W **121 F4**
Dolphin and Union Str. *Canada* 69°5N 114°45W **108 C8**
Dolphinton *U.K.* 55°42N 3°25W **21 C9**
Dolton *U.K.* 50°53N 4°2W **27 F5**
Dominica ■ *W. Indies* 15°20N 61°20W **115 D12**
Dominican Rep. ■ *W. Indies* 19°0N 70°30W **115 D10**
Don → *Russia* 47°4N 39°18E **73 E6**
Don → *Aberds., U.K.* 57°11N 2°5W **19 H13**
Don → *S. Yorks., U.K.* 53°41N 0°52W **23 E7**
Don Figuerero Mts. *Jamaica* 54°39N 5°33W **29 B10**
Donaghadee *U.K.* 54°39N 5°33W **29 B10**
Doncaster *U.K.* 53°32N 1°6W **23 E6**
Dondra Head *Sri Lanka* 5°55N 80°40E **84 S12**
Donegal *Ireland* 54°39N 8°5W **28 B5**
Donegal □ *Ireland* 54°53N 8°0W **28 B5**
Donegal B. *Ireland* 54°31N 8°49W **28 B4**
Donets → *Russia* 47°33N 40°55E **73 E7**
Donetsk *Ukraine* 48°0N 37°45E **73 E6**
Dong Hoi *Vietnam* 17°29N 106°36E **83 B2**
Dongola *Sudan* 19°9N 30°22E **95 E12**
Dongting Hu *China* 29°18N 112°45E **81 D6**
Donhead *U.K.* 51°1N 2°7W **24 D4**
Donington *U.K.* 52°54N 0°12W **23 G8**
Donna Nook *U.K.* 53°29N 0°8E **23 F9**
Donostia-San Sebastián *Spain* 43°17N 1°58W **69 A5**
Doon → *U.K.* 55°27N 4°39W **20 D6**
Dorchester *Dorset, U.K.* 50°42N 2°27W **24 E4**
Dorchester *Oxon., U.K.* 51°39N 1°10W **24 C6**
Dorchester, C. *Canada* 65°27N 77°27W **109 C12**
Dordogne → *France* 45°2N 0°36W **68 D3**
Dordrecht *Neths.* 51°48N 4°39E **65 C4**
Dores do Indaiá *Brazil* 19°27S 45°36W **122 C1**
Dorking *U.K.* 51°14N 0°19W **25 D8**
Dornie *U.K.* 57°17N 5°31W **18 H6**
Dornoch *U.K.* 57°53N 4°2W **19 G9**
Dornoch Firth *U.K.* 57°51N 4°4W **19 G9**
Döröö Nuur *Mongolia* 48°0N 93°0E **80 B4**
Dorset □ *U.K.* 50°45N 2°26W **24 E4**
Dorstone *U.K.* 52°3N 2°59W **24 B3**
Dortmund *Germany* 51°30N 7°28E **66 C4**
Dos Bahías, C. *Argentina* 44°58S 65°32W **121 G3**
Dos Hermanas *Spain* 37°16N 5°55W **69 D3**
Dothan *U.S.A.* 31°13N 85°24W **111 D9**
Douai *France* 50°21N 3°4E **68 A5**
Douala *Cameroon* 4°0N 9°45E **96 D1**
Doubs → *France* 46°53N 5°1E **68 C6**
Douglas *I. of Man* 54°10N 4°28W **29 C13**
Douglas *U.K.* 55°33N 3°50W **21 D8**
Douglas *U.S.A.* 31°21N 109°33W **110 D5**
Dounreay *U.K.* 58°35N 3°44W **19 E10**
Dourados *Brazil* 22°9S 54°50W **120 E4**
Douro → *Europe* 41°8N 8°40W **69 B1**
Dove → *Derby., U.K.* 52°51N 1°36W **23 G5**
Dove → *N. Yorks., U.K.* 54°15N 0°55W **22 D7**
Dove Dale *U.K.* 53°7N 1°46W **23 F5**
Dover *U.K.* 51°7N 1°19E **25 D11**
Dover *Del., U.S.A.* 39°10N 75°32W **113 F10**
Dover *N.H., U.S.A.* 43°12N 70°56W **113 D12**
Dover, Str. of *Europe* 51°0N 1°30E **64 F7**
Dover-Foxcroft *U.S.A.* 45°11N 69°13W **113 C13**
Doveridge *U.K.* 52°54N 1°49W **23 G5**
Dovrefjell *Norway* 62°15N 9°33E **63 E5**
Down □ *U.K.* 54°23N 6°2W **29 B9**
Downham *U.K.* 52°26N 0°14E **25 B9**
Downham Market *U.K.* 52°37N 0°23E **25 B9**
Downpatrick *U.K.* 54°20N 5°43W **29 C10**
Downpatrick Hd. *Ireland* 54°20N 9°21W **28 C3**
Downton *U.K.* 50°59N 1°44W **24 E5**
Drăa, Oued → *Morocco* 28°40N 11°10W **94 C3**
Draguignan *France* 43°32N 6°27E **68 E7**
Drake Passage *S. Ocean* 58°0S 68°0W **55 B17**
Drakensberg *S. Africa* 31°0S 28°0E **97 L5**
Drammen *Norway* 59°42N 10°12E **63 F6**
Drava → *Croatia* 45°33N 18°55E **71 B8**
Drenthe □ *Neths.* 52°52N 6°40E **65 B6**
Dresden *Germany* 51°3N 13°44E **66 C7**
Dreux *France* 48°44N 1°23E **68 B4**
Driffield *U.K.* 54°0N 0°26W **23 D8**
Drina → *Bos.-H.* 44°53N 19°21E **71 B8**
Drobeta-Turnu Severin *Romania* 44°39N 22°41E **67 F12**
Drogheda *Ireland* 53°43N 6°22W **29 D9**
Drohobych *Ukraine* 49°20N 23°30E **73 D3**
Droichead Nua *Ireland* 53°11N 6°48W **31 B9**
Droitwich *U.K.* 52°16N 2°8W **24 B4**
Dromore *U.K.* 54°31N 7°28W **28 B7**
Dromore West *Ireland* 54°15N 8°52W **28 B5**
Dronfield *U.K.* 53°19N 1°27W **23 F6**
Dronning Maud Land *Antarctica* 72°30S 12°0E **55 D3**
Drumheller *Canada* 51°25N 112°40W **108 D8**
Drummond I. *U.S.A.* 46°1N 83°39W **112 B5**
Drummondville *Canada* 45°55N 72°25W **113 C11**
Druridge B. *U.K.* 55°17N 1°32W **22 B5**
Dry Harbour Mts. *Jamaica* 18°19N 77°24W **114 a**
Dryden *Canada* 49°47N 92°50W **108 E10**
Drygalski I. *Antarctica* 66°0S 92°0E **55 C7**
Du Quoin *U.S.A.* 38°1N 89°14W **112 F3**
Dubà *Si. Arabia* 27°10N 35°40E **86 E3**
Dubai *U.A.E.* 25°18N 55°20E **87 E8**
Dubawnt → *Canada* 64°33N 100°6W **108 C9**
Dubawnt L. *Canada* 63°8N 101°28W **108 C9**
Dubbo *Australia* 32°11S 148°35E **98 G8**
Dublin *Ireland* 53°21N 6°15W **31 B10**
Dublin *U.S.A.* 32°32N 82°54W **111 D10**
Dublin □ *Ireland* 53°24N 6°20W **31 B10**
Dublin ✈ (DUB) *Ireland* 53°26N 6°15W **31 B10**
Dubrovnik *Croatia* 42°39N 18°6E **71 C8**

Dubuque *U.S.A.* 42°30N 90°41W **112 D2**
Duddington *U.K.* 52°36N 0°32W **25 A7**
Duddon → *U.K.* 54°12N 3°15W **22 D2**
Dudinka *Russia* 69°30N 86°13E **79 C10**
Dudley *U.K.* 52°31N 2°5W **23 G4**
Dufftown *U.K.* 57°27N 3°8W **19 H11**
Duffield *U.K.* 52°59N 1°29W **23 G6**
Dufourspitze *Switz.* 45°50N 7°53W **64 C4**
Dugi Otok *Croatia* 44°0N 15°3E **70 C6**
Duisburg *Germany* 51°26N 6°45E **66 C4**
Dukinfield *U.K.* 53°28N 2°6W **23 F4**
Dulce → *Argentina* 30°32S 62°33W **121 F3**
Duluth *U.S.A.* 46°47N 92°6W **112 B1**
Dulverton *U.K.* 51°2N 3°33W **27 E6**
Dumaguete *Phil.* 9°17N 123°15E **83 C4**
Dumbarton *U.K.* 55°57N 4°33W **20 C6**
Dumfries *U.K.* 55°4N 3°37W **21 D8**
Dumfries & Galloway □ *U.K.* 55°9N 3°58W **21 D8**
Dumyât *Egypt* 31°24N 31°48E **95 B12**
Dún Laoghaire *Ireland* 53°17N 6°8W **31 B10**
Dunbar *U.K.* 56°0N 2°31W **21 B10**
Dunblane *U.K.* 56°11N 3°58W **21 B8**
Duncan *U.S.A.* 34°30N 97°57W **111 D7**
Duncansby Head *U.K.* 58°38N 3°1W **19 E11**
Dunchurch *U.K.* 52°21N 1°17W **24 B6**
Dundalk *Ireland* 54°1N 6°24W **29 C9**
Dundalk Bay *Ireland* 53°55N 6°15W **29 D9**
Dundee *U.K.* 56°28N 2°59W **21 B10**
Dundrum *Ireland* 53°18N 6°14W **31 B10**
Dundrum *U.K.* 54°16N 5°52W **29 C10**
Dundrum B. *U.K.* 54°13N 5°47W **29 C10**
Dunedin *N.Z.* 45°50S 170°33E **99 K13**
Dunfermline *U.K.* 56°5N 3°27W **21 B9**
Dungannon *U.K.* 54°31N 6°46W **29 B8**
Dungarvan *Ireland* 52°5N 7°37W **31 D7**
Dungarvan Harbour *Ireland* 52°4N 7°35W **31 D7**
Dungeness *U.K.* 50°54N 0°59E **25 E10**
Dunhua *China* 43°20N 128°14E **81 B7**
Dunhuang *China* 40°8N 94°36E **80 B4**
Dunkeld *U.K.* 56°34N 3°35W **21 A8**
Dunkerque *France* 51°2N 2°20E **68 A5**
Dunkery Beacon *U.K.* 51°9N 3°36W **27 E6**
Dunkirk *U.K.* 42°29N 79°20W **112 D8**
Dunleer *Ireland* 53°50N 6°24W **29 D9**
Dunmanway *Ireland* 51°43N 9°6W **30 E4**
Dunmore *U.K.* 41°25N 75°38W **113 E10**
Dunnet Hd. *U.K.* 58°40N 3°21W **19 E11**
Dunoon *U.K.* 55°57N 4°56W **20 C6**
Duns *U.K.* 55°47N 2°20E **21 C10**
Dunsford *U.K.* 50°41N 3°42W **27 F6**
Dunstable *U.K.* 51°53N 0°32W **25 C7**
Dunster *U.K.* 51°11N 3°27W **24 D2**
Dunston *U.K.* 52°46N 2°7W **23 G4**
Dunvegan *U.K.* 57°27N 6°35W **18 H4**
Duque de Caxias *Brazil* 22°46S 43°18W **122 D2**
Durance → *France* 43°55N 4°45E **68 E6**
Durango *Mexico* 24°3N 104°39W **114 C4**
Durango *U.S.A.* 37°16N 107°53W **110 C5**
Durant *U.S.A.* 33°59N 96°25W **111 D7**
Durazno *Uruguay* 33°25S 56°31W **121 F4**
Durban *S. Africa* 29°49S 31°1E **97 K6**
Düren *Germany* 50°48N 6°29E **66 C4**
Durgapur *India* 23°30N 87°20E **85 H15**
Durham *U.K.* 54°47N 1°34W **22 C5**
Durham *U.S.A.* 35°59N 78°54W **111 C11**
Durham □ *U.K.* 54°42N 1°45W **22 C5**
Durlston Hd. *U.K.* 50°36N 1°57W **24 E5**
Durness *U.K.* 58°34N 4°45W **19 E8**
Durrës *Albania* 41°19N 19°28E **71 D8**
Durrington *U.K.* 51°12N 1°47W **24 D5**
Durrow *Ireland* 52°51N 7°24W **31 D8**
Dursey I. *Ireland* 51°36N 10°12W **30 E2**
Dursley *U.K.* 51°40N 2°21W **24 C4**
Dushanbe *Tajikistan* 38°33N 68°48E **87 B12**
Düsseldorf *Germany* 51°14N 6°47E **66 C4**
Dutch Harbor *U.S.A.* 53°53N 166°32W **108 D3**
Duyun *China* 26°18N 107°29E **80 D5**
Dvina, N. → *Russia* 64°32N 40°30E **72 B7**
Dvina B. *Russia* 65°0N 39°0E **72 B6**
Dwarka *India* 22°18N 69°8E **84 H6**
Dyce *U.K.* 57°13N 2°12W **19 H13**
Dyer, C. *Canada* 66°37N 61°16W **109 C13**
Dyersburg *U.S.A.* 36°3N 89°23W **111 C91**
Dyfi → *U.K.* 52°32N 4°3W **26 B5**
Dymchurch *U.K.* 51°1N 1°0E **25 D11**
Dymock *U.K.* 51°59N 2°26W **24 C4**
Dzerzhinsk *Russia* 56°14N 43°30E **72 C7**
Dzhankoy *Ukraine* 45°40N 34°20E **73 E5**
Dzhugdzhur Ra. *Russia* 57°30N 138°0E **79 D15**
Dzungarian Basin *China* 44°30N 86°0E **80 B3**
Dzuumod *Mongolia* 47°45N 106°58E **80 B5**

E

Eagle *U.S.A.* 64°47N 141°12W **108 C5**
Eagle L. *U.S.A.* 46°20N 69°22W **113 B13**
Eagle Pass *U.S.A.* 28°43N 100°30W **110 E6**
Eagle River *U.S.A.* 47°25N 88°18W **112 B3**
Eaglesfield *U.K.* 55°4N 3°12W **21 D9**
Eakring *U.K.* 53°9N 0°58W **23 F7**
Ealing *U.K.* 51°31N 0°20W **25 C8**
Earby *U.K.* 53°55N 2°7W **23 E4**
Eardisley *U.K.* 52°8N 3°1W **24 B2**
Earith *U.K.* 52°22N 0°2E **25 B9**
Earl Shilton *U.K.* 52°35N 1°18W **23 G6**
Earl Soham *U.K.* 52°14N 1°18E **25 B11**
Earls Barton *U.K.* 52°16N 0°45W **25 B7**
Earl's Colne *U.K.* 51°56N 0°43E **25 C10**
Earlston *U.K.* 55°39N 2°40W **21 C10**
Earn → *U.K.* 56°21N 3°18W **21 B9**
Earn, L. *U.K.* 56°23N 4°13W **20 B7**
Earsdon *U.K.* 55°3N 1°29W **22 B6**
Easebourne *U.K.* 51°0N 0°43W **25 D7**
Easington *Durham, U.K.* 54°47N 1°21W **22 C6**
Easington *E. Riding, U.K.* 53°39N 0°6E **23 E9**
Easington Colliery *U.K.* 54°48N 1°19W **22 C6**
Easingwold *U.K.* 54°8N 1°11W **22 D6**
East Ayrshire □ *U.K.* 55°26N 4°11W **20 C7**
East Bengal *Bangla.* 24°0N 90°0E **85 H17**

East Bergholt

East Bergholt U.K. 51°59N 1°3E 25 C11
East Beskids Europe 49°20N 22°0E 67 D11
East Brent U.K. 51°15N 2°56W 24 D3
East C. = Dezhneva, Mys. Russia 66°5N 169°40W 79 C20
East China Sea Asia 30°0N 126°0E 81 D7
East Cowes U.K. 50°45N 1°16W 24 E6
East Falkland Falk. Is. 51°30S 58°30W 121 H4
East Fen U.K. 53°4N 0°5E 23 F9
East Grinstead U.K. 51°7N 0°0 25 D9
East Harling U.K. 52°26N 0°56E 25 B10
East Ilsley U.K. 51°31N 1°16W 24 C6
East Indies Asia 0°0 120°0E 74 J14
East Kilbride U.K. 55°47N 4°11W 20 C7
East Lansing U.S.A. 42°44N 84°29W 112 D5
East London S. Africa 33°0S 27°55E 97 L5
East Lothian □ U.K. 55°58N 2°44W 21 C10
East Markham U.K. 53°15N 0°53W 23 F7
East Moor U.K. 53°16N 1°34W 23 F5
East Pacific Rise Pac. Oc. 15°0S 110°0W 103 J17
East Pt. Canada 46°27N 61°58W 113 C17
East Pt. Br. Virgin Is. 18°40N 64°18W 115 e
East St. Louis U.S.A. 38°37N 90°9W 112 F7
East Sea = Japan, Sea of Asia 40°0N 135°0E 82 D4
East Siberian Sea Russia 73°0N 160°0E 79 B18
East Sussex □ U.K. 50°56N 0°19E 25 E9
East Timor ■ Asia 8°50S 126°0E 83 D4
East Wittering U.K. 50°46N 0°52W 25 E7
East Woodhay U.K. 51°21N 1°25W 24 D6
Eastbourne U.K. 50°46N 0°18E 25 E9
Eastchurch U.K. 51°24N 0°53E 25 D10
Eastern Ghats India 14°0N 78°50E 84 N11
Eastern Group Fiji 17°0S 178°30W 99 D15
Eastleigh U.K. 50°58N 1°21W 24 E6
Eastmain Canada 52°10N 78°30W 109 D12
Eastmain → Canada 52°27N 78°26W 109 D12
Eastnor U.K. 52°2N 2°23W 24 B4
Easton Dorset, U.K. 50°33N 2°26W 24 E4
Easton Northants., U.K. 52°37N 0°31W 25 A7
Easton Md., U.S.A. 38°47N 76°5W 113 F9
Easton Pa., U.S.A. 40°41N 75°13W 113 E10
Easton-in-Gordano U.K. 51°28N 2°42W 24 D3
Eastport U.S.A. 44°56N 67°0W 113 C14
Eastry U.K. 51°14N 1°19E 25 D11
Eastwood U.K. 53°1N 1°18W 23 F6
Eaton U.K. 52°51N 0°49W 23 G7
Eaton Socon U.K. 52°14N 0°17W 25 B8
Eau Claire U.S.A. 44°49N 91°30W 112 C2
Eau Claire, L. à l' Canada 56°10N 74°25W 109 D12
Ebberston U.K. 54°14N 0°37W 22 D7
Ebbw Vale U.K. 51°46N 3°12W 26 D7
Eberswalde-Finow Germany 52°50N 13°49E 66 B7
Ebetsu Japan 43°7N 141°34E 82 B7
Ebinur Hu China 44°55N 82°55E 80 B3
Ebolowa Cameroon 2°55N 11°10E 96 D2
Ebro → Spain 40°43N 0°54E 69 B6
Ecclefechan U.K. 55°4N 3°16W 21 D9
Eccleshall U.K. 52°52N 2°15W 23 G4
Ech Chélif Algeria 36°10N 1°20E 94 A6
Echo Bay Canada 66°5N 117°55W 108 C8
Eckington U.K. 53°18N 1°22W 23 F6
Eclipse Sd. Canada 72°38N 79°0W 109 B12
Ecuador ■ S. Amer. 2°0S 78°0W 120 C2
Ed Damazin Sudan 11°46N 34°21E 95 F12
Edam Neths. 52°31N 5°3E 65 B5
Eday U.K. 59°11N 2°47W 19 D12
Eddrachillis B. U.K. 58°17N 5°14W 18 F7
Eddystone U.K. 50°11N 4°16W 27 G5
Eden → U.K. 54°57N 3°1W 22 C2
Edenbridge U.K. 51°12N 0°5E 25 D9
Edenderry Ireland 53°21N 7°4W 31 B8
Edge Hill U.K. 52°8N 1°26W 24 B6
Edinburgh U.K. 55°57N 3°13W 21 C9
Edinburgh ✈ (EDI) U.K. 55°54N 3°22W 21 C9
Edington U.K. 51°17N 2°5W 24 D4
Edirne Turkey 41°40N 26°34E 73 F4
Edmonton Canada 53°30N 113°30W 108 D8
Edmundbyers U.K. 54°50N 1°58W 22 C5
Edmundston Canada 47°23N 68°20W 109 E13
Edremit Turkey 39°34N 27°0E 86 B1
Edson Canada 53°35N 116°28W 108 D8
Edward, L. Africa 0°25S 29°40E 96 E5
Edward VII Land Antarctica 80°0S 150°0W 55 E13
Edwards Plateau U.S.A. 30°45N 101°20W 110 D6
Effingham U.S.A. 39°7N 88°33W 112 F3
Égadi, Ísole Italy 37°55N 12°16E 70 F5
Eganville Canada 45°32N 77°5W 112 C9
Eger Hungary 47°53N 20°27E 67 E11
Egham U.K. 51°26N 0°32W 25 D7
Eglinton I. Canada 75°48N 118°30W 109 B8
Egremont U.K. 54°29N 3°32W 22 D1
Eğridir Turkey 37°52N 30°51E 73 G5
Eğridir Gölü Turkey 37°53N 30°50E 73 G5
Egton U.K. 54°28N 0°44W 22 D7
Egypt ■ Africa 28°0N 31°0E 95 C12
Eifel Germany 50°15N 6°50E 66 C4
Eigg U.K. 56°54N 6°10W 18 J5
Eil, L. U.K. 56°51N 5°16W 18 J7
Eindhoven Neths. 51°26N 5°28E 65 C5
Eire = Ireland ■ Europe 53°50N 7°52W 64 E2
Eivissa Spain 38°54N 1°26E 69 C6
El Aaiún W. Sahara 27°9N 13°12W 94 C3
El 'Alamein Egypt 30°48N 28°58E 95 B11
El Centro U.S.A. 32°48N 115°34W 110 D3
El Djouf Mauritania 20°0N 9°0W 94 D4
El Dorado U.S.A. 33°12N 92°40W 111 D8
El Faiyûm Egypt 29°19N 30°50E 95 C12
El Fâsher Sudan 13°33N 25°26E 95 F11
El Fuerte Mexico 26°25N 108°39W 114 B3
El Geneina Sudan 13°27N 22°45E 95 F11
El Gezira □ Sudan 15°0N 33°0E 95 F12
El Gîza Egypt 30°0N 31°12E 95 C12
El Istiwa'iya Sudan 5°0N 28°0E 95 G11
El Jadida Morocco 33°11N 8°17W 94 B4
El Khârga Egypt 25°30N 30°33E 95 C12
El Mahalla el Kubra Egypt 31°0N 31°0E 95 B12
El Mansûra Egypt 31°0N 31°19E 95 B12
El Minyâ Egypt 28°7N 30°33E 95 C12

El Obeid Sudan 13°8N 30°10E 95 F12
El Oued Algeria 33°20N 6°58E 94 B7
El Paso U.S.A. 31°45N 106°29W 110 D5
El Puerto de Santa María Spain 36°36N 6°13W 69 D2
El Reno U.S.A. 35°32N 97°57W 110 C7
El Salvador ■ Cent. Amer. 13°50N 89°0W 114 E7
El Tigre Venezuela 8°44N 64°15W 120 B3
El Uqsur Egypt 25°41N 32°38E 95 C12
Elat Israel 29°30N 34°56E 86 D3
Elâzığ Turkey 38°37N 39°14E 73 G6
Elba Italy 42°46N 10°17E 70 C4
Elbasan Albania 41°9N 20°9E 71 D9
Elbe → Europe 53°50N 9°0E 66 B5
Elbert, Mt. U.S.A. 39°7N 106°27W 110 C5
Elbeuf France 49°17N 1°2E 68 B4
Elblag Poland 54°10N 19°25E 67 A10
Elbrus Asia 43°21N 42°30E 73 F7
Elburz Mts. Iran 36°0N 52°0E 87 B8
Elche Spain 38°15N 0°42W 69 C5
Elda Spain 38°29N 0°47W 69 C5
Eldoret Kenya 0°30N 35°17E 96 D7
Elektrostal Russia 55°41N 38°32E 72 C6
Elemi Triangle Africa 5°0N 35°20E 96 D7
Elephant Butte Res. U.S.A. 33°9N 107°11W 110 D5
Elephant I. Antarctica 61°0S 55°0W 55 C18
Eleuthera Bahamas 25°0N 76°20W 115 C9
Elgin U.K. 57°39N 3°19W 19 G11
Elgin U.S.A. 42°2N 88°17W 112 D3
Elgon, Mt. Africa 1°10N 34°30E 96 D6
Elham U.K. 51°9N 1°8E 25 D11
Elishaw U.K. 55°15N 2°14W 22 B4
Elista Russia 46°16N 44°14E 73 E7
Elizabeth U.S.A. 40°39N 74°12W 113 E10
Elizabeth City U.S.A. 36°18N 76°14W 111 C11
Elizabethtown U.S.A. 37°42N 85°52W 112 G5
Elkhart U.S.A. 41°41N 85°58W 112 E5
Elkins U.S.A. 38°55N 79°51W 112 F8
Elko U.S.A. 40°50N 115°46W 110 B3
Elland U.K. 53°41N 1°50W 23 E5
Ellef Ringnes I. Canada 78°30N 102°2W 109 B9
Ellen → U.K. 54°44N 3°30W 22 C2
Ellensburg U.S.A. 46°59N 120°34W 110 A2
Ellerton Barbados 13°7N 59°33W 115 g
Ellesmere U.K. 52°55N 2°53W 23 G3
Ellesmere I. Canada 79°30N 80°0W 109 B12
Ellesmere Port U.K. 53°17N 2°54W 23 F3
Ellington U.K. 55°14N 1°33W 22 B5
Elliot Lake Canada 46°25N 82°35W 109 E11
Ellon U.K. 57°22N 2°4W 19 H13
Ellsworth Land Antarctica 76°0S 89°0W 55 D16
Elmalı Turkey 36°44N 29°56E 73 G4
Elmswell U.K. 52°15N 0°55E 25 B10
Eluru India 16°48N 81°8E 85 L12
Ely U.K. 52°24N 0°16E 25 B9
Ely U.S.A. 39°15N 114°54W 110 C4
Elyria U.S.A. 41°22N 82°7W 112 E6
Emämrüd Iran 36°30N 55°0E 87 B8
Embarcación Argentina 23°10S 64°0W 121 E3
Embleton U.K. 55°29N 1°38W 22 B5
Emden Germany 53°21N 7°12E 66 B4
Emerald Australia 37°56S 145°29E 98 E8
Emmeloord Neths. 52°44N 5°46E 65 B5
Emmen Neths. 52°48N 6°57E 65 B6
Emmonak U.S.A. 62°47N 164°31W 108 C3
Empalme Mexico 27°58N 110°51W 114 B2
Empangeni S. Africa 28°50S 31°52E 97 K6
Empedrado Argentina 28°0S 58°46W 121 E4
Emperor Seamount Chain Pac. Oc. 40°0N 170°0E 102 D9
Emporia U.S.A. 38°25N 96°11W 111 C7
Emporium U.S.A. 41°31N 78°14W 112 E8
Empty Quarter = Rub' al Khāli Si. Arabia 19°0N 48°0E 88 D4
Ems → Germany 53°20N 7°12E 66 B4
En Nahud Sudan 12°45N 28°25E 95 F11
Enard B. U.K. 58°5N 5°20W 18 F7
Encarnación Paraguay 27°15S 55°50W 121 E4
Encounter B. Australia 35°45S 138°45E 98 H6
Ende Indonesia 8°45S 121°40E 83 D4
Enderbury I. Kiribati 3°8S 171°5W 102 H10
Enderby U.K. 52°36N 1°13W 23 G6
Enderby Land Antarctica 66°0S 53°0E 55 C5
Endicott U.S.A. 42°6N 76°4W 113 D9
Enewetak Atoll Marshall Is. 11°30N 162°15E 102 F8
Enez Turkey 40°45N 26°5E 73 F4
Enfer, Pte. d' Martinique 14°22N 60°54W 114 c
Enfield □ U.K. 51°38N 0°5W 25 C8
Engadin Switz. 46°45N 10°10E 66 E6
Engels Russia 51°28N 46°6E 73 D8
Enggano Indonesia 5°20S 102°40E 83 D2
England □ U.K. 53°0N 2°0W 64 E6
English → Canada 49°12N 91°5W 108 D10
English Channel Europe 50°0N 2°0W 64 F6
Enid U.S.A. 36°24N 97°53W 110 C7
Ennadai L. Canada 60°58N 101°20W 108 C9
Ennedi Chad 17°15N 22°0E 95 E10
Ennerdale Water U.K. 54°32N 3°24W 22 C2
Ennis Ireland 52°51N 8°59W 30 C5
Enniscorthy Ireland 52°30N 6°34W 31 D9
Enniskillen U.K. 54°21N 7°39W 28 C6
Ennistimon Ireland 52°57N 9°17W 30 C4
Enns → Austria 48°14N 14°32E 66 D8
Enschede Neths. 52°13N 6°53E 65 B6
Ensenada Mexico 31°52N 116°37W 114 A1
Enshi China 30°18N 109°29E 81 C5
Enstone U.K. 51°55N 1°27W 24 C6
Entebbe Uganda 0°4N 32°28E 96 D6
Entre Rios □ Argentina 30°30S 58°30W 121 F4
Enugu Nigeria 6°30N 7°30E 94 G7
Eólie, Ís. Italy 38°30N 14°57E 70 E6
Épernay France 49°3N 3°56E 68 B5
Épinal France 48°10N 6°27E 68 B7
Epping U.K. 51°41N 0°7E 25 C9
Epping Forest U.K. 51°40N 0°5E 25 C9
Epsom U.K. 51°19N 0°16W 25 D8
Epworth U.K. 53°32N 0°48W 23 E7

Equatorial Guinea ■ Africa 2°0N 8°0E 96 D1
Er Rachidia Morocco 31°58N 4°20W 94 B5
Ercıyaş Dağı Turkey 38°30N 35°30E 86 B3
Erdenet Mongolia 49°2N 104°5E 80 B5
Erebus, Mt. Antarctica 77°35S 167°0E 55 D11
Ereğli Konya, Turkey 37°31N 34°4E 73 G5
Ereğli Zonguldak, Turkey 41°15N 31°24E 73 F5
Erfurt Germany 50°58N 11°2E 66 C6
Ergeni Lowlands Russia 47°0N 44°0E 73 E7
Eriboll, L. U.K. 58°30N 4°42W 19 E8
Erie U.S.A. 42°8N 80°5W 112 D7
Erie, L. N. Amer. 42°15N 81°0W 112 D7
Eriskay U.K. 57°4N 7°18W 18 H3
Eritrea ■ Africa 14°0N 38°30E 88 D2
Erlangen Germany 49°36N 11°0E 66 D6
Ernakulam India 9°59N 76°22E 84 Q10
Erne → Ireland 54°30N 8°16W 28 C5
Erne, Lower L. U.K. 54°28N 7°47W 28 C6
Erne, Upper L. U.K. 54°14N 7°32W 28 C6
Erode India 11°24N 77°45E 84 P10
Erramala Hills India 15°30N 78°15E 84 M11
Errigal Ireland 55°2N 8°6W 28 A5
Erris Hd. Ireland 54°19N 10°0W 28 C1
Erromango Vanuatu 18°45S 169°5E 99 D12
Erzgebirge Germany 50°27N 12°55E 66 C7
Erzincan Turkey 39°46N 39°30E 73 G6
Erzurum Turkey 39°57N 41°15E 73 G7
Esbjerg Denmark 55°29N 8°29E 63 F5
Escada Brazil 8°22S 35°8W 122 A3
Escanaba U.S.A. 45°45N 87°4W 112 C4
Esch-sur-Alzette Lux. 49°32N 6°0E 65 E6
Escrick U.K. 53°53N 1°2W 23 E6
Escuinapa de Hidalgo Mexico 22°50N 105°50W 114 C3
Escuintla Guatemala 14°20N 90°48W 114 E6
Esfahān Iran 32°39N 51°43E 87 C7
Esha Ness U.K. 60°29N 1°38W 18 B14
Esil → Russia 57°45N 71°10E 79 D9
Esk → Cumb., U.K. 54°20N 3°24W 22 D2
Esk → Dumf. & Gall., U.K. 54°58N 3°2W 21 E9
Esk → N. Yorks., U.K. 54°30N 0°37W 22 D7
Eskdale U.K. 55°12N 3°4W 21 D9
Esker Canada 53°53N 66°25W 109 D13
Eskilstuna Sweden 59°22N 16°32E 63 F7
Eskişehir Turkey 39°50N 30°30E 73 G5
Eslāmābād-e Gharb Iran 34°10N 46°30E 86 C6
Esperance Australia 33°45S 121°55E 98 G3
Esperanza Puerto Rico 18°6N 65°28W 115 d
Espinhaço, Serra do Brazil 17°30S 43°30W 122 C2
Espírito Santo □ Brazil 20°0S 40°45W 122 C2
Espíritu Santo Vanuatu 15°15S 166°50E 99 D12
Espoo Finland 60°12N 24°40E 63 E8
Essaouira Morocco 31°32N 9°42W 94 B4
Essen Germany 51°28N 7°2E 66 C4
Essequibo → Guyana 6°50N 58°30W 120 B4
Essex □ U.K. 51°54N 0°27E 25 C9
Esslingen Germany 48°44N 9°18E 66 D5
Estados, I. de Los Argentina 54°40S 64°30W 121 H3
Estância Brazil 11°16S 37°26W 122 B3
Estevan Canada 49°10N 102°59W 108 E9
Eston U.K. 54°34N 1°8W 22 C6
Estonia ■ Europe 58°30N 25°30E 63 F8
Estrela, Serra da Portugal 40°10N 7°45W 69 B2
Estrondo, Serra do Brazil 7°20S 48°0W 120 C5
Etawah India 26°48N 79°6E 84 F11
Etchingham U.K. 51°0N 0°26E 25 D9
eThekwini = Durban S. Africa 29°49S 31°1E 97 K6
Ethiopia ■ Africa 8°0N 40°0E 88 F3
Ethiopian Highlands Ethiopia 10°0N 37°0E 88 F2
Etive, L. U.K. 56°29N 5°10W 20 B5
Etna Italy 37°50N 14°55E 70 F6
Eton U.K. 51°30N 0°36W 25 C7
Etosha Pan Namibia 18°40S 16°30E 97 H3
Ettington U.K. 52°8N 1°35W 24 B5
Ettrick Forest U.K. 55°30N 3°0W 21 D9
Ettrick Water → U.K. 55°31N 2°55W 21 C10
Euclid U.S.A. 41°34N 81°32W 112 E7
Eugene U.S.A. 44°5N 123°4W 110 B2
Euphrates → Asia 31°0N 47°25E 86 D6
Eureka Canada 80°0N 85°56W 109 B11
Eureka U.S.A. 40°47N 124°9W 110 B2
Europa, Île Ind. Oc. 22°20S 40°22E 97 J8
Europa, Picos de Spain 43°10N 4°49W 69 A3
Europe 50°0N 20°0E 56 E10
Euxton U.K. 53°41N 2°41W 23 E3
Evanston Ill., U.S.A. 42°3N 87°40W 112 D4
Evanston Wyo., U.S.A. 41°16N 110°58W 110 B4
Evansville U.S.A. 37°58N 87°35W 112 G4
Evercreech U.K. 51°9N 2°30W 24 D4
Everest, Mt. Nepal 28°5N 86°58E 85 E15
Everett U.S.A. 47°59N 122°12W 110 A2
Everglades, The U.S.A. 25°50N 81°0W 111 E10
Evesham U.K. 52°6N 1°56W 24 B5
Evia Greece 38°30N 24°0E 71 E11
Évora Portugal 38°33N 7°57W 69 C2
Évreux France 49°3N 1°8E 68 B4
Évros → Greece 41°40N 26°34E 71 D12
Ewe, L. U.K. 57°49N 5°38W 18 G6
Ewell U.K. 51°20N 0°14W 25 D8
Ewhurst U.K. 51°9N 0°25W 25 D8
Exe → U.K. 50°41N 3°29W 27 F7
Exeter U.K. 50°43N 3°31W 27 F6
Exminster U.K. 50°40N 3°29W 27 F7
Exmoor U.K. 51°12N 3°45W 27 E6
Exmoor △ U.K. 51°8N 3°42W 27 E6
Exmouth U.K. 50°37N 3°25W 27 F7
Exton U.K. 52°42N 0°38W 23 G7
Extremadura □ Spain 39°30N 6°5W 69 C2
Eyam U.K. 53°17N 1°40W 23 F5
Eyasi, L. Tanzania 3°30S 35°0E 96 E6
Eye Cambs., U.K. 52°37N 0°11W 25 B8
Eye Suffolk, U.K. 52°19N 1°9E 25 B11
Eye Pen. U.K. 58°13N 6°10W 18 F3
Eyemouth U.K. 55°52N 2°5W 21 C11
Eynsham U.K. 51°47N 1°22W 24 C6
Eyre, L. Australia 29°30S 137°26E 98 F6
Eyre Pen. Australia 33°30S 136°17E 98 G6

F

F.Y.R.O.M. = Macedonia ■ Europe 41°53N 21°40E 71 D9
Faenza Italy 44°17N 11°53E 70 B4
Fair Hd. U.K. 55°14N 6°9W 29 A9
Fair Isle U.K. 59°32N 1°38W 18 C14
Fairbanks U.S.A. 64°51N 147°43W 108 C5
Fairfield U.S.A. 38°23N 88°22W 112 F3
Fairford U.K. 51°43N 1°46W 24 C5
Fairlight U.K. 50°52N 0°40E 25 E10
Fairmont U.S.A. 39°29N 80°9W 112 F7
Fairweather, Mt. U.S.A. 58°55N 137°32W 108 D6
Faisalabad Pakistan 31°30N 73°5E 84 D8
Faizabad India 26°45N 82°10E 85 F13
Fakenham U.K. 52°51N 0°51E 25 A10
Falcon Res. U.S.A. 26°34N 99°10W 110 E7
Faldingworth U.K. 53°21N 0°24W 23 F8
Falkirk U.K. 56°0N 3°47W 21 C8
Falkland U.K. 56°16N 3°12W 21 B9
Falkland Is. ☐ Atl. Oc. 51°30S 59°0W 121 H4
Fall River U.S.A. 41°43N 71°10W 113 E12
Falmouth Jamaica 18°30N 77°40W 114 a
Falmouth U.K. 50°9N 5°5W 27 G3
Falmouth B. U.K. 50°6N 5°5W 27 G3
Falstone U.K. 55°11N 2°26W 22 B4
Falun Sweden 60°37N 15°37E 63 E7
Famagusta Cyprus 35°8N 33°55E 86 C3
Fanad Hd. Ireland 55°17N 7°38W 28 A6
Fannich, L. U.K. 57°38N 4°59W 19 G8
Fano Italy 43°50N 13°1E 70 C5
Far East Asia 40°0N 130°0E 74 E14
Farāh Afghan. 32°20N 62°7E 87 C10
Farasān Si. Arabia 16°45N 41°55E 88 D3
Fareham U.K. 50°51N 1°11W 24 E6
Farewell C. Greenland 59°48N 43°55W 54 D5
Fargo U.S.A. 46°53N 96°48W 111 A7
Faridabad India 28°26N 77°19E 84 E10
Faridkot India 51°39N 1°34W 24 C5
Farmington U.S.A. 36°44N 108°12W 110 C5
Farmville U.S.A. 37°18N 78°24W 112 G8
Farnborough U.K. 51°16N 0°45W 25 D7
Farne Is. U.K. 55°38N 1°37W 22 A5
Farnham U.K. 51°13N 0°47W 25 D7
Farnworth U.K. 53°34N 2°25W 23 E4
Faro Canada 62°11N 133°22W 108 C6
Faro Portugal 37°2N 7°55W 69 D2
Faroe Is. ☐ Atl. Oc. 62°0N 7°0W 57 C4
Färs □ Iran 29°30N 55°0E 87 D8
Fāryāb □ Afghan. 36°0N 65°0E 87 B11
Faslane U.K. 56°5N 4°49W 20 B6
Fataka Solomon Is. 11°55S 170°12E 99 C12
Fatehgarh India 27°25N 79°35E 84 F11
Fatehpur Raj., India 28°0N 74°40E 84 F9
Fatehpur Ut. P., India 25°56N 81°13E 85 G12
Fauldhouse U.K. 55°50N 3°43W 21 C8
Faversham U.K. 51°19N 0°56E 25 D10
Fawley U.K. 50°50N 1°20W 24 E6
Fayetteville Ark., U.S.A. 36°4N 94°10W 111 C8
Fayetteville N.C., U.S.A. 35°3N 78°53W 111 D11
Fazeley U.K. 52°37N 1°40W 23 G5
Fazilka India 30°27N 74°2E 84 D9
Fdérik Mauritania 22°40N 12°45W 94 D3
Feale → Ireland 52°27N 9°37W 30 D3
Fear, C. U.S.A. 33°50N 77°58W 111 D11
Fécamp France 49°45N 0°22E 68 B4
Fehmarn Germany 54°27N 11°7E 66 A6
Feira de Santana Brazil 12°15S 38°57W 122 B3
Felipe Carrillo Puerto Mexico 19°38N 88°3W 114 D7
Felixstowe U.K. 51°58N 1°23E 25 C11
Felton U.K. 55°18N 1°42W 22 B5
Feltwell U.K. 52°30N 0°32E 25 B10
Fenny Bentley U.K. 53°3N 1°45W 23 F5
Fenny Compton U.K. 52°10N 1°23W 24 B6
Fenny Stratford U.K. 52°0N 0°44W 25 C7
Fens, The U.K. 52°38N 0°2W 23 G8
Fenyang China 37°18N 111°48E 81 C6
Feodosiya Ukraine 45°2N 35°16E 73 E6
Fergus Falls U.S.A. 46°17N 96°4W 111 A7
Ferkéssédougou Ivory C. 9°35N 5°6W 94 G4
Fermanagh □ U.K. 54°21N 7°40W 28 C6
Fermont Canada 52°47N 67°5W 109 D13
Fermoy Ireland 52°9N 8°16W 30 D6
Fernhurst U.K. 51°3N 0°43W 25 D7
Ferrara Italy 44°50N 11°35E 70 B4
Ferret, C. France 44°38N 1°15W 68 D3
Ferrol Spain 43°29N 8°15W 69 A1
Fès Morocco 34°0N 5°0W 94 B5
Fethiye Turkey 36°36N 29°6E 73 G4
Fetlar U.K. 60°36N 0°52W 18 A16
Feuilles → Canada 58°47N 70°4W 109 D12
Feyzābād Afghan. 37°7N 70°33E 87 B12
Fezzan Libya 27°0N 13°0E 95 C8
Ffestiniog U.K. 52°57N 3°55W 26 B6
Fianarantsoa Madag. 21°26S 47°5E 97 J9
Fife □ U.K. 56°16N 3°1W 21 B9
Fife Ness U.K. 56°17N 2°35W 21 B10
Figeac France 44°37N 2°2E 68 D5
Figueres Spain 42°18N 2°58E 69 A7
Filby U.K. 52°40N 1°39E 25 A12
Filey U.K. 54°12N 0°18W 22 D8
Filey B. U.K. 54°12N 0°15W 22 D8
Filton U.K. 51°30N 2°34W 24 C3
Fincham U.K. 52°38N 0°30E 25 A9
Findhorn U.K. 57°38N 3°38W 19 G10
Findlay U.S.A. 41°2N 83°39W 112 E6
Finedon U.K. 52°21N 0°39W 25 B7
Finglas Ireland 53°23N 6°19W 31 B10
Finike Turkey 36°21N 30°10E 86 B2
Finland ■ Europe 63°0N 27°0E 63 E9
Finland, G. of Europe 60°0N 26°0E 63 F9
Finlay → Canada 57°0N 125°10W 108 D7
Finn → Ireland 54°51N 7°28W 28 B7
Firozabad India 27°10N 78°25E 84 F11

Firozpur India 30°55N 74°40E 84 D9
Fish → Namibia 28°7S 17°10E 97 K3
Fishguard U.K. 52°0N 4°58W 26 D4
Fishtoft U.K. 52°58N 0°1E 23 G9
Fisterra, C. Spain 42°50N 9°19W 69 A1
Fitchburg U.S.A. 42°35N 71°48W 113 D12
Flagstaff U.S.A. 35°12N 111°39W 110 C4
Flamborough U.K. 54°7N 0°7W 22 D8
Flamborough Hd. U.K. 54°7N 0°5W 22 D8
Flandre Europe 50°50N 2°30E 65 D2
Flathead L. U.S.A. 47°51N 114°8W 110 A4
Flattery, C. U.S.A. 48°23N 124°29W 110 A2
Fleet U.K. 51°17N 0°50W 25 D7
Fleetwood U.K. 53°55N 3°1W 23 E2
Flensburg Germany 54°47N 9°27E 66 A5
Flers France 48°47N 0°33W 68 B3
Flevoland □ Neths. 52°30N 5°30E 65 B5
Flimby U.K. 54°42N 3°30W 22 C2
Flin Flon Canada 54°46N 101°53W 108 D9
Flinders → Australia 17°36S 140°36E 98 D7
Flinders I. Australia 40°0S 148°0E 98 H8
Flinders Ranges Australia 31°30S 138°30E 98 G6
Flint U.K. 53°15N 3°8W 26 A7
Flint U.S.A. 43°1N 83°41W 112 D6
Flint → U.S.A. 30°57N 84°34W 111 D10
Flint I. Kiribati 11°26S 151°48W 103 J12
Flintshire □ U.K. 53°17N 3°17W 26 A7
Flitwick U.K. 52°0N 0°30W 25 C8
Flodden U.K. 55°37N 2°8W 22 A4
Flora U.S.A. 38°40N 88°29W 112 F3
Florence Italy 43°46N 11°15E 70 C4
Florence U.S.A. 34°12N 79°46N 111 D11
Florencia Colombia 1°36N 75°36W 120 B2
Flores Indonesia 8°35S 121°0E 83 D4
Flores Sea Indonesia 6°30S 120°0E 83 D4
Florianópolis Brazil 27°30S 48°30W 121 E5
Florida Uruguay 34°7S 56°10W 121 F4
Florida □ U.S.A. 28°0N 82°0W 111 E10
Florida, Straits of U.S.A. 25°0N 80°0W 115 C9
Florida Keys U.S.A. 24°40N 81°0W 111 F10
Florø Norway 61°35N 5°1E 63 E5
Fly → Papua N. G. 8°25S 143°0E 98 B7
Fochabers U.K. 57°37N 3°6W 19 G11
Focșani Romania 45°41N 27°15E 67 F14
Fóggia Italy 41°27N 15°34E 70 D6
Foix France 42°58N 1°38E 68 E4
Foligno Italy 42°57N 12°42E 70 C5
Folkestone U.K. 51°5N 1°12E 25 D11
Fond-du-Lac Canada 59°19N 107°12W 108 D9
Fond du Lac U.S.A. 43°47N 88°27W 112 D3
Fongafale Tuvalu 8°31S 179°13E 99 B14
Fontainebleau France 48°24N 2°40E 68 B5
Fontenay-le-Comte France 46°28N 0°48W 68 C3
Fordham U.K. 52°19N 0°23E 25 B9
Fordingbridge U.K. 50°56N 1°47W 24 E5
Forel, Mt. Greenland 66°52N 36°55W 54 C6
Forest Row U.K. 51°5N 0°3E 25 D9
Forfar U.K. 56°39N 2°53W 19 J12
Forli Italy 44°13N 12°3E 70 B5
Formartine U.K. 57°20N 2°15W 19 H13
Formby U.K. 53°34N 3°4W 23 E2
Formby Pt. U.K. 53°33N 3°6W 23 E2
Formentera Spain 38°43N 1°27E 69 C6
Formiga Brazil 20°27S 45°25W 122 D1
Formosa = Taiwan ■ Asia 23°30N 121°0E 81 D7
Formosa Argentina 26°15S 58°10W 121 E4
Formosa Brazil 15°32S 47°20W 122 C1
Forres U.K. 57°37N 3°37W 19 G10
Forsayth Australia 18°33S 143°34E 98 D7
Fort Albany Canada 52°15N 81°35W 109 D11
Fort Augustus U.K. 57°9N 4°42W 19 H8
Fort Chipewyan Canada 58°42N 111°8W 108 D8
Fort Collins U.S.A. 40°35N 105°5W 110 B5
Fort-Coulonge Canada 45°50N 76°45W 112 C9
Fort-de-France Martinique 14°36N 61°2W 114 c
Fort Dodge U.S.A. 42°30N 94°11W 111 B8
Fort Good Hope Canada 66°14N 128°40W 108 C7
Fort Kent U.S.A. 47°15N 68°36W 113 B13
Fort Lauderdale U.S.A. 26°7N 80°8W 111 E10
Fort Liard Canada 60°14N 123°30W 108 C7
Fort MacKay Canada 57°12N 111°41W 108 D8
Fort Macleod Canada 49°45N 113°30W 108 E8
Fort McMurray Canada 56°44N 111°7W 108 D8
Fort McPherson Canada 67°30N 134°55W 108 C6
Fort Morgan U.S.A. 40°15N 103°48W 110 B6
Fort Myers U.S.A. 26°39N 81°52W 111 E10
Fort Nelson Canada 58°50N 122°44W 108 D7
Fort Nelson → Canada 59°32N 124°0W 108 D7
Fort Peck L. U.S.A. 48°0N 106°26W 110 A5
Fort Providence Canada 61°3N 117°40W 108 C8
Fort Resolution Canada 61°10N 113°40W 108 C8
Fort St. John Canada 56°15N 120°50W 108 D7
Fort Scott U.S.A. 37°50N 94°42W 111 C8
Fort Shevchenko Kazakhstan 44°35N 50°23E 73 F9
Fort Simpson Canada 61°45N 121°15W 108 C7
Fort Smith Canada 60°0N 111°51W 108 B8
Fort Smith U.S.A. 35°23N 94°25W 111 C8
Fort Stockton U.S.A. 30°53N 102°53W 110 D6
Fort Wayne U.S.A. 41°4N 85°9W 112 E5
Fort William U.K. 56°49N 5°7W 18 J7
Fort Worth U.S.A. 32°43N 97°19W 111 D7
Fort Yukon U.S.A. 66°34N 145°16W 108 C5
Fortaleza Brazil 3°45S 38°35W 120 C6
Forth → U.K. 56°9N 3°50W 21 B9
Forth, Firth of U.K. 56°5N 2°55W 21 B10
Fortrose U.K. 57°35N 4°9W 19 G9
Foshan China 23°4N 113°5E 81 D6
Fostoria U.S.A. 41°10N 83°25W 112 E6
Fothergill U.K. 54°43N 3°29W 22 C2
Fotheringhay U.K. 52°32N 0°27W 25 A8
Fougères France 48°21N 1°14W 68 B3
Foula U.K. 60°10N 2°5W 18 B13
Foulness I. U.K. 51°36N 0°55E 25 C10
Foulness Pt. U.K. 51°37N 0°58E 25 C10
Foulsham U.K. 52°48N 0°59E 25 A10
Fountainhall U.K. 55°44N 2°53W 21 C10
Fouta Djalon Guinea 11°20N 12°10W 94 F3

Fovant

Fovant U.K. 51°4N 2°0W 24 D5

Fowey U.K. 50°20N 4°39W 27 G4
Fownhope U.K. 52°0N 2°36W 24 B3
Foxe Basin Canada 66°0N 77°0W 109 C12
Foxe Chan. Canada 65°0N 80°0W 109 C12
Foxe Pen. Canada 65°0N 76°0W 109 C12
Foyle → U.K. 55°3N 7°15W 29 A7
Foyle, Lough U.K. 55°7N 7°4W 29 A7
Foynes Ireland 52°37N 9°7W 30 C4
Foz do Iguaçu Brazil 25°30S 54°30W 121 E4
Fraddon U.K. 50°23N 4°58W 27 G4
Framlingham U.K. 52°14N 1°21E 25 B11
Franca Brazil 20°33S 47°30W 122 D1
France ■ Europe 47°0N 3°0E 68 C5
Franceville Gabon 1°40S 13°32E 96 E2
Franche-Comté □ France 46°50N 5°55E 68 C6
Francis Case, L. U.S.A. 43°4N 98°34W 110 B7
Francistown Botswana 21°7S 27°33E 97 J5
François L. Canada 54°0N 125°30W 108 D7
Frankfort Ind., U.S.A. 40°17N 86°31W 112 E4
Frankfort Ky., U.S.A. 38°12N 84°52W 112 F5
Frankfurt Brandenburg, Germany 52°20N 14°32E 66 B8
Frankfurt Hessen, Germany 50°7N 8°41E 66 C5
Fränkische Alb Germany 49°10N 11°23E 66 D6
Franklin N.H., U.S.A. 43°27N 71°39W 113 D12
Franklin Pa., U.S.A. 41°24N 79°50W 112 E8
Franklin B. Canada 69°45N 126°0W 108 C7
Franklin D. Roosevelt L. U.S.A. 48°18N 118°9W 110 A3
Franklin L. U.S.A. 40°25N 115°22W 110 B3
Franklin Mts. Canada 65°0N 125°0W 108 C7
Franklin Str. Canada 72°0N 96°0W 108 B10
Frant U.K. 51°5N 0°16E 25 D9
Franz Josef Land Russia 82°0N 55°0E 54 A10
Fraser → Canada 49°7N 123°11W 108 E7
Fraserburgh U.K. 57°42N 2°1W 19 G13
Frederick U.S.A. 39°25N 77°25W 112 F9
Fredericksburg U.S.A. 38°18N 77°28W 112 F9
Fredericktown U.S.A. 37°34N 90°18W 112 G2
Fredericton Canada 45°57N 66°40W 113 C14
Frederikshavn Denmark 57°28N 10°31E 63 F6
Fredonia U.S.A. 42°26N 79°20W 112 D8
Fredrikstad Norway 59°13N 10°57E 63 F6
Free State □ S. Africa 28°30S 27°0E 97 K5
Freeport Bahamas 26°30N 78°47W 115 B9
Freeport Ill., U.S.A. 42°17N 89°36W 112 D3
Freeport Tex., U.S.A. 28°57N 95°21W 111 E7
Freetown S. Leone 8°30N 13°17W 94 G3
Freiburg Germany 47°59N 7°51E 66 E4
Fréjus France 43°25N 6°44E 68 E7
Fremont U.S.A. 41°21N 83°7W 112 E6
French Creek → U.S.A. 41°24N 79°50W 112 E8
French Guiana ☒ S. Amer. 4°0N 53°0W 120 B4
French Polynesia ☒ Pac. Oc. 20°0S 145°0W 103 K13
Frenchman Cr. → N. Amer. 48°31N 107°10W 110 A5
Freshwater U.K. 50°41N 1°31W 24 E5
Fresnillo Mexico 23°10N 102°53W 114 C4
Fresno U.S.A. 36°44N 119°47W 110 C3
Fria, C. Namibia 18°0S 12°0E 90 H5
Fridaythorpe U.K. 54°2N 0°39W 23 D7
Friedrichshafen Germany 47°39N 9°30E 66 E5
Friesland □ Neths. 53°5N 5°50E 65 A5
Frimley U.K. 51°19N 0°44W 25 D7
Frinton-on-Sea U.K. 51°49N 1°15E 25 C11
Frio, C. Brazil 22°50S 41°50W 116 F6
Frizington U.K. 54°33N 3°28W 22 C2
Frobisher B. Canada 62°30N 66°0W 109 C13
Frobisher L. Canada 56°20N 108°15W 108 D9
Frodsham U.K. 53°18N 2°43W 23 F3
Frome U.K. 51°14N 2°19W 24 D4
Frome → U.K. 50°41N 2°6W 24 E4
Front Range U.S.A. 40°25N 105°45W 110 B5
Front Royal U.S.A. 38°55N 78°12W 112 F8
Frutal Brazil 20°0S 49°0W 122 C1
Frýdek-Místek Czech Rep. 49°40N 18°20E 67 D10
Fuchū Japan 34°34N 133°14E 82 F3
Fuengirola Spain 36°32N 4°41W 69 D3
Fuerte → Mexico 25°54N 109°22W 114 B3
Fuerteventura Canary Is. 28°30N 14°0W 94 C3
Fuhai China 47°2N 87°25E 80 B3
Fuji Japan 35°9N 138°39E 82 F6
Fuji-San Japan 35°22N 138°44E 82 F6
Fujian □ China 26°0N 118°0E 81 D6
Fukui Japan 36°5N 136°10E 82 E5
Fukuoka Japan 33°39N 130°21E 82 G2
Fukushima Japan 37°44N 140°28E 82 E7
Fukuyama Japan 34°35N 133°20E 82 F3
Fulda Germany 50°32N 9°40E 66 C5
Fulda → Germany 51°25N 9°39E 66 C5
Fulton U.S.A. 43°19N 76°25W 112 D9
Fulwood U.K. 53°47N 2°40W 23 E3
Funabashi Japan 35°45N 140°0E 82 F7
Funchal Madeira 32°38N 16°54W 94 B2
Fundy, B. of Canada 45°0N 66°0W 113 C15
Furnas, Représa de Brazil 20°50S 45°30W 122 D1
Furneaux Group Australia 40°10S 147°50E 98 J8
Fürth Germany 49°28N 10°59E 66 D6
Fury and Hecla Str. Canada 69°56N 84°0W 109 C11
Fushun China 41°50N 123°56E 81 B7
Fustic Barbados 13°16N 59°38W 115 g
Fuxin China 42°5N 121°48E 81 B7
Fuyang China 33°0N 115°48E 81 C6
Fuyu Heilongjiang, China 47°49N 124°27E 81 B7
Fuyu Jilin, China 45°12N 124°43E 81 B7
Fuyun China 47°0N 89°28E 80 B3
Fuzhou China 26°5N 119°16E 81 D6
Fylingdales Moor U.K. 54°25N 0°41W 22 D7
Fyn Denmark 55°20N 10°30E 63 F6
Fyne, L. U.K. 55°59N 5°23W 20 C5

G

Gabès Tunisia 33°53N 10°2E 95 B8
Gabès, G. de Tunisia 34°0N 10°30E 95 B8
Gabon ■ Africa 0°10S 10°0E 96 E2
Gaborone Botswana 24°45S 25°57E 97 J5
Gabrovo Bulgaria 42°52N 25°19E 71 C11
Gachsārān Iran 30°15N 50°45E 87 D7
Gadarwara India 22°50N 78°50E 84 H11
Gadsden U.S.A. 34°1N 86°1W 111 D9
Gafsa Tunisia 34°24N 8°43E 95 B7
Gagnoa Ivory C. 6°56N 5°16W 94 G4
Gagnon Canada 51°50N 68°5W 109 D13
Gainesville Fla., U.S.A. 29°40N 82°20W 111 E10
Gainesville Ga., U.S.A. 34°18N 83°50W 111 D10
Gainford U.K. 54°34N 1°43W 22 C5
Gainsborough U.K. 53°24N 0°46W 23 F7
Gairdner, L. Australia 31°30S 136°0E 98 G6
Gairloch U.K. 57°43N 5°41W 18 G6
Gairloch, L. U.K. 57°43N 5°45W 18 G6
Galapagos Ecuador 0°0 91°0W 116 D1
Galashiels U.K. 55°37N 2°49W 21 C10
Galaţi Romania 45°27N 28°2E 67 F15
Galcaio Somali Rep. 6°30N 47°30E 88 F4
Galdhøpiggen Norway 61°38N 8°18E 63 E5
Galena U.S.A. 64°44N 156°56W 108 C4
Galesburg U.S.A. 40°57N 90°22W 112 E2
Galgate U.K. 53°59N 2°46W 23 E3
Galicia □ Spain 42°43N 7°45W 69 A2
Galilee, Sea of Israel 32°45N 35°35E 86 C3
Galina Pt. Jamaica 18°24N 76°58W 114 a
Gallan Hd. U.K. 58°15N 7°2W 18 F3
Galle Sri Lanka 6°5N 80°10E 84 R12
Galley Hd. Ireland 51°32N 8°55W 30 E5
Gallinas, Pta. Colombia 12°28N 71°40W 120 A2
Gallipolis U.S.A. 38°49N 82°12W 112 F6
Gällivare Sweden 67°9N 20°40E 63 D8
Galloway U.K. 55°1N 4°29W 20 D7
Galloway, Mull of U.K. 54°39N 4°52W 20 E6
Gallup U.S.A. 35°32N 108°45W 110 C5
Galmpton U.K. 50°23N 3°35W 27 G6
Galston U.K. 55°36N 4°24W 20 C7
Galty Mts. Ireland 52°22N 8°10W 30 D6
Galtymore Ireland 52°21N 8°11W 30 D6
Galveston U.S.A. 29°18N 94°48W 111 E8
Galway Ireland 53°17N 9°3W 30 B4
Galway □ Ireland 53°22N 9°1W 30 B4
Galway B. Ireland 53°13N 9°10W 30 B4
Gambia ■ W. Afr. 13°25N 16°0W 94 F2
Gambia → W. Afr. 13°28N 16°34W 94 F2
Gamlingay U.K. 52°10N 0°11W 25 B8
Gan Jiang → China 29°15N 116°0E 81 D6
Gananoque Canada 44°20N 76°10W 113 C9
Gäncä Azerbaijan 40°45N 46°20E 73 F8
Gand = Gent Belgium 51°2N 3°42E 65 C3
Gandak → India 25°39N 85°13E 85 G14
Gander Canada 48°58N 54°35W 109 E14
Gandhi Sagar India 24°40N 75°40E 84 G9
Gandía Spain 38°58N 0°9W 69 C5
Ganganagar India 29°56N 73°56E 84 E8
Gangdisê Shan China 31°20N 81°0E 80 C3
Ganges → India 23°20N 90°30E 85 H17
Gangneung S. Korea 37°45N 128°54E 81 C7
Gangtok India 27°20N 88°37E 85 F16
Gannett Peak U.S.A. 43°11N 109°39W 110 B5
Gansu □ China 36°0N 104°0E 80 C5
Ganzhou China 25°51N 114°56E 81 D6
Gao Mali 16°15N 0°5W 94 E5
Gap France 44°33N 6°5E 68 D7
Gar China 32°10N 79°58E 80 C2
Garanhuns Brazil 8°50S 36°30W 122 A3
Garboldisham U.K. 52°23N 0°57E 25 B10
Garda, L. di Italy 45°40N 10°41E 70 B4
Garden City U.S.A. 37°58N 100°53W 110 C6
Gardēz Afghan. 33°37N 69°9E 87 C12
Gare L. U.K. 56°1N 4°50W 20 B6
Garforth U.K. 53°47N 1°24W 23 E6
Gargrave U.K. 53°59N 2°7W 23 E4
Garioch U.K. 57°18N 2°40W 19 H12
Garissa Kenya 0°25S 39°40E 96 E7
Garoe Somali Rep. 8°25N 48°33E 88 F4
Garonne → France 45°2N 0°36W 68 D3
Garoua Cameroon 9°19N 13°21E 95 G8
Garron Pt. U.K. 55°3N 5°59W 29 A10
Garry → U.K. 56°44N 3°47W 19 J10
Garry, L. Canada 65°58N 100°18W 108 C9
Garsdale Head U.K. 54°20N 2°20W 22 D4
Garstang U.K. 53°55N 2°46W 23 E3
Gary U.S.A. 41°36N 87°20W 112 E4
Garzê China 31°38N 100°1E 80 C5
Gascogne France 43°45N 0°20E 68 E4
Gascogne, G. de Europe 44°0N 2°0W 68 D2
Gashua Nigeria 12°54N 11°0E 95 F8
Gaspé Canada 48°52N 64°30W 109 E13
Gaspé, C. Canada 48°48N 64°7W 113 A15
Gaspésie, Pén. de la Canada 48°45N 65°40W 113 A15
Gata, Sierra de Spain 40°20N 6°45W 69 B2
Gatehouse of Fleet U.K. 54°53N 4°12W 20 E7
Gateshead U.K. 54°57N 1°35W 22 C5
Gatineau Canada 45°29N 75°39W 113 C10
Gatineau → Canada 45°27N 75°42W 113 C10
Gatley U.K. 53°24N 2°15W 23 F4
Gatwick, London ✈ (LGW) U.K. 51°10N 0°11W 25 D8
Gävle Sweden 60°40N 17°9E 63 E7
Gawilgarh Hills India 21°15N 76°45E 84 J10
Gawthwaite U.K. 54°16N 3°8W 22 D2
Gaxun Nur China 42°22N 100°30E 80 B5
Gaya India 24°47N 85°4E 85 G14
Gaylord U.S.A. 45°2N 84°41W 112 C5
Gayton U.K. 52°45N 0°36E 25 A10
Gaywood U.K. 52°46N 0°26E 25 A9
Gaza Gaza Strip 31°30N 34°28E 86 D3
Gaza Strip ■ Asia 31°29N 34°25E 86 D3
Gaziantep Turkey 37°6N 37°23E 73 G6
Gdańsk Poland 54°22N 18°40E 67 A10
Gdynia Poland 54°35N 18°33E 67 A10
Gebze Turkey 40°47N 29°25E 73 F4
Gedaref Sudan 14°2N 35°28E 95 F13
Gedney U.K. 52°48N 0°4E 23 G9
Gedser Denmark 54°35N 11°55E 63 G6
Geelong Australia 38°10S 144°22E 98 H7
Gejiu China 23°20N 103°10E 80 D5
Gela Italy 37°4N 14°15E 70 F6
Gelderland □ Neths. 52°5N 6°10E 65 B6
Gelib Somali Rep. 0°29N 42°46E 88 G3
Gelibolu Turkey 40°28N 26°43E 73 F4
Gelsenkirchen Germany 51°32N 7°6E 66 C4
General Acha Argentina 37°20S 64°38W 121 F3
General Alvear Argentina 35°0S 67°40W 121 F3
General Pico Argentina 35°45S 63°50W 121 F3
General Santos Phil. 6°5N 125°14E 83 C4
Geneva Switz. 46°12N 6°9E 66 E4
Geneva U.S.A. 42°52N 76°59W 112 D9
Geneva, L. = Léman, L. Europe 46°26N 6°30E 66 E4
Genk Belgium 50°58N 5°32E 65 D5
Gennargentu, Mti. del Italy 40°1N 9°19E 70 D3
Genoa Italy 44°25N 8°57E 70 B3
Génova, G. di Italy 44°0N 9°0E 70 C3
Gent Belgium 51°2N 3°42E 65 C3
George S. Africa 33°58S 22°29E 97 L4
George → Canada 58°49N 66°10W 109 D13
George, L. U.S.A. 29°17N 81°36W 111 E10
George Town Cayman Is. 19°20N 81°24W 115 D8
George Town Malaysia 5°25N 100°20E 83 C2
George V Land Antarctica 69°0S 148°0E 55 C10
Georgetown Guyana 6°50N 58°12W 120 B4
Georgetown Ky., U.S.A. 38°13N 84°33W 112 F5
Georgetown S.C., U.S.A. 33°23N 79°17W 111 D11
Georgia □ U.S.A. 32°50N 83°15W 111 D10
Georgia ■ Asia 42°0N 43°0E 73 F7
Georgian B. Canada 45°15N 81°0W 112 C7
Georgiyevsk Russia 44°12N 43°28E 73 F7
Gera Germany 50°53N 12°4E 66 C7
Geraldton Australia 28°48S 114°32E 98 F1
Germany ■ Europe 51°0N 10°0E 66 C6
Germiston S. Africa 26°13S 28°10E 97 K5
Gerrans B. U.K. 50°12N 4°57W 27 G4
Gerrards Cross U.K. 51°35N 0°33W 25 C7
Getafe Spain 40°18N 3°43W 69 B4
Ghadāmis Libya 30°11N 9°29E 95 B7
Ghaghara → India 25°45N 84°40E 85 G14
Ghana ■ W. Afr. 8°0N 1°0W 94 G5
Ghardaïa Algeria 32°20N 3°37E 94 B6
Gharyān Libya 32°10N 13°0E 95 B8
Ghats, Eastern India 14°0N 78°50E 84 N11
Ghats, Western India 14°0N 75°0E 84 N9
Ghazal, Bahr el → Chad 13°0N 15°47E 95 F9
Ghazâl, Bahr el → Sudan 9°31N 30°25E 95 G12
Ghaziabad India 28°42N 77°26E 84 E10
Ghazipur India 25°38N 83°35E 85 G13
Ghaznī Afghan. 33°30N 68°28E 87 C12
Ghent = Gent Belgium 51°2N 3°42E 65 C3
Ghowr □ Afghan. 34°0N 64°20E 87 C11
Giamama Somali Rep. 0°4N 42°44E 88 G3
Giants Causeway U.K. 55°16N 6°29W 29 A9
Gibraltar ☒ Europe 36°7N 5°22W 69 D3
Gibraltar, Str. of Medit. S. 35°55N 5°40W 69 E3
Gibraltar Pt. U.K. 53°6N 0°19E 23 F9
Gibson Desert Australia 24°0S 126°0E 98 E4
Gifu Japan 35°30N 136°45E 82 F5
Giggleswick U.K. 54°5N 2°17W 22 D4
Gigha U.K. 55°42N 5°44W 20 C4
Gijón Spain 43°32N 5°42W 69 A3
Gila → U.S.A. 32°43N 114°33W 110 D4
Gīlān □ Iran 37°0N 50°0E 86 B7
Gilbert Is. Kiribati 1°0N 172°0E 102 G9
Gilgit India 35°50N 74°15E 84 B9
Gillam Canada 56°20N 94°40W 108 D10
Gillette U.S.A. 44°18N 105°30W 110 B5
Gillingham Dorset, U.K. 51°2N 2°18W 24 D4
Gillingham Medway, U.K. 51°23N 0°33E 25 D10
Gilsland U.K. 55°0N 2°34W 22 C3
Gimie, Mt St. Lucia 13°54N 61°0W 115 f
Giohar Somali Rep. 2°48N 45°30E 88 G4
Girdle Ness U.K. 57°9N 2°3W 19 H13
Giresun Turkey 40°55N 38°30E 73 F6
Girga Egypt 26°17N 31°55E 95 C12
Girona Spain 41°58N 2°46E 69 B7
Gironde → France 45°32N 1°7W 68 D3
Girvan U.K. 55°14N 4°51W 20 D6
Gisborne N.Z. 38°39S 178°5E 99 H14
Gisburn U.K. 53°56N 2°16W 23 E4
Gitega Burundi 3°26S 29°56E 96 E5
Gizhiga Russia 62°3N 160°30E 79 C18
Gjoa Haven Canada 68°38N 95°53W 108 C10
Glace Bay Canada 46°11N 59°58W 113 B18
Glacier Nat. Park △ U.S.A. 48°42N 113°48W 110 A4
Gladstone Australia 23°52S 151°16E 98 E9
Gladstone U.S.A. 45°51N 87°1W 112 C4
Gladwin U.S.A. 43°59N 84°29W 112 D5
Glamorgan, Vale of □ U.K. 51°28N 3°25W 27 E7
Glanaruddery Mts. Ireland 52°20N 9°27W 30 D4
Glanton U.K. 55°26N 1°54W 22 B5
Glasgow U.K. 55°51N 4°15W 20 C7
Glasgow Ky., U.S.A. 37°0N 85°55W 112 G5
Glasgow Mont., U.S.A. 48°12N 106°38W 110 A5
Glasgow Int. ✈ (GLA) U.K. 55°51N 4°21W 20 C7
Glasnevin Ireland 53°22N 6°15W 31 B10
Glastonbury U.K. 51°9N 2°43W 24 D3
Glazov Russia 58°9N 52°40E 72 C9
Glemsford U.K. 52°6N 0°40E 25 B10
Glen → U.K. 52°51N 0°7W 23 G8
Glen Affric U.K. 57°17N 5°1W 18 H7
Glen Almond U.K. 56°28N 3°50W 21 B8
Glen Coe U.K. 56°40N 5°0W 18 J7
Glen Etive U.K. 56°37N 5°0W 20 A5
Glen Garry Highl., U.K. 57°3N 5°7W 18 H7
Glen Garry Perth & Kinr., U.K. 56°47N 4°5W 19 J9
Glen Mor U.K. 57°9N 4°37W 19 H8
Glen Moriston U.K. 57°11N 4°52W 19 H8
Glen Orchy U.K. 56°27N 4°52W 20 B6
Glen Orrin U.K. 57°31N 4°45W 19 G8
Glen Oykel U.K. 58°5N 4°50W 19 F8
Glen Roy U.K. 56°56N 4°50W 19 J8
Glen Shee U.K. 56°50N 3°28W 19 J11
Glen Shiel U.K. 57°9N 5°18W 18 H7
Glen Spean U.K. 56°53N 4°40W 19 J8
Glendale Ariz., U.S.A. 33°32N 112°11W 110 D4
Glendale Calif., U.S.A. 34°9N 118°15W 110 D3
Glendive U.S.A. 47°7N 104°43W 110 A6
Gleneagles U.K. 56°17N 3°43W 21 B8
Glenfinnan U.K. 56°53N 5°27W 18 J7
Glengarriff Ireland 51°45N 9°34W 30 E3
Glenkens, The U.K. 55°12N 4°12W 20 D7
Glenluce U.K. 54°52N 4°48W 20 E6
Glennallen U.S.A. 62°7N 145°33W 108 C5
Glennamaddy Ireland 53°37N 8°33W 28 D4
Glenrothes U.K. 56°12N 3°10W 21 B9
Glens Falls U.S.A. 43°19N 73°39W 113 D11
Glenties Ireland 54°49N 8°16W 28 B5
Glenveagh △ Ireland 55°3N 8°1W 28 A5
Gliwice Poland 50°22N 18°41E 67 C10
Globe U.S.A. 33°24N 110°47W 110 D4
Głogów Poland 51°37N 16°5E 66 C9
Glomma → Norway 59°12N 10°57E 63 F6
Glossop U.K. 53°27N 1°56W 23 F5
Gloucester U.K. 51°53N 2°15W 24 C4
Gloucestershire □ U.K. 51°46N 2°15W 24 C4
Gloversville U.S.A. 43°3N 74°21W 113 D10
Gniezno Poland 52°30N 17°35E 67 B9
Gnosall U.K. 52°48N 2°14W 23 G4
Goa India 15°33N 73°59E 84 M8
Goa □ India 15°33N 73°59E 84 M8
Goat Fell U.K. 55°38N 5°11W 20 C5
Gobi Asia 44°0N 110°0E 81 B5
Godalming U.K. 51°11N 0°36W 25 D7
Godavari → India 16°25N 82°18E 85 L13
Goderich Canada 43°45N 81°41W 112 D7
Godhra India 22°49N 73°40E 84 H8
Godmanchester U.K. 52°20N 0°11W 25 B8
Godoy Cruz Argentina 32°56S 68°52W 121 F3
Gods → Canada 56°22N 92°51W 108 D10
Gods L. Canada 54°40N 94°15W 108 D10
Godshill U.K. 50°38N 1°15W 24 E6
Godstone U.K. 51°14N 0°3W 25 D8
Gogama Canada 47°35N 81°43W 112 B7
Goiânia Brazil 16°43S 49°20W 122 C1
Goiás Brazil 15°55S 50°10W 120 D4
Goiás □ Brazil 12°10S 48°0W 120 D5
Goio-Erê Brazil 24°12S 53°1W 121 E4
Gold Coast Australia 28°0S 153°25E 98 F9
Gold Coast W. Afr. 4°0N 1°40W 94 H5
Golden Vale Ireland 52°33N 8°17W 30 C6
Goldsboro U.S.A. 35°23N 77°59W 111 C11
Golspie U.K. 57°58N 3°59W 19 G10
Goma Dem. Rep. of the Congo 1°37S 29°10E 96 E5
Gomel Belarus 52°28N 31°0E 67 B16
Gomera Canary Is. 28°7N 17°14W 94 C2
Gómez Palacio Mexico 25°34N 103°30W 114 B4
Gonābād Iran 34°15N 58°45E 87 C9
Gonaïves Haiti 19°20N 72°42W 115 D10
Gonbad-e Kāvūs Iran 37°20N 55°25E 87 B8
Gonda India 27°9N 81°58E 85 F12
Gonder Ethiopia 12°39N 37°30E 88 E2
Gonghe China 36°18N 100°32E 80 C5
Good Hope, C. of S. Africa 34°24S 18°30E 97 L3
Goodrich U.K. 51°52N 2°37W 24 C3
Goodwood U.K. 50°53N 0°44W 25 E7
Goole U.K. 53°42N 0°53W 23 E7
Goose L. U.S.A. 41°56N 120°26W 110 B2
Gorakhpur India 26°47N 83°23E 85 F13
Gordon U.K. 55°41N 2°34W 21 C10
Gore Ethiopia 8°12N 35°32E 88 F2
Gorebridge U.K. 55°50N 3°2W 21 C9
Gorey Ireland 52°41N 6°18W 31 C10
Gorgān Iran 36°55N 54°30E 87 B8
Goring U.K. 51°31N 1°7W 24 C6
Goring-by-Sea U.K. 50°49N 0°24W 25 E8
Gorleston U.K. 52°35N 1°44E 25 A12
Görlitz Germany 51°9N 14°58E 66 C8
Gorontalo Indonesia 0°35N 123°5E 83 C4
Gort Ireland 53°3N 8°49W 30 B5
Gorzów Wielkopolski Poland 52°43N 15°15E 66 B8
Gosberton U.K. 52°53N 0°9W 23 G8
Gosforth U.K. 54°26N 3°27W 22 D2
Gosport U.K. 50°48N 1°9W 24 E6
Göta kanal Sweden 58°30N 15°58E 63 F7
Götaland Sweden 57°30N 14°30E 63 F6
Göteborg Sweden 57°43N 11°59E 63 F6
Gotha Germany 50°56N 10°42E 66 C6
Gothenburg = Göteborg Sweden 57°43N 11°59E 63 F6
Gotland Sweden 57°30N 18°33E 63 F7
Gotō-Rettō Japan 32°55N 129°5E 82 G1
Göttingen Germany 51°31N 9°55E 66 C5
Gouda Neths. 52°1N 4°42E 65 B4
Goudhurst U.K. 51°6N 0°29E 25 D9
Gouin, Rés. Canada 48°35N 74°40W 113 A10
Goulburn Australia 34°44S 149°44E 98 G8
Goulimine Morocco 28°56N 10°0W 94 C3
Goundam Mali 16°27N 3°40W 94 E5
Gourock U.K. 55°57N 4°49W 20 C6
Governador Valadares Brazil 18°15S 41°57W 122 C2
Gower U.K. 51°35N 4°10W 27 D5
Gowna, L. Ireland 53°51N 7°34W 28 D6
Goya Argentina 29°10S 59°10W 121 E4
Gozo Malta 36°3N 14°15E 70 a
Graaff-Reinet S. Africa 32°13S 24°32E 97 L4
Gracias a Dios, C. Honduras 15°0N 83°10W 115 E8
Grafham Water U.K. 52°19N 0°18W 25 B8
Grafton Australia 29°38S 152°58E 98 F9
Grafton U.S.A. 48°25N 97°25W 111 A7
Graham Land Antarctica 65°0S 64°0W 55 C17
Grahamstown S. Africa 33°19S 26°31E 97 L5
Grain Coast W. Afr. 4°20N 10°0W 94 H3
Grainthorpe U.K. 53°27N 0°5E 23 F9
Grampian Mts. U.K. 56°50N 4°0W 19 J9
Gran Canaria Canary Is. 27°55N 15°35W 94 C2
Gran Chaco S. Amer. 25°0S 61°0W 121 E3
Gran Sasso d'Itália Italy 42°27N 13°42E 70 C5
Granada Nic. 11°58N 86°0W 114 E7
Granada Spain 37°10N 3°35W 69 D4
Granard Ireland 53°47N 7°30W 28 D6
Granby Canada 45°25N 72°45W 109 E12
Grand → U.S.A. 45°40N 100°45W 110 A6
Grand Bahama I. Bahamas 26°40N 78°30W 115 B9
Grand-Bourg Guadeloupe 15°53N 61°19W 114 b
Grand Canyon U.S.A. 36°3N 112°9W 110 C4
Grand Canyon Nat. Park △ U.S.A. 36°15N 112°30W 110 C4
Grand Cayman Cayman Is. 19°20N 81°20W 115 D8
Grand Erg de Bilma Niger 18°30N 14°0E 95 E8
Grand Falls Canada 47°3N 67°44W 109 E13
Grand Falls-Windsor Canada 48°56N 55°40W 109 E14
Grand Forks U.S.A. 47°55N 97°3W 111 A7
Grand Haven U.S.A. 43°4N 86°13W 112 D4
Grand Island U.S.A. 40°55N 98°21W 110 B7
Grand Junction U.S.A. 39°4N 108°33W 110 C5
Grand L. Canada 45°57N 66°7W 113 C14
Grand Manan I. Canada 44°45N 66°52W 113 C14
Grand-Mère Canada 46°36N 72°40W 113 B11
Grand Rapids Canada 53°12N 99°19W 108 D10
Grand Rapids U.S.A. 42°58N 85°40W 112 D4
Grand St-Bernard, Col du Europe 45°50N 7°10E 66 F4
Grand Teton U.S.A. 43°54N 110°50W 110 B4
Grande → Bolivia 15°51S 64°39W 120 D3
Grande → Brazil 11°30S 44°30W 122 B2
Grande, B. Argentina 50°30S 68°20W 121 H3
Grande, Rio → N. Amer. 25°58N 97°9W 111 E7
Grande Baleine, R. de la → Canada 55°16N 77°47W 109 D12
Grande Prairie Canada 55°10N 118°50W 108 D8
Grande-Terre Guadeloupe 16°20N 61°25W 114 b
Grande Vigie, Pte. de la Guadeloupe 16°32N 61°27W 114 b
Grange-over-Sands U.K. 54°12N 2°54W 22 D3
Grangemouth U.K. 56°1N 3°42W 21 B8
Grangeville U.S.A. 45°56N 116°7W 110 A3
Grantham U.K. 52°55N 0°38W 23 G7
Grantown-on-Spey U.K. 57°20N 3°36W 19 H10
Grants Pass U.S.A. 42°26N 123°19W 110 B2
Granville U.S.A. 43°24N 73°16W 113 D11
Grasmere U.K. 54°28N 3°1W 22 D2
Grasse France 43°38N 6°56E 68 E7
Grassington U.K. 54°5N 1°59W 22 D5
Graulhet France 43°45N 1°59E 68 E4
Gravatá Brazil 8°10S 35°29W 122 A3
Gravesend U.K. 51°26N 0°22E 25 D9
Grayling U.S.A. 44°40N 84°43W 112 C5
Grayrigg U.K. 54°23N 2°39W 22 D3
Grays U.K. 51°28N 0°21E 25 D9
Graz Austria 47°4N 15°27E 66 E8
Great Australian Bight Australia 33°30S 130°0E 98 G5
Great Ayton U.K. 54°30N 1°8W 22 D6
Great Baddow U.K. 51°43N 0°31E 25 C10
Great Barrier Reef Australia 18°0S 146°50E 98 D8
Great Basin U.S.A. 40°0N 117°0W 110 B3
Great Bear → Canada 65°0N 124°0W 108 C7
Great Bear L. Canada 65°30N 120°0W 108 B7
Great Bend U.S.A. 38°22N 98°46W 110 C7
Great Bentley U.K. 51°51N 1°4E 25 C11
Great Bernera U.K. 58°14N 6°50W 18 F4
Great Blasket I. Ireland 52°6N 10°32W 30 D1
Great Britain Europe 54°0N 2°15W 56 E5
Great Broughton U.K. 54°26N 1°9W 22 D6
Great Camanoe Br. Virgin Is. 18°30N 64°35W 115 e
Great Chesterford U.K. 52°4N 0°13E 25 B9
Great Clifton U.K. 54°39N 3°29W 22 C2
Great Dividing Ra. Australia 23°0S 146°0E 98 E8
Great Dunmow U.K. 51°52N 0°23E 25 C9
Great Exuma I. Bahamas 23°30N 75°50W 115 C9
Great Falls U.S.A. 47°30N 111°17W 110 A4
Great Harwood U.K. 53°47N 2°24W 23 E4
Great Inagua I. Bahamas 21°0N 73°20W 115 C10
Great Karoo S. Africa 31°55S 21°0E 97 L4
Great Khingan Mts. China 48°0N 121°0E 81 B7
Great Malvern U.K. 52°7N 2°18W 24 B4
Great Massingham U.K. 52°47N 0°40E 25 A10
Great Missenden U.K. 51°42N 0°41W 25 C7
Great Ormes Head U.K. 53°20N 3°52W 26 A6
Great Ouse → U.K. 52°48N 0°21E 25 A9
Great Pedro Bluff Jamaica 17°51N 77°44W 114 a
Great Plains N. Amer. 47°0N 105°0W 110 A6
Great Salt Desert Iran 34°30N 55°0E 87 C8
Great Salt L. U.S.A. 41°15N 112°40W 110 B4
Great Salt Lake Desert U.S.A. 40°50N 113°30W 110 B4
Great Sandy Desert Australia 21°0S 124°0E 98 E3
Great Sandy Desert U.S.A. 43°35N 120°15W 110 B2
Great Shefford U.K. 51°28N 1°28W 24 D6
Great Shelford U.K. 52°9N 0°8E 25 B9
Great Shunner Fell U.K. 54°22N 2°14W 22 D4
Great Skellig Ireland 51°47N 10°33W 30 E1
Great Slave L. Canada 61°23N 115°38W 108 C8
Great Snow Mt. Canada 57°26N 124°0W 108 D7
Great Torrington U.K. 50°57N 4°9W 27 F5
Great Victoria Desert Australia 29°30S 126°30E 98 F4
Great Wall China 38°30N 109°30E 81 C5
Great Waltham U.K. 51°47N 0°28E 25 C9
Great Whernside U.K. 54°10N 1°58W 22 D5
Great Yarmouth U.K. 52°37N 1°44E 25 A12
Greater Antilles W. Indies 17°40N 74°0W 115 D10
Greater London □ U.K. 51°31N 0°6W 25 C8
Greater Manchester □ U.K. 53°30N 2°15W 23 E4
Greater Sunda Is. Indonesia 7°0S 112°0E 83 D3
Greatham U.K. 54°39N 1°14W 22 C6
Greece ■ Europe 40°0N 23°0E 71 E9
Greeley U.S.A. 40°25N 104°42W 110 B6
Greely Fd. Canada 80°30N 85°0W 109 A11
Green → Ky., U.S.A. 37°54N 87°30W 112 G4
Green → Utah, U.S.A. 38°11N 109°53W 110 C5
Green B. U.S.A. 45°0N 87°30W 112 C4
Green Bay U.S.A. 44°31N 88°0W 112 C4
Green Hammerton U.K. 54°1N 1°18W 23 D6
Green River U.S.A. 41°32N 109°28W 110 B5
Greencastle U.S.A. 39°38N 86°52W 112 F4
Greenfield Ind., U.S.A. 39°47N 85°46W 112 F5
Greenfield Mass., U.S.A. 42°35N 72°36W 113 D11
Greenhead U.K. 54°59N 2°30W 22 C3
Greenland ☒ N. Amer. 66°0N 45°0W 54 C5
Greenland Sea Arctic 73°0N 10°0W 54 B7
Greenlaw U.K. 55°43N 2°27W 21 C11
Greenock U.K. 55°57N 4°46W 20 C6
Greenodd U.K. 54°14N 3°4W 22 D2

Greenore   Hounslow

Greenore *Ireland* 54°2N 6°8W 29 C9
Greenore Pt. *Ireland* 52°14N 6°19W 31 D10
Greensboro *U.S.A.* 36°4N 79°48W 111 C11
Greensburg *Ind., U.S.A.* 39°20N 85°29W 112 F3
Greensburg *Pa., U.S.A.* 40°18N 79°33W 112 E8
Greenstone Pt. *U.K.* 57°55N 5°37W 18 G6
Greenville *Ala., U.S.A.* 31°50N 86°38W 111 D9
Greenville *Maine, U.S.A.* 45°28N 69°35W 113 C13
Greenville *Mich., U.S.A.* 43°11N 85°15W 112 D5
Greenville *Miss., U.S.A.* 33°24N 91°4W 111 D8
Greenville *Ohio, U.S.A.* 40°6N 84°38W 112 E5
Greenville *S.C., U.S.A.* 34°51N 82°24W 111 D10
Greenwich □ *U.K.* 51°29N 0°1E 25 D9
Greenwood *U.S.A.* 33°31N 90°11W 111 D8
Gremikha *Russia* 67°59N 39°47E 72 A6
Grenada ■ *W. Indies* 12°10N 61°40W 115 E12
Grenoble *France* 45°12N 5°42E 68 D6
Greta → *U.K.* 54°9N 2°37W 22 D3
Gretna *U.K.* 55°0N 3°3W 21 E9
Gretna Green *U.K.* 55°1N 3°3W 21 D9
Gretton *U.K.* 52°33N 0°40W 25 A7
Grey Ra. *Australia* 27°0S 143°30E 98 F7
Greymouth *N.Z.* 42°29S 171°13E 99 J13
Greystoke *U.K.* 54°41N 2°51W 22 C3
Greystones *Ireland* 53°9N 6°5W 31 B10
Griffith *Australia* 34°18S 146°2E 98 G8
Grimsay *U.K.* 57°29N 7°14W 18 H3
Grimsby *U.K.* 53°34N 0°5W 23 E8
Gris-Nez, C. *France* 50°52N 1°35E 68 A4
Grise Fiord *Canada* 76°25N 82°57W 109 B11
Grizebeck *U.K.* 54°16N 3°10W 22 D2
Groningen *Neths.* 53°15N 6°35E 65 A6
Groote Eylandt *Australia* 14°0S 136°40E 98 C6
Gros Islet *St. Lucia* 14°5N 60°58W 115 f
Gros Piton *St. Lucia* 13°49N 61°5W 115 f
Gros Piton Pt. *St. Lucia* 13°49N 61°5W 115 f
Grosseto *Italy* 42°46N 11°8E 70 C4
Grossglockner *Austria* 47°5N 12°40E 66 E7
Groundhog → *Canada* 48°45N 82°58W 112 A6
Groznyy *Russia* 43°20N 45°45E 73 F8
Grudziądz *Poland* 53°30N 18°47E 67 B10
Gruinard B. *U.K.* 57°56N 5°35W 18 G6
Guadalajara *Mexico* 20°40N 103°20W 114 C4
Guadalajara *Spain* 40°37N 3°12W 69 B4
Guadalcanal *Solomon Is.* 9°32S 160°12E 99 B11
Guadalete → *Spain* 36°35N 6°13W 69 D2
Guadalquivir → *Spain* 36°47N 6°22W 69 D2
Guadarrama, Sierra de *Spain* 41°0N 4°0W 69 B4
Guadeloupe ☑ *W. Indies* 16°20N 61°40W 114 b
Guadiana → *Portugal* 37°14N 7°22W 69 D2
Guadix *Spain* 37°18N 3°11W 69 D4
Guafo, Boca del *Chile* 43°35S 74°0W 121 G2
Guajará-Mirim *Brazil* 10°50S 65°20W 120 D3
Guajira, Pen. de la *Colombia* 12°0N 72°0W 120 A2
Gualeguaychú *Argentina* 33°3S 59°31W 121 F4
Guam ☑ *Pac. Oc.* 13°27N 144°45E 102 F6
Guamúchil *Mexico* 25°28N 108°6W 114 B3
Guana I. *Br. Virgin Is.* 18°30N 64°30W 115 e
Guanajuato *Mexico* 21°1N 101°15W 114 C4
Guane *Cuba* 22°10N 84°7W 115 C8
Guangdong □ *China* 23°0N 113°0E 81 D6
Guangxi Zhuang □ *China* 24°0N 109°0E 81 D5
Guangzhou *China* 23°6N 113°13E 81 D6
Guanica *Puerto Rico* 17°58N 66°55W 115 d
Guantánamo *Cuba* 20°10N 75°14W 115 C9
Guantánamo B. *Cuba* 19°59N 75°10W 115 C9
Guaporé → *Brazil* 11°55S 65°4W 120 D3
Guaqui *Bolivia* 16°41S 68°54W 120 D3
Guarapuava *Brazil* 25°20S 51°30W 121 E4
Guaratinguetá *Brazil* 22°49S 45°9W 122 D1
Guarulhos *Brazil* 23°29S 46°33W 122 D1
Guarus *Brazil* 21°44S 41°20W 122 D2
Guatemala *Guatemala* 14°40N 90°22W 114 E6
Guatemala ■ *Cent. Amer.* 15°40N 90°30W 114 D6
Guaviare → *Colombia* 4°3N 67°44W 120 B3
Guaxupé *Brazil* 21°10S 47°5W 122 D1
Guayama *Puerto Rico* 17°59N 66°7W 115 d
Guayaquil *Ecuador* 2°15S 79°52W 120 C2
Guayaquil, G. de *Ecuador* 3°10S 81°0W 120 C1
Guaymas *Mexico* 27°56N 110°54W 114 B2
Gubkin *Russia* 51°17N 37°32E 73 D6
Guelph *Canada* 43°35N 80°20W 112 D7
Guéret *France* 46°11N 1°51E 68 C4
Guernsey *U.K.* 49°26N 2°35W 27 J8
Guestling Green *U.K.* 50°53N 0°39E 25 E10
Guia *China* 26°32N 106°40E 80 D5
Guiana Highlands *S. Amer.* 5°10N 60°40W 116 C4
Guidónia-Montecélio *Italy* 42°1N 12°45E 70 C5
Guildford *U.K.* 51°14N 0°34W 25 D7
Guilin *China* 25°18N 110°15E 81 D6
Guinea *Africa* 8°0N 8°0E 90 F4
Guinea ■ *W. Afr.* 10°20N 11°30W 94 F3
Guinea, Gulf of *Atl. Oc.* 3°0N 2°30W 90 F4
Guinea-Bissau ■ *Africa* 12°0N 15°0W 94 F3
Güines *Cuba* 22°50N 82°0W 115 C8
Guingamp *France* 48°34N 3°10W 68 B2
Guisborough *U.K.* 54°33N 1°4W 22 D6
Guiyang *China* 26°32N 106°40E 80 D5
Guizhou □ *China* 27°0N 107°0E 80 D5
Gujarat □ *India* 23°20N 71°0E 84 H7
Gujranwala *Pakistan* 32°10N 74°12E 84 C9
Gujrat *Pakistan* 32°40N 74°2E 84 C9
Gulbarga *India* 17°20N 76°50E 84 L10
Gulf, The = Persian Gulf *Asia* 27°0N 50°0E 87 E7
Gulfport *U.S.A.* 30°22N 89°6W 111 D9
Gulu *Uganda* 2°48N 32°17E 96 D6
Guna *India* 24°40N 77°19E 84 G10
Gunnison → *U.S.A.* 39°4N 108°35W 110 C5
Gunsan *S. Korea* 35°59N 126°45E 81 C7
Guntur *India* 16°23N 80°30E 85 L12
Gurgueia → *Brazil* 6°50S 43°24W 120 C5
Guri, Embalse de *Venezuela* 7°50N 62°52W 120 B3
Gurkha *Nepal* 28°5N 84°40E 85 E14
Gurnard's Hd. *U.K.* 50°11N 5°37W 27 G2
Gürün *Turkey* 38°43N 37°15E 73 G6
Gurupi *Brazil* 11°43S 49°4W 122 B1
Gurupi → *Brazil* 1°13S 46°6W 120 C5
Gurvan Sayhan Uul *Mongolia* 43°50N 104°0E 80 B5
Gusau *Nigeria* 12°12N 6°40E 94 F7

Guwahati *India* 26°10N 91°45E 85 F17
Guyana ■ *S. Amer.* 5°0N 59°0W 120 B4
Guyenne *France* 44°30N 0°40E 68 D4
Gwädar *Pakistan* 25°10N 62°18E 84 G3
Gwalchmai *U.K.* 53°16N 4°25W 26 A5
Gwalior *India* 26°12N 78°10E 84 F11
Gwanda *Zimbabwe* 20°55S 29°0E 97 J5
Gwangju *S. Korea* 35°9N 126°54E 81 C7
Gweebarra B. *Ireland* 54°51N 8°23W 28 B5
Gweedore *Ireland* 55°3N 8°13W 28 A5
Gweek *U.K.* 50°5N 5°13W 27 G3
Gwennap *U.K.* 50°12N 5°11W 27 G3
Gweru *Zimbabwe* 19°28S 29°45E 97 H5
Gwynedd □ *U.K.* 52°52N 4°10W 26 B6
Gyaring Hu *China* 34°50N 97°40E 80 C4
Gympie *Australia* 26°11S 152°38E 98 F9
Győr *Hungary* 47°41N 17°40E 67 E9
Gyumri *Armenia* 40°47N 43°50E 73 F7

H

Ha Tinh *Vietnam* 18°20N 105°54E 83 B2
Ha'apai Group *Tonga* 19°47S 174°27W 99 D16
Haarlem *Neths.* 52°23N 4°39E 65 B4
Habahe *China* 48°3N 86°23E 80 B3
Hachinohe *Japan* 40°30N 141°29E 82 C7
Hackney □ *U.K.* 51°33N 0°3W 25 C8
Hackthorpe *U.K.* 54°34N 2°42W 22 C3
Ḥadd, Ra's al *Oman* 22°35N 59°50E 87 F9
Haddenham *U.K.* 51°46N 0°55W 25 C7
Haddington *U.K.* 55°57N 2°47W 21 C10
Hadejia *Nigeria* 12°30N 10°5E 94 F7
Hadleigh *U.K.* 52°3N 0°58E 25 B10
Hadlow *U.K.* 51°13N 0°22E 25 D9
Ḥaḍramawt *Yemen* 15°30N 49°30E 88 D4
Haeju *N. Korea* 38°3N 125°45E 81 C7
Hafizabad *Pakistan* 32°5N 73°40E 84 C8
Hagen *Germany* 51°21N 7°27E 66 C4
Hagerstown *U.S.A.* 39°39N 77°43W 112 F9
Hags Hd. *Ireland* 52°57N 9°28W 30 C4
Hague, C. de la *France* 49°44N 1°56W 68 B3
Hague, The *Neths.* 52°7N 4°17E 65 B4
Haguenau *France* 48°49N 7°47E 68 B7
Haifa *Israel* 32°46N 35°0E 86 C3
Haikou *China* 20°1N 110°16E 81 D6
Ḥā'il *Si. Arabia* 27°28N 41°45E 86 E5
Hailar *China* 49°10N 119°38E 81 B6
Hailey *U.S.A.* 43°31N 114°19W 110 B4
Haileybury *Canada* 47°30N 79°38W 112 B8
Hailsham *U.K.* 50°52N 0°16E 25 E9
Hainan □ *China* 19°0N 109°30E 81 E5
Hainton *U.K.* 53°21N 0°14W 23 F8
Haiphong *Vietnam* 20°47N 106°41E 80 D5
Haiti ■ *W. Indies* 19°0N 72°30W 115 D10
Ḥajjah *Yemen* 15°42N 43°36E 88 D3
Hakodate *Japan* 41°45N 140°44E 82 C7
Halaib Triangle *Africa* 22°30N 35°20E 95 D13
Halberstadt *Germany* 51°54N 11°3E 66 C6
Halberton *U.K.* 50°54N 3°25W 27 F7
Halden *Norway* 59°9N 11°23E 63 F6
Haldia *India* 22°5N 88°3E 85 H16
Haldwani *India* 29°31N 79°30E 84 E11
Halesowen *U.K.* 52°27N 2°3W 23 H4
Halesworth *U.K.* 52°20N 1°31E 25 B12
Halifax *Canada* 44°38N 63°35W 113 C16
Halifax *U.K.* 53°43N 1°52W 23 E5
Halkirk *U.K.* 58°30N 3°29W 19 E11
Hall Pen. *Canada* 63°30N 66°0W 109 C13
Halle *Germany* 51°30N 11°56E 66 C6
Hallow *U.K.* 52°14N 2°15W 24 B4
Halls Creek *Australia* 18°16S 127°38E 98 D4
Hallworthy *U.K.* 50°39N 4°35W 27 F4
Halmahera *Indonesia* 0°40N 128°0E 83 C4
Halmstad *Sweden* 56°41N 12°52E 63 F6
Halstead *U.K.* 51°57N 0°40E 25 C10
Haltwhistle *U.K.* 54°58N 2°26W 22 C4
Hamadān *Iran* 34°52N 48°32E 86 C7
Ḥamāh *Syria* 35°5N 36°40E 86 C4
Hamamatsu *Japan* 34°45N 137°45E 82 F5
Hamar *Norway* 60°48N 11°7E 63 E6
Hambantota *Sri Lanka* 6°10N 81°10E 84 R12
Hambledon *U.K.* 50°55N 1°5W 24 E6
Hambleton Hills *U.K.* 54°17N 1°12W 22 D6
Hamburg *Germany* 53°33N 9°59E 66 B5
Hämeenlinna *Finland* 61°0N 24°28E 63 E8
Hameln *Germany* 52°6N 9°21E 66 B5
Hamersley Ra. *Australia* 22°0S 117°45E 98 E2
Hamhŭng *N. Korea* 39°54N 127°30E 81 C7
Hami *China* 42°55N 93°25E 80 B4
Hamilton *Canada* 43°15N 79°50W 109 E12
Hamilton *N.Z.* 37°47S 175°19E 99 H14
Hamilton *U.K.* 55°46N 4°2W 20 C7
Hamilton *U.S.A.* 39°24N 84°34W 112 F5
Hamm *Germany* 51°40N 7°50E 66 C4
Hammerfest *Norway* 70°39N 23°41E 63 A8
Hammersmith and Fulham □ *U.K.* 51°30N 0°14W 25 D8
Hammond *U.S.A.* 41°38N 87°30W 112 E4
Hammonton *U.S.A.* 39°39N 74°48W 113 F10
Hampshire □ *U.K.* 51°7N 1°23W 24 D6
Hampshire Downs *U.K.* 51°15N 1°10W 24 D6
Hampton in Arden *U.K.* 52°26N 1°41W 23 H5
Hancock *U.S.A.* 47°8N 88°35W 112 B31
Handan *China* 36°35N 114°28E 81 C6
Hanford *U.S.A.* 36°20N 119°39W 110 C3
Hangayn Nuruu *Mongolia* 47°30N 99°0E 80 B4
Hangzhou *China* 30°18N 120°11E 81 C7
Hangzhou Wan *China* 30°15N 120°45E 81 C7
Hankö *Finland* 59°50N 22°57E 63 F8
Hanna *Canada* 51°40N 111°54W 108 D8
Hannibal *U.S.A.* 39°42N 91°22W 111 C81
Hanningfield Res. *U.K.* 51°40N 0°31E 25 C10
Hannover *Germany* 52°22N 9°46E 66 B5
Hanoi *Vietnam* 21°5N 105°55E 80 B5
Hanover *Germany* 39°48N 76°59W 112 F9
Hanover, I. *Chile* 51°0S 74°50W 121 H2
Hans Lollik I. *U.S. Virgin Is.* 18°24N 64°53W 115 e
Hanzhong *China* 33°10N 107°1E 80 C5

Haora *India* 22°34N 88°18E 85 H16
Haparanda *Sweden* 65°52N 24°8E 63 D8
Happy Valley-Goose Bay *Canada* 53°15N 60°20W 109 D13
Har Hu *China* 38°20N 97°38E 80 C4
Har Us Nuur *Mongolia* 48°0N 92°0E 80 B4
Ḥaraḍ *Si. Arabia* 24°22N 49°0E 86 E7
Harare *Zimbabwe* 17°43S 31°2E 97 H6
Harbin *China* 45°48N 126°40E 81 B7
Harbor Beach *U.S.A.* 43°51N 82°39W 112 D6
Hardangerfjorden *Norway* 60°5N 6°0E 63 E5
Hardy, Pte. *St. Lucia* 14°6N 60°56W 115 f
Harer *Ethiopia* 9°20N 42°8E 88 F3
Harewood *U.K.* 53°54N 1°30W 23 E6
Hargeisa *Somali Rep.* 9°30N 44°2E 88 F3
Haridwar *India* 29°58N 78°9E 84 E11
Haringey □ *U.K.* 51°34N 0°5W 25 C8
Haringhata → *Bangla.* 22°0N 89°58E 85 J16
Harīrūd → *Asia* 37°24N 60°38E 87 B10
Harlech *U.K.* 52°52N 4°6W 26 B5
Harleston *U.K.* 52°24N 1°18E 25 B11
Harlingen *Neths.* 53°11N 5°25E 65 A5
Harlingen *U.S.A.* 26°12N 97°42W 110 E7
Harlow *U.K.* 51°46N 0°8E 25 C9
Harney L. *U.S.A.* 43°14N 119°8W 110 B3
Härnösand *Sweden* 62°38N 17°55E 63 E7
Haroldswick *U.K.* 60°48N 0°50W 18 A16
Harpenden *U.K.* 51°49N 0°21W 25 C8
Harricana → *Canada* 50°56N 79°32W 109 D12
Harrietsham *U.K.* 51°14N 0°41E 25 D10
Harrington *U.K.* 54°37N 3°33W 22 C1
Harris *U.K.* 57°50N 6°55W 18 G4
Harris, Sd. of *U.K.* 57°44N 7°6W 18 G3
Harrisburg *U.S.A.* 40°16N 76°53W 112 E9
Harrison, C. *Canada* 54°55N 57°55W 109 D14
Harrisonburg *U.S.A.* 38°27N 78°52W 112 F8
Harrisville *U.S.A.* 44°39N 83°17W 112 C6
Harrogate *U.K.* 54°0N 1°33W 23 D5
Harrow □ *U.K.* 51°35N 0°21W 25 C8
Hart *U.S.A.* 43°42N 86°22W 112 D4
Hartest *U.K.* 52°8N 0°40E 25 B10
Hartford *Conn., U.S.A.* 41°46N 72°41W 113 E11
Hartford *Ky., U.S.A.* 37°27N 86°55W 112 G4
Hartford *Wis., U.S.A.* 43°19N 88°22W 112 D3
Hartland *U.K.* 50°59N 4°29W 27 F5
Hartland Pt. *U.K.* 51°1N 4°32W 27 E4
Hartlebury *U.K.* 52°20N 2°14W 24 B4
Hartlepool *U.K.* 54°42N 1°13W 22 C6
Hartley *U.K.* 55°5N 1°28W 22 B6
Hartpury *U.K.* 51°55N 2°17W 24 C4
Harvey *U.S.A.* 41°36N 87°50W 112 E4
Harwell *U.K.* 51°36N 1°17W 24 C6
Harwich *U.K.* 51°56N 1°17E 25 C11
Haryana □ *India* 29°0N 76°10E 84 E10
Harz *Germany* 51°38N 10°44E 66 C6
Hasa *Si. Arabia* 25°50N 49°0E 86 E7
Haslemere *U.K.* 51°5N 0°43W 25 D7
Haslingden *U.K.* 53°42N 2°19W 23 E4
Hasselt *Belgium* 50°56N 5°21E 65 D5
Hastings *U.K.* 50°51N 0°35E 25 E10
Hastings *U.S.A.* 40°35N 98°23W 110 B7
Hat Yai *Thailand* 7°1N 100°27E 83 C2
Hatfield *U.K.* 51°46N 0°13W 25 C8
Hatgal *Mongolia* 50°26N 100°9E 80 A5
Hatherleigh *U.K.* 50°49N 4°5W 27 F5
Hathersage *U.K.* 53°20N 1°39W 23 F5
Hathras *India* 27°36N 78°6E 84 F11
Hatia *Bangla.* 22°30N 91°5E 85 H17
Hatteras, C. *U.S.A.* 35°14N 75°32W 111 C11
Hattiesburg *U.S.A.* 31°20N 89°17W 111 D9
Haugesund *Norway* 59°23N 5°13E 63 F5
Haughley *U.K.* 52°14N 0°57E 25 B10
Havana = La Habana *Cuba* 23°8N 82°22W 115 C8
Havant *U.K.* 50°51N 0°58W 25 E7
Havasu, L. *U.S.A.* 34°18N 114°28W 110 D4
Havel → *Germany* 52°50N 12°3E 66 B7
Haverfordwest *U.K.* 51°48N 4°58W 26 D4
Haverhill *U.K.* 52°5N 0°28E 25 B9
Haverhill *U.S.A.* 42°47N 71°5W 113 D12
Haverigg *U.K.* 54°13N 3°17W 22 D2
Havering □ *U.K.* 51°34N 0°13E 25 C9
Havre *U.S.A.* 48°33N 109°41W 110 A5
Havre-St.-Pierre *Canada* 50°18N 63°33W 109 D13
Hawai'i *U.S.A.* 19°30N 155°30W 110 J17
Hawai'i □ *U.S.A.* 19°30N 156°30W 110 J17
Hawaiian Is. *Pac. Oc.* 20°30N 156°0W 103 E12
Hawaiian Ridge *Pac. Oc.* 24°0N 165°0W 103 E11
Hawes *U.K.* 54°19N 2°12W 22 D4
Haweswater *U.K.* 54°31N 2°47W 22 C3
Hawick *U.K.* 55°26N 2°47W 21 D10
Hawkchurch *U.K.* 50°48N 2°56W 24 E3
Hawkesbury *Canada* 45°37N 74°37W 113 C10
Hawkesbury Upton *U.K.* 51°35N 2°19W 24 C4
Hawkhurst *U.K.* 51°2N 0°32E 25 D10
Hawkshead *U.K.* 54°23N 2°59W 22 D3
Hawksker *U.K.* 54°27N 0°34W 22 D7
Haxby *U.K.* 54°1N 1°4W 23 D6
Hay *Australia* 34°30S 144°51E 98 G8
Hay → *Canada* 60°50N 116°26W 108 C8
Hay-on-Wye *U.K.* 52°5N 3°8W 26 C7
Hay River *Canada* 60°51N 115°44W 108 C8
Haydon Bridge *U.K.* 54°58N 2°14W 22 C4
Hayes → *Canada* 57°3N 92°12W 108 D10
Hayle *U.K.* 50°11N 5°26W 27 G3
Hayton *U.K.* 54°55N 2°45W 22 C3
Hayward *U.S.A.* 46°1N 91°29W 112 B2
Haywards Heath *U.K.* 51°0N 0°5W 25 E8
Hazar *Turkmenistan* 39°34N 53°16E 73 G9
Hazard *U.S.A.* 37°15N 83°12W 112 G6
Hazaribag *India* 23°58N 85°26E 85 H14
Heacham *U.K.* 52°54N 0°29E 25 A9
Headcorn *U.K.* 51°10N 0°38E 25 D10
Heanor *U.K.* 53°1N 1°21W 23 F6
Heard I. *Ind. Oc.* 53°0S 74°0W 53 G13
Hearst *Canada* 49°40N 83°41W 109 E11
Heathfield *U.K.* 50°58N 0°16E 25 E9

Heathrow, London ✈ (LHR) *U.K.* 51°28N 0°27W 25 D8
Hebburn *U.K.* 54°59N 1°32W 22 C5
Hebden Bridge *U.K.* 53°45N 2°0W 23 E4
Hebei □ *China* 39°0N 116°0E 81 C6
Hebrides *U.K.* 57°30N 7°0W 56 H4
Hebrides, Sea of the *U.K.* 57°5N 7°0W 18 H4
Hebron *Canada* 58°5N 62°30W 109 D13
Hechi *China* 24°40N 108°2E 80 D5
Hechuan *China* 30°2N 106°12E 80 C5
Heckington *U.K.* 52°59N 0°17E 23 F8
Hednesford *U.K.* 52°43N 1°59W 23 G5
Hedon *U.K.* 53°44N 0°12W 23 E8
Heerlen *Neths.* 50°55N 5°58E 65 D5
Hefei *China* 31°52N 117°18E 81 C6
Hegang *China* 47°20N 130°19E 81 B8
Heidelberg *Germany* 49°24N 8°42E 66 D5
Heilbronn *Germany* 49°9N 9°13E 66 D5
Heilongjiang □ *China* 48°0N 126°0E 81 B7
Heimaey *Iceland* 63°26N 20°17W 63 B1
Hejaz *Si. Arabia* 24°0N 40°0E 86 E4
Hekou *China* 22°30N 103°59E 80 D5
Helena *U.S.A.* 46°36N 112°2W 110 A4
Helensburgh *U.K.* 56°1N 4°43W 20 B6
Helgoland *Germany* 54°10N 7°53E 66 A4
Hellifield *U.K.* 54°1N 2°12W 23 D4
Helmand □ *Afghan.* 31°12N 61°34E 87 D10
Helmond *Neths.* 51°29N 5°41E 65 C5
Helmsdale *U.K.* 58°7N 3°39W 19 F10
Helmsdale → *U.K.* 58°8N 3°43W 19 F10
Helmsley *U.K.* 54°15N 1°3W 22 D6
Helperby *U.K.* 54°8N 1°19W 22 D6
Helsby *U.K.* 53°17N 2°46W 23 F3
Helsingborg *Sweden* 56°3N 12°42E 63 F6
Helsinki *Finland* 60°10N 24°55E 63 E9
Helston *U.K.* 50°6N 5°17W 27 G3
Helvellyn *U.K.* 54°32N 3°1W 22 C2
Helwân *Egypt* 29°50N 31°20E 95 C12
Hemel Hempstead *U.K.* 51°44N 0°28W 25 C8
Hempton *U.K.* 52°50N 0°50E 25 A10
Hemsworth *U.K.* 53°37N 1°21W 23 E6
Hemyock *U.K.* 50°54N 3°15W 27 F7
Henan □ *China* 34°0N 114°0E 81 C6
Henares → *Spain* 40°24N 3°30W 69 B4
Henderson *Ky., U.S.A.* 37°50N 87°35W 112 G4
Henderson *Nev., U.S.A.* 36°2N 114°58W 110 C3
Hengelo *Neths.* 52°16N 6°48E 65 B6
Hengyang *China* 26°59N 112°22E 81 D6
Henley-in-Arden *U.K.* 52°18N 1°46W 24 B5
Henley-on-Thames *U.K.* 51°32N 0°54W 25 C7
Henlopen, C. *U.S.A.* 38°48N 75°6W 113 F10
Henlow *U.K.* 52°2N 0°17W 25 B8
Henrietta Maria, C. *Canada* 55°9N 82°20W 109 D11
Henstridge *U.K.* 50°58N 2°24W 24 E4
Hentiyn Nuruu *Mongolia* 48°30N 108°30E 81 B5
Herät *Afghan.* 34°20N 62°7E 87 C10
Hereford *U.K.* 52°4N 2°43W 24 B3
Herefordshire □ *U.K.* 52°8N 2°40W 24 B3
Herford *Germany* 52°7N 8°39E 66 B5
Herm *U.K.* 49°30N 2°28W 27 J9
Herma Ness *U.K.* 60°50N 0°54W 18 A16
Hermosillo *Mexico* 29°10N 111°0W 114 B2
Hernád → *Hungary* 47°56N 21°8E 67 D11
Herne *Germany* 51°32N 7°14E 66 C4
Herne Bay *U.K.* 51°21N 1°8E 25 D11
Herstmonceux *U.K.* 50°53N 0°20E 25 E9
Hertford *U.K.* 51°48N 0°4W 25 C8
Hertfordshire □ *U.K.* 51°51N 0°5W 25 C8
's-Hertogenbosch *Neths.* 51°42N 5°17E 65 C5
Hessen □ *Germany* 50°30N 9°0E 66 C5
Hessle *U.K.* 53°44N 0°24W 23 E8
Hethersett *U.K.* 52°36N 1°10E 25 A11
Hetton-le-Hole *U.K.* 54°49N 1°26W 22 C6
Hexham *U.K.* 54°58N 2°4W 22 C4
Heybridge *U.K.* 51°45N 0°42E 25 C10
Heysham *U.K.* 54°3N 2°53W 22 D3
Heytesbury *U.K.* 51°11N 2°6W 24 D4
Heywood *U.K.* 53°35N 2°12W 23 E4
Heze *China* 35°14N 115°20E 81 C6
Hibbing *U.S.A.* 47°25N 92°56W 111 A81
Hickman *U.S.A.* 36°34N 89°11W 112 G3
Hidalgo del Parral *Mexico* 26°56N 105°40W 114 B3
Hierro *Canary Is.* 27°44N 18°0W 94 C2
Higashiōsaka *Japan* 34°39N 135°37E 82 F4
High Atlas *Morocco* 32°30N 5°0W 94 B4
High Bentham *U.K.* 54°7N 2°28W 24 D4
High Ercall *U.K.* 52°45N 2°35W 23 G3
High Hesket *U.K.* 54°48N 2°49W 22 C3
High Level *Canada* 58°31N 117°8W 108 D8
High Pike *U.K.* 54°42N 3°4W 22 C2
High Plateaux *Algeria* 35°0N 1°0E 94 B6
High Prairie *Canada* 55°30N 116°30W 108 D8
High River *Canada* 50°30N 113°50W 108 D8
High Veld *Africa* 27°0S 27°0E 90 J6
High Willhays *U.K.* 50°40N 4°0W 27 F5
High Wycombe *U.K.* 51°37N 0°45W 25 C7
Higham Ferrers *U.K.* 52°18N 0°35W 25 B7
Highbridge *U.K.* 51°13N 2°58W 24 D3
Highclere *U.K.* 51°20N 1°21W 24 D6
Highland □ *U.K.* 57°17N 4°21W 18 H7
Highley *U.K.* 52°27N 2°23W 23 H4
Hightae *U.K.* 55°6N 3°26W 21 D9
Highworth *U.K.* 51°37N 1°43W 24 C5
Hiiumaa *Estonia* 58°50N 22°45E 63 F8
Hilgay *U.K.* 52°34N 0°24E 25 A9
Hillaby, Mt. *Barbados* 13°12N 59°35W 115 g
Hillcrest *Barbados* 13°13N 59°31W 115 g
Hillingdon □ *U.K.* 51°32N 0°27W 25 C8
Hillsborough *U.S.A.* 36°5N 79°6W 111 C11
Hillsdale *U.S.A.* 41°56N 84°38W 112 E5
Hilo *U.S.A.* 19°44N 155°5W 110 J17
Hilpsford Pt. *U.K.* 54°3N 3°12W 22 D2
Hilversum *Neths.* 52°14N 5°10E 65 B5
Himachal Pradesh □ *India* 31°30N 77°0E 84 D10
Himalaya *Asia* 29°0N 84°0E 85 E14
Himeji *Japan* 34°50N 134°40E 82 F4
Hinckley *U.K.* 52°33N 1°22W 23 G6
Hinderwell *U.K.* 54°32N 0°45W 22 C7

Hindhead *U.K.* 51°7N 0°43W 25 D7
Hindley *U.K.* 53°33N 2°35W 23 E3
Hindu Kush *Asia* 36°0N 71°0E 87 C12
Hingham *U.K.* 52°35N 0°59E 25 A10
Hingoli *India* 19°41N 77°15E 84 K10
Hinkley Pt. *U.K.* 51°12N 3°8W 24 D2
Hinstock *U.K.* 52°50N 2°27W 23 G3
Hinton *U.S.A.* 37°40N 80°54W 112 G7
Hirosaki *Japan* 40°34N 140°28E 82 C7
Hiroshima *Japan* 34°24N 132°30E 82 F3
Hisar *India* 29°12N 75°45E 84 E9
Hispaniola *W. Indies* 19°0N 71°0W 115 D10
Histon *U.K.* 52°16N 0°7E 25 B9
Hitachi *Japan* 36°36N 140°39E 82 E7
Hitchin *U.K.* 51°58N 0°16W 25 C8
Hjälmaren *Sweden* 59°18N 15°40E 63 F7
Hkakabo Razi *Burma* 28°25N 97°23E 85 A20
Ho Chi Minh City *Vietnam* 10°58N 106°40E 83 B2
Hoare B. *Canada* 65°17N 62°30W 109 C13
Hobart *Australia* 42°50S 147°21E 98 J8
Hobbs *U.S.A.* 32°42N 103°8W 110 D6
Hodder → *U.K.* 53°57N 2°27W 23 E4
Hoddesdon *U.K.* 51°45N 0°1W 25 C8
Hodge → *U.K.* 54°16N 0°56W 22 D7
Hodgson *Canada* 51°13N 97°36W 108 D10
Hódmezővásárhely *Hungary* 46°28N 20°22E 67 E11
Hodna, Chott el *Algeria* 35°26N 4°43E 94 A6
Hoff *U.K.* 54°34N 2°31W 22 C3
Hōfu *Japan* 34°3N 131°34E 82 F2
Hog's Back *U.K.* 51°13N 0°38W 25 D7
Hoh Xil Shan *China* 35°0N 89°0E 80 C3
Hoher Rhön *Germany* 50°24N 9°58E 66 C5
Hohhot *China* 40°52N 111°40E 81 B6
Hokkaido □ *Japan* 43°30N 143°0E 82 B8
Holbeach *U.K.* 52°48N 0°1E 23 G9
Holbeach Marsh *U.K.* 52°52N 0°5E 23 G9
Holderness *U.K.* 53°45N 0°5W 23 E8
Holetown *Barbados* 13°11N 59°38W 115 g
Holguín *Cuba* 20°50N 76°20W 115 C9
Holkham *U.K.* 52°57N 0°48E 25 A10
Holland *U.S.A.* 42°47N 86°7W 112 D4
Holland Fen *U.K.* 53°0N 0°8W 23 G8
Holland on Sea *U.K.* 51°48N 1°13E 25 C11
Holman *Canada* 70°44N 117°44W 108 B8
Holme *U.K.* 53°50N 0°46W 23 E8
Holmes Chapel *U.K.* 53°12N 2°21W 23 F4
Holmfirth *U.K.* 53°35N 1°46W 23 E5
Holstebro *Denmark* 56°22N 8°37E 63 F5
Holsworthy *U.K.* 50°48N 4°22W 27 F5
Holt *U.K.* 52°55N 1°6E 25 A11
Holy I. *Anglesey, U.K.* 53°17N 4°37W 26 A4
Holy I. *Northumberland, U.K.* 55°40N 1°47W 22 A5
Holyhead *U.K.* 53°18N 4°38W 26 A4
Holywell *U.K.* 53°16N 3°14W 26 A7
Home B. *Canada* 68°40N 67°10W 109 C13
Homer *U.S.A.* 59°39N 151°33W 108 D4
Homs *Syria* 34°40N 36°45E 86 C4
Honduras ■ *Cent. Amer.* 14°40N 86°30W 114 E7
Honduras, G. of *Caribbean* 16°50N 87°0W 114 D7
Honefoss *Norway* 60°10N 10°18E 63 E6
Honey L. *U.S.A.* 40°15N 120°19W 110 B2
Hong Gai *Vietnam* 20°57N 107°5E 80 D5
Hong Kong □ *China* 22°11N 114°14E 81 D6
Hongjiang *China* 27°7N 109°59E 81 D5
Hongshui He → *China* 23°48N 109°30E 81 D5
Hongze Hu *China* 33°15N 118°35E 81 C6
Honiara *Solomon Is.* 9°27S 159°57E 99 B10
Honington *U.K.* 52°59N 0°35W 23 G7
Honiton *U.K.* 50°47N 3°11W 27 F7
Honolulu *U.S.A.* 21°19N 157°52W 103 E12
Honshū *Japan* 36°0N 138°0E 82 F6
Hoo *U.K.* 51°25N 0°35E 25 D10
Hood, Mt. *U.S.A.* 45°23N 121°42W 110 A2
Hoogeveen *Neths.* 52°44N 6°28E 65 B6
Hook *U.K.* 51°17N 0°57W 25 D7
Hook Hd. *Ireland* 52°7N 6°56W 31 D9
Hooper Bay *U.S.A.* 61°32N 166°6W 108 C3
Hoopeston *U.S.A.* 40°28N 87°40W 112 E4
Hoorn *Neths.* 52°38N 5°4E 65 B5
Hoover Dam *U.S.A.* 36°1N 114°44W 110 C4
Hope *U.K.* 53°22N 3°2W 23 F2
Hopedale *Canada* 55°28N 60°13W 109 D13
Horden *U.K.* 54°46N 1°19W 22 C6
Horley *U.K.* 51°10N 0°10W 25 D8
Horlivka *Ukraine* 48°19N 38°5E 73 E6
Hormozgān □ *Iran* 27°30N 56°0E 87 E8
Hormuz, Str. of *The Gulf* 26°30N 56°30E 87 E8
Horn, C. = Hornos, C. de *Chile* 55°50S 67°30W 121 H3
Horn, Is. *Wall. & F. Is.* 14°16S 178°6W 99 C15
Horn Head *Ireland* 55°14N 8°0W 28 A6
Hornavan *Sweden* 66°15N 17°30E 63 D7
Horncastle *U.K.* 53°13N 0°7W 23 F8
Horndean *U.K.* 50°55N 1°1W 24 E6
Hornell *U.S.A.* 42°20N 77°40W 112 D9
Hornepayne *Canada* 49°14N 84°48W 112 A5
Horningsham *U.K.* 51°10N 2°15W 24 D4
Hornos, C. de *Chile* 55°50S 67°30W 121 H3
Hornsea *U.K.* 53°55N 0°11W 23 E8
Horqin Youyi Qianqi *China* 46°5N 122°3E 81 B7
Horsforth *U.K.* 53°50N 1°39W 23 E5
Horsham *Australia* 36°44S 142°13E 98 H7
Horsham *U.K.* 51°4N 0°20W 25 D8
Horsted Keynes *U.K.* 51°2N 0°1W 25 D8
Horton → *Canada* 69°56N 126°52W 108 C7
Horwich *U.K.* 53°36N 2°33W 23 E4
Hoste, I. *Chile* 55°0S 69°0W 121 H3
Hot Springs *Ark., U.S.A.* 34°31N 93°3W 111 D8
Hot Springs *S. Dak., U.S.A.* 43°26N 103°29W 110 B6
Hotan *China* 37°25N 79°55E 80 C2
Houghton *U.S.A.* 47°7N 88°34W 112 B31
Houghton L. *U.S.A.* 44°21N 84°44W 112 C5
Houghton-le-Spring *U.K.* 54°51N 1°28W 22 C6
Houghton Regis *U.K.* 51°54N 0°32W 25 C7
Houlton *U.S.A.* 46°8N 67°51W 113 B14
Houma *U.S.A.* 29°36N 90°43W 111 E8
Hounslow □ *U.K.* 51°28N 0°21W 25 D8

Hourn, L. U.K. 57°7N 5°35W 18 H6
Houston U.S.A. 29°45N 95°21W 111 E7
Hove U.K. 50°50N 0°10W 25 E8
Hoveton U.K. 52°45N 1°25E 25 A11
Hovingham U.K. 54°11N 0°58W 22 D7
Hövsgöl Nuur Mongolia 51°0N 100°30E 80 A5
Howden U.K. 53°45N 0°52W 23 E7
Howe, C. Australia 37°30S 150°0E 98 H9
Howell U.S.A. 42°36N 83°56W 112 D6
Howland I. Pac. Oc. 0°48N 176°38W 102 G10
Howth Ireland 53°23N 6°6W 31 B10
Howth Hd. Ireland 53°22N 6°3W 31 B10
Hoxne U.K. 52°21N 1°12E 25 B11
Hoy U.K. 58°50N 3°15W 19 E11
Høyanger Norway 61°13N 6°4E 63 E5
Hoylake U.K. 53°24N 3°10W 23 F2
Hradec Králové Czech Rep. 50°15N 15°50E 66 C8
Hrodna Belarus 53°42N 23°52E 67 B12
Hron → Slovak Rep. 47°49N 18°45E 67 E10
Hsinchu Taiwan 24°48N 120°58E 81 D7
Huacho Peru 11°10S 77°35W 120 D2
Huai He → China 33°0N 118°30E 81 C6
Huaibei China 34°0N 116°48E 81 C6
Huaihua China 27°32N 109°57E 81 D5
Huainan China 32°38N 116°58E 81 C6
Huallaga → Peru 5°15S 75°30W 120 C2
Huambo Angola 12°42S 15°54E 97 G3
Huancavelica Peru 12°50S 75°5W 120 D2
Huancayo Peru 12°5S 75°12W 120 D2
Huangshan China 29°42N 118°25E 81 D6
Huangshi China 30°10N 115°3E 81 C6
Huánuco Peru 9°55S 76°15W 120 C2
Huaraz Peru 9°30S 77°32W 120 C2
Huascarán, Nevado Peru 9°7S 77°37W 120 C2
Huasco Chile 28°30S 71°15W 121 E2
Huatabampo Mexico 26°50N 109°38W 114 B3
Hubei □ China 31°0N 112°0E 81 C6
Hubli India 15°22N 75°15E 84 M9
Hucknall U.K. 53°3N 1°13W 23 F6
Huddersfield U.K. 53°39N 1°47W 23 E5
Hudiksvall Sweden 61°43N 17°10E 63 E7
Hudson U.S.A. 40°42N 74°2W 113 E10
Hudson Bay Canada 60°0N 86°0W 109 D11
Hudson Falls U.S.A. 43°18N 73°35W 113 D11
Hudson Str. Canada 62°0N 70°0W 109 C13
Hue Vietnam 16°30N 107°35E 83 B2
Huelva Spain 37°18N 6°57W 69 D2
Huesca Spain 42°8N 0°25W 69 A5
Hughenden Australia 20°52S 144°10E 98 E7
Hugli → India 21°56N 88°4E 85 J16
Huila, Nevado del Colombia 3°0N 76°0W 120 B2
Huize China 26°24N 103°15E 80 D5
Hull = Kingston upon Hull U.K. 53°45N 0°21W 23 E8
Hull Canada 45°26N 75°43W 113 C10
Hull → U.K. 53°44N 0°20W 23 E8
Hullavington U.K. 51°32N 2°8W 24 C4
Hulme End U.K. 53°8N 1°50W 23 F5
Hulun Nur China 49°0N 117°30E 81 B6
Humacao Puerto Rico 18°9N 65°50W 115 d
Humaitá Brazil 7°35S 63°1W 120 C3
Humber → U.K. 53°42N 0°27W 23 E8
Humber, Mouth of the U.K. 53°32N 0°8E 23 E9
Humboldt Canada 52°15N 105°9W 108 D9
Humboldt → U.S.A. 39°59N 118°36W 110 B3
Humphreys Peak U.S.A. 35°21N 111°41W 110 C4
Humshaugh U.K. 55°3N 2°8W 22 B4
Húnaflói Iceland 65°50N 20°50W 63 A1
Hunan □ China 27°30N 112°0E 81 D6
Hungary ■ Europe 47°20N 19°20E 67 E10
Hungary, Plain of Europe 47°0N 20°0E 56 F10
Hungerford U.K. 51°25N 1°31W 24 D5
Hŭngnam N. Korea 39°49N 127°45E 81 C7
Hunmanby U.K. 54°10N 0°20W 22 D8
Hunsrück Germany 49°56N 7°27E 66 D4
Hunstanton U.K. 52°56N 0°29E 25 A9
Huntingdon Ind., U.S.A. 40°53N 85°30W 112 E5
Huntington W. Va., U.S.A. 38°25N 82°27W 112 F6
Huntly U.K. 57°27N 2°47W 19 H12
Huntsville Canada 45°20N 79°14W 109 E12
Huntsville Ala., U.S.A. 34°44N 86°35W 111 D9
Huntsville Tex., U.S.A. 30°43N 95°33W 111 D7
Hurghada Egypt 27°15N 33°50E 95 C12
Hurley U.S.A. 46°27N 90°11W 112 B2
Huron U.S.A. 44°22N 98°13W 110 B7
Huron, L. U.S.A. 44°30N 82°40W 112 C6
Hursley U.K. 51°2N 1°23W 24 D6
Hurstbourne Tarrant U.K. 51°17N 1°26W 24 D6
Hurstpierpoint U.K. 50°56N 0°11W 25 E8
Húsavík Iceland 66°3N 17°21W 63 A2
Husband's Bosworth U.K. 52°28N 1°4W 23 H6
Hutchinson U.S.A. 38°5N 97°56W 110 C7
Huyton U.K. 53°25N 2°51W 23 F3
Hvar Croatia 43°11N 16°28E 70 C7
Hwang Ho → China 37°55N 118°50E 81 C6
Hwange Zimbabwe 18°18S 26°30E 97 H5
Hyargas Nuur Mongolia 49°0N 93°0E 80 B4
Hyde U.K. 53°27N 2°4W 23 F4
Hyderabad India 17°22N 78°29E 84 L11
Hyderabad Pakistan 25°23N 68°24E 84 G6
Hyères France 43°8N 6°9E 68 E7
Hyères, Îs. d' France 43°0N 6°20E 68 E7
Hyndman Peak U.S.A. 43°45N 114°8W 110 B4
Hythe U.K. 51°4N 1°5E 25 D11

I
Ialomiţa → Romania 44°42N 27°51E 67 F14
Iaşi Romania 47°10N 27°40E 67 E14
Ibadan Nigeria 7°22N 3°58E 94 G6
Ibagué Colombia 4°20N 75°20W 120 B2
Ibb Yemen 14°2N 44°10E 88 E3
Iberian Peninsula Europe 40°0N 5°0W 56 H5
Ibiá Brazil 19°30S 46°30W 122 C1
Ibiapaba, Sa. da Brazil 4°0S 41°30W 120 C5
Ibicaraí Brazil 14°51S 39°36W 122 B3

Ibiza = Eivissa Spain 38°54N 1°26E 69 C6
Ibotirama Brazil 12°13S 43°12W 122 B2
Ibstock U.K. 52°42N 1°24W 23 G6
Ica Peru 14°0S 75°48W 120 D2
Ica → Brazil 2°55S 67°58W 120 C3
Içel Turkey 36°51N 34°36E 73 G5
Iceland ■ Europe 64°45N 19°0W 63 B2
Ichihara Japan 35°28N 140°5E 82 F7
Ichinomiya Japan 35°18N 136°48E 82 F5
Idaho □ U.S.A. 45°0N 115°0W 110 B4
Idaho Falls U.S.A. 43°30N 112°2W 110 B4
Idar-Oberstein Germany 49°43N 7°16E 66 D4
Idfû Egypt 24°55N 32°49E 95 D12
Idle → U.K. 53°27N 0°49W 23 F7
Idlib Syria 35°55N 36°36E 86 C4
Idmiston U.K. 51°9N 1°42W 24 D5
Ieper Belgium 50°51N 2°53E 65 D2
Ife Nigeria 7°30N 4°31E 94 G6
Iforas, Adrar des Africa 19°40N 1°40E 94 C5
Igarapava Brazil 20°3S 47°47W 122 D1
Igarka Russia 67°30N 86°33E 79 C10
Iglésias Italy 39°19N 8°32E 70 E3
Igloolik Canada 69°20N 81°49W 109 C11
Ignace Canada 49°30N 91°40W 112 A2
Igoumenitsa Greece 39°32N 20°18E 71 E9
Iguaçu → Brazil 25°36S 54°36W 121 B4
Iguaçu, Cat. del Brazil 25°41S 54°26W 121 B4
Iguala Mexico 18°21N 99°32W 114 D5
Iguatu Brazil 6°20S 39°18W 120 C6
Iguidi, Erg Africa 27°0N 7°0W 94 C4
Iisalmi Finland 63°32N 27°10E 63 E9
Ijebu-Ode Nigeria 6°47N 3°58E 94 G6
IJmuiden Neths. 52°28N 4°35E 65 B4
IJsselmeer Neths. 52°45N 5°20E 65 B5
Ikare Nigeria 7°32N 5°40E 94 G7
Ikaria Greece 37°35N 26°10E 71 F12
Ikeda Japan 34°1N 133°48E 82 F3
Ilagan Phil. 17°7N 121°53E 83 B4
Ilām Iran 33°36N 46°36E 86 C6
Ilchester U.K. 51°0N 2°41W 24 D3
Île-de-France □ France 49°0N 2°20E 68 B5
Ilebo Dem. Rep. of the Congo 4°17S 20°55E 96 E4
Ilesha Nigeria 7°37N 4°40E 94 G6
Ilfracombe U.K. 51°12N 4°8W 27 E5
Ilhéus Brazil 14°49S 39°2W 122 B3
Ili → Kazakhstan 45°53N 77°10E 79 E9
Iliamna L. U.S.A. 59°30N 155°0W 108 D4
Iligan Phil. 8°12N 124°13E 83 C4
Ilkeston U.K. 52°58N 1°19W 23 G6
Ilkley U.K. 53°56N 1°48W 23 E5
Illapel Chile 32°0S 71°10W 121 F2
Iller → Germany 48°23N 9°58E 66 D6
Illimani Bolivia 16°30S 67°50W 120 D3
Illinois □ U.S.A. 40°15N 89°30W 111 B9
Illinois → U.S.A. 38°58N 90°28W 111 C8
Ilmen, L. Russia 58°15N 31°10E 72 C5
Ilminster U.K. 50°55N 2°55W 24 E3
Iloilo Phil. 10°45N 122°33E 83 B4
Ilorin Nigeria 8°30N 4°35E 94 G6
Imabari Japan 34°4N 133°0E 82 F3
Imandra, L. Russia 67°30N 33°0E 72 A5
Imatra Finland 61°12N 28°48E 63 E9
Immingham U.K. 53°37N 0°13W 23 E8
Ímola Italy 44°20N 11°42E 70 B4
Imperatriz Brazil 5°30S 47°29W 120 C5
Impéria Italy 43°53N 8°3E 70 C3
Imphal India 24°48N 93°56E 85 G18
In Salah Algeria 27°10N 2°32E 94 C6
Inari Finland 68°54N 27°1E 63 D9
Inarijärvi Finland 69°0N 28°0E 63 D9
Ince Burun Turkey 42°7N 34°56E 73 F5
Incheon S. Korea 37°27N 126°40E 81 C7
Incomáti → Mozam. 25°46S 32°43E 97 K6
Indalsälven → Sweden 62°36N 17°30E 63 E7
India ■ Asia 20°0N 78°0E 84 K11
Indian Ocean 5°0S 75°0E 53 E13
Indiana U.S.A. 40°37N 79°9W 112 E8
Indiana □ U.S.A. 40°0N 86°0W 112 E4
Indianapolis U.S.A. 39°46N 86°9W 112 F4
Indigirka → Russia 70°48N 148°54E 79 B16
Indira Gandhi Canal India 28°0N 72°0E 84 F8
Indo-China Asia 15°0N 102°0E 74 G12
Indonesia ■ Asia 5°0S 115°0E 83 D3
Indore India 22°42N 75°53E 84 H9
Indre → France 47°16N 0°11E 68 C4
Indus → Pakistan 24°20N 67°47E 84 G5
Inebolu Turkey 41°55N 33°40E 73 F5
Ingatestone U.K. 51°40N 0°24E 25 C9
Ingleborough U.K. 54°10N 2°22W 22 D4
Ingleton U.K. 54°10N 2°27W 22 D4
Ingolstadt Germany 48°46N 11°26E 66 D6
Ingraj Bazar India 24°58N 88°10E 85 G16
Ingushetia □ Russia 43°20N 44°50E 73 F8
Inishbofin Ireland 53°37N 10°13W 28 D1
Inisheer Ireland 53°3N 9°32W 30 B3
Inishfree B. Ireland 55°4N 8°23W 28 A5
Inishkea North Ireland 54°9N 10°11W 28 C1
Inishkea South Ireland 54°7N 10°12W 28 C1
Inishmaan Ireland 53°5N 9°35W 30 B3
Inishmore Ireland 53°8N 9°45W 30 B3
Inishowen Pen. Ireland 55°14N 7°15W 29 A7
Inishshark Ireland 53°37N 10°16W 28 D1
Inishtrahull Ireland 55°26N 7°13W 29 A7
Inishturk Ireland 53°42N 10°7W 28 D1
Inishvickillane Ireland 52°3N 10°37W 30 D1
Inkberrow U.K. 52°13N 1°58W 24 B5
Inland Sea Japan 34°20N 133°30E 82 F3
Inn → Austria 48°35N 13°28E 66 D7
Inner Hebrides U.K. 57°0N 6°30W 18 J4
Inner Mongolia □ China 42°0N 112°0E 81 B6
Inner Sound U.K. 57°30N 5°55W 18 H6
Innerleithen U.K. 55°37N 3°4W 21 C9
Innsbruck Austria 47°16N 11°23E 66 E6
Inowrocław Poland 52°50N 18°12E 67 B10
Insein Burma 16°50N 96°5E 85 L20
Inta Russia 66°5N 60°8E 72 A11
Interlaken Switz. 46°41N 7°50E 66 E4
Inukjuak Canada 58°25N 78°15W 109 D12
Inuvik Canada 68°16N 133°40W 108 C6

Inveraray U.K. 56°14N 5°5W 20 B5
Inverbervie U.K. 56°51N 2°17W 19 J13
Invercargill N.Z. 46°24S 168°24E 99 K12
Invergordon U.K. 57°41N 4°10W 19 G9
Inverkeithing U.K. 56°2N 3°24W 21 B9
Inverness U.K. 57°29N 4°13W 19 H9
Inverurie U.K. 57°17N 2°23W 19 H13
Ioannina Greece 39°42N 20°47E 71 E9
Iona U.K. 56°20N 6°25W 20 B3
Ionia U.S.A. 42°59N 85°4W 112 D5
Ionian Is. Greece 38°40N 20°0E 71 E9
Ionian Sea Medit. S. 37°30N 17°30E 71 E7
Ios Greece 36°41N 25°20E 71 F11
Iowa □ U.S.A. 42°18N 93°30W 111 B8
Iowa City U.S.A. 41°40N 91°32W 111 B8
Ipameri Brazil 17°44S 48°9W 122 C1
Ipatinga Brazil 19°32S 42°30W 122 C2
Ipiales Colombia 0°50N 77°37W 120 B2
Ipoh Malaysia 4°35N 101°5E 83 D2
Ipswich Australia 27°35S 152°40E 98 F9
Ipswich U.K. 52°4N 1°10E 25 B11
Iqaluit Canada 63°44N 68°31W 109 C13
Iquique Chile 20°19S 70°5W 120 E2
Iquitos Peru 3°45S 73°10W 120 C2
Iraklio Greece 35°20N 25°12E 71 G11
Iran ■ Asia 33°0N 53°0E 87 C8
Irapuato Mexico 20°41N 101°28W 114 C4
Iraq ■ Asia 33°0N 44°0E 86 C5
Irazú, Vol. Costa Rica 10°10N 84°20W 115 E8
Irbil Iraq 36°15N 44°5E 86 B6
Irchester U.K. 52°18N 0°39W 25 B7
Ireland ■ Europe 53°50N 7°52W 64 E2
Ireland's Eye Ireland 53°24N 6°4W 31 B10
Iringa Tanzania 7°48S 35°43E 96 F7
Irish Republic ■ Europe 53°50N 7°52W 64 E2
Irish Sea Europe 53°38N 4°48W 64 E4
Irkutsk Russia 52°18N 104°20E 79 D12
Irlam U.K. 53°26N 2°26W 23 F4
Iron Gate Europe 44°44N 22°30E 67 F12
Iron Mountain U.S.A. 45°49N 88°4W 112 C3
Ironbridge U.K. 52°38N 2°30W 23 G3
Ironton U.S.A. 38°32N 82°41W 112 F6
Ironwood U.S.A. 46°27N 90°9W 112 B2
Irrawaddy → Burma 15°50N 95°6E 85 M19
Irt → U.K. 54°23N 3°26W 22 D2
Irthlingborough U.K. 52°20N 0°37W 25 B7
Irtysh → Russia 61°4N 68°52E 79 C8
Irún Spain 43°20N 1°52W 69 A5
Irvine U.K. 55°37N 4°41W 20 C6
Irvinestown U.K. 54°28N 7°39W 28 C6
Isabela Puerto Rico 18°30N 67°2W 115 d
Ísafjörður Iceland 66°5N 23°9W 63 A1
Isar → Germany 48°48N 12°57E 66 D7
Ischia Italy 40°44N 13°57E 70 D5
Isère → France 44°59N 4°51E 68 D6
Ishinomaki Japan 38°32N 141°20E 82 D7
Ishpeming U.S.A. 46°29N 87°40W 112 B4
Isiro Dem. Rep. of the Congo 2°53N 27°40E 96 D5
İskenderun Turkey 36°32N 36°10E 73 G6
Isla → U.K. 56°32N 3°20W 21 A9
Islamabad Pakistan 33°40N 73°10E 84 C8
Island L. Canada 53°47N 94°25W 108 D10
Island Pond U.S.A. 44°49N 71°53W 113 C12
Islay U.K. 55°46N 6°10W 20 C3
Isleham U.K. 52°21N 0°25E 25 B9
Islington □ U.K. 51°33N 0°5W 25 C8
Islip U.K. 51°50N 1°12W 24 C6
Ismâ'ilîya Egypt 30°37N 32°18E 95 B12
Isna Egypt 25°17N 32°30E 95 C12
Isparta Turkey 37°47N 30°30E 73 G5
Israel ■ Asia 32°0N 34°50E 86 C3
Issoire France 45°32N 3°15E 68 D5
Issyk Kul Kyrgyzstan 42°25N 77°15E 79 E9
İstanbul Turkey 41°0N 28°58E 73 F4
Istra Croatia 45°10N 14°0E 70 B5
Istres France 43°31N 4°59E 68 E6
Itaberaba Brazil 12°32S 40°18W 122 B2
Itabira Brazil 19°37S 43°13W 122 C2
Itabuna Brazil 14°48S 39°16W 122 B3
Itacoatiara Brazil 3°8S 58°25W 120 C4
Itajaí Brazil 27°50S 48°39W 121 E5
Itajubá Brazil 22°24S 45°30W 122 D1
Italy ■ Europe 42°0N 13°0E 70 C5
Itaperuna Brazil 21°10S 41°54W 122 D2
Itapetinga Brazil 15°15S 40°15W 122 C2
Itapetininga Brazil 23°36S 48°7W 122 D1
Itapicuru → Brazil 11°47S 37°32W 122 B3
Itaquari Brazil 20°20S 40°25W 122 D2
Itararé Brazil 24°6S 49°23W 122 D1
Itaúna Brazil 20°4S 44°34W 122 D2
Itchen → U.K. 50°55N 1°22W 24 E6
Ithaca U.S.A. 42°27N 76°30W 112 D9
Ittoqqortoormiit Greenland 70°20N 23°0W 54 B6
Itu Brazil 23°17S 47°15W 122 D1
Ivanava Belarus 52°7N 25°29E 67 B13
Ivano-Frankivsk Ukraine 48°40N 24°40E 67 D13
Ivanovo Russia 57°5N 41°0E 72 C7
Ivinghoe U.K. 51°50N 0°37W 25 C7
Ivory Coast ■ Africa 7°30N 5°0W 94 G4
Ivujivik Canada 62°24N 77°55W 109 C12
Ivybridge U.K. 50°23N 3°56W 27 G6
Iwaki Japan 37°3N 140°55E 82 E7
Iwakuni Japan 34°15N 132°8E 82 F3
Iwo Nigeria 7°39N 4°9E 94 G6
Ixworth U.K. 52°18N 0°51E 25 B10
Izhevsk Russia 56°51N 53°14E 72 C9
Izmayil Ukraine 45°22N 28°46E 73 E4
İzmir Turkey 38°25N 27°8E 73 G4
İznik Gölü Turkey 40°27N 29°30E 73 F4
Izumi-Sano Japan 34°23N 135°18E 82 F4

J
Jabalpur India 23°9N 79°58E 84 H11
Jaboatão Brazil 8°7S 35°1W 120 C6
Jaboticabal Brazil 21°15S 48°17W 122 D1
Jacareí Brazil 23°20S 46°0W 122 D1
Jackson Barbados 13°7N 59°36W 115 g
Jackson Ky., U.S.A. 37°33N 83°23W 112 G6

Jackson Mich., U.S.A. 42°15N 84°24W 112 D5
Jackson Miss., U.S.A. 32°18N 90°12W 111 D8
Jackson Mo., U.S.A. 37°23N 89°40W 112 G3
Jackson Tenn., U.S.A. 35°37N 88°49W 111 C9
Jacksonville Fla., U.S.A. 30°20N 81°39W 111 D10
Jacksonville Ill., U.S.A. 39°44N 90°14W 112 F2
Jacmel Haiti 18°14N 72°32W 115 D10
Jacobabad Pakistan 28°20N 68°29E 84 E6
Jacobina Brazil 11°11S 40°30W 122 B2
Jaén Spain 37°44N 3°43W 69 D4
Jaffna Sri Lanka 9°45N 80°2E 84 Q12
Jahrom Iran 28°30N 53°31E 87 D8
Jaipur India 27°0N 75°50E 84 F9
Jakarta Indonesia 6°9S 106°52E 83 D2
Jalālābād Afghan. 34°30N 70°29E 87 C12
Jalgaon India 21°0N 75°42E 84 J9
Jalna India 19°48N 75°38E 84 K9
Jalpaiguri India 26°32N 88°46E 85 F16
Jaluit I. Marshall Is. 6°0N 169°30E 102 G8
Jamaica ■ W. Indies 18°10N 77°30W 114 a
Jamalpur Bangla. 24°52N 89°56E 85 G16
Jamalpur India 25°18N 86°28E 85 G15
Jambi Indonesia 1°38S 103°30E 83 D2
James → U.S.A. 42°52N 97°18W 111 D7
James B. Canada 54°0N 80°0W 109 D12
Jamestown N. Dak., U.S.A. 46°54N 98°42W 110 A7
Jamestown N.Y., U.S.A. 42°6N 79°14W 112 D8
Jammu India 32°43N 74°54E 84 C9
Jammu & Kashmir □ India 34°25N 77°0E 84 B10
Jamnagar India 22°30N 70°6E 84 H7
Jamshedpur India 22°44N 86°12E 85 H15
Jan Mayen Arctic 71°0N 9°0W 54 B7
Janaúba Brazil 15°48S 43°19W 122 C2
Janesville U.S.A. 42°41N 89°1W 112 D3
Januária Brazil 15°25S 44°25W 122 C2
Jaora India 23°40N 75°10E 84 H9
Japan ■ Asia 36°0N 136°0E 82 F5
Japan, Sea of Asia 40°0N 135°0E 82 D4
Japan Trench Pac. Oc. 32°0N 142°0E 102 D6
Japurá → Brazil 3°8S 65°46W 120 C3
Jari → Brazil 1°9S 51°54W 120 C4
Jarrow U.K. 54°59N 1°28W 22 C6
Jarvis I. Pac. Oc. 0°15S 160°5W 103 H12
Jäsk Iran 25°38N 57°45E 87 E9
Jasper Canada 52°55N 118°5W 108 D8
Jaú Brazil 22°10S 48°30W 122 D1
Jauja Peru 11°45S 75°15W 120 D2
Jaunpur India 25°46N 82°44E 85 G13
Java Indonesia 7°0S 110°0E 83 D3
Java Sea Indonesia 4°35S 107°15E 83 D2
Java Trench Ind. Oc. 9°0S 105°0E 83 D2
Jaya, Puncak Indonesia 3°57S 137°17E 83 D5
Jebel, Bahr el → Sudan 9°30N 30°25E 95 G12
Jedburgh U.K. 55°29N 2°33W 21 D10
Jedda Si. Arabia 21°29N 39°10E 88 C2
Jeffersonville U.S.A. 38°17N 85°44W 112 F5
Jeju-do S. Korea 33°29N 126°34E 81 C7
Jelenia Góra Poland 50°50N 15°45E 66 C8
Jelgava Latvia 56°41N 23°49E 63 F8
Jena Germany 50°54N 11°35E 66 C6
Jeonju S. Korea 35°50N 127°4E 81 C7
Jequié Brazil 13°51S 40°5W 122 B2
Jequitinhonha Brazil 16°30S 41°0W 122 C2
Jequitinhonha → Brazil 15°51S 38°53W 122 C3
Jérémie Haiti 18°40N 74°10W 115 D10
Jerez de la Frontera Spain 36°41N 6°7W 69 D2
Jersey U.K. 49°11N 2°7W 27 J9
Jersey City U.S.A. 40°42N 74°4W 113 E10
Jerseyville U.S.A. 39°7N 90°20W 112 F2
Jerusalem Israel/West Bank 31°47N 35°10E 86 D3
Jervaulx U.K. 54°16N 1°43W 22 D5
Jessore Bangla. 23°10N 89°10E 85 H16
Jhang Maghiana Pakistan 31°15N 72°22E 84 D8
Jhansi India 25°30N 78°36E 84 G11
Jharkhand □ India 24°0N 85°50E 85 H14
Jhelum Pakistan 33°0N 73°45E 84 C8
Jhelum → Pakistan 31°20N 72°10E 84 D8
Jiamusi China 46°40N 130°26E 81 B8
Ji'an China 27°6N 114°59E 81 D6
Jiangmen China 22°32N 113°0E 81 D6
Jiangsu □ China 33°0N 120°0E 81 C7
Jiangxi □ China 27°30N 116°0E 81 D6
Jiaxing China 30°49N 120°45E 81 C7
Jihlava → Czech Rep. 48°55N 16°36E 67 D9
Jijiga Ethiopia 9°20N 42°50E 88 F3
Jilin China 43°44N 126°30E 81 B7
Jilin □ China 44°0N 127°0E 81 B7
Jima Ethiopia 7°40N 36°47E 88 F2
Jiménez Mexico 27°8N 104°54W 114 B4
Jinan China 36°38N 117°1E 81 C6
Jinchang China 38°30N 102°10E 80 C5
Jincheng China 35°29N 112°50E 81 C6
Jingdezhen China 29°20N 117°11E 81 D6
Jinggu China 23°35N 100°41E 80 D5
Jingmen China 31°0N 112°10E 81 C6
Jinhua China 29°8N 119°38E 81 D6
Jining Nei Monggol Zizhiqu, China 41°5N 113°0E 81 B6
Jining Shandong, China 35°22N 116°34E 81 C6
Jinja Uganda 0°25N 33°12E 96 D6
Jinxi China 40°52N 120°50E 81 B7
Jinzhou China 41°5N 121°3E 81 B7
Jipijapa Ecuador 1°0S 80°40W 120 C1
Jishou China 28°21N 109°43E 81 D5
Jiujiang China 29°42N 115°58E 81 D6
Jiwani Pakistan 25°1N 61°44E 87 E10
Jixi China 45°20N 130°50E 81 B8
Jīzān Si. Arabia 17°0N 42°20E 88 D3
João Pessoa Brazil 7°10S 34°52W 120 C6
Jodhpur India 26°23N 73°8E 84 F8
Joensuu Finland 62°37N 29°49E 63 E9
Johannesburg S. Africa 26°11S 28°2E 97 K5
John Crow Mts. Jamaica 18°5N 76°25W 114 a
John Day → U.S.A. 45°44N 120°39W 110 A2
John o' Groats U.K. 58°38N 3°4W 19 E11
Johnson City U.S.A. 36°19N 82°21W 112 G6
Johnston I. Pac. Oc. 17°10N 169°8W 103 F11
Johnstone U.K. 55°49N 4°31W 20 C6

Johnstown U.S.A. 40°20N 78°55W 112 E8
Johor Bahru Malaysia 1°28N 103°46E 83 C2
Joinville Brazil 26°15S 48°55W 121 E5
Joliet U.S.A. 41°32N 88°5W 112 E3
Joliette Canada 46°3N 73°24W 109 E12
Jolo Phil. 6°0N 121°0E 83 C4
Jones Sound Canada 76°0N 85°0W 109 B11
Jonesboro U.S.A. 35°50N 90°42W 111 C8
Jönköping Sweden 57°45N 14°8E 63 F6
Jonquière Canada 48°27N 71°14W 113 A12
Joplin U.S.A. 37°6N 94°31W 111 C8
Jordan ■ Asia 31°0N 36°0E 86 D4
Jordan → Asia 31°48N 35°32E 86 D3
Jos Nigeria 9°53N 8°51E 94 G7
Joseph Bonaparte G. Australia 14°35S 128°50E 98 C4
Jost Van Dyke I. Br. Virgin Is. 18°29N 64°47W 115 e
Jotunheimen Norway 61°35N 8°25E 63 E5
Jowzjān □ Afghan. 36°10N 66°0E 87 B11
Juan de Fuca, Str. of Canada 48°15N 124°0W 110 A2
Juan Fernández, Arch. de Pac. Oc. 33°50S 80°0W 103 L20
Juàzeiro Brazil 9°30S 40°30W 122 A2
Juàzeiro do Norte Brazil 7°10S 39°18W 120 C6
Jûbâ Sudan 4°50N 31°35E 95 H12
Juba → Somali Rep. 1°30N 42°35E 88 G3
Juchitán de Zaragoza Mexico 16°26N 95°1W 114 D5
Juiz de Fora Brazil 21°43S 43°19W 122 D2
Juliaca Peru 15°25S 70°10W 120 D2
Julianatop Suriname 3°40N 56°30W 120 B4
Jullundur India 31°20N 75°40E 84 D9
Junagadh India 21°30N 70°30E 84 J7
Jundiaí Brazil 24°30S 47°0W 122 D1
Juneau U.S.A. 58°18N 134°25W 108 D6
Junín Argentina 34°33S 60°57W 121 F3
Jur, Nahr el → Sudan 8°45N 29°15E 95 G11
Jura Europe 46°40N 6°5E 68 C6
Jura U.K. 56°0N 5°50W 20 C4
Jura, Sd. of U.K. 55°57N 5°45W 20 C4
Juruá → Brazil 2°37S 65°44W 120 C3
Juruena → Brazil 7°20S 58°3W 120 C4
Juticalpa Honduras 14°40N 86°12W 114 E7
Jutland Denmark 56°25N 9°30E 63 F5
Juventud, I. de la Cuba 21°40N 82°40W 115 C8
Jväskylä Finland 62°14N 25°50E 63 E9

K
K2 Pakistan 35°58N 76°32E 84 B10
Kabardino-Balkaria □ Russia 43°30N 43°30E 73 F7
Kābul Afghan. 34°28N 69°11E 87 C12
Kabwe Zambia 14°30S 28°29E 97 G5
Kachchh, Gulf of India 22°50N 69°15E 84 H6
Kachchh, Rann of India 24°0N 70°0E 84 H7
Kachin □ Burma 26°0N 97°30E 85 G20
Kaçkar Turkey 40°45N 41°10E 73 F7
Kadavu Fiji 19°0S 178°15E 99 E14
Kade Ghana 6°7N 0°56W 94 G5
Kadoma Zimbabwe 18°20S 29°52E 97 H5
Kaduna Nigeria 10°30N 7°21E 94 F7
Kaesŏng N. Korea 37°58N 126°35E 81 C7
Kafue → Zambia 15°30S 29°0E 97 H5
Kaga Bandoro C.A.R. 7°0N 19°10E 96 C3
Kagera → Uganda 0°57S 31°47E 96 E6
Kagoshima Japan 31°35N 130°33E 82 H2
Kaho'olawe U.S.A. 20°33N 156°37W 110 H16
Kahramanmaraş Turkey 37°37N 36°53E 73 G6
Kai, Kepulauan Indonesia 5°55S 132°45E 83 D5
Kaieteur Falls Guyana 5°1N 59°10W 120 B4
Kaifeng China 34°48N 114°21E 81 C6
Kailua U.S.A. 19°39N 155°59W 110 J17
Kainji Res. Nigeria 10°1N 4°40E 94 F6
Kairouan Tunisia 35°45N 10°5E 95 A8
Kaiserslautern Germany 49°26N 7°45E 66 D4
Kaitaia N.Z. 35°8S 173°17E 99 H13
Kaiyuan China 23°40N 103°12E 80 D5
Kajaani Finland 64°17N 27°46E 63 E9
Kajabbi Australia 20°0S 140°1E 98 E7
Kakamega Kenya 0°20N 34°46E 96 D6
Kakhovka Res. Ukraine 47°5N 34°0E 73 E5
Kakinada India 16°57N 82°11E 85 L13
Kalaallit Nunaat = Greenland □ N. Amer. 66°0N 45°0W 54 C5
Kalahari Africa 24°0S 21°30E 97 J4
Kalamata Greece 37°3N 22°10E 71 F10
Kalamazoo U.S.A. 42°17N 85°35W 112 D5
Kalamazoo → U.S.A. 42°40N 86°10W 112 D4
Kalemie Dem. Rep. of the Congo 5°55S 29°9E 96 F5
Kalgoorlie-Boulder Australia 30°40S 121°22E 98 G3
Kalimantan Indonesia 0°0 114°0E 83 D3
Kálimnos Greece 37°0N 27°0E 71 F12
Kaliningrad Russia 54°42N 20°32E 63 G8
Kalispell U.S.A. 48°12N 114°19W 110 A4
Kalisz Poland 51°45N 18°8E 67 C10
Kalkaska U.S.A. 44°44N 85°11W 112 C5
Kallsjön Sweden 63°38N 13°0E 63 E6
Kalmar Sweden 56°40N 16°20E 63 F7
Kalmykia □ Russia 46°5N 46°1E 73 E8
Kaluga Russia 54°35N 36°10E 72 D6
Kalutara Sri Lanka 6°35N 80°0E 84 R12
Kalyan India 19°15N 73°9E 84 K8
Kama → Russia 55°45N 52°0E 72 C9
Kamchatka Pen. Russia 57°0N 160°0E 79 D18
Kamina Dem. Rep. of the Congo 8°45S 25°0E 96 F5
Kamloops Canada 50°40N 120°20W 108 D7
Kampala Uganda 0°20N 32°30E 96 D6
Kampong Saom Cambodia 10°38N 103°30E 83 B2
Kamyanets-Podilskyy Ukraine 48°45N 26°40E 67 D14
Kamyshin Russia 50°10N 45°24E 73 D8
Kananga Dem. Rep. of the Congo 5°55S 22°18E 96 F4
Kanash Russia 55°30N 47°32E 72 C8
Kanawha → U.S.A. 38°50N 82°9W 112 F6
Kanazawa Japan 36°30N 136°38E 82 E5
Kanchenjunga Nepal 27°50N 88°10E 85 F16
Kanchipuram India 12°52N 79°45E 84 N11
Kandalaksha Russia 67°9N 32°30E 72 A5
Kandalaksha, G. of Russia 66°0N 35°0E 72 A6

Kandanghaur

La Grande

Kandanghaur *Indonesia* 6°21S 108°6E **83** D2
Kandi *Benin* 11°7N 2°55E **94** F6
Kandy *Sri Lanka* 7°18N 80°43E **84** R12
Kane *U.S.A.* 41°40N 78°49W **112** E8
Käne'ohe *U.S.A.* 21°25N 157°48W **110** H16
Kangaroo I. *Australia* 35°45S 137°0E **98** H6
Kangiqsualujjuaq *Canada* 58°30N 65°59W **109** D13
Kangiqsujuaq *Canada* 61°30N 72°0W **109** C12
Kangirsuk *Canada* 60°0N 70°0W **109** D13
Kanin Pen. *Russia* 68°0N 45°0E **72** A8
Kankakee *U.S.A.* 41°7N 87°52W **112** E4
Kankakee → *U.S.A.* 41°23N 88°15W **112** E3
Kankan *Guinea* 10°23N 9°15W **94** F4
Kano *Nigeria* 12°2N 8°30E **94** F7
Kanpur *India* 26°28N 80°20E **84** F12
Kansas □ *U.S.A.* 38°30N 99°0W **110** C7
Kansas → *U.S.A.* 39°7N 94°37W **111** C8
Kansas City *U.S.A.* 39°6N 94°35W **111** C8
Kanturk *Ireland* 52°11N 8°54W **30** D5
Kanye *Botswana* 24°55S 25°28E **97** J5
Kaohsiung *Taiwan* 22°35N 120°16E **81** D7
Kaolack *Senegal* 14°5N 16°8W **94** F2
Kapaa *U.S.A.* 22°5N 159°19W **110** G15
Kapiri Mposhi *Zambia* 13°59S 28°43E **97** G5
Käpisä □ *Afghan.* 35°0N 69°20E **87** C12
Kaposvár *Hungary* 46°25N 17°47E **67** E9
Kaptai L. *Bangla.* 22°40N 92°20E **85** H18
Kapuas → *Indonesia* 0°25S 109°20E **83** D2
Kapuskasing *Canada* 49°25N 82°30W **112** A6
Kara Bogaz Gol *Turkmenistan* 41°0N 53°30E **87** A8
Kara Kum *Turkmenistan* 39°30N 60°0E **87** B9
Kara Sea *Russia* 75°0N 70°0E **79** B8
Karabük *Turkey* 41°12N 32°37E **73** F5
Karachey-Cherkessia □
  Russia 43°40N 41°30E **73** F7
Karachi *Pakistan* 24°50N 67°0E **84** G5
Karaganda *Kazakhstan* 49°50N 73°10E **79** E9
Karagiye Depression
  Kazakhstan 43°27N 51°45E **73** F9
Karakalpakstan □ *Uzbekistan* 43°0N 58°0E **87** A9
Karakoram *Pakistan* 35°30N 77°0E **84** B10
Karaman *Turkey* 37°14N 33°13E **73** G5
Karamay *China* 45°30N 84°58E **80** B3
Karatax Shan *China* 35°57N 81°0E **80** C3
Karawang *Indonesia* 6°30S 107°15E **83** D2
Karayazı *Turkey* 39°41N 42°9E **73** G7
Karbalā' *Iraq* 32°36N 44°3E **86** C5
Karelia □ *Russia* 65°30N 32°30E **72** A5
Kariba, L. *Zimbabwe* 16°40S 28°25E **97** H5
Kariba Dam *Zimbabwe* 16°30S 28°35E **97** H5
Karimata, Str. of *Indonesia* 2°0S 108°40E **83** D2
Karlovac *Croatia* 45°31N 15°36E **70** B6
Karlskrona *Sweden* 56°10N 15°35E **63** F7
Karlsruhe *Germany* 49°0N 8°23E **66** D5
Karlstad *Sweden* 59°23N 13°30E **63** F6
Karnak *Egypt* 25°43N 32°39E **95** C12
Karnal *India* 29°42N 77°2E **84** E10
Karnataka □ *India* 13°15N 77°0E **84** N10
Kärnten □ *Austria* 46°52N 13°30E **66** E8
Karpathos *Greece* 35°37N 27°10E **71** G12
Kars *Turkey* 40°40N 43°5E **73** F7
Karwar *India* 14°55N 74°13E **84** M9
Kasai → *Dem. Rep. of the Congo* 3°30S 16°10E **96** E3
Kasaragod *India* 12°30N 74°58E **84** N9
Kasba L. *Canada* 60°20N 102°10W **108** C9
Käshän *Iran* 34°5N 51°30E **87** C7
Kashi *China* 39°30N 76°2E **80** C2
Kasongo *Dem. Rep. of the Congo* 4°30S 26°33E **96** E5
Kassalâ *Sudan* 15°30N 36°0E **95** E13
Kassel *Germany* 51°18N 9°26E **66** C5
Kastamonu *Turkey* 41°25N 33°43E **73** F5
Kasur *Pakistan* 31°5N 74°25E **84** D9
Katanga □ *Dem. Rep. of the Congo* 8°0S 25°0E **96** F4
Kathiawar *India* 22°20N 71°0E **84** H7
Katihar *India* 25°34N 87°36E **85** G15
Katima Mulilo *Zambia* 17°28S 24°13E **97** H4
Katiola *Ivory C.* 8°10N 5°10W **94** G4
Katmandu *Nepal* 27°45N 85°20E **85** F14
Katowice *Poland* 50°17N 19°5E **67** C10
Katrine, L. *U.K.* 56°15N 4°30W **20** B7
Katsina *Nigeria* 13°0N 7°32E **94** F7
Kattegat *Denmark* 56°40N 11°20E **63** F6
Kaua'i *U.S.A.* 22°3N 159°30W **110** H15
Kauai Channel *U.S.A.* 21°45N 158°50W **110** H15
Kaukauna *U.S.A.* 44°17N 88°17W **112** C3
Kaunakakai *U.S.A.* 21°6N 157°1W **110** H16
Kaunas *Lithuania* 54°54N 23°54E **63** G8
Kavala *Greece* 40°57N 24°28E **71** D11
Kavieng *Papua N. G.* 2°36S 150°51E **98** A9
Kawagoe *Japan* 35°55N 139°29E **82** F6
Kawaguchi *Japan* 35°52N 139°45E **82** F6
Kawardha *India* 22°0N 81°17E **85** J12
Kawasaki *Japan* 35°31N 139°43E **82** F6
Kawawachikamach
  Canada 54°48N 66°50W **109** D13
Kayah □ *Burma* 19°15N 97°15E **85** K20
Kayes *Mali* 14°25N 11°30W **94** F3
Kayin □ *Burma* 18°0N 97°30E **85** L20
Kayseri *Turkey* 38°45N 35°30E **73** G6
Kazakhstan ■ *Asia* 50°0N 70°0E **79** E8
Kazan *Russia* 55°50N 49°10E **72** C8
Kazan-Rettō *Pac. Oc.* 25°0N 141°0E **102** E6
Kazanlŭk *Bulgaria* 42°38N 25°20E **71** C11
Kea *Greece* 37°35N 24°22E **71** F11
Kea *U.K.* 50°14N 5°6W **27** G3
Keady *U.K.* 54°15N 6°42W **29** C8
Kearney *U.S.A.* 40°42N 99°5W **110** B7
Keban *Turkey* 38°50N 38°50E **73** G6
Keban Baraji *Turkey* 38°41N 38°33E **73** G6
Kebnekaise *Sweden* 67°53N 18°33E **63** E7
Kebri Dehar *Ethiopia* 6°45N 44°17E **88** F3
Kebumen *Indonesia* 7°42S 109°40E **83** D2
Kecskemét *Hungary* 46°57N 19°42E **67** E10
Kediri *Indonesia* 7°51S 112°1E **83** D3
Keelby *U.K.* 53°35N 0°16W **23** E8
Keele *U.K.* 53°0N 2°17W **23** F4
Keene *U.S.A.* 42°56N 72°17W **113** D11
Keeper Hill *Ireland* 52°45N 8°16W **30** C6

Keetmanshoop *Namibia* 26°35S 18°8E **97** K3
Kefalonia *Greece* 38°15N 20°30E **71** E9
Keflavík *Iceland* 64°2N 22°35W **63** B1
Kegworth *U.K.* 52°50N 1°17W **23** G6
Keighley *U.K.* 53°52N 1°54W **23** E5
Keith *U.K.* 57°32N 2°57W **19** G12
Keld *U.K.* 54°24N 2°10W **22** D4
Kelkit → *Turkey* 40°45N 36°32E **73** F6
Kellett, C. *Canada* 72°0N 126°0W **109** B7
Kellogg *U.S.A.* 47°32N 116°7W **110** A13
Kelowna *Canada* 49°50N 119°25W **108** E8
Kelsale *U.K.* 52°14N 1°31E **25** B12
Kelsall *U.K.* 53°13N 2°43W **23** F3
Kelso *U.K.* 55°36N 2°26W **21** C11
Kelvedon *U.K.* 51°50N 0°43E **25** C10
Kem *Russia* 65°0N 34°38E **72** B5
Kemble *U.K.* 51°40N 1°59W **24** C5
Kemerovo *Russia* 55°20N 86°5E **79** D10
Kemi *Finland* 65°44N 24°34E **63** D8
Kemijoki → *Finland* 65°47N 24°32E **63** D8
Kempsey *U.K.* 52°8N 2°12W **24** B4
Kempston *U.K.* 52°7N 0°30W **25** B7
Kempten *Germany* 47°45N 10°17E **66** E6
Kenai *U.S.A.* 60°33N 151°16W **108** C4
Kendal *U.K.* 54°20N 2°44W **22** D3
Kendari *Indonesia* 3°50S 122°30E **83** D4
Kenema *S. Leone* 7°50N 11°14W **94** G3
Kenilworth *U.K.* 52°21N 1°34W **24** B5
Kenmare *Ireland* 51°53N 9°36W **30** E3
Kenmare River *Ireland* 51°48N 9°51W **30** E3
Kennet → *U.K.* 51°27N 0°57W **25** D7
Kennewick *U.S.A.* 46°12N 119°7W **110** A3
Kenninghall *U.K.* 52°26N 1°0E **25** B11
Kenogami → *Canada* 51°6N 84°28W **109** D11
Kenora *Canada* 49°47N 94°29W **108** E10
Kenosha *U.S.A.* 42°35N 87°49W **112** D4
Kent □ *U.K.* 41°9N 81°22W **112** E7
Kent □ *U.K.* 51°12N 0°40E **25** D10
Kent Pen. *Canada* 68°30N 107°0W **108** C9
Kentisbeare *U.K.* 50°51N 3°20W **27** F7
Kenton *U.S.A.* 40°39N 83°37W **112** E6
Kentucky □ *U.S.A.* 37°0N 84°0W **112** G5
Kentucky → *U.S.A.* 38°41N 85°11W **112** F5
Kentville *Canada* 45°6N 64°29W **109** E13
Kenya ■ *Africa* 1°0N 38°0E **96** D7
Kenya, Mt. *Kenya* 0°10S 37°18E **96** E7
Kerala □ *India* 11°0N 76°15E **84** P10
Kerch *Ukraine* 45°20N 36°20E **73** E6
Kerguelen *Ind. Oc.* 49°15S 69°10E **53** G13
Kericho *Kenya* 0°22S 35°15E **96** E7
Kerinci *Indonesia* 1°40S 101°15E **83** D2
Kermadec Is. *Pac. Oc.* 30°0S 178°15W **99** G15
Kermadec Trench *Pac. Oc.* 30°30S 176°0W **99** G15
Kermān *Iran* 30°15N 57°1E **87** D9
Kermānshāh *Iran* 34°23N 47°0E **86** C6
Kerrera *U.K.* 56°24N 5°33W **20** B4
Kerrobert *Canada* 51°56N 109°8W **108** D9
Kerry □ *Ireland* 52°7N 9°35W **30** D3
Kerry Hd. *Ireland* 52°25N 9°56W **30** D3
Kerulen → *Asia* 48°48N 117°0E **81** B6
Kessingland *U.K.* 52°26N 1°43E **25** B12
Keswick *U.K.* 54°36N 3°8W **22** C2
Ketchikan *U.S.A.* 55°21N 131°39W **108** D6
Kettering *U.K.* 52°24N 0°43W **25** B7
Kettle Ness *U.K.* 54°33N 0°42W **22** C7
Kettlewell *U.K.* 54°9N 2°3W **22** D4
Kewaunee *U.S.A.* 44°27N 87°31W **112** C4
Keweenaw B. *U.S.A.* 47°0N 88°15W **112** B3
Keweenaw Pen. *U.S.A.* 47°15N 88°15W **112** B3
Keweenaw Pt. *U.S.A.* 47°25N 87°43W **112** B4
Kexby *U.K.* 53°22N 0°42W **23** F7
Key West *U.S.A.* 24°33N 81°48W **111** F10
Keyingham *U.K.* 53°43N 0°7W **23** E8
Keymer *U.K.* 50°55N 0°7W **25** E8
Keynsham *U.K.* 51°24N 2°29W **24** D4
Keyser *U.S.A.* 39°26N 78°59W **112** F8
Keyworth *U.K.* 52°52N 1°5W **23** G6
Khabarovsk *Russia* 48°30N 135°5E **79** E15
Khairpur *Pakistan* 27°32N 68°49E **84** F6
Khambhat *India* 22°23N 72°33E **84** H8
Khambhat, G. of *India* 20°45N 72°30E **84** J8
Khamis Mushayt *Si. Arabia* 18°18N 42°44E **88** D3
Khandyga *Russia* 62°42N 135°35E **79** C15
Khanewal *Pakistan* 30°20N 71°55E **84** D7
Kharagpur *India* 22°20N 87°25E **85** H15
Kharg *Iran* 29°15N 50°28E **86** D7
Khârga, El Wâhât-el *Egypt* 25°10N 30°35E **95** C12
Kharkov *Ukraine* 49°58N 36°20E **73** E6
Khartoum *Sudan* 15°31N 32°35E **95** E12
Khaskovo *Bulgaria* 41°56N 25°30E **71** D11
Khatanga *Russia* 72°0N 102°20E **79** B12
Khemisset *Morocco* 33°50N 6°1W **94** B4
Khenchela *Algeria* 35°28N 7°11E **94** A7
Kherson *Ukraine* 46°35N 32°35E **73** E5
Khmelnytskyy *Ukraine* 49°23N 27°0E **67** D14
Khojak Pass *Afghan.* 30°51N 66°34E **87** D11
Kholm *Afghan.* 36°45N 67°40E **87** B11
Khon Kaen *Thailand* 16°30N 102°47E **83** B2
Khorramābād *Iran* 33°30N 48°25E **86** C7
Khorrāmshahr *Iran* 30°29N 48°15E **86** D7
Khouribga *Morocco* 32°58N 6°57W **94** B4
Khudzhand *Tajikistan* 40°17N 69°37E **87** B12
Khulna *Bangla.* 22°45N 89°34E **85** H16
Khulna □ *Bangla.* 22°25N 89°35E **85** H16
Khunjerab Pass *Asia* 36°40N 75°25E **84** A9
Khushab *Pakistan* 32°20N 72°20E **84** C8
Khuzdar *Pakistan* 27°52N 66°30E **84** F5
Khvoy *Iran* 38°35N 45°0E **86** B6
Khyber Pass *Afghan.* 34°10N 71°8E **84** B7
Kibworth Beauchamp *U.K.* 52°33N 0°59W **23** G7
Kicking Horse Pass *Canada* 51°28N 116°16W **108** D8
Kidderminster *U.K.* 52°24N 2°15W **24** B4
Kidlington *U.K.* 51°50N 1°15W **24** C6
Kidsgrove *U.K.* 53°5N 2°14W **23** F4
Kidstones *U.K.* 54°13N 2°2W **22** D4
Kidwelly *U.K.* 51°44N 4°18W **26** D5

Kiel *Germany* 54°19N 10°8E **66** A6
Kiel Canal = Nord-Ostsee-Kanal
  Germany 54°12N 9°32E **66** A5
Kielce *Poland* 50°52N 20°42E **67** C11
Kielder *U.K.* 55°14N 2°35W **22** B3
Kieler Bucht *Germany* 54°35N 10°25E **66** A6
Kiev *Ukraine* 50°30N 30°28E **67** C16
Kigali *Rwanda* 1°59S 30°4E **96** E6
Kigoma-Ujiji *Tanzania* 4°55S 29°36E **96** E5
Kikwit *Dem. Rep. of the Congo* 5°0S 18°45E **96** E3
Kīlauea *U.S.A.* 19°25N 155°17W **110** J17
Kilbirnie *U.K.* 55°46N 4°41W **20** C6
Kilbrannan Sd. *U.K.* 55°37N 5°26W **20** C5
Kildare *Ireland* 53°9N 6°55W **31** B9
Kildare □ *Ireland* 53°10N 6°50W **31** B9
Kilfinnane *Ireland* 52°21N 8°28W **30** D6
Kilham *U.K.* 54°4N 0°23W **22** D8
Kilifi *Kenya* 3°40S 39°48E **96** E7
Kilimanjaro *Tanzania* 3°7S 37°20E **96** E7
Kilindini *Kenya* 4°4S 39°40E **96** E7
Kilkee *Ireland* 52°41N 9°39W **30** C3
Kilkeel *U.K.* 54°4N 6°0W **29** C10
Kilkenny *Ireland* 52°39N 7°15N **31** C8
Kilkenny □ *Ireland* 52°35N 7°15N **31** C8
Kilkhampton *U.K.* 50°52N 4°31W **27** F4
Kilkieran B. *Ireland* 53°20N 9°41W **30** B3
Killala *Ireland* 54°13N 9°12W **28** C2
Killala B. *Ireland* 54°16N 9°8W **28** C3
Killaloe *Ireland* 52°48N 8°28W **30** C6
Killarney *Ireland* 52°4N 9°30W **30** D4
Killarney △ *Ireland* 52°0N 9°33W **30** E3
Killary Harbour *Ireland* 53°38N 9°52W **28** D2
Killeen *U.S.A.* 31°7N 97°44W **110** D7
Killiney *Ireland* 53°15N 6°7W **31** B10
Killinghall *U.K.* 54°2N 1°33W **22** D5
Killorglin *Ireland* 52°6N 9°47W **30** D3
Killybegs *Ireland* 54°38N 8°26W **28** B5
Kilmarnock *U.K.* 55°37N 4°29W **20** C7
Kilrush *Ireland* 52°38N 9°29W **30** C4
Kilsby *U.K.* 52°20N 1°10W **24** B6
Kilsyth *U.K.* 55°59N 4°3W **20** C7
Kilwa Kivinje *Tanzania* 8°45S 39°25E **96** F7
Kilwinning *U.K.* 55°39N 4°43W **20** C6
Kimberley *Australia* 16°20S 127°0E **98** D4
Kimberley *S. Africa* 28°43S 24°46E **97** K4
Kimbolton *U.K.* 52°18N 0°24W **25** B8
Kimch'aek *N. Korea* 40°40N 129°10E **81** B7
Kimmirut *Canada* 62°50N 69°50W **109** C13
Kimry *Russia* 56°55N 37°15E **72** C6
Kinabalu, Gunung *Malaysia* 6°3N 116°14E **83** C3
Kincardine *Canada* 44°10N 81°40W **112** C7
Kincardine *Aberds., U.K.* 56°57N 2°25W **19** J13
Kincardine *Fife, U.K.* 56°4N 3°43W **21** B8
Kinder Scout *U.K.* 53°24N 1°52W **23** F5
Kindersley *Canada* 51°30N 109°10W **108** D9
Kindia *Guinea* 10°0N 12°52W **94** F3
Kindu *Dem. Rep. of the Congo* 2°55S 25°50E **96** E5
Kineshma *Russia* 57°30N 42°5E **72** C7
Kineton *U.K.* 52°10N 1°31W **24** B5
King George I. *Antarctica* 60°0S 60°0W **55** C18
King George Is. *Canada* 57°20N 80°30W **109** D11
King I. *Australia* 39°50S 144°0E **98** H7
King William I. *Canada* 69°10N 97°25W **108** C10
Kingman *U.S.A.* 35°12N 114°4W **110** C4
King's Lynn *U.K.* 52°45N 0°24E **25** A9
King's Sutton *U.K.* 52°2N 1°15W **24** B6
King's Worthy *U.K.* 51°6N 1°17W **24** D6
Kingsbridge *U.K.* 50°17N 3°47W **27** G6
Kingsbury *U.K.* 52°34N 1°40W **23** G5
Kingscourt *Ireland* 53°55N 6°48W **29** D8
Kingskerswell *U.K.* 50°29N 3°35W **27** G6
Kingsland *U.K.* 52°15N 2°48W **24** B3
Kingsteignton *U.K.* 50°33N 3°36W **27** F6
Kingston *Canada* 44°14N 76°30W **109** E12
Kingston *Jamaica* 18°0N 76°50W **114** a
Kingston *N.Y., U.S.A.* 41°56N 73°59W **113** E10
Kingston *Pa., U.S.A.* 41°16N 75°54W **113** E10
Kingston upon Hull *U.K.* 53°45N 0°21W **23** E8
Kingston-upon-Thames □
  U.K. 51°24N 0°17W **25** D8
Kingstown *St. Vincent* 13°10N 61°10W **115** E12
Kingsville *U.S.A.* 27°31N 97°52W **110** E7
Kingswear *U.K.* 50°21N 3°35W **27** G6
Kingswood *U.K.* 51°27N 2°31W **24** D3
Kington *U.K.* 52°13N 3°1W **24** B2
Kingussie *U.K.* 57°6N 4°2W **19** H9
Kinross *U.K.* 56°13N 3°25W **21** B9
Kinsale *Ireland* 51°42N 8°31W **30** E5
Kinsale, Old Hd. of *Ireland* 51°37N 8°33W **30** E5
Kinshasa *Dem. Rep. of the Congo* 4°20S 15°15E **96** E3
Kintore *U.K.* 57°14N 2°20W **19** H13
Kintyre *U.K.* 55°30N 5°35W **20** D4
Kintyre, Mull of *U.K.* 55°17N 5°47W **20** D4
Kippure *Ireland* 53°11N 6°21W **31** B10
Kirensk *Russia* 57°50N 107°55E **79** D12
Kirgiz Steppe *Eurasia* 50°0N 55°0E **73** E10
Kiribati ■ *Pac. Oc.* 3°0S 180°0E **102** H10
Kırıkkale *Turkey* 39°51N 33°32E **73** G5
Kiritimati *Kiribati* 1°58N 157°27W **103** G12
Kirkbean *U.K.* 54°55N 3°36W **21** E9
Kirkbride *U.K.* 54°54N 3°12W **22** C2
Kirkburton *U.K.* 53°37N 1°42W **23** E5
Kirkby *U.K.* 53°30N 2°54W **23** F3
Kirkby-in-Ashfield *U.K.* 53°6N 1°14W **23** F6
Kirkby Lonsdale *U.K.* 54°12N 2°36W **22** D3
Kirkby Malzeard *U.K.* 54°10N 1°37W **22** D5
Kirkby Stephen *U.K.* 54°29N 2°21W **22** D4
Kirkby Thore *U.K.* 54°38N 2°32W **22** C4
Kirkbymoorside *U.K.* 54°16N 0°56W **22** D7
Kirkcaldy *U.K.* 56°7N 3°9W **21** B9
Kirkcudbright *U.K.* 54°50N 4°2W **20** E7
Kirkham *U.K.* 53°47N 2°53W **23** E3
Kirkintilloch *U.K.* 55°56N 4°8W **20** C7
Kirkland Lake *Canada* 48°9N 80°2W **109** E11
Kırklareli *Turkey* 41°44N 27°15E **86** A1

Kirkoswald *U.K.* 54°46N 2°41W **22** C3
Kirksville *U.S.A.* 40°12N 92°35W **111** B8
Kirkūk *Iraq* 35°30N 44°21E **86** C6
Kirkwall *U.K.* 58°59N 2°58W **19** E12
Kirkwhelpington *U.K.* 55°9N 1°59W **22** B5
Kirov *Russia* 58°35N 49°40E **72** C8
Kirovohrad *Ukraine* 48°35N 32°20E **73** E5
Kirriemuir *U.K.* 56°41N 3°1W **19** J11
Kırşehir *Turkey* 39°14N 34°5E **73** G5
Kirthar Range *Pakistan* 27°0N 67°0E **84** F5
Kirtling *U.K.* 52°12N 0°28E **25** B9
Kirtlington *U.K.* 51°53N 1°15W **24** C6
Kirton *U.K.* 52°56N 0°3W **23** G8
Kirton in Lindsey *U.K.* 53°29N 0°34W **23** F7
Kiruna *Sweden* 67°52N 20°15E **63** E8
Kiryū *Japan* 36°24N 139°20E **82** E6
Kisangani
  Dem. Rep. of the Congo 0°35N 25°15E **96** D5
Kishanganj *India* 26°3N 88°14E **85** F16
Kishinev *Moldova* 47°2N 28°50E **67** E15
Kisii *Kenya* 0°40S 34°45E **96** E6
Kislovodsk *Russia* 43°50N 42°45E **73** F7
Kismayu *Somali Rep.* 0°22S 42°32E **88** H3
Kisumu *Kenya* 0°3S 34°45E **96** E6
Kitakyūshū *Japan* 33°50N 130°50E **82** G2
Kitale *Kenya* 1°0N 35°0E **96** D7
Kitami *Japan* 43°48N 143°54E **82** B8
Kitchener *Canada* 43°27N 80°29W **112** D7
Kithnos *Greece* 37°26N 24°27E **71** F11
Kitimat *Canada* 54°3N 128°38W **108** D7
Kittanning *U.S.A.* 40°49N 79°31W **112** E8
Kitwe *Zambia* 12°54S 28°13E **97** G5
Kivu, L. *Dem. Rep. of the Congo* 1°48S 29°0E **96** E5
Kızıl Irmak → *Turkey* 41°44N 35°58E **73** F6
Kizlyar *Russia* 43°51N 46°40E **73** F8
Kladno *Czech Rep.* 50°10N 14°7E **66** C8
Klagenfurt *Austria* 46°38N 14°20E **66** E8
Klaipėda *Lithuania* 55°43N 21°10E **63** F8
Klamath → *U.S.A.* 41°33N 124°5W **110** B2
Klamath Falls *U.S.A.* 42°13N 121°46W **110** B2
Klang *Malaysia* 3°2N 101°26E **83** C2
Klarälven → *Sweden* 59°23N 13°32E **63** F6
Klerksdorp *S. Africa* 26°53S 26°38E **97** K5
Kluane L. *Canada* 61°15N 138°40W **108** C6
Kluang *Malaysia* 2°3N 103°18E **83** C2
Klyuchevskaya, Gora
  Russia 55°50N 160°30E **79** D18
Knaresborough *U.K.* 54°1N 1°28W **23** D6
Knebworth *U.K.* 51°52N 0°11W **25** C8
Knighton *U.K.* 52°21N 3°3W **26** C7
Knock *Ireland* 53°48N 8°55W **28** D4
Knockmealdown Mts. *Ireland* 52°14N 7°56W **30** D7
Knossos *Greece* 35°16N 25°10E **71** G11
Knottingley *U.K.* 53°43N 1°16W **23** E6
Knowle *U.K.* 52°24N 1°44W **23** H5
Knoxville *U.S.A.* 35°58N 83°55W **111** C10
Knoydart *U.K.* 57°3N 5°33W **18** H6
Knutsford *U.K.* 53°18N 2°21W **23** F4
Kōbe *Japan* 34°41N 135°13E **82** F4
Koblenz *Germany* 50°21N 7°36E **66** C4
Kocaeli *Turkey* 40°45N 29°50E **73** F4
Koch Bihar *India* 26°22N 89°29E **85** F16
Kōchi *Japan* 33°30N 133°35E **82** G3
Kodiak *U.S.A.* 57°47N 152°24W **108** D4
Kodiak I. *U.S.A.* 57°30N 152°45W **108** D4
Koforidua *Ghana* 6°3N 0°17W **94** G5
Kōfu *Japan* 35°40N 138°30E **82** F6
Kohat *Pakistan* 33°40N 71°29E **84** C7
Kohima *India* 25°35N 94°10E **85** G19
Kohtla-Järve *Estonia* 59°20N 27°20E **63** F9
Kokkola *Finland* 63°50N 23°8E **63** E8
Koko Kyunzu *Burma* 14°10N 93°25E **85** M18
Kokomo *U.S.A.* 40°29N 86°8W **112** E4
Kokopo *Papua N. G.* 4°22S 152°19E **98** A9
Kōksoak → *Canada* 58°30N 68°10W **109** D13
Kola Pen. *Russia* 67°30N 38°0E **72** A6
Kolar Gold Fields *India* 12°58N 78°16E **84** N11
Kolguyev *Russia* 69°20N 48°30E **72** A8
Kolhapur *India* 16°43N 74°15E **84** L9
Kolkata *India* 22°34N 88°21E **85** H16
Kolomna *Russia* 55°8N 38°45E **72** C6
Kolomyya *Ukraine* 48°31N 25°2E **73** E4
Kolpino *Russia* 59°44N 30°39E **72** C5
Kolwezi *Dem. Rep. of the Congo* 10°40S 25°25E **96** G5
Kolyma → *Russia* 69°30N 161°0E **79** C18
Kolyma Ra. *Russia* 63°0N 157°0E **79** C17
Komatsu *Japan* 36°25N 136°30E **82** E5
Komi □ *Russia* 64°0N 55°0E **72** B10
Kompong Cham *Cambodia* 12°0N 105°30E **83** B2
Komsomolsk *Russia* 50°30N 137°0E **79** D15
Konarhā □ *Afghan.* 34°30N 71°3E **87** C12
Kongur Shan *China* 38°34N 75°18E **80** C2
Konin *Poland* 52°12N 18°15E **67** B10
Konosha *Russia* 61°0N 40°5E **72** B7
Konotop *Ukraine* 51°12N 33°7E **73** D5
Konqi He → *China* 41°0N 86°0E **80** B3
Konya *Turkey* 37°52N 32°35E **73** G5
Kootenay L. *Canada* 49°45N 116°50W **108** E8
Kopet Dagh *Asia* 38°0N 58°0E **87** B9
Korçë *Albania* 40°37N 20°50E **71** D9
Korčula *Croatia* 42°56N 16°57E **70** C7
Kordestān □ *Iran* 36°0N 47°0E **86** C6
Kordofân *Sudan* 13°0N 29°0E **95** F11
Korea, North ■ *Asia* 40°0N 127°0E **81** C7
Korea, South ■ *Asia* 36°0N 128°0E **81** C7
Korea Bay *Korea* 39°0N 124°0E **81** C7
Korea Strait *Asia* 34°0N 129°30E **81** C7
Korhogo *Ivory C.* 9°29N 5°28W **94** G4
Kōriyama *Japan* 37°24N 140°23E **82** E7
Korla *China* 41°45N 86°4E **80** B3
Körös → *Hungary* 46°43N 20°12E **67** E11
Korosten *Ukraine* 50°54N 28°36E **73** D4
Kortrijk *Belgium* 50°50N 3°17E **65** D3
Koryak Ra. *Russia* 61°0N 171°0E **79** C19
Kos *Greece* 36°50N 27°15E **71** F12
Kosciuszko, Mt. *Australia* 36°27S 148°16E **98** H8

Košice *Slovak Rep.* 48°42N 21°15E **67** D11
Kosovo ■ *Europe* 42°30N 21°0E **71** C9
Kosovska Mitrovica *Kosovo* 42°54N 20°52E **71** C9
Kôsti *Sudan* 13°8N 32°43E **95** F12
Kostroma *Russia* 57°50N 40°58E **72** C7
Koszalin *Poland* 54°11N 16°8E **66** A9
Kota *India* 25°14N 75°49E **84** G9
Kota Bharu *Malaysia* 6°7N 102°14E **83** C2
Kota Kinabalu *Malaysia* 6°0N 116°4E **83** C3
Kotabumi *Indonesia* 4°49S 104°54E **83** D2
Kotelnich *Russia* 58°22N 48°24E **72** C8
Kotka *Finland* 60°28N 26°58E **63** E9
Kotlas *Russia* 61°17N 46°43E **72** B8
Kotor *Montenegro* 42°25N 18°47E **71** C8
Kotri *Pakistan* 25°22N 68°22E **84** G6
Kotuy → *Russia* 71°54N 102°6E **79** B12
Kotzebue *U.S.A.* 66°53N 162°39W **108** C3
Koudougou *Burkina Faso* 12°10N 2°20W **94** F5
Koumra *Chad* 8°50N 17°35E **95** G9
Kovel *Ukraine* 51°11N 24°38E **72** D3
Kovrov *Russia* 56°25N 41°25E **72** C7
Kpalimé *Togo* 6°57N 0°44E **94** G6
Kra, Isthmus of *Thailand* 10°15N 99°30E **83** B1
Kragujevac *Serbia* 44°2N 20°56E **71** B9
Krakatoa *Indonesia* 6°10S 105°20E **83** D2
Kraków *Poland* 50°4N 19°57E **67** C10
Kraljevo *Serbia* 43°44N 20°41E **71** C9
Kramatorsk *Ukraine* 48°50N 37°30E **73** E6
Krasnodar *Russia* 45°5N 39°0E **73** E6
Krasnokamsk *Russia* 58°4N 55°48E **72** C10
Krasnoturinsk *Russia* 59°46N 60°12E **72** C11
Krasnoyarsk *Russia* 56°8N 93°0E **79** D11
Krasnyy Luch *Ukraine* 48°13N 39°0E **73** E6
Krefeld *Germany* 51°20N 6°33E **66** C4
Kremenchuk *Ukraine* 49°5N 33°25E **73** E5
Kribi *Cameroon* 2°57N 9°56E **96** D1
Krishna → *India* 15°57N 80°59E **85** M12
Kristiansand *Norway* 58°8N 8°1E **63** F5
Kristiansund *Norway* 63°7N 7°45E **63** E5
Krivoy Rog *Ukraine* 47°51N 33°20E **73** E5
Krk *Croatia* 45°8N 14°40E **70** B6
Kronshtadt *Russia* 59°57N 29°51E **72** B4
Kroonstad *S. Africa* 27°43S 27°19E **97** K5
Kropotkin *Russia* 45°28N 40°28E **73** E7
Krosno *Poland* 49°42N 21°46E **67** D11
Krugersdorp *S. Africa* 26°5S 27°46E **97** K5
Kruševac *Serbia* 43°35N 21°28E **71** C9
Ksar el Kebir *Morocco* 35°0N 6°0W **94** B4
Kuala Belait *Malaysia* 4°35N 114°11E **83** C3
Kuala Lumpur *Malaysia* 3°9N 101°41E **83** C2
Kuala Terengganu *Malaysia* 5°20N 103°8E **83** C2
Kuantan *Malaysia* 3°49N 103°20E **83** C2
Kuching *Malaysia* 1°33N 110°25E **83** C3
Kudymkar *Russia* 59°1N 54°39E **72** C9
Kugluktuk *Canada* 67°50N 115°5W **108** C8
Kuito *Angola* 12°22S 16°55E **97** G3
Kŭlob *Tajikistan* 37°55N 69°50E **87** B12
Kulsary *Kazakhstan* 46°59N 54°1E **73** E9
Kuma → *Russia* 44°55N 47°0E **73** F8
Kumagaya *Japan* 36°9N 139°22E **82** E6
Kumamoto *Japan* 32°45N 130°45E **82** G2
Kumanovo *Macedonia* 42°9N 21°42E **71** C9
Kumasi *Ghana* 6°41N 1°38W **94** G5
Kumba *Cameroon* 4°36N 9°24E **96** D1
Kumbakonam *India* 10°58N 79°25E **84** P11
Kumertau *Russia* 52°45N 55°57E **72** D10
Kungur *Russia* 57°25N 56°57E **72** C10
Kunlun Shan *Asia* 36°0N 86°30E **80** C3
Kunming *China* 25°1N 102°41E **80** D5
Kuopio *Finland* 62°53N 27°35E **63** E9
Kupang *Indonesia* 10°19S 123°39E **83** E4
Kuqa *China* 41°35N 82°30E **80** B3
Kür → *Azerbaijan* 39°29N 49°15E **73** G8
Kurdistan *Asia* 37°20N 43°30E **86** B5
Kure *Japan* 34°14N 132°32E **82** F3
Kurgan *Russia* 55°26N 65°18E **79** D8
Kuril Is. *Russia* 45°0N 150°0E **79** E17
Kuril-Kamchatka Trench
  Pac. Oc. 44°0N 153°0E **102** C7
Kurnool *India* 15°45N 78°0E **84** M11
Kursk *Russia* 51°42N 36°11E **72** D6
Kuruktag *China* 41°0N 89°0E **80** B3
Kurume *Japan* 33°15N 130°30E **82** G2
Kushiro *Japan* 43°0N 144°25E **82** B9
Kushtia *Bangla.* 23°55N 89°5E **85** H16
Kuskokwim B. *U.S.A.* 59°45N 162°25W **108** D3
Kütahya *Turkey* 39°30N 30°2E **73** G5
Kutaisi *Georgia* 42°19N 42°40E **73** F7
Kuujjuaq *Canada* 58°6N 68°15W **109** D13
Kuujjuarapik *Canada* 55°20N 77°35W **109** D12
Kuwait *Kuwait* 29°30N 48°0E **86** D7
Kuwait ■ *Asia* 29°30N 47°30E **86** D6
Kuybyshev Res. *Russia* 55°2N 49°30E **72** C8
Kuznetsk *Russia* 53°12N 46°40E **72** D8
Kuzomen *Russia* 66°22N 36°50E **72** A6
KwaMashu *S. Africa* 29°45S 30°58E **97** K6
KwaZulu Natal □ *S. Africa* 29°0S 30°0E **97** K6
Kwekwe *Zimbabwe* 18°58S 29°48E **97** H5
Kyle of Lochalsh *U.K.* 57°17N 5°44W **18** H6
Kyoga, L. *Uganda* 1°35N 33°0E **96** D6
Kyōto *Japan* 35°0N 135°45E **82** F4
Kyrenia *Cyprus* 35°20N 33°20E **86** C3
Kyrgyzstan ■ *Asia* 42°0N 75°0E **79** E9
Kythira *Greece* 36°8N 23°0E **71** F10
Kyūshū *Japan* 33°0N 131°0E **82** G2
Kyustendil *Bulgaria* 42°16N 22°41E **71** C10
Kyzyl Kum *Uzbekistan* 42°30N 65°0E **87** A10
Kyzyl-Orda *Kazakhstan* 44°48N 65°28E **79** E8

L

La Alcarria *Spain* 40°31N 2°45W **69** B4
La Ceiba *Honduras* 15°40N 86°50W **114** D7
La Coruña *Spain* 43°20N 8°25W **69** A1
La Crosse *U.S.A.* 43°48N 91°15W **112** D2
La Désirade *Guadeloupe* 16°18N 61°3W **114** b
La Grande *U.S.A.* 45°20N 118°5W **110** A4
La Grande → *Canada* 53°50N 79°0W **109** D12

La Grange

Lubumbashi

La Grange *U.S.A.* 33°2N 85°2W **111** D10
La Habana *Cuba* 23°8N 82°22W **115** C8
La Junta *U.S.A.* 37°59N 103°33W **110** C6
La Línea de la Concepción
 Spain 36°15N 5°23W **69** D3
La Loche *Canada* 56°29N 109°26W **108** D9
La Louvière *Belgium* 50°27N 4°10E **65** D4
La Mancha *Spain* 39°10N 2°54W **69** C4
La Oroya *Peru* 11°32S 75°54W **120** D2
La Palma *Canary Is.* 28°40N 17°50W **94** C2
La Paz *Bolivia* 16°20S 68°10W **120** D3
La Paz *Mexico* 24°10N 110°18W **114** C2
La Perouse Str. *Asia* 45°40N 142°0E **102** C6
La Plata *Argentina* 35°0S 57°55W **121** F4
La Quiaca *Argentina* 22°5S 65°35W **121** E3
La Rioja *Argentina* 29°20S 67°0W **121** E3
La Rioja □ *Spain* 42°20N 2°20W **69** A4
La Roche-sur-Yon *France* 46°40N 1°25W **68** C3
La Rochelle *France* 46°10N 1°9W **68** C3
La Romana *Dom. Rep.* 18°27N 68°57W **115** D11
La Ronge *Canada* 55°5N 105°20W **108** D9
La Sarre *Canada* 48°45N 79°15W **112** A8
La Serena *Chile* 29°55S 71°10W **121** E2
La Seyne-sur-Mer *France* 43°7N 5°52E **68** E6
La Spézia *Italy* 44°7N 9°50E **70** B3
La Tortuga *Venezuela* 11°0N 65°22W **120** A3
La Trinité *Martinique* 14°43N 60°58W **114** c
La Tuque *Canada* 47°30N 72°50W **109** E12
La Vega *Dom. Rep.* 19°20N 70°30W **115** D10
Labé *Guinea* 11°24N 12°16W **94** F3
Labinsk *Russia* 44°40N 40°48E **73** F7
Laborie *St. Lucia* 13°45N 61°2W **115** f
Labrador *Canada* 53°20N 61°0W **109** D13
Labrador City *Canada* 52°57N 66°55W **109** D13
Labrador Sea *Atl. Oc.* 57°0N 54°0W **109** D14
Labuan *Malaysia* 5°21N 115°13E **83** C3
Lac La Biche *Canada* 54°45N 111°58W **108** D8
Lac-Mégantic *Canada* 45°35N 70°53W **113** C12
Laccadive Is. = Lakshadweep Is.
 India 10°0N 72°30E **74** G9
Laceby *U.K.* 53°33N 0°10W **23** E8
Lacock *U.K.* 51°24N 2°7W **24** D4
Lacombe *Canada* 52°30N 113°44W **108** D8
Laconia *U.S.A.* 43°32N 71°28W **113** D12
Ladakh Ra. *India* 34°0N 78°0E **84** C11
Ladder Hills *U.K.* 57°13N 3°16W **19** H11
Ladock *U.K.* 50°19N 4°58W **27** G4
Ladoga, L. *Russia* 61°15N 30°30E **72** B5
Ladysmith *S. Africa* 28°32S 29°46E **97** K5
Ladysmith *U.S.A.* 45°28N 91°12W **112** C2
Lae *Papua N. G.* 6°40S 147°2E **98** B8
Lafayette *Ind., U.S.A.* 40°25N 86°54W **112** E4
Lafayette *La., U.S.A.* 30°14N 92°1W **111** D8
Lafia *Nigeria* 8°30N 8°34E **94** G7
Lagan → *U.K.* 54°36N 5°55W **29** B10
Lagarto *Brazil* 10°54S 37°41W **122** B3
Lagdo, Rés. de *Cameroon* 8°40N 14°0E **95** G8
Laghouat *Algeria* 33°50N 2°59E **94** B6
Lagos *Nigeria* 6°25N 3°27E **94** G6
Lagos *Portugal* 37°5N 8°41W **69** D1
Lahn → *Germany* 50°19N 7°37E **66** C4
Lahore *Pakistan* 31°32N 74°22E **84** D9
Lahti *Finland* 60°58N 25°40E **63** E9
Lairg *U.K.* 58°2N 4°24W **19** F9
Laizhou *China* 37°8N 119°57E **81** C6
Lake Charles *U.S.A.* 30°14N 93°13W **111** D8
Lake City *U.S.A.* 30°11N 82°38W **111** D10
Lake District △ *U.K.* 54°30N 3°21W **22** C2
Lake Havasu City *U.S.A.* 34°27N 114°22W **110** D4
Lakeland *U.S.A.* 28°3N 81°57W **111** E10
Lakenheath *U.K.* 52°25N 0°32E **25** B10
Lakewood *U.S.A.* 41°28N 81°47W **112** E7
Lakshadweep Is. *India* 10°0N 72°30E **74** G9
Lamar *U.S.A.* 38°5N 102°37W **110** C6
Lambaréné *Gabon* 0°41S 10°12E **96** E2
Lambay I. *Ireland* 53°29N 6°1W **31** B10
Lamberhurst *U.K.* 51°5N 0°24E **25** D9
Lambeth □ *U.K.* 51°28N 0°6W **25** D8
Lambley *U.K.* 54°56N 2°30W **22** C4
Lambourn *U.K.* 51°30N 1°32W **24** C5
Lamesa *U.S.A.* 32°44N 101°58W **110** D6
Lammermuir *U.K.* 55°50N 2°25W **21** C11
Lammermuir Hills *U.K.* 55°50N 2°40W **21** C10
Lamon B. *Phil.* 14°30N 122°20E **83** B4
Lampedusa *Medit. S.* 35°36N 12°40E **70** G5
Lampeter *U.K.* 52°7N 4°4W **26** D3
Lamu *Kenya* 2°16S 40°55E **96** E8
Lanark *U.K.* 55°40N 3°47W **21** C8
Lancashire □ *U.K.* 53°50N 2°48W **23** E3
Lancaster *U.K.* 54°3N 2°48W **22** D3
Lancaster *N.H., U.S.A.* 44°29N 71°34W **113** C12
Lancaster *Pa., U.S.A.* 40°2N 76°19W **112** E9
Lancaster *Wis., U.S.A.* 42°51N 90°43W **112** D2
Lancaster Sd. *Canada* 74°13N 84°0W **109** B11
Lanchester *U.K.* 54°50N 1°44W **22** C5
Lancing *U.K.* 50°49N 0°19W **25** E8
Landes *France* 44°0N 1°0W **68** D3
Landkey *U.K.* 51°3N 4°0W **27** E6
Land's End *U.K.* 50°4N 5°44W **27** G2
Langholm *U.K.* 55°9N 3°0W **21** D10
Langport *U.K.* 51°2N 2°50W **24** D3
Langreo *Spain* 43°18N 5°40W **69** A3
Langres *France* 47°52N 5°20E **68** C6
Langres, Plateau de *France* 47°45N 5°3E **68** C6
Langsa *Indonesia* 4°30N 97°57E **83** C1
Langstrothdale Chase *U.K.* 54°14N 2°13W **22** D4
Langtoft *U.K.* 52°42N 0°20W **23** G8
Langtree *U.K.* 50°55N 4°13W **27** F5
Languedoc *France* 43°58N 3°55E **68** E5
Lannion *France* 48°46N 3°29W **68** B2
L'Annonciation *Canada* 46°25N 74°55W **113** B10
L'Anse *U.S.A.* 46°45N 88°27W **112** B3
L'Anse la Raye *St. Lucia* 13°55N 61°3W **115** f
Lansing *U.S.A.* 42°44N 84°33W **112** D5
Lanzarote *Canary Is.* 29°0N 13°40W **94** C3
Lanzhou *China* 36°1N 103°52E **80** C5
Laoag *Phil.* 18°7N 120°34E **83** B4
Laois □ *Ireland* 52°57N 7°36W **31** D7

Laon *France* 49°33N 3°35E **68** B5
Laos ■ *Asia* 17°45N 105°0E **83** B2
Lapeer *U.S.A.* 43°3N 83°19W **112** D6
Lapford *U.K.* 50°51N 3°48W **27** F6
Lapland *Europe* 68°7N 24°0E **63** D8
LaPorte *U.S.A.* 41°36N 86°43W **112** E4
Laptev Sea *Russia* 76°0N 125°0E **79** B14
L'Áquila *Italy* 42°22N 13°22E **70** C5
Laramie *U.S.A.* 41°19N 105°35W **110** B5
Laramie Mts. *U.S.A.* 42°0N 105°30W **110** B5
Laredo *U.S.A.* 27°30N 99°30W **110** E7
Largs *U.K.* 55°47N 4°52W **20** C6
Larisa *Greece* 39°36N 22°27E **71** E10
Larnaca *Cyprus* 34°55N 33°38E **86** C3
Larne *U.K.* 54°51N 5°51W **29** B10
Larne L. *U.K.* 54°50N 5°48W **29** B10
Larrimah *Australia* 15°35S 133°12E **98** D5
Larsen Ice Shelf *Antarctica* 67°0S 62°0W **55** C17
Larvik *Norway* 59°4N 10°2E **63** F6
Las Cruces *U.S.A.* 32°19N 106°47W **110** D5
Las Palmas *Canary Is.* 28°7N 15°26W **94** C2
Las Tunas *Cuba* 20°58N 76°59W **115** C9
Las Vegas *N. Mex., U.S.A.* 35°36N 105°13W **110** C5
Las Vegas *Nev., U.S.A.* 36°10N 115°8W **110** C3
Lashio *Burma* 22°56N 97°45E **85** H20
Lassen Pk. *U.S.A.* 40°29N 121°30W **110** B2
Lastoursville *Gabon* 0°55S 12°38E **96** E2
Latacunga *Ecuador* 0°50S 78°35W **120** C2
Latakia *Syria* 35°30N 35°45E **86** C3
Latina *Italy* 41°28N 12°52E **70** D5
Latvia ■ *Europe* 56°50N 24°0E **63** F8
Lauder *U.K.* 55°43N 2°43W **21** C10
Lauderdale *U.K.* 55°44N 2°41W **21** C10
Launceston *Australia* 41°24S 147°8E **98** J8
Launceston *U.K.* 50°38N 4°22W **27** F5
Laune → *Ireland* 52°7N 9°47W **30** D3
Laurel *U.S.A.* 31°41N 89°8W **111** D9
Laurencekirk *U.K.* 56°50N 2°28W **19** J13
Lausanne *Switz.* 46°32N 6°38E **66** E4
Lavagh More *Ireland* 54°46N 8°6W **28** B5
Laval *Canada* 45°33N 73°42W **113** C11
Laval *France* 48°4N 0°48W **68** B3
Lavendon *U.K.* 52°11N 0°39W **25** B7
Lavenham *U.K.* 52°6N 0°48E **25** B10
Lavras *Brazil* 21°20S 45°0W **122** D2
Lawrence *Kans., U.S.A.* 38°58N 95°14W **111** C7
Lawrence *Mass., U.S.A.* 42°43N 71°10W **113** D12
Lawton *U.S.A.* 34°37N 98°25W **110** D7
Laxey *U.K.* 54°14N 4°23W **29** C13
Laxfield *U.K.* 52°18N 1°22E **25** B11
Laxford, L. *U.K.* 58°24N 5°6W **18** F7
Lazio □ *Italy* 42°10N 12°30E **70** C5
Lazonby *U.K.* 54°46N 2°42W **22** C3
Le Creusot *France* 46°48N 4°24E **68** C6
Le François *Martinique* 14°38N 60°57W **114** c
Le Gosier *Guadeloupe* 16°14N 61°29W **114** b
Le Havre *France* 49°30N 0°5E **68** B4
Le Lamentin *Martinique* 14°35N 61°2W **114** c
Le Mans *France* 48°0N 0°10E **68** C4
Le Marin *Martinique* 14°27N 60°55W **114** c
Le Moule *Guadeloupe* 16°20N 61°22W **114** b
Le Prêcheur *Martinique* 14°50N 61°12W **114** c
Le Puy-en-Velay *France* 45°3N 3°52E **68** D5
Le Robert *Martinique* 14°40N 60°56W **114** c
Le St-Esprit *Martinique* 14°34N 60°56W **114** c
Lea → *U.K.* 53°22N 0°45W **23** F7
Leadenham *U.K.* 51°31N 0°1E **25** D9
Leamington *Canada* 42°3N 82°36W **112** D6
Leane, L. *Ireland* 52°2N 9°32W **30** D3
Leatherhead *U.K.* 51°18N 0°20W **25** D8
Leavenworth *U.S.A.* 39°19N 94°55W **111** C8
Lebanon *Ind., U.S.A.* 40°3N 86°28W **112** E4
Lebanon *Ky., U.S.A.* 37°34N 85°15W **112** G5
Lebanon *Mo., U.S.A.* 37°41N 92°40W **111** C81
Lebanon *Pa., U.S.A.* 40°20N 76°26W **112** E9
Lebanon ■ *Asia* 34°0N 36°0E **86** C3
Lebu *Chile* 37°40S 73°47W **121** F2
Lecce *Italy* 40°23N 18°11E **71** D8
Lechlade *U.K.* 51°42N 1°41W **24** C5
Ledbury *U.K.* 52°2N 2°25W **24** B4
Lee → *Ireland* 51°53N 8°56W **30** E5
Lee-on-the-Solent *U.K.* 50°48N 1°12W **24** E6
Leech L. *U.S.A.* 47°10N 94°24W **111** A8
Leeds *U.K.* 53°48N 1°33W **23** E5
Leek *U.K.* 53°7N 2°1W **23** F4
Leeuwarden *Neths.* 53°15N 5°48E **65** A5
Leeuwin, C. *Australia* 34°20S 115°9E **98** G2
Leeward Is. *Atl. Oc.* 16°30N 63°30W **115** D12
Lefkada *Greece* 38°40N 20°43E **71** E9
Leganés *Spain* 40°19N 3°45W **69** B4
Legazpi *Phil.* 13°10N 123°45E **83** B4
Legionowo *Poland* 52°25N 20°50E **67** B11
Legnica *Poland* 51°12N 16°10E **66** C9
Leicester *U.K.* 52°38N 1°8W **23** G6
Leicestershire □ *U.K.* 52°41N 1°17W **23** G6
Leiden *Neths.* 52°9N 4°30E **65** B4
Leigh *Gt. Man., U.K.* 53°30N 2°32W **23** E3
Leigh *Hereford, U.K.* 52°11N 2°20W **24** B4
Leighton Buzzard *U.K.* 51°54N 0°38W **25** C7
Leine → *Germany* 52°43N 9°36E **66** B5
Leinster □ *Ireland* 53°3N 7°8W **31** B8
Leinster, Mt. *Ireland* 52°37N 6°46W **31** C9
Leintwardine *U.K.* 52°22N 2°51W **24** B3
Leipzig *Germany* 51°18N 12°22E **66** C7
Leiston *U.K.* 52°12N 1°36E **25** B12
Leith *U.K.* 55°59N 3°11W **21** C9
Leith Hill *U.K.* 51°11N 0°22W **25** D8
Leitholm *U.K.* 55°41N 2°20W **21** C11
Leitrim *Ireland* 54°0N 8°5W **28** C5
Leitrim □ *Ireland* 54°8N 8°0W **28** C5
Leixlip *Ireland* 53°22N 6°30W **31** B9
Leizhou Pen. *China* 21°0N 110°0E **81** D6
Lek → *Neths.* 51°54N 4°35E **65** C4
Lelant *U.K.* 50°11N 5°26W **27** G3
Lelystad *Neths.* 52°30N 5°25E **65** B5
Léman, L. *Europe* 46°26N 6°30E **66** E4
Lena → *Russia* 72°52N 126°40E **79** B14

Lenham *U.K.* 51°14N 0°44E **25** D10
Lennox Hills *U.K.* 56°3N 4°12W **20** B7
Lens *France* 50°26N 2°50E **68** A5
Leominster *U.K.* 52°14N 2°43W **24** B3
Leominster *U.S.A.* 42°32N 71°46W **113** D12
León *Mexico* 21°6N 101°41W **114** C4
León *Nic.* 12°20N 86°51W **114** E7
León *Spain* 42°38N 5°34W **69** A3
Leonora *Australia* 28°49S 121°19E **98** F3
Leopoldina *Brazil* 21°28S 42°40W **122** D2
Lerwick *U.K.* 60°9N 1°9W **18** B15
Les Cayes *Haiti* 18°15N 73°46W **115** D10
Les Sables-d'Olonne *France* 46°30N 1°45W **68** C3
Lesbos *Greece* 39°10N 26°20E **71** E12
Lesbury *U.K.* 55°25N 1°36W **22** B5
Leshan *China* 29°33N 103°41E **80** D5
Leskovac *Serbia* 43°0N 21°58E **71** C9
Lesotho ■ *Africa* 29°40S 28°0E **97** K5
Lesser Antilles *W. Indies* 15°0N 61°0W **115** D12
Lesser Slave L. *Canada* 55°30N 115°25W **108** D8
Lesser Sunda Is. *Indonesia* 8°0S 120°0E **83** D4
Leszno *Poland* 51°50N 16°30E **67** C9
Letchworth *U.K.* 51°59N 0°13W **25** C8
Lethbridge *Canada* 49°45N 112°45W **108** E8
Leti, Kepulauan *Indonesia* 8°10S 128°0E **83** D4
Leticia *Colombia* 4°9S 70°0W **120** C2
Letterkenny *Ireland* 54°57N 7°45W **28** B6
Leuchars *U.K.* 56°24N 2°53W **21** B10
Leuven *Belgium* 50°52N 4°42E **65** D4
Leven *E. Riding, U.K.* 53°53N 0°18W **23** E8
Leven *Fife, U.K.* 56°12N 3°0W **21** B10
Leven → *U.K.* 54°31N 1°19W **22** C6
Leven, L. *Highl., U.K.* 56°42N 5°6W **18** J7
Leven, L. *Perth & Kinr., U.K.* 56°12N 3°22W **21** B9
Lévis *Canada* 46°48N 71°9W **113** B12
Lewes *U.K.* 50°52N 0°1E **25** E9
Lewis *U.K.* 58°9N 6°40W **18** F4
Lewis, Butt of *U.K.* 58°31N 6°16W **18** E5
Lewisham □ *U.K.* 51°27N 0°1W **25** D8
Lewisporte *Canada* 49°15N 55°3W **109** E14
Lewiston *Idaho, U.S.A.* 46°25N 117°1W **110** A3
Lewiston *Maine, U.S.A.* 44°6N 70°13W **113** C12
Lewistown *Mont., U.S.A.* 47°4N 109°26W **110** A5
Lewistown *Pa., U.S.A.* 40°36N 77°34W **112** E9
Lexington *U.S.A.* 38°3N 84°30W **112** F5
Lexington Park *U.S.A.* 38°16N 76°27W **112** F9
Leyburn *U.K.* 54°19N 1°48W **22** C5
Leyland *U.K.* 53°42N 2°43W **23** E3
Leysdown on Sea *U.K.* 51°24N 0°56E **25** D10
Leyte □ *Phil.* 11°0N 125°0E **83** B4
Lhasa *China* 29°25N 90°58E **80** D4
Lhazê *China* 29°5N 87°38E **80** D3
L'Hospitalet de Llobregat *Spain* 41°21N 2°6E **69** B7
Lianyungang *China* 34°40N 119°11E **81** C6
Liaodong Pen. *China* 40°0N 122°30E **81** C7
Liaoning □ *China* 41°40N 122°30E **81** B7
Liaoyang *China* 41°15N 122°58E **81** B7
Liaoyuan *China* 42°58N 125°2E **81** B7
Liard → *Canada* 61°51N 121°18W **108** C7
Liberal *U.S.A.* 37°3N 100°55W **110** C6
Liberec *Czech Rep.* 50°47N 15°7E **66** C8
Liberia ■ *W. Afr.* 6°30N 9°30W **94** G4
Libourne *France* 44°55N 0°14W **68** D3
Libreville *Gabon* 0°25N 9°26E **96** D1
Libya ■ *N. Afr.* 27°0N 17°0E **95** C9
Libyan Desert *Africa* 25°0N 25°0E **95** C10
Libyan Plateau *Egypt* 30°40N 26°30E **95** B11
Lichfield *U.K.* 52°41N 1°49W **23** G5
Liddesdale *U.K.* 55°14N 2°50W **21** D10
Liechtenstein ■ *Europe* 47°8N 9°35E **66** E5
Liège *Belgium* 50°38N 5°35E **65** D5
Liepāja *Latvia* 56°30N 21°0E **63** F8
Liffey → *Ireland* 53°21N 6°13W **31** B10
Lifford *Ireland* 54°51N 7°29W **28** B7
Liguria □ *Italy* 44°30N 8°50E **70** B3
Ligurian Sea *Medit. S.* 43°20N 9°0E **70** C3
Lihue *U.S.A.* 21°59N 159°23W **110** H15
Lijiang *China* 26°55N 100°20E **80** D5
Likasi *Dem. Rep. of the Congo* 10°55S 26°48E **96** G5
Lille *France* 50°38N 3°3E **68** A5
Lillehammer *Norway* 61°8N 10°30E **63** E6
Lilleshall *U.K.* 52°44N 2°23W **23** G4
Lilongwe *Malawi* 14°0S 33°48E **97** G6
Lima *Peru* 12°3S 77°2W **120** D2
Lima *U.S.A.* 40°44N 84°6W **112** E5
Limassol *Cyprus* 34°42N 33°1E **86** C3
Limavady *U.K.* 55°3N 6°56W **29** A8
Limay → *Argentina* 39°0S 68°0W **121** F3
Limbe *Cameroon* 4°1N 9°10E **96** D1
Limburg □ *Neths.* 51°20N 5°55E **65** C5
Limeira *Brazil* 22°35S 47°28W **122** D1
Limerick *Ireland* 52°40N 8°37W **30** C5
Limerick □ *Ireland* 52°30N 8°50W **30** D5
Limfjorden *Denmark* 56°55N 9°0E **63** F5
Limnos *Greece* 39°50N 25°5E **71** E11
Limoges *France* 45°50N 1°15E **68** D4
Limón *Costa Rica* 10°0N 83°2W **115** F8
Limousin □ *France* 45°30N 1°30E **68** D4
Limoux *France* 43°4N 2°12E **68** E5
Limpopo → *Africa* 25°5S 33°30E **97** K6
Linares *Chile* 35°50S 71°40W **121** F2
Linares *Mexico* 24°52N 99°34W **114** C5
Linares *Spain* 38°10N 3°40W **69** C4
Linchuan *China* 27°57N 116°15E **81** D6
Lincoln *U.K.* 53°14N 0°32W **23** F7
Lincoln *Ill., U.S.A.* 40°9N 89°22W **112** E3
Lincoln *Maine, U.S.A.* 45°22N 68°30W **113** C13
Lincoln *Nebr., U.S.A.* 40°49N 96°41W **111** B7
Lincoln Sea *Arctic* 84°0N 55°0W **54** A5
Lincolnshire □ *U.K.* 53°14N 0°32W **23** F7
Lincolnshire Wolds *U.K.* 53°26N 0°13W **23** F8
Lindale *U.K.* 54°14N 2°53W **22** C3
Lindesnes *Norway* 57°58N 7°3E **63** F5
Lindsay *Canada* 44°22N 78°43W **112** C8
Linfen *China* 36°3N 111°30E **81** C6
Lingfield *U.K.* 51°11N 0°0 **25** D8
Lingga, Kepulauan *Indonesia* 0°10S 104°30E **83** D2
Linhai *China* 28°50N 121°8E **81** D7

Linhares *Brazil* 19°25S 40°4W **122** C2
Linhe *China* 40°48N 107°20E **80** B5
Linkinhorne *U.K.* 50°32N 4°24W **27** F5
Linköping *Sweden* 58°28N 15°36E **63** F7
Linnhe, L. *U.K.* 56°36N 5°25W **20** A5
Linqing *China* 36°50N 115°42E **81** C6
Linslade *U.K.* 51°54N 0°41W **25** C7
Linstead *Jamaica* 18°8N 77°2W **114** a
Linton *U.K.* 52°6N 0°17E **25** B9
Linton *U.S.A.* 39°2N 87°10W **112** F4
Linxia *China* 35°36N 103°10E **80** C5
Linyi *China* 35°5N 118°21E **81** C6
Linz *Austria* 48°18N 14°18E **66** D8
Lion, G. du *France* 43°10N 4°0E **68** E6
Lipa *Phil.* 13°57N 121°10E **83** B4
Lipari *Italy* 38°26N 14°58E **70** E6
Lipetsk *Russia* 52°37N 39°35E **72** D6
Lippe → *Germany* 51°39N 6°36E **66** C4
Liquillo, Sierra de *Puerto Rico* 18°20N 65°47W **115** d
Lisbon *Portugal* 38°42N 9°8W **69** C1
Lisburn *U.K.* 54°31N 6°3W **29** B9
Liscannor B. *Ireland* 52°55N 9°24W **30** C4
Lisianski I. *U.S.A.* 26°2N 174°0W **102** E10
Lisieux *France* 49°10N 0°12E **68** B4
Liskeard *U.K.* 50°27N 4°29W **27** G5
Liski *Russia* 51°3N 39°30E **73** D6
Lismore *Australia* 28°44S 153°21E **98** F9
Lismore *Ireland* 52°8N 7°55W **30** D7
Liss *U.K.* 51°2N 0°54W **25** D7
Listowel *Canada* 43°44N 80°58W **112** D7
Listowel *Ireland* 52°27N 9°29W **30** D4
Litani → *Lebanon* 33°20N 35°15E **86** C3
Litcham *U.K.* 52°44N 0°47E **25** A10
Litchfield *U.S.A.* 39°11N 89°39W **112** F3
Litherland *U.K.* 53°29N 2°59W **23** F3
Lithuania ■ *Europe* 55°30N 24°0E **63** F8
Little Current *Canada* 45°55N 82°0W **112** C7
Little Khingan Mts. *China* 49°0N 127°0E **81** B7
Little Minch *U.K.* 57°35N 6°45W **18** G4
Little Missouri → *U.S.A.* 47°36N 102°25W **110** A6
Little Ouse → *U.K.* 52°22N 1°12E **25** B11
Little Rock *U.S.A.* 34°45N 92°17W **111** D8
Little Walsingham *U.K.* 52°54N 0°52E **25** A10
Littlehampton *U.K.* 50°49N 0°32W **25** E7
Littleport *U.K.* 52°27N 0°19E **25** B9
Littlestone-on-Sea *U.K.* 50°58N 0°58E **25** E10
Liupanshui *China* 26°38N 104°48E **80** D5
Liuzhou *China* 24°22N 109°22E **81** D5
Liverpool *Canada* 44°5N 64°41W **109** E13
Liverpool *U.K.* 53°25N 3°0W **23** F2
Livingston *U.S.A.* 45°40N 110°34W **110** A4
Livingstone *Zambia* 17°46S 25°52E **97** H5
Livonia *U.S.A.* 42°23N 83°23W **112** D6
Livorno *Italy* 43°33N 10°19E **70** C4
Lizard *U.K.* 49°58N 5°13W **27** H3
Lizard Pt. *U.K.* 49°57N 5°13W **27** H3
Ljubljana *Slovenia* 46°4N 14°33E **66** E8
Llandeilo *U.K.* 51°53N 3°59W **26** D6
Llandovery *U.K.* 51°59N 3°48W **26** D6
Llandrindod Wells *U.K.* 52°14N 3°22W **26** B6
Llandudno *U.K.* 53°19N 3°50W **26** A6
Llanelli *U.K.* 51°41N 4°10W **26** D5
Llanerchymedd *U.K.* 53°20N 4°23W **26** A5
Llanfair Caereinion *U.K.* 52°39N 3°20W **26** B7
Llanfair Talhaiarn *U.K.* 53°13N 3°37W **26** A6
Llanfairfechan *U.K.* 53°15N 3°58W **26** A6
Llangefni *U.K.* 53°15N 4°18W **26** A5
Llangollen *U.K.* 52°58N 3°11W **26** B7
Llanidloes *U.K.* 52°27N 3°31W **26** C6
Llanllyfni *U.K.* 53°2N 4°17W **26** A5
Llano Estacado *U.S.A.* 33°30N 103°0W **110** D6
Llanos *S. Amer.* 5°0N 71°35W **120** B2
Llanquihue, L. *Chile* 41°10S 72°50W **121** G2
Llanrhystyd *U.K.* 52°19N 4°7W **26** C5
Llantrisant *U.K.* 51°32N 3°22W **27** D7
Llantwit-Major *U.K.* 51°24N 3°29W **27** E7
Llanwrtyd Wells *U.K.* 52°7N 3°38W **26** C6
Llanybydwel *U.K.* 52°48N 3°8W **26** B7
Llanymynech *U.K.* 52°47N 3°5W **26** B7
Lleida *Spain* 41°37N 0°39E **69** B6
Lleyn Peninsula *U.K.* 52°51N 4°36W **26** B4
Llobregat → *Spain* 41°19N 2°5E **69** B7
Lloret de Mar *Spain* 41°41N 2°53E **69** B7
Lloydminster *Canada* 53°17N 110°0W **108** D9
Llullaillaco, Volcán *S. Amer.* 24°43S 68°30W **121** E3
Lobatse *Botswana* 25°12S 25°40E **97** K5
Lobito *Angola* 12°18S 13°35E **97** G2
Loch Lomond and the Trossachs △
 U.K. 56°10N 4°40W **20** B6
Lochaber *U.K.* 56°59N 5°1W **18** J7
Locharbriggs *U.K.* 55°7N 3°35W **21** D8
Lochboisdale *U.K.* 57°9N 7°20W **18** H3
Loches *France* 47°7N 1°0E **68** C4
Lochgelly *U.K.* 56°7N 3°19W **21** B9
Lochgilphead *U.K.* 56°2N 5°26W **20** B5
Lochinver *U.K.* 58°9N 5°14W **18** F7
Lochmaben *U.K.* 55°8N 3°27W **21** D9
Lochmaddy *U.K.* 57°36N 7°10W **18** G3
Lochnagar *U.K.* 56°57N 3°15W **19** J11
Lochy, L. *U.K.* 57°0N 4°53W **19** J8
Lock Haven *U.S.A.* 41°8N 77°28W **112** E9
Lockerbie *U.K.* 55°7N 3°21W **21** D9
Loddon *U.K.* 52°32N 1°31E **25** A12
Lodwar *Kenya* 3°7N 35°36E **96** D7
Łódź *Poland* 51°45N 19°27E **67** C10
Lofoten *Norway* 68°30N 14°0E **63** D6
Loftus *U.K.* 54°34N 0°53W **22** C7
Logan *Ohio, U.S.A.* 39°32N 82°25W **112** F6
Logan *Utah, U.S.A.* 41°44N 111°50W **110** B4
Logan *W. Va., U.S.A.* 37°51N 81°59W **112** G7
Logan, Mt. *Canada* 60°34N 140°23W **108** C5
Logansport *U.S.A.* 40°45N 86°22W **112** E4
Logroño *Spain* 42°28N 2°27W **69** A4
Lohardaga *India* 23°27N 84°45E **85** H14
Loir → *France* 47°33N 0°32W **68** C3
Loire → *France* 47°16N 2°10W **68** C2

Loja *Ecuador* 3°59S 79°16W **120** C2
Lomami →
 Dem. Rep. of the Congo 0°46N 24°16E **96** D4
Lombárdia □ *Italy* 45°40N 9°30E **70** B3
Lomblen *Indonesia* 8°30S 123°32E **83** D4
Lombok *Indonesia* 8°45S 116°30E **83** D3
Lomé *Togo* 6°9N 1°20E **94** G6
Lomela →
 Dem. Rep. of the Congo 0°15S 20°40E **96** E4
Lomond, L. *U.K.* 56°8N 4°38W **20** B6
Łomża *Poland* 53°10N 22°2E **67** B12
London *Canada* 42°59N 81°15W **112** D7
London *U.K.* 51°30N 0°3W **25** D8
London Gatwick ✈ (LGW)
 U.K. 51°10N 0°11W **25** D8
London Heathrow ✈ (LHR)
 U.K. 51°28N 0°27W **25** D8
London Stansted ✈ (STN) *U.K.* 51°54N 0°14E **25** C9
Londonderry *U.K.* 55°0N 7°20W **28** A7
Londonderry □ *U.K.* 55°0N 7°20W **28** A7
Londonderry, C. *Australia* 13°45S 126°55E **98** C4
Londrina *Brazil* 23°18S 51°10W **121** E4
Long, L. *U.K.* 56°4N 4°50W **20** B6
Long Beach *U.S.A.* 33°46N 118°11W **110** D3
Long Bennington *U.K.* 52°59N 0°44W **23** G7
Long Branch *U.S.A.* 40°18N 74°0W **113** E11
Long Clawson *U.K.* 52°51N 0°55W **23** G7
Long Crendon *U.K.* 51°46N 0°59W **25** C7
Long Eaton *U.K.* 52°53N 1°15W **23** G6
Long I. *Bahamas* 23°20N 75°10W **115** C9
Long I. *Ireland* 51°30N 9°34W **30** F3
Long I. *U.S.A.* 40°45N 73°30W **113** E11
Long Itchington *U.K.* 52°16N 1°22W **24** B6
Long Melford *U.K.* 52°4N 0°45E **25** B10
Long Mynd, The *U.K.* 52°35N 2°50W **23** G3
Long Preston *U.K.* 54°2N 2°14W **23** D4
Long Sutton *U.K.* 52°48N 0°7E **23** G9
Long Xuyen *Vietnam* 10°19N 105°28E **83** B2
Longford *Ireland* 53°43N 7°49W **28** D6
Longford □ *Ireland* 53°42N 7°45W **28** D6
Longframlington *U.K.* 55°18N 1°47W **22** B5
Longhoughton *U.K.* 55°26N 1°37W **22** B5
Longlac *Canada* 49°45N 86°25W **112** A4
Longreach *Australia* 23°28S 144°14E **98** E7
Longridge *U.K.* 53°50N 2°35W **23** E3
Longton *U.K.* 53°44N 2°48W **23** E3
Longtown *Cumb., U.K.* 55°1N 2°58W **22** B3
Longtown *Hereford, U.K.* 51°58N 2°59W **24** C3
Longueuil *Canada* 45°31N 73°29W **113** C11
Longview *Tex., U.S.A.* 32°30N 94°44W **111** D8
Longview *Wash., U.S.A.* 46°8N 122°57W **110** A2
Lons-le-Saunier *France* 46°40N 5°31E **68** C6
Looe *U.K.* 50°22N 4°28W **27** G5
Loop Hd. *Ireland* 52°34N 9°56W **30** C3
Lop *China* 37°3N 80°11E **80** C3
Lop Nur *China* 40°20N 90°10E **80** B4
Lopez, C. *Gabon* 0°47S 8°40E **96** E1
Lorain *U.S.A.* 41°28N 82°11W **112** E6
Loralai *Pakistan* 30°20N 68°41E **84** D6
Lorca *Spain* 37°41N 1°42W **69** D5
Lord Howe I. *Pac. Oc.* 31°33S 159°6E **99** G10
Lord Howe Rise *Pac. Oc.* 30°0S 162°30E **99** H12
Lordsburg *U.S.A.* 32°21N 108°43W **110** D5
Lorestān □ *Iran* 33°30N 48°40E **86** C6
Lorient *France* 47°45N 3°23W **68** C2
Lorn *U.K.* 56°26N 5°10W **20** B5
Lorn, Firth of *U.K.* 56°20N 5°40W **20** B4
Lorraine □ *France* 48°53N 6°0E **68** B7
Los Alamos *U.S.A.* 35°53N 106°19W **110** C5
Los Andes *Chile* 32°50S 70°40W **121** F2
Los Angeles *Chile* 37°28S 72°23W **121** F2
Los Angeles *U.S.A.* 34°4N 118°15W **110** D3
Los Mochis *Mexico* 25°45N 108°57W **114** B3
Los Roques Is. *Venezuela* 11°50N 66°45W **120** A3
Lošinj *Croatia* 44°30N 14°30E **70** B6
Lossiemouth *U.K.* 57°42N 3°17W **19** G11
Lostwithiel *U.K.* 50°24N 4°41W **27** G4
Lot → *France* 44°18N 0°20E **68** D4
Lota *Chile* 37°5S 73°10W **121** F2
Loubomo *Congo* 4°9S 12°47E **96** E2
Loughborough *U.K.* 52°47N 1°11W **23** G6
Lougheed I. *Canada* 77°26N 105°6W **109** B9
Loughrea *Ireland* 53°12N 8°33W **30** B5
Loughros More B. *Ireland* 54°48N 8°32W **28** B4
Louis XIV, Pte. *Canada* 54°37N 79°45W **109** D12
Louisa *U.S.A.* 38°7N 82°36W **112** F6
Louisiade Arch. *Papua N. G.* 11°10S 153°0E **98** C9
Louisiana □ *U.S.A.* 30°50N 92°0W **111** D8
Louisville *U.S.A.* 38°15N 85°46W **112** F5
Lourdes *France* 43°6N 0°3W **68** E3
Louth *Ireland* 53°58N 6°32W **29** D8
Louth *U.K.* 53°22N 0°1W **23** F8
Louth □ *Ireland* 53°56N 6°34W **29** D8
Lovech *Bulgaria* 43°8N 24°42E **71** C11
Lowell *U.S.A.* 42°38N 71°19W **113** D12
Lower Beeding *U.K.* 51°2N 0°15W **25** D8
Lower Saxony = Niedersachsen □
 Germany 52°50N 9°0E **66** B5
Lower Tunguska → *Russia* 65°48N 88°4E **79** C10
Lowestoft *U.K.* 52°29N 1°45E **25** B12
Lowick *U.K.* 55°39N 1°57W **22** A5
Lowther Hills *U.K.* 55°20N 3°40W **21** D8
Lowville *U.S.A.* 43°47N 75°29W **113** D10
Loyauté, Îs. *N. Cal.* 20°50S 166°30E **99** E12
Lualaba →
 Dem. Rep. of the Congo 0°26N 25°20E **96** D5
Luanda *Angola* 8°50S 13°15E **96** F2
Luang Prabang *Laos* 19°52N 102°10E **83** B2
Luangwa → *Zambia* 14°25S 30°25E **97** G6
Luanshya *Zambia* 13°3S 28°28E **97** G5
Luapula → *Africa* 9°26S 28°33E **96** G5
Lubango *Angola* 14°55S 13°30E **97** G2
Lubbock *U.S.A.* 33°35N 101°51W **110** D6
Lübeck *Germany* 53°52N 10°40E **66** B6
Lublin *Poland* 51°12N 22°38E **67** C12
Lubumbashi
 Dem. Rep. of the Congo 11°40S 27°28E **97** G5

Lucan   Melaka

Lucan *Ireland* 53°22N 6°28W **31** B10
Lucania, Mt. *Canada* 61°1N 140°27W **108** C5
Lucca *Italy* 43°50N 10°29E **70** C4
Luce Bay *U.K.* 54°45N 4°48W **20** E6
Lucea *Jamaica* 18°27N 78°10W **114** a
Lucena *Phil.* 13°56N 121°37E **83** B4
Lucknow *India* 26°50N 81°0E **85** F12
Lüda = Dalian *China* 38°50N 121°40E **81** C7
Lüderitz *Namibia* 26°41S 15°8E **97** K3
Ludgershall *U.K.* 51°15N 1°37W **24** D5
Ludhiana *India* 30°57N 75°56E **84** D9
Ludington *U.S.A.* 43°57N 86°27W **112** D4
Ludlow *U.K.* 52°22N 2°42W **23** H3
Ludwigsburg *Germany* 48°53N 9°11E **66** D5
Ludwigshafen *Germany* 49°29N 8°26E **66** D5
Lufkin *U.S.A.* 31°21N 94°44W **111** D8
Luga *Russia* 58°40N 29°55E **72** C4
Lugano *Switz.* 46°1N 8°57E **66** E5
Lugansk *Ukraine* 48°38N 39°15E **73** E6
Lugnaquillia *Ireland* 52°58N 6°28W **31** C10
Lugo *Spain* 43°2N 7°35W **69** A2
Lugwardine *U.K.* 52°4N 2°39W **24** B3
Luing *U.K.* 56°14N 5°39W **20** D4
Luleå *Sweden* 65°35N 22°10E **63** D8
Luleälven → *Sweden* 65°35N 22°10E **63** D8
Lundy *U.K.* 51°10N 4°41W **27** E4
Lune → *U.K.* 54°0N 2°51W **23** D3
Lüneburger Heide *Germany* 53°10N 10°12E **66** B6
Lunéville *France* 48°36N 6°30E **68** B7
Luni → *India* 24°41N 71°14E **84** G7
Luofu *Dem. Rep. of the Congo* 0°1S 29°15E **96** E5
Luoyang *China* 34°40N 112°26E **81** C6
Luray *U.S.A.* 38°40N 78°28W **112** F8
Lurgan *U.K.* 54°28N 6°19W **29** C9
Lusaka *Zambia* 15°28S 28°16E **97** H5
Lūt, Dasht-e *Iran* 31°30N 58°0E **87** D9
Lutherstadt Wittenberg
  Germany 51°53N 12°39E **66** C7
Luton *U.K.* 51°53N 0°24W **25** C8
Łutselk'e *Canada* 62°24N 110°44W **108** C8
Lutsk *Ukraine* 50°50N 25°15E **67** C13
Lutterworth *U.K.* 52°28N 1°12W **23** H6
Luvua → *Dem. Rep. of the Congo* 6°50S 27°30E **90** G6
Luxembourg *Lux.* 49°37N 6°9E **65** E6
Luxembourg ■ *Europe* 49°45N 6°0E **65** E5
Luzern *Switz.* 47°3N 8°18E **66** E5
Luzhou *China* 28°52N 105°20E **80** D5
Luziânia *Brazil* 16°20S 48°0W **122** C1
Luzon *Phil.* 16°0N 121°0E **83** B4
Luzon Strait *Asia* 21°0N 120°40E **83** A4
Lvov *Ukraine* 49°50N 24°0E **67** D13
Lyakhov Is. *Russia* 73°40N 141°0E **79** B16
Lybster *U.K.* 58°18N 3°15W **19** F11
Lydd *U.K.* 50°57N 0°55E **25** E10
Lydford *U.K.* 50°38N 4°8W **27** F5
Lydham *U.K.* 52°31N 2°58W **23** G3
Lyme B. *U.K.* 50°42N 2°53W **24** E3
Lyme Regis *U.K.* 50°43N 2°57W **24** E3
Lyminge *U.K.* 51°7N 1°6E **25** D11
Lymington *U.K.* 50°45N 1°32W **24** E5
Lymm *U.K.* 53°23N 2°29W **23** F4
Lympne *U.K.* 51°4N 1°2E **25** D11
Lynchburg *U.S.A.* 37°25N 79°9W **112** G8
Lyndhurst *U.K.* 50°52N 1°35W **24** E5
Lyneham *U.K.* 51°30N 1°58W **24** D5
Lynmouth *U.K.* 51°13N 3°49W **27** E6
Lynn Lake *Canada* 56°51N 101°3W **108** D9
Lynton *U.K.* 51°13N 3°50W **27** E6
Lyonnais *France* 45°45N 4°15E **68** D6
Lyons *France* 45°46N 4°50E **68** D6
Lysva *Russia* 58°7N 57°49E **72** C10
Lysychansk *Ukraine* 48°55N 38°30E **73** E6
Lytchett Minster *U.K.* 50°44N 2°4W **24** E4
Lytham St. Anne's *U.K.* 53°45N 3°0W **23** E2
Lythe *U.K.* 54°31N 0°41W **22** C7
Lyubertsy *Russia* 55°40N 37°51E **72** C6

M

Ma-ubin *Burma* 16°44N 95°39E **85** L19
Ma'ān *Jordan* 30°12N 35°44E **86** D3
Ma'anshan *China* 31°44N 118°29E **81** C6
Maas → *Neths.* 51°45N 4°32E **65** C4
Maastricht *Neths.* 50°50N 5°40E **65** D5
Mablethorpe *U.K.* 53°20N 0°15E **23** F9
Macaé *Brazil* 22°20S 41°43W **122** D2
McAlester *U.S.A.* 34°56N 95°46W **111** D7
McAllen *U.S.A.* 26°12N 98°14W **110** E7
MacAlpine L. *Canada* 66°32N 102°45W **108** C9
Macapá *Brazil* 0°5N 51°4W **120** B4
Macau *Brazil* 5°15S 36°40W **120** C6
Macau *China* 22°12N 113°33E **81** D6
Macclesfield *U.K.* 53°15N 2°8W **23** F4
M'Clintock Chan. *Canada* 72°0N 102°0W **108** B9
M'Clure Str. *Canada* 75°0N 119°0W **109** B8
McComb *U.S.A.* 31°15N 90°27W **111** D8
McCook *U.S.A.* 40°12N 100°38W **110** B6
McDonald Is. *Ind. Oc.* 53°0S 73°0E **53** G13
MacDonnell Ranges *Australia* 23°40S 133°0E **98** E5
Macduff *U.K.* 57°40N 2°31W **19** G12
Macedonia □ *Greece* 40°39N 22°0E **71** D10
Macedonia ■ *Europe* 41°53N 21°40E **71** D9
Maceió *Brazil* 9°40S 35°41W **122** A3
Macgillycuddy's Reeks *Ireland* 51°58N 9°45W **30** E3
Mach *Pakistan* 29°50N 67°20E **84** E5
Machakos *Kenya* 1°30S 37°15E **96** E7
Machala *Ecuador* 3°20S 79°57W **120** D2
Machars, The *U.K.* 54°46N 4°30W **20** E6
Machias *U.S.A.* 44°43N 67°28W **113** C14
Machilipatnam *India* 16°12N 81°8E **85** L12
Machrihanish *U.K.* 55°25N 5°43W **20** D4
Machupicchu *Peru* 13°8S 72°30W **120** D2
Machynlleth *U.K.* 52°35N 3°50W **26** B6
Mackay *Australia* 21°8S 149°11E **98** E8
Mackay, L. *Australia* 22°30S 129°0E **98** E4
McKeesport *U.S.A.* 40°20N 79°51W **112** E8
Mackenzie *Canada* 55°20N 123°5W **108** D7

Mackenzie → *Canada* 69°10N 134°20W **108** C6
Mackenzie King I. *Canada* 77°45N 111°0W **109** B8
Mackenzie Mts. *Canada* 64°0N 130°0W **108** B6
Mackinaw City *U.S.A.* 45°47N 84°44W **112** C5
McKinley, Mt. *U.S.A.* 63°4N 151°0W **108** C4
McKinley Sea *Arctic* 82°0N 0°0 **54** A7
McMinnville *U.S.A.* 45°13N 123°12W **110** A2
McMurdo Sd. *Antarctica* 77°0S 170°0E **55** D11
Macomb *U.S.A.* 40°27N 90°40W **112** E2
Mâcon *France* 46°19N 4°50E **68** C6
Macon *U.S.A.* 32°51N 83°38W **111** D10
McPherson *U.S.A.* 38°22N 97°40W **110** C7
Macquarie Is. *Pac. Oc.* 54°36S 158°55E **102** N7
Macroom *Ireland* 51°54N 8°57W **30** E5
Madagascar ■ *Africa* 20°0S 47°0E **97** J9
Madang *Papua N. G.* 5°12S 145°49E **98** B8
Madeira *Atl. Oc.* 32°50N 17°0W **94** B2
Madeira → *Brazil* 3°22S 58°45W **120** C4
Madeleine, Îs. de la *Canada* 30°31N 61°40W **113** B17
Madeley *U.K.* 53°0N 2°20W **23** F4
Madhya Pradesh □ *India* 22°50N 78°0E **84** H11
Madison *Ind., U.S.A.* 38°44N 85°23W **112** F5
Madison *S. Dak., U.S.A.* 44°0N 97°7W **111** B7
Madison *Wis., U.S.A.* 43°4N 89°24W **112** D3
Madisonville *U.S.A.* 37°20N 87°30W **112** G4
Madiun *Indonesia* 7°38S 111°32E **83** D3
Madley *U.K.* 52°2N 2°51W **24** B3
Madras = Chennai *India* 13°8N 80°19E **84** N12
Madre de Dios → *Bolivia* 10°59S 66°8W **120** D3
Madre de Dios, I. *Chile* 50°20S 75°10W **121** H2
Madre Occidental, Sierra
  Mexico 27°0N 107°0W **114** B3
Madre Oriental, Sierra
  Mexico 25°0N 100°0W **114** C5
Madrid *Spain* 40°24N 3°42W **69** B4
Madura *Indonesia* 7°30S 114°0E **83** D3
Madurai *India* 9°55N 78°10E **84** Q11
Maebashi *Japan* 36°24N 139°4E **82** E6
Maesteg *U.K.* 51°36N 3°40W **27** D6
Mafeking *S. Africa* 25°50S 25°38E **97** K5
Mafia I. *Tanzania* 7°45S 39°50E **96** F7
Magadan *Russia* 59°38N 150°50E **79** D17
Magallanes, Estrecho de
  Chile 52°30S 75°0W **121** H2
Magangué *Colombia* 9°14N 74°45W **120** B2
Magdalena → *Colombia* 11°6N 74°51W **120** A2
Magdeburg *Germany* 52°7N 11°38E **66** B6
Magee, I. *U.K.* 54°48N 5°43W **29** B10
Magelang *Indonesia* 7°29S 110°13E **83** D3
Magellan's Str. = Magallanes,
  Estrecho de *Chile* 52°30S 75°0W **121** H2
Maggiore, Lago *Italy* 45°57N 8°39E **70** B3
Maggotty *Jamaica* 18°9N 77°46W **114** a
Maghâgha *Egypt* 28°38N 30°50E **95** C12
Magherafelt *U.K.* 54°45N 6°37W **29** B8
Maghreb *N. Afr.* 32°0N 4°0W **90** C3
Maghull *U.K.* 53°31N 2°57W **23** E3
Magnetic Pole (North)
  Canada 82°42N 114°24W **54** A2
Magnetic Pole (South)
  Antarctica 64°8S 138°8E **55** C9
Magnitogorsk *Russia* 53°27N 59°4E **72** D10
Magog *Canada* 45°18N 72°9W **113** C11
Magwe *Burma* 20°10N 95°0E **85** J19
Mahābād *Iran* 36°50N 45°45E **86** B6
Mahajanga *Madag.* 15°40S 46°25E **97** H9
Mahakam → *Indonesia* 0°35S 117°17E **83** D3
Mahalapye *Botswana* 23°1S 26°51E **97** J5
Maḥallāt *Iran* 33°55N 50°30E **87** C7
Mahanadi → *India* 20°20N 86°25E **85** J15
Maharashtra □ *India* 20°30N 75°30E **84** J9
Mahdia *Tunisia* 35°28N 11°0E **95** A8
Mahesana *India* 23°39N 72°26E **84** H8
Mahilyow *Belarus* 53°55N 30°18E **67** B16
Mai-Ndombe, L.
  Dem. Rep. of the Congo 2°0S 18°20E **96** E3
Maiden Bradley *U.K.* 51°9N 2°17W **24** D4
Maiden Newton *U.K.* 50°46N 2°34W **24** E3
Maidenhead *U.K.* 51°31N 0°42W **25** C7
Maidstone *U.K.* 51°16N 0°32E **25** D10
Maiduguri *Nigeria* 12°0N 13°20E **95** F8
Maijdi *Bangla.* 22°48N 91°10E **85** H17
Main → *Germany* 50°0N 8°18E **66** C5
Main → *U.K.* 54°48N 6°18W **29** B9
Maine *France* 48°20N 0°15W **68** C3
Maine □ *U.S.A.* 45°20N 69°0W **113** C13
Maine → *Ireland* 52°9N 9°45W **30** D3
Mainland *Orkney, U.K.* 58°59N 3°8W **19** E11
Mainland *Shet., U.K.* 60°15N 1°22W **18** B15
Mainz *Germany* 50°1N 8°14E **66** C5
Maiquetía *Venezuela* 10°36N 66°57W **120** A3
Majorca = Mallorca *Spain* 39°30N 3°0E **69** C7
Makale *Indonesia* 3°6S 119°51E **83** D3
Makasar, Str. of *Indonesia* 1°0S 118°20E **83** D3
Makgadikgadi Salt Pans
  Botswana 20°40S 25°45E **97** J5
Makhachkala *Russia* 43°0N 47°30E **73** F8
Makhado *S. Africa* 23°1S 29°43E **97** J5
Makran Coast Range *Pakistan* 25°40N 64°0E **84** G4
Makurdi *Nigeria* 7°43N 8°35E **94** G7
Mal B. *Ireland* 52°50N 9°30W **30** C4
Malabar Coast *India* 11°0N 75°0E **84** P9
Malacca, Straits of *Indonesia* 3°0N 101°0E **83** C2
Málaga *Spain* 36°43N 4°23W **69** D3
Malahide *Ireland* 53°26N 6°9W **31** B10
Malaita *Solomon Is.* 9°0S 161°0E **99** B11
Malakāl *Sudan* 9°33N 31°40E **95** G12
Malakula *Vanuatu* 16°15S 167°30E **99** D12
Malang *Indonesia* 7°59S 112°45E **83** D3
Malanje *Angola* 9°36S 16°17E **96** F3
Mälaren *Sweden* 59°30N 17°10E **63** F7
Malatya *Turkey* 38°25N 38°20E **73** G6
Malawi ■ *Africa* 11°55S 34°0E **97** G6
Malawi, L. *Africa* 12°30S 34°30E **97** G6
Malay Pen. *Asia* 7°25N 100°0E **74** H12
Malāyer *Iran* 34°19N 48°51E **86** C7
Malaysia ■ *Asia* 5°0N 110°0E **83** C3
Malden *U.S.A.* 36°34N 89°57W **112** G3

Malden I. *Kiribati* 4°3S 155°1W **103** H12
Maldives ■ *Ind. Oc.* 5°0N 73°0E **75** H9
Maldon *U.K.* 51°44N 0°42E **25** C10
Maldonado *Uruguay* 34°59S 55°0W **121** F4
Malegaon *India* 20°30N 74°38E **84** J9
Malham Tarn *U.K.* 54°6N 2°10W **22** C4
Malheur L. *U.S.A.* 43°20N 118°48W **110** B3
Mali ■ *Africa* 17°0N 3°0W **94** E5
Malin Hd. *Ireland* 55°23N 7°23W **28** A7
Malin Pen. *Ireland* 55°20N 7°17W **29** A7
Malindi *Kenya* 3°12S 40°5E **96** E8
Mallaig *U.K.* 57°0N 5°50W **18** H6
Mallawi *Egypt* 27°44N 30°44E **95** C12
Mallorca *Spain* 39°30N 3°0E **69** C7
Mallow *Ireland* 52°8N 8°39W **30** D5
Malmesbury *U.K.* 51°35N 2°5W **24** C4
Malmö *Sweden* 55°36N 12°59E **63** F6
Malone *U.S.A.* 44°51N 74°18W **113** C10
Malpas *U.K.* 53°1N 2°45W **23** F3
Malpelo, I. de *Colombia* 4°3N 81°35W **103** J19
Malta ■ *Europe* 35°55N 14°26E **70** a
Maltby *U.K.* 53°25N 1°12W **23** F6
Malton *U.K.* 54°8N 0°49W **22** D7
Malvinas, Is. = Falkland Is. ☑
  Atl. Oc. 51°30S 59°0W **121** H4
Mamoré → *Bolivia* 10°23S 65°53W **120** D3
Mamoudzou *Mayotte* 12°48S 45°14E **91** H8
Man *Ivory C.* 7°30N 7°40W **94** G4
Man, I. of *U.K.* 54°15N 4°30W **29** C12
Manado *Indonesia* 1°29N 124°51E **83** C4
Managua *Nic.* 12°6N 86°20W **114** E7
Manas *China* 44°17N 85°56E **80** B3
Manati *Puerto Rico* 18°26N 66°29W **115** d
Manaus *Brazil* 3°0S 60°0W **120** C3
Manby *U.K.* 53°21N 0°6E **23** F9
Manchester *U.K.* 53°29N 2°12W **23** F4
Manchester *U.S.A.* 42°59N 71°28W **113** D12
Manchester Int. ✈ (MAN)
  U.K. 53°21N 2°17W **23** F4
Manchuria *China* 45°0N 125°0E **81** B7
Manchurian Plain *China* 47°0N 124°0E **74** D14
Mandal *Norway* 58°2N 7°25E **63** F5
Mandalay *Burma* 22°0N 96°4E **85** J20
Mandalgovi *Mongolia* 45°45N 106°10E **80** B5
Mandan *U.S.A.* 46°50N 100°54W **110** A6
Mandeville *Jamaica* 18°2N 77°31W **114** a
Mandla *India* 22°39N 80°30E **85** H12
Mandsaur *India* 24°3N 75°8E **84** G9
Mandvi *India* 22°51N 69°22E **84** H6
Manea *U.K.* 52°29N 0°10E **25** B9
Manfalûṭ *Egypt* 27°20N 30°52E **95** C12
Manfredónia *Italy* 41°38N 15°55E **70** D6
Mangabeiras, Chapada das
  Brazil 10°0S 46°30W **122** B1
Mangalore *India* 12°55N 74°47E **84** N9
Mangnai *China* 37°52N 91°43E **80** C4
Mangole *Indonesia* 1°50S 125°55E **83** D4
Mangotsfield *U.K.* 51°29N 2°30W **24** D4
Manhattan *U.S.A.* 39°11N 96°35W **111** C7
Manhuaçu *Brazil* 20°15S 42°2W **122** D2
Manica *Mozam.* 18°58S 32°59E **97** H6
Manicoré *Brazil* 5°48S 61°16W **120** C3
Manicouagan → *Canada* 49°30N 68°30W **109** E13
Manicouagan, Rés. *Canada* 51°5N 68°40W **109** D13
Manihiki *Cook Is.* 10°24S 161°1W **103** J11
Manila *Phil.* 14°35N 120°58E **83** B4
Manipur □ *India* 25°0N 94°0E **85** G19
Manisa *Turkey* 38°38N 27°30E **73** G4
Manistee *U.S.A.* 44°15N 86°19W **112** C4
Manistee → *U.S.A.* 44°15N 86°21W **112** C4
Manistique *U.S.A.* 45°57N 86°15W **112** C4
Manitoba □ *Canada* 53°30N 97°0W **108** D10
Manitoba, L. *Canada* 51°0N 98°45W **108** D10
Manitou Is. *U.S.A.* 45°8N 86°0W **112** C4
Manitoulin I. *Canada* 45°40N 82°30W **112** C6
Manitowoc *U.S.A.* 44°5N 87°40W **112** C4
Manizales *Colombia* 5°5N 75°32W **120** B2
Mankato *U.S.A.* 44°10N 94°0W **111** B8
Mannar *Sri Lanka* 9°1N 79°54E **84** Q11
Mannar, G. of *Asia* 8°30N 79°0E **84** Q11
Mannheim *Germany* 49°29N 8°29E **66** D5
Manning *U.S.A.* 56°53N 117°39W **108** D8
Manningtree *U.K.* 51°56N 1°5E **25** C11
Manokwari *Indonesia* 0°54S 134°0E **83** D5
Manosque *France* 43°49N 5°47E **68** E6
Manresa *Spain* 41°48N 1°50E **69** B6
Mansel I. *Canada* 62°0N 80°0W **109** C12
Mansfield *U.K.* 53°9N 1°11W **23** F6
Mansfield *U.S.A.* 40°45N 82°31W **112** E6
Mansfield Woodhouse *U.K.* 53°11N 1°12W **23** F6
Manta *Ecuador* 1°0S 80°40W **120** C1
Mantes-la-Jolie *France* 48°58N 1°41E **68** B4
Mantiqueira, Serra da *Brazil* 22°0S 44°0W **116** F6
Manton *U.K.* 52°38N 0°41W **23** G7
Manton *U.S.A.* 44°25N 85°24W **112** C5
Mántova *Italy* 45°9N 10°48E **70** B4
Manuel Alves → *Brazil* 11°19S 48°28W **122** B1
Manzai *Pakistan* 32°12N 70°15E **84** C7
Manzanillo *Cuba* 20°20N 77°31W **115** C9
Manzanillo *Mexico* 19°3N 104°20W **114** D4
Manzhouli *China* 49°35N 117°25E **81** B6
Maó *Spain* 39°53N 4°16E **69** C8
Maoming *China* 21°50N 110°54E **81** D6
Mapam Yumco *China* 30°45N 81°28E **80** C3
Maputo *Mozam.* 25°58S 32°32E **97** K6
Maputo B. *Mozam.* 25°50S 32°45E **90** J7
Maquinchao *Argentina* 41°15S 68°50W **121** G3
Maquoketa *U.S.A.* 42°4N 90°40W **112** D2
Mar → *U.K.* 57°11S 16°17E **96** F2
Mar, Serra do *Brazil* 25°30S 49°0W **116** F6
Mar Chiquita, L. *Argentina* 30°40S 62°50W **121** F3
Mar del Plata *Argentina* 38°0S 57°30W **121** F4
Marabá *Brazil* 5°20S 49°5W **120** C5
Maracá, I. de *Brazil* 2°10N 50°30W **120** B4
Maracaibo *Venezuela* 10°40N 71°37W **120** A2
Maracaibo, L. de *Venezuela* 9°40N 71°30W **120** B2
Maracay *Venezuela* 10°15N 67°28W **120** A3

Maradi *Niger* 13°29N 7°20E **94** F7
Maragogipe *Brazil* 12°46S 38°55W **122** B3
Marajó, I. de *Brazil* 1°0S 49°30W **120** C5
Maranguape *Brazil* 3°55S 38°50W **120** C6
Maranhão □ *Brazil* 5°0S 46°0W **120** C5
Marañón → *Peru* 4°30S 73°35W **120** C2
Marazion *U.K.* 50°7N 5°29W **27** G3
Marbella *Spain* 36°30N 4°57W **69** D3
March *U.K.* 52°33N 0°5E **25** B9
Marche *France* 46°5N 1°20E **68** C4
Marcus I. *Pac. Oc.* 24°20N 153°58E **102** E7
Marden *U.K.* 52°7N 2°42W **24** B3
Mardin *Turkey* 37°20N 40°43E **73** G7
Maree, L. *U.K.* 57°40N 5°26W **18** G7
Mareham le Fen *U.K.* 53°8N 0°4W **23** F8
Marfleet *U.K.* 53°44N 0°17W **23** E8
Margarita, I. de *Venezuela* 11°0N 64°0W **120** A3
Margate *U.K.* 51°23N 1°23E **25** D11
Marghilon *Uzbekistan* 40°27N 71°42E **87** A12
Mārgow, Dasht-e *Afghan.* 30°40N 62°30E **87** D10
Mari El □ *Russia* 56°30N 48°0E **72** C8
Mariana Trench *Pac. Oc.* 13°0N 145°0E **102** F6
Marías, Is. *Mexico* 21°25N 106°28W **114** C3
Maribor *Slovenia* 46°36N 15°40E **66** E8
Marie Byrd Land *Antarctica* 79°30S 125°0W **55** D14
Marie-Galante *Guadeloupe* 15°56N 61°16W **114** b
Mariental *Namibia* 24°36S 18°0E **97** J3
Marietta *U.S.A.* 39°25N 81°27W **112** F7
Marília *Brazil* 22°13S 50°0W **120** E4
Marinette *U.S.A.* 45°6N 87°38W **112** C4
Marion *Ill., U.S.A.* 37°44N 88°56W **112** G3
Marion *Ind., U.S.A.* 40°32N 85°40W **112** E5
Marion *Ohio, U.S.A.* 40°35N 83°8W **112** E6
Mariupol *Ukraine* 47°5N 37°31E **73** E6
Markam *China* 29°42N 98°38E **80** D4
Market Bosworth *U.K.* 52°38N 1°24W **23** G6
Market Deeping *U.K.* 52°41N 0°19W **23** G8
Market Drayton *U.K.* 52°54N 2°29W **23** G4
Market Harborough *U.K.* 52°29N 0°55W **23** H7
Market Lavington *U.K.* 51°17N 1°58W **24** D5
Market Rasen *U.K.* 53°24N 0°20W **23** F8
Market Weighton *U.K.* 53°52N 0°40W **23** E7
Markfield *U.K.* 52°42N 1°17W **23** G6
Markham, Mt. *Antarctica* 83°0S 164°0E **55** E11
Marks Tey *U.K.* 51°52N 0°49E **25** C10
Marlborough *U.K.* 51°25N 1°43W **24** D5
Marlborough Downs *U.K.* 51°27N 1°53W **24** D5
Marlow *U.K.* 51°34N 0°46W **25** C7
Marmara, Sea of *Turkey* 40°45N 28°15E **73** F4
Marmaris *Turkey* 36°50N 28°14E **86** B2
Marmora *Canada* 44°28N 77°41W **112** C9
Marne → *France* 48°47N 2°29E **68** B5
Marnhull *U.K.* 50°57N 2°19W **24** E4
Maroua *Cameroon* 10°40N 14°20E **95** F8
Marple *U.K.* 53°24N 2°4W **23** F4
Marquette *U.S.A.* 46°33N 87°24W **112** B4
Marquis *St. Lucia* 14°2N 60°54W **115** f
Marquises, Îs.
  French Polynesia 9°30S 140°0W **103** H14
Marrakesh *Morocco* 31°9N 8°0W **94** B4
Marree *Australia* 29°39S 138°1E **98** F6
Marsá Matrûh *Egypt* 31°19N 27°9E **95** B11
Marsabit *Kenya* 2°18N 38°0E **96** D7
Marsala *Italy* 37°48N 12°26E **70** F5
Marseilles *France* 43°18N 5°23E **68** E6
Marsh I. *U.S.A.* 29°34N 91°53W **111** E8
Marshall *U.S.A.* 32°33N 94°23W **111** D8
Marshall Is. ■ *Pac. Oc.* 9°0N 171°0E **102** G9
Marshfield *U.K.* 51°28N 2°19W **24** D4
Marshfield *U.S.A.* 44°40N 90°10W **112** C2
Marske by the Sea *U.K.* 54°36N 1°0W **22** C7
Marston Moor *U.K.* 53°58N 1°17W **23** E6
Martaban *Burma* 16°30N 97°35E **85** L20
Martaban, G. of *Burma* 16°5N 96°30E **85** L20
Martapura *Indonesia* 3°22S 114°47E **83** D3
Martham *U.K.* 52°42N 1°37E **25** A12
Martha's Vineyard *U.S.A.* 41°25N 70°38W **113** E12
Martigues *France* 43°24N 5°4E **68** E6
Martinique ☑ *W. Indies* 14°40N 61°0W **114** c
Martin's Bay *Barbados* 13°12N 59°29E **115** g
Martinsville *U.S.A.* 39°26N 86°25W **112** F4
Martley *U.K.* 52°15N 2°21W **24** B4
Martock *U.K.* 50°58N 2°46W **24** E3
Marwar *India* 25°43N 73°45E **84** G8
Mary *Turkmenistan* 37°40N 61°50E **87** B10
Maryborough *Australia* 25°31S 152°37E **98** F9
Maryland □ *U.S.A.* 39°0N 76°30W **112** F9
Maryport *U.K.* 54°44N 3°28W **22** C2
Marystown *Canada* 47°10N 55°10W **109** E14
Marytavy *U.K.* 50°36N 4°7W **27** F5
Marzūq *Libya* 25°53N 13°57E **95** C8
Masai Steppe *Tanzania* 4°30S 36°30E **96** E7
Masan *S. Korea* 35°11N 128°32E **81** C7
Masandam, Ra's *Oman* 26°30N 56°30E **88** B6
Masaya *Nic.* 12°0N 86°7W **114** E7
Masbate *Phil.* 12°21N 123°36E **83** B4
Mascara *Algeria* 35°26N 0°6E **94** A6
Maseru *Lesotho* 29°18S 27°30E **97** K5
Masham *U.K.* 54°14N 1°39W **22** D5
Mashhad *Iran* 36°20N 59°35E **87** B9
Mashonaland *Zimbabwe* 16°30S 31°0E **97** H6
Maṣīrah *Oman* 21°0N 58°50E **88** C6
Masjed Soleyman *Iran* 31°55N 49°18E **86** D7
Mask, L. *Ireland* 53°36N 9°22W **28** D3
Mason City *U.S.A.* 43°9N 93°12W **111** B8
Massa *Italy* 44°1N 10°9E **70** B4
Massachusetts □ *U.S.A.* 42°30N 72°0W **113** D11
Massawa *Eritrea* 15°35N 39°25E **88** D2
Massena *U.S.A.* 44°56N 74°54W **113** C10
Massiah Street *Barbados* 13°9N 59°29E **115** g
Massif Central *France* 44°55N 3°0E **68** D5
Massillon *U.S.A.* 40°48N 81°32W **112** E7
Masurian Lakes *Poland* 53°50N 21°0E **67** B11
Masvingo *Zimbabwe* 20°8S 30°49E **97** J6
Mata-Utu *Wall. & F. Is.* 13°17S 176°8W **99** C15
Matabeleland *Zimbabwe* 18°0S 27°0E **97** H5

Matadi *Dem. Rep. of the Congo* 5°52S 13°31E **96** F2
Matagalpa *Nic.* 13°0N 85°58W **114** E7
Matagami *Canada* 49°45N 77°34W **109** E12
Matagami, L. *Canada* 49°50N 77°40W **109** E12
Matagorda I. *U.S.A.* 28°15N 96°30W **111** E7
Matamoros *Mexico* 25°32N 103°15W **114** B5
Matane *Canada* 48°50N 67°33W **109** E13
Matanzas *Cuba* 23°0N 81°40W **115** C8
Matara *Sri Lanka* 5°58N 80°30E **84** S12
Mataró *Spain* 41°32N 2°29E **69** B7
Matehuala *Mexico* 23°39N 100°39W **114** C4
Mateke Hills *Zimbabwe* 21°48S 31°0E **97** J6
Matera *Italy* 40°40N 16°36E **70** D7
Mathura *India* 27°30N 77°40E **84** F10
Mati *Phil.* 6°55N 126°15E **83** C4
Matlock *U.K.* 53°9N 1°33W **23** F5
Mato Grosso □ *Brazil* 14°0S 55°0W **120** D4
Mato Grosso, Planalto do
  Brazil 15°0S 55°0W **120** D4
Mato Grosso do Sul □ *Brazil* 18°0S 55°0W **120** D4
Matopo Hills *Zimbabwe* 20°36S 28°20E **97** J5
Maṭruḥ *Oman* 23°37N 58°30E **87** F9
Matsue *Japan* 35°25N 133°10E **82** F3
Matsumoto *Japan* 36°15N 138°0E **82** E6
Matsusaka *Japan* 34°34N 136°32E **82** F5
Matsuyama *Japan* 33°45N 132°45E **82** G3
Mattagami → *Canada* 50°43N 81°29W **109** D11
Mattancheri *India* 9°50N 76°15E **84** Q10
Mattawa *Canada* 46°20N 78°45W **112** B8
Matterhorn *Switz.* 45°58N 7°39E **66** F4
Matthew, Î. *N. Cal.* 22°29S 171°15E **99** E13
Mattoon *U.S.A.* 39°29N 88°23W **112** F3
Maturín *Venezuela* 9°45N 63°11W **120** B3
Maubeuge *France* 50°17N 3°57E **68** A6
Maudin Sun *Burma* 16°0N 94°30E **85** M19
Maui *U.S.A.* 20°48N 156°20W **110** H16
Maumee → *U.S.A.* 41°42N 83°28W **112** E6
Maumturk Mts. *Ireland* 53°32N 9°42W **28** D2
Maun *Botswana* 20°0S 23°26E **97** H4
Mauna Kea *U.S.A.* 19°50N 155°28W **110** J17
Mauna Loa *U.S.A.* 19°30N 155°35W **110** J17
Mauritania ■ *Africa* 20°50N 10°0W **94** E3
Mauritius ■ *Ind. Oc.* 20°0S 57°0E **91** J9
Mawgan *U.K.* 50°4N 5°13W **27** G3
Maxwellheugh *U.K.* 55°35N 2°26W **21** C11
May, I. of *U.K.* 56°11N 2°32W **21** B10
May Pen *Jamaica* 17°58N 77°15W **114** a
Mayaguana *Bahamas* 22°30N 72°44W **115** C10
Mayagüez *Puerto Rico* 18°12N 67°9W **115** d
Maybole *U.K.* 55°21N 4°42W **20** D6
Mayfield *E. Sussex, U.K.* 51°1N 0°17E **25** D9
Mayfield *Staffs., U.K.* 53°1N 1°47W **23** F5
Mayfield *U.S.A.* 36°44N 88°38W **112** G3
Maykop *Russia* 44°35N 40°10E **73** F7
Maynooth *Ireland* 53°23N 6°34W **31** B9
Mayo *Canada* 63°38N 135°57W **108** C6
Mayo □ *Ireland* 53°53N 9°3W **28** D3
Mayon Volcano *Phil.* 13°15N 123°41E **83** B4
Mayotte ☑ *Ind. Oc.* 12°50S 45°10E **97** G9
Maysville *U.S.A.* 38°39N 83°46W **112** F6
Māzandarān □ *Iran* 36°30N 52°0E **87** B8
Mazar *China* 36°32N 77°1E **80** C2
Mazār-e Sharīf *Afghan.* 36°41N 67°0E **87** B11
Mazaruni → *Guyana* 6°25N 58°35W **120** B4
Mazatlán *Mexico* 23°13N 106°25W **114** C3
Mazyr *Belarus* 51°59N 29°15E **72** D4
Mbabane *Swaziland* 26°18S 31°6E **97** K6
Mbaïki *C.A.R.* 3°53N 18°1E **96** D3
Mbala *Zambia* 8°46S 31°24E **96** F6
Mbale *Uganda* 1°8N 34°12E **96** D6
Mbandaka *Dem. Rep. of the Congo* 0°1N 18°18E **96** D3
Mbanza Ngungu
  Dem. Rep. of the Congo 5°12S 14°53E **96** F2
Mbeya *Tanzania* 8°54S 33°29E **96** F6
Mbour *Senegal* 14°22N 16°54W **94** F2
Mbuji-Mayi
  Dem. Rep. of the Congo 6°9S 23°40E **96** F4
Mdantsane *S. Africa* 32°56S 27°46E **97** L5
Mead, L. *U.S.A.* 36°0N 114°44W **110** C4
Meadow Lake *Canada* 54°10N 108°26W **108** D9
Meadville *U.S.A.* 41°39N 80°9W **112** E7
Meaford *Canada* 44°36N 80°35W **112** C7
Mealsgate *U.K.* 54°47N 3°13W **22** C2
Mearns, Howe of the *U.K.* 56°52N 2°26W **19** J13
Measham *U.K.* 52°43N 1°31W **23** G5
Meath □ *Ireland* 53°40N 6°57W **29** D8
Meaux *France* 48°58N 2°50E **68** B5
Mecca *Si. Arabia* 21°30N 39°54E **86** F4
Mechelen *Belgium* 51°2N 4°29E **65** C4
Mecklenburg *Germany* 53°33N 11°40E **66** B6
Mecklenburger Bucht
  Germany 54°20N 11°40E **66** A6
Medan *Indonesia* 3°40N 98°38E **83** C1
Médéa *Algeria* 36°12N 2°50E **94** A6
Medellín *Colombia* 6°15N 75°35W **120** B2
Medford *Oreg., U.S.A.* 42°19N 122°52W **110** B2
Medford *Wis., U.S.A.* 45°9N 90°20W **112** C2
Medicine Hat *Canada* 50°0N 110°45W **108** E8
Medina *Si. Arabia* 24°35N 39°52E **86** E4
Medina *U.S.A.* 43°13N 78°23W **112** D8
Mediterranean Sea *Europe* 35°0N 15°0E **90** C5
Médoc *France* 45°10N 0°50W **68** D3
Medstead *U.K.* 51°8N 1°3W **24** D6
Medvezhyegorsk *Russia* 63°0N 34°25E **72** B5
Medway → *U.K.* 51°27N 0°46E **25** D10
Meekatharra *Australia* 26°32S 118°29E **98** F2
Meerut *India* 29°1N 77°42E **84** E10
Meghalaya □ *India* 25°50N 91°0E **85** G17
Meghna → *Bangla.* 22°50N 90°50E **85** H17
Megisti *Greece* 36°8N 29°34E **86** B3
Meighen I. *Canada* 80°0N 99°30W **109** B10
Meiktila *Burma* 20°53N 95°54E **85** J19
Meizhou *China* 24°16N 116°6E **81** D6
Mejillones *Chile* 23°10S 70°30W **121** E2
Mekele *Ethiopia* 13°33N 39°30E **88** E2
Mekhtar *Pakistan* 30°30N 69°15E **84** D6
Meknès *Morocco* 33°57N 5°33W **94** B4
Mekong → *Asia* 9°30N 106°15E **83** C2
Melaka *Malaysia* 2°15N 102°15E **83** C2

Melanesia   Nanded

Melanesia *Pac. Oc.* 4°0S 155°0E 102 H7
Melbourn *U.K.* 52°4N 0°0 25 B9
Melbourne *Australia* 37°48S 144°58E 98 H8
Melbourne *U.K.* 52°50N 1°25W 23 G6
Melekeok *Palau* 7°27N 134°38E 102 G5
Mélèzes → *Canada* 57°40N 69°29W 109 D13
Melfort *Canada* 52°50N 104°37W 108 D9
Melilla *N. Afr.* 35°21N 2°57W 69 E4
Melitopol *Ukraine* 46°50N 35°22E 73 E6
Melksham *U.K.* 51°23N 2°8W 24 D4
Melmerby *U.K.* 54°45N 2°35W 22 C3
Melrose *U.K.* 55°36N 2°43W 21 C10
Melsonby *U.K.* 54°29N 1°42W 22 D5
Melton Constable *U.K.* 52°52N 1°2E 25 A11
Melton Mowbray *U.K.* 52°47N 0°54W 23 G7
Melun *France* 48°32N 2°39E 68 B5
Melville *Canada* 50°55N 102°50W 108 D9
Melville I. *Australia* 11°30S 131°0E 98 C5
Melville I. *Canada* 75°30N 112°0W 109 B8
Melville Pen. *Canada* 68°0N 84°0W 109 C11
Memphis *U.S.A.* 35°8N 90°2W 111 C9
Menai Bridge *U.K.* 53°14N 4°10W 26 A5
Menai Strait *U.K.* 53°11N 4°13W 26 A5
Mende *France* 44°31N 3°30E 68 D5
Mendip Hills *U.K.* 51°17N 2°40W 24 D3
Mendlesham *U.K.* 52°16N 1°6E 25 B11
Mendocino, C. *U.S.A.* 40°26N 124°25W 110 B2
Mendota *Argentina* 41°33N 89°7W 112 E3
Mendoza *Argentina* 32°50S 68°52W 121 F3
Mengzi *China* 23°20N 103°22E 80 D5
Menominee *U.S.A.* 45°6N 87°37W 112 C4
Menominee → *U.S.A.* 45°6N 87°35W 112 C4
Menomonie *U.S.A.* 44°53N 91°55W 112 C2
Menorca *Spain* 40°0N 4°0E 69 C8
Mentawai, Kepulauan *Indonesia* 2°0S 99°0E 83 D1
Merca *Somali Rep.* 1°48N 44°50E 88 G3
Merced *U.S.A.* 37°18N 120°29W 110 C2
Mercedes Corrientes, *Argentina* 29°10S 58°5W 121 E4
Mercedes San Luis, *Argentina* 33°40S 65°21W 121 F3
Mercedes *Uruguay* 33°12S 58°0W 121 F4
Mercy, C. *Canada* 65°0N 63°30W 109 C13
Mere *U.K.* 51°6N 2°16W 24 D4
Mergui *Burma* 12°26N 98°34E 83 B1
Mérida *Mexico* 20°58N 89°37W 114 C7
Mérida *Spain* 38°55N 6°25W 69 C2
Mérida *Venezuela* 8°24N 71°8W 120 B2
Mérida, Cord. de *Venezuela* 9°0N 71°0W 116 C3
Meriden *U.K.* 52°26N 1°38W 23 H5
Meriden *U.S.A.* 41°32N 72°48W 113 E11
Meridian *U.S.A.* 32°22N 88°42W 111 D9
Merrick *U.K.* 55°8N 4°28W 20 D7
Merrill *U.S.A.* 45°11N 89°41W 112 C3
Merritt *Canada* 50°10N 120°45W 108 D7
Merse *U.K.* 55°43N 2°16W 21 C11
Mersea I. *U.K.* 51°47N 0°58E 25 C10
Mersey → *U.K.* 53°25N 3°1W 23 F2
Merseyside □ *U.K.* 53°31N 3°2W 23 E2
Merthyr Tydfil *U.K.* 51°45N 3°22W 26 D7
Merton □ *U.K.* 51°25N 0°11W 25 D8
Meru *Kenya* 0°3N 37°40E 96 D7
Meru *Tanzania* 3°15S 36°46E 96 E7
Mesa *U.S.A.* 33°25N 111°50W 110 D4
Mesopotamia *Iraq* 33°30N 44°0E 86 C5
Messina *Italy* 38°11N 15°34E 70 E6
Messina, Str. di *Italy* 38°15N 15°35E 70 F6
Mestre, Espigão *Brazil* 12°30S 46°10W 122 B1
Meta → *S. Amer.* 6°12N 67°28W 120 B3
Meta Incognita Pen.
   Canada 62°45N 68°30W 109 C13
Metheringham *U.K.* 53°9N 0°23W 23 F8
Methwold *U.K.* 52°32N 0°33E 25 A10
Metlakatla *U.S.A.* 55°8N 131°35W 108 D6
Metropolis *U.S.A.* 37°9N 88°44W 112 G3
Metz *France* 49°8N 6°10E 68 B7
Meuse → *Europe* 50°45N 5°41E 65 D5
Mevagissey *U.S.A.* 50°16N 4°48W 27 G4
Mevagissey B. *U.K.* 50°17N 4°47W 27 G4
Mexborough *U.K.* 53°30N 1°15W 23 E6
Mexiana, I. *Brazil* 0°0 49°30W 120 B5
Mexicali *Mexico* 32°40N 115°30W 114 A1
México *Mexico* 19°24N 99°9W 114 D5
Mexico ■ *Cent. Amer.* 25°0N 105°0W 114 C4
Mexico, G. of *Cent. Amer.* 25°0N 90°0W 114 C7
Meymaneh *Afghan.* 35°53N 64°38E 87 C11
Mezen → *Russia* 65°44N 44°22E 72 A7
Miami *U.S.A.* 25°46N 80°11W 111 E10
Miándowāb *Iran* 37°0N 46°5E 86 B6
Mianeh *Iran* 37°30N 47°40E 86 B6
Mianwali *Pakistan* 32°38N 71°28E 84 C7
Mianyang *China* 31°22N 104°47E 80 C5
Miass *Russia* 54°59N 60°6E 72 D11
Micheldever *U.K.* 51°9N 1°14W 24 D6
Michigan □ *U.S.A.* 44°0N 85°0W 112 B4
Michigan, L. *U.S.A.* 44°0N 87°0W 112 D4
Michipicoten I. *Canada* 47°40N 85°40W 112 B5
Michurinsk *Russia* 52°58N 40°27E 72 D7
Mickle Fell *U.K.* 54°37N 2°18W 22 C4
Mickleover *U.K.* 52°55N 1°33W 23 G5
Micoud *St. Lucia* 13°49N 60°54W 115 f
Micronesia *Pac. Oc.* 11°0N 160°0E 102 G7
Micronesia, Federated States of ■
   Pac. Oc. 9°0N 150°0E 102 G7
Middelburg *Neths.* 51°30N 3°36E 65 C3
Middelburg *S. Africa* 31°30S 25°0E 97 L5
Middle Atlas *Morocco* 33°0N 5°0W 94 B4
Middle East *Asia* 35°0N 40°0E 74 E5
Middleham *U.K.* 54°17N 1°48W 22 D5
Middlemarsh *U.K.* 50°51N 2°28W 24 E4
Middlesbrough *U.K.* 54°35N 1°13W 22 C6
Middleton Gt. Man., *U.K.* 53°33N 2°12W 23 E4
Middleton Norfolk, *U.K.* 52°43N 0°29E 25 A9
Middleton Cheney *U.K.* 52°5N 1°16W 24 B6
Middleton in Teesdale *U.K.* 54°38N 2°4W 22 C4
Middleton on the Wolds *U.K.* 53°56N 0°35W 23 E7
Middletown *U.K.* 54°17N 6°51W 29 C8
Middletown N.Y., *U.S.A.* 41°27N 74°25W 113 E10

Middletown Ohio, *U.S.A.* 39°31N 84°24W 112 F5
Middlewich *U.K.* 53°12N 2°28W 23 F4
Middlezoy *U.K.* 51°5N 2°54W 24 D3
Midhurst *U.K.* 50°59N 0°44W 25 E7
Midi, Canal du → *France* 43°45N 1°21E 68 E4
Midland *Canada* 44°45N 79°50W 112 D8
Midland Mich., *U.S.A.* 43°37N 84°14W 112 D5
Midland Tex., *U.S.A.* 32°0N 102°3W 110 D6
Midleton *Ireland* 51°55N 8°10W 30 E6
Midsomer Norton *U.K.* 51°17N 2°28W 24 D4
Midway Is. *Pac. Oc.* 28°13N 177°22W 102 E10
Midwest *U.S.A.* 42°0N 90°0W 111 C9
Mieres *Spain* 43°18N 5°48W 69 A3
Mikhaylovka *Russia* 50°3N 43°5E 73 D7
Milan *Italy* 45°28N 9°10E 70 B3
Milborne Port *U.K.* 50°58N 2°28W 24 E4
Mildenhall *U.K.* 52°21N 0°32E 25 B10
Mildura *Australia* 34°13S 142°9E 98 G7
Miles City *U.S.A.* 46°25N 105°51W 110 A5
Milford *U.S.A.* 38°55N 75°26W 113 F10
Milford Haven *U.K.* 51°42N 5°7W 26 D3
Milford on Sea *U.K.* 50°43N 1°35W 24 E5
Milh, Bahr al *Iraq* 32°40N 43°35E 86 C5
Milk → *U.S.A.* 48°4N 106°19W 110 A5
Millau *France* 44°8N 3°4E 68 D5
Millbrook *U.K.* 50°20N 4°14W 27 G5
Millet *St. Lucia* 13°55N 60°59W 115 f
Millinocket *U.S.A.* 45°39N 68°43W 113 C13
Millom *U.K.* 54°13N 3°16W 22 D2
Milltown Malbay *Ireland* 52°52N 9°24W 30 C4
Millville *U.S.A.* 39°24N 75°2W 113 F10
Milngavie *U.K.* 55°56N 4°19W 20 C7
Milnthorpe *U.K.* 54°14N 2°45W 22 D3
Milos *Greece* 36°44N 24°25E 71 F11
Milton Abbot *U.K.* 50°35N 4°16W 27 F5
Milton Keynes *U.K.* 52°1N 0°44W 25 B7
Milverton *U.K.* 51°1N 3°16W 24 D2
Milwaukee *U.S.A.* 43°2N 87°54W 112 D4
Min Jiang → *Fujian, China* 26°0N 119°35E 81 D6
Min Jiang → *Sichuan, China* 28°45N 104°40E 80 D5
Minas *Uruguay* 34°20S 55°10W 121 F4
Minas Gerais □ *Brazil* 18°50S 46°0W 122 C1
Minatitlán *Mexico* 17°59N 94°31W 114 D6
Minchinhampton *U.K.* 51°42N 2°11W 24 C4
Mindanao *Phil.* 8°0N 125°0E 83 C4
Mindoro *Phil.* 13°0N 121°0E 83 B4
Mindoro Str. *Phil.* 12°30N 120°30E 83 B4
Minehead *U.K.* 51°12N 3°29W 24 D2
Mineral Wells *U.S.A.* 32°48N 98°7W 110 D7
Minfeng *China* 37°4N 82°46E 80 C3
Minginish *U.K.* 57°14N 6°15W 18 H5
Mingulay *U.K.* 56°49N 7°39W 18 J2
Minna *Nigeria* 9°37N 6°30E 94 G7
Minneapolis *U.S.A.* 44°57N 93°16W 111 B8
Minnesota □ *U.S.A.* 46°0N 94°15W 111 A8
Minorca = Menorca *Spain* 40°0N 4°0E 69 C8
Minot *U.S.A.* 48°14N 101°18W 110 A6
Minsk *Belarus* 53°52N 27°30E 67 B14
Minster Kent, *U.K.* 51°20N 1°20E 25 D11
Minster Kent, *U.K.* 51°25N 0°50E 25 D10
Minsterley *U.K.* 52°39N 2°54W 23 G3
Minto, L. *Canada* 57°13N 75°0W 109 D12
Miramichi B. *Canada* 47°15N 65°0W 113 C15
Mirim, L. *S. Amer.* 32°45S 52°50W 121 F4
Mirnyy *Russia* 62°33N 113°53E 79 C12
Mirpur Khas *Pakistan* 25°30N 69°0E 84 G6
Mirtoo Sea *Greece* 37°0N 23°20E 71 F10
Mirzapur *India* 25°10N 82°34E 85 G13
Mishan *China* 45°37N 131°48E 81 B8
Mishawaka *U.S.A.* 41°40N 86°11W 112 E4
Misool *Indonesia* 1°52S 130°10E 83 D5
Misrātah *Libya* 32°24N 15°3E 95 B9
Missinaibi → *Canada* 50°43N 81°29W 109 D11
Mississippi □ *U.S.A.* 33°0N 90°0W 111 D9
Mississippi → *U.S.A.* 29°9N 89°15W 111 E9
Mississippi River Delta
   U.S.A. 29°10N 89°15W 111 E9
Missoula *U.S.A.* 46°52N 114°1W 110 A4
Missouri □ *U.S.A.* 38°25N 92°30W 111 C8
Missouri → *U.S.A.* 38°49N 90°7W 111 C8
Mistassini, L. *Canada* 51°0N 73°30W 109 D12
Misterton Notts., *U.K.* 53°27N 0°50W 23 F7
Misterton Somst., *U.K.* 50°52N 2°47W 24 E3
Mitcheldean *U.K.* 51°51N 2°29W 24 C4
Mitchell → *Australia* 43°43N 98°2W 110 B7
Mitchell → *Australia* 15°12S 141°35E 98 D7
Mitchelstown *Ireland* 52°15N 8°16W 30 D6
Mito *Japan* 36°20N 140°30E 82 E7
Mitú *Colombia* 1°15N 70°13W 120 B2
Mitumba, Mts.
   Dem. Rep. of the Congo 7°0S 27°30E 96 F5
Miyakonojō *Japan* 31°40N 131°5E 82 H2
Miyazaki *Japan* 31°56N 131°30E 82 H2
Mizen Hd. Cork, *Ireland* 51°27N 9°50W 30 F3
Mizen Hd. Wicklow, *Ireland* 52°51N 6°4W 31 C10
Mizoram □ *India* 23°30N 92°40E 85 H18
Mjøsa *Norway* 60°40N 11°0E 63 E6
Mljet *Croatia* 42°43N 17°30E 70 C7
Mo i Rana *Norway* 66°20N 14°7E 63 D6
Moab *U.S.A.* 38°35N 109°33W 110 C5
Moate *Ireland* 53°24N 7°44W 28 E6
Mobaye *C.A.R.* 4°25N 21°5E 96 D4
Moberly *U.S.A.* 39°25N 92°26W 111 C81
Mobile *U.S.A.* 30°41N 88°3W 111 D9
Mobridge *U.S.A.* 45°32N 100°26W 110 A6
Moçâmbique *Mozam.* 15°3S 40°42E 97 H8
Mochudi *Botswana* 24°27S 26°7E 97 J5
Mocoa *Colombia* 1°7N 76°35W 120 B2
Mococa *Brazil* 21°28S 47°0W 122 D1
Mocuba *Mozam.* 16°54S 36°57E 97 H7
Modbury *U.K.* 50°21N 3°55W 27 G6
Módena *Italy* 44°40N 10°55E 70 B4
Modesto *U.S.A.* 37°39N 121°0W 110 C2
Moffat *U.K.* 55°21N 3°27W 21 D9
Mogadishu *Somali Rep.* 2°2N 45°25E 88 G4
Mogi das Cruzes *Brazil* 23°31S 46°11W 122 D1
Mogi-Mirim *Brazil* 22°29S 47°0W 122 D1

Mohammedia *Morocco* 33°44N 7°21W 94 B4
Moher, Cliffs of *Ireland* 52°58N 9°27W 30 C4
Moidart *U.K.* 56°49N 5°41W 18 J6
Moidart, L. *U.K.* 56°47N 5°52W 18 J6
Moisie → *Canada* 50°14N 66°5W 109 D13
Mojave Desert *U.S.A.* 35°0N 116°30W 110 D3
Mold *U.K.* 53°9N 3°8W 26 A7
Molde *Norway* 62°45N 7°9E 63 E5
Moldova ■ *Europe* 47°0N 28°0E 67 E15
Mole → *U.K.* 51°24N 0°21W 25 D8
Molepolole *Botswana* 24°28S 25°28E 97 J5
Moloka'i *U.S.A.* 21°8N 157°0W 110 H16
Molopo → *Africa* 28°30S 20°12E 97 K4
Molucca Sea *Indonesia* 0°0 125°0E 83 D4
Moluccas *Indonesia* 1°0S 127°0E 83 D4
Mombasa *Kenya* 4°3S 39°40E 96 E7
Mompós *Colombia* 9°14N 74°26W 120 B2
Mon □ *Burma* 16°0N 97°30E 85 L20
Mona Passage *W. Indies* 18°30N 67°45W 115 D11
Monach Is. *U.K.* 57°32N 7°40W 18 G2
Monaco ■ *Europe* 43°46N 7°23E 68 E7
Monadhliath Mts. *U.K.* 57°10N 4°4W 19 H9
Monaghan *Ireland* 54°15N 6°57W 29 C8
Monaghan □ *Ireland* 54°11N 6°56W 29 C8
Monar, L. *U.K.* 57°26N 5°8W 18 H7
Monar Forest *U.K.* 57°27N 5°10W 18 H7
Monasterevin *Ireland* 53°8N 7°4W 31 B8
Monavullagh Mts. *Ireland* 52°14N 7°35W 31 D7
Mönchengladbach *Germany* 51°11N 6°27E 66 C4
Monclova *Mexico* 26°54N 101°25W 114 B4
Moncton *Canada* 46°7N 64°51W 113 B15
Moneague *Jamaica* 18°16N 77°7W 114 a
Moneymore *U.K.* 54°41N 6°40W 29 B8
Mongolia ■ *Asia* 47°0N 103°0E 80 B5
Mongolia, Plateau of *Asia* 45°0N 105°0E 74 D12
Mongu *Zambia* 15°16S 23°12E 97 H4
Monifieth *U.K.* 56°30N 2°48W 21 B10
Monmouth *U.K.* 51°48N 2°42W 26 D8
Monmouth *U.S.A.* 40°55N 90°39W 112 E2
Monmouthshire □ *U.K.* 51°48N 2°54W 26 D8
Monnow → *U.K.* 51°49N 2°43W 24 C3
Monroe La., *U.S.A.* 32°30N 92°7W 111 D8
Monroe Mich., *U.S.A.* 41°55N 83°24W 112 E6
Monroe Wis., *U.S.A.* 42°36N 89°38W 112 D3
Monrovia *Liberia* 6°18N 10°47W 94 G3
Mons *Belgium* 50°27N 3°58E 65 D3
Mont-de-Marsan *France* 43°54N 0°31W 68 E3
Mont-Laurier *Canada* 46°35N 75°30W 109 E12
Montana *Bulgaria* 43°27N 23°16E 71 C10
Montaña *Peru* 6°0S 73°0W 120 C2
Montana □ *U.S.A.* 47°0N 110°0W 110 A5
Montargis *France* 47°59N 2°43E 68 C5
Montauban *France* 44°2N 1°21E 68 D4
Montbéliard *France* 47°31N 6°48E 68 C7
Montceau-les-Mines *France* 46°40N 4°23E 68 C6
Monte Azul *Brazil* 15°9S 42°53W 122 C2
Monte-Carlo *Monaco* 43°44N 7°25E 68 E7
Monte Caseros *Argentina* 30°10S 57°50W 121 F4
Monte Cristi *Dom. Rep.* 19°52N 71°39W 115 D10
Montego Bay *Jamaica* 18°28N 77°55W 114 a
Montélimar *France* 44°33N 4°45E 68 D6
Montello *U.S.A.* 43°48N 89°20W 112 D3
Montemorelos *Mexico* 25°12N 99°49W 114 B5
Montenegro ■ *Europe* 42°40N 19°20E 71 C8
Monterey *U.S.A.* 36°37N 121°55W 110 C2
Montería *Colombia* 8°46N 75°53W 120 B2
Monterrey *Mexico* 25°40N 100°19W 114 B4
Montes Claros *Brazil* 16°30S 43°50W 122 C2
Montevideo *Uruguay* 34°50S 56°11W 121 F4
Montgomery *U.K.* 52°34N 3°8W 26 B7
Montgomery *U.S.A.* 32°23N 86°19W 111 D9
Monticello *U.S.A.* 40°45N 86°46W 112 E4
Montluçon *France* 46°22N 2°36E 68 C5
Montmagny *Canada* 46°58N 70°34W 113 B12
Montpelier Idaho, *U.S.A.* 42°19N 111°18W 110 B4
Montpelier Vt., *U.S.A.* 44°16N 72°35W 113 C11
Montpellier *France* 43°37N 3°52E 68 E5
Montréal *Canada* 45°30N 73°33W 113 C11
Montreux *Switz.* 46°26N 6°55E 66 E4
Montrose *U.K.* 56°44N 2°27W 19 J13
Montrose *U.S.A.* 38°29N 107°53W 110 C5
Montserrat ☑ *W. Indies* 16°40N 62°10W 115 D12
Monywa *Burma* 22°7N 95°11E 85 H19
Monza *Italy* 45°35N 9°16E 70 B3
Monze, C. *Pakistan* 24°47N 66°37E 84 G5
Moorfoot Hills *U.K.* 55°44N 3°8W 21 D9
Moorhead *U.S.A.* 46°53N 96°45W 111 A7
Moose Jaw *Canada* 50°24N 105°30W 108 D9
Moosehead L. *U.S.A.* 45°38N 69°40W 113 C13
Moosomin *Canada* 50°9N 101°40W 108 D9
Moosonee *Canada* 51°17N 80°39W 109 D11
Mopti *Mali* 14°30N 4°0W 94 F5
Mora *Sweden* 61°2N 14°38E 63 E6
Moradabad *India* 28°50N 78°50E 84 E11
Morant Bay *Jamaica* 17°53N 76°25W 114 a
Morant Pt. *Jamaica* 17°55N 76°12W 114 a
Morar, L. *U.K.* 56°57N 5°40W 18 J6
Moratuwa *Sri Lanka* 6°45N 79°55E 84 R11
Morava → *Serbia* 44°36N 21°4E 71 B9
Morava → *Slovak Rep.* 48°10N 16°59E 67 D9
Moravian Hts. *Czech Rep.* 49°30N 15°40E 56 F9
Moray □ *U.K.* 57°31N 3°18W 19 G11
Moray Firth *U.K.* 57°40N 3°52W 19 G10
Morden *Canada* 49°15N 98°10W 108 E10
Mordvinia □ *Russia* 54°20N 44°30E 72 D7
Morea → *U.S.A.* 45°18N 100°43W 110 A6
Morebattle *U.K.* 55°31N 2°22W 21 C11
Morecambe *U.K.* 54°5N 2°52W 22 D3
Morecambe B. *U.K.* 54°7N 3°0W 22 D3
Moree *Australia* 29°28S 149°54E 98 F9
Morehead *U.S.A.* 38°11N 83°26W 112 F6
Morelia *Mexico* 19°42N 101°7W 114 D4
Morena, Sierra *Spain* 38°20N 4°0W 69 C3
Moresby I. *Canada* 52°30N 131°40W 108 D6
Moretonhampstead *U.K.* 50°39N 3°46W 27 F6
Morgan City *U.S.A.* 29°42N 91°12W 111 E8

Morgantown *U.S.A.* 39°38N 79°57W 112 F8
Morioka *Japan* 39°45N 141°8E 82 D7
Morlaix *France* 48°36N 3°52W 68 B2
Morley *U.K.* 53°45N 1°36W 23 E5
Morocco ■ *N. Afr.* 32°0N 5°50W 94 B4
Morogoro *Tanzania* 6°50S 37°40E 96 F7
Morón *Cuba* 22°8N 78°39W 115 C9
Morondava *Madag.* 20°17S 44°17E 97 J8
Moroni *Comoros Is.* 11°40S 43°16E 91 H8
Morotai *Indonesia* 2°10N 128°30E 83 C4
Morpeth *U.K.* 55°10N 1°41W 22 B5
Morphou *Cyprus* 35°12N 32°59E 86 C3
Morrinhos *Brazil* 17°45S 49°10W 122 C1
Morris *U.S.A.* 41°22N 88°26W 112 E31
Morte Bay *U.K.* 51°9N 4°14W 27 E5
Morte Pt. *U.K.* 51°11N 4°14W 27 E5
Mortehoe *U.K.* 51°11N 4°12W 27 E5
Mortimer's Cross *U.K.* 52°16N 2°50W 24 B3
Morton Fen *U.K.* 52°49N 0°20W 23 G8
Morvan *France* 47°5N 4°3E 68 C6
Morwenstow *U.K.* 50°54N 4°33W 27 F4
Moscos Is. *Burma* 14°0N 97°30E 85 N20
Moscow *Russia* 55°45N 37°37E 72 C6
Moscow *U.S.A.* 46°44N 117°0W 110 A3
Mosel → *Europe* 50°22N 7°36E 66 C4
Moses Lake *U.S.A.* 47°8N 119°17W 110 A3
Moshi *Tanzania* 3°22S 37°18E 96 E7
Mosjøen *Norway* 65°51N 13°12E 63 D6
Mosselbaai *S. Africa* 34°11S 22°8E 97 L4
Mossley *U.K.* 53°33N 2°1W 23 E4
Mossoró *Brazil* 5°10S 37°15W 120 C6
Most *Czech Rep.* 50°31N 13°38E 66 C7
Mostaganem *Algeria* 35°54N 0°5E 94 A6
Mostar *Bos.-H.* 43°22N 17°50E 71 C7
Mosul *Iraq* 36°15N 43°5E 86 B5
Motcombe *U.K.* 51°1N 2°13W 24 D4
Motherwell *U.K.* 55°47N 3°58W 21 D8
Motihari *India* 26°30N 84°55E 85 F14
Motril *Spain* 36°31N 3°37W 69 D4
Mottisfont *U.K.* 51°2N 1°32W 24 D5
Mouila *Gabon* 1°50S 11°0E 96 E2
Moule à Chique, C. *St. Lucia* 13°43N 60°57W 115 f
Moulins *France* 46°35N 3°19E 68 C5
Moulmein *Burma* 16°30N 97°40E 85 L20
Moulouya, O. → *Morocco* 35°5N 2°25W 94 B5
Moulton *U.K.* 52°17N 0°52W 25 B7
Moundou *Chad* 8°40N 16°10E 95 G9
Moundsville *U.S.A.* 39°55N 80°44W 112 F7
Mount Carmel *U.S.A.* 38°25N 87°46W 112 F4
Mount Desert I. *U.S.A.* 44°21N 68°20W 113 C13
Mount Gambier *Australia* 37°50S 140°46E 98 H7
Mount Hagen *Papua N. G.* 5°52S 144°16E 98 B7
Mount Isa *Australia* 20°42S 139°26E 98 E6
Mount Magnet *Australia* 28°2S 117°47E 98 F2
Mount Pleasant *U.S.A.* 43°36N 84°46W 112 D5
Mount Sterling *U.S.A.* 38°4N 83°56W 112 F6
Mount Vernon Ind., *U.S.A.* 37°56N 87°54W 112 F3
Mount Vernon Ohio, *U.S.A.* 40°23N 82°29W 112 E6
Mountain Ash *U.K.* 51°40N 3°23W 26 D7
Mountain Home *U.S.A.* 43°8N 115°41W 110 B3
Mountain View *U.S.A.* 19°33N 155°7W 110 J17
Mountmellick *Ireland* 53°7N 7°20W 31 B8
Mountrath *Ireland* 53°0N 7°28W 31 C8
Mount's Bay *U.K.* 50°5N 5°31W 27 G2
Mountsorrel *U.K.* 52°44N 1°8W 23 G6
Mourne → *U.K.* 54°52N 7°26W 28 B7
Mourne Mts. *U.K.* 54°10N 6°0W 29 C9
Mouscron *Belgium* 50°45N 3°12E 65 D3
Moville *Ireland* 55°11N 7°3W 29 A7
Moy → *Ireland* 54°8N 9°8W 28 C3
Mozambique ■ *Africa* 19°0S 35°0E 97 H7
Mozambique Chan. *Africa* 17°30S 42°30E 90 H8
Mozdok *Russia* 43°45N 44°48E 73 F7
Mpanda *Tanzania* 6°23S 31°1E 96 F6
Mpumalanga *S. Africa* 29°50S 30°33E 97 K6
Msaken *Tunisia* 35°49N 10°33E 95 A8
Mthatha *S. Africa* 31°36S 28°49E 97 L5
Mtwara-Mikindani *Tanzania* 10°20S 40°20E 96 G8
Muar *Malaysia* 2°3N 102°34E 83 C2
Mubi *Nigeria* 10°18N 13°16E 95 F8
Much Dewchurch *U.K.* 51°58N 2°45W 24 C3
Much Marcle *U.K.* 51°59N 2°29W 24 C4
Much Wenlock *U.K.* 52°35N 2°33W 23 G3
Muchinga Mts. *Zambia* 11°30S 31°30E 97 G6
Muck *U.K.* 56°50N 6°15W 18 J5
Muckle Flugga *U.K.* 60°51N 0°54W 18 A16
Muckle Roe *U.K.* 60°23N 1°27W 18 B15
Mucuri *Brazil* 18°0S 39°36W 122 C3
Mudanjiang *China* 44°38N 129°30E 81 B7
Mufulira *Zambia* 12°32S 28°15E 97 G5
Muğla *Turkey* 37°15N 28°22E 73 G4
Muine Bheag *Ireland* 52°42N 6°58W 31 C9
Muir of Ord *U.K.* 57°32N 4°28W 19 G9
Muktsar *India* 30°30N 74°30E 84 D9
Mulde → *Germany* 51°53N 12°15E 66 C7
Mulhacén *Spain* 37°4N 3°20W 69 D4
Mulhouse *France* 47°40N 7°20E 68 C7
Mull *U.K.* 56°25N 5°56W 20 B4
Mull, Sound of *U.K.* 56°30N 5°50W 20 B4
Mullaghareirk Mts. *Ireland* 52°20N 9°10W 30 D4
Mullet Pen. *Ireland* 54°13N 10°2W 28 C1
Mullingar *Ireland* 53°31N 7°21W 28 D7
Mullion *U.K.* 50°1N 5°16W 27 G3
Mulroy B. *Ireland* 55°15N 7°46W 28 A6
Multan *Pakistan* 30°15N 71°36E 84 D7
Mumbai *India* 18°56N 72°50E 84 K8
Mumbles Hd. *U.K.* 51°34N 3°59W 27 D6
Muna *Indonesia* 5°0S 122°30E 83 D4
Muncie *U.S.A.* 40°12N 85°23W 112 E5
Mundesley *U.K.* 52°53N 1°25E 25 A11
Mundo Novo *Brazil* 11°50S 40°29W 122 B2
Munger *India* 25°23N 86°30E 85 G15
Munich *Germany* 48°8N 11°34E 66 D6
Munising *U.S.A.* 46°25N 86°40W 112 B4
Münster *Germany* 51°58N 7°37E 66 C4
Munster □ *Ireland* 52°18N 8°44W 30 D5
Murashi *Russia* 59°30N 49°0E 72 C8
Murat → *Turkey* 38°46N 40°0E 73 G7

Murchison → *Australia* 27°45S 114°0E 98 F1
Murcia *Spain* 38°5N 1°10W 69 D5
Murcia □ *Spain* 37°50N 1°30W 69 D5
Mureş → *Romania* 46°15N 20°13E 67 E11
Murfreesboro *U.S.A.* 35°51N 86°24W 111 C9
Muriaé *Brazil* 21°8S 42°23W 122 D2
Müritz *Germany* 53°25N 12°42E 66 B7
Murmansk *Russia* 68°57N 33°10E 72 A5
Murom *Russia* 55°35N 42°3E 72 C7
Muroran *Japan* 42°25N 141°0E 82 B7
Murray → *U.S.A.* 36°37N 88°19W 112 G3
Murray → *Australia* 35°20S 139°22E 98 H6
Murton *U.K.* 54°50N 1°22W 22 C6
Mururoa *French Polynesia* 21°52S 138°55W 103 K14
Murwara *India* 23°46N 80°28E 85 H12
Muş *Turkey* 38°45N 41°30E 73 G7
Mûsa, Gebel *Egypt* 28°33N 33°59E 86 D3
Muscat *Oman* 23°37N 58°36E 87 F9
Musgrave Ranges *Australia* 26°0S 132°0E 98 F5
Musina *S. Africa* 22°20S 30°5E 97 J6
Muskegon *U.S.A.* 43°14N 86°16W 112 D4
Muskegon → *U.S.A.* 43°14N 86°21W 112 D4
Muskogee *U.S.A.* 35°45N 95°22W 111 C7
Musselburgh *U.K.* 55°57N 3°2W 21 C9
Musselshell → *U.S.A.* 47°21N 107°57W 110 A5
Mutare *Zimbabwe* 18°58S 32°38E 97 H6
Mutton I. *Ireland* 52°49N 9°32W 30 C3
Muynak *Uzbekistan* 43°44N 59°10E 87 A9
Muz Tag *China* 36°25N 87°25E 80 C3
Muzaffarabad *Pakistan* 34°25N 73°30E 84 B8
Muzaffarnagar *India* 29°26N 77°40E 84 E10
Muztagh-Ata *China* 38°17N 75°7E 80 C2
Mwanza *Tanzania* 2°30S 32°58E 96 E6
Mweelrea *Ireland* 53°39N 9°49W 28 D2
Mwene-Ditu
   Dem. Rep. of the Congo 6°35S 22°27E 96 F4
Mweru, L. *Zambia* 9°0S 28°40E 96 F5
My Tho *Vietnam* 10°29N 106°23E 83 B2
Myanmar = Burma ■ *Asia* 21°0N 96°30E 85 J20
Mycenæ *Greece* 37°43N 22°46E 71 F10
Myddle *U.K.* 52°49N 2°47W 23 G3
Myingyan *Burma* 21°30N 95°20E 85 J19
Myitkyina *Burma* 25°24N 97°26E 85 G20
Mymensingh *Bangla.* 24°45N 90°24E 85 G17
Mynydd Du *U.K.* 51°52N 3°50W 26 D6
Mynydd Preseli *U.K.* 51°57N 4°48W 26 D4
Mysore *India* 12°17N 76°41E 84 N10
Mytishchi *Russia* 55°50N 37°50E 72 C6

N

Naab → *Germany* 49°1N 12°2E 66 D6
Naas *Ireland* 53°12N 6°40W 31 B9
Naberezhnyye Chelny *Russia* 55°42N 52°19E 72 C9
Nabeul *Tunisia* 36°30N 10°44E 95 A8
Nābulus *West Bank* 32°14N 35°15E 86 C3
Nacala *Mozam.* 14°31S 40°34E 91 H8
Nacogdoches *U.S.A.* 31°36N 94°39W 111 D8
Nacozari de García *Mexico* 30°25N 109°38W 114 A3
Nadiad *India* 22°41N 72°56E 84 H8
Nador *Morocco* 35°14N 2°58W 94 B5
Nafferton *U.K.* 54°1N 0°23W 23 D8
Nafud Desert *Si. Arabia* 28°15N 41°0E 86 D5
Naga *Phil.* 13°38N 123°15E 83 B4
Nagaland □ *India* 26°0N 94°30E 85 G19
Nagano *Japan* 36°40N 138°10E 82 E6
Nagaoka *Japan* 37°27N 138°51E 82 E6
Nagappattinam *India* 10°46N 79°51E 84 P11
Nagasaki *Japan* 32°47N 129°50E 82 G1
Nagaur *India* 27°15N 73°45E 84 F8
Nagercoil *India* 8°12N 77°26E 84 Q10
Nagles Mts. *Ireland* 52°8N 8°30W 30 D6
Nagorno-Karabakh □
   Azerbaijan 39°55N 46°45E 73 F8
Nagoya *Japan* 35°10N 136°50E 82 F5
Nagpur *India* 21°8N 79°10E 84 J11
Naguabo *Puerto Rico* 18°13N 65°44W 115 d
Naha *Japan* 26°13N 127°42E 81 D7
Nailsea *U.K.* 51°26N 2°44W 24 D3
Nailsworth *U.K.* 51°41N 2°14W 24 C4
Nain *Canada* 56°34N 61°40W 109 D13
Nairn *U.K.* 57°35N 3°53W 19 G10
Nairobi *Kenya* 1°17S 36°48E 96 E7
Naivasha *Kenya* 0°40S 36°30E 96 E7
Najafābād *Iran* 32°40N 51°15E 87 C7
Najibabad *India* 29°40N 78°20E 84 E11
Najrān *Si. Arabia* 17°34N 44°18E 88 D3
Nakhon Ratchasima
   Thailand 14°59N 102°12E 83 B2
Nakhon Sawan *Thailand* 15°35N 100°10E 83 B2
Nakhon Si Thammarat
   Thailand 8°29N 100°0E 83 C2
Nakina *Canada* 50°10N 86°40W 109 D11
Nakuru *Kenya* 0°15S 36°4E 96 E7
Nalchik *Russia* 43°30N 43°33E 73 F7
Nallamalai Hills *India* 15°30N 78°50E 84 M11
Nam Co *China* 30°30N 90°45E 80 C4
Nam Dinh *Vietnam* 20°25N 106°5E 83 A2
Namak, Daryācheh-ye *Iran* 34°30N 52°0E 87 C8
Namaland *Namibia* 26°0S 17°0E 97 K3
Namangan *Uzbekistan* 41°0N 71°40E 87 A12
Namcha Barwa *China* 29°40N 95°10E 80 D4
Namib Desert *Namibia* 22°30S 15°0E 97 J3
Namibe *Angola* 15°7S 12°11E 97 H2
Namibia ■ *Africa* 22°0S 18°9E 97 J3
Nampa *U.S.A.* 43°34N 116°34W 110 B3
Nam'po *N. Korea* 38°52N 125°10E 81 C7
Nampula *Mozam.* 15°6S 39°15E 97 H7
Namumea *Tuvalu* 5°41S 176°9E 99 B14
Namur *Belgium* 50°27N 4°52E 65 D4
Nan-ch'ang *China* 28°42N 115°55E 81 D6
Nan Ling *China* 25°0N 112°30E 81 D6
Nanaimo *Canada* 49°10N 124°0W 108 E7
Nanchang *China* 30°43N 106°2E 80 C5
Nancy *France* 48°42N 6°12E 68 B7
Nanda Devi *India* 30°23N 79°59E 84 D11
Nanded *India* 19°10N 77°20E 84 K10

Nandurbar   Olsztyn

Nandurbar *India*   21°20N 74°15E **84** J9
Nanga Parbat *Pakistan*   35°10N 74°35E **84** B9
Nangarhār □ *Afghan.*   34°20N 70°0E **87** C12
Nanjing *China*   32°2N 118°47E **81** C6
Nanning *China*   22°48N 108°20E **80** D5
Nanping *China*   26°38N 118°10E **81** D6
Nansen Sd. *Canada*   81°0N 91°0W **109** A10
Nantes *France*   47°12N 1°33W **68** C3
Nantong *China*   32°1N 120°52E **81** C7
Nantucket I. *U.S.A.*   41°16N 70°5W **113** E12
Nantwich *U.K.*   53°4N 2°31W **23** F3
Nanuque *Brazil*   17°50S 40°21W **122** C2
Nanyang *China*   33°11N 112°30E **81** C6
Nanyuki *Kenya*   0°2N 37°4E **96** D7
Napa *U.S.A.*   38°18N 122°17W **110** C2
Napier *N.Z.*   39°30S 176°56E **99** H14
Naples *Italy*   40°50N 14°15E **70** D6
Napo → *Peru*   3°20S 72°40W **120** C2
Nappa *U.K.*   53°58N 2°13W **23** E4
Narayanganj *Bangla.*   23°40N 90°33E **85** H17
Narberth *U.K.*   51°47N 4°44W **26** D4
Narbonne *France*   43°11N 3°0E **68** E5
Narborough *U.K.*   52°34N 1°13W **23** G6
Nares Str. *Arctic*   80°0N 70°0W **109** A13
Narmada → *India*   21°38N 72°36E **84** J8
Narodnaya *Russia*   65°5N 59°58E **72** A10
Narva *Estonia*   59°23N 28°12E **63** F9
Narvik *Norway*   68°11N 17°26E **63** D7
Naryan-Mar *Russia*   67°42N 53°12E **72** A9
Naseby *U.K.*   52°24N 0°59W **25** B7
Nashua *U.S.A.*   42°45N 71°28W **113** D12
Nashville *U.S.A.*   36°10N 86°47W **111** C9
Nasik *India*   19°58N 73°50E **84** K8
Nasirabad *India*   26°15N 74°45E **84** F9
Nasiriyah *Iraq*   31°0N 46°15E **86** D6
Nassau *Bahamas*   25°5N 77°20W **115** B9
Nasser, L. *Egypt*   23°0N 32°30E **95** D12
Natal *Brazil*   5°47S 35°13W **120** C6
Natashquan *Canada*   50°14N 61°46W **109** D13
Natashquan → *Canada*   50°7N 61°50W **109** D13
Natchez *U.S.A.*   31°34N 91°24W **111** D8
Natchitoches *U.S.A.*   31°46N 93°5W **111** D8
Nathdwara *India*   24°55N 73°50E **84** G8
Natitingou *Benin*   10°20N 1°26E **94** F6
Natron, L. *Tanzania*   2°20S 36°0E **96** E7
Natuna Besar, Kepulauan *Indonesia*   4°0N 108°15E **83** C2
Nauru ■ *Pac. Oc.*   1°0S 166°0E **102** H8
Navarino, I. *Chile*   55°0S 67°40W **121** H3
Navarra □ *Spain*   42°40N 1°40W **69** A5
Navenby *U.K.*   53°6N 0°31W **23** F7
Naver → *U.K.*   58°32N 4°14W **19** E9
Navojoa *Mexico*   27°6N 109°26W **114** B3
Navsari *India*   20°57N 72°59E **84** J8
Nawabshah *Pakistan*   26°15N 68°25E **84** F6
Naxçıvan □ *Azerbaijan*   39°25N 45°26E **73** G8
Naxos *Greece*   37°8N 25°25E **71** F11
Naypyidaw *Burma*   19°44N 96°12E **85** K20
Nazaré *Brazil*   13°2S 39°0W **122** B3
Nazas → *Mexico*   25°12N 104°12W **114** B4
Nazca *Peru*   14°50S 74°57W **120** D2
Naze, The *U.K.*   51°53N 1°18E **25** C11
Nazret *Ethiopia*   8°32N 39°22E **88** F2
Ndjamena *Chad*   12°10N 14°59E **95** F8
Ndola *Zambia*   13°0S 28°34E **97** G5
Neagh, Lough *U.K.*   54°37N 6°25W **29** B9
Near Is. *U.S.A.*   52°30N 174°0E **108** D1
Neath *U.K.*   51°39N 3°48W **26** D6
Nebraska □ *U.S.A.*   41°30N 99°30W **110** B7
Nébrodi, Monti *Italy*   37°54N 14°35E **70** F6
Neckar → *Germany*   49°27N 8°29E **66** D5
Necochea *Argentina*   38°30S 58°50W **121** F4
Needham Market *U.K.*   52°9N 1°4E **25** B11
Needles, The *U.K.*   50°39N 1°35W **24** E5
Neenah *U.S.A.*   44°11N 88°28W **112** C3
Neepawa *Canada*   50°15N 99°30W **108** D10
Neftekumsk *Russia*   44°46N 44°50E **73** F7
Neftyugansk *Russia*   61°5N 72°42E **79** C9
Negaunee *U.S.A.*   46°30N 87°36W **112** B4
Negele *Ethiopia*   5°20N 39°36E **88** F2
Negombo *Sri Lanka*   7°12N 79°50E **84** R11
Negra, Pta. *Peru*   6°6S 81°10W **116** D2
Negril *Jamaica*   18°22N 78°20W **114** a
Negro → *Argentina*   41°2S 62°47W **121** G3
Negro → *Brazil*   3°0S 60°0W **120** C4
Negros *Phil.*   9°30N 122°40E **83** C4
Neijiang *China*   29°35N 104°55E **80** D5
Neisse → *Europe*   52°4N 14°46E **66** B8
Neiva *Colombia*   2°56N 75°18W **120** B2
Nellore *India*   14°27N 79°59E **84** M11
Nelson *Canada*   49°30N 117°20W **108** E8
Nelson *N.Z.*   41°18S 173°16E **99** J13
Nelson *U.K.*   53°50N 2°13W **23** E4
Nelson → *Canada*   54°33N 98°2W **108** D10
Neman → *Lithuania*   55°25N 21°10E **63** F8
Nenagh *Ireland*   52°52N 8°11W **30** C6
Nene → *U.K.*   52°49N 0°11E **25** A9
Nenjiang *China*   49°10N 125°10E **81** B7
Neosho → *U.S.A.*   36°48N 95°18W **111** C7
Nepal ■ *Asia*   28°0N 84°30E **85** F14
Nephi *U.S.A.*   39°43N 111°50W **110** C4
Nephin *Ireland*   54°1N 9°22W **28** C3
Nephin Beg Range *Ireland*   54°0N 9°40W **28** C2
Nerastro, Sarīr *Libya*   24°20N 20°37E **95** D10
Neryungri *Russia*   57°38N 124°28E **79** D14
Ness, L. *U.K.*   57°15N 4°32W **19** H8
Neston *U.K.*   53°17N 3°4W **23** F2
Netherbury *U.K.*   50°46N 2°45W **24** E3
Netherlands ■ *Europe*   52°0N 5°30E **65** C5
Netherlands Antilles ☑ *W. Indies*   12°15N 69°0W **115** E11
Netley *U.K.*   50°52N 1°20W **24** E5
Nettilling L. *Canada*   66°30N 71°0W **109** C12
Nettlebed *U.K.*   51°34N 0°59W **25** C7
Nettleham *U.K.*   53°16N 0°29W **23** F8
Neuchâtel *Switz.*   47°0N 6°55E **66** E4
Neuchâtel, Lac de *Switz.*   46°53N 6°50E **66** E4
Neuquén *Argentina*   38°55S 68°0W **121** F3

Neusiedler See *Austria*   47°50N 16°47E **67** E9
Neva → *Russia*   59°56N 30°20E **72** C5
Nevada □ *U.S.A.*   39°0N 117°0W **110** C3
Nevers *France*   47°0N 3°9E **68** C5
Nevinnomyssk *Russia*   44°40N 42°0E **73** F7
New Abbey *U.K.*   54°59N 3°37W **21** E9
New Alresford *U.K.*   51°5N 1°8W **24** D6
New Amsterdam *Guyana*   6°15N 57°36W **120** B4
New Bedford *U.S.A.*   41°38N 70°56W **113** E12
New Britain *Papua N. G.*   5°50S 150°20E **98** B9
New Britain *U.S.A.*   41°40N 72°47W **113** E11
New Brunswick *U.S.A.*   40°30N 74°27W **113** E10
New Brunswick □ *Canada*   46°50N 66°30W **113** B14
New Caledonia ☑ *Pac. Oc.*   21°0S 165°0E **99** E12
New Castle *Ind., U.S.A.*   39°55N 85°22W **112** F5
New Castle *Pa., U.S.A.*   41°0N 80°21W **112** E7
New Delhi *India*   28°36N 77°11E **84** E10
New England *U.S.A.*   43°0N 71°0W **111** B12
New Forest △ *U.K.*   50°53N 1°34W **24** E5
New Galloway *U.K.*   55°5N 4°9W **20** D7
New Georgia Is. *Solomon Is.*   8°15S 157°30E **99** B10
New Glasgow *Canada*   45°35N 62°36W **109** E13
New Guinea *Oceania*   4°0S 136°0E **98** B7
New Hampshire □ *U.S.A.*   44°0N 71°30W **113** D12
New Haven *U.S.A.*   41°18N 72°55W **113** E11
New Hebrides = Vanuatu ■ *Pac. Oc.*   15°0S 168°0E **99** D12
New Holland *U.K.*   53°42N 0°21W **23** E8
New Iberia *U.S.A.*   30°1N 91°49W **111** D8
New Ireland *Papua N. G.*   3°20S 151°50E **98** A9
New Jersey □ *U.S.A.*   40°0N 74°30W **113** E10
New Lexington *U.S.A.*   39°43N 82°13W **112** F6
New Liskeard *Canada*   47°31N 79°41W **109** E12
New London *U.S.A.*   41°22N 72°6W **113** E11
New Madrid *U.S.A.*   36°36N 89°32W **112** G3
New Mexico □ *U.S.A.*   34°30N 106°0W **110** D5
New Mills *U.K.*   53°23N 2°0W **23** F5
New Milton *U.K.*   50°45N 1°40W **24** E5
New Orleans *U.S.A.*   29°57N 90°4W **111** E8
New Philadelphia *U.S.A.*   40°30N 81°27W **112** E7
New Plymouth *N.Z.*   39°4S 174°5E **99** H13
New Providence *Bahamas*   25°25N 78°35W **115** B9
New Quay *U.K.*   52°13N 4°21W **26** C5
New Radnor *U.K.*   52°15N 3°9W **26** C7
New Romney *U.K.*   50°59N 0°57E **25** E10
New Ross *Ireland*   52°23N 6°57W **31** D9
New Rossington *U.K.*   53°29N 1°4W **23** F6
New Siberian Is. *Russia*   75°0N 142°0E **79** B15
New South Wales □ *Australia*   33°0S 146°0E **98** G8
New York *U.S.A.*   40°43N 74°0W **113** E11
New York □ *U.S.A.*   43°0N 75°0W **113** D9
New Zealand ■ *Oceania*   40°0S 176°0E **99** J14
Newark *Del., U.S.A.*   39°41N 75°46W **113** F10
Newark *N.J., U.S.A.*   40°44N 74°10W **113** E10
Newark *N.Y., U.S.A.*   43°3N 77°6W **112** D9
Newark *Ohio, U.S.A.*   40°3N 82°24W **112** E6
Newark-on-Trent *U.K.*   53°5N 0°48W **23** F7
Newberry *U.S.A.*   46°21N 85°30W **112** B5
Newbiggin-by-the-Sea *U.K.*   55°11N 1°31W **22** B5
Newbigging *U.K.*   55°42N 3°34W **21** C8
Newburgh *U.K.*   41°30N 74°1W **113** E10
Newburn *U.K.*   54°59N 1°43W **22** C5
Newbury *U.K.*   51°24N 1°20W **24** D6
Newburyport *U.S.A.*   42°49N 70°53W **113** D12
Newby Bridge *U.K.*   54°17N 2°57W **22** D3
Newcastle *Australia*   33°0S 151°46E **98** G9
Newcastle *Canada*   47°1N 65°38W **113** B15
Newcastle *S. Africa*   27°45S 29°58E **97** K5
Newcastle *U.S.A.*   54°13N 5°54W **29** C10
Newcastle Emlyn *U.K.*   52°2N 4°28W **26** C5
Newcastle-under-Lyme *U.K.*   53°1N 2°14W **23** F4
Newcastle-upon-Tyne *U.K.*   54°58N 1°36W **22** C5
Newcastle West *Ireland*   52°27N 9°3W **30** D4
Newcastleton *U.K.*   55°11N 2°49W **21** D10
Newent *U.K.*   51°56N 2°24W **24** C4
Newfoundland & Labrador □ *Canada*   53°0N 58°0W **109** D14
Newham □ *U.K.*   51°31N 0°3E **25** C9
Newhaven *U.K.*   50°47N 0°3E **25** E9
Newington *Kent, U.K.*   51°6N 1°7E **25** D11
Newington *Kent, U.K.*   51°21N 0°41E **25** D10
Newlyn *U.K.*   50°6N 5°34W **27** G2
Newlyn East *U.K.*   50°22N 5°5W **27** G3
Newman *Australia*   23°18S 119°45E **98** E2
Newmarket *Ireland*   52°13N 9°0W **30** D5
Newmarket *U.K.*   52°15N 0°25E **25** B9
Newnham *U.K.*   51°48N 2°27W **24** C4
Newport *Ireland*   53°53N 9°33W **28** D2
Newport *Essex, U.K.*   51°59N 0°14E **25** C9
Newport *I. of W., U.K.*   50°42N 1°17W **24** E6
Newport *Newport, U.K.*   51°35N 3°0W **27** D8
Newport *Pembs., U.K.*   52°1N 4°51W **26** C4
Newport *Telford & Wrekin, U.K.*   52°46N 2°22W **23** G4
Newport *Ark., U.S.A.*   35°37N 91°16W **111** C8
Newport *Ky., U.S.A.*   39°5N 84°29W **112** F5
Newport *R.I., U.S.A.*   41°29N 71°19W **113** E12
Newport *Vt., U.S.A.*   44°56N 72°13W **113** C11
Newport News *U.S.A.*   36°58N 76°25W **111** C11
Newport Pagnell *U.K.*   52°5N 0°43W **25** B7
Newquay *U.K.*   50°25N 5°6W **27** G3
Newry *U.K.*   54°11N 6°21W **29** C9
Newton Abbot *U.K.*   50°32N 3°37W **27** F6
Newton Arlosh *U.K.*   54°53N 3°14W **22** C2
Newton Aycliffe *U.K.*   54°37N 1°34W **22** C5
Newton Ferrers *U.K.*   50°19N 4°3W **27** G5
Newton le Willows *U.K.*   53°28N 2°38W **23** F3
Newton St. Cyres *U.K.*   50°46N 3°36W **27** F6
Newton Stewart *U.K.*   54°57N 4°30W **20** E6
Newtonmore *U.K.*   57°4N 4°8W **19** H9
Newtown *U.K.*   52°31N 3°19W **26** C7
Newtown St. Boswells *U.K.*   55°34N 2°39W **21** C10
Newtownabbey *U.K.*   54°40N 5°56W **29** B10
Newtownards *U.K.*   54°36N 5°42W **29** B10
Newtownstewart *U.K.*   54°43N 7°23W **28** B7
Neyshābūr *Iran*   36°10N 58°50E **87** B9
Nganglong Kangri *China*   33°0N 81°0E **80** D2
Ngaoundéré *Cameroon*   7°15N 13°35E **96** C1
Ngoring Hu *China*   34°55N 97°5E **80** C4

Ngorongoro *Tanzania*   3°11S 35°32E **96** E7
Nguru *Nigeria*   12°56N 10°29E **95** F8
Nha Trang *Vietnam*   12°16N 109°10E **83** B2
Nhamundá → *Brazil*   2°12S 56°41W **120** C4
Niagara Falls *Canada*   43°7N 79°5W **109** E12
Niagara Falls *U.S.A.*   43°5N 79°4W **112** D8
Niamey *Niger*   13°27N 2°6E **94** F6
Nias *Indonesia*   1°0N 97°30E **83** C1
Nicaragua ■ *Cent. Amer.*   11°40N 85°30W **114** E7
Nicaragua, L. de *Nic.*   12°0N 85°30W **114** E7
Nice *France*   43°42N 7°14E **68** E7
Nicholasville *U.S.A.*   37°53N 84°34W **112** G5
Nicobar Is. *Ind. Oc.*   8°0N 93°30E **83** C1
Nicosia *Cyprus*   35°10N 33°25E **86** C3
Nicoya, Pen. de *Costa Rica*   9°45N 85°40W **114** F7
Nidd → *U.K.*   53°59N 1°23W **23** E6
Nidderdale *U.K.*   54°5N 1°46W **22** D5
Niedersachsen □ *Germany*   52°50N 9°0E **66** B5
Niğde *Turkey*   37°58N 34°40E **86** B3
Niger ■ *W. Afr.*   17°30N 10°0E **94** E7
Niger → *W. Afr.*   5°33N 6°33E **94** G7
Nigeria ■ *W. Afr.*   8°30N 8°0E **94** G7
Niigata *Japan*   37°58N 139°0E **82** E6
Ni'ihau *U.S.A.*   21°54N 160°9W **110** H14
Nijmegen *Neths.*   51°50N 5°52E **65** C5
Nikolayev *Ukraine*   46°58N 32°0E **73** E5
Nikolayevsk-na-Amur *Russia*   53°8N 140°44E **79** D16
Nikopol *Ukraine*   47°35N 34°25E **73** E5
Nikšić *Montenegro*   42°50N 18°57E **71** C8
Nile → *Africa*   30°10N 31°6E **95** B12
Nimach *India*   24°30N 74°56E **84** G9
Nîmes *France*   43°50N 4°23E **68** E6
Nīmrūz □ *Afghan.*   30°0N 62°0E **87** D10
Nīnawá *Iraq*   36°25N 43°10E **86** B5
Ninfield *U.K.*   50°53N 0°26E **25** E9
Ningbo *China*   29°51N 121°28E **81** D7
Ningjing Shan *China*   30°0N 98°20E **80** C4
Ningxia Hui □ *China*   38°0N 106°0E **80** C5
Niobrara → *U.S.A.*   42°46N 98°3W **110** B7
Niort *France*   46°19N 0°29W **68** C3
Nipawin *Canada*   53°20N 104°0W **108** D9
Nipigon *Canada*   49°0N 88°17W **112** A3
Nipigon, L. *Canada*   49°50N 88°30W **109** E11
Nipissing, L. *Canada*   46°20N 80°0W **109** E12
Niquelândia *Brazil*   14°33S 48°23W **122** B1
Niš *Serbia*   43°19N 21°58E **71** C9
Niterói *Brazil*   22°53S 43°7W **122** D2
Nith → *U.K.*   55°14N 3°33W **21** D8
Nitra *Slovak Rep.*   48°19N 18°4E **67** D10
Nitra → *Slovak Rep.*   47°46N 18°10E **67** E10
Niuafo'ou *Tonga*   15°30S 175°58W **99** D15
Niue *Cook Is.*   19°2S 169°54W **99** D17
Nivernais *France*   47°15N 3°30E **68** C5
Nizamabad *India*   18°45N 78°7E **84** K11
Nizhnekamsk *Russia*   55°38N 51°49E **72** C9
Nizhnevartovsk *Russia*   60°56N 76°38E **79** C9
Nizhniy Novgorod *Russia*   56°20N 44°0E **72** C7
Nizhniy Tagil *Russia*   57°55N 59°57E **72** C10
Nizhyn *Ukraine*   51°5N 31°55E **73** D5
Nizwá *Oman*   22°56N 57°32E **88** C6
Nkawkaw *Ghana*   6°36N 0°49W **94** G5
Nkongsamba *Cameroon*   4°55N 9°55E **96** D1
Nobeoka *Japan*   32°36N 131°41E **82** G2
Noblesville *U.S.A.*   40°3N 86°1W **112** E5
Nogales *Mexico*   31°19N 110°56W **114** A2
Nogales *U.S.A.*   31°21N 110°56W **110** D4
Noirmoutier, Î. de *France*   46°58N 2°10W **68** C2
Nola *U.S.A.*   3°35N 16°4E **96** D3
Nome *U.S.A.*   64°30N 165°25W **108** C3
Nord-Ostsee-Kanal *Germany*   54°12N 9°32E **66** A5
Nordelph *U.K.*   52°35N 0°17E **25** A9
Norderstedt *Germany*   53°42N 10°1E **66** B5
Nordfriesische Inseln *Germany*   54°40N 8°20E **66** A5
Nordkapp *Norway*   71°10N 25°50E **63** C9
Nordrhein-Westfalen □ *Germany*   51°45N 7°30E **66** C4
Nordvik *Russia*   74°2N 111°32E **79** B13
Nore → *Ireland*   52°25N 6°58W **31** D9
Norfolk *Nebr., U.S.A.*   42°2N 97°25W **111** B7
Norfolk *Va., U.S.A.*   36°50N 76°17W **111** C11
Norfolk □ *U.K.*   52°39N 0°54E **25** A10
Norfolk Broads △ *U.K.*   52°45N 1°30E **25** A11
Norfolk I. *Pac. Oc.*   28°58S 168°3E **99** F12
Norham *U.K.*   55°43N 2°9W **22** A4
Norilsk *Russia*   69°20N 88°6E **79** C10
Normal *U.S.A.*   40°31N 88°59W **112** E3
Norman *U.S.A.*   35°13N 97°26W **110** C7
Norman Wells *Canada*   65°17N 126°51W **108** C7
Normandie *France*   48°45N 0°10E **68** B4
Normanton *Australia*   17°40S 141°10E **98** D7
Normanton *U.K.*   53°42N 1°24W **23** E6
Norristown *U.S.A.*   40°7N 75°21W **113** E10
Norrköping *Sweden*   58°37N 16°11E **63** F7
Norrland *Sweden*   62°15N 15°45E **63** E7
Norseman *Australia*   32°8S 121°43E **98** G3
Norte, Serra do *Brazil*   11°20S 59°0W **120** D4
North, C. *Canada*   47°2N 60°20W **113** B17
North Ayrshire □ *U.K.*   55°45N 4°44W **20** C6
North Battleford *Canada*   52°50N 108°17W **108** D9
North Bay *Canada*   46°20N 79°30W **109** E12
North Berwick *U.K.*   56°4N 2°42W **21** B10
North C. *Canada*   47°5N 64°0W **113** B15
North C. *N.Z.*   34°23S 173°4E **99** G13
North Canadian → *U.S.A.*   35°22N 95°37W **110** C7
North Carolina □ *U.S.A.*   35°30N 80°0W **111** C11
North Cerney *U.K.*   51°45N 1°57W **24** C5
North Channel *Canada*   46°0N 83°0W **112** B6
North Channel *U.K.*   55°13N 5°52W **20** D4
North Dakota □ *U.S.A.*   47°30N 100°15W **110** A7
North Dorset Downs *U.K.*   50°51N 2°30W **24** E4
North Downs *U.K.*   51°19N 0°21E **25** D9
North Esk → *U.K.*   56°46N 2°24E **19** J13
North European Plain *Europe*   55°0N 25°0E **56** E10
North Foreland *U.K.*   51°22N 1°28E **25** D11
North Harris *U.K.*   58°0N 6°55W **18** F4

North Hill *U.K.*   50°33N 4°27W **27** F5
North Hykeham *U.K.*   53°11N 0°35W **23** F7
North I. *N.Z.*   38°0S 175°0E **99** H14
North Korea ■ *Asia*   40°0N 127°0E **81** C7
North Magnetic Pole *Canada*   82°42N 114°24W **54** A2
North Minch *U.K.*   58°5N 5°55W **18** F7
North Molton *U.K.*   51°3N 3°49W **27** E6
North Ossetia □ *Russia*   43°30N 44°30E **73** F7
North Petherton *U.K.*   51°5N 3°1W **24** D2
North Platte *U.S.A.*   41°8N 100°46W **110** B6
North Platte → *U.S.A.*   41°7N 100°42W **110** B6
North Pole *Arctic*   90°0N 0°0W **54** A
North Pt. *Barbados*   13°20N 59°37W **115** g
North Ronaldsay *U.K.*   59°22N 2°26W **19** D13
North Saskatchewan → *Canada*   53°15N 105°5W **108** D9
North Sea *Europe*   56°0N 4°0E **64** C7
North Sea Canal = Nord-Ostsee-Kanal *Germany*   54°12N 9°32E **66** A5
North Somercotes *U.K.*   53°28N 0°9E **23** F9
North Sunderland *U.K.*   55°34N 1°40W **22** A5
North Tawton *U.K.*   50°48N 3°54W **27** F6
North Thompson → *Canada*   50°40N 120°20W **108** D7
North Thoresby *U.K.*   53°28N 0°4W **23** F8
North Tidworth *U.K.*   51°15N 1°40W **24** D5
North Tyne → *U.K.*   55°0N 2°8W **22** C4
North Uist *U.K.*   57°40N 7°15W **18** G3
North Vernon *U.S.A.*   39°0N 85°38W **112** F5
North Walsham *U.K.*   52°50N 1°22E **25** A11
North West C. *Australia*   21°45S 114°9E **98** E1
North West Frontier □ *Pakistan*   34°0N 72°0E **84** C7
North West Highlands *U.K.*   57°33N 4°58W **19** G8
North West River *Canada*   53°30N 60°10W **109** D13
North York Moors *U.K.*   54°23N 0°53W **22** D7
North York Moors △ *U.K.*   54°27N 0°51W **22** D7
North Yorkshire □ *U.K.*   54°15N 1°25W **22** D6
Northallerton *U.K.*   54°20N 1°26W **22** D6
Northam *Australia*   31°35S 116°42E **98** G2
Northam *U.K.*   51°2N 4°13W **27** E5
Northampton *U.K.*   52°15N 0°53W **25** B7
Northampton *U.S.A.*   42°19N 72°38W **113** D11
Northamptonshire □ *U.K.*   52°16N 0°55W **25** B7
Northern Areas □ *Pakistan*   36°30N 73°0E **84** B9
Northern Circars *India*   17°30N 82°30E **85** L13
Northern Ireland □ *U.K.*   54°45N 7°0W **29** B8
Northern Marianas ☑ *Pac. Oc.*   17°0N 145°0E **102** F6
Northern Sporades *Greece*   39°15N 23°30E **71** E10
Northern Territory □ *Australia*   20°0S 133°0E **98** E5
Northfleet *U.K.*   51°26N 0°20E **25** D9
Northiam *U.K.*   50°59N 0°36E **25** E10
Northleach *U.K.*   51°49N 1°50W **24** C5
Northrepps *U.K.*   52°54N 1°21E **25** A11
Northumberland □ *U.K.*   55°12N 2°0W **22** B4
Northumberland △ *Northumberland, U.K.*   55°15N 2°20W **22** B4
Northumberland Str. *Canada*   46°20N 64°0W **109** E13
Northwest Territories □ *Canada*   63°0N 118°0W **108** C9
Northwich *U.K.*   53°15N 2°31W **23** F3
Northwold *U.K.*   52°33N 0°36E **25** A10
Norton *N. Yorks., U.K.*   54°8N 0°47W **22** D7
Norton *Suffolk, U.K.*   52°16N 0°52E **25** B10
Norton Fitzwarren *U.K.*   51°1N 3°8W **24** D2
Norton Sd. *U.S.A.*   63°50N 164°0W **108** C3
Norwalk *U.S.A.*   41°15N 82°37W **112** E6
Norway ■ *Europe*   63°0N 11°0E **63** E6
Norway House *Canada*   53°59N 97°50W **108** D10
Norwegian B. *Canada*   77°30N 90°0W **109** B11
Norwegian Sea *Atl. Oc.*   66°0N 1°0E **54** C8
Norwich *U.K.*   52°38N 1°18E **25** A11
Norwich *U.S.A.*   42°32N 75°32W **113** D10
Noss Hd. *U.K.*   58°28N 3°3W **19** F11
Nossob → *S. Africa*   26°55S 20°45E **97** K4
Notre Dame B. *Canada*   49°45N 55°30W **109** E14
Nottaway → *Canada*   51°22N 78°55W **109** D12
Nottingham *U.K.*   52°58N 1°10W **23** G6
Nottingham □ *U.K.*   63°20N 77°55W **109** C12
Nottinghamshire □ *U.K.*   53°10N 1°3W **23** F6
Nouâdhibou *Mauritania*   20°54N 17°0W **94** D2
Nouâdhibou, Ras *Mauritania*   20°50N 17°0W **94** D2
Nouakchott *Mauritania*   18°9N 15°58W **94** E2
Nouméa *N. Cal.*   22°17S 166°30E **99** E12
Nova Casa Nova *Brazil*   9°25S 41°5W **122** A2
Nova Friburgo *Brazil*   22°16S 42°30E **122** D2
Nova Iguaçu *Brazil*   22°45S 43°28W **122** D2
Nova Lima *Brazil*   19°59S 43°51W **122** D2
Nova Scotia □ *Canada*   45°10N 63°0W **113** C16
Nova Venécia *Brazil*   18°45S 40°24W **122** C2
Novara *Italy*   45°28N 8°38E **70** B3
Novaya Zemlya *Russia*   75°0N 56°0E **79** B7
Novgorod *Russia*   58°30N 31°25E **72** C5
Novi Pazar *Serbia*   43°12N 20°28E **71** C9
Novi Sad *Serbia*   45°18N 19°52E **71** B8
Novo Remanso *Brazil*   9°41S 42°4W **122** A2
Novocherkassk *Russia*   47°27N 40°15E **73** E7
Novokuybyshevsk *Russia*   53°7N 49°58E **72** D8
Novomoskovsk *Russia*   54°5N 38°15E **72** D6
Novorossiysk *Russia*   44°43N 37°46E **73** F6
Novoshakhtinsk *Russia*   47°46N 39°58E **73** E6
Novosibirsk *Russia*   55°0N 83°5E **79** D10
Novotroitsk *Russia*   51°10N 58°15E **72** D10
Novyy Urengoy *Russia*   65°48N 76°52E **79** C9
Nowy Sącz *Poland*   49°40N 20°41E **67** D11
Nubia *Africa*   21°0N 32°0E **90** D7
Nubian Desert *Sudan*   21°30N 33°30E **95** D12
Nueces → *U.S.A.*   27°51N 97°30W **110** E7
Nueltin L. *Canada*   60°30N 99°30W **108** C10
Nueva Rosita *Mexico*   27°57N 101°13W **114** B4
Nuevitas *Cuba*   21°30N 77°20W **115** C9
Nuevo Laredo *Mexico*   27°30N 99°31W **114** B5
Nuku'alofa *Tonga*   21°10S 175°12W **99** E16
Nukulaelae *Tuvalu*   9°23S 179°52E **99** B14
Nukus *Uzbekistan*   42°27N 59°41E **87** A9
Nullarbor Plain *Australia*   31°10S 129°0E **98** G4
Numan *Nigeria*   9°29N 12°3E **95** G8

Numazu *Japan*   35°7N 138°51E **82** F6
Nunavut □ *Canada*   66°0N 85°0W **109** C11
Nuneaton *U.K.*   52°32N 1°27W **23** G6
Nunivak I. *U.S.A.*   60°10N 166°30W **108** B3
Nunney *U.K.*   51°12N 2°22W **24** D4
Núoro *Italy*   40°20N 9°20E **70** D3
Nuremberg *Germany*   49°27N 11°3E **66** D6
Nusaybin *Turkey*   37°3N 41°10E **73** G7
Nuuk *Greenland*   64°10N 51°35W **54** C5
Nuweveldberge *S. Africa*   32°10S 21°45E **97** L4
Nyahururu *Kenya*   0°2N 36°27E **96** D7
Nyainqentanglha Shan *China*   30°0N 90°0E **80** D3
Nyálá *Sudan*   12°2N 24°58E **95** F10
Nyíregyháza *Hungary*   47°58N 21°47E **67** E11
Nysa *Poland*   50°30N 17°22E **67** C9
Nzérékoré *Guinea*   7°49N 8°48W **94** G4

O

Oa, Mull of *U.K.*   55°35N 6°20W **20** C3
Oadby *U.K.*   52°36N 1°5W **23** G6
Oahe, L. *U.S.A.*   44°27N 100°24W **110** A6
O'ahu *U.S.A.*   21°28N 157°58W **110** H16
Oak Hill *U.S.A.*   37°59N 81°9W **112** G7
Oak Ridge *U.S.A.*   36°1N 84°16W **111** C10
Oakengates *U.K.*   52°41N 2°26W **23** G4
Oakham *U.K.*   52°40N 0°43W **23** G7
Oakland *U.S.A.*   37°48N 122°18W **110** C2
Oates Land *Antarctica*   69°0S 160°0E **55** C11
Oaxaca *Mexico*   17°3N 96°43W **114** D5
Ob → *Russia*   66°45N 69°30W **79** C8
Ob, G. of *Russia*   69°0N 73°0E **79** C9
Oba *Canada*   49°4N 84°7W **109** E11
Oban *U.K.*   56°25N 5°29W **20** B5
Oberhausen *Germany*   51°28N 6°51E **66** C4
Obi, Kepulauan *Indonesia*   1°23S 127°45E **83** D4
Óbidos *Brazil*   1°50S 55°30W **120** C4
Obihiro *Japan*   42°56N 143°12E **82** B8
Obozerskiy *Russia*   63°34N 40°21E **72** B7
Obshchi Syrt *Russia*   52°0N 53°0E **56** E16
Ocala *U.S.A.*   29°11N 82°8W **111** E10
Occidental, Cordillera *Colombia*   5°0N 76°0W **116** C3
Occidental, Grand Erg *Algeria*   30°20N 1°0E **94** B6
Ocean City *U.S.A.*   39°17N 74°35W **113** F10
Oceanside *U.S.A.*   33°12N 117°23W **110** D3
Ochil Hills *U.K.*   56°14N 3°40W **21** B8
Ocho Rios *Jamaica*   18°24N 77°6W **114** a
Oconto *U.S.A.*   44°53N 87°52W **112** C4
Odawara *Japan*   35°20N 139°6E **82** F6
Odense *Denmark*   55°22N 10°23E **63** F6
Oder → *Europe*   53°33N 14°38E **66** B8
Odessa *Ukraine*   46°30N 30°45E **73** E5
Odessa *U.S.A.*   31°52N 102°23W **110** D6
Odiham *U.K.*   51°15N 0°55W **25** D7
Odintsovo *Russia*   55°40N 37°16E **72** C6
Odzi *Zimbabwe*   19°0S 32°20E **97** H6
Offa *Nigeria*   8°13N 4°42E **94** G6
Offaly □ *Ireland*   53°15N 7°30W **31** B8
Offenbach *Germany*   50°6N 8°44E **66** C5
Ogaden *Ethiopia*   7°30N 45°30E **88** F3
Ōgaki *Japan*   35°21N 136°37E **82** F5
Ogasawara Gunto *Pac. Oc.*   27°0N 142°0E **102** E6
Ogbomosho *Nigeria*   8°1N 4°11E **94** G6
Ogden *U.S.A.*   41°13N 111°58W **110** B4
Ogdensburg *U.S.A.*   44°42N 75°30W **113** C10
Ogooué → *Gabon*   1°0S 9°0E **96** E1
Ohio □ *U.S.A.*   40°15N 82°45W **112** E5
Ohio → *U.S.A.*   36°59N 89°8W **111** C9
Ohře → *Czech Rep.*   50°30N 14°10E **66** C8
Ohrid, L. *Macedonia*   41°8N 20°52E **71** D9
Oil City *U.S.A.*   41°26N 79°42W **112** E8
Oise → *France*   49°0N 2°4E **68** B5
Oistins *Barbados*   13°4N 59°33W **115** g
Oistins B. *Barbados*   13°4N 59°33W **115** g
Ojos del Salado, Cerro *Argentina*   27°0S 68°40W **121** E3
Oka → *Russia*   56°20N 43°59E **72** C7
Okara *Pakistan*   30°50N 73°31E **84** D8
Okavango Delta *Botswana*   18°45S 22°45E **97** H4
Okayama *Japan*   34°40N 133°54E **82** F3
Okazaki *Japan*   34°57N 137°10E **82** F5
Okeechobee, L. *U.S.A.*   27°0N 80°50W **111** E10
Okehampton *U.K.*   50°44N 4°0W **27** F5
Okhotsk *Russia*   59°20N 143°10E **79** D16
Okhotsk, Sea of *Asia*   55°0N 145°0E **79** D16
Oki-Shotō *Japan*   36°5N 133°15E **82** E3
Okinawa-Jima *Japan*   26°32N 128°0E **81** D7
Oklahoma □ *U.S.A.*   35°20N 97°30W **110** C7
Oklahoma City *U.S.A.*   35°30N 97°30W **110** C7
Oktyabrsk *Kazakhstan*   49°28N 57°25E **73** E10
Oktyabrskiy *Russia*   54°28N 53°28E **72** D9
Öland *Sweden*   56°45N 16°38E **63** F7
Olavarría *Argentina*   36°55S 60°20W **121** F3
Ólbia *Italy*   40°55N 9°31E **70** D3
Old Basing *U.K.*   51°16N 1°3W **24** D6
Old Crow *Canada*   67°30N 139°55W **108** C6
Old Fletton *U.K.*   52°33N 0°14W **25** A8
Old Leake *U.K.*   53°2N 0°5E **23** F9
Old Town *U.S.A.*   44°56N 68°39W **113** C13
Oldbury *U.K.*   51°38N 2°33W **24** C3
Oldcastle *Ireland*   53°46N 7°10W **29** D7
Oldham *U.K.*   53°33N 2°7W **23** E4
Oldmeldrum *U.K.*   57°20N 2°19W **19** H13
Olean *U.S.A.*   42°5N 78°26W **112** D8
Olekminsk *Russia*   60°25N 120°30E **79** C14
Olenek → *Russia*   73°0N 120°10E **79** B14
Oléron, Î. d' *France*   45°55N 1°15W **68** D3
Ólgiy *Mongolia*   48°56N 89°57E **80** B3
Olímpia *Brazil*   20°44S 48°54W **122** D1
Oliveira *Brazil*   20°39S 44°50W **122** D2
Ollagüe *Chile*   21°15S 68°10W **120** E3
Ollerton *U.K.*   53°12N 1°1W **23** F6
Olney *U.K.*   52°9N 0°43W **25** B7
Olney *U.S.A.*   38°44N 88°5W **112** F3
Olomouc *Czech Rep.*   49°38N 17°12E **67** D9
Olsztyn *Poland*   53°48N 20°29E **67** B11

Olt · Placentia B.

Olt ➤ Romania	43°43N 24°51E **67** G13	Otterburn U.K.	55°14N 2°11W **22** B4	Palu Turkey	38°45N 40°0E **73** G7
Olympia Greece	37°39N 21°39E **71** F9	Ottery St. Mary U.K.	50°44N 3°17W **27** F7	Pamiers France	43°7N 1°39E **68** E4
Olympia U.S.A.	47°3N 122°53W **110** A2	Ottumwa U.S.A.	41°1N 92°25W **111** B81	Pamir Tajikistan	37°40N 73°0E **87** B13
Olympus, Mt. Greece	40°6N 22°23E **71** D10	Ouachita ➤ U.S.A.	31°38N 91°49W **111** D8	Pamlico Sd. U.S.A.	35°20N 76°0W **111** C11
Olympus, Mt. U.S.A.	47°48N 123°43W **110** A2	Ouachita Mts. U.S.A.	34°30N 94°30W **111** D8	Pampa U.S.A.	35°32N 100°58W **110** C6
Omagh U.K.	54°36N 7°19W **28** B7	Ouagadougou Burkina Faso	12°25N 1°30W **94** F5	Pampas Argentina	35°0S 63°0W **121** F3
Omaha U.S.A.	41°17N 95°58W **111** B7	Oubangi ➤		Pamplona Spain	42°48N 1°38W **69** A5
Oman ■ Asia	23°0N 58°0E **88** C6	Dem. Rep. of the Congo	0°30S 17°50E **96** E3	Pana U.S.A.	39°23N 89°5W **112** F3
Oman, G. of Asia	24°30N 58°30E **87** E9	Oudtshoorn S. Africa	33°35S 22°14E **97** L4	Panaji India	15°25N 73°50E **84** M8
Ombersley U.K.	52°16N 2°13W **24** B4	Ouezzane Morocco	34°51N 5°35W **94** B4	Panamá Panama	9°0N 79°25W **115** F9
Omdurmân Sudan	15°40N 32°28E **95** E12	Oughterard Ireland	53°26N 9°18W **30** B4	Panama ■ Cent. Amer.	8°48N 79°55W **115** F9
Ometepec Mexico	16°41N 98°25W **114** D5	Oujda Morocco	34°41N 1°55W **94** B5	Panamá, G. de Panama	8°4N 79°20W **115** F9
Omsk Russia	55°0N 73°12E **79** D9	Oulton U.K.	52°30N 1°43E **25** B12	Panama Canal Panama	9°10N 79°37W **115** F9
Ōmuta Japan	33°5N 130°26E **82** G2	Oulton Broad U.K.	52°28N 1°42E **25** B12	Panama City U.S.A.	30°10N 85°40W **111** D9
Ondangwa Namibia	17°57S 16°4E **97** H3	Oulu Finland	65°1N 25°29E **63** D9	Panay Phil.	11°10N 122°30E **83** B4
Onega ➤ Russia	63°58N 38°2E **72** B6	Oulujärvi Finland	64°25N 27°15E **63** E9	Pančevo Serbia	44°52N 20°41E **71** B9
Onega, L. Russia	61°44N 35°22E **72** B6	Oulujoki ➤ Finland	65°1N 25°30E **63** D9	Panevėžys Lithuania	55°42N 24°25E **63** F8
Onega B. Russia	64°24N 36°38E **72** B6	Oundle U.K.	52°29N 0°28W **25** B8	Pangani Tanzania	5°25S 38°58E **96** F7
Oneida U.S.A.	43°6N 75°39W **113** D10	Ourense Spain	42°19N 7°55W **69** A2	Pangbourne U.K.	51°29N 1°6W **24** D6
O'Neill U.S.A.	42°27N 98°39W **110** B7	Ouro Fino Brazil	22°16S 46°25W **122** D1	Pangkalpinang Indonesia	2°0S 106°0E **83** D2
Oneonta U.S.A.	42°27N 75°4W **113** D10	Ouro Prêto Brazil	20°20S 43°30W **122** D2	Pangnirtung Canada	66°8N 65°43W **109** C13
Onitsha Nigeria	6°6N 6°42E **94** G7	Ouse ➤ E. Sussex, U.K.	50°47N 0°4E **25** E9	Pantar Indonesia	8°28S 124°10E **83** D4
Onny ➤ U.K.	52°24N 2°47W **23** H3	Ouse ➤ N. Yorks., U.K.	53°44N 0°55W **23** E7	Pante Macassar E. Timor	9°30S 123°58E **83** D4
Onslow B. U.S.A.	34°20N 77°15W **111** D11	Outaouais ➤ Canada	45°27N 74°8W **109** E12	Pantelleria Italy	36°50N 11°57E **70** F4
Ontario U.S.A.	44°2N 116°58W **110** B3	Outer Hebrides U.K.	57°30N 7°40W **18** H2	Panzhihua China	26°33N 101°44E **80** D5
Ontario □ Canada	48°0N 83°0W **109** E11	Outjo Namibia	20°5S 16°7E **97** J3	Papa Stour U.K.	60°20N 1°42W **18** B14
Ontario, L. N. Amer.	43°20N 78°0W **112** D8	Outwell U.K.	52°37N 0°14E **25** A9	Papa Westray U.K.	59°20N 2°55W **19** D12
Ontonagon U.S.A.	46°52N 89°19W **112** B31	Ovalle Chile	30°33S 71°18W **121** F2	Papantla Mexico	20°27N 97°19W **114** C5
Oostende Belgium	51°15N 2°54E **65** C2	Ovamboland Namibia	18°30S 16°0E **97** H3	Papeete Tahiti	17°32S 149°34W **103** J13
Opava Czech Rep.	49°57N 17°58E **67** D9	Over Wallop U.K.	51°9N 1°36W **24** D5	Paphos Cyprus	34°46N 32°25E **86** C3
Opole Poland	50°42N 17°58E **67** C9	Overijssel □ Neths.	52°25N 6°35E **65** B6	Papua □ Indonesia	4°0S 137°0E **83** D5
Oradea Romania	47°2N 21°58E **67** E11	Overton U.K.	51°15N 1°15W **24** D6	Papua, G. of Papua N. G.	9°0S 144°50E **98** B7
Öræfajökull Iceland	64°2N 16°39W **63** B2	Oviedo Spain	43°25N 5°50W **69** A3	Papua New Guinea ■ Oceania	8°0S 145°0E **98** B8
Oral Kazakhstan	51°20N 51°20E **73** D9	Owatonna U.S.A.	44°5N 93°14W **111** B8	Pará □ Brazil	3°20S 52°0W **120** C4
Oran Algeria	35°45N 0°39W **94** A5	Owen Sound Canada	44°35N 80°55W **109** E11	Paracatu Brazil	17°10S 46°50W **122** C1
Orange Australia	33°15S 149°7E **98** G8	Owen Stanley Ra. Papua N. G.	8°30S 147°0E **98** B8	Paracel Is. S. China Sea	15°50N 112°0E **83** B3
Orange France	44°8N 4°47E **68** D6	Owens L. U.S.A.	36°26N 117°57W **110** C3	Paragould U.S.A.	36°3N 90°29W **111** C81
Orange U.S.A.	38°15N 78°7W **112** F8	Owensboro U.S.A.	37°46N 87°7W **112** G4	Paraguaçu ➤ Brazil	12°45S 38°54W **122** B1
Orange ➤ S. Africa	28°41S 16°28E **97** K3	Owo Nigeria	7°10N 5°39E **94** G7	Paraguaná, Pen. de Venezuela	12°0N 70°0W **120** A3
Orange, C. Brazil	4°20N 51°30W **120** B4	Owosso U.S.A.	43°0N 84°10W **112** D5	Paraguari Paraguay	25°36S 57°0W **121** E4
Orangeburg U.S.A.	33°30N 80°52W **111** D10	Owston Ferry U.K.	53°29N 0°47W **23** F7	Paraguay ■ S. Amer.	23°0S 57°0W **121** E4
Orangeville Canada	43°55N 80°5W **112** D7	Owyhee ➤ U.S.A.	43°49N 117°2W **110** B3	Paraguay ➤ Paraguay	27°18S 58°38W **121** E4
Ordos Desert China	39°0N 109°0E **81** C5	Oxford U.K.	51°46N 1°15W **24** C6	Paraíba □ Brazil	7°0S 36°0W **120** C6
Ordu Turkey	40°55N 37°53E **73** F6	Oxfordshire □ U.K.	51°48N 1°16W **24** C6	Parakou Benin	9°25N 2°40E **94** G6
Örebro Sweden	59°20N 15°18E **63** F7	Oxnard U.S.A.	34°12N 119°11W **110** D3	Paramaribo Suriname	5°50N 55°10W **120** B4
Oregon □ U.S.A.	44°0N 121°0W **110** B2	Oyama Japan	36°18N 139°48E **82** E6	Paraná Argentina	31°45S 60°30W **121** F3
Orekhovo-Zuyevo Russia	55°50N 38°55E **72** C6	Oyem Gabon	1°34N 11°31E **96** D2	Paraná Brazil	12°30S 47°48W **122** B1
Orel Russia	52°57N 36°3E **72** D6	Oykel ➤ U.K.	57°56N 4°26W **19** D9	Paraná □ Brazil	24°30S 51°0W **121** E4
Orem U.S.A.	40°19N 111°42W **110** B4	Oyo Nigeria	7°46N 3°56E **94** G6	Paraná ➤ Argentina	33°43S 59°15W **121** F4
Orenburg Russia	51°45N 55°6E **72** D10	Ozark Plateau U.S.A.	37°20N 91°40W **111** C81	Paranaguá Brazil	25°30S 48°30W **122** E1
Orford U.K.	52°6N 1°33E **25** B12	Ozarks, L. of the U.S.A.	38°12N 92°38W **111** C81	Paranaíba Brazil	20°6S 51°4W **120** D4
Orford Ness U.K.	52°5N 1°35E **25** B12			Paranaíba ➤ Brazil	20°6S 51°4W **120** D4
Orhon Gol ➤ Mongolia	50°21N 106°0E **80** A5	**P**		Paranapanema ➤ Brazil	22°40S 53°9W **121** E4
Oriental, Cordillera Colombia	6°0N 73°0W **116** C3			Parbhani India	19°8N 76°52E **84** K10
Oriental, Grand Erg Algeria	30°0N 6°30E **94** B7	Paarl S. Africa	33°45S 18°56E **97** L3	Pardo ➤ Brazil	15°40S 39°0W **122** C3
Orihuela Spain	38°7N 0°55W **69** C5	Pab Hills Pakistan	26°30N 66°45E **84** F5	Pardubice Czech Rep.	50°3N 15°45E **66** C8
Orinoco ➤ Venezuela	9°15N 61°30W **120** B3	Pabbay U.K.	57°46N 7°14W **18** G3	Parecis, Serra dos Brazil	13°0S 60°0W **120** D4
Orissa □ India	20°0N 84°0E **85** K14	Pabna Bangla.	24°1N 89°18E **85** G16	Parepare Indonesia	4°0S 119°40E **83** D3
Oristano Italy	39°54N 8°36E **70** E3	Pacaraima, Sa. S. Amer.	4°0N 62°30W **120** B3	Parima, Serra Brazil	2°30N 64°0W **120** B3
Orizaba Mexico	18°51N 97°6W **114** D5	Pacasmayo Peru	7°20S 79°35W **120** C2	Pariñas, Pta. S. Amer.	4°30S 82°0W **116** D2
Orizaba, Pico de Mexico	18°58N 97°15W **114** D5	Pachuca Mexico	20°7N 98°44W **114** C5	Parintins Brazil	2°40S 56°50W **120** C4
Orkney □ U.K.	59°2N 3°13W **19** D11	**Pacific Antarctic Ridge**		Pariparit Kyun Burma	14°55N 93°45E **85** M18
Orkney Is. U.K.	59°0N 3°0W **64** B5	Pac. Oc.	43°0S 115°0W **103** M16	Paris France	48°53N 2°20E **68** B5
Orlando U.S.A.	28°32N 81°22W **111** E10	**Pacific Ocean**	10°0N 140°0W **103** G14	Paris U.S.A.	33°40N 95°33W **111** D7
Orléanais France	48°0N 2°0E **68** C5	Padang Indonesia	1°0S 100°20E **83** D2	Park Falls U.S.A.	45°56N 90°27W **112** C1
Orléans France	47°54N 1°52E **68** C4	Padangsidempuan Indonesia	1°30N 99°15E **83** C1	Parkersburg U.S.A.	39°16N 81°34W **112** F7
Orléans, Î. d' Canada	46°54N 70°58W **113** B12	Paddock Wood U.K.	51°11N 0°24E **25** D9	Parkes Australia	33°9S 148°11E **98** G8
Ormara Pakistan	25°16N 64°33E **84** G4	Paderborn Germany	51°42N 8°45E **66** C5	Parla Spain	40°14N 3°46W **69** B4
Ormesby St. Margaret U.K.	52°41N 1°41E **25** A12	Padiham U.K.	53°48N 2°18W **23** E4	Parma Italy	44°48N 10°20E **70** B4
Ormoc Phil.	11°0N 124°37E **83** B4	Padre I. U.S.A.	27°10N 97°25W **111** E7	Parnaguá Brazil	10°10S 44°38W **122** B2
Ormskirk U.K.	53°35N 2°54W **23** E3	Padstow U.K.	50°33N 4°58W **27** F4	Parnaíba Brazil	2°54S 41°47W **120** C5
Örnsköldsvik Sweden	63°17N 18°40E **63** E7	Padstow B. U.K.	50°34N 4°57W **27** F4	Parnaíba ➤ Brazil	3°0S 41°50W **120** C5
Oronsay U.K.	56°1N 6°15W **20** B3	Padua Italy	45°25N 11°53E **70** B4	Pärnu Estonia	58°28N 24°33E **63** F8
Orsha Belarus	54°30N 30°25E **72** D5	Paducah U.S.A.	37°5N 88°37W **112** G3	Paros Greece	37°5N 25°12E **71** F11
Ortegal, C. Spain	43°43N 7°52W **69** A2	Pag Croatia	44°25N 15°3E **70** B6	Parracombe U.K.	51°11N 3°56W **27** E6
Oruro Bolivia	18°0S 67°9W **120** D3	Pagadian Phil.	7°55N 123°30E **83** C4	Parrett ➤ U.K.	51°12N 3°1W **24** D2
Oruzgān □ Afghan.	33°0N 66°0E **87** C11	Page U.S.A.	36°57N 111°27W **110** C4	Parry Is. Canada	77°0N 110°0W **109** B9
Orwell ➤ U.K.	51°59N 1°18E **25** C11	Pāhala U.S.A.	19°12N 155°29W **110** J17	Parry Sound Canada	45°20N 80°0W **109** E12
Ōsaka Japan	34°42N 135°30E **82** F4	Paignton U.K.	50°26N 3°35W **27** G6	Parsons U.S.A.	37°20N 95°16W **111** C7
Oshakati Namibia	17°45S 15°40E **97** H3	Paine, Cerro Chile	50°59S 73°4W **121** H2	Partney U.K.	53°12N 0°7E **23** F9
Oshawa Canada	43°50N 78°50W **109** E12	Painesville U.S.A.	41°43N 81°15W **112** E7	Parton U.K.	54°35N 3°33W **22** C1
Oshkosh U.S.A.	44°1N 88°33W **112** C3	Painswick U.K.	51°47N 2°10W **24** C4	Partry Mts. Ireland	53°40N 9°28W **28** D3
Oshogbo Nigeria	7°48N 4°37E **94** G6	Painted Desert U.S.A.	36°0N 111°0W **110** C4	Paru ➤ Brazil	1°33S 52°38W **120** C4
Osijek Croatia	45°34N 18°41E **71** B8	Paintsville U.S.A.	37°49N 82°48W **112** G6	Parvān □ Afghan.	35°0N 69°0E **87** C12
Osizweni S. Africa	27°49S 30°7E **97** K6	País Vasco □ Spain	42°50N 2°45W **69** A4	Pas, The Canada	53°45N 101°15W **108** D9
Oskaloosa U.S.A.	41°18N 92°39W **111** B81	Paisley U.K.	55°50N 4°25W **20** C7	Pasadena Calif., U.S.A.	34°9N 118°8W **110** D3
Oskarshamn Sweden	57°15N 16°27E **63** F7	Paita Peru	5°11S 81°9W **120** C1	Pasadena Tex., U.S.A.	29°43N 95°13W **111** E7
Öskemen Kazakhstan	50°0N 82°36E **79** D10	Pakistan ■ Asia	30°0N 70°0E **84** E7	Pasco, Cerro de Peru	10°45S 76°10W **120** D2
Oslo Norway	59°54N 10°43E **63** F6	Paktiā □ Afghan.	33°30N 69°15E **87** C12	Pascua, I. de Chile	27°7S 109°23W **103** K17
Oslofjorden Norway	59°20N 10°35E **63** F6	Pakxe Laos	15°5N 105°52E **83** B2	Paso Robles U.S.A.	35°38N 120°41W **110** C2
Osmaniye Turkey	37°5N 36°10E **73** G6	Palagruža Croatia	42°24N 16°15E **70** C7	Passage West Ireland	51°52N 8°21W **30** E6
Osmotherley U.K.	54°22N 1°18W **22** D6	Palani Hills India	10°14N 77°33E **84** P10	Passau Germany	48°34N 13°28E **66** D7
Osnabrück Germany	52°17N 8°3E **66** B5	Palanpur India	24°10N 72°25E **84** G8	Passo Fundo Brazil	28°10S 52°20W **121** E4
Osorno Chile	40°25S 73°0W **121** G2	Palapye Botswana	22°30S 27°7E **97** J5	Passos Brazil	20°45S 46°37W **122** D1
Ossa, Mt. Australia	41°52S 146°3E **98** J8	Palau ■ Palau	7°30N 134°30E **83** C5	Pastaza ➤ Peru	4°50S 76°52W **120** C2
Ossett U.K.	53°41N 1°34W **23** E5	Palawan Phil.	9°30N 118°30E **83** C3	Pasto Colombia	1°13N 77°17W **120** B2
Ostend = Oostende Belgium	51°15N 2°54E **65** C2	Palembang Indonesia	3°0S 104°50E **83** D2	Patagonia Argentina	45°0S 69°0W **121** G3
Österdalälven Sweden	61°30N 13°45E **63** E6	Palencia Spain	42°1N 4°34W **69** A3	Patan India	23°54N 72°14E **84** H8
Östersund Sweden	63°10N 14°38E **63** E6	Palermo Italy	38°7N 13°22E **70** E5	Pateley Bridge U.K.	54°5N 1°44W **22** D5
Ostfriesische Inseln Germany	53°42N 7°0E **66** B4	Palestine U.S.A.	31°46N 95°38W **111** D7	Paternò Italy	37°34N 14°54E **70** F6
Ostrava Czech Rep.	49°51N 18°18E **67** D10	Palghat India	10°46N 76°42E **84** P10	Paterson U.S.A.	40°54N 74°9W **113** E10
Ostrołęka Poland	53°4N 21°32E **67** B11	Palgrave U.K.	52°22N 1°6E **25** B11	Pathankot India	32°18N 75°45E **84** C9
Ostrów Wielkopolski Poland	51°36N 17°44E **67** C9	Pali India	25°50N 73°20E **84** G8	Pathfinder Res. U.S.A.	42°28N 106°51W **110** B5
Ostrowiec-Świętokrzyski		Palikir Micronesia	6°55N 158°9E **102** G7	Patkai Bum India	27°0N 95°30E **85** F19
Poland	50°55N 21°22E **67** C11	Palk Strait Asia	10°0N 79°45E **84** Q11	Patmos Greece	37°21N 26°36E **71** F12
Oswaldtwistle U.K.	53°43N 2°26W **23** E4	Palm Springs U.S.A.	33°50N 116°33W **110** D3	Patna India	25°35N 85°12E **85** G14
Oswego U.S.A.	43°27N 76°31W **112** D9	Palma de Mallorca Spain	39°35N 2°39E **69** C7	Patos Brazil	6°55S 37°16W **120** C6
Oswestry U.K.	52°52N 3°3W **23** G2	Palmares Brazil	8°41S 35°28W **122** A3	Patos, L. dos Brazil	31°20S 51°0W **121** F4
Otaru Japan	43°10N 141°0E **82** B7	Palmas, C. Liberia	4°27N 7°46W **94** H4	Patos de Minas Brazil	18°35S 46°32W **122** C1
Otjiwarongo Namibia	20°30S 16°33E **97** J3	Palmeira dos Índios Brazil	9°25S 36°37W **122** A3	Patra Greece	38°14N 21°47E **71** E9
Otley U.K.	53°54N 1°41W **23** E5	Palmira Colombia	3°32N 76°16W **120** B2	Patrington U.K.	53°41N 0°1W **23** E8
Otranto Italy	40°9N 18°28E **71** D8	Palmyra Syria	34°36N 38°15E **86** C4	Patrocínio Brazil	18°57S 47°0W **122** C1
Otranto, Str. of Italy	40°15N 18°40E **71** D8	Palmyra Is. Pac. Oc.	5°52N 162°5W **103** G11	Patten U.S.A.	46°0N 68°38W **113** C13
Ōtsu Japan	35°0N 135°50E **82** F4	Palopo Indonesia	3°0S 120°16E **83** D4	Patterdale U.K.	54°32N 2°56W **22** C3
Ottawa Canada	45°26N 75°42W **113** C10	Palu Indonesia	1°0S 119°52E **83** D3	Paulatuk Canada	69°25N 124°0W **108** C7
Ottawa U.S.A.	41°21N 88°51W **112** E3	Pavia Italy	45°7N 9°8E **70** B3	Paulistana Brazil	8°9S 41°9W **122** A2
Ottawa Is. Canada	59°35N 80°10W **109** D11	Pavlodar Kazakhstan	52°33N 77°0E **79** D9	Paull U.K.	53°44N 0°14W **23** E8
Otter ➤ U.K.	50°38N 3°19W **27** F7			Paulo Afonso Brazil	9°21S 38°15W **122** A3

Pavlohrad Ukraine	48°30N 35°52E **73** E6	Pervomaysk Ukraine	48°10N 30°46E **73** E5
Pavlovo Russia	55°58N 43°5E **72** C7	Pervouralsk Russia	56°59N 59°59E **72** C10
Pawtucket U.S.A.	41°53N 71°23W **113** E12	Pésaro Italy	43°54N 12°55E **70** C5
Paxton U.S.A.	40°27N 88°6W **112** E3	Pescara Italy	42°28N 14°13E **70** C6
Payakumbuh Indonesia	0°20S 100°58W **110** C6	Peshawar Pakistan	34°2N 71°37E **84** B7
Payette U.S.A.	44°5N 116°56W **110** B3	Pesqueira Brazil	8°20S 36°42W **122** A3
Payne L. Canada	59°30N 74°30W **109** D12	Petah Tiqwa Israel	32°6N 34°53E **86** C3
Paysandú Uruguay	32°19S 58°8W **121** F4	Peter I. Br. Virgin Is.	18°22N 64°35W **115** e
Payson U.S.A.	34°14N 111°20W **110** D4	Peterborough Canada	44°20N 78°20W **109** E12
Paz, B. de la Mexico	24°9N 110°25W **114** C2	Peterborough U.K.	52°35N 0°15W **25** B8
Pazardzhik Bulgaria	42°12N 24°20E **71** C11	Peterchurch U.K.	52°2N 2°56W **24** B3
Peace ➤ Canada	59°0N 111°25W **108** D8	Peterculter U.K.	57°6N 2°16W **19** H13
Peace River Canada	56°15N 117°18W **108** D8	Peterhead U.K.	57°31N 1°48W **19** G14
Peacehaven U.K.	50°48N 0°0 **25** E8	Peterlee U.K.	54°47N 1°20W **22** C6
Peak District △ U.K.	53°24N 1°46W **23** F5	Petersburg Alaska, U.S.A.	56°48N 132°58W **108** D6
Pearl City U.S.A.	21°24N 157°59W **110** H16	Petersburg Va., U.S.A.	37°14N 77°24W **112** G9
Pearl Harbor U.S.A.	21°21N 157°57W **110** H16	Petersfield U.K.	51°1N 0°56W **25** D7
Peasenhall U.K.	52°16N 1°27E **25** B11	Petit-Canal Guadeloupe	16°25N 61°31W **114** b
Peawanuck Canada	55°15N 85°12W **109** D11	Petit Piton St. Lucia	13°51N 61°5W **115** f
Peć Kosovo	42°40N 20°17E **71** C9	Petite Terre, Îles de la	
Pechora Russia	65°10N 57°11E **72** A10	Guadeloupe	16°13N 61°9W **114** b
Pechora ➤ Russia	68°13N 54°15E **72** A9	Petitot ➤ Canada	60°14N 123°29W **108** C7
Pechora B. Russia	68°40N 54°0E **72** A9	Petitsikapau L. Canada	54°37N 66°25W **109** D13
Pecos U.S.A.	31°26N 103°30W **110** D6	Peto Mexico	20°8N 88°55W **114** C7
Pecos ➤ U.S.A.	29°42N 101°22W **110** E6	Petoskey U.S.A.	45°22N 84°57W **112** C5
Pécs Hungary	46°5N 18°15E **67** E10	Petra Jordan	30°20N 35°22E **86** D3
Pedra Azul Brazil	16°2S 41°17W **122** C2	Petrolândia Brazil	9°5S 38°20W **122** A3
Pedro Afonso Brazil	9°0S 48°10W **122** A1	Petrolina Brazil	9°24S 40°30W **122** A2
Peebles U.K.	55°40N 3°11W **21** C9	Petropavlovsk-Kamchatskiy	
Peel I. of Man	54°13N 4°40W **29** C12	Russia	53°3N 158°43E **79** D17
Peel ➤ Canada	67°0N 135°0W **108** C6	Petrópolis Brazil	22°33S 43°9W **122** D2
Peel Fell U.K.	55°18N 2°34W **22** B3	Petrozavodsk Russia	61°41N 34°20E **72** B5
Peel Sd. Canada	73°0N 96°0W **108** B10	Petworth U.K.	51°0N 0°36W **25** E7
Pegswood U.K.	55°11N 1°39W **22** B5	Pevensey U.K.	50°49N 0°23E **25** E9
Pegu Burma	17°20N 96°29E **85** L20	Pevensey Levels U.K.	50°50N 0°20E **25** E9
Pegu Yoma Burma	19°0N 96°0E **85** K20	Pewsey U.K.	51°20N 1°45W **24** D5
Pegwell Bay U.K.	51°18N 1°24E **25** D11	Pewsey, Vale of U.K.	51°22N 1°40W **24** D5
Peixe Brazil	12°0S 48°40W **122** B1	Pforzheim Germany	48°52N 8°41E **66** D5
Pekalongan Indonesia	6°53S 109°40E **83** D2	Phalodi India	27°12N 72°24E **84** F8
Pekanbaru Indonesia	0°30N 101°15E **83** C2	Phan Rang Vietnam	11°34N 109°0E **83** B2
Pekin U.S.A.	40°35N 89°40W **112** E3	Phan Thiet Vietnam	11°1N 108°9E **83** B2
Peking = Beijing China	39°53N 116°21E **81** C6	Philadelphia U.S.A.	39°57N 75°9W **113** E10
Pelagie, Is. Italy	35°39N 12°33E **70** G5	Philippine Sea Pac. Oc.	18°0N 125°0E **74** G14
Pelée, Mt. Martinique	14°48N 61°10W **114** c	Philippine Trench Pac. Oc.	12°0N 126°6E **83** B4
Peleng Indonesia	1°20S 123°30E **83** D4	Philippines ■ Asia	12°0N 123°0E **83** B4
Pelješac Croatia	42°55N 17°25E **70** C7	Phillips U.S.A.	45°42N 90°24W **112** C2
Pelly ➤ Canada	62°47N 137°19W **108** C6	Phitsanulok Thailand	16°50N 100°12E **83** B2
Pelly Bay Canada	68°38N 89°50W **109** C11	Phnom Penh Cambodia	11°33N 104°55E **83** B2
Pelotas Brazil	31°42S 52°23W **121** F4	Phoenix U.S.A.	33°26N 112°4W **110** D4
Pelvoux, Massif du France	44°52N 6°20E **68** D7	Phoenix Is. Kiribati	3°30S 172°0W **99** A16
Pematangsiantar Indonesia	2°57N 99°5E **83** C1	Phra Nakhon Si Ayutthaya	
Pemba Mozam.	12°58S 40°30E **97** G8	Thailand	14°25N 100°30E **83** B2
Pemba I. Tanzania	5°0S 39°45E **96** F7	Phuket Thailand	7°53N 98°24E **83** C1
Pembridge U.K.	52°13N 2°52W **24** B3	Piacenza Italy	45°1N 9°40E **70** B3
Pembroke Canada	45°50N 77°7W **109** E12	Piatra Neamţ Romania	46°56N 26°21E **67** E14
Pembroke U.K.	51°41N 4°55W **26** D4	Piauí □ Brazil	7°0S 43°0W **120** C5
Pembrokeshire □ U.K.	51°52N 4°56W **26** D3	Piauí ➤ Brazil	6°38S 42°42W **120** C5
Pembrokeshire Coast △ U.K.	51°50N 5°2W **26** D3	Piave ➤ Italy	45°32N 12°44E **70** B5
Pembury U.K.	51°8N 0°20E **25** D9	Picardie □ France	49°50N 3°0E **68** B5
Pen-y-Ghent U.K.	54°10N 2°14W **22** D4	Pichilemu Chile	34°22S 72°0W **121** F2
Penarth U.K.	51°26N 3°11W **27** E7	Pickering U.K.	54°15N 0°46W **22** D7
Peñas, G. de Chile	47°0S 75°0W **121** G2	Pickering, Vale of U.K.	54°14N 0°45W **22** D7
Pend Oreille, L. U.S.A.	48°10N 116°21W **110** A3	Picos Brazil	7°5S 41°28W **120** C5
Pendeen U.K.	50°9N 5°41W **27** G2	Picton Canada	44°1N 77°9W **112** D9
Pendle Hill U.K.	53°52N 2°19W **23** E4	Pidley U.K.	52°23N 0°2W **25** B8
Pendleton U.S.A.	45°40N 118°47W **110** A3	Pidurutalagala Sri Lanka	7°10N 80°50E **84** R12
Penedo Brazil	10°15S 36°36W **122** B3	Piedmont U.S.A.	34°42N 82°28W **111** D10
Penetanguishene Canada	44°50N 79°55W **112** C8	Piedras Negras Mexico	28°42N 100°31W **114** B4
Penicuik U.K.	55°50N 3°13W **21** C9	Piemonte □ Italy	45°0N 8°0E **70** B2
Peninsular Malaysia □		Pierre U.S.A.	44°22N 100°21W **110** B6
Malaysia	4°0N 102°0E **83** C2	Pietermaritzburg S. Africa	29°35S 30°25E **97** K6
Penistone U.K.	53°31N 1°37W **23** E5	Pikes Peak U.S.A.	38°50N 105°3W **110** C5
Penkridge U.K.	52°44N 2°6W **23** G4	Pikeville U.S.A.	37°29N 82°31W **112** G6
Penmarch, Pte. de France	47°48N 4°22W **68** C1	Pilar Paraguay	26°50S 58°20W **121** E4
Penn Yan U.S.A.	42°40N 77°3W **112** D9	Pilcomayo ➤ Paraguay	25°21S 57°42W **121** E4
Pennines U.K.	54°45N 2°27W **22** C4	Pilibhit India	28°40N 79°50E **84** E11
Pennsylvania □ U.S.A.	40°45N 77°30W **112** E8	Pilica ➤ Poland	51°52N 21°17E **67** C11
Penong Australia	31°56S 133°1E **98** G5	Pilling U.K.	53°56N 2°54W **23** E3
Penrith Australia	33°43N 150°38E **98** G9	Pilton U.K.	51°10N 2°36W **24** D4
Penrith U.K.	54°40N 2°45W **22** C3	Pimentel Peru	6°45S 79°55W **120** C2
Penryn U.K.	50°9N 5°7W **27** G3	Pinar del Río Cuba	22°26N 83°40W **115** C8
Pensacola U.S.A.	30°25N 87°13W **111** D9	Pinatubo, Mt. Phil.	15°8N 120°21E **83** B4
Pensacola Mts. Antarctica	84°0S 40°0W **55** E1	Pinchbeck U.K.	52°50N 0°9W **23** G8
Penshurst U.K.	51°10N 0°12E **25** D9	Pinckneyville U.S.A.	38°5N 89°23W **112** F3
Penticton Canada	49°30N 119°38W **108** E8	Pindus Mts. Greece	40°0N 21°0E **71** E9
Pentire Pt. U.K.	50°35N 4°56W **27** F4	Pine Bluff U.S.A.	34°13N 92°1W **111** D8
Pentland Firth U.K.	58°43N 3°10W **19** E11	Pine Point Canada	60°50N 114°28W **108** C8
Pentland Hills U.K.	55°48N 3°25W **21** C9	Pinega ➤ Russia	64°30N 44°19E **72** B8
Penwortham U.K.	53°45N 2°46W **23** E3	Pingdingshan China	33°43N 113°27E **81** C6
Penygroes U.K.	53°3N 4°17W **26** A5	Pingliang China	35°35N 106°31E **80** C5
Penza Russia	53°15N 45°5E **72** D8	P'ingtung Taiwan	22°38N 120°30E **81** D7
Penzance U.K.	50°7N 5°33W **27** G2	Pingxiang China	22°6N 106°46E **80** D5
Peoria U.S.A.	40°42N 89°36W **112** E3	Pinheiro Brazil	2°31S 45°5W **120** C5
Perabumulih Indonesia	3°27S 104°15E **83** D2	Pinhoe U.K.	50°44N 3°28W **27** F7
Perdido, Mte. Spain	42°40N 0°5E **69** A6	Pinsk Belarus	52°10N 26°1E **72** D4
Pereira Colombia	4°49N 75°43W **120** B2	Piombino Italy	42°55N 10°32E **70** C4
Pergamino Argentina	33°52S 60°30W **121** F3	Piotrków Trybunalski	
Péribonka ➤ Canada	48°45N 72°5W **109** E12	Poland	51°23N 19°43E **67** C10
Périgueux France	45°10N 0°42E **68** D4	Pipmuacan, Rés. Canada	49°45N 70°30W **113** A12
Perm Russia	58°0N 56°10E **72** C10	Piracicaba Brazil	22°45S 47°40W **122** D1
Pernambuco □ Brazil	8°0S 37°0W **120** C6	Pirapora Brazil	17°20S 44°56W **122** C2
Pernik Bulgaria	42°35N 23°2E **71** C10	Pireas Greece	37°57N 23°42E **71** F10
Perpignan France	42°42N 2°53E **68** E5	Pirmasens Germany	49°12N 7°36E **66** D4
Perranporth U.K.	50°20N 5°11W **27** G3	Pisa Italy	43°43N 10°23E **70** C4
Perranzabuloe U.K.	50°19N 5°9W **27** G3	Pisagua Chile	19°40S 70°15W **120** D2
Perryton U.S.A.	36°24N 100°48W **110** C6	Pishan China	37°30N 78°33E **80** C2
Perryville U.S.A.	37°43N 89°52W **112** G3	Pistóia Italy	43°55N 10°54E **70** C4
Persepolis Iran	29°55N 52°50E **87** D8	Pit ➤ U.S.A.	40°47N 122°6W **110** B2
Pershore U.K.	52°7N 2°4W **24** B4	Pitcairn I. Pac. Oc.	25°5S 130°5W **103** K14
Persian Gulf Asia	27°0N 50°0E **87** E7	Piteå Sweden	65°20N 21°25E **63** D8
Perth Australia	31°57S 115°52E **98** G2	Piteşti Romania	44°52N 24°54E **67** F13
Perth Canada	44°55N 76°15W **113** C9	Pitlochry U.K.	56°42N 3°44W **19** J10
Perth U.K.	56°24N 3°26W **21** B9	Pittsburg U.S.A.	37°25N 94°42W **111** C7
Perth & Kinross □ U.K.	56°45N 3°55W **19** J9	Pittsburgh U.S.A.	40°26N 79°58W **112** E7
Peru U.S.A.	40°45N 86°4W **112** E4	Pittsfield U.S.A.	42°27N 73°15W **113** D11
Peru ■ S. Amer.	4°0S 75°0W **120** C2	Piura Peru	5°15S 80°38W **120** C1
Peru-Chile Trench Pac. Oc.	20°0S 72°0W **103** K20	Placentia Canada	47°20N 54°0W **109** E14
Perúgia Italy	43°7N 12°23E **70** C5	Placentia B. Canada	47°0N 54°40W **109** E14

Placetas Cuba 22°15N 79°44W 115 C9
Plainview U.S.A. 34°11N 101°43W 110 D6
Plata, Río de la → S. Amer. 34°45S 57°30W 121 F4
Platte → U.S.A. 39°16N 94°50W 111 C8
Plattsburgh U.S.A. 44°42N 73°28W 113 C11
Plauen Germany 50°30N 12°8E 66 C7
Plenty, B. of N.Z. 37°45S 177°0E 99 H14
Plessisville Canada 46°14N 71°47W 113 B12
Pleven Bulgaria 43°26N 24°37E 71 C11
Płock Poland 52°32N 19°40E 67 B10
Ploiești Romania 44°57N 26°5E 67 F14
Plovdiv Bulgaria 42°8N 24°44E 71 C11
Plymouth U.K. 50°22N 4°10W 27 G5
Plymouth Ind., U.S.A. 41°21N 86°19W 112 E4
Plymouth Wis., U.S.A. 43°45N 87°59W 112 D4
Plympton U.K. 50°23N 4°5W 27 G5
Plymstock U.K. 50°21N 4°7W 27 G5
Plzeň Czech Rep. 49°45N 13°22E 66 D7
Po → Italy 44°57N 12°4E 70 B5
Pobedy, Pik Kyrgyzstan 42°0N 79°58E 80 B2
Pocatello U.S.A. 42°52N 112°27W 110 B4
Pocklington U.K. 53°56N 0°46W 23 E7
Poços de Caldas Brazil 21°50S 46°33W 122 D1
Podgorica Montenegro 42°30N 19°19E 71 C8
Podolsk Russia 55°25N 37°30E 72 C6
Pohnpei Micronesia 6°55N 158°10E 102 G7
Point Hope U.S.A. 68°21N 166°47W 108 C3
Point L. Canada 65°15N 113°4W 108 C8
Point Pleasant U.S.A. 38°51N 82°8W 112 F6
Pointe-à-Pitre Guadeloupe 16°10N 61°32W 114 b
Pointe-Noire Congo 4°48S 11°53E 96 E2
Pointe-Noire Guadeloupe 16°14N 61°47W 114 b
Poitiers France 46°35N 0°20E 68 C4
Poitou France 46°40N 0°10W 68 C3
Pokhara Nepal 28°14N 83°58E 85 E13
Poland ■ Europe 52°0N 20°0E 67 C10
Polatsk Belarus 55°30N 28°50E 72 C4
Polden Hills U.K. 51°7N 2°50W 24 D3
Polegate U.K. 50°49N 0°16E 25 E9
Polesworth U.K. 52°37N 1°36W 23 G5
Polevskoy Russia 56°26N 60°11E 72 C11
Polokwane S. Africa 23°54S 29°25E 97 J5
Polperro U.K. 50°20N 4°32W 27 G4
Polruan U.K. 50°19N 4°38W 27 G4
Poltava Ukraine 49°35N 34°35E 73 E5
Polynesia Pac. Oc. 10°0S 162°0W 103 F11
Ponca City U.S.A. 36°42N 97°5W 111 C7
Ponce Puerto Rico 18°1N 66°37W 115 d
Pond Inlet Canada 72°40N 77°0W 109 B12
Pondicherry India 11°59N 79°50E 84 P11
Ponferrada Spain 42°32N 6°35W 69 A2
Ponta Grossa Brazil 25°7S 50°10W 121 E4
Pontardawe U.K. 51°43N 3°51W 26 D6
Pontardulais U.K. 51°43N 4°3W 26 D5
Pontarlier France 46°54N 6°20E 68 C7
Pontchartrain, L. U.S.A. 30°5N 90°5W 111 D9
Ponte Nova Brazil 20°25S 42°54W 122 D2
Pontefract U.K. 53°42N 1°18W 23 E6
Ponteland U.K. 55°3N 1°45W 22 B5
Pontevedra Spain 42°26N 8°40W 69 A1
Pontiac Ill., U.S.A. 40°53N 88°38W 112 E3
Pontiac Mich., U.S.A. 42°38N 83°18W 112 D6
Pontianak Indonesia 0°3S 109°15E 83 D2
Pontine Mts. Turkey 41°0N 36°45E 73 F6
Pontivy France 48°5N 2°58W 68 B2
Pontrilas U.K. 51°56N 2°52W 24 C3
Pontypool U.K. 51°42N 3°2W 26 D7
Pontypridd U.K. 51°36N 3°20W 27 D7
Ponziane, Ísole Italy 40°55N 12°57E 70 D5
Poole U.K. 50°43N 1°59W 24 E5
Poole Harbour U.K. 50°41N 2°0W 24 E5
Pooley Bridge U.K. 54°37N 2°48W 22 C3
Poopó, L. de Bolivia 18°30S 67°35W 120 D3
Popayán Colombia 2°27N 76°36W 120 B2
Poplar Bluff U.S.A. 36°46N 90°24W 111 C81
Popocatépetl, Volcán Mexico 19°2N 98°38W 114 D5
Porbandar India 21°44N 69°43E 84 J6
Porcupine → U.S.A. 66°34N 145°19W 108 C5
Pori Finland 61°29N 21°48E 63 E8
Porlock U.K. 51°13N 3°35W 27 E6
Port Alberni Canada 49°14N 124°50W 108 E7
Port Antonio Jamaica 18°10N 76°26W 114 a
Port Arthur U.S.A. 29°54N 93°56W 111 E8
Port-au-Prince Haiti 18°40N 72°20W 115 D10
Port Augusta Australia 32°30S 137°50E 98 G6
Port Carlisle U.K. 54°57N 3°11W 22 C2
Port-Cartier Canada 50°2N 66°50W 109 D13
Port-de-Paix Haiti 19°50N 72°50W 115 D10
Port Elgin Canada 44°25N 81°25W 112 C7
Port Elizabeth S. Africa 33°58S 25°40E 97 L5
Port Ellen U.K. 55°38N 6°11W 20 C3
Port Erin I. of Man 54°5N 4°45W 29 C12
Port-Gentil Gabon 0°40S 8°50E 96 E1
Port Glasgow U.K. 55°56N 4°41W 20 C6
Port Harcourt Nigeria 4°40N 7°10E 94 H7
Port Hawkesbury Canada 45°36N 61°22W 109 E13
Port Hedland Australia 20°25S 118°35E 98 E2
Port Hope Simpson Canada 52°33N 56°18W 109 D14
Port Huron U.S.A. 42°58N 82°26W 112 D6
Port Isaac U.K. 50°35N 4°50W 27 F4
Port Isaac B. U.K. 50°36N 4°50W 27 F4
Port Laoise Ireland 53°2N 7°18W 31 B8
Port Lincoln Australia 34°42S 135°52E 98 G6
Port-Louis Guadeloupe 16°28N 61°32W 114 b
Port Louis Mauritius 20°10S 57°30E 91 H9
Port McNeill Canada 50°35N 127°6W 108 D7
Port Macquarie Australia 31°25S 152°25E 98 G9
Port Maria Jamaica 18°22N 76°54W 114 a
Port Morant Jamaica 17°54N 76°19W 114 a
Port Moresby Papua N. G. 9°24S 147°8E 98 B8
Port Nolloth S. Africa 29°17S 16°52E 97 K3
Port of Spain Trin. & Tob. 10°40N 61°31W 120 A3
Port Pirie Australia 33°10S 138°1E 98 G6
Port Said Egypt 31°16N 32°18E 95 B12
Port St. Lucie U.S.A. 27°18N 80°21W 111 E10
Port St. Mary U.K. 54°5N 4°44W 29 C12
Port Shepstone S. Africa 30°44S 30°28E 97 L6
Port Sudan Sudan 19°32N 37°9E 95 E13
Port Talbot U.K. 51°35N 3°47W 27 D6
Port Vila Vanuatu 17°45S 168°18E 99 D12
Port Washington U.S.A. 43°23N 87°53W 112 D4
Port William U.K. 54°46N 4°35W 20 E6
Portadown U.K. 54°25N 6°27W 29 C9
Portaferry U.K. 54°23N 5°33W 29 C10
Portage U.S.A. 43°33N 89°28W 112 D3
Portage la Prairie Canada 49°58N 98°18W 108 E10
Portarlington Ireland 53°9N 7°14W 31 B8
Porthcawl U.K. 51°29N 3°42W 27 E6
Porthleven U.K. 50°4N 5°19W 27 G3
Porthmadog U.K. 52°55N 4°8W 26 B5
Portishead U.K. 51°29N 2°46W 24 D3
Portknockie U.K. 57°42N 2°51W 19 G12
Portland Maine, U.S.A. 43°39N 70°16W 113 D12
Portland Oreg., U.S.A. 45°32N 122°37W 110 A2
Portland, I. of U.K. 50°33N 2°26W 24 E4
Portland Bight Jamaica 17°52N 77°5W 114 a
Portland Bill U.K. 50°31N 2°28W 27 F9
Portland Pt. Jamaica 17°42N 77°11W 114 a
Portmarnock Ireland 53°26N 6°8W 31 B10
Portmore Jamaica 17°53N 77°53W 114 a
Porto Portugal 41°8N 8°40W 69 B1
Pôrto Alegre Brazil 30°5S 51°10W 121 F4
Pôrto Esperança Brazil 19°37S 57°29W 120 D4
Pôrto Nacional Brazil 10°40S 48°30W 122 B1
Porto-Novo Benin 6°23N 2°42E 94 G6
Pôrto Seguro Brazil 16°26S 39°5W 122 C3
Porto Tórres Italy 40°50N 8°24E 70 D3
Porto-Vecchio France 41°35N 9°16E 68 F8
Pôrto Velho Brazil 8°46S 63°54W 120 C3
Porton U.K. 51°8N 1°43W 24 D5
Portpatrick U.K. 54°51N 5°7W 20 E5
Portree U.K. 57°25N 6°12W 18 H5
Portrush U.K. 55°12N 6°40W 29 A8
Portslade U.K. 50°50N 0°12W 25 E8
Portsmouth U.K. 50°48N 1°6W 24 E6
Portsmouth N.H., U.S.A. 43°5N 70°45W 113 D12
Portsmouth Ohio, U.S.A. 38°44N 82°57W 112 F6
Portsmouth Va., U.S.A. 36°58N 76°23W 111 C11
Portsoy U.K. 57°41N 2°41W 19 G12
Portstewart U.K. 55°11N 6°43W 29 A8
Porttipahdan tekojärvi Finland 68°5N 26°40E 63 D9
Portugal ■ Europe 40°0N 8°0W 69 C1
Portumna Ireland 53°6N 8°14W 30 B6
Posadas Argentina 27°30S 55°50W 121 E4
Posse Brazil 14°4S 46°18W 122 B1
Postmasburg S. Africa 28°18S 23°5E 97 K4
Potchefstroom S. Africa 26°41S 27°7E 97 K5
Potenza Italy 40°38N 15°48E 70 D6
Poti Georgia 42°10N 41°38E 73 F7
Potiskum Nigeria 11°39N 11°2E 95 F8
Potomac → U.S.A. 38°0N 76°23W 112 F9
Potosí Bolivia 19°38S 65°50W 120 D3
Potsdam Germany 52°23N 13°3E 66 B7
Potsdam U.S.A. 44°40N 74°59W 113 C10
Potter Heigham U.K. 52°42N 1°34E 25 A12
Potterne U.K. 51°20N 2°0W 24 D4
Potters Bar U.K. 51°42N 0°11W 25 C8
Potterspury U.K. 52°5N 0°52W 25 B7
Pottstown U.S.A. 40°15N 75°39W 113 E10
Pottsville U.S.A. 40°41N 76°12W 113 E9
Pottuvil Sri Lanka 6°55N 81°50E 84 R12
Poughkeepsie U.S.A. 41°42N 73°56W 113 E11
Poulaphouca Res. Ireland 53°8N 6°30W 31 B10
Poulton-le-Fylde U.K. 53°51N 2°58W 23 E3
Poundstock U.K. 50°44N 4°36W 27 F4
Pouso Alegre Brazil 22°14S 45°57W 122 D1
Powder → U.S.A. 46°45N 105°26W 110 A5
Powell, L. U.S.A. 36°57N 111°29W 110 C4
Powell River Canada 49°50N 124°35W 108 E7
Powers U.S.A. 45°41N 87°32W 112 C4
Powick U.K. 52°10N 2°14W 24 B4
Powys □ U.K. 52°20N 3°20W 26 C7
Poyang Hu China 29°5N 116°20E 81 D6
Poza Rica Mexico 20°33N 97°27W 114 C5
Poznań Poland 52°25N 16°55E 67 B9
Pozzuoli Italy 40°49N 14°7E 70 D6
Prado Brazil 17°20S 39°13W 122 C3
Prague Czech Rep. 50°4N 14°25E 66 C8
Praia C. Verde Is. 15°2N 23°34W 91 E1
Prairie du Chien U.S.A. 43°3N 91°9W 112 D2
Prata Brazil 19°25S 48°54W 122 C1
Prato Italy 43°53N 11°6E 70 C4
Pratt U.S.A. 37°39N 98°44W 110 C7
Prawle Pt. U.K. 50°12N 3°44W 27 G6
Praya Indonesia 8°39S 116°17E 83 D3
Prees U.K. 52°54N 2°40W 23 G3
Preesall U.K. 53°55N 2°57W 23 E3
Prescott Canada 44°45N 75°30W 113 C10
Prescott U.S.A. 34°33N 112°28W 110 D4
Presidencia Roque Saenz Peña Argentina 26°45S 60°30W 121 E3
Presidente Prudente Brazil 22°5S 51°25W 120 E4
Presidio U.S.A. 29°34N 104°22W 110 E6
Prespa, L. Macedonia 40°55N 21°0E 71 D9
Presque Isle U.S.A. 46°41N 68°1W 113 B13
Prestatyn U.K. 53°20N 3°24W 26 A7
Prestbury U.K. 51°54N 2°2W 24 C4
Presteigne U.K. 52°17N 3°0W 26 C7
Preston Borders, U.K. 55°49N 2°19W 21 C11
Preston Dorset, U.K. 50°38N 2°26W 24 E4
Preston Lancs., U.K. 53°46N 2°42W 23 E3
Preston U.S.A. 42°6N 111°53W 110 B4
Prestonpans U.K. 55°58N 2°58W 21 C10
Prestwich U.K. 53°32N 2°17W 23 E4
Prestwick U.K. 55°29N 4°37W 20 D6
Pretoria S. Africa 25°44S 28°12E 97 K5
Pribilof Is. U.S.A. 57°0N 170°0W 108 D2
Price U.S.A. 39°36N 110°49W 110 C4
Prieska S. Africa 29°40S 22°42E 97 K4
Prilep Macedonia 41°21N 21°32E 71 D9
Prince Albert Canada 53°15N 105°50W 108 D9
Prince Albert Pen. Canada 72°30N 116°0W 108 B8
Prince Albert Sd. Canada 70°25N 115°0W 108 B8
Prince Alfred, C. Canada 74°20N 124°40W 109 B7
Prince Charles I. Canada 67°47N 76°12W 109 C12
Prince Charles Mts. Antarctica 72°0S 67°0E 55 D6
Prince Edward I. □ Canada 46°20N 63°20W 113 B16
Prince Edward Is. Ind. Oc. 46°35S 38°0E 53 G11
Prince George Canada 53°55N 122°50W 108 D7
Prince Gustaf Adolf Sea Canada 78°30N 107°0W 109 B9
Prince of Wales I. Canada 73°0N 99°0W 108 B10
Prince of Wales I. U.S.A. 55°47N 132°50W 108 D6
Prince Patrick I. Canada 77°0N 120°0W 109 B8
Prince Rupert Canada 54°20N 130°20W 108 D6
Princes Risborough U.K. 51°43N 0°49W 25 C7
Princeton Ill., U.S.A. 41°23N 89°28W 112 E3
Princeton Ind., U.S.A. 38°21N 87°34W 112 F4
Princeton Ky., U.S.A. 37°7N 87°53W 112 G4
Princeton W. Va., U.S.A. 37°22N 81°6W 112 G7
Princetown U.K. 50°33N 4°0W 27 F5
Príncipe, I. de Atl. Oc. 1°37N 7°27E 90 F4
Pripet → Europe 51°20N 30°15E 67 C16
Pripet Marshes Europe 52°10N 28°10E 67 B15
Priština Kosovo 42°40N 21°13E 71 C9
Privas France 44°45N 4°37E 68 D6
Prizren Kosovo 42°13N 20°45E 71 C9
Probolinggo Indonesia 7°46S 113°13E 83 D3
Probus U.K. 50°17N 4°58W 27 G4
Progreso Mexico 21°20N 89°40W 114 C7
Prome Burma 18°49N 95°13E 85 K19
Propriá Brazil 10°13S 36°51W 122 B3
Provence France 43°40N 5°46E 68 E6
Providence U.S.A. 41°49N 71°24W 113 E12
Providencia, I. de Colombia 13°25N 81°26W 115 E8
Provins France 48°33N 3°15E 68 B5
Provo U.S.A. 40°14N 111°39W 110 B4
Prudhoe U.K. 54°57N 1°52W 22 C5
Prudhoe Bay U.S.A. 70°18N 148°22W 108 B5
Pruszków Poland 52°9N 20°49E 67 B11
Prut → Romania 45°28N 28°10E 67 F15
Pryluky Ukraine 50°30N 32°24E 73 D5
Przemyśl Poland 49°50N 22°45E 67 D12
Pskov Russia 57°50N 28°25E 72 C4
Puddletown U.K. 50°44N 2°20W 24 E4
Pudsey U.K. 53°47N 1°40W 23 E5
Puebla Mexico 19°3N 98°12W 114 D5
Pueblo U.S.A. 38°16N 104°37W 110 C6
Puerca, Pta. Puerto Rico 18°13N 65°36W 115 d
Puerto Aisén Chile 45°27S 73°0W 121 G2
Puerto Barrios Guatemala 15°40N 88°32W 114 D7
Puerto Cabello Venezuela 10°28N 68°1W 120 A3
Puerto Cabezas Nic. 14°0N 83°30W 115 E8
Puerto Carreño Colombia 6°12N 67°22W 120 B3
Puerto Cortés Honduras 15°51N 88°0W 114 D7
Puerto Deseado Argentina 47°55S 66°0W 121 G3
Puerto La Cruz Venezuela 10°13N 64°38W 120 A3
Puerto Madryn Argentina 42°48S 65°4W 121 G3
Puerto Maldonado Peru 12°30S 69°10W 120 D3
Puerto Montt Chile 41°28S 73°0W 121 G2
Puerto Plata Dom. Rep. 19°48N 70°45W 115 D10
Puerto Princesa Phil. 9°46N 118°45E 83 C3
Puerto Rico ☑ W. Indies 18°15N 66°45W 115 d
Puerto San Julián Argentina 49°18S 67°43W 121 G3
Puerto Suárez Bolivia 18°58S 57°52W 120 D4
Puerto Wilches Colombia 7°21N 73°54W 120 B2
Puertollano Spain 38°43N 4°7W 69 C3
Puffin I. Ireland 51°50N 10°24W 30 E2
Puget Sound U.S.A. 47°50N 122°30W 110 A2
Pukapuka Cook Is. 10°53S 165°49W 103 J11
Pula Croatia 44°54N 13°57E 70 B5
Pulacayo Bolivia 20°25S 66°41W 120 E3
Pulaski U.S.A. 37°3N 80°47W 111 C10
Pulborough U.K. 50°58N 0°30W 25 E8
Pulham Market U.K. 52°26N 1°13E 25 B11
Pulham St. Mary U.K. 52°26N 1°16E 25 B11
Pullman U.S.A. 46°44N 117°10W 110 A3
Pumlumon Fawr U.K. 52°28N 3°46W 26 C6
Pune India 18°29N 73°57E 84 K8
Punjab □ India 31°0N 76°0E 84 D10
Punjab □ Pakistan 32°0N 72°30E 84 E9
Puno Peru 15°55S 70°3W 120 D2
Punta, Cerro de Puerto Rico 18°10N 66°37W 115 d
Punta Arenas Chile 53°10S 71°0W 121 H2
Punxsatawney U.S.A. 40°57N 78°59W 112 E8
Purbeck, Isle of U.K. 50°39N 1°59W 24 E5
Purfleet U.K. 51°29N 0°16E 25 D9
Puri India 19°50N 85°58E 85 K14
Purley on Thames U.K. 51°29N 1°3W 24 D6
Purnia India 25°45N 87°31E 85 G15
Puruliya India 23°17N 86°24E 85 H15
Purus → Brazil 3°42S 61°28W 120 C3
Putian China 25°23N 119°0E 81 D6
Putorana Russia 69°0N 95°0E 79 C11
Puttalam Sri Lanka 8°1N 79°55E 84 Q11
Putumayo → S. Amer. 3°7S 67°58W 120 C3
Puvirnituq Canada 60°2N 77°10W 109 C12
Puy-de-Dôme France 45°46N 2°57E 68 D5
Pwllheli U.K. 52°53N 4°25W 26 B5
Pyatigorsk Russia 44°2N 43°6E 73 F7
Pyinmana Burma 19°45N 96°12E 85 K20
P'yŏngyang N. Korea 39°0N 125°30E 81 C7
Pyramid L. U.S.A. 40°1N 119°35W 110 C3
Pyrénées Europe 42°45N 0°18E 68 E4

Q

Qaanaaq Greenland 77°40N 69°0W 54 B4
Qā'emshahr Iran 36°30N 52°53E 87 B8
Qaidam Basin China 37°0N 95°0E 80 C4
Qandahār Afghan. 31°32N 65°43E 87 D11
Qaqortoq Greenland 60°43N 46°0W 54 C5
Qarqan He → China 39°30N 88°30E 80 C3
Qarshi Uzbekistan 38°53N 65°48E 87 B11
Qatar ■ Asia 25°30N 51°15E 87 E7
Qattâra Depression Egypt 29°30N 27°30E 95 C11
Qazvīn Iran 36°15N 50°0E 86 B7
Qena Egypt 26°10N 32°43E 95 C12
Qeqertarsuaq Greenland 69°15N 53°38W 54 C5
Qeshm Iran 26°55N 56°10E 87 E9
Qiemo China 38°8N 85°32E 80 C3
Qijiaojing China 43°28N 91°36E 80 B4
Qikiqtarjuaq Canada 67°33N 63°0W 109 C13
Qilian Shan China 38°30N 96°0E 80 C4
Qingdao China 36°5N 120°20E 81 C7
Qinghai □ China 36°0N 98°0E 80 C4
Qinghai Hu China 36°40N 100°10E 80 C5
Qinhuangdao China 39°56N 119°30E 81 C6
Qinzhou China 21°58N 108°38E 80 D5
Qiqihar China 47°26N 124°0E 81 B7
Qira China 37°0N 80°48E 80 C3
Qitai China 44°2N 89°35E 80 B3
Qom Iran 34°40N 51°0E 87 C7
Qondūz Afghan. 36°50N 68°50E 87 B12
Quadring U.K. 52°54N 0°10W 23 G8
Quang Ngai Vietnam 15°13N 108°58E 83 B2
Quantock Hills U.K. 51°8N 3°10W 24 D2
Quanzhou China 24°55N 118°34E 81 D6
Quaqtaq Canada 60°55N 69°40W 109 C13
Quartu Sant'Élena Italy 39°15N 9°10E 70 E3
Québec Canada 46°52N 71°13W 113 B12
Québec □ Canada 48°0N 74°0W 109 E12
Queen Charlotte Is. Canada 53°20N 132°10W 108 D6
Queen Charlotte Sd. Canada 51°0N 128°0W 108 D7
Queen Elizabeth Is. Canada 76°0N 95°0W 109 B10
Queen Maud G. Canada 68°15N 102°30W 108 C9
Queenborough U.K. 51°25N 0°46E 25 D10
Queensbury U.K. 53°46N 1°50W 23 E5
Queensland □ Australia 22°0S 142°0E 98 E7
Queenstown N.Z. 45°1S 168°40E 99 K12
Queenstown S. Africa 31°52S 26°52E 97 L5
Queimadas Brazil 11°0S 39°38W 122 B3
Quelimane Mozam. 17°53S 36°58E 97 H7
Quendale, B. of U.K. 59°53N 1°20W 18 C15
Querétaro Mexico 20°36N 100°23W 114 C4
Quesnel Canada 53°0N 122°30W 108 D7
Quesnel L. Canada 52°30N 121°20W 108 D7
Quetta Pakistan 30°15N 66°55E 84 D5
Quezaltenango Guatemala 14°50N 91°30W 114 E6
Quezon City Phil. 14°37N 121°2E 83 B4
Qui Nhon Vietnam 13°40N 109°13E 83 B2
Quibdó Colombia 5°42N 76°40W 120 B2
Quilán, C. Chile 43°15S 74°30W 121 G2
Quilon India 8°50N 76°38E 84 Q10
Quilpie Australia 26°35S 144°11E 98 F7
Quimper France 48°0N 4°9W 68 B1
Quincy Ill., U.S.A. 39°56N 91°23W 111 C81
Quincy Mass., U.S.A. 42°14N 71°0W 113 D12
Quinte West Canada 44°10N 77°34W 112 C9
Quito Ecuador 0°15S 78°35W 120 C2
Qŭnghirot Uzbekistan 43°2N 58°50E 87 A9
Quorndon U.K. 52°46N 1°10W 23 G6
Qŭqon Uzbekistan 40°31N 70°56E 87 A12
Quseir Egypt 26°7N 34°16E 95 C12
Quzhou China 28°57N 118°54E 81 D6

R

Raahe Finland 64°40N 24°28E 63 E8
Raasay U.K. 57°25N 6°4W 18 H5
Raasay, Sd. of U.K. 57°30N 6°8W 18 H5
Raba Indonesia 8°36S 118°55E 83 D3
Rabat Morocco 34°2N 6°48W 94 B4
Rābigh Si. Arabia 22°50N 39°5E 88 C2
Race, C. Canada 46°40N 53°5W 109 E14
Rach Gia Vietnam 10°5N 105°5E 83 B2
Racine U.S.A. 42°44N 87°47W 112 D4
Rackheath U.K. 52°40N 1°22E 25 A11
Radcliffe U.K. 53°34N 2°18W 23 E4
Radcliffe-on-Trent U.K. 52°57N 1°2W 23 G6
Radford U.S.A. 37°8N 80°34W 112 G7
Radley U.K. 51°41N 1°14W 24 C6
Radnor Forest U.K. 52°17N 3°10W 26 C7
Radom Poland 51°23N 21°12E 67 C11
Radstock U.K. 51°17N 2°26W 24 D4
Rae Canada 62°50N 116°3W 108 C8
Rae Bareli India 26°18N 81°20E 85 F12
Rae Isthmus Canada 66°40N 87°30W 109 C11
Rafaela Argentina 31°10S 61°30W 121 F3
Rafsanjān Iran 30°30N 56°5E 87 D9
Ragusa Italy 36°55N 14°44E 70 F6
Rahimyar Khan Pakistan 28°30N 70°25E 84 E7
Raichur India 16°10N 77°20E 84 L10
Raigarh India 21°56N 83°25E 85 J13
Rainbow Lake Canada 58°30N 119°23W 108 D8
Rainham U.K. 51°22N 0°37E 25 D10
Rainier, Mt. U.S.A. 46°52N 121°46W 110 A2
Rainworth U.K. 53°7N 1°7W 23 F6
Rainy L. Canada 48°42N 93°10W 108 E10
Raipur India 21°17N 81°45E 85 J12
Raj Nandgaon India 21°5N 81°5E 85 J12
Rajahmundry India 17°1N 81°48E 85 L12
Rajapalaiyam India 9°25N 77°35E 84 Q10
Rajasthan □ India 26°45N 73°30E 84 F8
Rajkot India 22°15N 70°56E 84 H7
Rajshahi Bangla. 24°22N 88°39E 85 G16
Rajshahi □ Bangla. 25°0N 89°0E 85 G16
Raleigh U.S.A. 35°47N 78°39W 111 C11
Rame Head U.K. 50°19N 4°13W 27 G5
Ramgarh India 23°40N 85°35E 85 H14
Ramna Stacks U.K. 60°35N 1°24W 18 A15
Râmnicu Vâlcea Romania 45°9N 24°21E 67 F13
Rampside U.K. 54°6N 3°9W 22 D2
Rampur India 28°50N 79°5E 84 E11
Ramree I. Burma 19°0N 93°40E 85 K19
Ramsbottom U.K. 53°38N 2°19W 23 E4
Ramsbury U.K. 51°26N 1°36W 24 D5
Ramsey I. of Man 54°20N 4°22W 29 C13
Ramsey Cambs., U.K. 52°27N 0°7W 25 B8
Ramsey Essex, U.K. 51°55N 1°13E 25 C11
Ramsgate U.K. 51°20N 1°25E 25 D11
Rancagua Chile 34°10S 70°50W 121 F2
Ranchi India 23°19N 85°27E 85 H14
Randalstown U.K. 54°45N 6°19W 29 B9
Randers Denmark 56°29N 10°1E 63 F6
Rangoon Burma 16°45N 96°20E 85 L20
Rangpur Bangla. 25°42N 89°22E 85 G16
Rankin Inlet Canada 62°30N 93°0W 108 C10
Rannoch U.K. 56°40N 4°20W 19 J9
Rannoch, L. U.K. 56°41N 4°20W 19 J9
Rannoch Moor U.K. 56°38N 4°48W 19 J8
Rantoul U.S.A. 40°19N 88°9W 112 E3
Rapa French Polynesia 27°35S 144°20W 103 K13
Rapallo Italy 44°21N 9°14E 70 B3
Raper, C. Canada 69°44N 67°6W 109 C13
Rapid City U.S.A. 44°5N 103°14W 110 B6
Rarotonga Cook Is. 21°30S 160°0W 103 K12
Ra's al Khaymah U.A.E. 25°50N 55°59E 87 E9
Rasht Iran 37°20N 49°40E 86 B7
Rat Islands U.S.A. 52°0N 178°0E 108 D1
Ratangarh India 28°5N 74°35E 84 E9
Rath Luirc Ireland 52°21N 8°40W 30 D5
Rathcoole Ireland 53°17N 6°29W 31 B10
Rathdrum Ireland 52°56N 6°14W 31 C10
Rathkeale Ireland 52°32N 8°56W 30 C5
Rathlin I. U.K. 55°18N 6°14W 29 A9
Rathmelton Ireland 55°2N 7°38W 28 A6
Ratlam India 23°20N 75°0E 84 H9
Ratnagiri India 16°57N 73°18E 84 L8
Raton U.S.A. 36°54N 104°24W 110 C6
Rattray Hd. U.K. 57°38N 1°50W 19 G14
Rauma Finland 61°10N 21°30E 63 E8
Raunds U.K. 52°21N 0°32W 25 B7
Raurkela India 22°14N 84°50E 85 H14
Ravenglass U.K. 54°22N 3°24W 22 D2
Ravenna Italy 44°25N 12°12E 70 B5
Ravenstonedale U.K. 54°26N 2°25W 22 D4
Ravi → Pakistan 30°35N 71°49E 84 D7
Rawalpindi Pakistan 33°38N 73°8E 84 C8
Rawāndūz Iraq 36°40N 44°30E 86 B6
Rawlins U.S.A. 41°47N 107°14W 110 B5
Rawmarsh U.K. 53°27N 1°21W 23 F6
Rawson Argentina 43°15S 65°5W 121 G3
Rawtenstall U.K. 53°42N 2°17W 23 E4
Ray, C. Canada 47°33N 59°15W 109 E14
Rayleigh U.K. 51°36N 0°37E 25 C10
Rayong Thailand 12°40N 101°20E 83 B2
Raz, Pte. du France 48°2N 4°47W 68 C1
Razazah, L. Iraq 32°40N 43°35E 86 C5
Ré, Î. de France 46°12N 1°30W 68 C3
Reading U.K. 51°27N 0°58W 25 D7
Reading U.S.A. 40°20N 75°56W 113 E10
Reay Forest U.K. 58°22N 4°55W 19 F8
Rebiana Desert Libya 24°30N 21°0E 95 D10
Recife Brazil 8°0S 35°0W 122 A3
Reconquista Argentina 29°10S 59°45W 121 E4
Red → U.S.A. 31°1N 91°45W 111 D8
Red Bluff U.S.A. 40°11N 122°15W 110 B2
Red Deer Canada 52°20N 113°50W 108 D8
Red Dial U.K. 54°49N 3°10W 22 C2
Red L. U.S.A. 48°8N 94°45W 111 A8
Red Lake Canada 51°3N 93°49W 108 D10
Red Oak U.S.A. 41°1N 95°14W 111 B7
Red River of the North → N. Amer. 49°0N 97°15W 108 D10
Red Sea Asia 25°0N 36°0E 88 C2
Red Wing U.S.A. 44°34N 92°31W 111 B81
Redbridge □ U.K. 51°35N 0°7E 25 C9
Redcar U.K. 54°37N 1°4W 22 C6
Redding U.S.A. 40°35N 122°24W 110 B2
Redditch U.K. 52°18N 1°55W 24 B5
Rede → U.K. 55°9N 2°13W 22 B4
Redesmouth U.K. 55°8N 2°13W 22 B4
Redhill U.K. 51°14N 0°9W 25 D8
Redlynch U.K. 50°59N 1°41W 24 E5
Redmile U.K. 52°55N 0°48W 23 G7
Redmire U.K. 54°19N 1°55W 22 D5
Redon France 47°40N 2°6W 68 C2
Redruth U.K. 50°14N 5°14W 27 G3
Ree, L. Ireland 53°35N 8°0W 28 D6
Reedham U.K. 52°34N 1°34E 25 A12
Reepham U.K. 52°46N 1°6E 25 A11
Reese → U.S.A. 40°48N 117°4W 110 B3
Reeth U.K. 54°23N 1°56W 22 D5
Regensburg Germany 49°1N 12°6E 66 D7
Réggio di Calábria Italy 38°6N 15°39E 70 E6
Réggio nell'Emília Italy 44°43N 10°36E 70 B4
Regina Canada 50°27N 104°35W 108 D9
Reichenbach Germany 50°37N 12°17E 66 C7
Reigate U.K. 51°14N 0°12W 25 D8
Reims France 49°15N 4°1E 68 B6
Reina Adelaida, Arch. Chile 52°20S 74°0W 121 H2
Reindeer L. Canada 57°15N 102°15W 108 D9
Remscheid Germany 51°11N 7°12E 65 C7
Renfrew Canada 45°30N 76°40W 112 C9
Renfrew U.K. 55°52N 4°24W 20 C7
Rennell Solomon Is. 11°40S 160°10E 99 C11
Rennes France 48°7N 1°41W 68 B3
Reno U.S.A. 39°31N 119°48W 110 C3
Repton U.K. 52°50N 1°33W 23 G5
Republican → U.S.A. 39°4N 96°48W 111 C7
Repulse Bay Canada 66°30N 86°30W 109 C11
Resistencia Argentina 27°30S 59°0W 121 E4
Resolute Canada 74°42N 94°54W 109 B10
Resolution I. Canada 61°30N 65°0W 109 C13
Reston U.K. 55°51N 2°10W 21 C11
Retford U.K. 53°19N 0°56W 23 F7
Rethimno Greece 35°18N 24°30E 71 G11
Réunion ☑ Ind. Oc. 21°0S 56°0E 91 J9
Reus Spain 41°10N 1°5E 69 B6
Reutlingen Germany 48°29N 9°12E 66 D5
Revda Russia 56°48N 59°57E 72 C10
Revelstoke Canada 51°0N 118°10W 108 D8
Revillagigedo, Is. de Pac. Oc. 18°40N 112°0W 114 D2
Rewa India 24°33N 81°25E 85 G12
Rexburg U.S.A. 43°49N 111°47W 110 B4
Rey Malabo Eq. Guin. 3°45N 8°50E 96 D1
Reykjavík Iceland 64°10N 21°57W 63 B1
Reynosa Mexico 26°7N 98°18W 114 B5
Rēzekne Latvia 56°30N 27°17E 63 F9
Rhayader U.K. 52°18N 3°29W 26 C7
Rheidol → U.K. 52°25N 4°5W 26 C5
Rheine Germany 52°17N 7°26E 66 B4
Rheinland-Pfalz □ Germany 50°0N 7°0E 66 C4
Rhine → Europe 51°52N 6°2E 65 C6
Rhinelander U.S.A. 45°38N 89°25W 112 C3
Rhinns Pt. U.K. 55°40N 6°29W 20 C3
Rhins, The U.K. 54°52N 5°3W 20 E5
Rhode Island □ U.S.A. 41°40N 71°30W 113 E12
Rhodes Greece 36°15N 28°10E 71 F13

Rhodope Mts. *Bulgaria* 41°40N 24°20E 71 D11
Rhondda *U.K.* 51°39N 3°31W 26 D6
Rhône → *France* 43°28N 4°42E 68 E6
Rhoslanerchrugog *U.K.* 53°1N 3°3W 26 A7
Rhossili *U.K.* 51°34N 4°17W 27 D5
Rhossili B. *U.K.* 51°32N 4°14W 27 D5
Rhum *U.K.* 57°0N 6°20W 18 J5
Rhum, Sound of *U.K.* 56°55N 6°14W 18 J5
Rhyl *U.K.* 53°20N 3°29W 26 A7
Rhymney *U.K.* 51°46N 3°17W 26 D7
Riau, Kepulauan *Indonesia* 0°30N 104°20E 83 C2
Ribble → *U.K.* 53°52N 2°25W 23 E4
Ribeirão Prêto *Brazil* 21°10S 47°50W 122 D1
Riberalta *Bolivia* 11°0S 66°0W 120 D3
Riccall *U.K.* 53°50N 1°3W 23 E6
Rice Lake *U.S.A.* 45°30N 91°44W 112 C2
Richards Bay *S. Africa* 28°48S 32°6E 97 K6
Richfield *U.S.A.* 38°46N 112°5W 110 C4
Richland *U.S.A.* 46°17N 119°18W 110 A3
Richland Center *U.S.A.* 43°21N 90°23W 112 D2
Richlands *U.S.A.* 37°6N 81°48W 112 G7
Richmond *U.K.* 54°25N 1°43W 22 D5
Richmond *Ind., U.S.A.* 39°50N 84°53W 112 F5
Richmond *Ky., U.S.A.* 37°45N 84°18W 112 G5
Richmond *Va., U.S.A.* 37°33N 77°27W 112 G9
Richmond-upon-Thames □ *U.K.* 51°27N 0°17W 25 D8
Rickmansworth *U.K.* 51°38N 0°29W 25 C8
Ridgecrest *U.S.A.* 35°38N 117°40W 110 C3
Ridgway *U.S.A.* 41°25N 78°44W 112 E8
Ridsdale *U.K.* 55°9N 2°9W 22 B4
Rievaulx *U.K.* 54°16N 1°7W 22 D6
Rift Valley *Africa* 7°0N 30°0E 90 G7
Rīga *Latvia* 56°53N 24°8E 63 F8
Riga, G. of *Latvia* 57°40N 23°45E 63 F8
Rigestān *Afghan.* 30°15N 65°0E 87 D11
Rigolet *Canada* 54°10N 58°23W 109 D14
Rijeka *Croatia* 45°20N 14°21E 70 B6
Rillington *U.K.* 54°9N 0°42W 22 D7
Rímini *Italy* 44°3N 12°33E 70 B5
Rimouski *Canada* 48°27N 68°30W 109 E13
Ringmer *U.K.* 50°53N 0°5E 25 E9
Ringwood *U.K.* 50°50N 1°47W 24 E5
Rio Branco *Brazil* 9°58S 67°49W 120 C3
Rio Claro *Brazil* 22°19S 47°35W 122 D1
Rio Cuarto *Argentina* 33°10S 64°25W 121 F3
Rio de Janeiro *Brazil* 22°54S 43°12W 122 D2
Rio de Janeiro □ *Brazil* 22°50S 43°0W 122 D2
Rio Gallegos *Argentina* 51°35S 69°15W 121 H3
Rio Grande *Brazil* 32°0S 52°20W 121 F4
Rio Grande *Nic.* 12°54N 83°33W 115 E8
Rio Grande *Puerto Rico* 18°23N 65°50W 115 d
Rio Grande → *N. Amer.* 25°58N 97°9W 111 E7
Rio Grande de Santiago → *Mexico* 21°36N 105°26W 114 C3
Rio Grande do Norte □ *Brazil* 5°40S 36°0W 120 C6
Rio Grande do Sul □ *Brazil* 30°0S 53°0W 121 E4
Rio Largo *Brazil* 9°28S 35°50W 122 A3
Río Muni □ *Eq. Guin.* 1°30N 10°0E 96 D2
Riohacha *Colombia* 11°33N 72°55W 120 A2
Ripley *Derby, U.K.* 53°3N 1°24W 23 F6
Ripley *N. Yorks., U.K.* 54°3N 1°34W 22 D5
Ripon *U.K.* 54°9N 1°31W 22 D5
Ripon *U.S.A.* 43°51N 88°50W 112 D3
Risca *U.K.* 51°37N 3°5W 27 D7
Rishton *U.K.* 53°46N 2°26W 23 E4
Rivera *Uruguay* 31°0S 55°50W 121 F4
Riverhead *U.S.A.* 40°55N 72°40W 113 E11
Riverside *U.S.A.* 33°59N 117°22W 110 D3
Riverton *U.S.A.* 43°2N 108°23W 110 B5
Rivière-du-Loup *Canada* 47°50N 69°30W 109 E13
Rivière-Pilote *Martinique* 14°26N 60°53W 114 c
Rivière-Salée *Martinique* 14°31N 61°0W 114 c
Rivne *Ukraine* 50°40N 26°10E 67 C14
Riyadh *Si. Arabia* 24°41N 46°42E 86 E6
Rize *Turkey* 41°0N 40°30E 73 F7
Rizhao *China* 35°25N 119°30E 81 C6
Road Town *Br. Virgin Is.* 18°27N 64°37W 115 e
Roade *U.K.* 52°9N 0°53W 25 B7
Roanne *France* 46°3N 4°4E 68 C6
Roanoke *U.S.A.* 37°16N 79°56W 112 G8
Roanoke → *U.S.A.* 35°57N 76°42W 111 C11
Roberton *U.K.* 55°25N 2°54W 21 D10
Roberval *Canada* 48°32N 72°15W 109 E12
Robin Hood's Bay *U.K.* 54°27N 0°32W 22 D7
Robson, Mt. *Canada* 53°10N 119°10W 108 D8
Roca, C. da *Portugal* 38°40N 9°31W 69 C1
Rocester *U.K.* 52°57N 1°50W 23 G5
Rocha *Uruguay* 34°30S 54°25W 121 F4
Rochdale *U.K.* 53°38N 2°9W 23 E4
Roche *U.K.* 50°24N 4°50W 27 G4
Rochefort *France* 45°56N 0°57W 68 D3
Rochester *Medway, U.K.* 51°23N 0°31E 25 D10
Rochester *Northumberland, U.K.* 55°17N 2°17W 22 B4
Rochester *Ind., U.S.A.* 41°4N 86°13W 112 E4
Rochester *Minn., U.S.A.* 44°1N 92°28W 111 B81
Rochester *N.H., U.S.A.* 43°18N 70°59W 113 D12
Rochester *N.Y., U.S.A.* 43°10N 77°37W 112 D9
Rochford *U.K.* 51°34N 0°43E 25 C10
Rock Hill *U.S.A.* 34°56N 81°1W 111 D10
Rock Island *U.S.A.* 41°30N 90°34W 112 E2
Rock Springs *U.S.A.* 41°35N 109°14W 110 B5
Rockall *Atl. Oc.* 57°37N 13°42W 56 D3
Rockcliffe *U.K.* 54°57N 3°0W 22 C3
Rockford *U.S.A.* 42°16N 89°6W 112 D3
Rockhampton *Australia* 23°22S 150°32E 98 E9
Rockingham *U.K.* 52°31N 0°43W 25 B7
Rockingham Forest *U.K.* 52°29N 0°42W 25 B7
Rockland *U.S.A.* 44°6N 69°7W 113 C13
Rocky Mount *U.S.A.* 35°57N 77°48W 111 C11
Rocky Mts. *N. Amer.* 49°0N 115°0W 108 D7
Rodez *France* 44°21N 2°33E 68 D5
Roding → *U.K.* 51°31N 0°6E 25 C9
Rodríguez *Ind. Oc.* 19°45S 63°20E 53 E13
Roe → *U.K.* 55°6N 6°59W 29 A8
Roermond *Neths.* 51°12N 6°0E 65 C6
Roes Welcome Sd. *Canada* 65°0N 87°0W 109 C11

Roeselare *Belgium* 50°57N 3°7E 65 D3
Rogans Seat *U.K.* 54°25N 2°6W 22 D4
Rogate *U.K.* 51°0N 0°50W 25 D7
Rogers City *U.S.A.* 45°25N 83°49W 112 C6
Rohri *Pakistan* 27°45N 68°51E 84 F6
Rojo, C. *Mexico* 21°33N 97°20W 114 C5
Rolla *U.S.A.* 37°57N 91°46W 111 C81
Roma *Australia* 26°32S 148°49E 98 F8
Romaine → *Canada* 50°18N 63°47W 109 D13
Romania ■ *Europe* 46°0N 25°0E 67 F12
Romans-sur-Isère *France* 45°3N 5°3E 68 D6
Rome *Italy* 41°54N 12°28E 70 D5
Rome *Ga., U.S.A.* 34°15N 85°10W 111 D9
Rome *N.Y., U.S.A.* 43°13N 75°27W 113 D10
Romney *U.K.* 39°21N 78°45W 112 F8
Romney Marsh *U.K.* 51°2N 0°54E 25 D10
Romorantin-Lanthenay *France* 47°21N 1°45E 68 C4
Romsey *U.K.* 51°0N 1°29W 24 E6
Rona *U.K.* 57°34N 5°59W 18 G6
Roncador, Serra do *Brazil* 12°30S 52°30W 120 D4
Rondônia □ *Brazil* 11°0S 63°0W 120 D3
Rondonópolis *Brazil* 16°28S 54°38W 120 D4
Ronge, L. la *Canada* 55°6N 105°17W 108 D9
Ronne Ice Shelf *Antarctica* 77°30S 60°0W 55 D18
Roosendaal *Neths.* 51°32N 4°29E 65 C4
Roosevelt → *Brazil* 7°35S 60°20W 120 C3
Roosevelt I. *Antarctica* 79°30S 162°0W 55 D12
Ropsley *U.K.* 52°54N 0°30W 23 G8
Roquetas de Mar *Spain* 36°46N 2°36W 69 D4
Roraima □ *Brazil* 2°0N 61°30W 120 B3
Roraima, Mt. *Venezuela* 5°10N 60°40W 120 B3
Rosario *Argentina* 33°0S 60°40W 121 F3
Rosario *Mexico* 22°58N 105°53W 114 C3
Rosario de la Frontera *Argentina* 25°50S 65°0W 121 E3
Roscommon *Ireland* 53°38N 8°11W 28 D5
Roscommon □ *Ireland* 53°49N 8°23W 28 D5
Roscrea *Ireland* 52°57N 7°49W 30 C7
Roseau *Dominica* 15°17N 61°24W 115 D12
Roseburg *U.S.A.* 43°13N 123°20W 110 B2
Rosedale Abbey *U.K.* 54°21N 0°52W 22 D7
Rosehearty *U.K.* 57°42N 2°7W 19 G13
Rosenheim *Germany* 47°51N 12°7E 66 E7
Rosetown *Canada* 51°35N 107°59W 108 D9
Roseville *U.S.A.* 38°45N 121°17W 110 C2
Roslavl *Russia* 53°57N 32°55E 72 D5
Ross Ice Shelf *Antarctica* 80°0S 180°0E 55 E12
Ross-on-Wye *U.K.* 51°54N 2°34W 24 C3
Ross River *Canada* 62°30N 131°30W 108 C6
Ross Sea *Antarctica* 74°0S 178°0E 55 D11
Rossall Pt. *U.K.* 53°55N 3°3W 23 E2
Rossan Pt. *Ireland* 54°42N 8°47W 28 B4
Rosses, The *Ireland* 55°2N 8°20W 28 A5
Rossignol L. *Canada* 44°12N 65°10W 113 C15
Rosslare *Ireland* 52°17N 6°24W 31 D10
Rosslare Harbour *Ireland* 52°15N 6°20W 31 D10
Rossosh *Russia* 50°15N 39°28E 73 D6
Rostock *Germany* 54°5N 12°8E 66 A7
Rostov *Russia* 47°15N 39°45E 73 E6
Roswell *Ga., U.S.A.* 34°2N 84°22W 111 D10
Roswell *N. Mex., U.S.A.* 33°24N 104°32W 110 D6
Rothbury *U.K.* 55°19N 1°58W 22 B5
Rothbury Forest *U.K.* 55°19N 1°50W 22 B5
Rother → *U.K.* 50°59N 0°45E 25 E10
Rotherham *U.K.* 53°26N 1°20W 23 F6
Rothes *U.K.* 57°32N 3°13W 19 G11
Rothesay *U.K.* 55°50N 5°3W 20 C5
Rothwell *Northants., U.K.* 52°25N 0°48W 25 B7
Rothwell *W. Yorks., U.K.* 53°45N 1°28W 23 E6
Roti *Indonesia* 10°50S 123°0E 83 E4
Rotorua *N.Z.* 38°9S 176°16E 99 H14
Rotterdam *Neths.* 51°55N 4°30E 65 C4
Rottingdean *U.K.* 50°48N 0°4E 25 E8
Rotuma *Fiji* 12°25S 177°5E 99 C14
Roubaix *France* 50°40N 3°10E 68 A5
Rouen *France* 49°27N 1°4E 68 B4
Round Mt. *Australia* 30°26S 152°16E 98 G9
Rousay *U.K.* 59°10N 3°2W 19 D11
Roussillon *France* 42°30N 2°35E 68 E5
Rouyn-Noranda *Canada* 48°20N 79°0W 109 E12
Rovaniemi *Finland* 66°29N 25°41E 63 D9
Rovigo *Italy* 45°4N 11°47E 70 B4
Rowanburn *U.K.* 55°5N 2°55W 21 D10
Roxas *Phil.* 11°36N 122°49E 83 B4
Roxburgh *U.K.* 55°35N 2°28W 21 C11
Roxby *U.K.* 53°38N 0°38W 23 E7
Royal Canal *Ireland* 53°30N 7°13W 31 B8
Royal Leamington Spa *U.K.* 52°18N 1°31W 24 B5
Royal Tunbridge Wells *U.K.* 51°7N 0°16E 25 D9
Royale, Isle *U.S.A.* 48°0N 88°54W 112 B3
Royan *France* 45°37N 1°2W 68 D3
Royston *U.K.* 52°3N 0°0 25 B8
Royton *U.K.* 53°34N 2°8W 23 E4
Rub' al Khālī *Si. Arabia* 19°0N 48°0E 88 D4
Rubery *U.K.* 52°24N 2°1W 24 B4
Rubh a' Mhail *U.K.* 55°56N 6°8W 20 C3
Rubha Hunish *U.K.* 57°42N 6°20W 18 G5
Ruby L. *U.S.A.* 40°10N 115°28W 110 B3
Rudston *U.K.* 54°6N 0°20W 22 D8
Ruffling Pt. *Br. Virgin Is.* 18°44N 64°27W 115 e
Rufford *U.K.* 53°38N 2°50W 23 E4
Rufiji → *Tanzania* 7°50S 39°15E 96 F7
Rugby *U.K.* 52°23N 1°16W 24 B6
Rugeley *U.K.* 52°46N 1°55W 23 G5
Rügen *Germany* 54°22N 13°24E 66 A7
Ruhr → *Germany* 51°27N 6°43E 66 C4
Ruki → *Dem. Rep. of the Congo* 0°5N 18°17E 96 E3
Rukwa, L. *Tanzania* 8°0S 32°20E 96 F6
Rumania = Romania ■ *Europe* 46°0N 25°0E 67 F12
Rumford *U.S.A.* 44°33N 70°33W 113 C12
Runaway Bay *Jamaica* 18°27N 77°20W 114 a
Runcorn *U.K.* 53°21N 2°44W 23 F3
Rundu *Namibia* 17°52S 19°43E 97 H3
Rungwe *Tanzania* 9°11S 33°32E 90 G7
Ruoqiang *China* 38°55N 88°10E 80 C3
Rupert → *U.S.A.* 42°37N 113°41W 110 B4
Rupert → *Canada* 51°29N 78°45W 109 D12

Ruse *Bulgaria* 43°48N 25°59E 71 C12
Rush *Ireland* 53°31N 6°6W 31 A10
Rushden *U.K.* 52°18N 0°35W 25 B7
Rushville *Ill., U.S.A.* 40°7N 90°34W 112 E2
Rushville *Ind., U.S.A.* 39°37N 85°27W 112 F5
Russellville *U.S.A.* 35°17N 93°8W 111 C8
Russia ■ *Eurasia* 62°0N 105°0E 79 C12
Rustavi *Georgia* 41°30N 45°0E 73 F8
Rustenburg *S. Africa* 25°41S 27°14E 97 K5
Rutherglen *U.K.* 55°49N 4°13W 20 C7
Ruthin *U.K.* 53°6N 3°19W 26 A7
Ruthwell *U.K.* 55°0N 3°25W 21 E9
Rutog *China* 33°27N 79°42E 80 C2
Ruvuma → *Tanzania* 10°29S 40°28E 96 G8
Ruwenzori *Africa* 0°30N 29°55E 96 D5
Rwanda ■ *Africa* 2°0S 30°0E 96 E5
Ryan, L. *U.K.* 55°0N 5°2W 20 E5
Ryazan *Russia* 54°40N 39°40E 72 D6
Rybachi Pen. *Russia* 69°43N 32°0E 72 A5
Rybinsk *Russia* 58°5N 38°50E 72 C6
Rybinsk Res. *Russia* 58°30N 38°25E 72 C6
Rydal *U.K.* 54°27N 2°59W 22 D3
Ryde *U.K.* 50°43N 1°9W 24 E6
Rye *U.K.* 50°57N 0°45E 25 E10
Rye → *U.K.* 54°11N 0°44W 22 D7
Rye Bay *U.K.* 50°52N 0°49E 25 E10
Ryhope *U.K.* 54°53N 1°21W 22 C6
Ryton *U.K.* 52°22N 1°25W 24 B6
Ryukyu Is. *Japan* 26°0N 126°0E 81 D7
Rzeszów *Poland* 50°5N 21°58E 67 C11
Rzhev *Russia* 56°20N 34°20E 72 C5

S

Saale → *Germany* 51°56N 11°54E 66 C6
Saar → *Europe* 49°41N 6°32E 65 E6
Saarbrücken *Germany* 49°14N 6°59E 66 D4
Saaremaa *Estonia* 58°30N 22°30E 63 F8
Sabadell *Spain* 41°28N 2°7E 69 B7
Sabah □ *Malaysia* 6°0N 117°0E 83 C3
Sabará *Brazil* 19°55S 43°46W 122 C2
Sabhā *Libya* 27°9N 14°29E 95 C8
Sabinas *Mexico* 27°51N 101°7W 114 B4
Sabinas Hidalgo *Mexico* 26°30N 100°10W 114 B4
Sabine → *U.S.A.* 29°59N 93°47W 111 E8
Sable, C. *Canada* 43°29N 65°38W 113 D15
Sable, C. *U.S.A.* 25°9N 81°8W 111 E10
Sable I. *Canada* 44°0N 60°0W 109 E14
Sachsen □ *Germany* 50°55N 13°10E 66 C7
Sachsen-Anhalt □ *Germany* 52°0N 12°0E 66 C7
Saco *U.S.A.* 43°30N 70°27W 113 D12
Sacramento *U.S.A.* 38°35N 121°29W 110 C2
Sacramento → *U.S.A.* 38°3N 121°56W 110 C2
Sacramento Mts. *U.S.A.* 32°30N 105°30W 110 D5
Sado *Japan* 38°0N 138°25E 82 D6
Safford *U.S.A.* 32°50N 109°43W 110 D5
Saffron Walden *U.K.* 52°1N 0°16E 25 B9
Safi *Morocco* 32°18N 9°20W 94 B4
Saga *Japan* 33°15N 130°16E 82 G2
Sagaing *Burma* 21°52N 95°59E 85 J19
Sagar *India* 23°50N 78°44E 84 H11
Saginaw *U.S.A.* 43°26N 83°56W 112 D6
Saginaw B. *U.S.A.* 43°50N 83°40W 112 D6
Sagua la Grande *Cuba* 22°50N 80°10W 115 C8
Saguenay → *Canada* 48°22N 71°0W 113 A12
Sagunt *Spain* 39°42N 0°18W 69 C5
Sahara *Africa* 23°0N 5°0E 94 D6
Saharan Atlas *Algeria* 33°30N 1°0E 94 B6
Saharanpur *India* 29°58N 77°33E 84 E10
Sahel *Africa* 16°0N 5°0E 94 E5
Sahiwal *Pakistan* 30°45N 73°8E 84 D8
Saidpur *Bangla.* 25°48N 89°0E 85 G16
St. Abb's Head *U.K.* 55°55N 2°8W 21 C10
St. Agnes *Corn., U.K.* 50°19N 5°13W 27 G3
St. Agnes *Corn., U.K.* 49°54N 6°21W 27 H1
St. Agnes Hd. *U.K.* 50°19N 5°15W 27 G3
St. Albans *U.K.* 51°45N 0°19W 25 C8
St. Albans *Vt., U.S.A.* 44°49N 73°5W 113 C11
St. Albans *W. Va., U.S.A.* 38°23N 81°50W 112 F7
St. Alban's Head *U.K.* 50°34N 2°4W 24 E4
St. Andrews *U.K.* 56°20N 2°47W 21 B10
St. Ann's *U.K.* 55°14N 3°28W 21 D9
St. Ann's Bay *Jamaica* 18°26N 77°12W 114 a
St. Anthony *Canada* 51°22N 55°35W 109 D14
St. Asaph *U.K.* 53°15N 3°27W 26 A7
St-Augustin *Canada* 51°13N 58°38W 109 D14
St. Augustine *U.S.A.* 29°54N 81°19W 111 E10
St. Austell *U.K.* 50°20N 4°47W 27 G4
St. Bees *U.K.* 54°30N 3°35W 22 C1
St. Bees Hd. *U.K.* 54°31N 3°38W 22 C1
St. Blazey *U.K.* 50°22N 4°43W 27 G4
St. Brides B. *U.K.* 51°49N 5°9W 26 D3
St-Brieuc *France* 48°30N 2°46W 68 B2
St. Buryan *U.K.* 50°4N 5°37W 27 G2
St. Catharines *Canada* 43°10N 79°15W 112 D8
St. Catherine's Pt. *U.K.* 50°34N 1°18W 24 E6
St. Charles *U.S.A.* 38°47N 90°29W 112 F2
St. Clair, L. *N. Amer.* 42°27N 82°39W 112 D6
St. Clears *U.K.* 51°49N 4°31W 26 D4
St. Cloud *U.S.A.* 45°34N 94°10W 111 A8
St. Columb Major *U.K.* 50°26N 4°58W 27 G4
St. Croix *U.S. Virgin Is.* 17°45N 64°45W 115 D12
St. David's *U.K.* 51°53N 5°16W 26 D3
St. David's Head *U.K.* 51°54N 5°19W 26 D3
St-Denis *France* 48°56N 2°20E 68 B5
St. Dennis *U.K.* 50°23N 4°53W 27 G4
St-Dizier *France* 48°38N 4°56E 68 B6
St. Dominick *U.K.* 50°29N 4°15W 27 G3
St. Elias, Mt. *U.S.A.* 60°18N 140°56W 108 C5
St. Elias Mts. *N. Amer.* 60°33N 139°28W 108 D6
St. Enoder *U.K.* 50°22N 4°57W 27 G4
St. Erth *U.K.* 50°9N 5°26W 27 G3
St-Étienne *France* 45°27N 4°22E 68 D6
St-Félicien *Canada* 48°40N 72°25W 113 A11
St-Flour *France* 45°2N 3°6E 68 D5
St. Gallen *Switz.* 47°26N 9°22E 66 E5
St-Gaudens *France* 43°6N 0°44E 68 E4

St. George *U.S.A.* 37°6N 113°35W 110 C4
St-Georges *Canada* 46°8N 70°40W 113 B12
St. George's *Grenada* 12°5N 61°43W 115 E12
St. George's Channel *Europe* 52°0N 6°0W 31 E11
St. Germans *U.K.* 50°23N 4°19W 27 G5
St. Helena *Atl. Oc.* 15°58S 5°42W 52 E9
St. Helens *U.K.* 53°27N 2°44W 23 F3
St. Helens, Mt. *U.S.A.* 46°12N 122°12W 110 A2
St. Helier *U.K.* 49°10N 2°7W 27 J9
St-Hyacinthe *Canada* 45°40N 72°58W 109 E12
St. Ignace *U.S.A.* 45°52N 84°44W 112 C5
St. Issey *U.K.* 50°30N 4°57W 27 G4
St. Ives *Cambs., U.K.* 52°20N 0°4W 25 B8
St. Ives *Corn., U.K.* 50°12N 5°30W 27 G3
St. Ives B. *U.K.* 50°13N 5°27W 27 G3
St-Jean, L. *Canada* 48°40N 72°0W 113 A12
St-Jérôme *Canada* 45°47N 74°0W 113 C11
St. John *Canada* 45°20N 66°8W 109 E13
St. John *U.S. Virgin Is.* 18°20N 64°42W 115 e
St. John's *Antigua & B.* 17°6N 61°51W 115 D12
St. John's *Canada* 47°35N 52°40W 109 E14
St. Johns *U.S.A.* 43°0N 84°33W 112 D5
St. Johns → *U.S.A.* 30°24N 81°24W 111 D10
St. Johns Chapel *U.K.* 54°44N 2°10W 22 C4
St. John's Pt. *Ireland* 54°34N 8°27W 28 B5
St. Johnsbury *U.S.A.* 44°25N 72°1W 113 C11
St-Joseph *Martinique* 14°39N 61°4W 114 c
St. Joseph *Mich., U.S.A.* 42°6N 86°29W 112 D4
St. Joseph *Mo., U.S.A.* 39°46N 94°50W 111 C8
St. Joseph, L. *Canada* 51°10N 90°35W 109 D10
St. Just *U.K.* 50°7N 5°42W 27 G2
St. Keverne *U.K.* 50°3N 5°6W 27 G3
St. Kilda *U.K.* 57°49N 8°34W 64 C2
St. Kitts & Nevis ■ *W. Indies* 17°20N 62°40W 115 D12
St. Lawrence → *Canada* 49°30N 66°0W 109 E13
St. Lawrence, Gulf of *Canada* 48°25N 62°0W 109 E13
St. Lawrence I. *U.S.A.* 63°30N 170°30W 108 C3
St. Levan *U.K.* 50°2N 5°41W 27 G2
St-Lô *France* 49°7N 1°5W 68 B3
St-Louis *Guadeloupe* 15°56N 61°19W 114 b
St. Louis *Senegal* 16°8N 16°27W 94 E2
St. Louis *U.S.A.* 38°37N 90°11W 112 F2
St. Lucia ■ *W. Indies* 14°0N 60°57W 115 f
St. Mabyn *U.K.* 50°30N 4°47W 27 F4
St. Magnus B. *U.K.* 60°25N 1°35W 18 B14
St-Malo *France* 48°39N 2°1W 68 B2
St-Marc *Haiti* 19°10N 72°41W 115 D10
St. Margaret's-at-Cliffe *U.K.* 51°9N 1°23E 25 D11
St-Martin ☑ *W. Indies* 18°0N 63°0W 115 D12
St-Martin, C. *Martinique* 14°52N 61°14W 114 c
St. Martins *Barbados* 13°5N 59°28W 115 g
St. Martin's *U.K.* 49°58N 6°17W 27 H1
St. Mary Bourne *U.K.* 51°15N 1°24W 24 D6
St. Mary's *Corn., U.K.* 49°55N 6°18W 27 H1
St. Mary's *Orkney, U.K.* 58°54N 2°54W 19 E12
St. Marys *U.S.A.* 41°26N 78°34W 112 E8
St. Mary's Sd. *U.K.* 49°54N 6°20W 27 H1
St. Matthew I. *U.S.A.* 60°24N 172°42W 108 C2
St. Mawes *U.K.* 50°10N 5°2W 27 G3
St. Merryn *U.K.* 50°32N 5°1W 27 F3
St. Michael's Mount *U.K.* 50°7N 5°29W 27 G3
St. Minver *U.K.* 50°33N 4°53W 27 F4
St. Moritz *Switz.* 46°30N 9°51E 66 E5
St-Nazaire *France* 47°17N 2°12W 68 C2
St. Neots *U.K.* 52°14N 0°15W 25 B8
St-Niklaas *Belgium* 51°10N 4°8E 65 C4
St-Omer *France* 50°45N 2°15E 68 A5
St. Osyth *U.K.* 51°47N 1°5E 25 C11
St. Paul, I. *Ind. Oc.* 38°55N 77°34E 53 F13
St. Peter Port *U.K.* 49°26N 2°33W 27 J8
St. Petersburg *Russia* 59°55N 30°20E 72 C5
St. Petersburg *U.S.A.* 27°46N 82°40W 111 E10
St-Pierre *Martinique* 14°45N 61°10W 114 c
St-Pierre-et-Miquelon ☑ *N. Amer.* 46°55N 56°10W 109 E14
St-Quentin *France* 49°50N 3°16E 68 B5
St. Stephen *Canada* 45°16N 67°17W 113 C14
St. Stephen *U.K.* 50°21N 4°53W 27 G4
St. Teath *U.K.* 50°35N 4°45W 27 F4
St. Thomas *Canada* 42°45N 81°10W 112 D7
St. Thomas I. *U.S. Virgin Is.* 18°20N 64°55W 115 e
St-Tropez *France* 43°17N 6°38E 68 E7
St. Tudy *U.K.* 50°33N 4°45W 27 F4
St. Vincent, G. *Australia* 35°0S 138°0E 98 G6
St. Vincent & the Grenadines ■ *W. Indies* 13°0N 61°10W 115 e
Ste-Anne *Guadeloupe* 16°13N 61°24W 114 b
Ste. Genevieve *U.S.A.* 37°59N 90°2W 112 G2
Ste-Marie *Canada* 46°26N 71°0W 113 B12
Ste-Marie *Martinique* 14°48N 61°1W 114 c
Ste-Rose *Guadeloupe* 16°20N 61°45W 114 b
Saintes *France* 45°45N 0°37W 68 D3
Saintes, Îs. des *Guadeloupe* 15°50N 61°35W 114 b
Saintfield *U.K.* 54°28N 5°49W 29 C10
Saintonge *France* 45°40N 0°50W 68 D3
Saipan *N. Marianas* 15°12N 145°45E 102 F6
Sajama *Bolivia* 18°7S 69°0W 120 D3
Sakakawea, L. *U.S.A.* 47°30N 101°25W 110 A6
Sakarya *Turkey* 40°48N 30°25E 73 F5
Sakata *Japan* 38°55N 139°50E 82 D6
Sakhalin *Russia* 51°0N 143°0E 79 D16
Sala *Sweden* 59°58N 16°35E 63 F7
Sala-y-Gómez *Pac. Oc.* 26°28S 105°28W 103 K17
Salado → *La Pampa, Argentina* 37°30S 67°0W 121 F3
Salado → *Santa Fe, Argentina* 31°40S 60°41W 121 F3
Salālah *Oman* 16°56N 53°59E 88 D5
Salamanca *Spain* 40°58N 5°39W 69 B3
Salamanca *U.S.A.* 42°10N 78°43W 112 D8
Salar de Uyuni *Bolivia* 20°30S 67°45W 120 E3
Salavat *Russia* 53°21N 55°55E 72 D10
Salaverry *Peru* 8°15S 79°0W 120 C2
Salayar *Indonesia* 6°7S 120°30E 83 D4
Salcombe *U.K.* 50°14N 3°47W 27 H6
Saldanha *S. Africa* 33°0S 17°58E 97 L3
Sale *Australia* 38°6S 147°6E 98 H8
Salé *Morocco* 34°3N 6°48W 94 B4

Sale *U.K.* 53°26N 2°19W 23 F4
Salekhard *Russia* 66°30N 66°35E 79 C8
Salem *India* 11°40N 78°11E 84 P11
Salem *Ind., U.S.A.* 38°36N 86°6W 112 F4
Salem *Mass., U.S.A.* 42°31N 70°53W 113 D12
Salem *Ohio, U.S.A.* 40°54N 80°52W 112 E7
Salem *Oreg., U.S.A.* 44°56N 123°2W 110 B2
Salem *Va., U.S.A.* 37°18N 80°3W 112 G7
Salerno *Italy* 40°41N 14°47E 70 D6
Salford *U.K.* 53°30N 2°18W 23 F4
Salford Priors *U.K.* 52°10N 1°53W 24 B5
Salida *U.S.A.* 38°32N 106°0W 110 C5
Salina *U.S.A.* 38°50N 97°37W 110 C7
Salina Cruz *Mexico* 16°10N 95°12W 114 D5
Salinas *Ecuador* 2°10S 80°58W 120 C1
Salinas *U.S.A.* 36°40N 121°39W 110 C2
Salinas → *U.S.A.* 36°45N 121°48W 110 C2
Salinas Grandes *Argentina* 30°0S 65°0W 121 E3
Salisbury *U.K.* 51°4N 1°47W 24 D5
Salisbury *U.S.A.* 38°22N 75°36W 113 F10
Salisbury I. *Canada* 63°30N 77°0W 109 C12
Salisbury Plain *U.K.* 51°14N 1°55W 24 D5
Salmon *U.S.A.* 45°11N 113°54W 110 A4
Salmon → *U.S.A.* 45°51N 116°47W 110 A3
Salmon Arm *Canada* 50°40N 119°15W 108 D8
Salmon River Mts. *U.S.A.* 45°0N 114°30W 110 B4
Salon-de-Provence *France* 43°39N 5°6E 68 E6
Salsk *Russia* 46°28N 41°30E 73 E7
Salt → *U.S.A.* 33°23N 112°19W 110 D4
Salt Lake City *U.S.A.* 40°45N 111°53W 110 B4
Salta *Argentina* 24°57S 65°25W 121 E3
Saltash *U.K.* 50°24N 4°14W 27 G5
Saltburn by the Sea *U.K.* 54°35N 0°58W 22 C7
Saltcoats *U.K.* 55°38N 4°47W 20 C6
Saltee Is. *Ireland* 52°7N 6°37W 31 D10
Saltfleet *U.K.* 53°25N 0°11E 23 F9
Saltfleetby *U.K.* 53°23N 0°10E 23 F9
Saltillo *Mexico* 25°25N 101°0W 114 B4
Salton Sea *U.S.A.* 33°15N 115°45W 110 D3
Saltwood *U.K.* 51°4N 1°2E 25 D11
Salvador *Brazil* 13°0S 38°30W 122 B3
Salvador, El ■ *Cent. Amer.* 13°50N 89°0W 114 E7
Salween → *Burma* 16°31N 97°37E 85 L20
Salyan *Azerbaijan* 39°33N 48°59E 73 G8
Salzburg *Austria* 47°48N 13°2E 66 E7
Salzgitter *Germany* 52°9N 10°19E 66 B6
Samangān □ *Afghan.* 36°15N 68°3E 87 B12
Samar *Phil.* 12°0N 125°0E 83 B4
Samara *Russia* 53°8N 50°6E 72 D9
Samarinda *Indonesia* 0°30S 117°9E 83 D3
Samarkand *Uzbekistan* 39°40N 66°55E 87 B11
Sambalpur *India* 21°28N 84°4E 85 J14
Sambhal *India* 28°35N 78°37E 84 E11
Sambhar *India* 26°52N 75°6E 84 F9
Samoa ■ *Pac. Oc.* 14°0S 172°0W 99 C16
Samos *Greece* 37°45N 26°50E 71 F12
Samothraki *Greece* 40°28N 25°28E 71 D11
Sampford Courtenay *U.K.* 50°47N 3°58W 27 F6
Samsun *Turkey* 41°15N 36°22E 73 F6
Samui, Ko *Thailand* 9°30N 100°0E 83 C2
San Ambrosio *Pac. Oc.* 26°28S 79°53W 103 K20
San Andrés, I. de *Caribbean* 12°42N 81°46W 115 E8
San Andres Mts. *U.S.A.* 33°0N 106°30W 110 D5
San Andrés Tuxtla *Mexico* 18°27N 95°13W 114 D5
San Angelo *U.S.A.* 31°28N 100°26W 110 D6
San Antonio *Chile* 33°40S 71°40W 121 F2
San Antonio *U.S.A.* 29°25N 98°29W 110 E7
San Antonio → *U.S.A.* 28°30N 96°54W 111 E7
San Antonio Oeste *Argentina* 40°40S 65°0W 121 G3
San Bernardino *U.S.A.* 34°7N 117°19W 110 D3
San Bernardino Str. *Phil.* 13°0N 125°0E 83 B4
San Bernardo *Chile* 33°40S 70°50W 121 F2
San Blas, C. *U.S.A.* 29°40N 85°21W 111 E9
San Carlos *Phil.* 10°29N 123°25E 83 B4
San Carlos de Bariloche *Argentina* 41°10S 71°25W 121 G2
San Carlos de Bolívar *Argentina* 36°15S 61°6W 121 F3
San Cristóbal *Argentina* 30°20S 61°10W 121 F3
San Cristóbal *Solomon Is.* 10°30S 161°0E 99 C11
San Cristóbal *Venezuela* 7°46N 72°14W 120 B2
San Cristóbal de las Casas *Mexico* 16°45N 92°38W 114 D6
San Diego *U.S.A.* 32°42N 117°9W 110 D3
San Felipe *Venezuela* 10°20N 68°44W 120 A3
San Félix *Pac. Oc.* 26°23S 80°0W 103 K20
San Fernando *Chile* 34°30S 71°0W 121 F2
San Fernando *Spain* 36°28N 6°17W 69 D2
San Fernando de Apure *Venezuela* 7°54N 67°15W 120 B3
San Francisco *U.S.A.* 37°46N 122°23W 110 C2
San Francisco, C. de *Colombia* 6°18N 77°29W 116 C3
San Francisco de Macorís *Dom. Rep.* 19°19N 70°15W 115 D10
San German *Puerto Rico* 18°4N 67°4W 115 d
San Gottardo, P. del *Switz.* 46°33N 8°33E 66 E5
San Ignacio *Bolivia* 16°20S 60°55W 120 D3
San Joaquín → *U.S.A.* 38°4N 121°51W 110 C2
San Jorge, G. *Argentina* 46°0S 66°0W 121 G3
San José *Costa Rica* 9°55N 84°2W 115 F8
San Jose *Phil.* 12°27N 121°4E 83 B4
San Jose *U.S.A.* 37°20N 121°53W 110 C2
San Jose → *U.S.A.* 34°25N 106°45W 110 C5
San José de Chiquitos *Bolivia* 17°53S 60°50W 120 D3
San José de Jáchal *Argentina* 30°15S 68°46W 121 F3
San José de Mayo *Uruguay* 34°27S 56°40W 121 F4
San Juan *Argentina* 31°30S 68°30W 121 F3
San Juan *Puerto Rico* 18°28N 66°7W 115 d
San Juan → *Nic.* 10°56N 83°42W 115 E8
San Juan → *U.S.A.* 37°16N 110°26W 110 C4
San Juan de los Morros *Venezuela* 9°55N 67°21W 120 B3
San Juan Mts. *U.S.A.* 37°30N 107°0W 110 C5
San Lorenzo, Mte. *Argentina* 47°40S 72°20W 121 G2
San Lucas, C. *Mexico* 22°52N 109°53W 114 C3
San Luis *Argentina* 33°20S 66°20W 121 F3

San Luis Obispo   Skeleton Coast

San Luis Obispo *U.S.A.* 35°17N 120°40W **110** C2
San Luis Potosí *Mexico* 22°9N 100°59W **114** C4
San Marcos *U.S.A.* 29°53N 97°56W **110** E7
San Marino ■ *Europe* 43°56N 12°25E **70** C5
San Matías, G. *Argentina* 41°30S 64°0W **121** G3
San Miguel *El Salv.* 13°30N 88°12W **114** E7
San Miguel de Tucumán
  Argentina 26°50S 65°20W **121** E3
San Nicolás *Argentina* 33°25S 60°10W **121** F3
San Pédro *Ivory C.* 4°50N 6°33W **94** H4
San Pedro de las Colonias
  Mexico 25°45N 102°59W **114** B4
San Pedro de Macoris
  Dom. Rep. 18°30N 69°18W **115** D11
San Pedro Sula *Honduras* 15°30N 88°0W **114** D7
San Pietro *Italy* 39°8N 8°17E **70** E3
San Rafael *Argentina* 34°40S 68°21W **121** F3
San Remo *Italy* 43°49N 7°46E **70** C2
San Salvador *El Salv.* 13°40N 89°10W **114** E7
San Salvador de Jujuy
  Argentina 24°10S 64°48W **121** E3
San Salvador I. *Bahamas* 24°0N 74°40W **115** C10
San Sebastián *Puerto Rico* 18°20N 66°59W **115** d
San Severo *Italy* 41°41N 15°23E **70** D6
San Valentín. Mte. *Chile* 46°30S 73°30W **121** G2
Sana' *Yemen* 15°27N 44°12E **88** D3
Sanaga → *Cameroon* 3°35N 9°38E **96** D1
Sanandaj *Iran* 35°18N 47°1E **86** C6
Sancti Spíritus *Cuba* 21°52N 79°33W **115** C9
Sancy, Puy de *France* 45°32N 2°50E **68** D5
Sandakan *Malaysia* 5°53N 118°4E **83** C3
Sanday *U.K.* 59°16N 2°31W **19** D12
Sandbach *U.K.* 53°9N 2°21W **23** F4
Sandgate *U.K.* 51°4N 1°10E **25** D11
Sandhurst *U.K.* 51°21N 0°48W **25** D7
Sandown *U.K.* 50°40N 1°10W **24** E6
Sandpoint *U.S.A.* 48°17N 116°33W **110** A3
Sandray *U.K.* 56°53N 7°31W **18** J2
Sandringham *U.K.* 52°51N 0°31E **25** A10
Sandusky *U.S.A.* 41°27N 82°42W **112** E6
Sandwich *U.K.* 51°16N 1°21E **25** D11
Sandy *U.K.* 52°8N 0°17W **25** B8
Sandy *U.S.A.* 40°32N 111°50W **110** B4
Sandy L. *Canada* 53°2N 93°0W **108** D10
Sanford, Mt. *U.S.A.* 62°13N 144°8W **108** C5
Sangihe, Pulau *Indonesia* 3°35N 125°30E **83** C4
Sangli *India* 16°55N 74°33E **84** L9
Sangre de Cristo Mts.
  U.S.A. 37°30N 105°20W **110** C5
Sanikiluaq *Canada* 56°32N 79°14W **109** D12
Sanirajak *Canada* 68°46N 81°12W **109** C11
Sankt Pölten *Austria* 48°12N 15°38E **66** D8
Sankuru →
  Dem. Rep. of the Congo 4°17S 20°25E **96** E4
Sanliurfa *Turkey* 37°12N 38°50E **73** G6
Sanlúcar de Barrameda *Spain* 36°46N 6°21W **69** D2
Sanmenxia *China* 34°47N 111°12E **81** C6
Sanming *China* 26°15N 117°40E **81** D6
Sanquhar *U.K.* 55°22N 3°54W **21** D8
Sant Feliu de Guíxols *Spain* 41°45N 3°1E **69** B7
Santa Ana *El Salv.* 14°0N 89°31W **114** E7
Santa Ana *U.S.A.* 33°46N 117°52W **110** D3
Sant' Antíoco *Italy* 39°4N 8°27E **70** E3
Santa Barbara *U.S.A.* 34°25N 119°42W **110** D3
Santa Catarina □ *Brazil* 27°25S 48°30W **121** E5
Santa Clara *Cuba* 22°20N 80°0W **115** C9
Santa Clarita *U.S.A.* 34°24N 118°33W **110** D3
Santa Coloma de Gramenet
  Spain 41°27N 2°13E **69** B7
Santa Cruz *Bolivia* 17°43S 63°10W **120** D3
Santa Cruz *U.S.A.* 36°58N 122°1W **110** C2
Santa Cruz de Tenerife
  Canary Is. 28°28N 16°15W **94** C2
Santa Cruz Is. *Solomon Is.* 10°30S 166°0E **99** C12
Santa Cruz Mts. *Jamaica* 17°58N 77°43W **114** a
Santa Fé *Argentina* 31°35S 60°41W **121** F3
Santa Fe *U.S.A.* 35°41N 105°57W **110** C5
Santa Inés, I. *Chile* 54°0S 73°0W **121** H2
Santa Isabel *Solomon Is.* 8°0S 159°0E **99** B10
Santa Maria *Brazil* 29°40S 53°48W **121** E4
Santa Maria *U.S.A.* 34°57N 120°26W **110** D2
Santa María → *Mexico* 31°0N 107°14W **114** A3
Santa Marta *Colombia* 11°15N 74°13W **120** A2
Santa Marta, Sierra Nevada de
  Colombia 10°55N 73°50W **120** A2
Santa Rosa *Argentina* 36°40S 64°17W **121** F3
Santa Rosa *U.S.A.* 38°26N 122°43W **110** C2
Santai *China* 31°5N 104°58E **80** C5
Santana do Livramento
  Brazil 30°55S 55°30W **121** F4
Santander *Spain* 43°27N 3°51W **69** A4
Santarém *Brazil* 2°25S 54°42W **120** C4
Santarém *Portugal* 39°12N 8°42W **69** C1
Santiago *Chile* 33°26S 70°40W **121** F2
Santiago de Compostela *Spain* 42°52N 8°37W **69** A1
Santiago de Cuba *Cuba* 20°0N 75°49W **115** D9
Santiago de los Caballeros
  Dom. Rep. 19°30N 70°40W **115** D10
Santiago del Estero
  Argentina 27°50S 64°15W **121** E3
Santo Amaro *Brazil* 12°30S 38°43W **122** B3
Santo André *Brazil* 23°39S 46°29W **122** D1
Santo Antônio de Jesus
  Brazil 12°58S 39°16W **122** B3
Santo Domingo *Dom. Rep.* 18°30N 69°59W **115** D11
Santo Domingo de los Colorados
  Ecuador 0°15S 79°9W **120** C2
Santorini *Greece* 36°23N 25°27E **71** F11
Santos *Brazil* 24°0S 46°20W **122** D1
Santos Dumont *Brazil* 22°55S 43°10W **122** D2
Sanya *China* 18°14N 109°29E **81** E5
São Bernardo do Campo
  Brazil 23°45S 46°34W **122** D1
São Borja *Brazil* 28°39S 56°0W **121** E4
São Caitano *Brazil* 8°21S 36°6W **122** A3
São Carlos *Brazil* 22°0S 47°50W **122** D1
São Francisco → *Brazil* 10°30S 36°24W **122** B3
São Gonçalo *Brazil* 22°48S 43°5W **122** D2

São João da Boa Vista *Brazil* 22°0S 46°52W **122** D1
São João del Rei *Brazil* 21°8S 44°15W **122** D2
São João do Piauí *Brazil* 8°21S 42°15W **122** A2
São José do Rio Prêto *Brazil* 20°50S 49°20W **122** D1
São José dos Campos *Brazil* 23°7S 45°52W **122** D1
São Lourenço *Brazil* 22°7S 45°3W **122** D1
São Luís *Brazil* 2°39S 44°15W **120** C5
São Marcos → *Brazil* 18°15S 47°37W **122** C1
São Marcos, B. de *Brazil* 2°0S 44°0W **120** C5
São Mateus *Brazil* 18°44S 39°50W **122** C3
São Paulo *Brazil* 23°32S 46°38W **122** D1
São Paulo □ *Brazil* 22°0S 49°0W **120** E5
São Roque, C. de *Brazil* 5°30S 35°16W **120** C6
São Sebastião do Paraíso
  Brazil 20°54S 46°59W **122** D1
São Tomé *São Tomé & Príncipe* 0°10N 6°39E **90** F4
São Tomé & Príncipe ■ *Africa* 0°12N 6°39E **91** F4
São Vicente *Brazil* 23°57S 46°23W **122** D1
São Vicente, C. de *Portugal* 37°0N 9°0W **69** D1
Saône → *France* 45°44N 4°50E **68** D6
Sapele *Nigeria* 5°50N 5°40E **94** G7
Sapporo *Japan* 43°0N 141°21E **82** B7
Saqqez *Iran* 36°15N 46°20E **86** B6
Sar-e Pol *Afghan.* 36°10N 66°0E **87** B11
Sarajevo *Bos.-H.* 43°52N 18°26E **71** C8
Saranac Lakes *U.S.A.* 44°20N 74°28W **113** C10
Saransk *Russia* 54°10N 45°10E **72** D8
Sarapul *Russia* 56°28N 53°48E **72** D9
Sarasota *U.S.A.* 27°20N 82°32W **111** E10
Saratoga Springs *U.S.A.* 43°5N 73°47W **113** D11
Saratov *Russia* 51°30N 46°2E **73** D8
Sarawak □ *Malaysia* 2°0N 113°0E **83** C3
Sarda → *India* 27°21N 81°23E **85** F12
Sardinia □ *Italy* 40°0N 9°0E **70** D3
Sargasso Sea *Atl. Oc.* 27°0N 72°0W **103** D20
Sargodha *Pakistan* 32°10N 72°40E **84** C8
Sarh *Chad* 9°5N 18°23E **95** G9
Sári *Iran* 36°30N 53°4E **87** B8
Sark *U.K.* 49°25N 2°22W **27** F9
Sarlat-la-Canéda *France* 44°54N 1°13E **68** D4
Sarmiento *Argentina* 45°35S 69°5W **121** G3
Sarnia *Canada* 42°58N 82°23W **109** E11
Sarreguemines *France* 49°5N 7°4E **68** B7
Sarthe → *France* 47°33N 0°31W **68** C3
Sasebo *Japan* 33°10N 129°43E **82** G1
Saskatchewan □ *Canada* 54°40N 106°0W **108** D9
Saskatchewan → *Canada* 53°37N 100°40W **108** D9
Saskatoon *Canada* 52°10N 106°38W **108** D9
Sássari *Italy* 40°43N 8°34E **70** D3
Sassnitz *Germany* 54°29N 13°39E **66** A7
Satmala Hills *Andhra Pradesh,
  India* 19°45N 78°45E **84** K11
Satmala Hills *Maharashtra,
  India* 20°15N 74°40E **84** J9
Satna *India* 24°35N 80°50E **85** G12
Satpura Ra. *India* 21°25N 76°10E **84** J10
Satu Mare *Romania* 47°46N 22°55E **67** E12
Saudi Arabia ■ *Asia* 26°0N 44°0E **88** B3
Sault Ste. Marie *Canada* 46°30N 84°20W **112** B5
Saumur *France* 47°15N 0°5W **68** C3
Saundersfoot *U.K.* 51°43N 4°42W **26** D4
Saurimo *Angola* 9°40S 20°12E **96** F4
Sava → *Serbia* 44°50N 20°26E **71** B9
Savai'i *Samoa* 13°28S 172°24W **99** C16
Savanna-la-Mar *Jamaica* 18°10N 78°10W **114** a
Savannah *U.S.A.* 32°5N 81°6W **111** D10
Savannah → *U.S.A.* 32°2N 80°53W **111** D10
Savannakhet *Laos* 16°30N 104°49E **83** B2
Savoie □ *France* 45°26N 6°25E **68** D7
Savona *Italy* 44°17N 8°30E **70** B3
Sawatch Range *U.S.A.* 39°0N 106°30W **110** C5
Sawbridgeworth *U.K.* 51°48N 0°9E **25** C9
Sawel Mt. *U.K.* 54°50N 7°2W **29** B7
Sawston *U.K.* 52°8N 0°10E **25** B9
Sawtry *U.K.* 52°27N 0°17W **25** B8
Sawu *Indonesia* 10°35S 121°50E **83** F4
Sawu Sea *Indonesia* 9°30S 121°50E **83** D4
Saxilby *U.K.* 53°16N 0°38W **23** F7
Saxlingham Nethergate *U.K.* 52°32N 1°18E **25** A11
Saxmundham *U.K.* 52°13N 1°30E **25** B12
Sayan Mts. *Russia* 54°0N 96°0E **79** D11
Saydā *Lebanon* 33°35N 35°25E **86** C3
Sayre *U.S.A.* 41°59N 76°32W **112** D9
Sázava → *Czech Rep.* 49°53N 14°24E **66** D8
Scafell Pike *U.K.* 54°27N 3°14W **22** D2
Scalby *U.K.* 54°18N 0°26W **22** D8
Scalloway *U.K.* 60°9N 1°17W **18** B15
Scalpay *Highl., U.K.* 57°18N 6°0W **18** H6
Scalpay *W. Isles, U.K.* 57°52N 6°40W **18** G4
Scamblesby *U.K.* 53°17N 0°5W **23** F8
Scandicci *Italy* 43°45N 11°11E **70** C4
Scandinavia *Europe* 64°0N 12°0E **56** C8
Scapa Flow *U.K.* 58°53N 3°3W **19** E11
Scarba *U.K.* 56°11N 5°43W **20** A4
Scarborough *U.K.* 54°17N 0°24W **22** D8
Scarning *U.K.* 52°41N 0°54E **25** A10
Scarp *U.K.* 58°1N 7°8W **18** F3
Scebeli, Wabi → *Somali Rep.* 2°0N 44°0E **88** G3
Schaffhausen *Switz.* 47°42N 8°39E **66** E5
Schelde → *Belgium* 51°15N 4°16E **65** C4
Schenectady *U.S.A.* 42°49N 73°57W **113** D11
Schiedam *Neths.* 51°55N 4°25E **65** C4
Schiehallion *U.K.* 56°40N 4°6W **20** A7
Schiphol, Amsterdam ✈ (AMS)
  Neths. 52°18N 4°45E **65** B4
Schleswig *Germany* 54°31N 9°34E **66** A5
Schleswig-Holstein □ *Germany* 54°30N 9°30E **66** A5
Schœlcher *Martinique* 14°36N 61°7W **114** c
Schreiber *Canada* 48°45N 87°20W **112** A4
Schwäbische Alb *Germany* 48°20N 9°30E **66** D5
Schwarzwald *Germany* 48°30N 8°20E **66** D5
Schwerin *Germany* 53°36N 11°22E **66** B6
Schwyz *Switz.* 47°2N 8°39E **66** E5
Scilly Is. *U.K.* 49°56N 6°22W **27** H1
Scioto → *U.S.A.* 38°44N 83°1W **112** F6
Scole *U.K.* 52°22N 1°10E **25** B11

Scone *U.K.* 56°25N 3°24W **21** B9
Scopwick *U.K.* 53°8N 0°24W **23** F8
Scotia Sea *Antarctica* 56°5S 56°0W **55** B18
Scotland □ *U.K.* 57°0N 4°0W **64** C5
Scott I. *Antarctica* 67°0S 179°0E **55** C11
Scottish Borders □ *U.K.* 55°35N 2°50W **21** C10
Scottsbluff *U.S.A.* 41°52N 103°40W **110** B6
Scottsburg *U.S.A.* 38°41N 85°47W **112** F5
Scrabster *U.K.* 58°36N 3°33W **19** E10
Scranton *U.S.A.* 41°25N 75°40W **113** E10
Scremerston *U.K.* 55°44N 2°0W **22** A5
Scunthorpe *U.K.* 53°36N 0°39W **23** E7
Scutari *Albania* 42°4N 19°32E **71** C8
Scutari *Turkey* 41°1N 29°0E **86** A2
Seaford *U.K.* 50°47N 0°7E **25** E9
Seaford *U.S.A.* 38°39N 75°37W **113** F10
Seaforth, L. *U.K.* 57°52N 6°36W **18** G4
Seaham *U.K.* 54°50N 1°20E **22** C6
Seahouses *U.K.* 55°34N 1°39W **22** A5
Seal → *Canada* 59°4N 94°48W **108** D10
Seamer *U.K.* 54°15N 0°26W **22** D8
Seascale *U.K.* 54°24N 3°29W **22** D2
Seaton *Cumb., U.K.* 54°40N 3°31W **22** C1
Seaton *Devon, U.K.* 50°42N 3°5W **27** F7
Seaton Delaval *U.K.* 55°5N 1°33W **22** B5
Seattle *U.S.A.* 47°36N 122°19W **110** A2
Sebastián Vizcaíno, B.
  Mexico 28°0N 114°30W **114** B2
Şebinkarahisar *Turkey* 40°22N 38°28E **73** F6
Sedalia *U.S.A.* 38°42N 93°14W **111** C8
Sedan *France* 49°43N 4°57E **68** B6
Sedbergh *U.K.* 54°20N 2°31W **22** D3
Sedgefield *U.K.* 54°40N 1°26W **22** C6
Sedgemoor *U.K.* 51°12N 2°58E **24** D3
Seend *U.K.* 51°21N 2°4W **24** D4
Segesta *Italy* 37°56N 12°50E **70** F5
Ségou *Mali* 13°30N 6°16W **94** F4
Segovia *Spain* 40°57N 4°10W **69** B3
Séguéla *Ivory C.* 7°55N 6°40W **94** G4
Sehore *India* 23°10N 77°5E **84** H10
Seil *U.K.* 56°18N 5°38W **20** B4
Seine → *France* 49°26N 0°26E **68** B4
Sekondi-Takoradi *Ghana* 4°58N 1°45W **94** H5
Selborne *U.K.* 51°6N 0°56W **25** D7
Selby *U.K.* 53°47N 1°5W **23** E6
Selebi-Pikwe *Botswana* 21°58S 27°48E **97** J5
Selenge Mörön → *Asia* 52°16N 106°16E **80** A5
Selkirk *Canada* 50°10N 96°55W **108** D10
Selkirk *U.K.* 55°33N 2°50W **21** C10
Selkirk Mts. *Canada* 51°15N 117°40W **108** D8
Selma *U.S.A.* 32°25N 87°1W **111** D9
Selsey *U.K.* 50°44N 0°47W **25** E7
Selsey Bill *U.K.* 50°43N 0°47W **25** E7
Selvas *Brazil* 6°30S 67°0W **120** C3
Selwyn L. *Canada* 60°0N 104°30W **108** C9
Selwyn Mts. *Canada* 63°0N 130°0W **108** C6
Semarang *Indonesia* 7°0S 110°26E **83** D3
Semey *Kazakhstan* 50°30N 80°10E **79** D10
Semnān *Iran* 35°40N 53°23E **87** C8
Sena Madureira *Brazil* 9°5S 68°45W **120** C3
Sendai *Japan* 38°15N 140°53E **82** D7
Seneca L. *U.S.A.* 42°40N 76°54W **112** D9
Senegal ■ *W. Afr.* 14°30N 14°30W **94** F3
Sénégal → *W. Afr.* 15°48N 16°32W **94** E2
Senegambia *Africa* 12°45N 12°0W **90** E2
Senhor-do-Bonfim *Brazil* 10°30S 40°10W **122** B2
Senja *Norway* 69°25N 17°30E **63** D7
Senlis *France* 49°13N 2°35E **68** B5
Sennen *U.K.* 50°4N 5°42W **27** G2
Sens *France* 48°11N 3°15E **68** B5
Seoul *S. Korea* 37°31N 126°58E **81** C7
Seph → *U.K.* 54°18N 1°8W **22** D6
Sept-Îles *Canada* 50°13N 66°22W **109** D13
Seram *Indonesia* 3°10S 129°0E **83** D4
Seram Sea *Indonesia* 2°30S 128°30E **83** D4
Serang *Indonesia* 6°8S 106°10E **83** D2
Serbia ■ *Europe* 43°20N 20°0E **71** B9
Serdar *Turkmenistan* 39°4N 56°23E **87** B9
Seremban *Malaysia* 2°43N 101°53E **83** C2
Serengeti Plain *Tanzania* 2°40S 35°0E **96** E7
Sergipe □ *Brazil* 10°30S 37°30W **122** B3
Sergiyev Posad *Russia* 56°20N 38°10E **72** C6
Serhetabat *Turkmenistan* 35°20N 62°18E **87** C10
Serifos *Greece* 37°9N 24°30E **71** F11
Serov *Russia* 59°29N 60°35E **72** C11
Serowe *Botswana* 22°25S 26°43E **97** J5
Serpukhov *Russia* 54°55N 37°28E **72** D6
Serra de Mesa, Barragem de
  Brazil 14°30S 49°10W **122** B1
Serrinha *Brazil* 11°39S 39°0W **122** B3
Sète *France* 43°25N 3°42E **68** E5
Sete Lagôas *Brazil* 19°27S 44°16W **122** C2
Sétif *Algeria* 36°9N 5°26E **94** A7
Settat *Morocco* 33°0N 7°40W **94** B4
Settle *U.K.* 54°5N 2°16W **22** D4
Settlement, The *Br. Virgin Is.* 18°43N 64°22W **115** e
Setúbal *Portugal* 38°30N 8°58W **69** C1
Setúbal, B. de *Portugal* 38°40N 8°56W **69** C1
Seul, Lac *Canada* 50°20N 92°30W **108** D10
Sevan, L. *Armenia* 40°30N 45°20E **73** F8
Sevastopol *Ukraine* 44°35N 33°30E **73** F5
Seven → *U.K.* 54°12N 0°52W **22** D7
Sevenoaks *U.K.* 51°16N 0°11E **25** D9
Severn → *Canada* 56°2N 87°36W **109** D11
Severn → *U.K.* 51°35N 2°40W **24** C3
Severn Beach *U.K.* 51°33N 2°39W **24** C3
Severn Stoke *U.K.* 52°6N 2°12W **24** B4
Severnaya Zemlya *Russia* 79°0N 100°0E **79** B11
Severodvinsk *Russia* 64°27N 39°58E **72** B6
Severomorsk *Russia* 69°5N 33°27E **72** A5
Sevier → *U.S.A.* 39°4N 113°6W **110** C4
Sevier L. *U.S.A.* 38°54N 113°9W **110** C4
Seville *Spain* 37°23N 5°58W **69** D2
Seward *U.S.A.* 60°7N 149°27W **108** C5
Seward Peninsula *U.S.A.* 65°30N 166°0W **108** C3
Seychelles ■ *Ind. Oc.* 5°0S 56°0E **53** E12
Seyðisfjörður *Iceland* 65°16N 13°57W **63** A3
Seydişehir *Turkey* 37°25N 31°51E **73** G5
Seymour *U.S.A.* 38°58N 85°53W **112** F5

Sfântu Gheorghe *Romania* 45°52N 25°48E **67** F13
Sfax *Tunisia* 34°49N 10°48E **95** B8
Shaanxi □ *China* 35°0N 109°0E **81** C5
Shache *China* 38°20N 77°10E **80** C2
Shaftesbury *U.K.* 51°0N 2°11W **24** D4
Shahjahanpur *India* 27°54N 79°57E **84** F11
Shakhty *Russia* 47°40N 40°16E **73** E7
Shaki *Nigeria* 8°41N 3°21E **94** G6
Shaldon *U.K.* 50°32N 3°31W **27** F6
Shaluli Shan *China* 30°40N 99°55E **80** C4
Shamo, L. *Ethiopia* 5°45N 37°30E **88** F2
Shan □ *Burma* 21°30N 98°30E **85** J21
Shandong □ *China* 36°0N 118°0E **81** C6
Shandong Pen. *China* 37°0N 121°0E **81** C7
Shanghai *China* 31°15N 121°26E **81** C7
Shangqiu *China* 34°26N 115°36E **81** C6
Shangrao *China* 28°25N 117°59E **81** D6
Shangshui *China* 33°42N 114°35E **81** C6
Shanklin *U.K.* 50°38N 1°11W **24** E6
Shannon → *Ireland* 52°35N 9°30W **30** C4
Shannon ✈ (SNN) *Ireland* 52°42N 8°57W **30** C5
Shannon, Mouth of the
  Ireland 52°30N 9°55W **30** D3
Shantou *China* 23°18N 116°40E **81** D6
Shanxi □ *China* 37°0N 112°0E **81** C6
Shaoguan *China* 24°48N 113°35E **81** D6
Shaoxing *China* 30°0N 120°35E **81** D7
Shaoyang *China* 27°14N 111°25E **81** D6
Shap *U.K.* 54°32N 2°40W **22** C3
Shapinsay *U.K.* 59°3N 2°51W **19** D12
Shaqra *Si. Arabia* 25°15N 45°16E **86** E6
Shaqrā' *Yemen* 13°22N 45°44E **88** E4
Sharjah *U.A.E.* 25°23N 55°26E **87** E8
Shark B. *Australia* 25°30S 113°32E **98** F1
Sharon *U.S.A.* 41°14N 80°31W **112** E7
Sharpness *U.K.* 51°43N 2°28W **24** C4
Sharya *Russia* 58°22N 45°20E **72** C8
Shashi *China* 30°25N 112°14E **81** C6
Shasta, Mt. *U.S.A.* 41°25N 122°12W **110** B2
Shatt al Arab *Asia* 29°57N 48°34E **86** D7
Shawano *U.S.A.* 44°47N 88°36W **112** C3
Shawbury *U.K.* 52°48N 2°39W **23** G3
Shawinigan *Canada* 46°35N 72°50W **109** E12
Shawnee *U.S.A.* 35°20N 96°55W **111** C7
Shebbear *U.K.* 50°51N 4°15W **27** F5
Sheboygan *U.S.A.* 43°46N 87°45W **112** D4
Shechen □ *U.S.A.* 39°19N 77°44W **113** F9
Sheelin, L. *Ireland* 53°48N 7°20W **28** D7
Sheep Haven *Ireland* 55°11N 7°52W **28** A6
Sheerness *U.K.* 51°26N 0°47E **25** D10
Sheffield *U.K.* 53°23N 1°28W **23** F6
Shefford *U.K.* 52°2N 0°20W **25** B8
Shehy Mts. *Ireland* 51°47N 9°15W **30** E4
Shelburne *Canada* 43°47N 65°20W **113** D15
Shelby *U.S.A.* 48°30N 111°51W **110** A4
Shelbyville *Ill., U.S.A.* 39°24N 88°48W **112** F3
Shelbyville *Ind., U.S.A.* 39°31N 85°47W **112** F5
Shelekhov G. *Russia* 59°30N 157°0E **79** D17
Shenandoah *U.S.A.* 40°49N 76°12W **113** E9
Shenandoah → *U.S.A.* 39°19N 77°44W **113** F9
Shendî *Sudan* 16°46N 33°22E **95** E12
Shenfield *U.K.* 51°38N 0°22E **25** C9
Shenyang *China* 41°48N 123°27E **81** B7
Shenzhen *China* 22°32N 114°5E **81** D6
Shepparton *Australia* 36°23S 145°26E **98** H8
Sheppey, I. of *U.K.* 51°25N 0°48E **25** D10
Shepshed *U.K.* 52°47N 1°18W **23** G6
Shepton Mallet *U.K.* 51°11N 2°33W **24** D3
Sherborne *U.K.* 50°57N 2°31W **24** E3
Sherborne St. John *U.K.* 51°17N 1°7W **24** D6
Sherbrooke *Canada* 45°28N 71°57W **113** C12
Sherburn *N. Yorks., U.K.* 54°11N 0°32W **22** D7
Sherburn *N. Yorks., U.K.* 53°48N 1°15W **23** E6
Shere *U.K.* 51°13N 0°27W **25** D8
Sherfield English *U.K.* 51°1N 1°34W **24** D5
Sheridan *U.S.A.* 44°48N 106°58W **110** B5
Sheriff Hutton *U.K.* 54°5N 1°0W **22** D7
Sheringham *U.K.* 52°56N 1°13E **25** A11
Sherkin I. *Ireland* 51°28N 9°26W **30** F4
Sherman *U.S.A.* 33°38N 96°36W **111** D7
Sherston *U.K.* 51°34N 2°14W **24** C4
Sherwood Forest *U.K.* 53°6N 1°7W **23** F6
Shetland □ *U.K.* 60°30N 1°30W **18** B15
Shetland Is. *U.K.* 60°30N 1°30W **64** B6
Sheyenne → *U.S.A.* 47°2N 96°50W **111** A7
Shiant Is. *U.K.* 57°54N 6°22W **18** G5
Shibām *Yemen* 15°59N 48°36E **88** D4
Shiel, L. *U.K.* 56°48N 5°34W **18** J6
Shifnal *U.K.* 52°39N 2°23W **23** G4
Shihezi *China* 44°15N 86°2E **80** B3
Shijiazhuang *China* 38°2N 114°28E **81** C6
Shikarpur *Pakistan* 27°57N 68°39E **84** F6
Shikoku □ *Japan* 33°30N 133°30E **82** G3
Shildon *U.K.* 54°38N 1°38W **22** C5
Shiliguri *India* 26°45N 88°25E **85** F16
Shillelagh *Ireland* 52°45N 6°32W **31** C9
Shillingstone *U.K.* 50°53N 2°15W **24** E4
Shillong *India* 25°35N 91°53E **85** G17
Shimla *India* 31°2N 77°9E **84** D10
Shimoga *India* 13°57N 75°32E **84** N9
Shimonoseki *Japan* 33°58N 130°55E **82** G2
Shin, L. *U.K.* 58°5N 4°30W **19** F8
Shinyanga *Tanzania* 3°45S 33°27E **96** E6
Shipdham *U.K.* 52°38N 0°54E **25** A10
Shipley *U.K.* 53°50N 1°47W **23** E5
Shipston-on-Stour *U.K.* 52°3N 1°37W **24** B5
Shipton under Wychwood
  U.K. 51°51N 1°36W **24** C5
Shīrāz *Iran* 29°42N 52°30E **87** D8
Shire → *Africa* 17°42S 35°19E **97** H7
Shirebrook *U.K.* 53°12N 1°13W **23** F6
Shivpuri *India* 25°26N 77°42E **84** G10
Shiyan *China* 32°42N 113°56E **81** D6
Shizuishan *China* 39°15N 106°50E **80** C5
Shizuoka *Japan* 34°57N 138°24E **82** G6
Shoeburyness *U.K.* 51°32N 0°49E **25** C10
Shoreham by Sea *U.K.* 50°50N 0°16W **25** E8

Shreveport *U.S.A.* 32°31N 93°45W **111** D8
Shrewsbury *U.K.* 52°43N 2°45W **23** G3
Shrewton *U.K.* 51°12N 1°54W **24** D5
Shrirampur *India* 22°44N 88°21E **85** H16
Shrivenham *U.K.* 51°36N 1°38W **24** C5
Shropshire □ *U.K.* 52°36N 2°45W **23** G3
Shuangliao *China* 43°29N 123°30E **81** B7
Shuangyashan *China* 46°28N 131°5E **81** B8
Shule *China* 39°25N 76°3E **80** C2
Shumagin Is. *U.S.A.* 55°7N 160°30W **108** D4
Shumen *Bulgaria* 43°18N 26°55E **71** C12
Shwebo *Burma* 22°30N 95°45E **85** H19
Si Kiang → *China* 22°5N 113°20E **81** D6
Siahan Range *Pakistan* 27°30N 64°40E **84** F4
Sialkot *Pakistan* 32°32N 74°30E **84** C9
Šiauliai *Lithuania* 55°56N 23°15E **63** F8
Šibenik *Croatia* 43°48N 15°54E **70** C6
Siberia *Russia* 60°0N 100°0E **79** C11
Siberut *Indonesia* 1°30S 99°0E **83** D1
Sibi *Pakistan* 29°30N 67°54E **84** E5
Sibiu *Romania* 45°45N 24°9E **67** F13
Sible Hedingham *U.K.* 51°59N 0°37E **25** C10
Sibolga *Indonesia* 1°42N 98°45E **83** C1
Sibsey *U.K.* 53°2N 0°1E **23** F9
Sibu *Malaysia* 2°18N 111°49E **83** C3
Sibuyan Sea *Phil.* 12°30N 122°20E **83** B4
Sichuan □ *China* 30°30N 103°0E **80** C5
Sicily *Italy* 37°30N 14°30E **70** F6
Sicuani *Peru* 14°21S 71°10W **120** D2
Sidbury *U.K.* 50°42N 3°14W **27** F7
Sidi-bel-Abbès *Algeria* 35°13N 0°39W **94** A5
Sidlaw Hills *U.K.* 56°32N 3°2W **21** A9
Sidlesham *U.K.* 50°47N 0°47W **25** E7
Sidmouth *U.K.* 50°40N 3°15W **27** F7
Sidney *Nebr., U.S.A.* 41°8N 102°59W **110** B6
Sidney *Ohio, U.S.A.* 40°17N 84°9W **112** E5
Sidra, G. of *Libya* 31°40N 18°30E **95** B9
Siedlce *Poland* 52°10N 22°20E **67** B12
Siegen *Germany* 50°51N 8°0E **66** C5
Siena *Italy* 43°19N 11°21E **70** C4
Sierra Blanca Peak *U.S.A.* 33°23N 105°49W **110** D5
Sierra Leone ■ *W. Afr.* 9°0N 12°0W **94** G3
Sierra Madre Occidental
  Mexico 27°0N 107°0W **114** B3
Sierra Madre Oriental *Mexico* 25°0N 100°0W **114** C5
Sierra Nevada *Spain* 37°3N 3°15W **69** D4
Sierra Nevada *U.S.A.* 39°0N 120°30W **110** C2
Sierra Vista *U.S.A.* 31°33N 110°18W **110** D4
Sifnos *Greece* 37°0N 24°45E **71** F11
Sighty Crag *U.K.* 55°7N 2°38W **22** B3
Sikar *India* 27°33N 75°10E **84** F9
Sikasso *Mali* 11°18N 5°35W **94** F4
Sikeston *U.S.A.* 36°53N 89°35W **112** G3
Sikhote Alin Ra. *Russia* 45°0N 136°0E **79** E15
Sikkim □ *India* 27°50N 88°30E **85** F16
Silesia *Poland* 51°0N 16°30E **66** C9
Silifke *Turkey* 36°22N 33°58E **73** G5
Siling Co *China* 31°50N 89°20E **80** C3
Silloth *U.K.* 54°52N 3°23W **22** C2
Silsden *U.K.* 53°55N 1°55W **23** E5
Silver City *U.S.A.* 32°46N 108°17W **110** D5
Silvermine Mts. *Ireland* 52°47N 8°15W **30** C6
Silverstone *U.K.* 52°5N 1°2W **24** B6
Silverton *U.K.* 50°49N 3°29W **27** F7
Simcoe, L. *Canada* 44°25N 79°20W **112** C8
Simeulue *Indonesia* 2°45N 95°45E **83** C1
Simferopol *Ukraine* 44°55N 34°3E **73** F5
Simi *Greece* 36°35N 27°50E **71** F12
Simonsbath *U.K.* 51°8N 3°46W **27** E6
Simonside *U.K.* 55°17N 1°59W **22** B5
Simplonpass *Switz.* 46°15N 8°3E **66** E5
Simpson Desert *Australia* 25°0S 137°0E **98** F6
Simpson Pen. *Canada* 68°34N 88°45W **109** C11
Sinai *Egypt* 29°0N 34°0E **95** C12
Sincelejo *Colombia* 9°18N 75°24W **120** B2
Sinclair's B. *U.K.* 58°31N 3°5W **19** E11
Sind Sagar Doab *Pakistan* 32°0N 71°30E **84** D7
Sindh □ *Pakistan* 26°0N 69°0E **84** G6
Sines *Portugal* 37°56N 8°51W **69** D1
Singapore ■ *Asia* 1°17N 103°51E **83** C2
Singaraja *Indonesia* 8°7S 115°6E **83** D3
Singida *Tanzania* 4°49S 34°48E **96** E6
Singkawang *Indonesia* 1°0N 108°57E **83** C2
Singleton *U.K.* 50°55N 0°46W **25** E7
Sinkiang □ *China* 42°0N 86°0E **80** B3
Sinop *Turkey* 42°1N 35°11E **73** F6
Sintra *Portugal* 38°47N 9°25W **69** C1
Sion *Switz.* 46°14N 7°20E **66** E4
Sion Mills *U.K.* 54°48N 7°29W **28** B7
Sioux City *U.S.A.* 42°30N 96°24W **111** B7
Sioux Falls *U.S.A.* 43°33N 96°44W **111** B7
Sioux Lookout *Canada* 50°10N 91°50W **108** D10
Siping *China* 43°8N 124°21E **81** B7
Sir James MacBrien, Mt.
  Canada 62°7N 127°41W **108** C7
Siracusa *Italy* 37°4N 15°17E **70** F6
Sirajganj *Bangla.* 24°25N 89°47E **85** G16
Sirsa *India* 29°33N 75°4E **84** E9
Šištán *Asia* 30°50N 61°0E **87** D10
Sitapur *India* 27°38N 80°45E **85** F12
Sitges *Spain* 41°17N 1°47E **69** B6
Sitka *U.S.A.* 57°3N 135°20W **108** D6
Sittingbourne *U.K.* 51°21N 0°45E **25** D10
Sittwe *Burma* 20°18N 92°45E **85** J18
Sivas *Turkey* 39°43N 36°58E **73** G6
Sivrihisar *Turkey* 39°30N 31°35E **73** G5
Sîwa *Egypt* 29°11N 25°31E **95** C11
Siwalik Range *Nepal* 28°0N 83°0E **85** F13
Six Cross Roads *Barbados* 13°8N 59°28W **114** c
Sixmilebridge *Ireland* 52°44N 8°46W **30** C5
Sizewell *U.K.* 52°12N 1°37E **25** B12
Själland *Denmark* 55°30N 11°30E **63** F6
Skagerrak *Denmark* 57°30N 9°0E **63** F5
Skagway *U.S.A.* 59°28N 135°19W **108** D6
Skeena → *Canada* 54°9N 130°5W **108** D6
Skegness *U.K.* 53°9N 0°20E **23** F9
Skeleton Coast *Namibia* 20°0S 13°0E **97** J2

Skellefteå   Talgarth

Skellefteå Sweden 64°45N 20°50E 63 E8
Skellefteälven → Sweden 64°45N 21°10E 63 E8
Skellingthorpe U.K. 53°15N 0°37W 23 F7
Skelmersdale U.K. 53°33N 2°48W 23 E3
Skelmorlie U.K. 55°52N 4°53W 20 C6
Skelton Cleve., U.K. 54°34N 0°58W 22 C7
Skelton Cumb., U.K. 54°43N 2°51W 22 C3
Skerries, The U.K. 53°25N 4°36W 26 A4
Skiathos Greece 39°12N 23°30E 71 E10
Skibbereen Ireland 51°33N 9°16W 30 E4
Skiddaw U.K. 54°39N 3°9W 22 C2
Skien Norway 59°12N 9°35E 63 F5
Skikda Algeria 36°50N 6°58E 94 A7
Skipsea U.K. 53°58N 0°13W 23 E8
Skipton U.K. 53°58N 2°3W 23 E4
Skopelos Greece 39°9N 23°47E 71 E10
Skopje Macedonia 42°1N 21°26E 71 C9
Skovorodino Russia 54°0N 124°0E 79 D14
Skowhegan U.S.A. 44°46N 69°43W 113 C13
Skull Ireland 51°32N 9°34W 30 E3
Skye U.K. 57°15N 6°10W 18 H5
Skyros Greece 38°55N 24°34E 71 E11
Slaidburn U.K. 53°58N 2°26W 23 E4
Slaney → Ireland 52°26N 6°33W 31 D9
Slatina Romania 44°28N 24°22E 67 F13
Slave → Canada 61°18N 113°39W 108 C8
Slave Coast W. Afr. 6°0N 2°30E 94 G6
Slave Lake Canada 55°17N 114°43W 108 D8
Sleaford U.K. 53°0N 0°24W 23 F8
Sleat, Sd. of U.K. 57°5N 5°47W 18 H6
Sledmere U.K. 54°4N 0°35W 22 D7
Sleeper Is. Canada 58°30N 81°0W 109 D11
Sleights U.K. 54°27N 0°40W 22 D7
Slieve Aughty Ireland 53°4N 8°30W 30 B5
Slieve Bloom Ireland 53°4N 7°40W 31 B7
Slieve Donard U.K. 54°11N 5°55W 29 C10
Slieve Gamph Ireland 54°6N 9°0W 28 C4
Slieve Gullion Ireland 54°7N 6°26W 29 C9
Slieve League Ireland 54°40N 8°42W 28 B4
Slieve Mish Ireland 52°12N 9°50W 30 D3
Slievenamon Ireland 52°25N 7°34W 31 D7
Sligo Ireland 54°16N 8°28W 28 C5
Sligo □ Ireland 54°8N 8°42W 28 C4
Sligo B. Ireland 54°18N 8°40W 28 C4
Sliven Bulgaria 42°42N 26°19E 71 C12
Slough U.K. 51°30N 0°36W 25 C7
Slovak Rep. ■ Europe 48°30N 20°0E 67 D10
Slovenia ■ Europe 45°58N 14°30E 66 B6
Slovyansk Ukraine 48°55N 37°36E 73 E6
Slupsk Poland 54°30N 17°3E 67 A9
Slutsk Belarus 53°2N 27°31E 72 D4
Slyne Hd. Ireland 53°25N 10°10W 28 C1
Smallwood Res. Canada 54°5N 64°30W 109 D13
Smederevo Serbia 44°40N 20°57E 71 B9
Smerwick Harbour Ireland 52°12N 10°23W 30 D2
Smethwick U.K. 52°30N 1°57W 23 G5
Smithfield U.K. 54°59N 2°51W 22 C3
Smiths Falls Canada 44°55N 76°0W 113 C9
Smoky → Canada 56°10N 117°21W 108 D8
Smoky Hill → U.S.A. 39°4N 96°48W 111 C7
Smolensk Russia 54°45N 32°5E 72 D5
Snaefell I. of Man 54°16N 4°27W 29 C13
Snainton U.K. 54°14N 0°33W 22 D7
Snaith U.K. 53°42N 1°1W 23 E6
Snake → U.S.A. 46°12N 119°2W 110 A3
Snape U.K. 52°10N 1°30E 25 B12
Snettisham U.K. 52°53N 0°31E 25 A10
Snizort, L. U.K. 57°33N 6°28W 18 G5
Snøhetta Norway 62°19N 9°16E 63 E5
Snow Hill U.S.A. 38°11N 75°24W 113 F10
Snowdon U.K. 53°4N 4°5W 26 A5
Snowdonia △ U.K. 53°7N 3°59W 26 A6
Snowy Mts. Australia 36°30S 148°20E 98 H8
Sobat, Nahr → Sudan 9°22N 31°33E 95 G12
Sobradinho, Reprêsa de Brazil 9°30S 42°0W 122 A2
Sobral Brazil 3°50S 40°20W 120 C5
Soc Trang Vietnam 9°37N 105°50E 83 C2
Sochi Russia 43°35N 39°40E 73 F6
Société, Îs. de la French Polynesia 17°0S 151°0W 103 J12
Socorro U.S.A. 34°4N 106°54W 110 D5
Socotra Yemen 12°30N 54°0E 88 E5
Söderhamn Sweden 61°18N 17°10E 63 E7
Sofia Bulgaria 42°45N 23°20E 71 C10
Sognefjorden Norway 61°10N 5°50E 63 E5
Sohâg Egypt 26°33N 31°43E 95 C12
Soham U.K. 52°21N 0°21E 25 B9
Soissons France 49°25N 3°19E 68 B5
Sokhumi Georgia 43°0N 41°0E 73 F7
Sokodé Togo 9°0N 1°11E 94 G6
Sokoto Nigeria 13°2N 5°16E 94 F7
Solapur India 17°43N 75°56E 84 L9
Soldotna U.S.A. 60°29N 151°3W 108 C4
Soledad Colombia 10°55N 74°46W 120 A2
Solent, The U.K. 50°45N 1°25W 24 E6
Solihull U.K. 52°26N 1°47W 23 H5
Solikamsk Russia 59°38N 56°50E 72 C10
Solingen Germany 51°10N 7°5E 66 C4
Söller Spain 39°46N 2°43E 69 C7
Sologne France 47°40N 1°45E 68 C4
Solomon Is. ■ Pac. Oc. 6°0S 155°0E 99 B10
Solomon Sea Papua N. G. 7°0S 150°0E 98 B9
Solon China 46°32N 121°10E 81 B7
Solothurn Switz. 47°13N 7°32E 66 E4
Solway Firth U.K. 54°49N 3°35W 22 C1
Somali Pen. Africa 7°0N 46°0E 90 F8
Somali Rep. ■ Africa 7°0N 47°0E 88 F4
Somaliland □ Somali Rep. 9°0N 46°0E 88 F4
Sombrerete Mexico 23°38N 103°39W 114 C4
Somerby U.K. 52°42N 0°49W 23 G7
Somerset U.S.A. 37°5N 84°36W 112 G5
Somerset □ U.K. 51°9N 3°0W 24 D2
Somerset I. Canada 73°30N 93°0W 108 A10
Somerton U.K. 51°2N 2°43W 24 D3
Somme → France 50°11N 1°38E 68 A4
Songhua Hu China 43°35N 126°50E 81 B7
Songhua Jiang → China 47°45N 132°30E 81 B8
Songkhla Thailand 7°13N 100°37E 83 C2

Songpan China 32°40N 103°30E 80 C5
Sonning U.K. 51°28N 0°54W 25 D7
Sonora → Mexico 29°5N 110°55W 114 B2
Sonoran Desert U.S.A. 33°40N 113°30W 110 D4
Sonoyta Mexico 31°51N 112°50W 114 A2
Sonsonate El Salv. 13°43N 89°44W 114 E7
Sopot Poland 54°27N 18°31E 67 A10
Sorel-Tracy Canada 46°0N 73°10W 113 C11
Soria Spain 41°43N 2°32W 69 B4
Sorocaba Brazil 23°31S 47°27W 122 D1
Sørøya Norway 70°40N 22°30E 63 C8
Sosnowiec Poland 50°20N 19°10E 67 C10
Soufrière Guadeloupe 16°5N 61°40W 114 b
Soufrière St. Lucia 13°51N 61°3W 115 f
Soufrière Bay St. Lucia 11°50N 61°21W 115 f
Sound, The U.K. 50°20N 4°10W 27 G5
Souris → Canada 49°40N 99°34W 108 E9
Sousse Tunisia 35°50N 10°38E 95 A8
South Africa ■ Africa 32°0S 23°0E 97 L4
South America 10°0S 60°0W 116 E5
South Australia □ Australia 32°0S 139°0E 98 G6
South Ayrshire □ U.K. 55°18N 4°41W 20 D6
South Bend U.S.A. 41°41N 86°15W 112 E4
South Benfleet U.K. 51°33N 0°36E 25 C10
South Brent U.K. 50°25N 3°51W 27 G6
South Carolina □ U.S.A. 34°0N 81°0W 111 D10
South Cave U.K. 53°46N 0°37W 23 E7
South Charleston U.S.A. 38°22N 81°44W 112 F7
South China Sea Asia 10°0N 113°0E 83 C3
South Dakota □ U.S.A. 44°15N 100°0W 110 B7
South Dorset Downs U.K. 50°40N 2°26W 24 E4
South Downs U.K. 50°52N 0°25W 25 E8
South East C. Australia 43°40S 146°50E 98 J8
South Elkington U.K. 53°23N 0°4W 23 F8
South Esk → U.K. 56°43N 2°31W 19 J12
South Foreland U.K. 51°8N 1°24E 25 D11
South Georgia Antarctica 54°30S 37°0W 55 B1
South Harris U.K. 57°50N 7°0W 18 G4
South Hayling U.K. 50°47N 0°58W 25 E7
South Honshu Ridge Pac. Oc. 23°0N 143°0E 102 E6
South I. N.Z. 44°0S 170°0E 99 J13
South Korea ■ Asia 36°0N 128°0E 81 C7
South Lanarkshire □ U.K. 55°37N 3°53W 21 C8
South Magnetic Pole Antarctica 64°8S 138°8E 55 C9
South Molton U.K. 51°1N 3°51W 27 E6
South Nahanni → Canada 61°3N 123°21W 108 C7
South Negril Pt. Jamaica 18°16N 78°22W 114 a
South Orkney Is. Antarctica 63°0S 45°0W 55 C18
South Ossetia □ Georgia 42°21N 44°2E 73 F7
South Petherton U.K. 50°57N 2°46W 24 E3
South Petherwin U.K. 50°36N 4°24W 27 F5
South Platte → U.S.A. 41°7N 100°42W 110 B6
South Pole Antarctica 90°0S 0°0 55 E
South Pt. Barbados 13°2N 59°32W 115 g
South Queensferry U.K. 56°0N 3°23W 21 C9
South Ronaldsay U.K. 58°48N 2°58W 19 E12
South Sandwich Is. Antarctica 57°0S 27°0W 55 B1
South Saskatchewan → Canada 53°15N 105°5W 108 D9
South Shetland Is. Antarctica 62°0S 59°0W 55 C18
South Shields U.K. 55°0N 1°25W 22 C6
South Tawton U.K. 50°44N 3°55W 27 F6
South Tyne → U.K. 54°59N 2°8W 22 C4
South Uist U.K. 57°20N 7°15W 18 H3
South Woodham Ferrers U.K. 51°39N 0°37E 25 C10
South Yorkshire □ U.K. 53°27N 1°36W 23 F5
Southam U.K. 52°18N 1°23W 24 B6
Southampton U.K. 50°54N 1°23W 24 E6
Southampton I. Canada 64°30N 84°0W 109 C11
Southborough U.K. 51°9N 0°16E 25 D9
Southend-on-Sea U.K. 51°32N 0°44E 25 C10
Southern Alps N.Z. 43°41S 170°11E 99 J13
Southern Indian L. Canada 57°10N 98°30W 108 D10
Southern Ocean Antarctica 62°0S 60°0E 53 H13
Southern Uplands U.K. 55°28N 3°52W 21 D8
Southery U.K. 52°31N 0°24E 25 A9
Southminster U.K. 51°40N 0°51E 25 C10
Southport U.K. 53°39N 3°0W 23 E2
Southwark □ U.K. 51°29N 0°6W 25 D8
Southwell U.K. 53°4N 0°57W 23 F7
Southwick U.K. 50°50N 0°13W 25 E8
Southwold U.K. 52°20N 1°41E 25 B12
Sovetsk Russia 55°6N 21°50E 63 F8
Sowerby U.K. 54°14N 1°21W 22 D6
Soweto S. Africa 26°14S 27°52E 97 K5
Spain ■ Europe 39°0N 4°0W 69 B4
Spalding U.K. 52°48N 0°9W 23 G8
Spanish Canada 46°12N 82°20W 112 B6
Spanish Town Br. Virgin Is. 17°43N 64°26W 115 e
Spanish Town Jamaica 18°0N 76°57W 114 a
Sparkford U.K. 51°2N 2°33W 24 D3
Sparks U.S.A. 39°32N 119°45W 110 C3
Sparta Greece 37°5N 22°25E 71 F10
Sparta U.S.A. 43°56N 90°49W 112 D2
Spartanburg U.S.A. 34°56N 81°57W 111 D10
Spartivento, C. Italy 37°55N 16°4E 70 F7
Speightstown Barbados 13°15N 59°39W 115 g
Speke U.K. 53°21N 2°52W 23 F3
Spencer U.S.A. 43°9N 95°9W 111 B7
Spencer G. Australia 34°0S 137°20E 98 G6
Spennymoor U.K. 54°42N 1°36W 22 C5
Sperrin Mts. U.K. 54°50N 7°0W 29 B7
Spey → U.K. 57°40N 3°6W 19 G11
Spilsby U.K. 53°10N 0°6E 23 F9
Spithead U.K. 50°45N 1°10W 24 E6
Split Croatia 43°31N 16°26E 70 C7
Spofforth U.K. 53°57N 1°27W 23 E6
Spokane U.S.A. 47°40N 117°24W 110 A3
Spooner U.S.A. 45°50N 91°53W 112 C2
Spratly Is. S. China Sea 8°20N 112°0E 83 C3
Spree → Germany 52°32N 13°12E 66 B7
Spring Hall Barbados 13°18N 59°36W 115 g
Springbok S. Africa 29°42S 17°54E 97 K3
Springfield Ill., U.S.A. 39°48N 89°39W 112 F3
Springfield Mass., U.S.A. 42°6N 72°35W 113 D11
Springfield Mo., U.S.A. 37°13N 93°17W 111 C8
Springfield Ohio, U.S.A. 39°55N 83°49W 112 F6
Springfield Oreg., U.S.A. 44°3N 123°1W 110 B2

Springhill Canada 45°40N 64°4W 113 C15
Springs S. Africa 26°13S 28°25E 97 K5
Sproatley U.K. 53°47N 0°11W 23 E8
Spurn Hd. U.K. 53°35N 0°8E 23 E9
Srebrenica Bos.-H. 44°6N 19°18E 71 B8
Sredinny Ra. Russia 57°0N 160°0E 79 D18
Sri Lanka ■ Asia 7°30N 80°50E 84 R12
Srikakulam India 18°14N 83°58E 85 K13
Srinagar India 34°5N 74°50E 84 B9
Stacks Mts. Ireland 52°20N 9°34W 30 D3
Staffa U.K. 56°27N 6°21W 20 B3
Stafford U.K. 52°49N 2°7W 23 G4
Staffordshire □ U.K. 52°53N 2°10W 23 G4
Staindrop U.K. 54°36N 1°47W 22 C5
Staines U.K. 51°26N 0°29W 25 D8
Stainforth U.K. 53°37N 1°0W 23 E7
Stainmore Forest U.K. 54°29N 2°4W 22 C4
Stainton U.K. 53°18N 0°24W 23 F8
Staithes U.K. 54°34N 0°46W 22 C7
Stakhanov Ukraine 48°35N 38°40E 73 E6
Stalbridge U.K. 50°57N 2°23W 24 E4
Stalham U.K. 52°47N 1°31E 25 A12
Stallingborough U.K. 53°35N 0°12W 23 E8
Stalybridge U.K. 53°28N 2°3W 23 F4
Stamford U.K. 52°39N 0°29W 23 G8
Stamford U.S.A. 41°3N 73°32W 113 E11
Stamford Bridge U.K. 53°59N 0°54W 23 E7
Stamfordham U.K. 55°3N 1°53W 22 B5
Standish U.K. 53°35N 2°41W 23 E3
Standish U.S.A. 43°59N 83°57W 112 D6
Stanford on Teme U.K. 52°16N 2°25W 24 B4
Stanhope U.K. 54°45N 2°1W 22 C4
Stanley Falk. Is. 51°40S 59°51W 121 H4
Stanley U.K. 54°53N 1°41W 22 C5
Stannington U.K. 55°7N 1°40W 22 B5
Stanovoy Ra. Russia 55°0N 130°0E 79 D14
Stansted, London × (STN) U.K. 51°54N 0°14E 25 C9
Stansted Mountfitchet U.K. 51°52N 0°11E 25 C9
Stanwix U.K. 54°55N 2°56W 22 C3
Stapleford U.K. 52°57N 1°16W 23 G6
Staplehurst U.K. 51°9N 0°34E 25 D10
Stara Zagora Bulgaria 42°26N 25°39E 71 C11
Staraya Russa Russia 57°58N 31°23E 72 C5
Starbuck I. Kiribati 5°37S 155°55W 103 H12
Start B. U.K. 50°15N 3°39W 27 G6
Start Pt. U.K. 50°13N 3°39W 27 G6
Staryy Oskol Russia 51°19N 37°55E 73 D6
State College U.S.A. 40°48N 77°52W 112 E9
Staten, I. = Estados, I. de los Argentina 54°40S 64°30W 121 H3
Staunton U.K. 51°57N 2°17W 24 C4
Staunton U.S.A. 38°9N 79°4W 112 F8
Stavanger Norway 58°57N 5°40E 63 F5
Staveley Cumb., U.K. 54°23N 2°48W 22 D3
Staveley Derby, U.K. 53°16N 1°21W 23 F6
Stavropol Russia 45°5N 42°0E 73 E7
Steiermark □ Austria 47°26N 15°0E 66 E8
Steinkjer Norway 64°1N 11°31E 63 E6
Stellarton Canada 45°32N 62°30W 113 C16
Stellenbosch S. Africa 33°58S 18°50E 97 L3
Stenhousemuir U.K. 56°2N 3°48W 21 B8
Stephenville Canada 48°31N 58°35W 109 E14
Steppe Asia 50°0N 50°0E 74 C7
Sterling Colo., U.S.A. 40°37N 103°13W 110 B6
Sterling Ill., U.S.A. 41°48N 89°42W 112 E3
Sterlitamak Russia 53°40N 56°0E 72 D10
Stettiner Haff Germany 53°47N 14°15E 66 B8
Stettler Canada 52°19N 112°40W 108 D8
Steubenville U.S.A. 40°22N 80°37W 112 E7
Stevenage U.K. 51°55N 0°13W 25 C8
Stevens Point U.S.A. 44°31N 89°34W 112 C3
Stevenston U.K. 55°39N 4°45W 20 C6
Stewart Canada 55°56N 129°57W 108 D7
Stewart → Canada 63°19N 139°26W 108 C6
Stewart I. N.Z. 46°58S 167°54E 99 K12
Stewarton U.K. 55°40N 4°32W 20 C6
Steyning U.K. 50°53N 0°18W 25 E8
Steyr Austria 48°3N 14°25E 66 D8
Stikine → Canada 56°40N 132°30W 108 D6
Stillington U.K. 54°6N 1°2W 22 D6
Stillwater U.S.A. 36°7N 97°4W 111 A8
Stiperstones U.K. 52°36N 2°55W 23 G3
Stirling Canada 44°18N 77°33W 113 C9
Stirling U.K. 56°8N 3°57W 21 B8
Stirling □ U.K. 56°12N 4°18W 20 B7
Stobo U.K. 55°38N 3°17W 21 C9
Stockbridge U.K. 51°7N 1°29W 24 D6
Stockholm Sweden 59°19N 18°4E 63 F7
Stockport U.K. 53°25N 2°9W 23 F4
Stocksbridge U.K. 53°29N 1°35W 23 F5
Stockton U.S.A. 37°58N 121°17W 110 C2
Stockton-on-Tees U.K. 54°35N 1°19W 22 C6
Stoer, Pt. of U.K. 58°16N 5°23W 18 F7
Stoke U.K. 51°26N 0°41E 25 D10
Stoke Ferry U.K. 52°34N 0°31E 25 A10
Stoke Fleming U.K. 50°19N 3°37W 27 G6
Stoke Mandeville U.K. 51°47N 0°47W 25 C7
Stoke-on-Trent U.K. 53°1N 2°11W 23 F4
Stoke Prior U.K. 52°19N 2°4W 24 B4
Stokesley U.K. 54°28N 1°12W 22 D6
Stone Bucks., U.K. 51°48N 0°52W 25 C7
Stone Staffs., U.K. 52°55N 2°9W 23 G4
Stonehaven U.K. 56°59N 2°12W 19 J13
Stonehouse U.K. 51°45N 2°16W 24 C4
Stonham Aspal U.K. 52°12N 1°8E 25 B11
Stony Stratford U.K. 52°3N 0°50W 25 B7
Stony Tunguska → Russia 61°50N 90°13E 79 C11
Stora Lulevatten Sweden 67°10N 19°30E 63 D7
Storavan Sweden 65°45N 18°10E 63 D7
Store Bælt Denmark 55°20N 11°0E 63 F6
Stormberge S. Africa 31°16S 26°17E 97 L5
Stornoway U.K. 58°13N 6°23W 18 F5
Storsjön Sweden 63°9N 14°30E 63 E6
Stort → U.K. 51°46N 0°2E 25 C9
Storuman Sweden 65°5N 17°10E 63 D7
Stotfold U.K. 52°1N 0°13W 25 B8
Stour → Dorset, U.K. 50°43N 1°47W 24 E6
Stour → Kent, U.K. 51°18N 1°22E 25 D11
Stour → Suffolk, U.K. 51°57N 1°4E 25 C11

Stour → Worcs., U.K. 52°21N 2°17W 24 B4
Stourbridge U.K. 52°28N 2°8W 23 H4
Stourport-on-Severn U.K. 52°21N 2°17W 24 B4
Stow U.K. 55°42N 2°50W 21 C10
Stow Bardolph U.K. 52°38N 0°24E 25 A9
Stow-on-the-Wold U.K. 51°56N 1°42W 24 C5
Stowmarket U.K. 52°12N 1°0E 25 B10
Strabane U.K. 54°50N 7°27W 28 B7
Stradbroke U.K. 52°19N 1°16E 25 B11
Stralsund Germany 54°18N 13°4E 66 A7
Strangford L. U.K. 54°30N 5°37W 29 C10
Stranraer U.K. 54°54N 5°1W 20 E5
Strasbourg France 48°35N 7°42E 68 B7
Stratford Canada 43°23N 81°0W 112 D7
Stratford St. Mary U.K. 51°58N 1°0E 25 C10
Stratford-upon-Avon U.K. 52°12N 1°42W 24 B5
Strath Avon U.K. 57°18N 3°23W 19 H11
Strath Dearn U.K. 57°20N 4°0W 19 H9
Strath Glass U.K. 57°22N 4°42W 19 H8
Strath Halladale U.K. 58°30N 3°51W 19 F10
Strath Naver U.K. 58°24N 4°12W 19 F9
Strath of Kildonan U.K. 58°14N 3°56W 19 F10
Strath Spey U.K. 57°9N 3°49W 19 H10
Strath Tay U.K. 56°40N 3°48W 21 A8
Strathaven U.K. 55°40N 4°5W 20 C7
Strathbogie U.K. 57°25N 2°45W 19 H12
Strathmore Angus, U.K. 56°37N 3°7W 19 J11
Strathmore Highl., U.K. 58°22N 4°40W 19 F8
Strathpeffer U.K. 57°35N 4°32W 19 G8
Strathroy Canada 42°58N 81°38W 112 D7
Strathy Pt. U.K. 58°36N 4°1W 19 E9
Stratton U.K. 50°49N 4°32W 27 F4
Stratton St. Margaret U.K. 51°35N 1°44W 24 C5
Streatley U.K. 51°31N 1°8W 24 C6
Street U.K. 51°8N 2°44W 24 D3
Strensall U.K. 54°3N 1°4W 22 D6
Stretford U.K. 53°28N 2°17W 23 F4
Stroma U.K. 58°41N 3°7W 19 E11
Strömboli Italy 38°47N 15°13E 70 E6
Stromeferry U.K. 57°21N 5°33W 18 H6
Stromness U.K. 58°58N 3°17W 19 E11
Stronsay U.K. 59°7N 2°35W 19 D12
Stroud U.K. 51°45N 2°13W 24 C4
Sturt L. Canada 54°0N 124°30W 108 D7
Studland U.K. 50°39N 1°58W 24 E5
Studley U.K. 52°16N 1°53W 24 B5
Sturgeon Bay U.S.A. 44°50N 87°23W 112 C4
Sturgeon Falls Canada 46°25N 79°57W 112 B8
Sturminster Marshall U.K. 50°47N 2°5W 24 E4
Sturminster Newton U.K. 50°55N 2°18W 24 E4
Sturt Stony Desert Australia 28°30S 141°0E 98 F6
Sturton U.K. 53°19N 0°39W 23 F7
Stuttgart Germany 48°48N 9°11E 66 D5
Stuttgart U.S.A. 34°30N 91°33W 111 D8
Suakin Sudan 19°8N 37°20E 95 E13
Subotica Serbia 46°6N 19°39E 71 A8
Suceava Romania 47°38N 26°16E 67 E14
Suck → Ireland 53°17N 8°3W 30 B6
Sucre Bolivia 19°0S 65°15W 120 D3
Sudan ■ Africa 15°0N 30°0E 95 E11
Sudbury Canada 46°30N 81°0W 112 B7
Sudbury Derby, U.K. 52°54N 1°45W 23 G5
Sudbury Suffolk, U.K. 52°2N 0°45E 25 B10
Sûdd Sudan 8°20N 30°0E 95 G12
Sudeten Europe 50°20N 16°45E 67 C9
Suez Egypt 29°58N 32°31E 95 C12
Suez, G. of Egypt 28°40N 33°0E 95 C12
Suez Canal Egypt 31°0N 32°20E 95 B12
Suffolk □ U.K. 52°16N 1°0E 25 B11
Sugluk Canada 62°14N 75°38W 109 C12
Şuḩār Oman 24°20N 56°40E 87 E9
Suihua China 46°32N 126°55E 81 B7
Suining China 30°26N 105°35E 80 C5
Suir → Ireland 52°16N 7°9W 31 D8
Sukabumi Indonesia 6°56S 106°50E 83 D2
Sukhona → Russia 61°15N 46°39E 72 C8
Sukkur Pakistan 27°42N 68°54E 84 F6
Sulaiman Range Pakistan 30°30N 69°50E 84 D6
Sulawesi Indonesia 2°0S 120°0E 83 D4
Sullana Peru 4°52S 80°39W 120 C1
Sullom Voe U.K. 60°27N 1°20W 18 B15
Sulu Arch. Phil. 6°0N 121°0E 83 C4
Sulu Sea E. Indies 8°0N 120°0E 83 C4
Sumatra Indonesia 0°40N 100°20E 83 C2
Sumba Indonesia 9°45S 119°35E 83 D3
Sumbawa Indonesia 8°26S 117°30E 83 D3
Sumburgh Hd. U.K. 59°52N 1°17W 18 C15
Sumenep Indonesia 7°1S 113°52E 83 D3
Summer L. U.S.A. 42°50N 120°45W 110 B2
Summerside Canada 46°24N 63°47W 109 E13
Sumqayıt Azerbaijan 40°34N 49°38E 73 F8
Sumter U.S.A. 33°55N 80°21W 111 D10
Sumy Ukraine 50°57N 34°50E 73 D5
Sun Valley U.S.A. 43°42N 114°21W 110 B4
Sunart, L. U.K. 56°43N 5°43W 18 J6
Sunart, L. U.K. 56°42N 5°43W 18 J6
Sunbury U.S.A. 40°52N 76°48W 112 E9
Sunda, Selat Indonesia 6°20S 105°30E 83 D2
Sunda Is. Indonesia 5°0S 105°0E 102 H2
Sundarbans Asia 22°0N 89°0E 85 J16
Sunderland U.K. 54°55N 1°23W 22 C6
Sundsvall Sweden 62°23N 17°17E 63 E7
Sungaipenuh Indonesia 2°1S 101°20E 83 D2
Sunk Island U.K. 53°39N 0°6W 23 E8
Sunninghill U.K. 51°24N 0°39W 25 D7
Sunshine Coast Australia 26°30S 153°0E 98 F9
Superior U.S.A. 46°44N 92°6W 112 B1
Superior, L. N. Amer. 47°0N 87°0W 112 B4
Sūr Lebanon 33°19N 35°16E 86 C3
Sura → Russia 56°6N 46°0E 72 C8
Surabaya Indonesia 7°17S 112°45E 83 D3
Surakarta Indonesia 7°35S 110°48E 83 D3
Surat India 21°12N 72°55E 84 J8
Surgut Russia 61°14N 73°20E 79 C9
Surigao Phil. 9°47N 125°29E 83 C4
Suriname ■ S. Amer. 4°0N 56°0W 120 B4
Surrey □ U.K. 51°15N 0°31W 25 D8
Surt Libya 31°11N 16°39E 95 B9
Surtsey Iceland 63°20N 20°30W 63 B1

Susquehanna → U.S.A. 39°33N 76°5W 112 F9
Sussex Canada 45°45N 65°37W 113 C15
Sutherland U.K. 58°12N 4°50W 19 F8
Sutlej → Pakistan 29°23N 71°3E 84 E7
Sutterton U.K. 52°55N 0°6W 23 G8
Sutton □ U.K. 51°21N 0°11W 25 D8
Sutton Bridge U.K. 52°47N 0°10E 23 G9
Sutton Coldfield U.K. 52°35N 1°49W 23 G5
Sutton Courtenay U.K. 51°39N 1°16W 24 C6
Sutton in Ashfield U.K. 53°8N 1°16W 23 F6
Sutton-on-Sea U.K. 53°18N 0°16E 23 F9
Sutton Scotney U.K. 51°9N 1°20W 24 D6
Suva Fiji 18°6S 178°30E 99 D14
Suvorov Is. Cook Is. 13°15S 163°5W 103 J11
Suwałki Poland 54°8N 22°59E 67 A12
Suzhou China 31°19N 120°38E 81 C7
Svalbard Arctic 78°0N 17°0E 54 B8
Svealand □ Sweden 60°20N 15°0E 63 E7
Sverdrup Chan. Canada 79°56N 96°25W 109 B10
Sverdrup Is. Canada 79°0N 97°0W 109 B10
Svir → Russia 60°30N 32°48E 72 B5
Swadlincote U.K. 52°47N 1°33W 23 G5
Swaffham U.K. 52°39N 0°42E 25 A10
Swakopmund Namibia 22°37S 14°30E 97 J2
Swale → U.K. 54°5N 1°20W 25 D11
Swan Hill Australia 35°20S 143°33E 98 H7
Swan River Canada 52°10N 101°16W 108 D9
Swanage U.K. 50°36N 1°58W 24 E5
Swansea U.K. 51°37N 3°57W 27 D6
Swansea B. U.K. 51°32N 3°57W 27 D6
Swartberge S. Africa 33°20S 22°0E 90 K6
Swaziland ■ Africa 26°30S 31°30E 97 K6
Sweden ■ Europe 57°0N 15°0E 63 F7
Sweetwater U.S.A. 32°28N 100°25W 110 D6
Swellendam S. Africa 34°1S 20°26E 97 L4
Swift Current Canada 50°20N 107°45W 108 D9
Swilly, L. Ireland 55°12N 7°33W 28 A6
Swindon U.K. 51°34N 1°46W 24 C5
Swineshead U.K. 52°57N 0°10W 23 G8
Swinford Ireland 53°57N 8°58W 28 D4
Swinton Borders, U.K. 55°43N 2°15W 21 C11
Swinton Gt. Man., U.K. 53°31N 2°20W 23 E4
Swinton S. Yorks., U.K. 53°29N 1°20W 23 F6
Switzerland ■ Europe 46°30N 8°0E 66 E5
Swords Ireland 53°28N 6°13W 31 B10
Sydney Australia 33°52S 151°12E 98 G9
Sydney Canada 46°7N 60°7W 113 B17
Syktyvkar Russia 61°45N 50°40E 72 B9
Sylhet Bangla. 24°54N 91°52E 85 G17
Sylhet □ Bangla. 24°50N 91°50E 85 G17
Symington U.K. 55°36N 3°36W 21 C8
Symonds Yat U.K. 51°51N 2°38W 24 C3
Syracuse U.S.A. 43°3N 76°9W 113 D9
Syrdarya → Kazakhstan 46°3N 61°0E 79 E8
Syria ■ Asia 35°0N 38°0E 86 C4
Syrian Desert Asia 32°0N 40°0E 86 C4
Syros Greece 37°28N 24°57E 71 F11
Syston U.K. 52°42N 1°3W 23 G6
Syzran Russia 53°12N 48°30E 72 D8
Szczecin Poland 53°27N 14°27E 66 B8
Szechwan = Sichuan □ China 30°30N 103°0E 80 C5
Szeged Hungary 46°16N 20°10E 67 E11
Székesfehérvár Hungary 47°15N 18°25E 67 E10
Szekszárd Hungary 46°22N 18°42E 67 E10
Szolnok Hungary 47°10N 20°15E 67 E11
Szombathely Hungary 47°14N 16°38E 67 E9

T
Tabas Iran 33°35N 56°55E 87 C9
Tablas Phil. 12°25N 122°2E 83 B4
Table B. S. Africa 33°35S 18°25E 97 L3
Table Mt. S. Africa 34°0S 18°22E 97 L3
Tabora Tanzania 5°2S 32°50E 96 F6
Tabriz Iran 38°7N 46°20E 86 B6
Tabuaeran Kiribati 3°51N 159°22W 103 G12
Tacheng China 46°40N 82°58E 80 B3
Tacloban Phil. 11°15N 124°58E 83 B4
Tacna Peru 18°0S 70°20W 120 D2
Tacoma U.S.A. 47°14N 122°26W 110 A2
Tacuarembó Uruguay 31°45S 56°0W 121 F4
Tadcaster U.K. 53°53N 1°16W 23 E6
Tademaït, Plateau du Algeria 28°30N 2°30E 94 C6
Tadley U.K. 51°21N 1°7W 24 D6
Taganrog Russia 47°12N 38°50E 73 E6
Taguatinga Brazil 12°27S 46°22E 122 B1
Tagus → Europe 38°40N 9°24W 69 C1
Tahiti French Polynesia 17°37S 149°27W 103 J13
Tahoe, L. U.S.A. 39°6N 120°2W 110 C2
Tahoua Niger 14°57N 5°16E 94 F7
Tahta Egypt 26°44N 31°32E 95 C12
Taichung Taiwan 24°9N 120°37E 81 D7
Taimyr, L. Russia 74°20N 102°0E 79 B12
Taimyr Peninsula Russia 75°0N 100°0E 79 B11
Tain U.K. 57°49N 4°4W 19 G8
T'ainan Taiwan 23°0N 120°10E 81 D7
Taipei Taiwan 25°4N 121°29E 81 D7
Taiping Malaysia 4°51N 100°44E 83 C2
Taitao, Pen. de Chile 46°30S 75°0W 121 G2
T'aitung Taiwan 22°43N 121°4E 81 D7
Taiwan ■ Asia 23°30N 121°0E 81 D7
Taiyuan China 37°52N 112°33E 81 C6
Ta'izz Yemen 13°35N 44°2E 88 E3
Tajikistan ■ Asia 38°30N 70°0E 87 B12
Tak Thailand 16°52N 99°8E 83 B1
Takamatsu Japan 34°20N 134°5E 82 F4
Takaoka Japan 36°47N 137°0E 82 E5
Takasaki Japan 36°20N 139°0E 82 E6
Takeshima = Tokdo Asia 37°15N 131°52E 82 E2
Takhâr □ Afghan. 36°40N 70°0E 87 B12
Takla Makan China 38°0N 83°0E 80 C3
Talara Peru 4°38S 81°18W 120 C1
Talaud, Kepulauan Indonesia 4°30N 126°50E 83 C4
Talavera de la Reina Spain 39°55N 4°46W 69 C3
Talca Chile 35°28S 71°40W 121 F2
Talcahuano Chile 36°40S 73°10W 121 F2
Taldyqorghan Kazakhstan 45°10N 78°45E 79 E9
Talgarth U.K. 52°0N 3°14W 26 D7

Taliabu   Tuticorin

Taliabu *Indonesia* 1°50S 125°0E **83** D4
Tallaght *Ireland* 53°17N 6°22W **31** B10
Tallahassee *U.S.A.* 30°27N 84°17W **111** D10
Taloyoak *Canada* 69°32N 93°32W **108** C10
Tallinn *Estonia* 59°22N 24°48E **63** F8
Taltal *Chile* 25°23S 70°33W **121** E2
Tamale *Ghana* 9°22N 0°50W **94** G5
Tamana *Kiribati* 2°30S 175°59E **99** A13
Tamanrasset *Algeria* 22°50N 5°30E **94** D7
Tamar → *U.K.* 50°27N 4°15W **27** G5
Tambov *Russia* 52°45N 41°28E **72** D7
Tame → *U.K.* 52°44N 1°43W **23** G5
Tamerton Foliot *U.K.* 50°25N 4°11W **27** G5
Tamil Nadu □ *India* 11°0N 77°0E **84** P10
Tampa *U.S.A.* 27°56N 82°27W **111** E10
Tampa B. *U.S.A.* 27°50N 82°30W **111** E10
Tampere *Finland* 61°30N 23°50E **63** E8
Tampico *Mexico* 22°13N 97°51W **114** C5
Tamworth *Australia* 31°7S 150°58E **98** G9
Tamworth *U.K.* 52°39N 1°41W **23** G5
Tana → *Kenya* 2°32S 40°31E **96** E8
Tana → *Norway* 70°30N 28°14E **63** C9
Tana, L. *Ethiopia* 13°5N 37°30E **88** E2
Tanami Desert *Australia* 18°50S 132°0E **98** D5
Tanana → *U.S.A.* 65°10N 151°58W **108** C4
Tandil *Argentina* 37°15S 59°6W **121** F4
Tandragee *U.K.* 54°21N 6°24W **29** C9
Tanezrouft *Algeria* 23°9N 0°11E **94** D6
Tanga *Tanzania* 5°5S 39°2E **96** F7
Tanganyika, L. *Africa* 6°40S 30°0E **96** F6
Tanggula Shan *China* 32°40N 92°10E **80** C4
Tangier *Morocco* 35°50N 5°49W **94** A4
Tangshan *China* 39°38N 118°10E **81** C6
Tanimbar, Kepulauan *Indonesia* 7°30S 131°30E **83** D5
Tanjungbalai *Indonesia* 2°55N 99°44E **83** C1
Tanjungpandan *Indonesia* 2°43S 107°38E **83** D2
Tanjungredeb *Indonesia* 2°9N 117°29E **83** C3
Tanna *Vanuatu* 19°30S 169°20E **99** D12
Tanta *Egypt* 30°45N 30°57E **95** B12
Tanworth *U.K.* 52°20N 1°50W **24** B5
Tanzania ■ *Africa* 6°0S 34°0E **96** F6
Taolanaro *Madag.* 25°2S 47°0E **97** K9
Taos *U.S.A.* 36°24N 105°35W **110** C5
Tapachula *Mexico* 14°54N 92°17W **114** E6
Tapajós → *Brazil* 2°24S 54°41W **120** C4
Tapti → *India* 21°8N 72°41E **84** J8
Taquaritinga *Brazil* 21°24S 48°30W **122** D1
Tarakan *Indonesia* 3°20N 117°35E **83** C3
Taransay *U.K.* 57°54N 7°0W **18** G3
Táranto *Italy* 40°28N 17°14E **70** D7
Táranto, G. di *Italy* 40°8N 17°20E **70** D7
Tarawa *Kiribati* 1°30N 173°0E **102** G9
Taraz *Kazakhstan* 42°54N 71°22E **87** A12
Tarbagatai Ra. *Kazakhstan* 48°0N 83°0E **79** E10
Tarbat Ness *U.K.* 57°52N 3°47W **19** G10
Tarbert *Argyll & Bute, U.K.* 55°52N 5°25W **20** C5
Tarbert *W. Isles, U.K.* 57°54N 6°49W **18** G4
Tarbes *France* 43°15N 0°3E **68** E4
Tarcoola *Australia* 30°44S 134°36E **98** G5
Taree *Australia* 31°50S 152°30E **98** G9
Tarfaya *Morocco* 27°55N 12°55W **94** C3
Târgoviște *Romania* 44°55N 25°27E **67** F13
Târgu-Jiu *Romania* 45°5N 23°19E **67** F12
Târgu Mureș *Romania* 46°31N 24°38E **67** E13
Tarija *Bolivia* 21°30S 64°40W **120** E3
Tarim Basin *China* 40°0N 84°0E **80** B3
Tarim He → *China* 39°30N 88°30E **80** C3
Tarleton *U.K.* 53°41N 2°50W **23** E3
Tarn → *France* 44°5N 1°6E **68** E4
Tarnów *Poland* 50°3N 21°0E **67** C11
Taroudannt *Morocco* 30°30N 8°52W **94** B4
Tarporley *U.K.* 53°10N 2°40W **23** F3
Tarragona *Spain* 41°5N 1°17E **69** B6
Tarsus *Turkey* 36°58N 34°55E **73** G5
Tartu *Estonia* 58°20N 26°44E **63** F9
Ţarţūs *Syria* 34°55N 35°55E **86** C3
Tashkent *Uzbekistan* 41°20N 69°10E **87** A12
Tasiilaq *Greenland* 65°40N 37°20W **54** C6
Tasikmalaya *Indonesia* 7°18S 108°12E **83** D2
Tasman Sea *Pac. Oc.* 36°0S 160°0E **99** H10
Tasmania □ *Australia* 42°0S 146°30E **98** J4
Tassili n' Ajjer *Algeria* 25°47N 8°1E **94** C7
Tatarstan □ *Russia* 55°30N 51°30E **72** D9
Tatnam, C. *Canada* 57°16N 91°0W **109** D10
Tatra *Slovak Rep.* 49°20N 20°0E **67** D11
Tatta *Pakistan* 24°42N 67°55E **84** G5
Tattenhall *U.K.* 53°7N 2°46W **23** F3
Tatuí *Brazil* 23°25S 47°53W **122** D1
Tatvan *Turkey* 38°31N 42°15E **73** G7
Taubaté *Brazil* 23°0S 45°36W **122** D1
Tauern *Austria* 47°15N 12°40E **66** E7
Taunggyi *Burma* 20°50N 97°0E **85** J20
Taunton *U.K.* 51°1N 3°5W **24** D2
Taunton *U.S.A.* 41°54N 71°6W **113** E12
Taunus *Germany* 50°13N 8°34E **66** C5
Taurus Mts. *Turkey* 37°0N 32°30E **73** G5
Tavan Bogd Uul *Mongolia* 49°10N 87°49E **80** B3
Tavistock *U.K.* 50°33N 4°9W **27** F5
Taw → *U.K.* 51°4N 4°4W **27** F5
Tawas City *U.S.A.* 44°16N 83°31W **112** C6
Tawau *Malaysia* 4°20N 117°55E **83** C3
Taxkorgan Tajik Zizhixian *China* 37°49N 75°14E **80** C2
Tay → *U.K.* 56°37N 3°38W **21** A8
Tay, Firth of *U.K.* 56°25N 3°8W **21** B9
Tay, L. *U.K.* 56°32N 4°8W **20** A7
Taylor, Mt. *U.S.A.* 35°14N 107°37W **110** C5
Taylorville *U.S.A.* 39°33N 89°18W **112** F3
Tayport *U.K.* 56°27N 2°52W **21** B10
Taz → *Russia* 67°32N 78°40E **79** C9
Taza *Morocco* 34°16N 4°6W **94** B5
Tbilisi *Georgia* 41°43N 44°50E **73** F7
Tébay *U.K.* 54°26N 2°35W **22** D3
Tébessa *Algeria* 35°22N 8°8E **94** A7
Tees → *U.K.* 54°37N 1°10W **22** C6
Teesdale *U.K.* 54°37N 2°10W **22** C5
Teesside *U.K.* 54°36N 1°15W **22** C6
Tegal *Indonesia* 6°52S 109°8E **83** D2

Tegucigalpa *Honduras* 14°5N 87°14W **114** E7
Tehrān *Iran* 35°41N 51°25E **87** C7
Tehuantepec *Mexico* 16°21N 95°13W **114** D5
Tehuantepec, G. de *Mexico* 15°50N 95°12W **114** D5
Tehuantepec, Istmo de *Mexico* 17°15N 94°30W **114** D6
Teifi → *U.K.* 52°5N 4°41W **26** C4
Teign → *U.K.* 50°32N 3°32W **27** F6
Teignmouth *U.K.* 50°33N 3°31W **27** F6
Tejen *Turkmenistan* 37°23N 60°31E **87** B10
Tekirdağ *Turkey* 40°58N 27°30E **73** D11
Tel Aviv-Jaffa *Israel* 32°4N 34°48E **86** C3
Tela *Honduras* 15°40N 87°28W **114** D7
Telegraph Creek *Canada* 58°0N 131°10W **108** D6
Teles Pires → *Brazil* 7°21S 58°3W **120** C4
Telford *U.K.* 52°40N 2°27W **23** G4
Tell City *U.S.A.* 37°57N 86°46W **112** G4
Tellicherry *India* 11°45N 75°30E **84** P9
Telpos Iz *Russia* 63°16N 59°13E **72** B10
Teluk Intan *Malaysia* 4°3N 101°0E **83** C2
Tema *Ghana* 5°41N 0°0 **94** G5
Teme → *U.K.* 52°11N 2°13W **24** B4
Témiscaming *Canada* 46°44N 79°5W **112** B8
Temple *U.S.A.* 31°6N 97°21W **111** D7
Temple Combe *U.K.* 51°0N 2°24W **24** D4
Temple Ewell *U.K.* 51°8N 1°17E **25** D11
Temple Sowerby *U.K.* 54°38N 2°36W **22** C3
Templemore *Ireland* 52°47N 7°51W **30** C7
Temuco *Chile* 38°45S 72°40W **121** F2
Tenali *India* 16°15N 80°35E **85** L12
Tenbury Wells *U.K.* 52°19N 2°35W **24** B3
Tenby *U.K.* 51°40N 4°42W **26** D4
Tenerife *Canary Is.* 28°15N 16°35W **94** C2
Tengchong *China* 25°0N 98°28E **80** D4
Tengger Desert *China* 38°0N 104°0E **80** C5
Tennant Creek *Australia* 19°30S 134°15E **98** D5
Tenneswell *U.K.* 36°0N 86°30W **111** C9
Tennessee □ *U.S.A.* 36°0N 86°30W **111** C9
Tennessee → *U.S.A.* 37°4N 88°34W **111** C9
Tenterden *U.K.* 51°4N 0°42E **25** D10
Teófilo Otoni *Brazil* 17°50S 41°30W **122** C2
Tepic *Mexico* 21°30N 104°54W **114** C4
Teraina *Kiribati* 4°43N 160°25W **103** G11
Téramo *Italy* 42°39N 13°42E **70** C5
Teresina *Brazil* 5°9S 42°45W **120** C5
Termiz *Uzbekistan* 37°15N 67°15E **87** B11
Ternate *Indonesia* 0°45N 127°25E **83** C4
Terni *Italy* 42°34N 12°37E **70** C5
Ternopil *Ukraine* 49°30N 25°40E **67** D13
Terrace *Canada* 54°30N 128°35W **108** D7
Terrassa *Spain* 41°34N 2°1E **69** B7
Terre Haute *U.S.A.* 39°28N 87°25W **112** F4
Teruel *Spain* 40°22N 1°8W **69** B5
Tesiyn Gol → *Mongolia* 50°40N 93°20E **80** A4
Teslin *Canada* 60°10N 132°43W **108** C6
Test → *U.K.* 50°56N 1°29W **24** E6
Tetbury *U.K.* 51°38N 2°10W **24** C4
Tete *Mozam.* 16°13S 33°33E **97** H6
Tetney *U.K.* 53°29N 0°1W **23** F8
Tétouan *Morocco* 35°35N 5°21W **94** A4
Tetovo *Macedonia* 42°1N 20°59E **71** C9
Teuco → *Argentina* 25°35S 60°11W **121** E3
Teutoburger Wald *Germany* 52°5N 8°22E **66** B5
Tevere → *U.K.* 55°29N 2°38W **21** D10
Teviotdale *U.K.* 55°25N 2°50W **21** D10
Teviothead *U.K.* 55°20N 2°56W **21** D10
Tewkesbury *U.K.* 51°59N 2°9W **24** C4
Texarkana *U.S.A.* 33°26N 94°3W **111** D8
Texas □ *U.S.A.* 31°40N 98°30W **110** D7
Texel *Neths.* 53°5N 4°50E **65** A4
Teynham *U.K.* 51°20N 0°50E **25** D10
Tezpur *India* 26°40N 92°45E **85** F18
Thabana Ntlenyana *Lesotho* 29°30S 29°16E **97** K5
Thabazimbi *S. Africa* 24°40S 27°21E **97** J5
Thailand ■ *Asia* 16°0N 102°0E **83** B2
Thailand, G. of *Asia* 11°30N 101°0E **83** B2
Thal Desert *Pakistan* 31°10N 71°30E **84** D7
Thame → *U.K.* 51°45N 0°58W **25** C7
Thame *U.K.* 51°39N 1°9W **24** C6
Thames → *Canada* 42°20N 82°25W **112** D6
Thames → *U.K.* 51°29N 0°34E **25** D10
Thane *India* 19°12N 72°59E **84** K8
Thanet, I. of *U.K.* 51°21N 1°20E **25** D11
Thanh Hoa *Vietnam* 19°48N 105°46E **83** B2
Thanjavur *India* 10°48N 79°12E **84** P11
Thar Desert *India* 28°0N 72°0E **84** F8
Thargomindah *Australia* 27°58S 143°46E **98** F7
Thasos *Greece* 40°40N 24°40E **71** D11
Thatcham *U.K.* 51°24N 1°15W **24** D6
Thatta *Pakistan* 24°42N 67°55E **84** G5
The Everglades *U.S.A.* 25°50N 81°0W **111** E10
The Pas *Canada* 53°45N 101°15W **108** D9
The Wash *U.K.* 52°58N 0°20E **25** A9
The Weald *U.K.* 51°4N 0°20E **25** D9
Theale *U.K.* 51°26N 1°5W **24** D6
Thebes *Egypt* 25°40N 32°35E **95** C12
Thelon → *Canada* 64°16N 96°4W **108** C9
Thermopolis *U.S.A.* 43°39N 108°13W **110** B5
Thessalon *Canada* 46°20N 83°30W **112** B6
Thessaloníki *Greece* 40°38N 22°58E **71** D10
Thetford *U.K.* 52°25N 0°45E **25** B10
Thetford Mines *Canada* 46°8N 71°18W **109** E12
Thiers *France* 45°52N 3°33E **68** D5
Thiès *Senegal* 14°50N 16°51W **94** F2
Thika *Kenya* 1°1S 37°5E **96** E7
Thimphu *Bhutan* 27°31N 89°45E **85** F16
Thionville *France* 49°20N 6°10E **68** B7
Thira = Santorini *Greece* 36°23N 25°27E **71** F11
Thirlmere *U.K.* 54°32N 3°4W **22** C2
Thirsk *U.K.* 54°14N 1°19W **22** D6
Thlewiaza → *Canada* 60°29N 94°40W **108** C9
Thomasville *U.S.A.* 30°50N 83°59W **111** D10
Thompson *Canada* 55°45N 97°52W **108** D10
Thornaby on Tees *U.K.* 54°33N 1°18W **22** C6
Thornbury *U.K.* 51°36N 2°31W **24** C3
Thorndon *U.K.* 52°17N 1°9E **25** B11
Thorne *U.K.* 53°37N 0°57W **23** E7
Thorney *U.K.* 52°37N 0°6W **25** A8
Thornham *U.K.* 52°58N 0°35E **25** A10
Thornthwaite *U.K.* 54°39N 3°13W **22** C2

Thornton *U.K.* 53°52N 2°59W **23** E3
Thornton Dale *U.K.* 54°15N 0°42W **22** D7
Thorpe *U.K.* 52°38N 1°22E **25** A11
Thorpe le Soken *U.K.* 51°51N 1°11E **25** C11
Thrace *Turkey* 41°0N 27°0E **71** D12
Thrapston *U.K.* 52°24N 0°32W **25** B7
Three Gorges Dam *China* 30°45N 111°15E **81** C6
Threlkeld *U.K.* 54°37N 3°3W **22** C2
Threshfield *U.K.* 54°4N 2°1W **22** D4
Thunder B. *U.S.A.* 45°0N 83°20W **112** C6
Thunder Bay *Canada* 48°20N 89°15W **112** A3
Thüringer Wald *Germany* 50°35N 11°0E **66** C6
Thurlby *U.K.* 52°45N 0°23W **23** G8
Thurles *Ireland* 52°41N 7°49W **30** C7
Thurmaston *U.K.* 52°40N 1°5W **23** G6
Thursby *U.K.* 54°51N 3°2W **22** C2
Thurso *U.K.* 58°36N 3°32W **19** E10
Thurso → *U.K.* 58°36N 3°32W **19** E10
Thurston I. *Antarctica* 72°0S 100°0W **55** D16
Tian Shan *Asia* 40°30N 76°0E **80** B3
Tianjin *China* 39°7N 117°12E **81** C6
Tianmen *China* 30°39N 113°9E **81** C6
Tianshui *China* 34°32N 105°40E **80** C5
Tiaret *Algeria* 35°20N 1°21E **94** A6
Tibasti, Sarīr *Libya* 22°50N 18°30E **95** D9
Tiber = Tevere → *Italy* 41°44N 12°14E **70** D5
Tiberias, L. = Galilee, Sea of *Israel* 32°45N 35°35E **86** C3
Tibesti *Chad* 21°0N 17°30E **95** D9
Tibet □ *China* 32°0N 88°0E **80** C3
Tibet, Plateau of *Asia* 32°0N 86°0E **74** D10
Tiburón, I. *Mexico* 29°0N 112°25W **114** B2
Ticehurst *U.K.* 51°3N 0°25E **25** D9
Ticino → *Italy* 45°9N 9°14E **70** B3
Tickhill *U.K.* 53°26N 1°6W **23** F6
Ticonderoga *U.S.A.* 43°51N 73°26W **113** D11
Tideswell *U.K.* 53°17N 1°47W **23** F5
Tieling *China* 42°20N 123°55E **81** B7
Tierra de Campos *Spain* 42°10N 4°50W **69** A3
Tierra del Fuego, I. Gr. de *Argentina* 54°0S 69°0W **121** H3
Tiffin *U.S.A.* 41°7N 83°11W **112** E6
Tighina *Moldova* 46°50N 29°30E **67** E15
Tignish *Canada* 46°58N 64°2W **113** B15
Tigris → *Asia* 31°0N 47°25E **86** D6
Tijuana *Mexico* 32°32N 117°1W **114** A1
Tikhoretsk *Russia* 45°56N 40°5E **73** E7
Tikhvin *Russia* 59°35N 33°30E **72** C5
Tikrīt *Iraq* 34°35N 43°37E **86** C5
Tiksi *Russia* 71°40N 128°45E **79** B14
Tilburg *Neths.* 51°31N 5°6E **65** C5
Tilbury *U.K.* 51°27N 0°22E **25** D9
Till → *U.K.* 55°41N 2°13W **22** A4
Tillicoultry *U.K.* 56°9N 3°45W **21** B9
Tilmanstone *U.K.* 51°12N 1°18E **25** D11
Tilt → *U.K.* 56°46N 3°51W **19** J10
Timaru *N.Z.* 44°23S 171°14E **99** J13
Timișoara *Romania* 45°43N 21°15E **67** F11
Timmins *Canada* 48°28N 81°25W **109** E11
Timor *Asia* 9°0S 125°0E **83** D4
Timor Leste = East Timor ■ *Asia* 8°50S 126°0E **83** D4
Timor Sea *Ind. Oc.* 12°0S 127°0E **83** E4
Tingewick *U.K.* 51°59N 1°2W **24** C6
Tinogasta *Argentina* 28°5S 67°32W **121** E3
Tinos *Greece* 37°33N 25°8E **71** F11
Tintagel *U.K.* 50°39N 4°46W **27** F4
Tintagel Hd. *U.K.* 50°40N 4°47W **27** F4
Tipperary *Ireland* 52°28N 8°10W **30** D6
Tipperary □ *Ireland* 52°37N 7°55W **30** C7
Tipton *U.K.* 52°32N 2°4W **23** G4
Tipton *U.S.A.* 41°46N 91°8W **112** E2
Tiptree *U.K.* 51°48N 0°46E **25** C10
Tiranë *Albania* 41°18N 19°49E **71** D8
Tiraspol *Moldova* 46°55N 29°35E **67** E15
Tirebolu *Turkey* 40°58N 38°45E **73** F6
Tiree *U.K.* 56°31N 6°55W **20** A2
Tiree, Passage of *U.K.* 56°30N 6°30W **20** A2
Tirich Mir *Pakistan* 36°15N 71°55E **84** A7
Tirol □ *Austria* 47°3N 10°43E **66** E6
Tiruchchirappalli *India* 10°45N 78°45E **84** P11
Tirunelveli *India* 8°45N 77°45E **84** Q10
Tiruppur *India* 11°5N 77°22E **84** P10
Tisa → *Serbia* 45°15N 20°17E **71** B9
Tisbury *U.K.* 51°4N 2°5W **24** D4
Tisdale *Canada* 52°50N 104°0W **108** D9
Titchfield *U.K.* 50°50N 1°15W **24** E6
Titicaca, L. *S. Amer.* 15°30S 69°30W **120** D3
Titusville *U.S.A.* 41°38N 79°41W **112** E8
Tiverton *U.K.* 50°54N 3°29W **27** F7
Tivoli *Italy* 41°58N 12°45E **70** D5
Tizi-Ouzou *Algeria* 36°42N 4°3E **94** A6
Tlaxiaco *Mexico* 17°25N 97°35W **114** D5
Tlemcen *Algeria* 34°52N 1°21W **94** B5
Toamasina *Madag.* 18°10S 49°25E **97** H9
Toba, Danau *Indonesia* 2°30N 97°30E **83** C1
Toba Kakar *Pakistan* 31°30N 69°0E **84** D6
Tobago *Trin. & Tob.* 11°10N 60°30W **120** A3
Tobermory *Canada* 45°12N 81°40W **112** C7
Tobermory *U.K.* 56°38N 6°5W **20** A2
Tocantins → *Brazil* 1°45S 49°10W **120** C5
Toddington *U.K.* 51°57N 0°32W **25** C7
Todmorden *U.K.* 53°43N 2°6W **23** E4
Todos os Santos, B. de *Brazil* 12°48S 38°38W **122** B3
Toe Hd. *U.K.* 57°50N 7°8W **18** G3
Togliatti *Russia* 53°32N 49°24E **72** D8
Togo ■ *W. Afr.* 8°30N 1°35E **94** G6
Tok *U.S.A.* 63°20N 142°59W **108** C5
Tokat *Turkey* 40°22N 36°35E **73** F6
Tokdo *Asia* 37°15N 131°52E **82** E2
Tokelau Is. *Pac. Oc.* 9°0S 171°45W **99** B16
Tokushima *Japan* 34°4N 134°34E **82** F4
Tokuyama *Japan* 34°3N 131°50E **82** F2
Tōkyō *Japan* 35°43N 139°45E **82** F6
Toledo *Spain* 39°50N 4°2W **69** C3
Toledo *U.S.A.* 41°39N 83°33W **112** E6
Toledo, Montes de *Spain* 39°33N 4°20W **69** C3
Toliara *Madag.* 23°21S 43°40E **97** J8
Tolima *Colombia* 4°40N 75°19W **120** B2

Tollesbury *U.K.* 51°45N 0°51E **25** C10
Toluca *Mexico* 19°17N 99°40W **114** D5
Tomah *U.S.A.* 43°59N 90°30W **112** D2
Tomakomai *Japan* 42°38N 141°36E **82** B7
Tombador, Serra do *Brazil* 12°0S 58°0W **120** D4
Tombigbee → *U.S.A.* 31°8N 87°57W **111** D9
Tombouctou *Mali* 16°50N 3°0W **94** E5
Tomini, Teluk *Indonesia* 0°10S 121°0E **83** D4
Tomintoul *U.K.* 57°15N 3°23W **19** H11
Tomsk *Russia* 56°30N 85°5E **79** D9
Tonbridge *U.K.* 51°11N 0°17E **25** D9
Tone → *U.K.* 50°58N 3°20W **27** F7
Tong *U.K.* 52°40N 2°17W **23** G4
Tonga ■ *Pac. Oc.* 19°50S 174°30W **99** D16
Tonga Trench *Pac. Oc.* 18°0S 173°0W **99** D16
Tongareva *Cook Is.* 9°0S 158°0W **103** H12
Tongatapu Group *Tonga* 21°0S 175°0W **99** E16
Tongchuan *China* 35°6N 109°3E **81** C5
Tonghua *China* 41°42N 125°58E **81** B7
Tongliao *China* 43°38N 122°18E **81** B7
Tongling *China* 30°55N 117°48E **81** C6
Tongue *U.K.* 58°29N 4°25W **19** F9
Tongue → *U.S.A.* 46°25N 105°52W **110** A5
Tonk *India* 26°6N 75°54E **84** F9
Tonkin, G. of *Asia* 20°0N 108°0E **80** E5
Tonle Sap *Cambodia* 13°0N 104°0E **83** B2
Tonopah *U.S.A.* 38°4N 117°14W **110** C3
Toowoomba *Australia* 27°32S 151°56E **98** F9
Topeka *U.S.A.* 39°3N 95°40W **111** C7
Topolobampo *Mexico* 25°36N 109°3W **114** B3
Topsham *U.K.* 50°41N 3°28W **27** F7
Tor B. *U.K.* 50°25N 3°33W **27** G6
Torbay *U.K.* 50°26N 3°31W **27** G6
Torbay □ *U.K.* 50°26N 3°32W **23** F5
Torne älven → *Europe* 65°50N 24°12E **63** D8
Torneträsk *Sweden* 68°24N 19°15E **63** D7
Tornio *Finland* 65°50N 24°12E **63** D8
Toro, Cerro del *Chile* 29°10S 69°50W **121** E3
Toronto *Canada* 43°39N 79°20W **112** D8
Torpoint *U.K.* 50°23N 4°13W **27** G5
Torquay *U.K.* 50°27N 3°32W **27** G6
Torre del Greco *Italy* 40°47N 14°22E **70** D6
Torrejón de Ardoz *Spain* 40°27N 3°29W **69** B4
Torrelavega *Spain* 43°20N 4°5W **69** A3
Torremolinos *Spain* 36°38N 4°30W **69** D3
Torrens, L. *Australia* 31°0S 137°50E **98** G6
Torrent *Spain* 39°27N 0°28W **69** C5
Torreón *Mexico* 25°33N 103°26W **114** B4
Torres Strait *Australia* 9°50S 142°20E **98** C7
Torridge → *U.K.* 51°0N 4°13W **27** E5
Torridon, L. *U.K.* 57°35N 5°50W **18** G6
Torthorwald *U.K.* 55°6N 3°32W **21** D8
Tortola *Br. Virgin Is.* 18°19N 64°45W **115** e
Tórtosa *Spain* 40°49N 0°31E **69** B6
Toruń *Poland* 53°2N 18°39E **67** B10
Torver *U.K.* 54°20N 3°6W **22** D2
Tory I. *Ireland* 55°16N 8°14W **28** A5
Toscana □ *Italy* 43°25N 11°0E **70** C4
Toshka Lakes *Egypt* 22°50N 31°0E **95** D12
Totland *U.K.* 50°41N 1°32W **24** E5
Totnes *U.K.* 50°26N 3°42W **27** G6
Totton *U.K.* 50°55N 1°29W **24** E6
Tottori *Japan* 35°30N 134°15E **82** F4
Toubkal, Djebel *Morocco* 31°0N 8°0W **94** B4
Touggourt *Algeria* 33°6N 6°4E **94** B7
Toul *France* 48°40N 5°53E **68** B6
Toulon *France* 43°10N 5°55E **68** E6
Toulouse *France* 43°37N 1°27E **68** E4
Touraine *France* 47°20N 0°30E **68** C4
Tournai *Belgium* 50°35N 3°25E **65** D3
Tournon-sur-Rhône *France* 45°4N 4°50E **68** D6
Tours *France* 47°22N 0°40E **68** C4
Towanda *U.S.A.* 41°46N 76°27W **112** E9
Towcester *U.K.* 52°8N 0°59W **25** B7
Town Yetholm *U.K.* 55°33N 2°17W **21** C11
Townsville *Australia* 19°15S 146°45E **98** D8
Towraghondi *Afghan.* 35°13N 62°16E **84** B3
Towson *U.S.A.* 39°24N 76°36W **112** F9
Toyama *Japan* 36°40N 137°15E **82** E5
Toyohashi *Japan* 34°45N 137°25E **82** F5
Toyota *Japan* 35°3N 137°7E **82** F5
Trabzon *Turkey* 41°0N 39°45E **73** F6
Trafalgar, C. *Spain* 36°10N 6°2W **69** D2
Trail *Canada* 49°5N 117°40W **108** E8
Tralee *Ireland* 52°16N 9°42W **30** D3
Tralee B. *Ireland* 52°17N 9°55W **30** D2
Tramore *Ireland* 52°10N 7°10W **31** D8
Tramore B. *Ireland* 52°9N 7°10W **31** D8
Tranent *U.K.* 55°57N 2°57W **21** C10
Trang *Thailand* 7°33N 99°38E **83** C1
Transantarctic Mts. *Antarctica* 85°0S 170°0W **55** E12
Transylvania *Romania* 46°30N 24°0E **67** E13
Transylvanian Alps *Romania* 45°30N 25°0E **67** F13
Trápani *Italy* 38°1N 12°29E **70** E5
Trasimeno, L. *Italy* 43°8N 12°6E **70** C5
Traverse City *U.S.A.* 44°46N 85°38W **112** C5
Trawbreaga B. *Ireland* 55°20N 7°25W **28** A7
Trawsfynydd *U.K.* 52°54N 3°55W **26** B5
Tredegar *U.K.* 51°47N 3°14W **26** D5
Tregaron *U.K.* 52°14N 3°56W **26** C5
Treinta y Tres *Uruguay* 33°16S 54°17W **121** F4
Trelew *Argentina* 43°10S 65°20W **121** G3
Trent → *U.K.* 53°41N 0°42W **23** E7
Trentham *U.K.* 52°58N 2°11W **23** G4
Trento *Italy* 46°4N 11°8E **70** A4
Trenton *U.S.A.* 40°14N 74°46W **113** E10
Tres Arroyos *Argentina* 38°26S 60°20W **121** F3
Três Corações *Brazil* 21°44S 45°15W **122** D1
Três Lagoas *Brazil* 20°50S 51°43W **120** D4
Tres Pontas *Brazil* 21°23S 45°29W **122** D1
Tres Puntas, C. *Argentina* 47°0S 66°0W **121** G3
Três Rios *Brazil* 22°6S 43°15E **122** D2
Tresco *U.K.* 49°57N 6°20W **27** H1
Treviso *Italy* 45°40N 12°15E **70** B5
Trevose Hd. *U.K.* 50°32N 5°3W **27** F3
Tribal Areas □ *Pakistan* 33°0N 70°0E **84** C7

Trichur *India* 10°30N 76°18E **84** P10
Trier *Germany* 49°45N 6°38E **66** D4
Trieste *Italy* 45°40N 13°46E **70** B5
Trim *Ireland* 53°33N 6°48W **29** D8
Trimdon *U.K.* 54°42N 1°24W **22** C6
Trimley *U.K.* 51°59N 1°20E **25** C11
Trincomalee *Sri Lanka* 8°38N 81°15E **84** Q12
Trindade, I. Atl. Oc. 20°20S 29°50W **52** F8
Trinidad *Bolivia* 14°46S 64°50W **120** D3
Trinidad *Cuba* 21°48N 80°0W **115** C9
Trinidad *U.S.A.* 37°10N 104°31W **110** C6
Trinidad & Tobago ■ *W. Indies* 10°30N 61°20W **115** E12
Trinity → *U.S.A.* 29°45N 94°43W **111** E8
Trinity B. *Canada* 48°20N 53°10W **109** E14
Trinity Is. *U.S.A.* 56°33N 154°25W **108** D4
Trípoli *Lebanon* 34°31N 35°50E **86** C3
Tripoli *Libya* 32°49N 13°7E **95** B8
Tripolitania N. *Afr.* 31°0N 13°0E **95** B8
Tripura □ *India* 24°0N 92°0E **85** H18
Tristan da Cunha *Atl. Oc.* 37°6S 12°20W **52** F9
Trivandrum *India* 8°41N 77°0E **84** Q10
Trnava *Slovak Rep.* 48°23N 17°35E **67** D9
Trois-Rivières *Canada* 46°25N 72°34W **109** E12
Trois-Rivières *Guadeloupe* 15°57N 61°40W **114** b
Trollhättan *Sweden* 58°17N 12°20E **63** F6
Trombetas → *Brazil* 1°55S 55°35W **120** C4
Tromsø *Norway* 69°40N 18°56E **63** D7
Tronador *Argentina* 41°10S 71°50W **121** G2
Trondheim *Norway* 63°36N 10°25E **63** E6
Trondheimsfjorden *Norway* 63°35N 10°30E **63** E6
Troon *U.K.* 55°33N 4°39W **20** D6
Trossachs, The *U.K.* 56°14N 4°24W **20** B7
Trostan *U.K.* 55°3N 6°10W **29** A9
Trotternish *U.K.* 57°32N 6°15W **18** G5
Trou Gras Pt. *St. Lucia* 13°51N 60°53W **115** f
Trout L. N.W.T., *Canada* 60°40N 121°14W **108** C7
Trout L. Ont., *Canada* 51°20N 93°15W **108** D10
Trowbridge *U.K.* 51°18N 2°12W **24** D4
Troy *Turkey* 39°57N 26°12E **73** G4
Troy *Ala., U.S.A.* 31°48N 85°58W **111** D9
Troy *N.Y., U.S.A.* 42°44N 73°41W **113** D11
Troy *Ohio, U.S.A.* 40°2N 84°12W **112** E5
Troyes *France* 48°19N 4°3E **68** B6
Trujillo *Honduras* 16°0N 86°0W **114** D7
Trujillo *Peru* 8°6S 79°0W **120** C2
Trujillo *Venezuela* 9°22N 70°38W **120** B2
Trull *U.K.* 51°0N 3°6W **24** E2
Trumpington *U.K.* 52°10N 0°7E **25** B9
Truro *Canada* 45°21N 63°14W **109** E13
Truro *U.K.* 50°16N 5°4W **27** G3
Tsavo *Kenya* 2°59S 38°28E **96** E7
Tsetserleg *Mongolia* 47°36N 101°32E **80** B5
Tshikapa *Dem. Rep. of the Congo* 6°28S 20°48E **96** F4
Tsiigehtchic *Canada* 67°15N 134°0W **108** C6
Tsimlyansk Res. *Russia* 48°0N 43°0E **73** E7
Tskhinvali *Georgia* 42°14N 44°1E **73** F7
Tsuchiura *Japan* 36°5N 140°15E **82** E7
Tsugaru Str. *Japan* 41°35N 141°0E **82** C7
Tsumeb *Namibia* 19°9S 17°44E **97** H3
Tsuruoka *Japan* 38°44N 139°50E **82** D6
Tsushima *Japan* 34°20N 129°20E **82** F1
Tuam *Ireland* 53°31N 8°51W **28** D4
Tuamotu, Îs. *French Polynesia* 17°0S 144°0W **103** J13
Tuamotu Ridge *Pac. Oc.* 20°0S 138°0W **103** K14
Tuapse *Russia* 44°5N 39°10E **73** F6
Tubarão *Brazil* 28°30S 49°0W **121** E5
Tübingen *Germany* 48°31N 9°4E **66** D5
Tubruq *Libya* 32°7N 23°55E **95** B10
Tubuai, Îs. *French Polynesia* 25°0S 150°0W **103** K13
Tucson *U.S.A.* 32°13N 110°58W **110** D4
Tucumcari *U.S.A.* 35°10N 103°44W **110** C6
Tucupita *Venezuela* 9°2N 62°3W **120** B3
Tucuruí *Brazil* 3°42S 49°44W **120** C5
Tucuruí, Reprêsa de *Brazil* 4°0S 49°30W **120** C5
Tuguegarao *Phil.* 17°35N 121°42E **83** B4
Tuktoyaktuk *Canada* 69°27N 133°2W **108** C6
Tula *Russia* 54°13N 37°38E **72** D6
Tulancingo *Mexico* 20°5N 98°22W **114** C5
Tulare *U.S.A.* 36°13N 119°21W **110** C3
Tulcán *Ecuador* 0°48N 77°43W **120** B2
Tulcea *Romania* 45°13N 28°46E **67** F15
Tulita *Canada* 64°57N 125°30W **108** C7
Tulla *Ireland* 52°53N 8°46W **30** D5
Tullamore *Ireland* 53°16N 7°31W **31** B7
Tulle *France* 45°16N 1°46E **68** D4
Tullow *Ireland* 52°49N 6°45W **31** D9
Tulsa *U.S.A.* 36°10N 95°55W **111** C7
Tumaco *Colombia* 1°50N 78°45W **120** B2
Tumbes *Peru* 3°37S 80°27W **120** C1
Tummel → *U.K.* 56°42N 4°5W **19** J9
Tummel, L. *U.K.* 56°43N 3°55W **19** J10
Tumucumaque, Serra *Brazil* 2°0N 55°0W **120** B4
Tunis *Tunisia* 36°50N 10°11E **95** A8
Tunisia ■ *Africa* 33°30N 9°10E **95** A7
Tunja *Colombia* 5°33N 73°25W **120** B2
Tunstall *U.K.* 52°9N 1°27E **25** B11
Tupaciguara *Brazil* 18°35S 48°42W **122** C1
Tupelo *U.S.A.* 34°16N 88°43W **111** D9
Tupiza *Bolivia* 21°30S 65°40W **120** E3
Turfan Basin *China* 42°40N 89°25E **80** B3
Turgutlu *Turkey* 38°30N 27°43E **73** E4
Turin *Italy* 45°3N 7°40E **70** B2
Turkana, L. *Africa* 3°30N 36°5E **96** D7
Turkey ■ *Eurasia* 39°0N 36°0E **73** G5
Türkmenabat *Turkmenistan* 39°6N 63°34E **87** B10
Türkmenbashi *Turkmenistan* 40°5N 53°5E **87** A8
Turkmenistan ■ *Asia* 39°0N 59°0E **87** B9
Turks & Caicos Is. ☑ *W. Indies* 21°20N 71°20W **115** C10
Turku *Finland* 60°30N 22°19E **63** E8
Turnberry *U.K.* 55°18N 4°49W **20** D6
Turneffe Is. *Belize* 17°20N 87°50W **114** D7
Turpan *China* 43°58N 89°10E **80** B3
Turriff *U.K.* 57°32N 2°27W **19** H12
Tuscaloosa *U.S.A.* 33°12N 87°34W **111** D9
Tuscany = Toscana □ *Italy* 43°25N 11°0E **70** C4
Tutbury *U.K.* 52°51N 1°41W **23** G5
Tuticorin *India* 8°50N 78°12E **84** Q11

Tutuila   Wells

Tutuila *Amer. Samoa* 14°19S 170°50W 99 C16
Tutume *Botswana* 20°30S 27°5E 97 J5
Tuvalu ■ *Pac. Oc.* 8°0S 178°0E 99 B14
Tuxford *U.K.* 53°14N 0°54W 23 F7
Tuxpan *Mexico* 20°57N 97°24W 114 C5
Tuxtla Gutiérrez *Mexico* 16°45N 93°7W 114 D6
Tuz Gölü *Turkey* 38°42N 33°18E 73 G5
Tuzla *Bos.-H.* 44°34N 18°41E 71 B8
Tver *Russia* 56°55N 35°55E 72 C6
Tweed ➤ *U.K.* 55°45N 2°0W 22 C5
Tweedmouth *U.K.* 55°45N 2°0W 22 A5
Tweedshaws *U.K.* 55°27N 3°29W 21 D9
Twenty *U.K.* 52°47N 0°17W 23 G8
Twin Falls *U.S.A.* 42°34N 114°28W 110 B4
Two Harbors *U.S.A.* 47°2N 91°40W 112 B2
Two Rivers *U.S.A.* 44°9N 87°34W 112 C4
Twyford *Hants., U.K.* 51°1N 1°19W 24 D6
Twyford *Wokingham, U.K.* 51°28N 0°51W 25 D7
Tychy *Poland* 50°9N 18°59E 67 C10
Tydd St. Mary *U.K.* 52°45N 0°7E 23 G9
Tyler *U.S.A.* 32°21N 95°18W 111 D7
Tyndrum *U.K.* 56°26N 4°42W 20 B6
Tyne ➤ *U.K.* 54°59N 1°32W 22 C5
Tyne & Wear □ *U.K.* 55°6N 1°17W 22 B6
Tynemouth *U.K.* 55°1N 1°26W 22 B6
Tyrol = Tirol □ *Austria* 47°3N 10°43E 66 E6
Tyrone □ *U.K.* 54°38N 7°11W 29 B7
Tyrrhenian Sea *Medit. S.* 40°0N 12°30E 70 E5
Tyumen *Russia* 57°11N 65°29E 78 D8
Tywardreath *U.K.* 50°21N 4°42W 27 G4
Tywi ➤ *U.K.* 51°48N 4°21W 26 D5
Tywyn *U.K.* 52°35N 4°5W 26 B5
Tzaneen *S. Africa* 23°47S 30°9E 97 J6

U

U.S.A. = United States of America ■
N. Amer. 37°0N 96°0W 110 C7
U.S. Virgin Is. ☑ *W. Indies* 18°20N 65°0W 115 e
Uanle Uen *Somali Rep.* 2°37N 44°54E 88 G3
Uaupés ➤ *Brazil* 0°2N 67°16W 120 B3
Ubá *Brazil* 21°8S 43°0W 122 D2
Ubaitaba *Brazil* 14°18S 39°20W 122 B3
Ube *Japan* 33°56N 131°15E 82 G2
Uberaba *Brazil* 19°50S 47°55W 122 C1
Uberlândia *Brazil* 19°0S 48°20W 122 C1
Ubon Ratchathani *Thailand* 15°15N 104°50E 83 B2
Ucayali ➤ *Peru* 4°30S 73°30W 120 C2
Uckfield *U.K.* 50°58N 0°7E 25 E9
Udagamandalam *India* 11°30N 76°44E 84 P10
Udaipur *India* 24°36N 73°44E 84 G8
Uddingston *U.K.* 55°49N 4°5W 20 D7
Údine *Italy* 46°3N 13°14E 70 A5
Udmurtia □ *Russia* 57°30N 52°30E 72 C9
Udon Thani *Thailand* 17°29N 102°46E 83 B2
Udupi *India* 13°25N 74°42E 84 N9
Uele ➤ *Dem. Rep. of the Congo* 3°45N 24°45E 96 D4
Ufa *Russia* 54°45N 55°55E 72 D10
Uffculme *U.K.* 50°54N 3°20W 27 F7
Ufford *U.K.* 52°8N 1°23E 25 B11
Uganda ■ *Africa* 2°0N 32°0E 96 D6
Ugborough *U.K.* 50°22N 3°53W 27 G6
Uig *U.K.* 57°35N 6°21W 18 G5
Uinta Mts. *U.S.A.* 40°45N 110°30W 110 B4
Uitenhage *S. Africa* 33°40S 25°28E 97 L5
Ujjain *India* 23°9N 75°43E 84 H9
Ujung Pandang *Indonesia* 5°10S 119°20E 83 D3
Ukhta *Russia* 63°34N 53°41E 72 B9
Ukiah *U.S.A.* 39°9N 123°13W 110 C2
Ukraine ■ *Europe* 49°0N 32°0E 73 E5
Ulaanbaatar *Mongolia* 47°55N 106°53E 80 B5
Ulaangom *Mongolia* 50°5N 92°10E 80 A4
Ulaanjirem *Mongolia* 45°5N 105°30E 80 B5
Ulan Ude *Russia* 51°45N 107°40E 79 D12
Ulceby Cross *U.K.* 53°15N 0°7E 23 F9
Ulhasnagar *India* 19°15N 73°10E 84 K8
Ullapool *U.K.* 57°54N 5°9W 18 G7
Ulleungdo *S. Korea* 37°30N 130°30E 82 E2
Ullswater *U.K.* 54°34N 2°52W 22 C3
Ulm *Germany* 48°23N 9°58E 66 D5
Ulster □ *U.K.* 54°35N 6°30W 29 B9
Ulungur He ➤ *China* 47°1N 87°24E 80 B3
Uluru *Australia* 25°23S 131°5E 98 F5
Ulva *U.K.* 56°29N 6°13W 20 B3
Ulverston *U.K.* 54°13N 3°5W 22 D2
Ulyanovsk *Russia* 54°20N 48°25E 72 D8
Ulyasutay *Mongolia* 47°56N 97°28E 80 B4
Uman *Ukraine* 48°40N 30°12E 73 E5
Umeå *Sweden* 63°45N 20°20E 63 E8
Umeälven ➤ *Sweden* 63°45N 20°20E 63 E8
Umlazi *S. Africa* 29°59S 30°54E 97 L6
Umm al Qaywayn *U.A.E.* 25°30N 55°35E 87 E8
Umnak I. *U.S.A.* 53°15N 168°20W 108 D3
Umuarama *Brazil* 23°45S 53°20W 121 E4
Unalakleet *U.S.A.* 63°52N 160°47W 108 C3
Unalaska *U.S.A.* 53°53N 166°32W 108 D3
Unalaska I. *U.S.A.* 53°35N 166°50W 108 D3
'Unayzah *Si. Arabia* 26°6N 43°58E 86 E5
Uncía *Bolivia* 18°25S 66°40W 120 D3
Ungava, Pén. d' *Canada* 60°0N 74°0W 109 D12
Ungava B. *Canada* 59°30N 67°30W 109 D13
União dos Palmares *Brazil* 9°10S 36°2W 122 A3
Unimak I. *U.S.A.* 54°45N 164°0W 108 D3
Union City *U.S.A.* 36°26N 89°3W 112 G3
Uniontown *U.S.A.* 39°54N 79°44W 112 F8
United Arab Emirates ■ *Asia* 23°50N 54°0E 87 F8
United Kingdom ■ *Europe* 53°0N 2°0W 64 E6
United States of America ■
N. Amer. 37°0N 96°0W 110 C7
Unst *U.K.* 60°44N 0°53W 18 A16
Upavon *U.K.* 51°18N 1°48W 24 D5
Upington *S. Africa* 28°25S 21°15E 97 K4
'Upolu *Samoa* 13°58S 172°0W 99 C16
Upper Heyford *U.K.* 51°56N 1°15W 24 C6
Upper Klamath L. *U.S.A.* 42°25N 121°55W 110 B2
Uppingham *U.K.* 52°36N 0°43W 23 G7
Uppsala *Sweden* 59°53N 17°38E 63 F7
Upton *U.K.* 53°13N 2°53W 23 F3
Upton-upon-Severn *U.K.* 52°3N 2°12W 24 B4

Upwey *U.K.* 50°39N 2°29W 24 E4
Ur *Iraq* 30°55N 46°25E 86 D6
Ural ➤ *Kazakhstan* 47°0N 51°48E 73 E9
Ural Mts. *Eurasia* 60°0N 59°0E 72 C10
Uranium City *Canada* 59°34N 108°37W 108 D9
Uraricoera ➤ *Brazil* 3°2N 60°30W 120 B3
Urbana *Ill., U.S.A.* 40°7N 88°12W 112 E3
Urbana *Ohio, U.S.A.* 40°7N 83°45W 112 E6
Ure ➤ *U.K.* 54°5N 1°20W 22 D5
Urganch *Uzbekistan* 41°40N 60°41E 87 A10
Urmia *Iran* 37°40N 45°0E 86 B6
Urmia, L. *Iran* 37°50N 45°30E 86 B6
Urmston *U.K.* 53°27N 2°21W 23 F4
Uroyan, Mts. de *Puerto Rico* 18°12N 67°0W 115 d
Uruaçu *Brazil* 14°30S 49°10W 122 B1
Uruapan *Mexico* 19°24N 102°3W 114 D4
Urubamba ➤ *Peru* 10°43S 73°48W 120 D2
Uruguai ➤ *Brazil* 26°0S 53°30W 121 E4
Uruguaiana *Brazil* 29°50S 57°0W 121 E4
Uruguay ■ *S. Amer.* 32°30S 56°30W 121 F4
Uruguay ➤ *S. Amer.* 34°12S 58°18W 116 G5
Ürümqi *China* 43°45N 87°45E 80 B3
Usa ➤ *Russia* 66°16N 59°49E 72 A10
Uşak *Turkey* 38°43N 29°28E 73 G4
Usakos *Namibia* 21°54S 15°31E 97 J3
Usedom *Germany* 53°55N 14°2E 66 B8
Ushant *France* 48°28N 5°6W 68 B1
Ushuaia *Argentina* 54°50S 68°23W 121 H3
Usk ➤ *U.K.* 51°33N 2°58W 27 D8
Usselby *U.K.* 53°26N 0°21W 23 F8
Ussuriysk *Russia* 43°48N 131°59E 82 B2
Ust-Ilimsk *Russia* 58°3N 102°39E 79 D12
Ústí nad Labem *Czech Rep.* 50°41N 14°3E 66 C8
Ústica *Italy* 38°42N 13°11E 70 E5
Ustyurt Plateau *Asia* 44°0N 55°0E 79 E7
Usu *China* 44°27N 84°40E 80 B3
Usumacinta ➤ *Mexico* 18°24N 92°38W 114 D6
Utah □ *U.S.A.* 39°20N 111°30W 110 C4
Utah L. *U.S.A.* 40°12N 111°48W 110 B4
Utica *U.S.A.* 43°6N 75°14W 113 D10
Utrecht *Neths.* 52°5N 5°8E 65 B5
Utsunomiya *Japan* 36°30N 139°50E 82 E6
Uttar Pradesh □ *India* 27°0N 80°0E 84 F12
Uttaradit *Thailand* 17°36N 100°5E 83 B2
Uttarakhand □ *India* 30°0N 79°30E 84 D11
Uttoxeter *U.K.* 52°54N 1°52W 23 G5
Utuado *Puerto Rico* 18°16N 66°42W 115 d
Uusikaupunki *Finland* 60°47N 21°25E 63 E8
Uvalde *U.S.A.* 29°13N 99°47W 110 E7
Uvira *Dem. Rep. of the Congo* 3°22S 29°3E 96 E5
Uvs Nuur *Mongolia* 50°20N 92°30E 80 A4
Uyuni *Bolivia* 20°28S 66°47W 120 E3
Uzbekistan ■ *Asia* 41°30N 65°0E 87 A10
Uzhhorod *Ukraine* 48°36N 22°18E 67 D12

V

Vaal ➤ *S. Africa* 29°4S 23°38E 97 K4
Vaasa *Finland* 63°6N 21°38E 63 E8
Vadodara *India* 22°20N 73°10E 84 H8
Vadsø *Norway* 70°3N 29°50E 63 C9
Vaduz *Liech.* 47°8N 9°31E 66 E5
Váh ➤ *Slovak Rep.* 47°43N 18°7E 67 D9
Vail *U.S.A.* 39°40N 106°20W 110 C5
Vaila *U.K.* 60°12N 1°36W 18 B14
Val-d'Or *Canada* 48°7N 77°47W 109 E12
Valahia *Romania* 44°35N 25°0E 67 F13
Valdai Hills *Russia* 57°0N 33°30E 72 C5
Valdés, Pen. *Argentina* 42°30S 63°45W 121 G3
Valdez *U.S.A.* 61°7N 146°16W 108 C5
Valdivia *Chile* 39°50S 73°14W 121 F2
Valdosta *U.S.A.* 30°50N 83°17W 111 D10
Vale of Glamorgan □ *U.K.* 51°28N 3°25W 27 E7
Valença *Brazil* 13°20S 39°5W 122 B3
Valence *France* 44°57N 4°54E 68 D6
Valencia *Spain* 39°27N 0°23W 69 C5
Valencia *Venezuela* 10°11N 68°0W 120 A3
Valencia □ *Spain* 39°20N 0°40W 69 C5
Valencia, G. de *Spain* 39°30N 0°20E 69 C6
Valencia I. *Ireland* 51°54N 10°22W 30 E2
Valenciennes *France* 50°20N 3°34E 68 A5
Valera *Venezuela* 9°19N 70°37W 120 B2
Valladolid *Mexico* 20°41N 88°12W 114 C7
Valladolid *Spain* 41°38N 4°43W 69 B3
Valledupar *Colombia* 10°29N 73°15W 120 A2
Vallejo *U.S.A.* 38°7N 122°14W 110 C2
Vallenar *Chile* 28°30S 70°50W 121 E2
Valletta *Malta* 35°54N 14°31E 70 G6
Valley *U.K.* 53°16N 4°34W 26 A4
Valley City *U.S.A.* 46°55N 98°0W 110 A7
Valparaíso *Chile* 33°2S 71°40W 121 F2
Van *Turkey* 38°30N 43°20E 73 G7
Van, L. *Turkey* 38°30N 43°0E 73 G7
Van Buren *U.S.A.* 47°10N 67°58W 113 B13
Van Wert *U.S.A.* 40°52N 84°35W 112 E5
Vanadzor *Armenia* 40°48N 44°30E 73 F7
Vancouver *Canada* 49°15N 123°7W 108 E7
Vancouver *U.S.A.* 45°38N 122°40W 110 A2
Vancouver I. *Canada* 49°50N 126°0W 108 E7
Vandalia *U.S.A.* 38°58N 89°6W 112 F3
Vanderhoof *Canada* 54°0N 124°0W 108 D7
Vänern *Sweden* 58°47N 13°30E 63 F6
Vanino *Russia* 48°50N 140°5E 79 E16
Vännäs *Sweden* 63°58N 19°48E 63 E7
Vannes *France* 47°40N 2°47W 68 C2
Vanrhynsdorp *S. Africa* 31°36S 18°44E 97 L3
Vantaa *Finland* 60°18N 24°56E 63 E8
Vanua Levu *Fiji* 16°33S 179°15E 99 D14
Vanuatu ■ *Pac. Oc.* 15°0S 168°0E 99 D12
Varanasi *India* 25°22N 83°8E 85 G13
Varangerfjorden *Norway* 70°3N 29°25E 63 C9
Varberg *Sweden* 57°6N 12°20E 63 F6
Vardak □ *Afghan.* 34°0N 68°0E 87 C12
Vardø *Norway* 70°23N 31°5E 63 C10
Varese *Italy* 45°48N 8°50E 70 B3
Varginha *Brazil* 21°33S 45°25W 122 D1
Varna *Bulgaria* 43°13N 27°56E 71 C12
Vasa Barris ➤ *Brazil* 11°10S 37°10W 122 B3

Västerås *Sweden* 59°37N 16°38E 63 F7
Västervik *Sweden* 57°43N 16°33E 63 F7
Vaté *Vanuatu* 17°40S 168°25E 99 D12
Vatersay *U.K.* 56°55N 7°32W 18 J2
Vatican City ■ *Europe* 41°54N 12°27E 70 D5
Vatnajökull *Iceland* 64°30N 16°48W 63 B2
Vättern *Sweden* 58°25N 14°30E 63 F6
Vaughn *U.S.A.* 34°36N 105°13W 110 D5
Vava'u Group *Tonga* 18°40S 174°0W 99 D16
Vega *Norway* 65°40N 11°55E 63 D6
Vega Baja *Puerto Rico* 18°27N 66°23W 115 d
Vegreville *Canada* 53°30N 112°5W 108 D8
Vélez-Málaga *Spain* 36°48N 4°5W 69 D3
Velhas ➤ *Brazil* 17°13S 44°49W 122 C2
Velikiye Luki *Russia* 56°25N 30°32E 72 C5
Veliko Tŭrnovo *Bulgaria* 43°5N 25°41E 71 C11
Velikonda Range *India* 14°45N 79°10E 84 M11
Vellore *India* 12°57N 79°10E 84 N11
Velsk *Russia* 61°10N 42°5E 72 B7
Vendée □ *France* 46°50N 1°35W 68 C3
Vendôme *France* 47°47N 1°3E 68 C4
Venézia, G. di *Italy* 45°15N 13°0E 70 B5
Venezuela ■ *S. Amer.* 8°0N 66°0W 120 B3
Venezuela, G. de *Venezuela* 11°30N 71°0W 120 A2
Vengurla *India* 15°53N 73°45E 84 M8
Venice *Italy* 45°27N 12°21E 70 B5
Venlo *Neths.* 51°22N 6°11E 65 C6
Ventnor *U.K.* 50°36N 1°12W 24 E6
Ventoux, Mt. *France* 44°10N 5°17E 68 D6
Ventspils *Latvia* 57°25N 21°32E 63 F8
Veracruz *Mexico* 19°11N 96°8W 114 D5
Veraval *India* 20°53N 70°27E 84 J7
Vercelli *Italy* 45°19N 8°25E 70 B3
Verde ➤ *U.S.A.* 33°33N 111°40W 110 D4
Verdun *France* 49°9N 5°24E 68 B6
Vereeniging *S. Africa* 26°38S 27°57E 97 K5
Verkhoyansk *Russia* 67°35N 133°25E 79 C15
Verkhoyansk Ra. *Russia* 66°0N 129°0E 79 C14
Vermont □ *U.S.A.* 44°0N 73°0W 113 D11
Vernal *U.S.A.* 40°27N 109°32W 110 B5
Vernon *Canada* 50°20N 119°15W 108 D8
Vernon *U.S.A.* 34°9N 99°17W 110 D7
Verona *Italy* 45°27N 10°59E 70 B4
Versailles *France* 48°48N 2°7E 68 B5
Vert, C. *Senegal* 14°45N 17°30W 94 F2
Verviers *Belgium* 50°37N 5°52E 65 D5
Verwood *U.K.* 50°52N 1°52W 24 E5
Veryan *U.K.* 50°13N 4°56W 27 G4
Veryan B. *U.K.* 50°13N 4°51W 27 G4
Vesoul *France* 47°40N 6°11E 68 C7
Vesterålen *Norway* 68°45N 15°0E 63 D7
Vestfjorden *Norway* 67°55N 14°0E 63 D6
Vesuvio *Italy* 40°49N 14°26E 70 D6
Veszprém *Hungary* 47°8N 17°57E 67 E9
Vianópolis *Brazil* 16°40S 48°35W 122 C1
Viaréggio *Italy* 43°52N 10°14E 70 C4
Vicenza *Italy* 45°33N 11°33E 70 B4
Vichada ➤ *Colombia* 4°55N 67°50W 120 B3
Vichy *France* 46°9N 3°26E 68 C5
Vickerstown *U.K.* 54°6N 3°15W 22 D2
Vicksburg *U.S.A.* 32°21N 90°53W 111 D8
Victoria *Canada* 48°30N 123°25W 108 E7
Victoria □ *Australia* 37°0S 144°0E 98 H7
Victoria *L., Africa* 1°0S 33°0E 96 E6
Victoria Falls *Zimbabwe* 17°58S 25°52E 97 H5
Victoria I. *Canada* 71°0N 111°0W 108 B8
Victoria Ld. *Antarctica* 75°0S 160°0E 55 D11
Victoria Str. *Canada* 69°31N 100°30W 108 C9
Victoriaville *Canada* 46°4N 71°56W 113 B12
Vidin *Bulgaria* 43°59N 22°50E 71 C10
Viedma, L. *Argentina* 49°30S 72°30W 121 G2
Vienna *Austria* 48°12N 16°22E 66 D9
Vienne *France* 45°31N 4°53E 68 D6
Vienne ➤ *France* 47°13N 0°5E 68 C4
Vientiane *Laos* 17°58N 102°36E 83 B2
Vieques *Puerto Rico* 18°8N 65°25W 115 d
Vierge Pt. *St. Lucia* 13°49N 60°53W 115 f
Vierzon *France* 47°13N 2°5E 68 C5
Vietnam ■ *Asia* 19°0N 106°0E 83 B2
Vieux Fort *St. Lucia* 13°46N 60°58W 115 f
Vigévano *Italy* 45°19N 8°51E 70 B3
Vigo *Spain* 42°12N 8°41W 69 A1
Vijayawada *India* 16°31N 80°39E 85 L12
Vikna *Norway* 64°55N 10°58E 63 E6
Vila Nova de Gaia *Portugal* 41°8N 8°37W 69 B1
Vila Velha *Brazil* 20°20S 40°17W 122 D2
Vilaine ➤ *France* 47°30N 2°27W 68 C2
Vilhelmina *Sweden* 64°35N 16°39E 63 E7
Vilhena *Brazil* 12°40S 60°5W 120 D3
Vilkitski Str. *Russia* 78°0N 103°0E 79 B12
Villa Bella *Bolivia* 10°25S 65°22W 120 D3
Villa Maria *Argentina* 32°20S 63°10W 121 F3
Villach *Austria* 46°37N 13°51E 66 E7
Villahermosa *Mexico* 17°59N 92°55W 114 D6
Villajoyosa *Spain* 38°30N 0°12W 69 C5
Villarrica *Paraguay* 25°40S 56°30W 121 E4
Villavicencio *Colombia* 4°9N 73°37W 120 B2
Ville-Marie *Canada* 47°20N 79°30W 112 B8
Villeneuve-sur-Lot *France* 44°24N 0°42E 68 D4
Vilnius *Lithuania* 54°38N 25°19E 63 G9
Vilyuy ➤ *Russia* 64°24N 126°26E 79 C14
Vilyuysk *Russia* 63°40N 121°35E 79 C14
Viña del Mar *Chile* 33°0S 71°30W 121 F2
Vincennes *U.S.A.* 38°41N 87°32W 112 F4
Vindhya Ra. *India* 22°50N 77°0E 84 H10
Vineland *U.S.A.* 39°29N 75°2W 113 F10
Vinnytsya *Ukraine* 49°15N 28°30E 73 E4
Virden *Canada* 49°50N 100°56W 108 E9
Vire *France* 48°50N 0°53W 68 B3
Virgenes, C. *Argentina* 52°19S 68°21W 121 H3
Virgin ➤ *U.S.A.* 36°28N 114°21W 110 C4
Virgin Is. (British) ☑
W. Indies 18°30N 64°30W 115 e
Virgin Is. (U.S.) ☑ *W. Indies* 18°20N 65°0W 115 e
Virginia *S. Africa* 28°8S 26°55E 97 K5
Virginia □ *U.S.A.* 37°30N 78°45W 112 G8

Virginia Beach *U.S.A.* 36°44N 76°0W 111 C11
Viroqua *U.S.A.* 43°34N 90°53W 112 D2
Vis *Croatia* 43°4N 16°10E 70 C7
Visalia *U.S.A.* 36°20N 119°18W 110 C3
Visby *Sweden* 57°37N 18°18E 63 F7
Viscount Melville Sd.
Canada 74°10N 108°0W 109 B9
Vishakhapatnam *India* 17°45N 83°20E 85 L13
Vistula ➤ *Poland* 54°22N 18°55E 67 A10
Vitebsk *Belarus* 55°10N 30°15E 72 C5
Viterbo *Italy* 42°25N 12°6E 70 C5
Viti Levu *Fiji* 17°30S 177°30E 99 D14
Vitim ➤ *Russia* 59°26N 112°34E 79 D13
Vitória *Brazil* 20°20S 40°22W 122 D2
Vitória da Conquista *Brazil* 14°51S 40°51W 122 B2
Vitoria-Gasteiz *Spain* 42°50N 2°41W 69 A4
Vittória *Italy* 36°57N 14°32E 70 F6
Vizianagaram *India* 18°6N 83°30E 85 K13
Vlaardingen *Neths.* 51°55N 4°21E 65 C4
Vladikavkaz *Russia* 43°0N 44°35E 73 F7
Vladimir *Russia* 56°15N 40°30E 72 C7
Vladivostok *Russia* 43°10N 131°53E 79 E15
Vlissingen *Neths.* 51°26N 3°34E 65 C3
Vlorë *Albania* 40°32N 19°28E 71 D8
Vltava ➤ *Czech Rep.* 50°21N 14°30E 66 D8
Voe *U.K.* 60°21N 1°16W 18 B15
Vogelsberg *Germany* 50°31N 9°12E 66 C5
Vohimena, Tanjon' i *Madag.* 25°36S 45°8E 97 K9
Voi *Kenya* 3°25S 38°32E 96 E7
Vojvodina □ *Serbia* 45°20N 20°0E 71 B9
Volga ➤ *Russia* 46°0N 48°30E 73 E8
Volga Hts. *Russia* 51°0N 46°0E 73 D8
Volgodonsk *Russia* 47°33N 42°5E 73 E7
Volgograd *Russia* 48°40N 44°25E 73 E7
Volgograd Res. *Russia* 50°0N 45°20E 73 D8
Vologda *Russia* 59°10N 39°45E 72 C6
Volos *Greece* 39°24N 22°59E 71 E10
Volsk *Russia* 52°5N 47°22E 72 D8
Volta ➤ *Ghana* 5°46N 0°41E 94 G6
Volta, L. *Ghana* 7°30N 0°0 94 G6
Volta Redonda *Brazil* 22°31S 44°5W 122 D2
Volzhskiy *Russia* 48°56N 44°46E 73 E7
Vorkuta *Russia* 67°48N 64°20E 72 A11
Voronezh *Russia* 51°40N 39°10E 73 D6
Vosges *France* 48°20N 7°10E 68 B7
Vostok I. *Kiribati* 10°5S 152°23W 103 J12
Votkinsk *Russia* 57°0N 53°55E 72 C9
Vratsa *Bulgaria* 43°15N 23°30E 71 C10
Vryburg *S. Africa* 26°55S 24°45E 97 K4
Vryheid *S. Africa* 27°45S 30°47E 97 K6
Vulcano *Italy* 38°24N 14°58E 70 E6
Vung Tau *Vietnam* 10°21N 107°4E 83 B2
Vyazma *Russia* 55°10N 34°15E 72 C5
Vyborg *Russia* 60°43N 28°47E 72 B4
Vychegda ➤ *Russia* 61°18N 46°36E 72 B8
Vyrnwy, L. *U.K.* 52°48N 3°31W 26 B6
Vyshniy Volochek *Russia* 57°30N 34°30E 72 C5

W

Waal ➤ *Neths.* 51°37N 5°0E 65 C5
Wabasca ➤ *Canada* 58°22N 115°20W 108 D8
Wabash *U.S.A.* 40°48N 85°49W 112 E5
Wabash ➤ *U.S.A.* 37°48N 88°2W 112 G3
Waco *U.S.A.* 31°33N 97°9W 111 D7
Wad Medanī *Sudan* 14°28N 33°30E 95 F12
Waddenzee *Neths.* 53°6N 5°10E 65 A5
Waddesdon *U.K.* 51°51N 0°55W 25 C7
Waddingham *U.K.* 53°27N 0°32W 23 F7
Waddington *U.K.* 53°10N 0°32W 23 F7
Waddington, Mt. *Canada* 51°23N 125°15W 108 D7
Wadebridge *U.K.* 50°31N 4°51W 27 F4
Wadhurst *U.K.* 51°3N 0°20E 25 D9
Wadi Halfa *Sudan* 21°53N 31°19E 95 D12
Wager B. *Canada* 65°26N 88°40W 109 C11
Wagga Wagga *Australia* 35°7S 147°24E 98 H8
Wah *Pakistan* 33°45N 72°40E 84 C8
Wahiawā *U.S.A.* 21°30N 158°2W 110 H15
Waigeo *Indonesia* 0°20S 130°40E 83 D5
Wailuku *U.S.A.* 20°53N 156°30W 110 H16
Wainfleet All Saints *U.K.* 53°7N 0°15E 23 F9
Wakayama *Japan* 34°15N 135°15E 82 F4
Wake I. *Pac. Oc.* 19°18N 166°36E 102 F8
Wakefield *Jamaica* 18°26N 77°42W 114 a
Wakefield *U.K.* 53°41N 1°29W 23 E6
Wakkanai *Japan* 45°28N 141°35E 82 A7
Walberswick *U.K.* 52°19N 1°40E 25 B12
Walbrzych *Poland* 50°45N 16°18E 66 C9
Walbury Hill *U.K.* 51°21N 1°28W 24 D6
Walcheren *Neths.* 51°30N 3°35E 65 C3
Waldron *U.S.A.* 50°56N 0°13E 25 E9
Wales □ *U.K.* 52°19N 4°43W 26 C4
Walgett *Australia* 30°0S 148°5E 98 G8
Walker L. *U.S.A.* 38°42N 118°43W 110 C3
Walla Walla *U.S.A.* 46°4N 118°20W 110 A3
Wallaceburg *Canada* 42°34N 82°23W 112 D6
Wallachia = Valahia *Romania* 44°35N 25°0E 67 F13
Wallasey *U.K.* 53°25N 3°2W 23 F2
Wallingford *U.K.* 51°35N 1°8W 24 C6
Wallis & Futuna, Is.
Pac. Oc. 13°18S 176°10W 99 C15
Walls *U.K.* 60°14N 1°33W 18 B14
Wallsend *U.K.* 54°59N 1°31W 22 C5
Walmer *U.K.* 51°11N 1°25E 25 D11
Walney, I. of *U.K.* 54°6N 3°15W 22 D2
Walpole *U.K.* 52°45N 0°13E 25 B9
Walsall *U.K.* 52°35N 1°58W 23 G5
Walsenburg *U.S.A.* 37°38N 104°47W 110 C6
Walsoken *U.K.* 52°41N 0°11E 25 B9
Waltham *U.S.A.* 42°23N 71°14W 113 D12
Waltham *U.K.* 53°31N 0°7W 23 E8
Waltham Abbey *U.K.* 51°41N 0°1E 25 C9
Waltham Forest □ *U.K.* 51°35N 0°0 25 C9
Waltham on the Wolds *U.K.* 52°50N 0°48W 23 G7
Walton-on-the-Naze *U.K.* 51°51N 1°17E 25 C11
Walvis Bay *Namibia* 23°0S 14°28E 97 J2
Wamba *Dem. Rep. of the Congo* 2°10N 27°57E 96 D5
Wanborough *U.K.* 51°33N 1°42W 24 C5
Wandsworth □ *U.K.* 51°27N 0°11W 25 D8

Wanganui *N.Z.* 39°56S 175°3E 99 H14
Wansbeck ➤ *U.K.* 55°10N 1°32W 22 B5
Wantage *U.K.* 51°35N 1°25W 24 C6
Wanxian *China* 30°42N 108°20E 80 C5
Wapakoneta *U.S.A.* 40°34N 84°12W 112 E5
Warangal *India* 17°58N 79°35E 84 L11
Warboys *U.K.* 52°24N 0°4W 25 B8
Ward *Ireland* 53°26N 6°20W 31 B10
Wardha *India* 20°45N 78°39E 84 J11
Wardington *U.K.* 52°7N 1°17W 24 B6
Wardle *U.K.* 53°7N 2°35W 23 F3
Ward's Stone *U.K.* 54°1N 2°36W 23 D3
Ware *U.K.* 51°49N 0°0 25 C8
Wareham *U.K.* 50°42N 2°7W 24 E4
Wark *U.K.* 55°6N 2°14W 22 B4
Warkworth *U.K.* 55°21N 1°37W 22 B5
Warley *U.K.* 52°30N 1°59W 23 H5
Warminster *U.K.* 51°12N 2°10W 24 D4
Warrego ➤ *Australia* 30°24S 145°21E 98 G8
Warren *Mich., U.S.A.* 42°28N 83°1W 112 D6
Warren *Ohio, U.S.A.* 41°14N 80°49W 112 E7
Warren *Pa., U.S.A.* 41°51N 79°9W 112 E8
Warrenpoint *U.K.* 54°6N 6°15W 29 C9
Warri *Nigeria* 5°30N 5°41E 94 G7
Warrington *U.K.* 53°24N 2°35W 23 F3
Warrnambool *Australia* 38°25S 142°30E 98 H7
Warsaw *Poland* 52°14N 21°0E 67 B11
Warsop *U.K.* 41°14N 85°51W 112 E5
Warta ➤ *Poland* 52°35N 14°39E 66 B8
Warwick *U.K.* 52°18N 1°35W 24 B5
Warwick *U.S.A.* 41°42N 71°28W 113 E12
Warwickshire □ *U.K.* 52°14N 1°38W 24 B5
Wasatch Ra. *U.S.A.* 40°0N 111°30W 110 B4
Wash, The *U.K.* 52°58N 0°20E 23 E9
Washburn *U.S.A.* 46°40N 90°54W 112 B2
Washford *U.K.* 51°9N 3°21W 24 D2
Washington *U.K.* 54°55N 1°30W 22 C6
Washington *D.C., U.S.A.* 38°53N 77°2W 112 F9
Washington *Ind., U.S.A.* 38°40N 87°10W 112 F4
Washington *Pa., U.S.A.* 40°10N 80°15W 112 E7
Washington □ *U.S.A.* 47°30N 120°30W 110 A2
Washington, Mt. *U.S.A.* 44°16N 71°18W 113 C12
Washington I. *U.S.A.* 45°23N 86°54W 112 C4
Wasilla *U.S.A.* 61°35N 149°26W 108 C5
Waskaganish *Canada* 51°30N 78°40W 109 D12
Wast Water *U.K.* 54°26N 3°18W 22 D2
Watampone *Indonesia* 4°29S 120°25E 83 D4
Watchet *U.K.* 51°10N 3°19W 24 D2
Waterbeach *U.K.* 52°16N 0°12E 25 B9
Waterbury *U.S.A.* 41°33N 73°3W 113 E11
Waterford *Ireland* 52°15N 7°8W 31 D8
Waterford □ *Ireland* 52°10N 7°40W 31 D7
Waterford Harbour *Ireland* 52°8N 6°58W 31 D9
Watergate B. *U.K.* 50°26N 5°4W 27 G3
Waterloo *Belgium* 50°43N 4°25E 65 D4
Waterloo *Canada* 43°30N 80°32W 112 D7
Waterloo *Ill., U.S.A.* 38°20N 90°9W 112 F2
Waterloo *Iowa, U.S.A.* 42°30N 92°21W 111 B8
Watersmeet *U.S.A.* 46°16N 89°11W 112 B3
Watertown *N.Y., U.S.A.* 43°59N 75°55W 113 D10
Watertown *S. Dak., U.S.A.* 44°54N 97°7W 111 B7
Watertown *Wis., U.S.A.* 43°12N 88°43W 112 D3
Waterville *U.S.A.* 44°33N 69°38W 113 C13
Watford *U.K.* 51°40N 0°24W 25 C8
Watlington *Norfolk, U.K.* 52°40N 0°24E 25 B9
Watlington *Oxon., U.K.* 51°38N 1°0W 24 C6
Watrous *Canada* 51°40N 105°25W 108 D9
Watsa *Dem. Rep. of the Congo* 3°4N 29°30E 96 D5
Watseka *U.S.A.* 40°47N 87°44W 112 E4
Watson Lake *Canada* 60°6N 128°49W 108 C7
Watton *U.K.* 52°34N 0°51E 25 A10
Waukegan *U.S.A.* 42°22N 87°50W 112 D4
Waukesha *U.S.A.* 43°1N 88°14W 112 D3
Waupaca *U.S.A.* 44°21N 89°5W 112 C3
Waupun *U.S.A.* 43°38N 88°44W 112 D3
Wausau *U.S.A.* 44°58N 89°38W 112 C3
Wautoma *U.S.A.* 44°4N 89°18W 112 C3
Wauwatosa *U.S.A.* 43°2N 88°0W 112 D4
Waveney ➤ *U.K.* 52°35N 1°39E 25 A12
Waver ➤ *U.K.* 54°50N 3°15W 22 C2
Wâw *Sudan* 7°45N 28°1E 95 G11
Wawa *Canada* 47°59N 84°47W 112 B5
Waycross *U.S.A.* 31°13N 82°21W 111 D10
Wayne *U.S.A.* 38°13N 82°27W 112 F6
Waynesboro *U.S.A.* 38°4N 78°53W 112 F8
Waynesburg *U.S.A.* 39°54N 80°11W 112 F7
Wazirabad *Pakistan* 32°30N 74°8E 84 C9
Weald, The *U.K.* 51°4N 0°20E 25 D9
Wear ➤ *U.K.* 54°55N 1°22W 22 C6
Weardale *U.K.* 54°44N 2°5W 22 C4
Wearhead *U.K.* 54°45N 2°13W 22 C4
Weaver ➤ *U.K.* 53°17N 2°35W 23 F3
Weaverham *U.K.* 53°16N 2°35W 23 F3
Webster Springs *U.S.A.* 38°29N 80°25W 112 F7
Weddell Sea *Antarctica* 72°30S 40°0W 55 D1
Wednesbury *U.K.* 52°33N 2°1W 23 G4
Wednesfield *U.K.* 52°37N 2°2W 23 G4
Weedon Bec *U.K.* 52°15N 1°5W 24 B6
Weifang *China* 36°44N 119°7E 81 C6
Weipa *Australia* 12°40S 141°50E 98 C7
Welch *U.S.A.* 37°26N 81°35W 112 G7
Weldon *U.K.* 55°17N 1°45W 22 B5
Welford *Northants., U.K.* 52°26N 1°0W 24 B6
Welford *W. Berkshire, U.K.* 51°27N 1°24W 24 D6
Welkom *S. Africa* 28°0S 26°46E 97 K5
Welland *Canada* 43°0N 79°15W 112 D8
Welland ➤ *U.K.* 52°51N 0°5W 23 G8
Wellesley Is. *Australia* 16°42S 139°30E 98 D6
Wellingborough *U.K.* 52°19N 0°41W 25 B7
Wellington *Telford & Wrekin,
U.K.* 52°42N 2°30W 23 G3
Wellington *Somst., U.K.* 50°58N 3°13W 24 E2
Wellington & Chan. *Canada* 75°0N 93°0W 109 B10
Wells *U.K.* 51°13N 2°39W 24 D3

Wells-next-the-Sea U.K. 52°57N 0°51E 25 A10
Wellsboro U.S.A. 41°45N 77°18W 112 E9
Wellsville U.S.A. 42°7N 77°57W 112 D9
Welney U.K. 52°31N 0°15E 25 A9
Wels Austria 48°9N 14°1E 66 D8
Welshpool U.K. 52°39N 3°8W 26 B7
Welton U.K. 53°18N 0°29W 23 F8
Welwyn Garden City U.K. 51°48N 0°12W 25 C8
Wem U.K. 52°52N 2°44W 23 G3
Wemindji Canada 53°0N 78°49W 109 D12
Wemyss Bay U.K. 55°53N 4°53W 20 C6
Wenatchee U.S.A. 47°25N 120°19W 110 A2
Wendover U.K. 51°45N 0°44W 25 C7
Wenlock Edge U.K. 52°30N 2°43W 23 H3
Wensleydale U.K. 54°17N 2°0W 22 D4
Wensu China 41°15N 80°10E 80 B3
Wensum → U.K. 52°40N 1°15E 25 A11
Wenzhou China 28°0N 120°38E 81 D7
Weobley U.K. 52°11N 2°50W 24 B3
Werrington U.K. 50°39N 4°23W 27 F5
Weser → Germany 53°36N 8°28E 66 B5
West Antarctica Antarctica 80°0S 90°0W 55 D15
West Auckland U.K. 54°38N 1°43W 22 C5
West Bank ■ Asia 32°6N 35°13E 86 C3
West Bend U.S.A. 43°25N 88°11W 112 D3
West Bengal □ India 23°0N 88°0E 85 H16
West Berkshire □ U.K. 51°25N 1°17W 24 D6
West Beskids Europe 49°30N 19°0E 67 D10
West Bridgford U.K. 52°55N 1°8W 23 G6
West Bromwich U.K. 52°32N 1°59W 23 G5
West Burra U.K. 60°5N 1°21W 18 B15
West Calder U.K. 55°51N 3°33W 21 C8
West Coker U.K. 50°55N 2°40W 24 E3
West Falkland Falk. Is. 51°40S 60°0W 121 H3
West Fen U.K. 53°5N 0°5W 23 F8
West Frankfort U.S.A. 37°54N 88°55W 111 G9
West Grinstead U.K. 50°58N 0°19W 25 E8
West Haddon U.K. 52°20N 1°3W 24 B6
West Kirby U.K. 53°23N 3°11W 23 F2
West Linton U.K. 55°46N 3°21W 21 C9
West Lulworth U.K. 50°37N 2°14W 24 E4
West Malling U.K. 51°17N 0°26E 25 D9
West Meon U.K. 51°1N 1°5W 24 D6
West Mersea U.K. 51°46N 0°56E 25 C10
West Midlands □ U.K. 52°26N 2°0W 23 H5
West Moors U.K. 50°49N 1°53W 24 E5
West Palm Beach U.S.A. 26°43N 80°3W 111 E10
West Point U.S.A. 37°32N 76°48W 112 G9
West Rasen U.K. 53°23N 0°24W 23 F7
West Seneca U.S.A. 42°51N 78°48W 112 D8
West Siberian Plain Russia 62°0N 75°0E 74 B9
West Sussex □ U.K. 50°55N 0°30W 25 E8
West Virginia □ U.S.A. 38°45N 80°30W 112 F7
West Yorkshire □ U.K. 53°45N 1°40W 23 E5
Westbourne U.K. 50°52N 0°55W 25 E7
Westbrook U.S.A. 43°41N 70°22W 113 D12
Westbury Shrops., U.K. 52°41N 2°55W 23 G3
Westbury Wilts., U.K. 51°15N 2°11W 24 D4
Westbury-on-Severn U.K. 51°50N 2°25W 24 C4
Wester Ross U.K. 57°37N 4°51W 19 G8
Westerham U.K. 51°16N 0°5E 25 D9
Western Australia □ Australia 25°0S 118°0E 98 F2
Western Ghats India 14°0N 75°0E 84 N9
Western Isles □ U.K. 57°30N 7°10W 18 G3
Western Sahara ■ Africa 25°0N 13°0W 94 D3
Westerschelde → Neths. 51°25N 3°25E 64 C3
Westerwald Germany 50°38N 7°56E 66 C4
Westfield U.K. 50°55N 0°35E 25 E10
Westhill U.K. 57°9N 2°19W 19 H13
Westhoughton U.K. 53°33N 2°31W 23 E3
Westmeath □ Ireland 53°33N 7°34W 28 D6
Westminster U.K. 39°34N 76°59W 112 F9
Westmoreland Barbados 13°13N 59°37W 115 g
Weston U.K. 52°51N 2°1W 23 G4
Weston U.S.A. 39°2N 80°28W 112 F7
Weston-super-Mare U.K. 51°21N 2°58W 24 D3
Westport Ireland 53°48N 9°31W 28 D2
Westray U.K. 59°18N 3°0W 19 D11
Westruther U.K. 55°45N 2°35W 21 C10
Westward Ho! U.K. 51°2N 4°15W 27 E5
Wetar Indonesia 7°48S 126°30E 83 D4
Wetaskiwin Canada 52°55N 113°24W 108 D8
Wetherby U.K. 53°56N 1°23W 23 E6
Wetwang U.K. 54°1N 0°35W 23 D7
Wewak Papua N. G. 3°38S 143°41E 98 A7
Wexford Ireland 52°20N 6°28W 31 D10
Wexford □ Ireland 52°20N 6°25W 31 D10
Wexford Harbour Ireland 52°20N 6°25W 31 D10
Wey → U.K. 51°22N 0°27W 25 D8
Weybourne U.K. 52°57N 1°9E 25 A11
Weybridge U.K. 51°22N 0°27W 25 D8
Weyburn Canada 49°40N 103°50W 108 E9
Weymouth U.K. 50°37N 2°28W 24 E4
Wha Ti Canada 63°8N 117°16W 108 C8
Whale Cove Canada 62°10N 92°34W 108 C10
Whales, B. of Antarctica 78°0S 160°0W 55 D12
Whalley U.K. 53°49N 2°24W 23 E4
Whalsay U.K. 60°22N 0°59W 18 B16
Whalton U.K. 55°8N 1°46W 22 B5
Whangarei N.Z. 35°43S 174°21E 99 H13
Whaplode U.K. 52°42N 0°3W 23 G8
Wharfe → U.K. 53°51N 1°9W 23 E6
Wharfedale U.K. 54°6N 2°1W 22 D4
Wheatley Hill U.K. 54°45N 1°23W 22 C6
Wheeler Pk. U.S.A. 38°57N 114°15W 110 C4
Wheeling U.S.A. 40°4N 80°43W 112 E7
Whernside U.K. 54°14N 2°24W 22 D4
Whicham U.K. 54°15N 3°21W 22 D2
Whimple U.K. 50°46N 3°20W 27 F7
Whipsnade U.K. 51°51N 0°32W 25 C7
Whissendine U.K. 52°43N 0°46W 23 G7
Whitburn U.K. 55°52N 3°40W 21 C8
Whitby U.K. 54°29N 0°37W 22 D7
Whitchurch Devon., U.K. 50°32N 4°7W 27 F5
Whitchurch Hants., U.K. 51°14N 1°20W 24 D6
Whitchurch Hereford, U.K. 51°51N 2°39W 24 C3
Whitchurch Shrops., U.K. 52°59N 2°40W 23 G3

White → Ark., U.S.A. 33°57N 91°5W 111 D8
White → Ind., U.S.A. 38°25N 87°45W 112 F4
White → Utah, U.S.A. 40°4N 109°41W 110 B5
White Esk → U.K. 55°13N 3°11W 21 D9
White Horse, Vale of U.K. 51°37N 1°30W 24 C5
White Horse Hill U.K. 51°34N 1°33W 24 C5
White Mts. Calif., U.S.A. 37°30N 118°15W 110 C3
White Mts. N.H., U.S.A. 44°15N 71°15W 111 B12
White Nile → Sudan 15°38N 32°31E 95 E12
White Sea Russia 66°30N 38°0E 72 A6
Whiteadder Water → U.K. 55°51N 2°25W 21 C11
Whitecourt Canada 54°10N 115°45W 108 D8
Whitefish Point U.S.A. 46°45N 84°59W 112 B5
Whitehall U.S.A. 44°22N 91°19W 112 C2
Whitehaven U.K. 54°33N 3°35W 22 C1
Whitehorse Canada 60°43N 135°3W 108 C6
Whitesand B. U.K. 50°21N 4°18W 27 G5
Whitewater U.K. 42°50N 88°44W 112 D3
Whithorn U.K. 54°44N 4°26W 20 E7
Whitley Bay U.K. 55°4N 1°27W 22 B6
Whitney, Mt. U.S.A. 36°35N 118°18W 110 C3
Whitstable U.K. 51°21N 1°3E 25 D11
Whittington Derby., U.K. 53°16N 1°26W 23 F6
Whittington Shrops., U.K. 52°52N 3°0W 23 G3
Whittlesey U.K. 52°33N 0°0W 25 A8
Whittlesford U.K. 52°7N 0°9E 25 B9
Whitwell Derby., U.K. 53°17N 1°12W 23 F6
Whitwell I. of W., U.K. 50°36N 1°15W 24 E6
Whitwick U.K. 52°45N 1°22W 23 G6
Whitworth U.K. 53°39N 2°11W 23 E4
Wholdaia L. Canada 60°43N 104°20W 108 C9
Whyalla Australia 33°2S 137°30E 98 G6
Wiarton Canada 44°40N 81°10W 112 C7
Wiay U.K. 57°24N 7°13W 18 H3
Wichita U.S.A. 37°42N 97°20W 111 C7
Wichita Falls U.S.A. 33°54N 98°30W 110 D7
Wick U.K. 58°26N 3°5W 19 F11
Wickford U.K. 51°36N 0°33E 25 C10
Wickham U.K. 50°54N 1°11W 24 E6
Wickham Market U.K. 52°9N 1°23E 25 B11
Wicklow Ireland 52°59N 6°3W 31 C10
Wicklow □ Ireland 52°57N 6°25W 31 C10
Wicklow Hd. Ireland 52°58N 6°0W 31 C11
Wicklow Mts. Ireland 52°58N 6°26W 31 C10
Wicklow Mts. △ Ireland 53°6N 6°21W 31 B11
Wickwar U.K. 51°36N 2°23W 24 C4
Widdrington U.K. 55°15N 1°35W 22 B5
Widecombe U.K. 50°34N 3°49W 27 F6
Widemouth U.K. 50°47N 4°34W 27 F4
Widnes U.K. 53°23N 2°45W 23 F3
Wiener Neustadt Austria 47°49N 16°16E 66 E9
Wiesbaden Germany 50°4N 8°14E 66 C5
Wigan U.K. 53°33N 2°38W 23 E3
Wight, I. of U.K. 50°41N 1°17W 24 E6
Wight, Isle of □ U.K. 50°41N 1°17W 24 E6
Wigmore U.K. 52°19N 2°51W 24 B3
Wigston U.K. 52°35N 1°6W 23 G6
Wigton U.K. 54°50N 3°10W 22 C2
Wigtown U.K. 54°53N 4°27W 20 E7
Wigtown B. U.K. 54°46N 4°15W 20 E7
Wilhelm, Mt. Papua N. G. 5°50S 145°1E 98 B8
Wilhelmshaven Germany 53°31N 8°7E 66 B5
Wilkes-Barre U.S.A. 41°15N 75°53W 113 E10
Wilkes Land Antarctica 69°0S 120°0E 55 D9
Willemstad Neth. Ant. 12°5N 68°55W 115 E11
Willenhall U.K. 52°36N 2°2W 23 G4
Willesborough U.K. 51°8N 0°56E 25 D10
Williams Lake Canada 52°10N 122°10W 108 D7
Williamsburg U.S.A. 37°16N 76°43W 112 G9
Williamson U.S.A. 37°41N 82°17W 112 G6
Williamsport U.S.A. 41°15N 77°1W 112 E9
Willingdon U.K. 50°47N 0°17E 25 E9
Willingham U.K. 52°19N 0°4E 25 B9
Williston U.S.A. 48°9N 103°37W 110 A6
Williston L. Canada 56°0N 124°0W 108 D7
Williton U.K. 51°9N 3°19W 24 D2
Willmar U.S.A. 45°7N 95°3W 111 A7
Willoughby U.K. 53°13N 0°12E 23 F9
Wilmington Del., U.S.A. 39°45N 75°33W 113 F10
Wilmington N.C., U.S.A. 34°14N 77°55W 111 D11
Wilmslow U.K. 53°19N 2°13W 23 F4
Wilnecote U.K. 52°36N 1°39W 23 G5
Wilton U.K. 51°5N 1°51W 24 D5
Wiltshire □ U.K. 51°18N 1°53W 24 D5
Wimblington U.K. 52°31N 0°4E 25 A9
Wimborne Minster U.K. 50°48N 1°59W 24 E5
Wincanton U.K. 51°3N 2°24W 24 D4
Winchelsea U.K. 50°55N 0°43E 25 E10
Winchester U.K. 51°4N 1°18W 24 D6
Winchester Ky., U.S.A. 37°59N 84°11W 112 G6
Winchester Va., U.S.A. 39°11N 78°10W 112 F8
Wind → U.S.A. 43°12N 108°12W 110 B5
Wind River Range U.S.A. 43°0N 109°30W 110 B5
Windermere U.K. 54°23N 2°55W 22 D3
Windhoek Namibia 22°35S 17°4E 97 J3
Windrush → U.K. 51°43N 1°24W 24 C6
Windsor Canada 42°18N 83°0W 109 E11
Windsor U.K. 51°29N 0°36W 25 D7
Windward Is. W. Indies 13°0N 61°0W 115 D12
Windward Passage Caribbean 20°0N 74°0W 115 D10
Wing U.K. 51°53N 0°43W 25 C7
Wingham U.K. 51°16N 1°13E 25 D11
Winisk → Canada 55°17N 85°5W 109 D11
Winkleigh U.K. 50°50N 3°58W 27 F6
Winkler Canada 49°10N 97°56W 108 E10
Winneba Ghana 5°25N 0°36W 94 G5
Winnebago, L. U.S.A. 44°0N 88°26W 112 D3
Winnemucca U.S.A. 40°58N 117°44W 110 B3
Winnipeg Canada 49°54N 97°9W 108 E10
Winnipeg, L. Canada 52°0N 97°0W 108 D10
Winnipegosis L. Canada 52°30N 100°0W 108 C9
Winona U.S.A. 44°3N 91°39W 111 B8
Winooski U.S.A. 44°29N 73°11W 113 C11
Winsford U.K. 53°12N 2°31W 23 F3
Winslow U.K. 51°57N 0°52W 25 C7
Winslow U.S.A. 35°2N 110°42W 110 C4
Winster U.K. 53°9N 1°39W 23 F5
Winston-Salem U.S.A. 36°6N 80°15W 111 C10

Winterborne Abbas U.K. 50°42N 2°33W 24 E3
Winterthur Switz. 47°30N 8°44E 66 E5
Winterton N. Lincs., U.K. 53°39N 0°37W 23 E7
Winterton Norfolk, U.K. 52°43N 1°41E 25 A12
Winton Australia 22°24S 143°3E 98 E7
Wirksworth U.K. 53°6N 1°35W 23 F5
Wirral U.K. 53°25N 3°0W 23 F2
Wisbech U.K. 52°41N 0°9E 25 A9
Wisborough Green U.K. 51°2N 0°30W 25 D7
Wisconsin □ U.S.A. 44°45N 89°30W 111 B9
Wisconsin Rapids U.S.A. 44°23N 89°49W 112 C3
Wishaw U.K. 55°46N 3°54W 21 C8
Wiske → U.K. 54°19N 1°27W 22 D6
Witbank S. Africa 25°51S 29°14E 97 K5
Witham U.K. 51°48N 0°40E 25 C10
Witham → U.K. 52°59N 0°2W 23 G8
Withern U.K. 53°18N 0°8E 23 F9
Withernsea U.K. 53°44N 0°1E 23 E9
Witley U.K. 51°9N 0°39W 25 D7
Witney U.K. 51°48N 1°28W 24 C6
Wittersham U.K. 51°0N 0°43E 25 D10
Wiveliscombe U.K. 51°2N 3°19W 24 D2
Wivenhoe U.K. 51°51N 0°59E 25 C10
Wkra → Poland 52°27N 20°44E 67 B11
Wloclawek Poland 52°40N 19°3E 67 B10
Woburn U.K. 51°59N 0°36W 25 C7
Woburn Sands U.K. 52°1N 0°39W 25 B7
Wodonga Australia 36°5S 146°50E 98 H8
Woking U.K. 51°19N 0°34W 25 D7
Wokingham U.K. 51°24N 0°49W 25 D7
Wolf Rock U.K. 49°57N 5°49W 27 H2
Wolfsburg Germany 52°25N 10°48E 66 B6
Wolin Poland 53°50N 14°37E 66 B8
Wollaston L. Canada 58°7N 103°10W 108 D9
Wollaston Pen. Canada 69°30N 115°0W 108 C8
Wollongong Australia 34°25S 150°54E 98 G9
Wolsingham U.K. 54°44N 1°52W 22 C5
Wolverhampton U.K. 52°35N 2°7W 23 G4
Wolverton U.K. 52°3N 0°47W 25 B7
Wolviston U.K. 54°38N 1°18W 22 C6
Wombwell U.K. 53°32N 1°25W 23 E6
Wŏnsan N. Korea 39°11N 127°27E 81 C7
Wonston U.K. 51°8N 1°18W 24 D6
Woodbridge U.K. 52°6N 1°20E 25 B11
Woodbury U.K. 50°41N 3°24W 27 F7
Woodhall Spa U.K. 53°10N 0°12W 23 F8
Woodhouse U.K. 53°22N 1°21W 23 F6
Woodley U.K. 51°27N 0°54W 25 D7
Woodroffe, Mt. Australia 26°20S 131°45E 98 F5
Woods, L. of the Canada 49°15N 94°45W 108 E10
Woodstock N.B., Canada 46°11N 67°37W 109 E13
Woodstock Ont., Canada 43°10N 80°45W 112 D7
Woodstock U.K. 51°51N 1°20W 24 C6
Woodstock U.S.A. 42°19N 88°27W 112 D3
Wookey U.K. 51°13N 2°41W 24 D3
Wookey Hole U.K. 51°14N 2°40W 24 D3
Wool U.K. 50°40N 2°12W 24 E4
Woolacombe U.K. 51°10N 4°13W 27 E5
Wooler U.K. 55°33N 2°1W 22 A4
Woonsocket U.S.A. 42°0N 71°31W 113 E11
Wootton Bassett U.K. 51°32N 1°54W 24 C5
Wootton Wawen U.K. 52°16N 1°47W 24 B5
Worcester S. Africa 33°39S 19°27E 97 L3
Worcester U.K. 52°11N 2°12W 24 B4
Worcester U.S.A. 42°16N 71°48W 113 D12
Worcestershire □ U.K. 52°13N 2°10W 24 B4
Worfield U.K. 52°34N 2°21W 23 G4
Workington U.K. 54°39N 3°33W 22 C1
Worksop U.K. 53°18N 1°7W 23 F6
Worms Germany 49°37N 8°21E 66 D5
Wortham U.K. 52°21N 1°3E 25 B11
Worthing Barbados 13°5N 59°35W 115 g
Worthing U.K. 50°49N 0°21W 25 E8
Worthington U.S.A. 43°37N 95°36W 111 B7
Wotton under Edge U.K. 51°37N 2°20W 24 C4
Wragby U.K. 53°18N 0°17W 23 F8
Wrangel I. Russia 71°0N 180°0E 79 B19
Wrangell U.S.A. 56°28N 132°23W 108 D6
Wrangell Mts. U.S.A. 61°30N 142°0W 108 C5
Wrangle U.K. 53°3N 0°7E 23 F9
Wrath, C. U.K. 58°38N 5°1W 18 E7
Wrekin, The U.K. 52°41N 2°32W 23 G3
Wrentham U.K. 52°23N 1°40E 25 B12
Wrexham U.K. 53°3N 3°0W 26 A8
Wrexham □ U.K. 53°1N 2°58W 26 D3
Wrigley Canada 63°16N 123°37W 108 C7
Writtle U.K. 51°44N 0°27E 25 C9
Wroclaw Poland 51°5N 17°5E 67 C9
Wroughton U.K. 51°31N 1°47W 24 C5
Wroxham U.K. 52°42N 1°24E 25 A11
Wu Jiang → China 29°40N 107°20E 80 D5
Wuhai China 39°47N 106°52E 80 C5
Wuhan China 30°31N 114°18E 81 C6
Wuhu China 31°22N 118°21E 81 C6
Wuppertal Germany 51°16N 7°12E 66 C4
Würzburg Germany 49°46N 9°55E 66 D5
Wushi China 41°9N 79°13E 80 B2
Wutongqiao China 29°22N 103°50E 80 D5
Wuwei China 37°57N 102°34E 80 C5
Wuxi China 31°33N 120°18E 81 C7
Wuyi Shan China 27°0N 117°0E 81 D6
Wuzhong China 38°2N 106°12E 80 C5
Wuzhou China 23°30N 111°18E 81 D6
Wye U.K. 51°10N 0°57E 25 D10
Wye → U.K. 51°38N 2°40W 24 C3
Wylye → U.K. 51°5N 1°51W 24 D5
Wymondham Leics., U.K. 52°45N 0°43W 23 G7
Wymondham Norfolk, U.K. 52°35N 1°7E 25 A11
Wyndham Australia 15°33S 128°3E 98 D4
Wyoming □ U.S.A. 43°0N 107°30W 110 B5
Wyre → U.K. 53°52N 2°57W 23 E3
Wyre Forest U.K. 52°24N 2°24W 23 H4

X
Xaçmaz Azerbaijan 41°31N 48°42E 73 F8
Xainza China 30°58N 88°35E 80 C3
Xalapa Mexico 19°32N 96°55W 114 D5

Xankändi Azerbaijan 39°52N 46°49E 73 G8
Xenia U.S.A. 39°41N 83°56W 112 F6
Xiaguan China 25°32N 100°16E 80 D5
Xiamen China 24°25N 118°4E 81 D6
Xi'an China 34°15N 109°0E 81 C5
Xiang Jiang → China 28°55N 112°50E 81 D6
Xiangfan China 32°2N 112°8E 81 C6
Xiangtan China 27°51N 112°54E 81 D6
Xianyang China 34°20N 108°40E 81 C5
Xichang China 27°51N 102°19E 80 D5
Xigazê China 29°5N 88°45E 80 D3
Xing'an China 25°38N 110°40E 81 D6
Xinghua China 32°58N 119°48E 81 C6
Xingu → Brazil 1°30S 51°53W 120 C4
Xining China 36°34N 101°40E 80 C5
Xinxiang China 35°18N 113°50E 81 C6
Xinyang China 32°6N 114°3E 81 C6
Xique-Xique Brazil 10°50S 42°40W 122 B2
Xuanhua China 40°40N 115°2E 81 B6
Xuzhou China 34°18N 117°10E 81 C6

Y
Yablonovyy Ra. Russia 53°0N 114°0E 79 D13
Yabucoa Puerto Rico 18°3N 65°53W 115 d
Yacuiba Bolivia 22°0S 63°43W 120 E3
Yakima U.S.A. 46°36N 120°31W 110 A2
Yakutat U.S.A. 59°33N 139°44W 108 D6
Yakutsk Russia 62°5N 129°50E 79 C14
Yala Thailand 6°33N 101°18E 83 C2
Yalong Jiang → China 26°40N 101°55E 80 D5
Yalta Ukraine 44°30N 34°10E 73 F5
Yalu Jiang → China 39°55N 124°19E 81 C7
Yamagata Japan 38°15N 140°15E 82 D7
Yamal Pen. Russia 71°0N 70°0E 79 B8
Yambol Bulgaria 42°30N 26°30E 71 C12
Yamethin Burma 20°29N 96°18E 85 J20
Yamoussoukro Ivory C. 6°49N 5°17W 94 G4
Yampa → U.S.A. 40°32N 108°59W 110 B5
Yamuna → India 25°30N 81°53E 85 G12
Yamzho Yumco China 28°48N 90°35E 80 D4
Yan'an China 36°35N 109°26E 81 C5
Yanbu 'al Baḥr Si. Arabia 24°0N 38°5E 86 E4
Yancheng China 33°23N 120°8E 81 C7
Yangambi Dem. Rep. of the Congo 0°47N 24°24E 96 D4
Yangjiang China 21°50N 111°59E 81 D6
Yangquan China 37°58N 113°31E 81 C6
Yangtze → China 31°48N 121°10E 81 C7
Yangzhou China 32°21N 119°26E 81 C6
Yanji China 42°59N 129°30E 81 B7
Yankton U.S.A. 42°53N 97°23W 111 B7
Yanqi China 42°5N 86°35E 80 B3
Yantai China 37°34N 121°22E 81 C7
Yaoundé Cameroon 3°50N 11°35E 96 D2
Yap Pac. Oc. 9°30N 138°10E 102 G5
Yapen Indonesia 1°50S 136°0E 83 D5
Yaqui → Mexico 27°37N 110°39W 114 B2
Yaraka Australia 24°53S 144°3E 98 E7
Yarcombe U.K. 50°51N 3°5W 27 F7
Yare → U.K. 52°35N 1°38E 25 A12
Yarkant He → China 40°26N 80°59E 80 B3
Yarkhun → Pakistan 36°17N 72°30E 84 A8
Yarm U.K. 54°31N 1°21W 22 C6
Yarmouth Canada 43°50N 66°7W 109 E13
Yarmouth U.K. 50°42N 1°29W 24 E6
Yaroslavl Russia 57°35N 39°55E 72 C6
Yarrow U.K. 55°33N 3°1W 21 C9
Yarumal Colombia 6°58N 75°24W 120 B2
Yate U.K. 51°32N 2°25W 24 C4
Yathkyed L. Canada 62°40N 98°0W 108 C10
Yatsushiro Japan 32°30N 130°40E 82 G2
Yatton U.K. 51°23N 2°49W 24 D3
Yauco Puerto Rico 18°2N 66°51W 115 d
Yavari → Peru 4°21S 70°2W 120 C2
Yaxley U.K. 52°31N 0°16W 25 A8
Yazd Iran 31°55N 54°27E 87 D8
Yazoo → U.S.A. 32°22N 90°54W 111 D8
Yazoo City U.S.A. 32°51N 90°25W 111 D8
Yealmpton U.K. 50°21N 4°1W 27 G5
Yecheng China 37°54N 77°26E 80 C2
Yekaterinburg Russia 56°50N 60°30E 79 D8
Yelets Russia 52°40N 38°30E 72 D6
Yell U.K. 60°35N 1°5W 18 A15
Yell Sd. U.K. 60°33N 1°15W 18 A15
Yellow Sea China 35°0N 123°0E 81 C7
Yellowhead Pass Canada 52°53N 118°25W 108 D8
Yellowknife Canada 62°27N 114°29W 108 C8
Yellowstone → U.S.A. 47°59N 103°59W 110 A6
Yellowstone Nat. Park △ U.S.A. 44°40N 110°30W 110 B5
Yemen ■ Asia 15°0N 44°0E 88 E3
Yenisey → Russia 71°50N 82°40E 79 B10
Yeo → U.K. 51°24N 2°54W 24 D3
Yeola India 20°2N 74°30E 84 J9
Yeovil U.K. 50°57N 2°38W 24 E3
Yes Tor U.K. 50°41N 4°0W 27 F5
Yeu, Î. d' France 46°42N 2°20W 68 C2
Yevpatoriya Ukraine 45°15N 33°20E 73 E5
Yeysk Russia 46°40N 38°12E 73 E6
Yibin China 28°45N 104°32E 80 D5
Yichang China 30°40N 111°20E 81 C6
Yichun China 47°44N 128°52E 81 B7
Yinchuan China 38°30N 106°15E 80 C5
Yining China 43°58N 81°10E 80 B3
Yishan China 24°28N 108°38E 80 D5
Yiyang China 28°35N 112°18E 81 D6
Yogyakarta Indonesia 7°49S 110°22E 83 D3
Yokkaichi Japan 34°55N 136°38E 82 F5
Yokohama Japan 35°27N 139°28E 82 F6
Yonago Japan 35°25N 133°19E 82 F3
Yong'an China 25°59N 117°25E 81 D6
Yongzhou China 26°17N 111°37E 81 D6
Yonkers U.S.A. 40°56N 73°52W 113 E11
Yonne → France 48°23N 2°58E 68 B5

York U.K. 53°58N 1°6W 23 E6
York, C. Australia 10°42S 142°31E 98 C7
York, Vale of U.K. 54°15N 1°25W 22 D6
Yorkshire Dales △ U.K. 54°12N 2°10W 22 D4
Yorkshire Wolds U.K. 54°8N 0°31W 23 D6
Yorkton Canada 51°11N 102°28W 108 D9
Yosemite Nat. Park △ U.S.A. 37°45N 119°40W 110 C3
Yoshkar Ola Russia 56°38N 47°55E 72 C8
Youghal Ireland 51°56N 7°52W 30 E7
Youghal B. Ireland 51°55N 7°49W 30 E7
Youlgreave U.K. 53°11N 1°40W 23 F5
Youngstown U.S.A. 41°6N 80°39W 112 E7
Yoxall U.K. 52°46N 1°47W 23 G5
Yoxford U.K. 52°16N 1°31E 25 B12
Yozgat Turkey 39°51N 34°47E 73 G5
Yreka U.S.A. 41°44N 122°38W 110 B2
Ystalyfera U.K. 51°46N 3°48W 26 D6
Ythan → U.K. 57°19N 1°59W 19 H14
Yu Jiang → China 23°22N 110°3E 81 D6
Yuan Jiang → China 28°55N 111°50E 81 D6
Yuba City U.S.A. 39°8N 121°37W 110 C2
Yucatán Mexico 19°30N 89°0W 114 C7
Yucatan Channel Caribbean 22°0N 86°30W 114 C7
Yuci China 37°42N 112°46E 81 C6
Yueyang China 29°21N 113°5E 81 D6
Yugoslavia = Serbia ■ Europe 43°20N 20°0E 71 B9
Yukon → U.S.A. 62°32N 163°54W 108 C3
Yukon Territory □ Canada 63°0N 135°0W 108 C6
Yulin China 38°20N 109°30E 81 C5
Yuma U.S.A. 32°43N 114°37W 110 D4
Yumen China 39°50N 97°30E 80 C4
Yungas Bolivia 17°0S 66°0W 120 D3
Yunnan □ China 25°0N 102°0E 80 D5
Yurimaguas Peru 5°55S 76°7W 120 C2
Yushu China 33°5N 96°55E 80 C4
Yutian China 36°52N 81°42E 80 C3
Yuzhno-Sakhalinsk Russia 46°58N 142°45E 79 E16
Yuzhou China 34°10N 113°28E 81 C6
Yvetot France 49°37N 0°44E 68 B4

Z
Zāb al Kabīr → Iraq 36°1N 43°24E 86 B5
Zābol □ Afghan. 32°0N 67°0E 87 D11
Zabrze Poland 50°18N 18°50E 67 C10
Zacatecas Mexico 22°47N 102°35W 114 C4
Zadar Croatia 44°8N 15°14E 70 B6
Zagaoua Chad 15°30N 22°24E 95 E10
Zagazig Egypt 30°40N 31°30E 95 B12
Zagreb Croatia 45°50N 15°58E 70 B7
Zagros Mts. Iran 33°45N 48°5E 86 C7
Zāhedān Iran 29°30N 60°50E 87 D10
Zahlah Lebanon 33°52N 35°50E 86 C3
Zakynthos Greece 37°47N 20°54E 71 F9
Zambezi → Africa 18°35S 36°20E 97 H7
Zambia ■ Africa 15°0S 28°0E 97 G5
Zamboanga Phil. 6°59N 122°3E 83 C4
Zamora Mexico 19°59N 102°16W 114 D4
Zamora Spain 41°30N 5°45W 69 B3
Zamość Poland 50°43N 23°15E 67 C12
Zanesville U.S.A. 39°56N 82°1W 112 F6
Zanjan Iran 36°40N 48°35E 86 B7
Zanzibar Tanzania 6°12S 39°12E 96 F7
Zaouiet Reggâne Algeria 26°32N 0°3E 94 C6
Zaoyang China 32°10N 112°45E 81 C6
Zaozhuang China 34°50N 117°35E 81 C6
Zapala Argentina 39°0S 70°5W 121 F2
Zaporozhye Ukraine 47°50N 35°10E 73 E6
Zaragoza Spain 41°39N 0°53W 69 B5
Zaranj Afghan. 30°55N 61°55E 87 D10
Zárate Argentina 34°7S 59°0W 121 F4
Zaria Nigeria 11°0N 7°40E 94 F7
Zarzis Tunisia 33°31N 11°2E 95 B8
Zaskar Mts. India 33°15N 77°30E 84 C10
Zāwiyat al Bayḍā Libya 32°50N 21°44E 95 B10
Zeebrugge Belgium 51°19N 3°12E 65 C3
Zeeland □ Neths. 51°30N 3°50E 65 C3
Zeil, Mt. Australia 23°30S 132°23E 98 E5
Zeist Neths. 52°5N 5°15E 65 B5
Zelenograd Russia 56°1N 37°12E 72 C6
Zenica Bos.-H. 44°10N 17°57E 71 B7
Zhangjiakou China 40°48N 114°55E 81 B6
Zhangye China 38°50N 100°23E 80 C5
Zhangzhou China 24°30N 117°35E 81 D6
Zhanjiang China 21°15N 110°20E 81 D6
Zhanyi China 25°38N 103°48E 80 D5
Zhaoqing China 23°0N 112°20E 81 D6
Zhaotong China 27°20N 103°44E 80 D5
Zhejiang □ China 29°0N 120°0E 81 D7
Zhengzhou China 34°45N 113°34E 81 C6
Zhezqazghan Kazakhstan 47°44N 67°40E 79 E8
Zhigansk Russia 66°48N 123°27E 79 C13
Zhlobin Belarus 52°55N 30°0E 72 D5
Zhob Pakistan 31°20N 69°31E 84 D6
Zhongdian China 27°48N 99°42E 80 D4
Zhumadian China 32°59N 114°2E 81 C6
Zhytomyr Ukraine 50°20N 28°40E 67 C15
Zibo China 36°47N 118°3E 81 C6
Zielona Góra Poland 51°57N 15°31E 66 C8
Zigong China 29°15N 104°48E 80 D5
Ziguinchor Senegal 12°35N 16°20W 94 F2
Žilina Slovak Rep. 49°12N 18°42E 67 D10
Zimbabwe ■ Africa 19°0S 30°0E 97 H5
Zinder Niger 13°48N 8°50E 94 F7
Ziway, L. Ethiopia 8°0N 38°50E 88 F2
Zlatoust Russia 55°10N 59°40E 72 C10
Zlín Czech Rep. 49°14N 17°40E 67 D9
Zonguldak Turkey 41°28N 31°50E 73 F5
Zrenjanin Serbia 45°22N 20°23E 71 B9
Zug Switz. 47°10N 8°31E 66 E5
Zunyi China 27°42N 106°53E 80 D5
Zürich Switz. 47°22N 8°32E 66 E5
Zuwārah Libya 32°58N 12°1E 95 B8
Zvishavane Zimbabwe 20°17S 30°2E 97 J6
Zwelitsha S. Africa 32°55S 27°22E 97 L5
Zwickau Germany 50°44N 12°30E 66 C7

SATELLITE IMAGE OF THE SEVERN ESTUARY

This Landsat false-colour composite image was captured in October. The cities of Bristol and Cardiff are clearly visible, as are the Black Mountains and the Brecon Beacons in Wales. Images such as this are used for recording and monitoring land use. *(EROS)*